Oracle Press™

Oracle Database 12c
Oracle RMAN Backup
and Recovery

Oracle Press™

Oracle Database 12c Oracle RMAN Backup and Recovery

Robert G. Freeman
Matthew Hart

New York   Chicago   San Francisco
Athens   London   Madrid   Mexico City
Milan   New Delhi   Singapore   Sydney   Toronto

Cataloging-in-Publication Data is on file with the Library of Congress

McGraw-Hill Education books are available at special quantity discounts to use as premiums and sales promotions, or for use in corporate training programs. To contact a representative, please visit the Contact Us pages at www.mhprofessional.com.

Oracle Database 12c Oracle RMAN Backup and Recovery

1 2 3 4 5 6 7 8 9 0   DOC DOC   1 0 9 8 7 6

ISBN   978-0-07-184743-8
MHID   0-07-184743-X

Sponsoring Editor	**Copy Editor**	**Composition**
Brandi Shailer	Bart Reed	Cenveo® Publisher Services
Editorial Supervisor	**Proofreader**	**Illustration**
Janet Walden	Lisa McCoy	Cenveo Publisher Services
Project Editor	**Indexer**	**Art Director, Cover**
LeeAnn Pickrell	Karin Arrigoni	Jeff Weeks
Technical Editor	**Production Supervisor**	
Matthew Arrocha	Lynn M. Messina	

For Carrie and all my kids, whom I love more than life itself.
—RF

About the Authors

Robert G. Freeman is the senior DBA at Businessolver, Inc., in Des Moines, Iowa. Robert has worked with Oracle databases for well over two decades, including working for Oracle Corporation for five years. In this long career Robert has worked in a number of different Oracle environments, from the mini to some of the largest in the world, and many in between. He loves working with Oracle databases and playing with his two-year old, Amy.

   Matthew Hart is the coauthor of six books for Oracle Press, most recently *Oracle 10g High Availability with RAC, Flashback, and DataGuard; Oracle Enterprise Manager 10g Grid Control Handbook;* and the tome you now hold in your hands. He has worked with high availability technologies in Oracle since version 7.3, and has worked with RMAN since its inception. Matthew currently works and lives in Kansas City, Missouri.

About the Contributors

Emre Baransel holds two master's degrees in information systems and business administration, and has worked in IT for 11 years. He has worked for the largest fixed-line, GSM telco companies and Oracle Corp. in Turkey. He was awarded as an Oracle ACE in 2012. He authored *Oracle Data Guard 11gR2 Administration: Beginner's Guide* and contributed to the *Oracle RMAN 11g Backup and Recovery* book. He's an Oracle Certified Professional (OCP), a founding member of TROUG (Turkish Oracle User Group), and a blogger at emrebaransel.blogspot.com. He has spoken at Oracle Open World in the United States and at user group conferences across Europe.

   E. Craig Brown is a Senior Database Engineer for Commvault, specializing in Oracle database solutions. Mr. Brown has been a database administrator for 20 years, primarily with Oracle as well as others. His work with Commvault for the past eight years consists of consulting multiple companies across many industries, including healthcare, telecommunications, public utilities, engineering, and government, in planning for backup and disaster recovery.

   Scott Black has over 15 years of experience in the technology field, with almost the past 5 years at Oracle helping public sector, healthcare, and higher education clients get the most value out of their data and Oracle products.

   Tim Chien is a product manager with Oracle's High Availability and Storage Management Group, focusing on Backup and Recovery, including Zero Data Loss Recovery Appliance, Recovery Manager (RMAN), and Flashback technologies. His extensive product management and marketing experience includes both application server and database products, and he has presented at numerous Oracle and industry conferences around the world. Tim received his bachelor's and master's degrees in computer science from the Massachusetts Institute of Technology.

Rao Chelli is a Senior Principal Consultant at Oracle USA. Rao has 15+ years of experience in technology consulting, solution architecture, and making customers successful with their Oracle product investments. He is one of the first-generation Oracle-engineered systems experts and Oracle MAA solutions delivery leaders at Oracle. Prior to Oracle, Rao worked at GE (USA), GOTEVOT (Saudi Arabia), and Frontier (India). Rao holds a master's degree (M.Sc.Tech) in Electronics Technology from Andhra University, India, and is currently enrolled as an Executive MBA student (A16) at New York University's Stern Business School.

Marcus Vinicius Miguel Pedro is a Principal Advanced Support Engineer at Oracle ACS Brazil. Marcus Vinicius has more than 10 years working with Oracle technologies and is a consultant focusing and specializing in high availability solutions; he is also responsible for designing HA solutions for the most important corporations in Brazil. He was nominated as an Oracle ACE in 2010. He also maintains his Oracle-related blog and speaks at user group events in Brazil.

Ramesh Raghav is a Principal Sales Engineer at Oracle Corporation. He is an accomplished Oracle database professional with extensive expertise in implementation and administration of technologies spanning Database (versions 5–12c), RMAN, Recovery Appliance, Exadata, RAC, and DataGuard. Ramesh has recovered many critical production databases for various enterprise clients using RMAN. He is an Oracle 12c Certified Professional (OCP) DBA, a RAC-certified expert, and author of *Oracle 10gR2 Recovery Manager*.

Pete Sharman is a database architect in the Database as a Service team for Enterprise Manager with Oracle. He is also a member of the OakTable Network and has presented at earlier RMOUG Training Days, Hotsos Symposia, Oracle OpenWorld conferences, and other user group events. He has co-authored the *Expert Oracle Enterprise Manager 12*c and *Practical Oracle Database Appliance* books published by Apress.

About the Technical Editor

Matthew Arrocha has been with Oracle for 20 years and started working with RMAN when it was released in Oracle Database 8.0.3. Over the years he has provided support and training to Oracle internal and external audiences. Matthew is the Oracle RMAN Global Technical Lead and Backup & Recovery Lead for the United States and Canada, and also provides Advanced Resolution support and BDE bug screening for development. This is the fourth RMAN Oracle Press book he has reviewed. Matthew thanks Robert Freeman for inviting him on the project, and Jennifer Dittman for the support in helping him concentrate on this book review.

Contents at a Glance

Contents

PART I
Getting Started with RMAN in Oracle Database 12c

PART II
RMAN Configuration, Backup, and Recovery Essentials

PART III
RMAN Maintenance and Administration

PART IV
RMAN in a Highly Available Architecture

PART V
RMAN Media Management

PART VI
Appendixes

Acknowledgments

A book of this size is a monumental challenge. Additionally, with each book I write the fact is that there are so many people to thank, I always worry I'll forget someone. So, I'm going to keep this very simple. Thanks to my uber-supportive wife, Carrie, and my entire family, who has always been behind me. Thanks to those folks at Oracle I worked with while I was writing this book, and the folks at Businessolver, too. Further, thanks also to all the contributors and those at Oracle Press who have contributed to the production of this book. I could not do this without all of you.

Introduction

When it comes to databases, there are few things more important than backup and recovery. Many times when I speak publicly, one of the things I say is that if you don't have a database with the data the business needs in it, what good are skillful tuning, writing awesome SQL, and building out RAC clusters anyway. It's all about the data and protecting it.

As a result, using RMAN really goes hand in hand with using the Oracle Database. While there may be other solutions, these solutions are bereft of the options that RMAN offers. That's why, in almost every case I've seen, RMAN is the tool that is used to perform the actual backup of the database tasked with being the backup used when the database needs to be restored. It's true that there are cases where other solutions are used to provide solutions for specific needs. For example, snapshot technologies may be used to quickly clone databases (something that Oracle Database 12*c* Multitenant may well do away with). However, RMAN is always the front-line recovery tool for both on-site and disaster recovery situations.

What This Book Covers

This book covers using both basic and advanced RMAN functionality. It covers all the information on RMAN you will need to know to use RMAN to provide a robust and complete backup and recovery solution to your database. This book is also designed to help you build your RMAN skills and apply them to your databases.

How This Book Is Organized

In an effort to give you the RMAN skills you need, we first introduce you to the basics of RMAN. We discuss how to set RMAN up, configure it, and use it for backups and restores of all kinds. We then discuss the management and administration of RMAN backups and RMAN-related metadata. Next, we turn our attention to using RMAN to augment your highly available (HA) architecture. Finally, we deal with the question of the various media management layers available for you to use with RMAN. These are the vendors that provide the media you can put your backups on and, later, use those backups to restore your databases.

This is a big book, and it was a big project. We have updated the book for the new functionality in Oracle Database 12c, and at the same time reviewed the content in previous versions of this book and modified it as required. In some cases, we decided to remove some content as well—we felt like this book really shouldn't cause your bookshelf to inadvertently exceed its weight design limitations.

Who Should Read This Book

This book is designed to be read by every Oracle DBA who is responsible for the backup and recovery of an Oracle database. In this book, we will take the beginner, hold their hand, and help them learn about backup and recovery of Oracle databases. For the more advanced DBA, this book is designed to help them develop more advanced skills, and it also provides a helpful reference during their DBA work.

PART
I

Getting Started
with RMAN in
Oracle Database 12c

CHAPTER
1

Quick-Start Guide
for RMAN and
Oracle Database 12c

Welcome to *Oracle Database 12c Oracle RMAN Backup and Recovery*. If you purchased our previous RMAN books, you have an idea of what to expect from this text. However, we have added a number of things, changed a number of things, and updated a great deal to help you use RMAN 12c.

Many people we've talked to wished that this book came with a quick-start guide. We really debated how good of an idea adding such a chapter to the book would be. Our concern is that you will use the quick-start chapter and simply stop there and assume that we have covered all of the features, best practices, and all of the knowledge you really need to use RMAN in the most efficient way.

At the same time, we want you to get your feet wet with RMAN so you can see some indication of how useful the tool really is. Also, when you use something, it makes it easier to follow what you're reading and reduces the learning curve a bit. With that in mind, we have added this chapter, which is a quick RMAN primer.

In this chapter we show you how to quickly set up your database and then back it up using RMAN. We then quickly demonstrate a full recovery. We will not be using all the bells and whistles of RMAN; instead, this is a basic, quick "how do I back up my database safely" demonstration of RMAN.

This chapter covers the following topics:

- Preliminary steps
- Configuring the database for RMAN operations
- Backing up the database
- Restoring the database

Also, in this chapter we are going to limit the output of the various commands. This will help keep the chapter clean and really highlight the format of the commands themselves. As we progress through the remaining chapters of the book, you will see more and more detailed output and learn what it means. So, let's get down to using RMAN for the first time.

Preliminary Steps

Before we can do anything, you have to understand where we are starting from. In this quick-start guide we expect the following:

- That you have installed the Oracle database software
- That you have created an Oracle database. We assume its name is orcl throughout this quick-start chapter
- That the database is currently in NOARCHIVELOG mode
- That you have sufficient disk space to create backups of the database

All of these are basic DBA tasks, and, as such, are not covered in this book. Once you have met these prerequisites, we are ready to move on to the next steps.

Configuring the Database for RMAN Operations

Before you can use RMAN, you need to do a few things to configure the database for RMAN operations. The tasks you need to complete are listed next. We have also listed what chapter these tasks are in so you can go look in that chapter for additional information.

1. Put the database in ARCHIVELOG mode (more detail in Chapter 5).
2. Configure RMAN parameters from the RMAN command line (more detail in Chapter 5).

Note that although RMAN can run in NOARCHIVELOG mode, we feel this quick-start guide would better serve you if your database was in ARCHIVELOG mode. So, here's what you need to do:

1. Determine where the FRA should be located and create it.
2. Log into the database and configure it to use the FRA.
3. Put the database in ARCHIVELOG mode.

Determine Where the FRA Should Be Located and Create It

You need to decide where the database backups are going to be located. To do this, we use a feature of RMAN called the Fast Recovery Area (FRA) to simplify the backup process. We discuss the FRA in great detail in Chapter 5. So, let's say that you decide to put all backups in a directory called /u01/FRA. Make sure you check file system permissions. For example, you would need to make sure that the /u01/FRA directories you create are owned by the Oracle software–owning account (called oracle in our example), as seen here:

```
[root@server12c]# cd /u01
[root@server12c]# mkdir FRA
[root@server12c]# chown oracle:dba FRA
```

Note that you only need to create the directory FRA. Oracle will manage all the other directories under FRA for you. You will be able to see this in greater detail after you have performed your first backup!

Log Into the Database and Configure It to Use the FRA

Next, you need to log into the database and configure two database parameters so that the database will use the newly created FRA:

```
[root@server12c]# su - oracle
[oracle@server12c]#. oraenv
ORACLE_SID=[oracle] ? orcl
The Oracle base has been set to /u01/app/oracle
[oracle@server12c]# sqlplus / as sysdba
```

Now that you have logged into the database, you need to configure the database to use the FRA directory in /u01/FRA created earlier. This requires two commands:

```
SQL> alter system set db_recovery_file_dest_size=2G;
System altered.
SQL> alter system set db_recovery_file_dest='/u01/FRA';
System altered.
```

You have now configured the database to write its backups to the FRA (/u01/FRA) by default. This is the location of the FRA we mentioned earlier. You have also allocated 2GB of logical space within the FRA to this database for use. Now it's time to put the database in ARCHIVELOG mode so you can perform inconsistent backups.

Put the Database in ARCHIVELOG Mode

Putting the database in ARCHIVELOG mode (assuming that it is not already) is a simple process, but it does require shutting down the database and then restarting it. Here are the steps for putting the database in ARCHIVELOG mode:

1. Shut down the database:

   ```
   SQL> shutdown immediate
   Database closed.
   Database dismounted.
   ORACLE instance shut down.
   ```

2. Mount the database:

   ```
   SQL> startup mount
   ```

3. Put the database in ARCHIVELOG mode:

   ```
   SQL> alter database archivelog;
   Database altered.
   ```

4. Open the database:

   ```
   SQL> alter database open;
   Database altered.
   ```

You are now ready to start doing backups of your database. Exit SQL*Plus at this time to get back to the command prompt.

Backing Up the Database

Backing up the database with RMAN is now quite easy. You simply start the RMAN tool and execute the backup. First, however, you need to make sure that the environment is set correctly for the database you want to back up:

```
[root@server12c]# su - oracle
[oracle@server12c]#. oraenv
ORACLE_SID=[oracle] ? orcl
The Oracle base has been set to /u01/app/oracle
```

Now start RMAN. RMAN should be in the path already, so it's easy to start:

```
[oracle@server12c]# rman target=/
```

Note that you have invoked the RMAN command using the **target** parameter. This indicates the user and password you will use to connect to the database you are backing up, which is called the *target* database. In this case, the target database is the database the ORACLE_SID environment variable is set for (which is database orcl). You will now see the RMAN banner and the RMAN prompt, which looks like this:

```
[oracle@server12c]# rman>
```

You are now ready to back up your database for the first time. Here is the command you need to run to back up your database:

```
[oracle@server12c]# rman>backup database plus archivelog delete input;
```

In this case, you will be backing up the entire database, including all of the archived redo logs. The backup files will be created in the Fast Recovery Area and will contain all the database datafiles and the archived redo logs.

From the RMAN prompt, you can now create a report that provides information on the backup you have just taken. Use the **list** command to look at both the database backups and the archivelog backups:

```
[oracle@server12c]# rman>list backup of database summary;
[oracle@server12c]# rman>list backup of archivelog all summary;
```

Note that the information output from these commands is coming from the control file of the database to which you are connected. Most RMAN-related metadata is stored in the database control file. A number of database views and RMAN commands are available that provide access to that metadata, just as the **list** command has done in the preceding example.

Now that you have confirmed that the backups are actually listed in the RMAN metadata, let's go to the FRA directory and look at the files and directories that have been added:

```
[oracle@server12c]# cd /FRA/orcl
[oracle@server12c]# ls -alR
```

You will see a number of files that were created by the backup process. The files that RMAN created in this case are called backup set pieces. We discuss the backup set pieces in Chapter 3.

Restoring the Database

Now that you have backed up the database, you can restore it if need be. A number of kinds of restores can be performed, and we will discuss them throughout the book. One example is a complete restore of the database, including a recovery of the database using the archived redo logs. Here is an example of this kind of recovery:

```
[oracle@server12c]# rman>restore database;
[oracle@server12c]# rman>recover database;
[oracle@server12c]# rman>alter database open;
```

When running the **restore database** command, RMAN will restore the datafiles from the backups and put them into their correct place. The **recover database** command then extracts the archived redo logs and applies them to the database. Finally, the **alter database open** command will open the database, which applies any redo in the online redo log files. After the final command, the database will be open and ready for operations. We discuss restore- and recovery-related topics and options throughout this book.

Summary

In this chapter we have quickly run through a basic setup of RMAN and showed you how to back up and then restore your database. This is just a quick-and-dirty basic introduction to RMAN and really does not begin to show you the power that is in your backup-hungry hands. Please don't look at this chapter as an example of how to configure your production backups, because that is not what this chapter is meant for. This chapter simply lets you get your hands a little bit dirty with RMAN. As you move through the next few chapters of the book, we will dig into a number of RMAN features and settings that you will want to be aware of before you truly implement a production version of your RMAN backup and recovery solution.

CHAPTER
2

Oracle Database 12c
Backup and Recovery
Architecture Tour

N ow that you have a taste for how RMAN works, it's time to start moving into the engine room of RMAN and see what really makes it tick. We want to take you through the RMAN landscape from the bottom up because we believe it's not enough to just know, generally, how something as important as backup and recovery works. In this chapter we introduce you to the basic backup and recovery concepts of Oracle that RMAN is built around.

Before we do that, though, we want to take a moment to tell you what we really think this book is about and explain the approach we are taking. In previous editions, we suggested that if you considered yourself to be an Oracle backup and recovery architecture expert, then maybe you could skip this chapter. We have changed our minds about this, and we will take a few paragraphs to tell you why we think it's important that you read this chapter, even if you are an expert.

NOTE
You may be aware of the Multitenant option for the Oracle Database. This chapter does not cover Oracle Multitenant—we have saved that for Chapter 4. However, most of the concepts presented in this chapter do apply to Oracle Multitenant.

Then, after that, it's time to kick off our tour of the Oracle Database Backup and Recovery architecture. We hope you find this tour useful and educational. We also hope you find it fun. Don't worry, there are little surprises around every corner, but nothing that can hurt you.

So, please line up and watch the screen as some previously famous and now washed-up, semi-well-known actor or actress gives you our pre-tour briefing. Your ride will begin shortly afterward.

What This Book Is About

Greetings! Backup and recovery is at the heart of an enterprise's strategy for business continuity. That is to say, without the data that enables enterprise operations and decision making, what is left to make the enterprise go? Therefore, one of the most important jobs, if not *the* most important job, of the DBA is to provide *expertise* with respect to backup and recovery.

Now, a particular dictionary describes "expertise" this way:

Expert skill or knowledge; expertness; know-how: business expertise.

What does it mean then to be an expert at backup and recovery? Well, we can tell you that it's more than knowing a few "recipes" on how to do this or that. Granted, having a formalized process (or checklist) is important, but with backup and recovery of an Oracle database, your knowledge has to go way beyond a set of formulistic approaches to things. Why is this?

First, Oracle database backups provide a multitude of options when it comes to formulating a solution to meet your needs. It might be that in your case a weekly full offline consistent backup will meet your needs. It might be that your needs require a much more complex set of solutions, such as incremental backups. If you are versed in recipes, then you might not be versed in all of the options available to you beyond just the basic backup methodologies. If you don't know the product and its features well, how can you hope to really craft the backup strategy that is right for your organization?

This is even more critical when it comes to recovering a database after a failure. The different permutations of things that can go wrong at one time can be astounding. These permutations lead to different kinds of restore and recovery situations that no set of recipes can begin to cover. Recipes can prepare you for the expected, but if you don't understand how things work, you will find recipes sorely lacking when the problem is of the unexpected variety.

So, the difference between the recipe approach and ours is a bit like the difference between putting monkeys into space and sending astronauts. Monkeys could go through the motions and follow a basic set of tricks, encoded in response to stimuli. However, when things go wrong, no monkey is able to reason the problem out and craft a solution knowing what was available to them. If monkeys had been on Apollo 13 instead of men, there is no way they would have made it back to Earth. The reason Apollo 13 made it home safely is that engineers on the ground and astronauts in space all understood the hardware and software they had to deal with, how it worked, and its limitations. Understanding this key bit of information, they crafted solutions that no monkey could ever have completed.

A DBA who is prepared to build a database "carbon dioxide scrubber" on the fly from a piece of this and a piece of that is truly one in whom you can put your faith. One who is versed only in recipes, checklists, and responses to a static set of problems is a dangerous DBA indeed in our opinion.

As a result of this philosophy, our approach in this book is to make you an expert on Oracle Backup and Recovery with an emphasis on RMAN. In this book we approach RMAN from the bottom up. This chapter, as a result, is more about the foundations of core Oracle backup and restore functionality, and little of RMAN is introduced at this point. Why is that? After all, this is a book about RMAN, isn't it?

Well, the fact is that RMAN is dependent on the database architecture designed to ensure that a database is recoverable. RMAN uses the mechanisms built into the database to ensure your transactions are recoverable to also make sure you can restore and recover a database and those transactions.

So, to truly understand RMAN and, more importantly perhaps, to understand Oracle Database Backup and Recovery, you must understand the Oracle database. That is what this chapter is about then—understanding the Oracle database with a particular emphasis on the architecture and processes that make the backup and recovery of an Oracle database possible. Without knowing this stuff, you cannot really understand Oracle Backup and Recovery or RMAN. You can go through the basic motions, but when the real challenge presents itself, you will be lost—without a recipe.

I'm Already an RMAN Expert—Why Do I Need This Book or This Chapter?

This is a fair question if you have been working with RMAN for some time. You might have read an earlier copy of this book and, as a result, you feel comfortable with RMAN and database backup and recovery. This might make you wonder what more you might glean from this updated book. We can tell you when it comes to Oracle Database 12c and RMAN, there is a lot to gain from reading this book, and the content of this chapter in particular. First, Oracle Database 12c has changed a lot.

The introduction of Oracle Multitenant Database itself justifies reading this chapter and also the next, where we present Oracle Multitenant Database. Oracle Multitenant is probably one of the single biggest changes to the Oracle architecture, and how that impacts RMAN is important. Yet, a lot of the basic architectural concepts remain the same. So although the chapter on Oracle Multitenant is important, this chapter is just as important. Think you won't be working with Oracle Multitenant? Think again. Sometime in the future Oracle will only support the Multitenant architecture, so if you are truly going to be an Oracle DBA of the future, now is the time to start understanding just what Oracle Multitenant is all about.

Beyond Oracle Multitenant, there are a number of new Oracle Database 12*c* features that might well impact how you use RMAN. We discuss all of these new features in this book, which has been completely revised for Oracle Database 12c–related features. If you're an old-timer, re-reading this book might well show you something new that will change how you want to perform backups of your Oracle database, or we might clue you into new restore and recovery techniques that will help you to look at your recovery plans in the future.

If you are already using RMAN and are concerned that the changes in Oracle Database 12*c* will adversely affect your backup and recovery strategies, don't worry. RMAN is fully backward compatible, so your existing backup and recovery strategies will not have to change when you move to Oracle Database 12*c*. That being said, as you read this book you might well find some good reasons to change your backup or restore strategy to take advantage of a new feature, or a feature you didn't know existed (which happens sometimes when you just use someone else's recipes).

Let's Kick Off the Tour

Okay, now that we have provided you with the Disneyesque pre-ride briefing, it's about time to load up on our tour bus, which is pulling up. Quickly, let's review what you are going to see on the tour. In this chapter a number of great stops are in store for you. You will encounter the following:

- Backup and recovery essentials
- A few Oracle terms to know
- Oracle database architecture in the pre-Multitenant era
- The combined picture
- More Oracle Database internals
- ARCHIVELOG versus NOARCHIVELOG mode operation
- Entering the Oracle Multitenant era
- Controlling the database software
- Oracle Backup and Recovery primer

As we proceed, you will learn the importance of understanding how the Oracle product works so that you can properly apply the techniques documented in this book to bring your wayward database back to life. You will also see that there is more to backing up and recovering a database than just entering a few commands and putting tapes in the tape drive.

The direct results of misapplying a technique or not understanding a principle of the architecture may be an extended outage or even loss of data.

Each of the authors has seen a number of cases where serious mistakes in planning and understanding have led to serious problems in recovering databases. We have each seen cases where databases were not fully recoverable because of simple mistakes that could have been avoided if best practices had been followed. So, in this book we talk about best practices a lot.

Finally, in this chapter and the next, we are going to cover only database internals and any additional information that you need to know with regard to backup, recovery, and RMAN. If you need more information on other subject areas, such as performance tuning, database modeling, or connecting your database to your favorite gaming platform, you might want to look elsewhere. Many books on these subject areas are available from Oracle Press, and you can find these titles at www.oraclepressbooks.com. (We're not sure they have anything on connecting gaming platforms to Oracle databases, though.)

Ah, the tour bus has arrived. Please get in, move all the way to the end of the row you are in, and then have a seat. Buckle yourself in and make sure you keep your hands and legs in the vehicle at all times. Have a great tour of the Oracle Database Backup and Recovery landscape!

Backup and Recovery Essentials

Our first stop is backup and recovery essentials. Two different areas need to be dealt with when crafting a plan to execute in the event your database goes bottom up. The first architectural question is one of high availability, which is loosely coupled with the second question, which is one of backup and recovery. Let's look at these questions of high availability and backup and recovery in more detail.

High Availability

High availability (HA) implies an architecture that attempts to remove single points of failure that can cause systems to experience outages. In our opinion, HA solutions are sometimes incorrectly lumped in with disaster recovery (DR) solutions. This seems natural because they provide similar services, but they are two completely different animals and, as such, should be treated differently.

HA solutions are *local* solutions implemented to provide redundancy for local resources that are identified as potential single points of failure. This might include a RAC cluster to protect the system from the loss of a compute node, or it might include redundant disk controllers or power supplies. HA solutions can also include such elements as mirrored drives, RAID architectures, database clustering, database failover schemes, and, of course, backup and recovery. HA adds costs to the overall database architectural solution.

The main idea with HA solutions is that the application and/or user is as unaware of local failures as possible. Generally this means that if a single resource fails, the user or application simply fails over to an active and redundant resource and uses it. In our mind, in a true HA solution, the user should never know that the resource they are using has had an outage. At most, they might experience some delay in the processing of their query, but they should never see an error, have to re-execute a query, or be denied access to the system. Most HA solutions we have seen do not provide this level of redundancy for many reasons.

HA solutions are not just about providing redundancy from failure of a given resource (such as a database). HA solutions usually provide a given resource the ability to scale up or down as demand requires. That is, HA solutions should prevent users from seeing any system slowdowns because those solutions should enact rules that provide for scalability of those resources. Given these definitions of HA, it's clear that RMAN is not a high availability solution, though sometimes it is mistakenly clumped into the family of HA solutions.

Because HA options are really a separate topic from RMAN, we do not cover them in great detail in this book unless they are related to RMAN (for example, we do cover RMAN backups on Oracle RAC databases). Oracle Press does offer a book that includes coverage of HA solutions: *Oracle 12*c

Oracle Real Application Clusters Handbook (McGraw-Hill Professional, 2011), by my friend K. Gopalakrishnan. This is a great book! Also, *Oracle Data Guard 12c Handbook* (McGraw-Hill Professional, 2009), by Larry Carpenter and Joseph Meeks, provides information on Oracle Data Guard as part of an overall HA solution.

When HA solutions fail, the family of disaster recovery (DR) solutions comes into play. The term *disaster recovery* is usually associated with catastrophic loss, and so we sometimes do not see RMAN as a DR solution, but that is exactly what RMAN is. Loss of any data is a disaster of the highest order, and when you have to pull out RMAN to recover lost data, you should treat that incident as a disaster. Any unexpected database restore should always be followed by a post-mortem to figure out what happened, what the impact was, and how the problem can be avoided in the future. Beyond RMAN, the most common DR solutions include Oracle Data Guard and Oracle GoldenGate. Each of these has its place in the enterprise.

As with HA solutions, we don't really touch on DR solutions a great deal in this book, except for those solutions that have an RMAN hook into them. For example, you can create an Oracle Data Guard database using RMAN. As a result, we provide pretty good coverage of that kind of operation. However, we don't get into the nitty-gritty of Oracle Data Guard in this book.

Backup and Recovery

As we continue our tour, we move to backup and recovery, which is getting us close to the main topic of this book, RMAN. We will talk in detail throughout this chapter about the different kinds of backups that can be done in Oracle, but for now, let's talk about the primary types of backups: offline (cold) and online (hot). We also sometimes talk about backups as being consistent or inconsistent. Let's define each of these terms a bit more before we proceed.

Offline backups are done with the database down, which means that it is also unavailable to users. *Online* backups, on the other hand, are done with the database up and running, so users can continue with their business. Online backups require the database to be properly configured so that recovery information can be properly applied (we will discuss this concept as we progress through this chapter).

RMAN supports both online and offline backups. In fact, as you will see in later chapters, some of the features of RMAN make it the preferable method for performing online database backups.

Beyond online and offline backups, you need to be aware that database backups can occur while the database is in one of two different states: consistent or inconsistent. When backups are made in one of these two states, they are known as either consistent backups or inconsistent backups, respectively. The state the database is in when the backup was taken is critical to understand because it impacts your recovery options.

How can a database be inconsistent? That seems worrying. We discuss the particulars in greater detail later in this chapter, but for now you should know that when a database is running normally there are two different kinds of storage: persistent and transient. The *persistent storage* would be the information stored on disk because it persists through shutdowns of the database. Information that is persistent is information in the database datafiles and in the online redo logs (and archived redo logs).

Transient storage, on the other hand, is the memory that is allocated to the SGA (the PGA too, but for our purposes the SGA is sufficient). The SGA resides in memory areas that no longer exist after the database is shut down, and once that memory is gone, anything that was in it is gone as well.

Oracle uses a combination of transient and persistent storage to store database data. When the database is shut down using the **shutdown**, **shutdown immediate**, or **shutdown transactional** command, Oracle will update the persistent storage with the information from the transient storage.

Thus, the two storage areas are consistent with each other before the SGA is deallocated. Additionally, the data and synch points within the datafiles, control files, and online redo logs are all aligned, so those persistent storage mechanisms are all consistent. Any backup that is made under these specific conditions would be considered a *consistent backup*.

If the **shutdown abort** command was used to shut down the database, then the database datafiles, control files, and online redo logs will all be inconsistent with each other. Thus, a database backup in this state would be considered an *inconsistent backup*. Also, if the database just crashed due to a bug or someone pulling the power on that database, it would also be in an inconsistent state.

In fact, the database when it's running normally is always in an inconsistent state. This is because Oracle does not update the database datafiles every time data is changed. Thus, any database backup taken during the time that the database is running would be an inconsistent backup.

Throughout this book we will discuss inconsistent and consistent backups. There are rules that need to be followed when making each kind of backup to ensure that it can be recovered successfully. You need to make sure you understand those rules when you design your backup and recovery strategy.

Now that we have given you a quick introduction to the notion of offline, online, consistent, and inconsistent backups, it's time to start looking at the things that need to be considered when designing a backup strategy. Users (and the owners of corporate policy, systems, data, and applications, who we often call *stakeholders*) have certain levels of expectations for the protection of their data. Before you decide when and how to back up your database, you should gather some of the requirements that these folks have and make sure that your backup plans mesh with their needs. Only after you have gathered those requirements can you craft that backup plan, and perhaps justify the cost of that plan. Let's look in more detail at how you gather those requirements.

Backup and Recovery Strategy Requirements Gathering

In gathering user requirements, you really want to find out from them what their needs are. Users need to be asked a number of questions, and as the database administrator (DBA), you should take the lead in asking them. To collect backup and recovery requirements, you should ask your customers questions like the following:

- How much data loss can you afford in the event of a database failure? This is called the *recovery point objective* (RPO).

- What is the maximum length of time you are able to allow for recovery of your database? This is called the *recovery time objective* (RTO).

- How much are you willing to spend to ensure that your data is recoverable?

- Can the system be down during the backup?

- How much time will it take to get damaged hardware replaced?

Let's quickly look at each of these questions in more detail.

How Much Data Loss Can You Afford?   This is probably the most important question of all. All backup and recovery plans have some risk of data loss associated with them, and as you move closer to a zero data loss solution, the costs of the backup and recovery plan can skyrocket. Therefore, it's important to clearly define the recovery point objectives with your customers.

As was the case with HA, the organization needs to quantify the cost of data loss and, based on that cost, craft a cost-effective backup and recovery plan in light of the RPO they have selected. It is critical that the customer understand how much data loss risk they are taking with the chosen backup and recovery plan. Of course, each database has an allowable amount of loss, too, and one database may be much more tolerant of data loss than another.

What Is the Maximum Length of Time You Are Able to Allow for Recovery? Stakeholders can be very concerned about how long the recovery of their database will take. It's important to define the restore point objective with the customer because, again, this makes it easier to translate the customers' expectations into the cost of meeting those expectations. Different technologies perform in different ways and vary widely in price. Generally, the faster you wish your recovery to go, the more expensive the technology ends up being. For example, recoveries directly from disk tend to be a bit more expensive than recoveries from tape, but also tend to be faster. It is important that the customer understand how long recovery of the database will take in the event of a complete outage.

As these discussions ensure, it may become clear that the stakeholders' objectives are not feasible, or that they will require more infrastructure and architecture work than was originally believed to be the case. It may well be that the stakeholders' requirements will lead to a discussion of HA or DR requirements in association with backup and recovery requirements. You should be able to address and articulate all of these possibilities in your planning meetings with the stakeholders.

How Much Can You Spend on Recovery? There is a direct relationship between RPO and RTO and how much it will cost to provide a specific service level. It is important early on to understand just how much the customer is willing to spend on architecture to support your proposed backup and recovery plan. Nothing is more embarrassing than proposing a massive architecture with a high dollar cost and then having the customer look at you and laugh at the projected expense.

Can the System Be Down During the Backup? Another key piece of information to determine is what the state of the database needs to be during the backup. Can an outage be afforded when performing the backups, or do those backups need to be done online? The answer to this question impacts your total overall cost and your decisions in choosing a backup strategy.

How Much Time Will It Take to Get Damaged Hardware Replaced? This is a key consideration. Often it's not the database that fails, but some piece of hardware. Hardware failure can considerably impact the time it takes to get your database running again. You need to make sure the system stakeholders understand the impact of hardware failures and consider architectures that can help protect them from hardware failures, such as Oracle Real Application Clusters.

Growth and Scale Considerations Sure, the development database is only 20GB in size, or the production database is only 40GB in size now, but what about six months from now, a year from now, or five years from now? The solution you craft for a 40GB database with a steady state of growth will be very different from a solution you will craft for a database that is going to grow, very quickly, to terabytes in size, or even larger.

Additionally, external factors can impact your backups, such as increases in concurrent usage of the database. Oftentimes database usage grows over time as new releases of existing applications are rolled out, new functionality is added, or groups of users are added during a long rollout. Therefore, you need to look toward the future, not the now, when planning your backup strategy and infrastructure.

Backup and Recovery: Crafting the Plan

Now that you have gathered your requirements, you can begin to craft your backup and recovery plan. You need to make a number of decisions:

- Based on the user (and business) requirements, do you need to perform offline or online backups of the database?

- If you are going to use online backups, how often do you need to back up archived redo logs? How will you protect the archived redo logs from loss between backup sessions?

- What are the company policies and standards with regard to recoverability?

- How are you going to ensure that your system is recoverable in the event of a disaster?

- Are there any architectural decisions that need to be made?

Each of these questions is important. Disasters need to be planned for because they do happen. Company policies may well supersede the needs of the users. Backup policies and standards are important to implement and enforce. Managing one database backup and recovery policy is easy. Managing many different databases with different methods of doing backup and recovery becomes cumbersome and dangerous.

Managing archived redo logs is important because they are critical to recovery, and you want to be able to support your users as much as you can. After all, the users are the reason you are there! To really determine how to craft your backup strategy, you need to understand how Oracle works and how Oracle backup and recovery works; we will talk about that shortly. First, just to make sure we are all on the same page, let's discuss some basic Oracle terms.

A Few Oracle Terms to Know

It is always a bit hard to decide where to start when discussing the Oracle architecture, because so many of the different components are interrelated. This makes it hard to talk about one without referring to the other. So that we can have a common point of reference for some basic terms, in this section we quickly define those terms. We will be using these terms throughout the rest of this book, so it is really important that you clearly understand them (we also define them in more depth as this chapter progresses). So, if you are a bit hazy on Oracle internal terms, please review the following list until you know without hesitation what they are:

- **Alert log**   A text log file in which the database maintains error and status messages. The alert log can be a critical structure when trying to determine the nature of a database failure. Typically, the alert log is in the background dump destination directory, as defined by the database parameter DIAGNOSTIC_DEST, and is called alert<sid>.log.

- **Archived redo logs**   When the database is in ARCHIVELOG mode, archived redo logs are generated each time Oracle switches online redo logs by the LGWR process. Archived redo logs are used during database recovery. Copies of the archived redo logs can be written to as many as ten different directories, defined by the Oracle parameter LOG_ARCHIVE_DEST_*n* in the database parameter file. Also, Oracle Database 12c allows you to store archived redo logs in a new location called the Fast Recovery Area, which we discuss in more detail in Chapter 5.

- **Backup control file** A backup of the control file generated as the result of using the **alter database backup controlfile to 'file_name'** command or the **alter database backup control file to trace** command.

- **Block** The most atomic unit of storage in Oracle. The default block size is determined by the parameter DB_BLOCK_SIZE in the database parameter file, and it is set permanently when a database is created. Oracle Database 12c allows tablespaces to be different block sizes than the default.

- **Checkpoint** A database event that causes the database to flush dirty (used) blocks from memory and write them to disk.

- **Database** Consists of the different components that make up an Oracle database (tablespaces, redo logs, and so forth). A database is much different from an instance. A database is where the data lives, and it's what you will be backing up and recovering with RMAN.

- **Database consistency** Implies that each object in the database is consistent to the same point in time. This means that the data in the database datafiles is consistent to the same point in time. This also means that the database control files are synchronized with the database datafile headers.

- **Database control file** A database control file stores several kinds of metadata related to the database. This includes information on the database datafiles, archived redo logs, RMAN backups, and other internal database information.

- **Database datafile** A physical entity that is related to a tablespace. A database consists of at least one database datafile (which would be assigned to the SYSTEM tablespace), and most databases consist of many different database datafiles. Whereas a tablespace can have many different database datafiles associated with it, a given database datafile can have only one tablespace associated with it.

- **Database parameter file** Contains instance and database configuration information and comes in two mutually exclusive flavors: init.ora, which is a text file, and spfile.ora, which allows for persistent settings of database parameters via the **alter system** command.

- **Fast Recovery Area (FRA)** An optionally configured area of disk that is used to store various recovery-related files. RMAN backup files, archived redo logs, online redo logs, and control files can be stored in this area. We will cover the FRA in great detail in later chapters of this book. Most examples that you will see in this book assume the configuration and use of the FRA.

- **Granule** A unit of Oracle contiguous memory. All System Global Area (SGA) memory allocations are rounded to the nearest granule units. The size of a granule depends on the overall expected size of the SGA, and it may be 4MB or 16MB. An SGA size of greater than 128MB tends to be the break point when Oracle uses the larger granule sizes. The number of granules allocated to the database is determined at database startup.

- **Instance** The collection of Oracle memory and processes. When the SGA (memory) is allocated and each of the required Oracle processes is up and running successfully, then the Oracle instance is considered started. Note that just because the Oracle instance is running, this does not mean that the database itself is open. An instance is associated with one, and only one, database at any given time.

- **Online redo logs**   When redo is generated, it is physically stored in the online redo logs of the database. Oracle requires that at least two online redo logs be created for a database to operate. These online redo logs can have multiple mirrored copies for protection of the redo. This is known as *multiplexing* the redo log. As an online redo log fills with redo, Oracle switches to the next online redo log, which is known as a *log switch* operation.

  Each online redo log file has a *log sequence number* associated with it that uniquely identifies it and, if it's archived, its associated archived redo log file. You can find the log sequence number of the online redo logs by querying the V$LOG view. The sequence number of a given archived redo log can be found in the V$ARCHIVED_LOG view or the V$LOG_HISTORY view.

  Additionally, an online redo log (and an archived redo log) contains a range of database System Change Numbers (SCNs) that is unique to that redo log. During recovery, Oracle applies the undo in the archived/online redo logs in order of log sequence number.

- **Processes**   The programs that do the actual work of the Oracle database. Oracle Database 12c has five required processes, among others.

- **Redo**   A record of all changes made to a given database. For almost any change in the database, an associated redo record is generated.

- **Schema**   Owns the various logical objects in Oracle, such as tables and indexes, and is synonymous with the user.

- **SGA (System Global Area)**   An area of shared memory that is allocated by Oracle as it is started. Memory in the SGA can be shared by all Oracle processes.

- **System Change Number (SCN)**   A counter that represents the current state of the database at a given time. As with the counter on a VCR, as time progresses, the SCN increases. Each SCN atomically represents a point in the life of the database. Thus, at 11 A.M., the database SCN might be 10ffx0 (4351 decimal), and at 12 P.M., it might be 11f0x0 (4592 decimal).

- **Tablespace**   A physi-logical entity. It is a logical entity because it is the place that Oracle logical objects (such as tables and indexes) are stored. It is a physical entity because it is made up of one or more database datafiles. A database must contain at least one tablespace, the SYSTEM tablespace, but most databases consist of many different tablespaces.

- **Trace files**   Generated by the database in a number of different situations, including process errors. Each database process also generates its own trace file. Trace files can be important when you're trying to resolve the nature of a database failure.

Oracle Database Architecture in the Pre-Multitenant Age

Our tour continues as we begin looking at the physical components of Oracle. First, we take a look at the processes that make up an Oracle database. Then, we look at Oracle memory structures and the different logical, physical, and physi-logical structures that make up an Oracle database. Finally, we discuss the differences between an instance and an Oracle database.

The Oracle Processes

When the **startup nomount** command is issued, Oracle attempts to start an Oracle *instance*. An Oracle instance is started after several required operating system processes (programs) are started and the SGA memory area is allocated. In this section, we are going to look at the processes that get Oracle started. First, we look at the basic Oracle processes required for any Oracle database to be functional. Next, we look at user and server processes. Finally, we look at other, optional Oracle processes that you might see from time to time.

> **NOTE**
> *This is just a basic introduction to the Oracle processes. If you want more in-depth detail on them, please refer to the Oracle documentation.*

Background Oracle Processes

The first kind of processes that run in an Oracle database are the background processes. These are processes that are started when an Oracle Database 12*c* instance has successfully started. The background processes are critical to database functionality because they provide the various tasks required for the database to operate, such as maintenance tasks, writing to database datafiles, writing to the online redo logs, and providing crash recovery services. So, you can see, in the context of backup and recovery, how understanding these processes and how they work might be important.

There can be any number of processes started for a given database (my Oracle 12*c* Database is running some 49 right now). Often, as a place to discuss the various processes in Oracle we start with what might be considered the mandatory background database processes. These are the processes that are automatically started and run for almost any Oracle database. There used to be five processes on this list in the beginning, but now the list has grown to nine processes.

Most of these processes are required by the Oracle database for it to function at all, and the instances will terminate if they fail for any reason. Some processes will be restarted if the database fails. In this section we introduce you to these important Oracle database processes.

PMON   Also known as the Process Monitor process (and one of what some call the "Jamaican processes"), the PMON process monitors the other background processes and is responsible for process recovery for parallel processes (server and dispatcher processes) that might fail. PMON manages the cleanup of the database buffer cache and other resources after user processes are exited normally or terminated abnormally. The database will crash and burn should the PMON process die an unexpected death. Mourning will ensue, and you will need to start the database backup and figure out why PMON failed. Note that while PMON might fail, the remaining database processes might still stay up for some time. However, the database will still not be accessible, and the processes will eventually shut down.

SMON   Also known as the System Monitor process (and the other "Jamaican process"), SMON has a lot of jobs to do, including performing instance recovery, crash recovery, recovery of terminated transactions on read-only or missing tablespaces during recovery, cleaning up unused temporary segments, and managing free extents on dictionary-managed tablespaces. Loss of the SMON process tends to cause all of the processes related to the database to shut down without delay.

LREG   This process is known as the Listener Registration (LREG) process and is new in Oracle Database 12*c* (the tasks LREG is responsible for used to be performed by PMON). This process is responsible for registering information about the database instance with the Oracle listener process(es). If the listener is running, then LREG will communicate the needed information to the listener so that the database will be registered for network connectivity. If the listener is not running, the LREG process will re-poll the listener on a regular basis to determine when it is running. Once the listener can be communicated with, LREG will register the database. If the LREG process is terminated, the entire database instance will be terminated.

DBW (or DBWn, Since There Can Be More Than One of These Processes)   The Database Writer (DBW) process is responsible for writing the contents of the data buffers from the SGA (volatile storage) to the database data files (persistent storage). Once the database blocks have been written to persistent storage, then the dirty blocks in the SGA can be used for other purposes.

Because the writing of database blocks can be I/O intensive, the DBW process does not immediately write the blocks after a transaction is committed. Instead, the persistence mechanism used by the database is the online redo logs, which are written to by the LGWR process. As a result, the version of the database in the database datafiles, and the version that is current to the most recent point in time, are often very different. You need to clearly understand this if you are to understand Oracle Backup and Recovery.

Even more interesting is that DBW can, in certain circumstances, write blocks that are part of uncommitted transactions to the database datafiles. If you think about this, it makes sense because a long-running DML transaction could easily require more SGA memory than is available. Once the dirty SGA blocks start piling up, they have to go somewhere, and it's the DBW process that moves them to disk. You might be asking, "What is it that indicates to Oracle if the database block is valid then?" The answer is in the online redo stream that gets created.

Once the transaction is committed, a commit vector is created in the redo log stream. The commit vector is associated with the specific point in time that the commit was executed. Once the commit is completed, the blocks associated with that transaction will be considered valid blocks. Thus, read consistency is assured. Until the commit vector is issued, Oracle will use the read-consistent mechanism of the database (in the form of the undo records) to reconstruct the blocks for queries that are executed prior to the commit.

This also explains another DBW rule that is little known. That is, before the database can reuse an online redo log, the blocks that were dirtied as a part of any transaction in that redo log have to have been written to the persistent media before a log switch can occur (note that this is different from the more common cause of being unable to write to an archived redo log). If you see waits for log file switches, this might indicate that the DBW process is not writing to the database datafiles quickly enough, thus freeing up an online redo log. For more on the online redo logs, see information on the LGWR process.

When the DBW needs to flush dirty blocks in the SGA to persistent storage, it has some options available to it on how it can do that operation. The DBW process can use a "lazy" checkpoint method, it can use a more prioritized method (with less consideration given to performance), or it can use a panic type of operation where it writes to the datafiles as quickly as it can (this panic mode is used, for example, when you issue the **shutdown abort** command).

Normally DBW will write dirty buffers in a "lazy" manner, such that it will not impact the overall performance of the system. It will continue to try to advance the checkpoint over time to reduce the time that crash recovery might require. The parameter FAST_START_MTTR_TARGET controls the manner in which the DBW process writes to a degree in that it provides a target for the DBW to meet with respect to divergence between the copy of the data in the buffer cache and the data on physical disk.

FAST_START_MTTR_TARGET defaults to a setting of 0, which means that the DBW process tries to reduce the divergence between the data in memory and on disk to a minimum. This might not be the most efficient thing if you are concerned about database performance or the performance of RMAN. As a result, you might want to explore various settings for the parameter. Another consideration to setting this parameter is one of instance recovery. This parameter is designed to balance performance against availability—the lower it's set, the faster your database should come up after a crash. However, the lower it's set, the more likely it is to cause database performance issues. Therefore, it's important to define which is more important: performance or recovery time.

Other tasks include the DBW process handling its checkpoint-related operations (such as updating datafile headers), synchronization of the opening of data files, and logging of blog-written records.

In Oracle Database 12c, there can be up to 100 DBW processes running at any one time (this number varies by Oracle Database version). The number of DBW processes that should be running is configured using the parameter DB_WRITER_PROCESSES. In Oracle Database 12c, the default is either 1 or CPU_COUNT/8, whichever is higher (there are some other outlier conditions that we won't consider here). Usually the default value is more than sufficient.

LGWR   The Log Writer (LGWR) process is responsible for writing generated redo to the database online redo logs from the log buffer. LGWR is signaled to do these writes during a number of different conditions, including the following:

- A user commit is issued.
- An online redo log switch occurs.
- Three seconds have passed since LGWR last wrote redo data.
- The redo log buffer is one-third full or contains 1MB of data.
- DBW must write modified buffers to disk.

As with the DBW process, note that it is very possible for uncommitted data to be written to the online redo logs (and also the archived redo logs). Again, it is the presence of the commit vector that will indicate whether or not that data should eventually be committed.

Note that LGWR writes redo records to the online redo logs. Redo records are much smaller and at a much finer grain with respect to the transaction. Thus, the online redo writes are much quicker in nature than the DBW writes are. For this reason, it is the online redo logs that provide the persistent record of transactional activity that is required to ensure a database recovery. This means that the LGWR process can, at times, be a single point of serialization with respect to overall database operations. This being the case, you can see why it's important that the online redo logs be put on the fastest media possible. This also has implications for restoring databases, which we will discuss in later chapters of this book.

There is a symbiotic relationship between the LGWR and DBW processes. Before the DBW process can write a dirty buffer to disk, the redo data must have been flushed to the online redo logs first. If this has not happened, the DBW process will signal LGWR to flush these buffers, and DBW will wait for LGWR to complete the flush before it will write its blocks to disk. There can be significant performance issues if this kind of situation occurs. We will discuss properly configuring online redo logs in an effort to reduce this kind of contention in later chapters of this book.

The System Change Number (SCN) is also very interconnected between the DBW process, the LGWR process, and the database itself. The SCN figures importantly into backup, restore, and recovery of the Oracle database because it is the means by which all database operations are properly ordered, and thus recovered. We will address the SCN later in this chapter, but we wanted to give you a quick heads-up that it's coming.

Finally, it probably seems obvious, but if the LGWR process fails then the database will crash as well. That's what we call a bad day in the Oracle world. A really bad day.

CKPT   During a checkpoint operation, the CKPT process will update datafile headers and the control file with checkpoint information. The CKPT process also notifies DBW of the checkpoint, signaling that DBW should start writing blocks to disk. Note, though, that the CKPT process does not actually write any database data blocks or redo records.

In earlier versions of Oracle the job of the CKPT process was allocated to the DBWR process, and the CKPT process was optional. In those days if the CKPT process died, the database would survive without it. In Oracle Database 12c, if the CKPT process dies, then the rest of the database will die as well.

RECO   The Recoverer (RECO) process comes into play if your database is involved in any kind of distributed transactions. RECO is responsible for resolving in-doubt distributed transactions. If the RECO process should fail, it will usually not result in the entire database shutting itself down. The RECO process will usually restart itself if it crashes or is killed inadvertently. (No one kills RECO on purpose, surely!)

MMON   The Manageability Monitor (MMON) process is responsible for managing tasks related to the Active Workload Repository (AWR) of the Oracle Database. This includes such things as taking snapshots and monitoring various database-related thresholds. It has a first cousin (who has been known to get out of hand at times) called the MMNL process, which maintains Active Session History (ASH)–related Oracle data. The death of the MML process is not a harbinger of the death of the database. In fact, the process will usually restart if it crashes (or is killed).

MMNL   As just stated, the first cousin to the MML process, the Manageability Monitor Lite (MMNL) process, maintains Active Session History (ASH)–related Oracle data. Items such as the capture of session history information and the metrics computation of that information are done by the MMNL process. MMNL is a process that can die or be killed but will not cause the database to crash; in fact, the process will restart should it be killed or crash for some reason.

Other Optional Oracle Processes

A number of other Oracle processes may also be launched when the Oracle instance is started (and in some cases, optional processes may actually be started much later on demand), depending on the configuration of the Oracle database parameter file. Most of these processes have little bearing on RMAN and database backup and recovery (unless the failure of one of the processes causes the database to crash, which is rare), and there are a large number of them. As a result, we won't spend much time on them. All of the optional processes are described in the Oracle documentation, online at docs.oracle.com, as well as in several Oracle Press books. Perhaps the best description of them is in Appendix F of the Oracle Database Reference manual.

One set of optional processes that does have some bearing on RMAN and backup and recovery are the ARCH*n* processes. These processes (one or many of them) are critical to the backup and recovery process if you are doing online backups. See the section titled "ARCHIVELOG Mode vs. NOARCHIVELOG Mode," later in the chapter, for more on the ARCH*n* process(es).

There may be other processes to contend with. For example, if you are restoring a database to an ASM managed disk group, it's possible that the ASM rebalance process might kick in and start rebalancing your ASM disk group. This could cause performance problems that you might want to address. We will discuss performance considerations like this throughout the book.

The User and Server Processes

When a user connects to the database, a user process is spawned (or a new thread is started on Windows NT) that connects to a separately spawned server process. These processes communicate with each other using various protocols, such as Bequeath or TCP/IP. Note that these processes all have their own memory area called the PGA. The PGA typically is fairly small for a given process, but it can also grow quite large. SQL statements that include operations such as **order by** and **group by** may well use a lot of PGA. Therefore, when considering how much memory your database server has, you need to include the fixed components (for example, the SGA, which we will consider to be a fixed memory area for the sake of this discussion) and also the variable components (the PGA).

We often find that SGA memory tends to be overallocated on a given database server. Often, when we put a database into production we don't know how much memory it's really going to need, so we throw a lot of memory at the instance, with the rationale that we will come back later and justify that instance's memory allocations later. Unfortunately, later never comes. Then, more databases get added and memory becomes a scarce commodity. Therefore, carefully manage memory because it can impact RMAN performance over time.

Finally, with respect to processes, RMAN backup and recovery operations can be done in parallel, using more than one process. We often find that RMAN backup operations are based on using a single processor. Often this is a great waste of resources when a database server has lots of memory and available CPU as well as the network and/or I/O bandwidth to handle the additional load. Particularly with RAC configurations, we rarely see anyone taking advantage of more than one node in a cluster to facilitate backup operations. We will discuss these issues further throughout this book.

Oracle Database 12*c*—Processes or Threads

We have mentioned Oracle processes, which are essentially individual programs that run independently of each other. They communicate with each other, this is true; however, they are all in their own unique run space, memory space (excepting shared memory access, of course), and so on.

In an effort to gain additional performance benefits, Oracle Database 12*c* now offers a multithreaded option to the database. Some operating systems such as Windows already run Oracle using multithreading. Others, such as various versions of Unix, run each Oracle process as just that, an OS process on the system. Thus, the common processes we talk about, DBWR, LGWR, and so on, are individual programs assigned a process ID running in their own space.

By default, operating systems that ran Oracle using a process model in previous releases will see no change in how the processes run. They will use the process model by default. To use the multithreaded model, set the THREADED_EXECUTION to TRUE. This parameter is not a dynamic parameter, so you must adjust the value in the SPFILE first and then restart the database.

When you restart the database, you will see that the number of processes now running is significantly less. (In our case, we went from some 50 processes down to 7.) When running in the multithreaded Oracle model, the DBW, PMON, PSP, U*n*, and VKTM background processes will run as operating system processes. We have described a couple of these processes already. Here are the ones we have not:

- **PSP**   This is the Process Spawner Process (PSP). PSP is responsible for spawning Oracle background processes after the instance has started.

- **U*n***   These processes (two of them on the databases we are using, called u001 and u002) are the ones used to spawn various threads for other Oracle background processes such as MMAN, LGWR, and CKPT. These processes might have different numbers to them based on when they are spawned.

- **VKTM**   This is the Virtual Keeper of Time (VKTM) process. This process provides time measurement management for the database.

Note that the use of the Oracle multithreaded model does not change anything in how RMAN works. However, if you have scripts that use OS authentication to log into any database that is using the multithreaded model (that is, using "/"), you will need to revise these scripts because OS authentication is not allowed when using the Oracle multithreaded mode.

Oracle Memory and RMAN

In this section, we look at the memory areas we need to be concerned with in relationship to RMAN. As with any process, RMAN does require memory for its own operations and as a part of its database interactions. First, we describe the Oracle SGA in more detail, and then we look at the Program Global Area (PGA).

The Oracle System Global Area

The principal memory structure we are concerned with in terms of RMAN and backup and recovery is the System Global Area (SGA). The SGA consists of one large allocation of shared memory that can be broken down into several memory substructures:

- The database buffer cache
- The shared pool
- The redo log buffer
- The large pool
- The Java pool
- The Streams pool

A number of different memory models are available for use by an Oracle database instance. Which model is used depends on various constraints (for example, HugePages used in Linux disallows the use of Automatic Memory Management). Here are the different memory models available within Oracle:

- Force Full Database Caching Mode
- Automatic Memory Management (AMM)
- Automatic Shared Memory Management (ASMM)
- Manual Shared Memory Management

- PGA Automatic Memory Management
- PGA Manual Memory Management

It's really beyond the scope of this book to compare and contrast the benefits of these models. RMAN typically will use these memory areas in the same way.

Typically, RMAN uses a relatively small part of the SGA for its overall operations. RMAN also uses the shared pool quite a bit since RMAN uses several Oracle PL/SQL packages as it goes through its paces. These packages are like any other Oracle PL/SQL packages in that they must be loaded into the shared pool. If the shared pool is not large enough, or if it becomes fragmented, it is possible that the RMAN packages will not be able to execute. Therefore, it is important to allocate enough memory to the shared pool for RMAN operations.

During backup operations, RMAN will allocate memory buffers and move the data from the database datafiles on disk to that memory area. The data is then moved to the backup storage medium. When restores are occurring, memory is again allocated to support the transfer of restored data from the restore media and then to the location where that data needs to be restored to.

Typically these memory buffers are allocated from the Program Global Area (PGA) that is assigned to the various RMAN backup or restore processes. The exception to this is when the operating system that RMAN operations are occurring on does not have asynchronous I/O facilities. In these cases, for best performance, you can use a feature of RMAN called I/O slaves. When I/O slaves are in use, RMAN will use the large pool to allocate backup buffer memory if the large pool is allocated. If the large pool is not allocated, then memory from the SGA proper will be allocated for the memory buffers. Most systems that are supported today offer asynchronous I/O, and as a result the use of I/O slaves is rare. If you are configuring I/O slaves, you might want to make sure that you really need to be using this feature. It might well be causing performance issues if your OS supports asynchronous I/O operations, and you could be allocating memory to the large pool that you will never use.

Defining SGA Memory Allocations and Choosing Memory Models

The individual sizes of the SGA components are allocated based on the settings of parameters in the database parameter file. Depending on the version of the database you are using, these parameters include MEMORY_MAX_SIZE, MEMORY_TARGET, SGA_MAX_SIZE, SGA_TARGET, SHARED_POOL_SIZE, DB_CACHE_SIZE, DB_*n*K_CACHE_SIZE, LOG_BUFFER, LARGE_POOL_SIZE, and JAVA_POOL_SIZE (and several others). Each of these is defined in the Oracle documentation, so refer to it if you need more information on them. We will also address these various parameters throughout this book when required.

Other Kinds of Memory to Be Aware Of

Although we talk about the SGA and the PGA a lot, there are other kinds of memory we might well run into. Probably the most typical of these are various kinds of memory caching systems. Very often disks are fronted by large amounts of cache memory. Keep in mind that backup procedures can flush cache memory and end up removing hot blocks. This is a good argument for an incremental backup strategy because it will reduce the amount of memory required overall by the backup process.

This is one nice thing about Oracle's Exadata product. Its Smart Flash Cache features eliminate the problem of flooding the cache with blocks that do not need to be cached. Thus, backup operations will never age out data from the cache as the result of a backup.

Our Take on Change, Best Practices, and Standards

We find change just for the sake of change itself, without any real empirical evidence to support making that change, to be a really bad idea. Way too many people get swept up in this feature or that feature. Often they rush to implement something with a promise of better performance or cheaper operating costs. Sometimes it works. Sometimes it's a disaster.

In this same light, we always are very careful about best practices or silver bullets that some people might espouse. Treat such things with caution. Remember, everyone has an opinion. However, this is your system, and it is unique. As such, no one can possibly outline best practices that cover every possible situation. Remember that best practices are really just guidelines. They are worth paying attention to, but they don't replace actual thought and application of your real-world situation when you develop operating policies and standards.

The bottom line is that if you have a stable environment, you need to be very cautious about any change. Stand your ground, and if someone suggests a change, make them clearly and convincingly quantify the expected return and justify that in the face of the risk any change has on a production system. What does this have to do with RMAN and backup and recovery? Everything. The best backup and recovery plan is the one that you never ever have to use to recover because your architecture is well designed and wisely managed.

To recap quickly, we have discussed the makings of an Oracle instance over the last several pages. We have talked about the different Oracle processes and the different Oracle memory structures. When the processes and the memory all come together, an Oracle instance is formed. Now that we have an instance, we are ready for a database. In the next section, we discuss the various structures that make up an Oracle database.

The Oracle Database

On our tour, we now turn our attention to the Oracle database architecture itself. An Oracle database is made up of a number of different structures—some physical, some logical, and some physi-logical. In this section, we look at each of these types of structures and discuss each of the individual components of the Oracle database. We will conclude this section by looking at the Fast Recovery Area (FRA) and Automatic Storage Management (ASM).

Oracle Physical Components   The Oracle database physical architecture includes the following components:

- Database datafiles
- Online redo logs
- Archived redo logs
- Database control files
- Oracle tablespaces
- Flashback logs (optional)

Each of these items is physically located on a storage device that is connected to your computer. These objects make up the physical existence of your Oracle database, and to recover your database, you may need to restore and recover one or more of these objects from a backup (except the flashback log). Let's look at each of these objects in a bit more detail.

Database Datafiles   The database datafiles are the data storage medium of the database and are related to tablespaces, as you will see shortly. When information is stored in the database, it ultimately gets stored in these physical files. Each database datafile contains a *datafile header* that contains information to help track the current state of that datafile. This datafile header is updated during checkpoint operations to reflect the current state of the datafile. As you might have suspected, database datafiles contain database data as well as temporary data and undo data.

Database datafiles can have a number of different statuses assigned to them. The primary statuses we are interested in are ONLINE, which is the normal status, and OFFLINE, which is generally an abnormal status. A database datafile might take on the RECOVER status as well, indicating that there is a problem with the datafile and that recovery is required.

If the database is in ARCHIVELOG mode (more on this later), you can take a datafile offline, which may be required for certain recovery operations. If the database is in NOARCHIVELOG mode, you can only take the database datafile offline by dropping it. Offline dropping of a datafile can have some nasty effects on your database (such as loss of data), so drop datafiles with care.

Online Redo Logs   If the Oracle SCN can be likened to the counter on a VCR, then the redo logs can be likened to the videotape. (This analogy becomes harder and harder as DVRs replace VCRs!) The online redo logs are responsible for recording every single atomic change that occurs in the database. Each Oracle database must have a minimum of two different online redo log groups, and most databases generally have many more than that for performance and data preservation reasons.

Each online redo log group can have multiple members located on different disk drives for protection purposes. Oracle writes to the different members in parallel, making the write process more efficient. Oracle writes to one redo log group at a time, in round-robin fashion. When the group has been filled, the LGWR process closes those redo logs and then opens the next online redo log for processing.

Within redo logs are records called *change vectors*. Each change vector represents an atomic database change, in SCN order. During recovery (RMAN or manual), Oracle applies those change vectors to the database. This has the effect of applying all change records to the database in order, thus recovering it to the point in time of the failure (or another, earlier time if required). The LGWR process is responsible for writing the change vectors (cumulatively known as redo) to the online redo logs from the redo log buffer. We discuss this in more detail shortly in the section, "The Combined Picture."

Archived Redo Logs   A *log switch* occurs when Oracle stops writing to one online redo log and begins to write to another. As the result of a log switch, if the database is in ARCHIVELOG mode and the ARCH process is running, a copy of the online redo log will be made. This copy of the online redo log is called an archived redo log. Oracle can actually copy the archived redo log files to up to ten different destinations. During media recovery, the archived redo logs are applied to the database to recover it. We discuss this in more detail in "The Combined Picture."

Database Control Files   Each Oracle database has one or more database control files. The control file contains various database information, such as the current SCN, the state of the database datafiles, and the status of the database. Of interest to the RMAN DBA is the fact that the control file also stores critical information on various RMAN operations, such as the backup status of each database datafile. If you lose your control file, you will need to follow specific procedures to re-create the RMAN catalog within it. Also of interest might be the fact that the checkpoint SCN (or the SCN of the last update of a given datafile) is stored in the control file. Oracle will cross-check this checkpoint SCN with the checkpoint SCNs stored in the datafile headers. If they all match, the database requires no recovery whatsoever. If the SCNs do not match, then some form of recovery will be required. Typically this will be crash recovery, which is automated. Sometimes, for example if a data file is missing, media recovery will be required.

Oracle Tablespaces   Our tour continues into a somewhat metaphysical part of Oracle. Tablespaces link the physical world of Oracle (in the form of database datafiles) to the logical world of the tablespace. Often, we refer to a tablespace as a physi-logical structure. Oracle stores objects within tablespaces, such as tables and indexes.

A tablespace is physically made up of one or more Oracle database datafiles. Therefore, the overall space allocation available in a tablespace depends on the overall allocated size of these database datafiles. There are different kinds of tablespaces. These include normal data tablespaces, bigfile tablespaces, temporary tablespaces (these use tempfiles rather than normal datafiles), and undo tablespaces.

Normal, undo, and temporary tablespaces have a one-to-many relationship with the database datafiles or tempfiles. If you create a bigfile tablespace, then there will be only one datafile. The benefit of using a bigfile tablespace is that these tablespaces can get quite a bit larger than non-bigfile tablespaces, and as a result they can store more data and take advantage of large file systems.

The bad thing about a bigfile tablespace is that it is a single, large datafile. This was a problem when bigfile tablespaces first came out, but this problem has since been addressed by RMAN through the use of the **section-size** parameter of the **backup** command. So, now you can parallelize the backup of a bigfile tablespace during your backups.

A tablespace can have a number of different statuses. It can be OFFLINE or ONLINE, and may also be in either READ WRITE or READ ONLY mode. If a tablespace is in READ ONLY mode, the contents of the tablespace will not change. Because the contents of a READ ONLY tablespace do not change, DBAs often only back up READ ONLY tablespace database datafiles once, immediately after they are made read-only. Of course, if the tablespace is ever taken out of READ ONLY mode, you need to start backing up the tablespace again.

Flashback Logs   Oracle Database 10g introduced the capability to flash back the Oracle database to a time other than the current time. This capability is facilitated through the use of flashback logs. Flashback logs are stored in the FRA. Oracle is solely responsible for the management of flashback logs, so it will create, remove, and resize them as required. Also note that flashback logs are not archived by Oracle and are not needed for recovery. RMAN supports flashback recovery.

The Fast Recovery Area

Oracle Database 10g introduced the concept of the FRA (originally called the Flash Recovery Area and later renamed the Fast Recovery Area). The FRA defines a central area of disk space for recovery-related files such as RMAN backups and archived redo logs. The Fast Recovery Area should not be confused with Oracle's Flashback Database features, though the FRA does participate in Flashback Database operations. The FRA does more than just support Flashback Database operations, though. The following structures can be stored in the FRA:

- Archived redo logs
- RMAN backup set pieces

- RMAN datafile copies
- Flashback logs
- A copy of the database control file
- One member of each redo log group
- Control file autobackups and copies

We will discuss the FRA in much more detail throughout this book.

Oracle Automatic Storage Management

Oracle ASM is Oracle's answer to the need for an integrated system to manage database files. ASM supports a number of different file system types, from cooked disk drives, to raw disk drives, to NetFiler devices. The idea of ASM is to simplify the life of the DBA by making Oracle responsible for basic disk management operations such as load balancing and data protection. RMAN supports the ASM infrastructure in that you can place your database FRA on ASM disks, or you can back up directly to ASM disks.

ASM has really found its place in the Oracle world, and we are finding it being put to use more and more. At one time, we felt that ASM might be overkill, but now we feel that ASM is an integral part of any stable Oracle database configuration. Even if you are just using one database, the features of ASM are significant enough to consider using.

Starting in Oracle Database 12*c*R2, ASM became integrated into Oracle Clusterware rather than being a separately installable component. However, you can install Oracle Clusterware and ASM without a license, so you can use ASM with the normal Oracle Database license. It is well beyond the scope of this book to get into the specifics of installing and configuring ASM.

NOTE
ASM is a major part of an overall tiered RMAN backup strategy. We discuss RMAN backup strategies in Chapter 13.

More About the Oracle Redo Logs

We have talked about the Oracle redo logs somewhat already, but they are such important things, even when talking about RMAN, that we wanted to dive into a bit more detail. You might ask, "But doesn't RMAN take care of everything for me?" RMAN certainly tries to take care of everything for you, but you will find times when it's your knowledge that gives you the insight to truly save the day. Indeed, just having a recipe to follow might well not be enough. You need to understand the whys and mechanics behind Oracle Backup and Recovery. As Carl Jung said, "The shoe that fits one person pinches another; there is no recipe for living that suits all cases." Just knowing the rudiments of backup and recovery does not prepare you for all potential problems you will face.

Redo logs are typically created when the database is first created, and as the database changes, you may find that you need to modify the online redo log files by creating more of them, making them larger, or perhaps renaming them. Because you are an enlightened DBA and want to know everything you can about the backup and recovery of your database, you will want to understand online and archived redo logs. In this section, we talk about redo logs in a bit more detail. First, we look at redo logs in general. Next, we look at the multiplexing of online redo log groups and the redo log sequence number. Finally, we address administration of online redo logs.

An Overview of Redo Logs

Oracle redo logs come in two flavors:

- Online redo logs
- Archived redo logs

Redo logs are one of the most critical components when restoring and recovering an Oracle database. This is because redo logs store a history of almost everything that happens in your database. During normal database operations, the Oracle LGWR process will write to an online redo log, creating a change record that you really hope you never have to use.

The LGWR process will write information called "redo" to the online redo log files as the redo is generated by Oracle transactions. *Redo* is simply a record of what occurs in the database and the order in which those events happen. Redo is generated by almost every Oracle operation, including DML, DDL, and transactional commit operations. During recovery, Oracle will read the redo and essentially replay the redo in the order it was generated to recover the database. Sometimes this recovery is behind the scenes and requires no DBA activity (as with crash recovery), but sometimes, such as in the case of database or datafile recovery, the DBA has to get involved.

Online redo log files are fixed in size. Once the LGWR process has reached the end of a given online redo log file, it will close that file and try to find another online redo log file to write to. This process is called a *log switch*. A log switch is a serial process, and is potentially very expensive from a performance point of view. This isn't a performance book, though, so we won't go into the performance aspects of a log switch.

During a log switch, LGWR will look for an available online redo log file that it can write to. If it finds an available online redo log file, it will open that file and begin to write to it. If LGWR cannot find an available file, it will wait for an online redo log to become available. While it's waiting, LGWR will be busy writing complaining messages to the alert log and other places, and database operations will be suspended. Database managers typically are not too happy if the databases stop, so we want to avoid that if at all possible!

Each online redo log file that is created is assigned to an *online redo log group*. In a nonclustered configuration, Oracle will only write to one redo log group at a time. If you are running Real Application Clusters (RAC), each RAC instance will write to its own set of redo log groups.

Online redo log groups can have one of several different statuses:

- **Current**   This is the online redo log that is in use.
- **Active**   This is an online redo log that is not in the current redo log file group, but it's still waiting for the ARCH process to finish copying redo to the archived redo logs.
- **Inactive**   This is an online redo log that isn't active and has been archived.
- **Unused**   This is an online redo log that has yet to be used by the Oracle database.

The status of an online redo log group can be seen by querying the V$LOG view, as seen here:

```
SQL> select group#, status from v$Log;
    GROUP# STATUS
---------- ----------------
         1 INACTIVE
         2 INACTIVE
         3 INACTIVE
         4 CURRENT
```

Multiplexing Online Redo Logs

If you want to have a really bad day, then just try losing your active online redo log. If you do, it's pretty likely that your database is about to come crashing down and that you will have experienced some data loss. This is because recovery to the point of failure in an Oracle database is dependent on the availability of the online redo log. As you can see, the online redo log makes the database vulnerable to loss of a disk device, mistaken administrative delete commands, and other kinds of errors. To address this concern, you can create mirrors of each online redo log. When you have created more than one copy of an online redo log, the group that log is a member of is called a *multiplexed online redo log group*. Typically these multiplexed copies are put on different physical devices to provide additional protection for the online redo log groups. For highest availability, we recommend that you separate the members of each online redo log group onto different disk devices, different everything. Here is an example of creating a multiplexed online redo log group:

```
alter database add logfile group 4
('C:\ORACLE\ORADATA\BETA1\REDO04a.LOG','C:\ORACLE\ORADATA\BETA1\REDO04b.LOG')
size 100m reuse;
```

Each member of a multiplexed online redo log group is written to in parallel, and having multiple members in each group rarely causes performance problems.

The Log Sequence Number

As each online redo log group is written to, that group is assigned a number. This is the *log sequence number*. The first log sequence number for a new database is always 1. As the online redo log groups are written to, the number will increment by one during each log switch operation. So, the next online redo log being written to will be log sequence 2, and so on.

During normal database operations, Oracle will open an available online redo log, write redo to it, and then close it once it has filled the online redo log. Once the online redo log has filled, the LGWR process switches to another online redo log group. At that time, if the database is in ARCHIVELOG mode, LGWR also signals ARCH to wake up and start working. This round-robin style of writing to online redo logs is shown in Figure 2-1.

ARCH responds to the call from LGWR by making copies of the online redo log in the locations defined by the Oracle database parameter LOG_ARCHIVE_DEST_*n* and/or to the defined FRA. Until the ARCH process has successfully completed the creation of at least one archived redo log, the related online redo log file cannot be reused by Oracle. Depending on your system configuration, more than one archived redo log may need to be created before the associated online redo log can be reused. As archived redo logs are created, they maintain the log sequence number assigned to the parent online redo log. That log sequence number will remain unique for that database until the database is opened using the **resetlogs** operation. Once a **resetlogs** operation is executed, the log sequence number is reset to 1.

Another note about opening the database using the **resetlogs** command when performing recovery: If you are using Oracle Database 10g and later Oracle provides the ability to restore the database using a backup taken before the point in time that you issued the **resetlogs** command, when you issue the **resetlogs** command, Oracle will archive any remaining unarchived online redo logs before the online redo logs are reset. This provides the ability to restore the database from a backup taken before the issuance of the **resetlogs** command. Using these backup files, and all the archived redo logs, you can now restore beyond the point of the **resetlogs** command. The ability to restore past the point of the **resetlogs** command relieves the DBA from the urgency of performing a backup after a **resetlogs**-based recovery (though such a backup is still important).

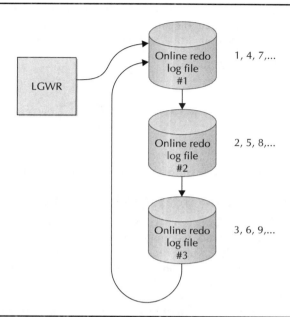

FIGURE 2-1.   *Writing to online redo logs*

This also provides for reduced mean-time-to-recover because you can open the database to users after the restore, rather than having a requirement to back up the database first.

Finally, you should be aware that when the database opens with the **resetlogs** command, the archivelog sequence numbers will be reset. The SCN of the database is not reset, however. This can have impacts on future recoveries by SCN or log sequence number.

Management of Online Redo Logs

The **alter database** command is used to add or remove online redo logs. In this example, we are adding a new online redo log group to the database. The new logfile group will be group 4, and we define its size as 100m:

```
alter database add logfile group 4
'C:\ORACLE\ORADATA\BETA1\REDO04.LOG' size 100m;
```

You can see the resulting logfile group in the V$LOG and V$LOGFILE views:

```
SQL> select group#, sequence#, bytes, members from v$log
  2  where group#=4;
   GROUP#  SEQUENCE#       BYTES    MEMBERS
---------- ---------- ---------- ----------
        4          0 104,857,600          1
SQL> select group#, member from v$logfile
  2  where group#=4;
   GROUP# MEMBER
---------- -------------------------------------------------------------
        4 C:\ORACLE\ORADATA\BETA1\REDO04.LOG
```

In this next example, we remove redo logfile group 4 from the database. Note that this does not physically remove the physical files. You will still have to perform this function after removing the logfile group. This can be dangerous, so be careful when doing so:

```
alter database drop logfile group 4;
```

NOTE
*If you are using the FRA or have set the DB_CREATE_ONLINE_LOG_*
DEST_n parameter, Oracle will remove online redo logs for you after
you drop them.

To resize a logfile group, you will need to drop and then re-create it with the bigger file size.

ARCHIVELOG Mode vs. NOARCHIVELOG Mode

An Oracle database can run in one of two modes. By default, the database is created in NOARCHIVELOG mode. This mode permits normal database operations, but does not provide the capability to perform point-in-time recovery operations or online backups. If you want to do online (or hot) backups, then run the database in ARCHIVELOG mode. In ARCHIVELOG mode, the database makes copies of all online redo logs via the ARCH process to one or more archive log destination directories.

The use of ARCHIVELOG mode requires some configuration of the database beyond simply putting it in ARCHIVELOG mode. You must also configure the ARCH process and prepare the archived redo log destination directories. Note that once an Oracle database is in ARCHIVELOG mode, that database activity will be suspended once all available online redo logs have been used. The database will remain suspended until those online redo logs have been archived. Thus, incorrect configuration of the database when it is in ARCHIVELOG mode can eventually lead to the database suspending operations because it cannot archive the current online redo logs. This might sound menacing, but really it just boils down to a few basic things:

- Configure your database properly (we cover configuration of your database for backup and recovery in this book quite well).

- Make sure you have enough space available.

- Make sure that things are working as you expect them to. For example, if you define a Fast Recovery Area (FRA) in your ARCHIVELOG mode database, make sure the archived redo logs are being successfully written to that directory.

More coverage on the implications of ARCHIVELOG mode, how to implement it (and disable it), and the configuration for ARCHIVELOG operations can be found in Chapter 5.

Oracle Logical Structures

There are several different logical structures within Oracle. These structures include tables, indexes, views, clusters, user-defined objects, and other objects within the database. Schemas own these objects, and if storage is required for the objects, that storage is allocated from a tablespace.

It is the ultimate goal of an Oracle backup and recovery strategy to be able to recover these logical structures to a given point in time. Also, it is important to recover the data in these different objects in such a way that the state of the data is consistent to a given point in time. Consider the impact, for example, if you were to recover a table as it looked at 10 A.M., but only recover its associated index as it looked at 9 A.M. The impact of such an inconsistent recovery could be awful. It is this idea of a consistent recovery that really drives Oracle's backup and recovery mechanism, and RMAN fits nicely into this backup and recovery architectural framework.

The Combined Picture

Now that we have introduced you to the various components of the Oracle database, let's quickly put together a couple of narratives that demonstrate how they all work together. First, we look at the overall database startup process, which is followed by a narrative of the basic operational use of the database.

Startup and Shutdown of the Database

Our DBA, Eliza, has just finished some work on the database, and it's time to restart it. She starts SQL*Plus and connects as SYS using the SYSDBA account. At the SQL prompt, Eliza issues the **startup** command to open the database. The following shows an example of the results of this command:

```
SQL> startup
ORACLE instance started.
Total System Global Area     84700976 bytes
Fixed Size                     282416 bytes
Variable Size                71303168 bytes
Database Buffers             12582912 bytes
Redo Buffers                   532480 bytes
Database mounted.
Database opened.
```

Recall the different phases that occur after the **startup** command is issued: instance startup, database mount, and then database open. Let's look at each of these stages now in a bit more detail.

Instance Startup (startup nomount)

The first thing that occurs when starting the database is instance startup. It is here that Oracle parses the database parameter file and makes sure that the instance is not already running by trying to acquire an instance lock. Then, the various database processes (as described in "The Oracle Processes," earlier in this chapter), such as DBWn and LGWR, are started. Also, Oracle allocates memory needed for the SGA. Once the instance has been started, Oracle reports to the user who has started it that the instance has been started back and how much memory has been allocated to the SGA.

Had Eliza issued the command **startup nomount**, then Oracle would have stopped the database startup process after the instance was started. She might have started the instance in order to perform certain types of recovery, such as control file re-creation.

Mounting the Database (startup mount)

The next stage in the startup process is the mount stage. As Oracle passes through the mount stage, it opens the database control file. Having done that successfully, Oracle extracts the database datafile names from the control file in preparation for opening them. Note that Oracle does not actually check for the existence of the datafiles at this point, but only identifies their location from the control file. Having completed this step, Oracle reports back that it has mounted the database.

At this point, had Eliza issued the command **startup mount**, Oracle would have stopped opening the database and waited for further direction. When the Oracle instance is started and the database is mounted but not open, certain types of recovery operations may be performed, including renaming the location of database datafiles and recovery system tablespace datafiles.

Opening the Database

Eliza issued the **startup** command, however, so Oracle moves on and tries to open the database. During this stage, Oracle verifies the presence of the database datafiles and opens them. As it opens them, it checks the datafile headers and compares the SCN information contained in those headers with the SCN stored in the control files. Let's talk about these SCNs for a second.

SCNs are Oracle's method of tracking the state of the database. As changes occur in the database, they are associated with a given SCN. As these changes are flushed to the database datafiles (which occurs during a *checkpoint* operation), the headers of the datafiles are updated with the current SCN. The current SCN is also recorded in the database control file.

When Oracle tries to open a database, it checks the SCNs in each datafile and in the database control file. If the SCNs are the same and the bitmapped flags are set correctly, then the database is considered to be consistent, and the database is opened for use.

NOTE
Think of SCNs as being like the counter on a VCR. As time goes on, the counter continues to increment, indicating a temporal point in time where the tape currently is. So, if you want to watch a program on the tape, you can simply rewind (or fast forward) the tape to the counter number, and there is the beginning of the program. SCNs are the same way. When Oracle needs to recover a database, it "rewinds" to the SCN it needs to start with and then replays all of the transactions after that SCN until the database is recovered.

If the SCNs are different, then Oracle automatically performs *crash or instance recovery,* if possible. Crash or instance recovery occurs if the redo needed to generate a consistent image is in the online redo log files. If crash or instance recovery is not possible because of a corrupted datafile or because the redo required to recover is not in the online redo logs, then Oracle requests that the DBA perform *media recovery.* Media recovery involves recovering one or more database datafiles from a backup taken of the database and is a manual process, unlike instance recovery. Assisting in media recovery is where RMAN comes in, as you will see in later chapters. Once the database open process is completed successfully (with no recovery, crash recovery, or media recovery), then the database is open for business.

Shutting Down the Database

Of course, Eliza will probably want to shut down the database at some point in time. To do so, she could issue the **shutdown** command. This command closes the database, unmounts it, and then shuts down the instance in almost the reverse order as the startup process already discussed. There are several options to the **shutdown** command.

Note in particular that a **shutdown abort** of a database is basically like simulating a database crash. This command is used often, and it rarely causes problems. Oracle generally recommends that your database be shut down in a consistent manner, if at all possible.

If you must use the **shutdown abort** command to shut down the database (and in the real world, this does happen frequently because of outage constraints), then you should reopen the database with the **startup** command (or even better, **startup restrict**). Following this, do the final shutdown on the database using the **shutdown immediate** command before performing any offline backup operations. Note that even this method may result in delays shutting down the database because of the time it takes to roll back transactions during the shutdown process.

> **NOTE**
> As long as your backup and recovery strategy is correct, it really doesn't matter whether the database is in a consistent state (as with a normal **shutdown**) or an inconsistent state (as with a **shutdown abort**) when an offline backup occurs. Oracle does recommend that you do cold backups with the database in a consistent state, and we recommend that, too (because the online redo logs will not be getting backed up by RMAN). Finally, note that online backups eliminate this issue completely!

More Oracle Database Internals

In this section, we are going to follow some users performing different transactions in an Oracle database. First, we provide you with a graphical roadmap that puts together all the processes, memory structures, and other components of the database for you. Then, we follow a user as the user makes changes to the database. We then look at commits and how they operate. Finally, we look at database checkpoints and how they work.

Process and Database Relationships

We have discussed a number of different processes, memory structures, and other objects that make up the Oracle database. We have also discussed the use of multithreaded Oracle. Figure 2-2 provides a graphic of the Oracle database processes that might help you better understand the interrelationships between the different components in Oracle. Even in multithreaded mode, these processes exist, but just as a thread as opposed to individual processes.

Changing Data in the Database

Now, assume the database is open. Let's say that Fred needs to add a new record to the DEPT table for the janitorial department. So, Fred might issue a SQL statement like this:

```
INSERT INTO DEPT VALUES (60, 'JANITOR','DALLAS');
```

The **insert** statements (as well as **update** and **delete** commands) are collectively known as Data Manipulation Language (DML). As a statement is executed, redo is generated and stored in the redo log buffer in the Oracle SGA. Note that redo is generated by this command, regardless of the presence of the **commit** command. The **delete** and **update** commands work generally the same way with respect to redo generation.

One of the results of DML is that undo is generated and stored in *rollback segments*. Undo consists of instructions that allow Oracle to undo (or roll back) the statement being executed. Using undo, Oracle can roll back the database changes and provide *read consistent images* (also known as read consistency) to other users. Let's look a bit more at the **commit** command and read consistency.

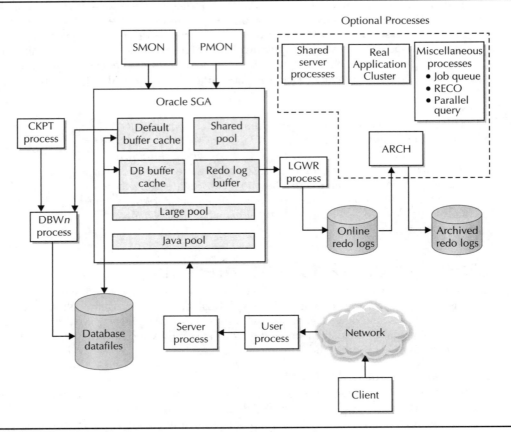

FIGURE 2-2. *Architecture of a typical Oracle database*

Committing the Change

Having issued the **insert** command, Fred wants to ensure that this change is committed to the database, so he issues the **commit** command:

```
COMMIT;
```

The effects of issuing the **commit** command include the following:

- The change becomes visible to all users who query the table at a point in time after the commit occurs. If Eliza queries the DEPT table after the commit occurs, then she will see department 60. However, if Eliza had already started a query before the commit, then this query would not see the changes to the table.

- The change is recoverable if the database is in NOARCHIVELOG mode and if crash or instance recovery is required.

- ■ The change is recoverable if the database is in ARCHIVELOG mode (assuming a valid backup and recovery strategy) and media recovery is required, and if all archived and online redo logs are available.

The **commit** command causes the Oracle LGWR process to flush the online redo log buffer to the online redo logs. Uncommitted redo is flushed to the online redo logs regardless of a commit (in fact, uncommitted changes can be written to the datafiles, too). When a **commit** is issued, Oracle writes a *commit vector* to the redo log buffer, and the buffer is flushed to disk before the commit returns. It is this commit vector, and the fact that the commit issued by Fred's session will not return until his redo has been flushed to the online redo logs successfully, that will ensure that Fred's changes will be recoverable.

The commit Command and Read Consistency   Did you notice that Eliza was not able to see Fred's change until he issued the **commit** command? This is known as *read consistency*. Another example of read consistency would be a case where Eliza started a report before Fred committed his change. Assume that Fred committed the change during Eliza's report. In this case, it would be inconsistent for department 60 to show up in Eliza's report because it did not exist at the time that her report started. As Eliza's report continues to run, Oracle checks the start SCN of the report query against the SCNs of the blocks being read in Oracle to produce the report output. If the time of the report is earlier than the current SCN on the data block, Oracle goes to the rollback segments and finds undo for that block that will allow Oracle to construct an image consistent with the time that the report started.

As Fred continues other work on the database, the LGWR process writes to the online redo logs on a regular basis. At some point in time, an online redo log will fill up, and LGWR will close that log file, open the next log file, and begin writing to it. During this transition period, LGWR also signals the ARCH process to begin copying the log file that it just finished using to the archive log backup directories.

Checkpoints

Now, you might be wondering, when does this data actually get written out to the database datafiles? Recall that a checkpoint is an event in which Oracle (through DBWR) writes data out to the datafiles. There are several different kinds of checkpoints. Some of the events that result in a checkpoint are the following:

- ■ A redo log switch
- ■ Normal database shutdowns
- ■ When a tablespace is taken in or out of online backup mode (see "Oracle Physical Backup and Recovery" later in this chapter)

Note that ongoing incremental checkpoints occur throughout the lifetime of the database, providing a method for Oracle to decrease the overall time required when performing crash recovery. As the database operates, Oracle is constantly writing out streams of data to the database datafiles. These writes occur in such a way as to not impede performance of the database. Oracle provides certain database parameters to assist in determining how frequently Oracle must process incremental checkpoints.

NOTE
You might have heard of Oracle Multitenant, which we will cover in detail in Chapter 4. Even though there are a number of changes in the way you manage the Oracle database when using Oracle Multitenant, the way that many of the backup and recovery structures work, as described in this chapter, largely have not changed. Where there are slight differences, we will cover them in Chapter 4. What has changed is how you back up and recover the multitenant database structures. We will be discussing that throughout this book.

Controlling the Database Software

During various recovery operations, you need to control the state of the Oracle database and its associated instance. Let's quickly review how to start and stop Oracle databases.

To start the Oracle Database 12*c* database, you use the SQL*Plus Oracle utility. Log in as the user system by using the SYSDBA login ID. At the SQL*Plus prompt, issue the **startup** command, as you can see in this example:

```
/usr/oracle>sqlplus / as sysdba
Connected to an idle instance.
SQL> startup
```

When you start an Oracle database with the **startup** command, the operation goes through three different phases:

- **Instance startup**   The Oracle database instance is started.
- **Database mount**   The Oracle database is mounted.
- **Database open**   The Oracle database is opened for user activity.

NOTE
*You should be aware that the RMAN client, which we will discuss in later chapters, has the ability to shut down and start up the Oracle database on its own. You will not need to move from RMAN to SQL*Plus during a recovery operation in most cases.*

The **startup** command has several different variations (which are important to know for several different RMAN operations), including the following:

- **startup**   Causes Oracle to go through each of the three startup phases and to open to the user community.
- **startup restrict**   Causes Oracle to go through each of the three startup phases and to open in restricted mode. Only those users with restricted privileges can access the database.
- **startup nomount**   Causes the startup process to stop after it has successfully started the database instance. You will often use this command to start the database instance prior to actually creating a database. This command is also handy to have if you need to re-create

the control file. Note that to use RMAN with a given database, you must be able to successfully start the instance with the **startup nomount** command.

- **startup mount** Causes the startup process to stop after it has successfully started the database instance and then mounted it. This command is helpful if you need to recover the SYSTEM tablespace.

- **startup read only** Causes your Oracle database (or standby database) to open in READ ONLY mode. Therefore, DML operations are not supported, but you can query the database. This is handy if you are doing point-in-time recovery and you want to make sure you have recovered the database to the correct point in time before you commit to the new database incarnation with the **resetlogs** command.

- **startup force** Causes the database to be shut down with a **shutdown abort** (discussed in the next list). This command can be followed by the mode you wish the database to be opened in again. Examples include

  - **startup force restrict**
  - **startup force mount**
  - **startup force nomount**

Of course, now that you know how to start up the database, you need to know how to shut it down. Again, from SQL*Plus, you can use the **shutdown** command, which comes in these flavors:

- **shutdown** (also **shutdown normal**) Causes Oracle to wait for all user processes to disconnect from the database. Once this has occurred, the database will be completely shut down. Use of this option avoids instance recovery. After the **shutdown** command is executed, no new user processes are able to connect to the database.

- **shutdown immediate** Kills all existing user sessions and rolls back all uncommitted transactions. Use of this option avoids instance recovery. After **shutdown immediate** is executed, no new user processes are able to connect to the database.

- **shutdown abort** Basically, this crashes the database. Use of this option requires instance (but not media) recovery. After **shutdown abort** is executed, no new user processes are able to connect to the database.

- **shutdown transactional** Causes Oracle to wait for all user processes to commit their current transactions and then disconnects the user processes and shuts down the database. While Oracle is waiting for these transactions to complete, no new user sessions are allowed to connect to the database.

As we proceed through this book, we use many of these commands, and it is important to understand what state the database and its associated instance are in when the command has completed.

NOTE
Within Oracle Multitenant are a number of additional commands you would use to manage the database. We cover these in Chapter 4.

Oracle Backup and Recovery Primer

Before you use RMAN, you should understand some general backup and recovery concepts in Oracle. Backups in Oracle come in two general categories: logical and physical. In the following sections, we quickly look at logical backup and recovery and then give Oracle physical backup and recovery a full treatment.

Logical Backup and Recovery

Oracle Database 12*c* uses the Oracle Data Pump architecture to support logical backup and recovery. These utilities include the Data Pump Export program (**expdp**) and the Data Pump Import program (**impdp**). With logical backups, point-in-time recovery is not possible. RMAN does not do logical backup and recovery, so this topic is beyond the scope of this book.

Oracle Physical Backup and Recovery

Physical backups are what RMAN is all about. Before we really delve into RMAN in the remaining chapters of this book, let's first look at what is required to manually do physical backups and recoveries of an Oracle database. Although RMAN removes you from much of the work involved in backup and recovery, some of the principles remain the same. Understanding the basics of manual backup and recovery will help you understand what is going on with RMAN and will help us contrast the benefits of RMAN versus previous methods of backing up Oracle.

We have already discussed ARCHIVELOG mode and NOARCHIVELOG mode in Oracle. In either mode, Oracle can do an offline backup. Further, if the database is in ARCHIVELOG mode, then Oracle can do offline or online backups. We will cover the specifics of these operations with RMAN in later chapters of this book.

Of course, if you back up a database, it would be nice to be able to recover it. Following the sections on online and offline backups, we will discuss the different Oracle recovery options available. Finally, in these sections, we take a very quick, cursory look at Oracle manual backup and recovery.

NOARCHIVELOG Mode Physical Backups

We have already discussed NOARCHIVELOG mode in the Oracle database. This mode of database operations supports backups of the database only when the database is shut down. Also, only full recovery of the database up to the point of the backup is possible in NOARCHIVELOG mode. To perform a manual backup of a database in NOARCHIVELOG mode, follow these steps (note that these steps are different if you are using RMAN, which we will cover in later chapters):

1. Shut down the database completely.
2. Back up all database datafiles, the control files, and the online redo logs.
3. Restart the database.

ARCHIVELOG Mode Physical Backups

If you are running your database in ARCHIVELOG mode, you can continue to perform full backups of your database with the database either running or shut down. Even if you perform the backup with the database shut down, you will want to use a slightly different cold backup procedure:

1. Shut down the database completely.
2. Back up all database datafiles.

3. Restart the database.

4. Force an online redo log switch with the **alter system switch logfile** command. Once the online redo logs have been archived, back up all archived redo logs.

5. Create a backup of the control file using the **alter database backup control file to trace** and **alter database backup controlfile to 'file_name'** commands.

Of course, with your database in ARCHIVELOG mode, you may well want to do online, or hot, backups of your database. With the database in ARCHIVELOG mode, Oracle allows you to back up each individual tablespace and its datafiles while the database is up and running. The nice thing about this is that you can back up selective parts of your database at different times. To do an online backup of your tablespaces, follow this procedure:

1. Use the **alter tablespace begin backup** command to put the tablespaces and datafiles that you wish to back up in online backup mode. If you want to back up the entire database, you can use the **alter database begin backup** command to put all the database tablespaces in hot backup mode.

2. Back up the datafiles associated with the tablespace you have just put in hot backup mode. (You can opt to just back up specific datafiles.)

3. Take the tablespaces out of hot backup mode by issuing the **alter tablespace end backup** command for each tablespace you put in online backup mode in Step 1. If you want to take all tablespaces out of hot backup mode, use the **alter database end backup** command.

4. Force an online redo log switch with the **alter system switch logfile** command.

5. Once the log switch has completed and the current online redo log has been archived, back up all the archived redo logs.

Note the log switch and backup of archived redo logs in Step 5. This is required, because all redo generated during the backup must be available to apply should a recovery be required. While Oracle continues to physically update the datafiles during the online backup (except for the datafile headers), there is a possibility of block splitting during backup operations, which will make the backed-up datafile inconsistent. Further, since a database datafile might be written after it has been backed up but before the end of the overall backup process, it is important to have the redo generated during the backup to apply during recovery because each datafile on the backup might well be current as of a different SCN, and thus the datafile backup images will be inconsistent.

Redo generation changes when you issue the **alter tablespace begin backup** command or **alter database begin backup** command. Typically, Oracle only stores change vectors as redo records. These are small records that just define the change that has taken place. When a datafile is in online backup mode, Oracle will record the entire block that is being changed rather than just the change vectors. This means total redo generation during online backups can increase significantly. This can impact disk space requirements and CPU overhead during the hot backup process. RMAN enables you to perform hot backups without having to put a tablespace in hot backup mode, thus eliminating the additional I/O you would otherwise experience. Things return to normal when you end the online backup status of the datafiles.

Note that in both backups in ARCHIVELOG mode (online and offline), we do not back up the online redo logs, and instead back up the archived redo logs of the database. In addition, we do not back up the control file, but rather create backup control files. We do this because we never want to run the risk of overwriting the online redo logs or control files during a recovery.

You might wonder why we don't want to recover the online redo logs. During a recovery in ARCHIVELOG mode, the most current redo is likely to be available in the online redo logs, and thus the current online redo log will be required for full point-in-time recovery. Because of this, we do not overwrite the online redo logs during a recovery of a database that is in ARCHIVELOG mode. If the online redo logs are lost as a result of the loss of the database (and hopefully this will not be the case), you will have to do point-in-time recovery with all available archived redo logs.

For much the same reason that we don't back up the online redo logs, we don't back up the control files. Because the current control file contains the latest online and archived redo log information, we do not want to overwrite that information with earlier information on these objects. In case we lose all of our control files, we will use a backup control file to recover the database.

Finally, consider performing supplemental backups of archived redo log files and other means of protecting the archived redo logs from loss. Loss of an archived redo log directly impacts your ability to recover your database to the point of failure. If you lose an archived redo log and that log sequence number is no longer part of the online redo log groups, you will not be able to recover your database beyond the archived redo log sequence prior to the sequence number of the lost archived redo log.

NOARCHIVELOG Mode Recoveries

If you need to recover a backup taken in NOARCHIVELOG mode, doing so is as simple as recovering all the database datafiles, the control files, and the online redo logs and starting the database. Of course, a total recovery may require such things as recovering the Oracle RDBMS software, the parameter file, and other required Oracle items, which we will discuss in the last section of this chapter.

Note that a recovery in NOARCHIVELOG mode is only possible to the point in time that you took your last backup. If you are recovering a database backed up in NOARCHIVELOG mode, you can only recover the database to the point of the backup. No database changes after the point of the backup can be recovered if your database is in NOARCHIVELOG mode.

ARCHIVELOG Mode Recoveries

A database that is in ARCHIVELOG mode can be backed up using online or offline backups. The fortunate thing about ARCHIVELOG mode, as opposed to NOARCHIVELOG mode, is that you can recover the database to the point of the failure that occurred. In addition, you can choose to recover the database to a specific point in time, or to a specific point in time based on the change number.

ARCHIVELOG mode recoveries also allow you to do specific recoveries on datafiles, tablespaces, or the entire database. In addition, you can do point-in-time recovery or recovery to a specific SCN. Let's quickly look at each of these options.

In this section, we briefly cover full database recoveries in ARCHIVELOG mode. We then look at tablespace and datafile recoveries, followed by point-in-time recoveries.

ARCHIVELOG Mode Full Recovery   You can recover a database backup in ARCHIVELOG mode up to the point of failure, assuming that the failure of the database did not compromise at least one member of each of your current online redo log groups and any archived redo logs that were not backed up. If you have lost your archived redo logs or online redo logs, you will need to perform some form of point-in-time recovery, as discussed later in this section. Also, if you have lost all copies of your current control file, you will need to recover it and perform an incomplete recovery.

To perform a full database recovery from a backup of a database in ARCHIVELOG mode, follow this procedure:

1. Restore all the database datafiles from your backup.

2. Restore all backed up archived redo logs.

3. Mount the database **(startup mount)**.

4. Recover the database **(recover database)**.

5. Oracle prompts you to apply redo from the archived redo logs. Simply enter **AUTO** at the prompt, and Oracle will automatically apply all redo logs.

6. Once all redo logs have been applied, open the recovered database **(alter database open)**.

ARCHIVELOG Tablespace and Datafile Recovery   Tablespace and datafile recovery can be performed with the database mounted or open. To perform a recovery of a tablespace in Oracle with the database open, follow these steps:

1. Take the tablespace offline **(alter tablespace offline)**.

2. Restore all datafiles associated with the tablespace to be recovered.

3. Recover the tablespace **(recover tablespace)** online.

4. Once recovery has completed, bring the tablespace online **(alter tablespace online)**.

Just as you can recover a tablespace, you can also recover specific datafiles. This has the benefit of leaving the tablespace online. Only data that resides in the offline datafiles will be unavailable during the recovery process. The rest of the database will remain available during the recovery. Here is a basic outline of a datafile recovery:

1. Take the datafile offline **(alter database datafile 'file_name' offline)**.

2. Restore all datafiles to be recovered.

3. Recover the tablespace **(recover datafile)** online.

4. Once recovery has completed, bring the datafile online **(alter database datafile 'file_name' online)**.

ARCHIVELOG Point-in-Time Recoveries   Another benefit of ARCHIVELOG mode is the capability to recover a database to a given point in time rather than to the point of failure. This capability is used often when creating a clone database (perhaps for testing or reporting purposes) or in the event of major application or user error. You can recover a database to either a specific point in time or a specific database SCN.

If you want to recover a tablespace to a point in time, you need to recover the entire database to the same point in time (unless you perform tablespace point-in-time recovery, which is a different topic). For example, assume that you have an accounting database, that most of your data is in the ACCT tablespace, and that you wish to recover the database back in time two days. You cannot just restore the ACCT tablespace and recover it to a point in time two days ago, because the remaining tablespaces (SYSTEM, TEMP, and RBS, for example) will still be consistent to the current point in time, and the database will fail to open because it will be inconsistent.

To recover a database to a point in time, follow these steps:

1. Recover all database datafiles from a backup that ended before the point in time to which you want to recover the database.

2. Recover the database to the desired point in time. Use the command **recover database until time '01-01-2010 21:00:00'** and apply the redo logs as required.

3. Once the recovery is complete, open the database using the **alter database open resetlogs** command.

You can also choose to recover the database using an SCN number:

1. Recover all database datafiles from a backup that ended before the point in time to which you want to recover the database.

2. Recover the database to the desired SCN. Use the command **recover database until change '221122'** and apply the redo logs as required.

3. Once the recovery is complete, open the database.

Further, you can apply changes to the database and manually cancel the process after a specific archived redo log has been applied:

1. Recover all database datafiles from a backup that ended before the point in time to which you want to recover the database.

2. Recover the database to the desired point in time. Use the command **recover database until cancel** and apply the redo logs as required. When you have applied the last archived redo log, simply issue the **cancel** command to finish applying redo.

3. Once the recovery is complete, open the database.

Keep in mind the concept of database consistency when doing point-in-time recovery (or any recovery, for that matter). If you are going to recover a database to a given point in time, you must do so with a backup that finished before the point in time to which you wish to recover. Also, you must have all the archived redo logs (and possibly the remaining online redo logs) available to complete recovery.

A Word About Flashback Database   Another recovery method available to you is the use of Oracle's flashback features. We cover Oracle's flashback features in more depth in Chapter 16, but know that with the varied flashback functionality, you can significantly reduce the overall time it takes to recover your database from user- and application-level errors. RMAN supports some of the Oracle Database 12*c* flashback features, so it is most appropriate to cover those in this book.

Backing Up Other Oracle Components

We have quickly covered the essentials of backup and recovery for Oracle. One last issue that remains to be covered is the items that need to be backed up. These generally are backed up with less frequency because they change rarely. These items include the following:

- The Oracle RDBMS software (Oracle Home and the Oracle Inventory).

- Network parameter files (names.ora, sqlnet.ora, and tnsnames.ora).

- Database parameter files (init.ora, INI files, and so forth). Note that RMAN does allow you to back up the database parameter file (only if it's a SPFILE) along with the control file!

- The system oratab file and other system Oracle-related files (for example, all rc startup scripts for Oracle).

It is important that these items be backed up regularly as a part of your backup and recovery process. You need to plan to back up these items regardless of whether you do manual backups or RMAN backups, because RMAN does not back up these items either.

As you can see, the process of backup and recovery of an Oracle database can involve a number of steps. Because DBAs want to make sure they do backups correctly every time, they generally write a number of scripts for this purpose. There are a few problems with this practice, however. First of all, scripts can break. When the script breaks, who is going to support it, particularly when the DBA who wrote it moves to a new position somewhere in the inaccessible tundra in northern Alaska? Second, either you have to write the script to keep track of when you add or remove datafiles, or you have to manually add or remove datafiles from the script as required.

With RMAN, you get a backup and recovery product that is included with the base database product for free, and that reduces the complexity of the backup and recovery process. Also, you get the benefit of Oracle support when you run into a problem. Finally, with RMAN, you get additional features that no other backup and recovery process can match. We will look at those features in coming chapters.

Summary

We didn't discuss RMAN much in this chapter, but we laid some important groundwork for future discussions of RMAN that you will find in later chapters. As promised, we covered some essential backup and recovery concepts, such as high availability and backup and recovery planning, that are central to the purpose of RMAN. We then defined several Oracle terms that you need to be familiar with later in this text. We also reviewed the Oracle database architecture and internal operations. We cannot stress enough how important it is to have an understanding of how Oracle works inside when it comes time to actually recover your database in an emergency situation. Finally, we discussed manual backup and recovery operations in Oracle. Contrast these to the same RMAN operations in later chapters, and you will find that RMAN is ultimately an easy solution for backing up and recovering your Oracle database.

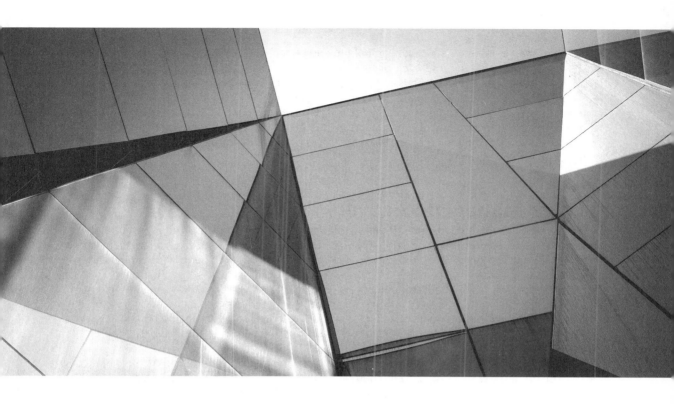

CHAPTER
3

Introduction to the
RMAN Architecture

This chapter takes you through each of the components in the RMAN architecture, one by one, explaining the role each plays in a successful backup or recovery of the Oracle database. Most of this discussion assumes that you have a good understanding of the Oracle RDBMS architecture. If you are not familiar at a basic level with the different components of an Oracle database, you might want to read the brief introduction in Chapter 2, or pick up a beginner's guide to database administration, before continuing. After we discuss the different components for backup and recovery, we walk through a simple backup procedure to disk and talk about each component in action.

Server-Managed Recovery

In the previous chapter, you learned the principles and practices of backup and recovery in the old world. It involved creating and running scripts to capture the filenames, associate them with tablespaces, get the tablespaces into backup mode, get an OS utility to perform the copy, and then stop backup mode.

But this book is really about using Recovery Manager (RMAN). Recovery Manager implements a type of *server-managed recovery* (SMR). SMR refers to the ability of the database to perform the operations required to keep itself backed up successfully. It does so by relying on built-in code in the Oracle RDBMS kernel. Who knows more about the schematics of the database than the database itself?

The power of SMR comes from what details it can eliminate on your behalf. As the degree of enterprise complexity increases and the number of databases that a single DBA is responsible for increases, personally troubleshooting dozens or even hundreds of individual scripts becomes too burdensome. In other words, as the move to "grid computing" becomes more mainstream, the days of personally eyeballing all the little details of each database backup become a thing of the past. Instead, many of the nitpicky details of backup management get handled by the database itself, allowing us to take a step back from the day-to-day upkeep and to concentrate on more important things. Granted, the utilization of RMAN introduces certain complexities that overshadow the complete level of ease that might be promised by SMR—why else would you be reading this book? But the blood, sweat, and tears you pour into RMAN will give you huge payoffs. You'll see.

The RMAN Utility

RMAN is the specific implementation of SMR provided by Oracle. RMAN is a stand-alone application (not unlike SQL*Plus) that makes a client connection to the Oracle database. To perform its duties, RMAN has to be able to access internal backup and recovery packages. These internal RMAN packages are built into the Oracle Database kernel, so they are available even if the database is not open. These packages are available as soon as the database instance is started in NOMOUNT mode. There are some basic procedures to follow if you can't get the Oracle database instance to start, which we will describe in this book when we discuss backup and recovery.

The result is that RMAN is, at its very core, nothing more than a command interpreter that takes simplified commands you type, submits them to the database, and turns those commands into remote procedure calls (RPCs) that are executed at the database. We point this out primarily to make one thing very clear: RMAN does very little work. The real work of actually backing up and recovering a database is performed by programs and the spawned processes of those programs within the target database itself. The *target database* refers to the database that is being backed up.

You can actually see the internal PL/SQL packages that RMAN uses in the database, and in the early days of RMAN there were rare cases that you actually had to access those packages to be able to restore your database. Those days are long past, though. The last time I had to do any kind of manual restore with the PL/SQL packages was back in the Oracle 8*i* days. Since then, RMAN has added some commands that have removed almost any need to access these packages. In very rare situations you might need to use them to reset some setting, but these cases are well documented on Metalink Oracle Support (MOS), and by and large they are not something to worry about.

The RMAN utility is automatically installed when the database software is installed, just like Data Pump or SQL*Loader is. RMAN is included with Enterprise and Standard Editions, although there are restrictions if you have a license only for Standard Edition: without Enterprise Edition, for example, RMAN can only allocate a single channel for backups. As of Oracle Database 12*c*, the current database family consists of the following editions:

- Oracle Database Standard Edition Two
- Oracle Database Enterprise Edition
- Oracle Database Express Edition
- Oracle Database Personal Edition

Oracle Enterprise Edition has the largest number of supported features, and the two versions of Standard Edition have restricted feature sets. The feature differences are pretty wide, and they change from time to time. We recommend that you review Chapter 1 of the Oracle Database Licensing Information documentation for Oracle Database 12*c*R1 if you wish to determine what features in your version of the database are supported. In this book, we assume you are using Oracle Enterprise Edition; therefore, all the features of that version of the database product will be supported.

Although we won't provide an exhaustive list of features not supported, here are some of the main RMAN features we discuss that are only supported by Oracle Database Enterprise Edition:

- Multitenant
- Oracle Data Guard features
- Parallelized and duplexed backup sets
- Block change tracking for incremental backups
- Unused block compression in RMAN backups
- Block-level recovery via RMAN
- Automatic block repair
- Tablespace point-in-time recovery
- Trial recoveries
- Flashback Database features
- Cross-platform backup and recovery

You can also install RMAN as part of the Oracle client install. If you wish to install RMAN during the client install, you need to choose the Administrator option instead of the Runtime client option.

The RMAN utility is made up of several pieces of code, including the following:

- **The RMAN executable**   The client used to interface with RMAN.
- **The $ORACLE_HOME/rdbms/admin/recover.bsq file**   This file almost provides a script for what the commands you issue from RMAN do. It shows you the procedures being called and other process-related information.
- **The $ORACLE_HOME/rdbms/admin/dbmsrman.sql file**   This file contains the header files for the wrapped **dbms_rcvman** PL/SQL package that is loaded into the database. This package is mostly dedicated to the management of the RMAN metadata records.
- **The $ORACLE_HOME/rdbms/admin/dbmsbkrs.sql file**   This is the header file for the **dbms_backup_restore**-wrapped PL/SQL package that is loaded in the database. A great deal of commentary related to RMAN is contained in this file. If you truly want to understand the guts of RMAN, this is a long file to look through.
- **The Oracle database stored packages dbms_backup_restore and dbms_rcvcat**   These wrapped packages are really the guts of RMAN. Most RMAN operations consist of calls to one of these two packages, which do the actual work.

Needless to say, you should never change any of these files, but we thought it would be nice to show you where the interesting stuff resides (in case you like to go spelunking).

Of all of these files, the recover.bsq file is probably the brains of the whole operation. It coordinates the commands from the RMAN client to the database packages. So, RMAN is kind of like the Godfather—he gives the basic order: "restore the database." The recover.bsq file is his lieutenant, who designs the plan and implements it. This file then gets the strong-armed RDBMS packages to do the heavy lifting. Think about it: the Godfather can even say "drop database" and it will mysteriously disappear... probably to be found buried somewhere in the Nevada desert.

The RMAN utility serves a distinct, orderly, and predictable purpose: it interprets commands you provide into PL/SQL calls that are remotely executed at the target database. The command language is unique to RMAN, and using it takes a little practice. It is essentially a stripped-down list of all the things you need to do to back up, restore, or recover databases, or to manipulate those backups in some way. These commands are interpreted by the executable translator, then matched to PL/SQL blocks in the recover.bsq file. RMAN then passes these RPCs to the database to gather information based on what you have requested. If your command requires an I/O operation (in other words, a backup command or a restore command), then when this information is returned, RMAN prepares another block of procedures and passes it back to the target database. These blocks are responsible for engaging the system calls to the OS for specific read or write operations.

RMAN and Database Privileges

Just like SQL*Plus, RMAN is a client. Just like with SQL*Plus, you need to have the correct privileges to log into the database using RMAN. Prior to Oracle Database 12*c*, RMAN required SYSDBA or SYSOPER privilege for whatever account it logged into. This makes sense because RMAN needs to have the privileges necessary to start up, shut down, and—during restore operations—create the target database and so on. So, if you have an account with SYSDBA privileges, RMAN can connect to it as shown here:

```
RMAN> connect target sys/password
connected to target database: PROD (DBID=4159396170)
```

Note that you don't need to use the "as sysdba" part of the connection string. RMAN always assumes that you intend to connect using the SYSDBA privileges.

In Oracle Database 12c, a new privilege called SYSBACKUP has been added. Now a user can have either SYSDBA or SYSBACKUP privilege to use RMAN. The SYSBACKUP privilege is more restrictive than SYSDBA. When you connect as SYSBACKUP, your current schema will be the SYS schema, but the current user will be SYSBACKUP (as opposed to SYSDBA).

The SYSBACKUP privilege has a number of system-level privileges associated with it. You can find these privileges documented in Chapter 4 of the Oracle Database Security Guide 12c.

If you try to connect as someone who does not have the appropriate privileges, RMAN will give you an error:

```
RMAN> connect target /
RMAN-00571: ===========================================================
RMAN-00569: =============== ERROR MESSAGE STACK FOLLOWS =============
RMAN-00571: ===========================================================
ORA-01031: insufficient privileges
```

This is a common error during the setup and configuration phase of RMAN. It is encountered when you are not logged into your server in such a way that you do not have sufficient privileges to perform RMAN operations. This can be due to many different reasons. You may have OS authenticated logins disabled, you may not have a password file properly configured, or your user might not have the right permissions. Any number of reasons can cause your login to be rejected. In Chapter 7 we walk through examples of properly setting up RMAN privileges so that you can use the product.

The Network Topology of RMAN Backups

When it comes to using RMAN over the network, just think of it like using SQL*Plus. If you are using RMAN on the backup server, then all you need to do is set the Oracle environment as you would for SQL*Plus and carry on executing RMAN commands.

Additionally, just like with SQL*Plus, if you want to run RMAN remotely, you use TNS services to connect to the database. When you connect remotely via TNS to a privileged account (such as SYSDBA), the database must have a password file. The same is true if you are using RMAN. All the RMAN connections have to use privileged accounts, so to use RMAN via Oracle TNS, the database must have a password file.

RMAN and Scale

True story. One evening this author had a call from one of the higher-ups of the company I was working for. A real disaster had occurred at a company we did business with, and they were in deep trouble. I was on a red-eye flight that night and landed the next morning. When I got to the company data center, I arrived to see a number of people with long faces—they were not happy.

As I dove into the problem, I found the following:

- A disk controller had failed.
- Around 200 databases were impacted.
- They had replaced the disk controller, and when they spun up the disks, they discovered that there was a lot of corrupted blocks on those disks.
- As a result of the corruption, some 75 percent of the databases would not start.

This was a huge problem, of course. However, there was this sense of calm as everyone was sure that backups were available to restore these databases. Then the calm turned into desperation as we discovered the following:

- There was no standardized way used to back up the databases. Some DBAs used their own home-grown scripts, some used RMAN, and some used one of two tools that the organization owned. Worse yet, three of the DBAs were away on vacation.

- We discovered that the sole location where the most current backups were stored was on the disk array that had failed. Many of the backups and/or archived redo logs were therefore unavailable to perform full restores.

- There were offsite backups, but at best they were a week old.

As you can imagine, the restore exercise was a long and painful one, and in many cases it was not a complete one. The team I was working with literally spent three days combing through how they were doing backups for each individual database, where those backups were, what kind of restore needed to be done, and then scrambling to see if the recovery was even possible. I had not spent sleepless nights like that for many years.

A lot of lessons can be learned from this experience, to be sure. Some of these lessons we discuss in Chapter 15, in which we discuss architecting an enterprise-worthy backup and recovery strategy. The other lesson, which I think is relevant for this chapter, is one of consistency and standardization. Particularly with backup and recovery, it's important to have a single, enterprise-wide solution that everyone else knows about. This is the only way you can scale as your organization grows. This is also how you reduce risk and downtime.

That being said, we strongly suggest that you consolidate all of your Oracle database backup jobs using RMAN as your sole platform. Further, as we will discuss in Chapters 14, we strongly recommend using the Oracle Cloud Control infrastructure to manage all of your RMAN backups, including scheduling them. This architecture provides an easy-to-use, single pane of glass from which to manage your backups and restores.

Frankly, the growth of data and the proliferation of databases is not going to stop. It's just going to become harder and harder to manage the sprawl. Therefore, cron jobs and home-baked shell scripts just don't cut it anymore. There is a significant cost to these things—they might be fun to do, but they cost money and they don't scale for many reasons. You should avoid them and instead look to OEM to help you centrally manage your needs using a single, reliable, repeatable method.

This all being said, we also want to make it crystal clear that an RMAN recovery catalog is, in most cases, no longer an optional item. The RMAN recovery catalog stores RMAN metadata. So everything you wanted to know about an RMAN backup is stored in the recovery catalog. If you only have one or two databases to manage, you might well be able to live without it. However, in a true enterprise architecture, you will want to implement and use a recovery catalog. We discuss the recovery catalog throughout this book.

RMAN and Shared Servers

If you will be making a remote connection from RMAN to a target database that is running the Oracle Database Shared Server option, you need to create a tnsnames.ora entry that can connect you to the target database with a dedicated server process. RMAN cannot use Shared Servers (formerly known as Multi-Threaded Servers, or MTS) to make a database connection. So if you use Shared Servers, you need to create a separate Oracle Net alias that uses a dedicated server process.

The difference between the two can be seen in the following sample tsnames.ora file. Note that the first alias entry is for dedicated server processes, and the second uses the Shared Servers architecture.

```
PROD_RMAN =
  (DESCRIPTION =
    (ADDRESS_LIST =
      (ADDRESS = (PROTOCOL = TCP)(HOST = cervantes)(PORT = 1521))
    )
    (CONNECT_DATA =
      (SERVER = DEDICATED)
      (SERVICE_NAME = prod)
    )
  )
PROD =
  (DESCRIPTION =
    (ADDRESS_LIST =
      (ADDRESS = (PROTOCOL = TCP)(HOST = cervantes)(PORT = 1521))
    )
    (CONNECT_DATA =
      (SERVER = SHARED)
      (SERVICE_NAME = prod)
    )
  )
```

Running RMAN Locally from the Target Database's ORACLE_HOME

Of course, you can run RMAN locally on the server where your target database is located. This might be required at times for very specific reasons. Although our recommendation in previous versions of this book has been to run your backups on the local servers, we now feel confident enough with Cloud Control 12c that we strongly advise that you use that tool to run your backups rather than run them on the servers themselves through some scheduling facility such as cron. Using Cloud Control really removes a lot of the headaches from managing numerous databases across many servers. We discuss these issues in Chapters 14 in a lot more detail and provide you with a nice list of the benefits when you run your RMAN backups from Cloud Control.

When you do run RMAN locally, you will almost always make a bequeath connection to the database rather than going through the TNS networking stack. This then potentially requires no password file setup and no tnsnames.ora configuration. Bear in mind that the simplicity of this option is also its drawback: as soon as you want to introduce a recovery catalog or perform a database duplication operation, you introduce all the elements you were trying to avoid in the first place. Also, we abhor the notion of OS authenticated logins to the database.

Yes, you will find that our opinion on the optimal RMAN architecture has changed a great deal in this book. Database Cloud Control 12c is a wonderful and stable product. It now has become our platform of choice for RMAN backup administration.

NOTE
Oracle Database 12c has removed all support for Oracle Database Control and replaced it with a new product called Database Express. When we talk about Oracle Database Cloud Control, we are not talking about Oracle Database Express in any way. See Chapter 14 for more information on Oracle Database Cloud Control.

The Database Control File

So far, we have discussed the RMAN executable and its role in the process of using server-managed recovery with Oracle 12*c*. As we said, the real work is being done at the target database—it's backing itself up. Next, we must discuss the role of the control file in an RMAN backup or recovery process.

The control file has a day job already; it is responsible for the physical schematics of the database. The name says it all: the control file controls where the physical files of a database can be found and what header information each file currently contains (or should contain). Its contents include datafile information, redo log information, and archive log information. It has a snapshot of each file header for the critical files associated with the database. Because of this wealth of information, the control file has been the primary component of any recovery operation prior to RMAN (Chapter 2 discusses this in greater detail).

Because of the control file's role as the repository of database file information, it makes sense that RMAN would utilize the control file to pull information about what needs to be backed up. And that's just what it does: RMAN uses the control file to compile file lists, obtain checkpoint information, and determine recoverability. By accessing the control file directly, RMAN can compile file lists without a user having to create the list herself, thus eliminating one of the most tiresome steps of backup scripting. And RMAN does not require that the script be modified when a new file is added. It already knows about your new file. RMAN knows this because the control file knows this.

The control file also moonlights as an RMAN data repository. After RMAN completes a backup of any portion of the database, it writes a record of that backup to the control file, along with checkpoint information about when the backup was started and completed. This is one of the primary reasons that the control file grew exponentially in size between Oracle version 7 and Oracle version 8—RMAN tables in the control file. These records are often referred to as *metadata*—data about the data recorded in the actual backup. This metadata will also be stored in a recovery catalog when one is used.

Record Reuse in the Control File

The control file can grow to meet space demands. When a new record is added for a new datafile, a new log file, or a new RMAN backup, the control file can expand to meet these demands. However, there are limitations. Because most databases can live for years, during which time thousands of redo logs switch and thousands of checkpoints occur, the control file has to be able to eliminate some data that is no longer necessary. Therefore, it ages out information as it needs space and reuses certain "slots" in tables in round-robin fashion. However, some information cannot be eliminated—for instance, the list of datafiles. This information is critical for the minute-to-minute database operation, and new space *must* be made available for these records.

The control file thus separates its internal data into two types of records: circular reuse records and noncircular reuse records. *Circular reuse records* are records that include information that can be aged out of the control file if push comes to shove. This includes, for instance, archive log history information, which can be removed without affecting the production database. *Noncircular reuse records* are those records that cannot be sacrificed. If the control file runs out of space for these records, the file expands to make more room. These records include datafile and log file lists.

The record of RMAN backups in the control file falls into the category of circular reuse records, meaning that the records will get aged out if the control file section that contains them becomes full. This can be catastrophic to a recovery situation: without the record of the backups in the control file, it is as though the backups never took place. Remember this: if the control file does not have a record of your RMAN backup, the backup cannot easily be used by RMAN for recovery. There is a command called **catalog** that makes it possible to refresh the control file records, so all is not lost (we discuss the **catalog** command in later chapters of this book). This makes the control file a critical piece in the RMAN equation. Without one, we have nothing. If records get aged out, then we have created a lot of manual labor to rediscover the backups.

Fear not, though. Often, we can take steps to ensure that important records don't get aged out. First, it usually takes some time for the control file to fill up in the first place. By the time it has, there are backups that are already obsolete and can be removed.

Second, you can set the CONTROL_FILE_RECORD_KEEP_TIME parameter to make sure that the control file does not age out records prematurely. By default, this parameter is set to 7 (in days). This means that if a record is less than seven days old, the control file will not delete it, but rather expand the control file section. If the record is over seven days old, the record would be deleted rather than the control file expanded.

You can set the CONTROL_FILE_RECORD_KEEP_TIME parameter to a higher value (say, 30 days) so that the control file always expands until only records older than a month will be overwritten when necessary. Setting this to a higher day value is a good idea, but the reverse is not true. Setting this parameter to 0 means that the record section never expands, in which case you are flirting with disaster.

If you need to retain records over 365 days, or if you will be using archival backups (which we discuss in Chapter 8), you must have a recovery catalog. In this case, you won't need to worry about records disappearing in the control file. Whereas the control file will age out records based on the CONTROL_FILE_RECORD_KEEP_TIME parameter, the control file will not.

The Snapshot Control File

As you probably know, the control file is a busy little file. It's responsible for storing all sorts of metadata about your database, and it's changing all the time, updating SCN records, file locations, and so on. This activity is critical to the livelihood of your database, so the control file must be available for usage by the RDBMS on a constant basis.

Like many things Oracle, RMAN needs to work with a consistent image. The fact that the control file is this little demon of business then causes issues. Because the control file does not have the benefit of its own UNDO tablespace, RMAN needs a way to manage a consistent view of the control file. Sure, RMAN could take a latch against the control file for the duration of the backup, but that would mean the database could not advance the checkpoint, switch logs, or produce new archive logs. Impossible.

To get around this, RMAN uses the *snapshot control file,* an exact copy of your control file that is only used by RMAN during backup and resync operations. At the beginning of these operations, RMAN refreshes the snapshot control file from the actual control file, thus putting a momentary lock on the control file. Then, RMAN switches to the snapshot and uses it for the duration of the backup; in this way, it has read consistency without holding up database activity.

By default, the snapshot control file exists in the ORACLE_HOME/dbs directory on Unix platforms and in the ORACLE_HOME/database directory on Windows. It has a default name of SNCF<ORACLE_SID>.ORA. This can be modified or changed at any time by using the **configure snapshot controlfile** command:

```
configure snapshot controlfile name to '<location\file_name>';
```

Certain conditions might lead to the following error on the snapshot control file, which is typically the first time a person ever notices the file even exists:

```
RMAN-08512: waiting for snapshot controlfile enqueue
```

This error happens when the snapshot control file header is locked by a process other than the one requesting the enqueue. If you have multiple backup jobs, it may be that you are trying to run two backup jobs simultaneously from two different RMAN sessions. To troubleshoot this error, open a SQL*Plus session and run the following SQL statement:

```
SELECT s.sid, username AS "User", program, module, action, logon_time
"Logon", l.*
FROM v$session s, v$enqueue_lock l
WHERE l.sid = s.sid and l.type = 'CF' AND l.id1 = 0 and l.id2 = 2;
```

Rebuilding the Control File

There may be occasions when you need to rebuild or restore the control file. Often you will use RMAN to perform this operation, and this is described in Chapter 7. You can also manually rebuild the control file with the **create control file** command. There are generally two ways of doing this. One is to handcraft the **create control file** command yourself, and the second is to use the **create control file** command contained in the trace file that is created with the **alter database backup controlfile to trace** command. We cover these conditions in Chapter 7 in much more detail.

The RMAN Server Processes

RMAN makes a client connection to the target database, and two server processes are spawned. The primary process is used to make calls to packages in the SYS schema in order to perform the backup or recovery operations. This process coordinates the work of the channel processes during backups and restores.

The secondary, or shadow, process polls any long-running transactions in RMAN and then logs the information internally. You can view the results of this polling in the view V$SESSION_LONGOPS:

```
SELECT SID, SERIAL#, CONTEXT, SOFAR, TOTALWORK,
       ROUND(SOFAR/TOTALWORK*100,2) "%_COMPLETE"
FROM V$SESSION_LONGOPS
WHERE OPNAME LIKE 'RMAN%'
AND OPNAME NOT LIKE '%aggregate%'
AND TOTALWORK != 0
AND SOFAR <> TOTALWORK
/
```

You can also view these processes in the V$SESSION view. When RMAN allocates a channel, it provides the session ID information in the output:

```
allocated channel: ORA_DISK_1
channel ORA_DISK_1: sid=16 devtype=DISK
```

The "sid" information corresponds to the SID column in V$SESSION. So you could construct a query such as this:

```
SQL> column client_info format a30
SQL> column program format a15
SQL> select sid, saddr, paddr, program, client_info
     from v$session where sid=16;
     SID SADDR    PADDR    PROGRAM         CLIENT_INFO
---------- -------- -------- --------------- -----------------------
      16 682144E8 681E82BC RMAN.EXE        rman channel=ORA_DISK_1
```

RMAN Channel Processes

In addition to the two default processes, an individual process is created for every channel that you allocate during a backup or restore operation. In RMAN lingo, the *channel* is the server process at the target database that coordinates the reads from the datafiles and the writes to the specified location during backup. During a restore, the channel coordinates reads from the backup location and the writing of data blocks to the datafile locations. There are only two kinds of channels: disk channels and tape channels. You cannot allocate both kinds of channels for a single backup operation—you are writing the backup either to disk or to tape. Like the background RMAN process, the channel processes can be tracked from the data dictionary, and then correlated with an SID at the OS level. It is the activity of these channel processes that gets logged by the polling shadow process into the V$SESSION_LONGOPS view.

RMAN and I/O Slaves

Some people confuse the idea of I/O slaves and think that they need to be configured for RMAN to work properly. If your OS supports asynchronous I/O, and pretty much all of them do today, then you do not need to configure disk I/O slaves. Disk I/O slaves were designed to mimic asynchronous I/O for RMAN in systems that do not provide this feature. RMAN supports two different kinds of I/O slaves: disk I/O slaves and tape I/O slaves.

Tape I/O slaves assist with server process access to the tape device. If you have the parameter BACKUP_TAPE_IO_SLAVES set to TRUE, then RMAN will allocate a single I/O slave per tape channel process to assist with writes to the tape location. Unlike with disk I/O slaves, this parameter affects no part of the database other than RMAN tape backups. Because there is no native asynchronous I/O-to-tape devices, we recommend you set this parameter to TRUE. It will help keep your tape drives streaming, meaning better performance on backups and restores. Chapter 11 discusses tape streaming in more depth.

The SYS Packages Used by RMAN

The RMAN server process that coordinates the work of the channels has access to two packages in the SYS schema: DBMS_RCVMAN and DBMS_BACKUP_RESTORE. These two packages compose the entirety of the RMAN functionality in the target database.

SYS.DBMS_RCVMAN

SYS.DBMS_RCVMAN is the package that is used to access the tables in the control file and pass this information to RMAN so it can build backup and restore operations that accurately reflect the database schematics. This package is responsible for setting TIME operators and verifying checkpoint information in the datafile headers prior to running any operation. It also checks file locations and sizes, along with other information concerning node affinity (in a RAC environment) and disk affinity. This kind of information affects performance, and RMAN has automatic load-balancing and performance-enhancing algorithms that it runs through prior to building the actual backup/restore commands. Chapter 11 talks in depth about these performance gains. Stay tuned.

SYS.DBMS_BACKUP_RESTORE

SYS.DBMS_RCVMAN accesses the control file and verifies all the requisite information. It passes this information back to the RMAN server process, which can then create PL/SQL blocks based on code in the recover.bsq file. These PL/SQL blocks are made up of calls to the package DBMS_BACKUP_RESTORE, the true workhorse of RMAN. DBMS_BACKUP_RESTORE is the actual package that creates system calls to back up datafiles, control files, and archived redo logs. RMAN takes the information returned from DBMS_RCVMAN, divvies out the work among the channels based on the load-balancing algorithm, and then creates a series of calls to DBMS_BACKUP_RESTORE.

It is the work of DBMS_BACKUP_RESTORE that you can track in V$SESSION_LONGOPS. It performs the backup and restore operations. In addition, it accesses the control file, but only in a very limited way. It accesses it to back it up (actually, it backs up the snapshot control file) and to write backup information to it after backups have completed. Once it has completed a backup set, it writes to tables in the control file the information about when the backup was taken, how long it took to complete, and the size and name of the backup.

RMAN Packages in the Kernel

Both of these RMAN packages are installed by default by running the catproc.sql script when the database is created. There is no way to omit them during database creation, and therefore they exist in every Oracle database since version 8.0.3. What this means to you is that no configuration by you is required for RMAN to work. You can run RMAN right now and start backing up your database.

These packages have another important trait: they are hard-coded into the Oracle software library files, so they can be called even when the database is not open. Most packages, as you know, would only be available when the database is open. However, RMAN can write calls to DBMS_BACKUP_RESTORE when the database instance is in either NOMOUNT or MOUNT mode. This is a critical element, and the reason is clear: we need to be able to back up and restore the database even when it is not open.

Which brings us to an interesting point: What state must the target be in if we are to connect to it using RMAN? Does the instance need to be started, or do we need to mount it, or must it be open? The answer is that RMAN can connect to the target database in any of these three states, but it must at least be in NOMOUNT mode (otherwise, there's no *there* there!) for RMAN to do much more than issue a **startup** command.

Backing Up the Data Block

When you used manual (non-RMAN) techniques for backups, you are backing up the database at the file level. As a result of this, there is very little integrity checking that goes on within the database datafiles. If a block in the datafile is corrupted, then guess what—your backup is corrupted. This same problem applies to "snapshot" kinds of backups where the file system mirror is broken and the snapshot is backed up by some OS utility. I've seen more than one case where the snapshot backups were all unable to be used because of block corruption that was not able to be corrected. RMAN, however, is different. Because RMAN is integrated into the RDBMS, it has access to your data at the same level that the database itself uses: the data block.

Block-level access is what distinguishes RMAN from any other backup utility. This is an extremely powerful level of access that provides nearly all the benefits that you will get from using RMAN. It is because of this access that we can utilize the data block for more efficient backup and recovery. In backing up at the block level, we can validate the block. In backing up at the block level, we can actually restore individual corrupted blocks. Block-level access provides a great deal of flexibility when it comes time for things such as incremental backups and other operations that exist at the block level.

The Data Block Backup Overview

Here's how it works: RMAN compiles the list of files to be backed up, based on the backup algorithm rules. Based on the number of channels and the number of files being simultaneously backed up, RMAN creates memory buffers in the Oracle shared memory segment. This is typically in the Private Global Area (PGA) of the individual RMAN processes (a single process is spawned off for each channel that is backing up the database). There are circumstances that will push the memory buffers into the Shared Global Area (SGA), but this is rare.

The channel server process then begins reading the datafiles, block by block, filling the RMAN memory buffers with these blocks. When a buffer is full, it pushes the blocks from an input buffer into an output buffer. With a full backup, or incremental backup without block change tracking enabled, this memory-to-memory write occurs for each individual used data block in the datafiles. In the case of an incremental backup where block change tracking is enabled, only blocks marked to be read in the tracking file would be read. If the block meets the criteria for being backed up and the memory-to-memory write detected no corruption, then the block remains in the output buffer until the output buffer is full. Once full, the output buffer is pushed to the backup location—a disk or a tape, whichever it may be.

Once the entire set of files has been filtered through the memory buffers, the backup piece is finished, and RMAN writes the completion time and name of the backup piece to the target database control file.

The Benefits of Block-Level Backups

Several benefits are realized with RMAN block-level backups. We have already described how the block is checked for corruption. Other benefits include the ability to implement various kinds of compression of the backup image. Finally, backing up at the block level can provide performance benefits. Let's look at each of these issues in more detail.

Null Block Compression

Null block compression becomes an option when we have access to the data block. We can eliminate blocks that have never been used (have a zeroed header) and discard them during the memory-to-memory write. Therefore, we only back up blocks that have been used and that have a more efficient backup.

This is a good place to mention the different misconceptions related to null block compression. The first misconception is that null compression eliminates empty blocks. The null compression algorithm has only two access points that RMAN has to the database: the file header and the block header. RMAN can only draw conclusions about the contents of a block from its header or from the file header information. Why no space management information? Space management information is only available when the database is open, and RMAN null compression cannot rely on the database being open. We must rely only on that information that we can get without an open database: namely, file headers and block headers. So, if you truncate a table, all the blocks that had information in them but are now empty will be backed up, because RMAN only knows that the block has been initialized by a segment. It does not know that the block is empty.

The second common misconception about null block compression is that null compression saves time during the backup because less is being backed up. This is true, to a certain extent, but only if your backup device is an extremely bad bottleneck. If you stream very quickly to your disk or tape backup location, then the act of eliminating blocks in memory saves little time because RMAN is still reading every block in the file into memory—it just is not writing every block to the output device. Even during incremental backups, which eliminate blocks based on an incremental checkpoint SCN, we still have to check the header of each block to discover if it has changed since the last incremental backup. Incremental backups, then, save space in our backup location, and they provide a faster form of recovery, but they are not meant to be a significant or reliable timesaver during the actual backup.

Unused Block Compression

Unused block compression is another mechanism for skipping unused blocks. It matches null block compression in its outcome: namely, never-initialized blocks will not be backed up. However, after version 10.2.0.3, it also can exclude used-but-empty blocks. This algorithm lends itself to saved time during backup, because it accesses space management information and checks the bitmaps for each segment. From this information, it builds the lists of initialized blocks and does not even attempt to back up the others. This means there is less total data read into memory, which translates into saved time.

Unused block compression is automatically used, but it cannot be used for all blocks in a database. There are architectural limits to the approach, and it requires the following be true:

- The backup requested is a full or level 0 incremental backup.
- The backup is going to disk (or Oracle Secure Backup).
- The **COMPATIBLE init** parameter is set to 10.2 or higher.
- There are no guaranteed restore points for the database.
- The datafile is locally managed (that is, the space management info is in the file header, not in the data dictionary).

It is this final element, locally managed datafiles, that allows RMAN to get the bitmap info it requires for successful unused block compression because it does not require a round trip through the (perhaps unavailable) data dictionary.

Binary Compression

In version 10g, RMAN finally made available a version of whitespace compression, as would be done by a ZIP utility. This provides actual compression of the backed-up blocks themselves. In addition, the new block-change tracking file allows RMAN to skip some blocks during backup without reading them into a memory buffer—so incremental backups begin to save time if the change tracking is turned on. For more on compression and block-change tracking, see the full coverage in Chapter 7.

Starting with version 11*g*, you can enable Oracle Advanced Compression, which provides three different levels of compression, so you can match the binary compression to your environment. The levels are High, Medium, and Low: High, for bandwidth-bound environments where limiting access to the network resources is the highest priority; Medium, for a combination of compression ratio to CPU utilization; and Low, where CPU utilization is the limiting factor over network bandwidth or total size of the backup piece.

Backup Performance with Block-Level Backup

Block-level backup also provides performance gains from the perspective of redo generation. As you learned in Chapter 2, if you use the old-school hot backup methodology, the amount of redo that you generate while you are running with a tablespace in hot backup mode can sometimes grow exponentially. This causes excess redo log switching, checkpoint failure, and massive amounts of archive log generation that can further cascade into space management challenges in your log archive destination.

RMAN, on the other hand, does not require hot backup mode because it does not need to guarantee block consistency during a backup. RMAN's access to the data block allows it to coordinate with DBWR processes writing dirty buffers, and it can wait until the block is consistent before it reads the block into memory. So, blocks aren't being dumped to redo, and we always have consistent blocks in our backup.

RMAN does require ARCHIVELOG mode, of course. In fact, RMAN will not allow you to back up a datafile while the database is open unless you are in ARCHIVELOG mode. It gives you the following polite error:

```
ORA-19602: cannot backup or copy active file in NOARCHIVELOG mode
```

RMAN also leverages block-level backups to provide an often-overlooked but extremely useful recovery option: block media recovery. Now, if you were to receive the stomach-turning "ora-1578: block corruption detected" error, instead of recovering the entire file and performing recovery, RMAN can simply recover the bad block and perform recovery, meaning the rest of the data in the datafile is available during the recovery. More information on this appears in Chapter 8.

Another nice feature of RMAN is multisection backups. Because RMAN handles backups at the block level, it can segment off very large datafiles (like those associated with bigfile tablespaces) and back up and restore those segments in parallel. This can make backup and restore much faster because it allows you to take advantage of as much parallelism as possible.

This just touches the surface of all the benefits you get from RMAN, but you get the point. The payoff is enormous when RMAN is utilized for block-level backups. The rest of this book is dedicated to utilizing this to your advantage.

RMAN in Memory

RMAN builds buffers in memory through which it streams data blocks for potential backup. This memory utilization counts against the total size of the PGA and, sometimes, the SGA. There are two kinds of memory buffers. *Input buffers* are the buffers that are filled with data blocks read from files that are being backed up. *Output buffers* are the buffers that are filled when the memory-to-memory write occurs to determine whether a particular block needs to be backed up. When the output buffer is filled, it is written to the backup location. The memory buffers differ depending on whether you are backing up to or restoring from disk or tape. Figure 3-1 illustrates

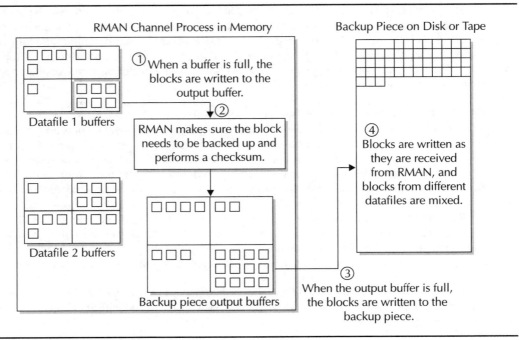

RMAN Channel Process in Memory

Backup Piece on Disk or Tape

Datafile 1 buffers

① When a buffer is full, the blocks are written to the output buffer.

② RMAN makes sure the block needs to be backed up and performs a checksum.

Datafile 2 buffers

Backup piece output buffers

③ When the output buffer is full, the blocks are written to the backup piece.

④ Blocks are written as they are received from RMAN, and blocks from different datafiles are mixed.

FIGURE 3-1. *Input and output buffers in memory*

input and output buffer allocation. It illustrates a backup of two datafiles being multiplexed into a single backup set.

Input Memory Buffers

When you are backing up the database, the size and number of input memory buffers depend on the exact backup command being executed. Primarily, they depend on the number of files being multiplexed into a single backup. *Multiplexing* refers to the number of files that will have their blocks backed up to the same backup piece. To keep the memory allocation within reason, the following rules are applied to the memory buffer sizes based on the number of files being backed up together (this is known as multiplexing):

- If the number of files going into the backup set is four or less, then RMAN allocates four buffers per file at 1MB per buffer. The total will be 16MB or less.

- If the number of files going into the backup set is greater than four but no greater than eight, then each file gets four buffers, each of 512KB. This ensures that the total remains at 16MB or less.

- If the number of files being multiplexed is greater than eight, then RMAN allocates four buffers of size 128KB. This ensures that each file being backed up will account for 512KB of buffer memory.

Bear in mind that these memory amounts are on a per-channel basis. So, if you allocate two channels to back up a database with 32 datafiles, for instance, then RMAN will load-balance the files between the two channels and may not end up with 16 files per channel. If some files are significantly larger than others, you may end up with only 8 files going into one backup set and 24 files going into the other. If this were the case, then the buffers for the first channel with eight files would allocate 16MB of memory for input buffers (four buffers multiplied by 512KB each, multiplied by eight files), and the second channel would allocate 12MB of memory buffers (512KB per file multiplied by 24 files).

The formula for the number of input buffers is slightly different if you are using ASM. In this case the number of buffers that will be created is the same as the number of physical disks in the ASM disk group. In this case, the size of these buffers is dependent on the operating system that the database is running on. Additionally, ASM will autotune the buffers related to a backup, so when you are running ASM you really don't need to worry about the input buffers that much.

You can use the following query to monitor the size of buffers on a per-file basis while the backup is running:

```
SELECT set_count, device_type, type, filename,
buffer_size, buffer_count, open_time, close_time
FROM v$backup_async_io
ORDER BY set_count,type, open_time, close_time;
```

Output Buffers When Backing Up to Disk

In addition to input buffers, RMAN allocates output buffers, depending on what the output source is. If you are backing up to disk, then RMAN allocates output buffers that must fill up with data blocks from the input buffers before being flushed to the backup destination on your file system. Per channel, there will be four output buffers, each of which is 1MB. Therefore, the memory footprint per channel will always be 4MB.

The movement of blocks from the input buffers to the output buffers is also where some critical RMAN processing occurs, including validation, compression, and encryption of the data blocks. Note that there are varying levels of validation available, which we will discuss in later chapters of this book.

Output Memory Buffers When Backing Up to Tape

Memory allocation is different when backing up to tape, to account for the slower I/O rates that we expect from tape devices. When you are backing up to or restoring from tape, RMAN typically allocates four buffers per channel process, each of which is 256KB, so that the total memory footprint per channel is 1MB. These values can be platform dependent and can also be adjusted when allocating the RMAN channels. We discuss allocating RMAN channels starting in Chapter 11 of this book and then really throughout many of the remaining chapters.

Memory Buffers on Restore

During a restore from a disk backup, the input buffers will be 1MB, and RMAN will allocate four buffers per channel. When restoring from tape, RMAN allocates four input buffers with a size of BLKSIZE, which defaults to 256KB. The output buffers on restore are always 128KB, and there will be four of them per channel.

Multisection Backups and Memory

Starting in Oracle Database 11g, Oracle introduced a new feature that allows RMAN to use multiple channels to back up a single large file. This means that the memory input/output buffer conversation earlier still holds true, but the buffers are per channel, not necessarily per file.

Therefore, each channel opens the four input buffers for each section of the file it will be backing up. The output buffers remain the same as the preceding algorithm per backup piece.

RMAN Memory Utilization: PGA vs. SGA

Backups to disk use PGA memory space for backup buffers, which is allocated out of the memory space for the channel processes. If your operating system is not configured for native asynchronous I/O, you can utilize the parameter DBWR_IO_SLAVES to use I/O slaves for filling up the input buffers in memory. If this parameter is set to any nonzero value, RMAN automatically allocates four I/O slaves to coordinate the load of blocks into the input memory buffer. To coordinate this work, RMAN must utilize a shared memory location. Therefore, the memory buffers for disk backups are pushed into the shared pool, or the large pool if one exists.

Memory for tape output buffers is allocated in the PGA, unless you are using tape I/O slaves. To enable tape I/O slaves, you set the init.ora parameter BACKUP_TAPE_IO_SLAVES to TRUE. This can be done dynamically and set in the SPFILE if you desire. When this is set to TRUE, RMAN creates a single slave process per channel to assist with the backup workload. To coordinate this work, RMAN pushes the memory allocation into the SGA.

If either of these I/O slave options is configured, memory will be pulled from the shared pool area in the SGA, unless you have a large pool configured. If you do not have a large pool configured and you expect to use I/O slaves, we highly recommend that you create a large pool with a size based on the total number of channels you expect to allocate for your backups, plus 1MB for overhead. If you already have a large pool for Shared Servers (formerly MTS), JDBC connection pooling, or because you have PARALLEL_AUTOMATIC_TUNING set to TRUE, then increase the size of the pool to account for the RMAN memory buffers.

This introduction to the RMAN memory architecture does not include much information on tuning your system to cope with RMAN backups. Obviously, a resource hit takes place while RMAN is running. In fact, you can tune RMAN to use more or less resources, depending on your needs. Chapter 16 discusses how to do this in greater detail.

One last note on memory utilization: If you are backing up to tape, you will be using a media management server product. If you are running your media manager from the same system as your target database, you will need additional system resources for the tape subsystem. Be sure to factor this in when tuning for backups.

The Large Pool in the Oracle SGA

The large pool is a specific area in the SGA of Oracle's memory space. It is configured using the LARGE_POOL_SIZE parameter in your init.ora or SPFILE, and the value is specified in bytes. The large pool is utilized for certain memory activities that require shared space but tend to walk all over the usual operations in the shared pool. Its occupants are primarily restricted to RMAN memory buffers if I/O slaves are used, and Shared Servers for connection pooling. Sometimes the large pool is used for Java connections, and it will also house parallel query slaves if you set PARALLEL_AUTOMATIC_TUNING to TRUE (this is deprecated in 10g).

Do you need a large pool? No. Without one, all of its potential occupants simply take up space in the shared pool. This is not the end of the world, but it's highly desirable to separate out RMAN buffers into their own space in the PGA. That way, SQL and PL/SQL parsing and other normal shared pool operations are not affected by RMAN backups, and vice versa. It also makes tuning the Oracle memory space for RMAN simpler and more straightforward.

The Recovery Catalog

So far, we have discussed the two most important RMAN components: the RMAN client utility and the internal database packages. However, another component is involved with RMAN backups, although its usage is entirely optional: the recovery catalog. Our advice, use the recovery catalog!

The recovery catalog is a repository for metadata about RMAN backups. In a sense, you can think of the recovery catalog as merely a copy of the pertinent information out of the control file that RMAN requires for backup and recovery purposes. You create the recovery catalog in a user's schema in an Oracle database, and it is no more than a few packages, tables, indexes, and views. These tables contain data that is refreshed from the target database control file upon a resync command from within RMAN. The difference, of course, is that the recovery catalog can contain information about all the databases in your enterprise—and the control file holds only information about its own database.

To use a recovery catalog, you first connect from RMAN to the target database. Then, you make a second Oracle Net connection to the recovery catalog from within RMAN, like this:

```
rman>connect target /
rman>connect catalog rman/password@rcat
```

In the connect string to the catalog, you pass the username and password for the user who owns the RMAN catalog. Unlike with the target, the connection to the catalog is not a sysdba connection and does not need this privilege granted to it.

Once connected, you can manually resync the catalog, or it will be implicitly resynchronized on any backup or restore operation. A *resync* refers to the refreshing of the information from the target database control file to the tables in the recovery catalog.

A recovery catalog can serve as a repository for more than one target database, and as such can help centralize the administration of backups of many different databases. It has views that can be queried from SQL*Plus to determine the number, size, and range of backups for each target database that has been registered in that catalog.

Figure 3-2 details the network topology when a catalog is used. Two Oracle packages are used to manage the recovery catalog: DBMS_RCVMAN and DBMS_RCVCAT. It is in this way that

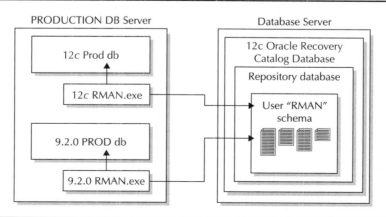

FIGURE 3-2. *Connecting to a recovery catalog*

the RMAN utility can use either the recovery catalog or the target database control file for information about backup and recovery, and not worry about different implementations.

The package name DBMS_RCVMAN in the recovery catalog can lead to some confusion on the database that houses the recovery catalog. This database is usually referred to as the *catalog database*. The catalog database is also a potential target database, so it also has a package in the SYS schema called DBMS_RCVMAN; thus, if you select from DBA_OBJECTS on your catalog database, there are two packages with the same name, in two different schemas. This is not a mistake or a problem. One of them is built by the catproc.sql at the time of database creation (in the SYS schema), and the other is built when we create the recovery catalog (in a regular user schema).

The second package in the recovery catalog is DBMS_RCVCAT, and it is only used to perform operations specific to the recovery catalog during RMAN operations. In essence, you can think of this package as being the recovery catalog implementation of DBMS_BACKUP_RESTORE; whereas DBMS_BACKUP_RESTORE writes backup completion information to the target database control file, DBMS_RCVCAT does this in the recovery catalog.

The base tables that contain information in the recovery catalog are unimportant because you do not want to manually modify them. Instead, for the catalog's protection, Oracle created a series of views, all prefixed with RC_, that can be used to extract information from the catalog. Manually issuing any DML against catalog objects is a dangerous prospect, and we don't recommend it. The RC_* views, and what you can get from them, are outlined in Chapter 11. As noted there, these views are different implementations of corresponding v$views in the database control file.

The Auxiliary Database

The *auxiliary database* refers to the instance that will become host to restored files from the target database in the event of a tablespace point-in-time recovery (TSPITR), a duplication operation (cloning the database), or the creation of a standby database using RMAN backups. Also, the auxiliary database is used for new features in Oracle Database 12c such as the ability to extract individual tables from backups (discussed in Chapter 9). When you perform any of these tasks, you will be connecting to the target database and the auxiliary database at the same time from within RMAN. In this way, you can utilize the information about the backups in the target database control file to coordinate the restore of those backups to the auxiliary database location. The following shows the connection to both the target database (locally) and the auxiliary database (using an Oracle Net connection):

```
rman>connect target /
rman>connect auxiliary sys/pwd@aux1
```

RMAN makes a simultaneous connection to each database and requires access to the SYS .DBMS_BACKUP_RESTORE and SYS.DBMS_RCVMAN packages in both the target database and the auxiliary database. As such, RMAN requires SYSDBA, SYSOPER, or SYSBACKUP privilege at the auxiliary, just as it does at the target. Because you have to connect to both databases using privileged accounts, you should configure both of them with a password file so that you can make a privileged Oracle Net connection to it. This is a requirement, especially if you want to use OEM to manage your backups and use a recovery catalog.

We discuss the auxiliary database setup in great detail in Chapter 21. Figure 3-3 shows the network topology of an RMAN configuration when an auxiliary database is used.

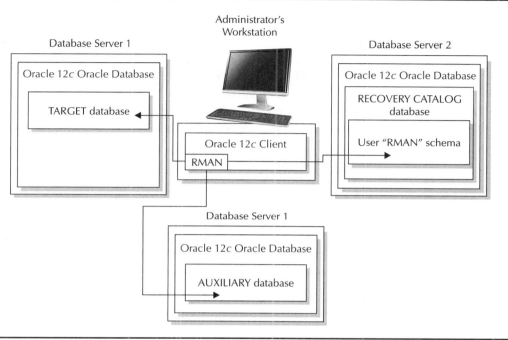

FIGURE 3-3.   *Network topology with an auxiliary database in the mix*

Compatibility Issues

Given the number of different components that we have to work with, you must stick with database version restrictions when working with RMAN. There are five different pieces to the compatibility puzzle, each of which has a version number:

- The RMAN executable version (the client utility)
- The target database
- The recovery catalog schema
- The recovery catalog database
- The auxiliary database (for duplication, TSPITR, and standby creation)

The easiest answer, of course, is to make sure all of these components are on the latest version of the database. If they are all at the same level, then there is no problem, right? Of course, in the world where all of your databases are at the same level, everyone has their very own pony, fairies roam the earth, babies never cry, and no one ever has to take backups because failures never occur. But for the world we live in, there are some things to understand about RMAN version compatibility.

Some general rules must be considered when it comes to compatibility. Let's take a look at those.

Target/Auxiliary Database Version	RMAN Client Version	Recovery Catalog Database Version	Recovery Catalog Schema Version
10.1.0.5	>=10.1.0.5 and <= target database executable	>=10.1.0.5	>= RMAN client version
10.2.0	>=10.1.0.5 and <= target database executable	>=10.1.0.5	>= RMAN client version
11.1.0	>=10.1.0.5 and <= target database executable	>=10.2.0.3	>= RMAN client version
11.2.0	>=10.1.0.5 and <= target database executable	>=10.2.0.3	>= RMAN client version
12.1.0.x	= 12.1.0.x	>= 10.2.0.3	= RMAN client version (Also note that you must create your recovery catalog using Oracle Enterprise Edition. Oracle no longer supports creating a recovery catalog when using Standard Edition.)

TABLE 3-1. *RMAN Compatibility Matrix*

The RMAN General Compatibility Rules

A general set of rules apply to RMAN compatibility issues. The version of the RMAN client should be equal to the following:

- The version of the target database.
- The version of the auxiliary database.
- The version of the recovery catalog.
- Any release of the Oracle database can restore backup sets or image copies that were created be any earlier version of the Oracle database. Thus, an 12.1.0.2 Oracle database RMAN client can be used to restore an 11.2.0.4 database.

Table 3-1 provides a copy of the RMAN compatibility matrix you can use to refer to the supported versions of the various components of RMAN.

The RMAN Process: From Start to Finish

So far, we have discussed the different architectural components of taking a backup using Recovery Manager. As you may have noticed, there are a number of pieces to keep straight. To put it into a little perspective, we will run through a typical backup operation and explain the underlying

RMAN activity at every step. That way, you should be able to associate the lengthy exposition in this chapter to the actual steps that you will take to perform a backup.

The following example illustrates a backup of a database called PROD. The backup will be going to a disk location; the discussion of setting up and utilizing a media manager for backups to tape will be deferred to Chapters 4 through 8. The target database PROD has 20 datafiles and is running in ARCHIVELOG mode. The database is up and running during this operation. Here is our backup command:

```
C$>rman
rman>connect target /
rman>backup database;
```

That's it. That's all it takes. The following discussion explains what happens.

RMAN makes the bequeath connection to the target database that we have set up in our environment. This means it checks the variable ORACLE_SID for an instance name, then spawns a server process at that instance, logging in as a sysdba user. This connects as the internal database user SYS. RMAN immediately spawns the channel processes that will be used to perform the backup. In this case, we are using default settings, so only one channel is allocated. We are not using I/O slaves, so the process allocates memory in the PGA.

Next, RMAN compiles a call to SYS.DBMS_RCVMAN to request database schematic information from the target database control file, starting with a determination of the target database version. It gathers version information from the control file, along with control file information itself: What type of control file is it? What is the sequence number current in it? When was it created?

Because we have specified a full database backup, RMAN requests information for each datafile in the database and determines if any files are offline. As part of this information, it gathers which disk each file is on and how to dole out the work. Because we are using default settings, there will be only one channel and only one backup set. Therefore, RMAN ignores all disk affinity information and concentrates on compiling the list of files for inclusion in the backup set.

After the list is compiled, RMAN is ready to begin the backup process itself. To guarantee consistency, it then builds the snapshot control file. If one already exists, it overwrites it with a new one. Then RMAN creates the call to the DBMS_BACKUP_RESTORE package to create the backup piece. The backup piece will be built in the default file location; on Unix, this is ORACLE_HOME/dbs, and on Windows, it is ORACLE_HOME/database. RMAN has the file list, so it can allocate the memory buffers for performing the read from disk. With 20 files, RMAN allocates input buffers of size 128KB. There will be four buffers per file, for a total memory utilization of 10MB for input buffers. RMAN will only allocate four output buffers, each of 1MB. This brings our total memory utilization to 14MB for the backup.

After the memory is allocated, RMAN initializes the backup piece. The backup piece will be given a default name that guarantees uniqueness. RMAN then begins the backup. In database versions 9.2, 10.1, and 10.2, RMAN allocates disk space in 50MB increments: 50MB is allocated on disk and filled with output buffers; when full, another 50MB is grabbed, until the last block is dumped to the backup piece. When the backup is complete, any remaining space in the final 50MB chunk is freed. It is worth pointing out that RMAN no longer does a check to see if there is enough space to complete the entire backup at the onset. This is due to the fact that null compression, and also whitespace compression, will significantly reduce the backup from being the size of the datafiles. Instead, RMAN will run its backup until it runs out of space and then fail.

Once the backup piece is initiated, the channel process can begin the database backup process. RMAN determines if you are using an SPFILE, and if so, it backs it up automatically as part of your backup set. Then RMAN will back up the current control file to the backup set. This control file backup is automatic whenever the SYSTEM tablespace is backed up; this behavior is changed if you have control file autobackup turned on (see Chapter 11).

So, we have the SPFILE and the control file backed up, it is time to begin the datafile reads to pull data blocks into memory. The channel process does this by doing a read-ahead on the disk and pulling several blocks into memory at the same time. Then, the memory-to-memory write from input buffer to output buffer occurs. During this write, RMAN determines if the block has ever been initialized or if the block header information is still zeroed out. If it is an unused block, the write to the output buffer never occurs and the block is discarded. If the block has been used, RMAN performs a checksum on the block. If the header and footer of the block do not match, RMAN indicates a corrupt block and aborts the backup. If the block has been initialized and it passes the checksum, then that block is written to the output buffer.

Once the output buffer fills to capacity, we dump the buffer to the backup file location. The RMAN buffers are being filled up with blocks from all of the datafiles, so there is no order to the blocks in the dump file. The file is merely a bucket, and only RMAN will be able to restore the blocks to their proper location upon restore. While the blocks are being written out to the backup piece, the status of the backup is being polled by the RMAN shadow process. It checks in on the RPCs at the target and passes that information to V$SESSION_LONGOPS for your review. Based on the information gathered at the beginning of the backup operation, RMAN has an estimated completion percentage for each channel process. This can be viewed in V$SESSION_LONGOPS:

```
SELECT SID, SERIAL#, CONTEXT, SOFAR, TOTALWORK,
       ROUND(SOFAR/TOTALWORK*100,2) "%_COMPLETE"
FROM V$SESSION_LONGOPS
WHERE OPNAME LIKE 'RMAN%'
AND OPNAME NOT LIKE '%aggregate%'
AND TOTALWORK != 0
AND SOFAR <> TOTALWORK
/
       SID    SERIAL#    CONTEXT      SOFAR  TOTALWORK %_COMPLETE
---------- ---------- ---------- ---------- ---------- ----------
        17        167          1       4784     116328       4.11
```

You can reissue this query throughout the backup process to get an update on the work still needing to be completed:

```
       SID    SERIAL#    CONTEXT      SOFAR  TOTALWORK %_COMPLETE
---------- ---------- ---------- ---------- ---------- ----------
        17        167          1      96999     116328      83.38
```

Once every block in a datafile has been read into an input buffer and its status determined, then RMAN completes the file backup by writing the datafile header out to the backup piece. After all the files have their file headers written to the backup piece, RMAN makes a final call to SYS.DBMS_BACKUP_RESTORE, which writes backup information to the control file. This information includes the name of the backup piece, the checkpoint SCN at the time it started, and the time it completed.

And that is the entire process. Obviously, it gets more complex if we exercise more backup options, such as using multiple channels, using the FILESPERSET parameter, and backing up to tape. But each of these configurations shares the same fundamental process as previously described. If at any time during your study or testing of RMAN you want a more intimate look at the internal steps RMAN takes during backup, you can turn the debug option on for the backup and get a complete list of the entire process:

```
rman target / debug trace=/u02/oradata/trace/rmanbkup.out
```

Be warned, though, that this output is extremely verbose, and it can hamper backup performance. Only use debug for learning purposes on TEST instances, unless otherwise instructed to do so by Oracle Support Services when you are troubleshooting a production backup problem.

The Fast Recovery Area

The Fast Recovery Area (FRA) is not a requirement for using RMAN, but it should be. The FRA was introduced in Oracle Database version 10g. It was first called the Flash Recovery Area but was then renamed to the Fast Recovery Area. The term *recovery files* refers to all files that might be required for a media recovery operation: full datafile backups, incremental backups, datafile copies, backup control files, and archive logs. The FRA also functions as a repository for mirrored copies of online redo log files, the block-change tracking file, and for a current control file. If set up, flashback logs for using the flashback database option also live in the FRA.

The concept behind the FRA is to simplify the management of your backup and recovery duties by consolidating the requisite files into a single location that Oracle and RMAN can then micromanage, while the DBA moves on to other important duties. The FRA really is part of an overall backup and recovery architecture strategy that is designed to ensure that the database is recoverable, with a minimum of work on the part of the DBA. We discuss this architecture in more detail in Chapter 5.

The FRA that you set up can be either a directory on a normal disk volume or an Automatic Storage Management (ASM) disk group. The FRA is determined by two initialization parameters: DB_RECOVERY_FILE_DEST and DB_RECOVERY_FILE_DEST_SIZE. The first determines the location; the second, the size. These can be set in your init.ora file, if you still use one, or in the SPFILE via an **alter system set** command. We will discuss configuring the FRA in more detail in Chapter 5.

With an FRA configured, you are not required to set any other LOG_ARCHIVE_DEST_*n* parameter for archive logs; by default, with an FRA, Oracle will default the setting for LOG_ARCHIVE_DEST_10 to use the FRA. There may be some cases where you will want to set other log archived destination directories—for example, with standby databases. We will discuss those specific cases as we come to them in the different chapters of this book.

It should also be noted that with an FRA in use, the parameters LOG_ARCHIVE_DEST or LOG_ARCHIVE_DUPLEX_DEST are mutually exclusive, but you certainly rid yourself of these outdated parameters long ago, right?

The FRA manages recovery files internally, first based on database name, then on types of files, and then by the dates when the files are generated. The files themselves are named according to the Oracle Managed Files (OMF) format. Significant internal directory structures exist for file management. However, the point of an FRA is that you don't need to spend much time worrying about the files.

The same FRA can be used by multiple databases. This can provide significant advantages, particularly for a Data Guard configuration, but also if you have a large ASM disk group and multiple databases on the same system. It can come in handy, as well, when it comes time to clone production for test purposes.

Summary

In this chapter, we have covered the basic RMAN architecture. We talked about server-managed recovery and then we started a discussion on the RMAN utility. We also talked about RMAN and some networking considerations, and we discussed the control file and its importance related to RMAN operations. We then discussed the various RMAN processes and how RMAN backs up database blocks. We also discussed how RMAN uses memory, the RMAN recovery catalog, and the RMAN auxiliary database. We finished this chapter by discussing how RMAN backups work in general, followed by a discussion on compatibility and finally the Fast Recovery Area. That's a lot of ground to cover in a few pages! Time to move on to the next chapter and learn even more about RMAN!

CHAPTER
4

Oracle Database 12c Multitenant

One of the truly defining new features of Oracle Database 12*c* is the introduction of *Oracle Multitenant* (and it's my intent to use the acronym OM for Oracle Multitenant—it's not official, but my goodness it saves a lot of typing!). In fact, OM may perhaps be the biggest architectural change to the Oracle database ever. OM is designed to add a number of database efficiencies to your environment, including the following:

- Quick and efficient provisioning of databases
- Easier database patching
- Easier database consolidation efforts
- More robust and efficient resource utilization

In this chapter we want to introduce you to this new architecture. We won't discuss anything really specific to RMAN here, but what we do discuss will be relevant to RMAN operations that you will learn about later in this book. Thus, we are teaching you about how OM works here, and we will save the RMAN goodies relative to OM for the chapters they most appropriately belong in. For example, backing up an Oracle Multitenant database with RMAN is covered in Chapter 7, where we discuss RMAN backups. For the most part, you will find that many things don't change a great deal. However, some things are different, and we will make sure to point those out to you.

Also, let's be clear that for right now, using Oracle Multitenant is wholly optional; in fact, it's a separate licensed product. You can upgrade your pre-12*c* database to Oracle Database 12*c* and it will look, act, and feel just the same as it did before. The good news, then, is that you do not need to move all of your Oracle databases into a multitenant model—yet. However, I suspect that someday this will be the only model available for use. As a result, it's a good idea to get a leg up on what's coming in the future and learn how to use the features of OM now when you have the time rather than when it's forced upon you.

Therefore, this chapter is designed to be an introduction to OM so that you can be prepared to integrate RMAN backup strategies into the OM architecture. The goal of this chapter is that once you have finished it, you should understand the following:

- The basic architecture of OM databases
- How OM databases differ from non-OM databases
- What a CDB is, and what a PDB is
- The different kinds of users/schemas present in an OM database architecture and the basic security model for these different kinds of users/schemas
- A review of features in OM databases that are related to overall backup, recovery, and similar operations in an Oracle database

So, let's get started and see what all this OM stuff is all about.

Introducing Oracle Multitenant

Oracle Database 12*c* has introduced a new feature called *Oracle Multitenant*. This one feature is perhaps the biggest change in the Oracle database ever, so it's important to know about it.

Oracle Multitenant introduces some interesting changes to the traditional architecture of the Oracle Database from both the physical and logical points of view. Until now, it has always been a given that a particular Oracle Database instance (or set of instances, in the case of an Oracle RAC database) is always associated with only one database. With the introduction of Oracle Multitenant, that basic assumption is no longer always true. Now, one database instance can have many databases attached to it. We know, we might well have already sent your head spinning.

Oracle Multitenant provides the ability to create multiple Oracle databases (called *pluggable databases,* or PDBs) within the confines of a single main database called the *container database* (CDB). These PDBs then share the various computing resources of the CDB, which makes the overall data processing system much more efficient.

Typical use cases for OM databases are several. Consolidation of a large number of disparate databases often rises to the top of the list. Oracle Multitenant is a great tool for database consolidation. Beyond the typical use cases for consolidation (reduction in power usage, cooling costs, space requirements, and so on) using Oracle Multitenant Database can be a much more efficient platform to run multiple databases on from a performance and resource utilization point of view. It is simply more efficient to run more databases as PDBs in an Oracle Multitenant database than to run them individually on the same machine. Also, the OM database environment provides powerful features that make it quick and easy to clone databases within a CDB or over to another CDB.

In this section then, we introduce you to the principal actors in the Oracle Multitenant Database play. First, we discuss the CDB in some more detail, and then we discuss the PDB in more detail. Finally, we talk a little bit about how Oracle Multitenant impacts backup and recovery with RMAN.

The CDB

At the core of the Oracle Multitenant architecture is what is called the *container database* (CDB), which is the parent, or *root,* structure within the OM architecture. The container database is the overarching owner of an OM database. It is a database in its own right, and when you start an OM database instance, what you are really starting is the instance associated with the container database. Therefore, the processes (or threads) and SGA memory that are allocated when the OM database is started belong to that one container database. Let's look at the CDB in a bit more detail then. In the following sections we will look at the following:

- The architecture of the CDB
- Naming the CDB
- CDB creation
- The CDB root container

Architecture of the CDB

The CDB is very much like an Oracle database. One might say it's an "Oracle database on steroids." As we discuss the architecture of the CDB in this section, you will find that it is very familiar. As we progress through the different components of the CDB, use Figure 4-1 as a reference to help you put all the pieces together. The components of the CDB are as follows:

- **The instance**   As with normal Oracle databases, the CDB is associated with an Oracle instance. Obviously if the CDB is an Oracle RAC database, it will have one or more instances associated with it. The CDB and all of the PDBs associated with that CDB share the same instance. Therefore, they share all of the same SGA memory structures, and there is just one set of parameters that is used to configure memory.

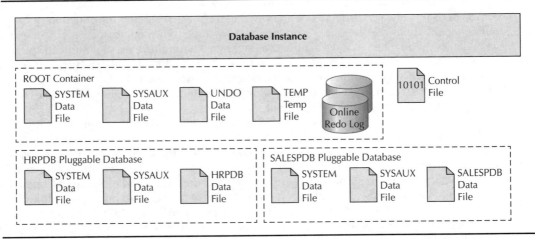

FIGURE 4-1. *The CDB architecture*

- **The CDB** The CDB represents the database as a whole. The CDB contains multiple containers that store metadata and database data. The database instance is directly tied to the CDB.

- **Containers or pluggable databases (PDBs)** The container is the principal storage unit for system metadata and system schema information (see the root container). It can also be a unique and isolated storage location for specific database metadata and schema data. Containers are also known as *pluggable databases,* or PDBs. A CDB can contain one or more PDBs.

  One thing you will want to be aware of is that the Oracle database does not consider CDB$ROOT to be a PDB, but it does consider it to be a container. Therefore, if you are querying the data dictionary views (which we will discuss later in this chapter), keep in mind that if you want to see everything, including the CDB$ROOT container, you will need to use the various container views rather than the PDB views. This is important, as you will see in a moment, because if you use the wrong views, you very well might miss something important.

  Figure 4-2 provides an example of how CDBs and PDBs work together.

- **Root container** Each CDB has exactly one root container. This container provides a location for schemas, schema objects, and non schema objects that belong to the CDB as a whole. System metadata required for the database to manage the individual PDBs is stored in the root container. The root container is named CDB$ROOT.

- **Seed PDB** Each CDB has an Oracle-supplied container called PDB$SEED that is used as a template to create new PDBs within the CDB. You cannot add or modify objects in PDB$SEED.

- **PDB** See *Containers or pluggable databases (PDBs)*.

- **Oracle Database instance** This includes the normal instance-related items such as the instance parameter files, System Global Area (SGA), and background processes.

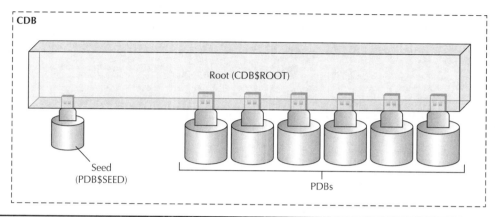

FIGURE 4-2.   *The Oracle Multitenant CDB and PDBs*

- **At least one control file**   As with a non-CDB, you would typically multiplex the control file. This control file supports the CDB and all PDBs that are plugged into that CDB.

- **Two or more online redo log groups**   As with a non-CDB, you would typically create several groups and multiplex them. These redo logs support the entire CDB, along with all the PDBs that are plugged into it. Because the online redo logs serve the entire CDB and all associated PDBs, they need to be large enough and sufficiently numerous to avoid performance problems. If you add PDBs to a CDB, you may need to analyze the online redo log requirements for the CDB and determine if you need to enlarge the size of or increase the number of online redo logs. The online redo logs are considered to be stored as a part of the root container. If the CDB instance/database is in ARCHIVELOG mode, then archived redo logs will also be created by the CDB via the normal ARCH process. The configuration of ARCHIVELOG mode itself is done at the level of the CDB. You cannot opt to disable ARCHIVELOG mode for individual PDBs.

- **One or more sets of temporary files**   A CDB has a minimum of a single temporary tablespace, called TEMP by default. This tablespace is contained in the root container and supports the temporary tablespace needs of the root CDB and all the attached PDBs. You can create and define a different default temporary tablespace for the CDB, if you choose. You can also give individual PDBs their own individual temporary tablespaces.

- **An UNDO tablespace and related tempfiles**   A single UNDO tablespace and its tempfiles reside in the root container of the CDB in a non-RAC configuration. In a RAC configuration, you will have an UNDO tablespace for each thread. The UNDO tablespace supports the entire CDB and all PDBs.

- **SYSTEM and SYSAUX**   These CDB system-related tablespace datafiles contain the data dictionary for the root container. These tablespaces also contain pointers to data dictionary information associated with attached PDBs (more on this later). The CDB has no user tablespaces or related datafiles. No data should ever be stored in the CDB. Though it's possible to create objects in the SYSTEM and SYSAUX tablespaces, as always, those tablespaces are reserved for Oracle only.

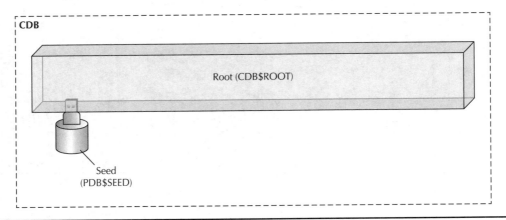

FIGURE 4-3. *The freshly created CDB*

It's clear that the CDB itself is a database. That is, it has its own tablespaces, data dictionary, UNDO tablespace, TEMP tablespace, control files, and online redo logs, just like a regular database. You can create objects in the CDB, just like any other database, but please do not do this—this is bad form, and the CDB police will come looking for you and subject you to hours of watching Jim Carrey making the world's most obnoxious noise on YouTube until you promise that you will never again create objects in the CDB without support telling you to.

Figure 4-3 provides an example of what a typical CDB looks like just after it's created for the first time.

Naming the CDB

You might have more than one Oracle database instance running on your database server right now. In the same way that you can run many database instances, you can run many CDB database instances. That being the case, it follows that just like Oracle database instances have database names (or SIDs), so, too, do CDB database instances.

Just as a given database server can host many non-CDB Oracle databases, it can also host many CDBs. Like a regular Oracle database, each CDB has its own ORACLE_SID that identifies that CDB uniquely from every other database (CDB or not) on that database server. For example, on my Oracle Database 12*c* server I currently have two database SIDs. One is a non-CDB (called orcl) and one is a CDB (called contdb). The following example shows the two LGWR processes running:

```
ps -ef|grep lgwr
oracle    4135    1   0 18:52 ?        00:00:00 ora_lgwr_contdb
oracle    5127    1   0 19:30 ?        00:00:00 ora_lgwr_orcl
```

Because not all Oracle databases are CDBs, you will want to be able to determine whether you are dealing with a CDB or not. For example, you might need to know this information if you want to be able to create or plug in a PDB because the related database must have been created as a CDB. To see if your database has been created as a CDB, you can query the V$DATABASE view column named CDB, as shown here:

```
select name, cdb from v$database;
NAME       CDB
---------  ---
CONTDB     YES
```

The preceding output shows that a database called CONTDB has been created as an OM container database. Also note that the same instance- and database-naming restrictions on non-CDBs apply to CDBs.

CDB Creation

You create a CDB in almost the same way you create a regular Oracle database, except that you indicate that the database to be created is a container database. This is done by adding the **enable pluggable database** clause to the **create database** command or by clicking a button and adding some additional information within the Database Configuration Assistant (DBCA) when creating a database. You must take into account a number of different considerations when creating a CDB, and this book isn't really about creating Oracle databases. Therefore, we refer you to the Oracle Database Documentation (really, several books within that set) for planning considerations, details, and specifics on creating CDBs.

Oracle supports running a CDB only on Oracle Database version 12*c* and later. The COMPATIBLE parameter must be set to 12.0.0.0 or greater to be able to create a CDB. The version of the CDB and the PDBs that you will plug into the CDB must be the same. Thus, you cannot have an Oracle Database 11*g* PDB plugged into an Oracle 12*c* CDB. This also means you can't restore an 11*g* database to a 12*c* CDB (which is true also for a non-CDB database).

Another thing to note is that you cannot convert a CDB into a non-CDB. You cannot change an existing non-CDB into a CDB. Methods are available to move the PDBs in a CDB out of a CDB and make them their own stand-alone database. There are also methods available to take an existing database and move it into a CDB environment as a PDB. We address these methods in several chapters of this book as they become relevant.

The CDB Root Container

After you have created the CDB, it contains what is called the *root container* (introduced earlier in the section "Architecture of the CDB"). Each CDB has only one root container, which is open in read-only mode whenever the CDB itself is open. The root container is used to store system information about the CDB itself and to store all the metadata required for PDBs that will later become part of the CDB. The root container is a single PDB called CDB$ROOT.

The CDB$ROOT container essentially stores all the CDB-related metadata. Therefore, the object definitions for all of the data dictionary tables and the underlying tables of the data dictionary with all of its associated data is there. We will talk about pluggable databases shortly, but in a CDB the pluggable database may actually store data relevant to that PDB as opposed to it being stored in CDB$ROOT. In this case, there are often pointers in the CDB$ROOT container that point to that data so it can be accessed when logged into the CDB$ROOT container. Figure 4-4 provides a graphic look at the root container and its contents.

So, you might be thinking, "If I can't put objects in a CDB, what good is it? Where do I put data and create schemas and do other kinds of DBA things?" I'm glad you asked. That's where the pluggable databases (PDBs) come in.

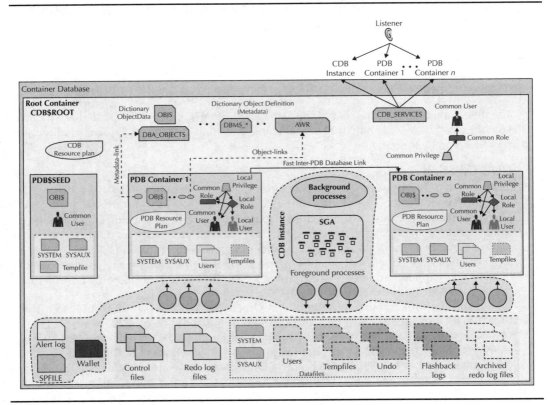

FIGURE 4-4. *The root container*

Pluggable Databases

I love the movie *Independence Day*. In this movie there is this huge alien ship that's the mother ship of many smaller, but still quite large and scary-looking, baby ships. This mother ship sends these baby ships out to go blow up things all over the earth. The CDB is kind of like a more peaceful version of that mother ship.

Think of the CDB as the mother ship. The little baby ships of this CDB are the pluggable databases (PDBs). When we say little, we only mean it metaphorically, because a PDB is an Oracle database—thus, it can store lots of data. So the main job of the CDB is to provide an environment in which anywhere from 0 to 253 PDBs can live, run, and thrive. Fortunately, they are not known to blow the smithereens out of Los Angeles and Washington, D.C., like the aliens do in *Independence Day!*

Each PDB is a wholly contained database in and of itself. Each PDB is separated from any other PDB within a CDB. Each PDB has the following:

- Its own container database name
- One or more unique service names

- Users and schema namespaces
- Tablespaces and datafiles
- A unique security domain

The application connects to a PDB through a service provided by that PDB that is registered to a listener process. This works just like any other individual Oracle database, and indeed in many ways that is what a PDB is—just another Oracle database simply sharing the resources of one instance instead of many. As a result, the PDB looks no different to the application than if it had been connected to a non-OM database. Thus, the application is abstracted from the architecture completely. This abstraction is taken a level deeper, even when you add Oracle RAC and the SCAN listener into the mix.

For the DBA, you should know that within the Oracle data dictionary the PDBs are often referred to as *containers,* and in this book we use both names interchangeably. Each PDB is assigned a unique identifier called the container ID, which displays as a column called CON_ID. This column is also found in many of the Oracle database data dictionary views of a CDB.

In Figure 4-5, we have taken the simple CDB we showed you in Figure 4-1 and have added PDBs to it.

Notice that every PDB has a name associated with it. When the PDB is created, a service with the name of the PDB is also created automatically. This service is registered with the listener process servicing that CDB. One thing to be careful about is service name collisions at the listener level. If you have two CDBs using the same listener service and they have two PDBs that are named the same, all sorts of issues will arise with your networking. One way around this is to have a separate listener for each CDB, or just make sure you don't name PDBs the same!

As a DBA, you will love the new CDB/PDB architecture because it makes many common DBA tasks much easier. The CDB/PDB architecture makes database cloning much easier, it makes moving databases between CDBs much easier, and it makes upgrading databases much easier. The CDB makes it easier to monitor your databases because they are centralized into one location.

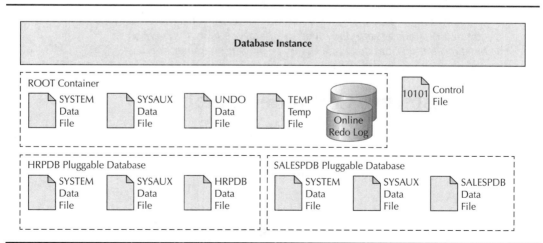

FIGURE 4-5. *A CDB and many PDBs*

Further, the PDBs share the memory and processor resources of the CDB. This results in a significant performance improvement and better resource utilization in environments where there are many databases. Memory is more efficiently utilized, and CPU utilization is typically much improved. Oracle has done significant testing and has demonstrated that you can efficiently run many more databases within the CDB architecture than outside of it.

How Does Oracle Multitenant Impact RMAN Backup and Recovery?

Since you are reading this book, you are probably wondering how backup and recovery operations change with the CDB and PDB architecture, and in large part they do not. As you will see in future chapters, you can back up all the databases of the CDB at once, or you can back up specific PDBs whenever you wish. You can back up datafiles and tablespaces, as well as perform all the other backup operations you are used to.

Recovery has not really changed much either. You can recover the whole CDB, or just an individual PDB, or a tablespace or datafile within a PDB. Not much difference there. Also slightly different is that fact that the redo logs for all PDBs within the CDB are common to the CDB, so there aren't individual online redo logs or archived redo logs for the PDBs. Therefore, when you restore a PDB, you will be using the CDB's redo logs.

The control file is also owned by the CDB. It now contains information about all the PDBs in the CDB, including RMAN-related backup information, as we'll discuss in later chapters.

The fact that the online redo logs and the control file are owned by the CDB do make for a couple of differences to specific backup and restore processes. These differences are minor, and we will point them out in the appropriate chapters when we come to them. Don't worry, though. You'll be able to sleep quite soundly at night in spite of these little differences.

Now that we have given you a higher-level introduction to Oracle Multitenant, let's circle back and look at things in a bit more detail.

NOTE
Oracle Multitenant is a separately licensed product that you need to purchase if you are going to take advantage of its features. At the time of this writing, the normal Oracle license will allow you to create a container database with one pluggable database in it. If you wish to have more than one pluggable database in your container database, you need to purchase Oracle Multitenant.

Administering Container Databases

With respect to RMAN backup and recovery, you will need to understand some of the subtle differences that exist with respect to administering CDBs and their PDBs. In this section we discuss the following topics:

- Starting and stopping the CDB
- Common users

Starting and Stopping the CDB

Starting and stopping the CDB is just like starting and stopping a normal Oracle database. In this section we demonstrate how to start and stop a CDB.

Starting the CDB

Starting the CDB itself is pretty much the same as starting a non-OM database, really. You simply log into the root of the CDB with a user who has the appropriate privileges and issue the **startup** command, as shown in this example:

```
-- set your Oracle environment for the CDB name (contdb in our case).
sqlplus sys/robert as sysdba
startup
```

All the various options of the **startup** command are available, including **startup nomount** and **startup mount**. When you start the CDB, the PDBs may or may not start automatically, depending on what version of Oracle 12*c* you are running and the state those PDBs were last in. Oracle 12.1.0.2 and later versions support the automated opening of PDBs when the CDB is opened. We discuss opening and closing PDBs later in this chapter.

Stopping the CDB

All the various **shutdown** commands are available for you to use when shutting down a CDB, including **shutdown abort, shutdown transactional**, and **shutdown immediate**. Here is an example of shutting down a CDB with the **shutdown immediate** command:

```
-- set your Oracle environment for the CDB name (contdb in our case).
sqlplus sys/robert as sysdba
SQL> shutdown immediate
Database closed.
Database dismounted.
ORACLE instance shut down.
```

Common Users

A *common user* is a new type of user created at the CDB level only. It is kind of a super user for the CDB, of sorts, but its access privileges can still be finely controlled. The common user exists throughout the CDB and can also be assigned to one or more PDBs, or to all PDBs. A PDB common user is local to that PDB.

When the CDB is created, common users are created that allow the DBA to administer not only the CDB but also all PDBs that are part of the CDB. Although these users are called "common," they are actually very powerful users. They have access not only to the CDB itself, but also to every PDB. The most powerful common user is the SYS user.

Common users can log into the CDB directly by setting the ORACLE_SID and simply logging into the database, as shown in the following example, where we are logging into the CDB CONTDB as the user c##robert using the **sysdba** privilege:

```
sqlplus c##robert/robert as sysdba
```

That looks pretty normal—well, except for the "c##" business.

Common users have the same identity in the root container and in every PDB attached (or that will be attached) to the database. A common user can log into any container, but the privileges of a common user can be administered separately within each PDB. For example, a common user might have the privilege to create a table in one PDB but not in another.

You can also create your own common users (which we will discuss in more detail next). Each common user account must be prefixed by the naming convention c##, followed by the common user name (for example, c##robert). Of course, Oracle-supplied user accounts such as SYS and

SYSTEM are exempt from this rule. The namespace for a given common user exists across all the containers of the CDB. Thus, if you create a c##robert user, that user exists in all containers in that database. This means you cannot have a local user c##robert in any individual PDB.

It is often the case that when you are logged into a CDB or any of its PDBs that you will want to know which one you are actually logged into. This is especially true for administrators who may move between different containers in SQL*Plus. To find out which container you are in, you can use the SQL*Plus **show con_name** command, as shown here:

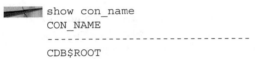

```
show con_name
CON_NAME
------------------------------
CDB$ROOT
```

In this case, the user is logged into a container (PDB) called CDB$ROOT, which is the root container.

Creating a Common User

Creating a common user is very similar to creating a normal user. You use the **create user** command to create the user. The following rules apply:

- You must be logged in with a user account that has the following privileges: **create user** and **set container**. The **set container** privilege is new, and it allows you to traverse containers using the **alter session set container** command. We show you an example of this in just a moment.

- Your current container must be the root container (CDB$ROOT):

  ```
  show con_name
  CON_NAME
  ------------------------------
  CDB$ROOT
  ```

  If you are logged in as a privileged user and need to change to the CDB$ROOT container, you can use the SQL command **alter session set container**, as mentioned earlier.

- Use the **create user** command to create the common user using the **container=all** option. Remember that the common user's name must start with c## or C##.

- When creating a common user, if you define default tablespaces, temporary tablespaces, quotas, and profiles when issuing the **create user** command, those objects must exist in all containers attached to the CDB. Otherwise, the **create user** command will fail.

NOTE
If you create a schema-level object as a common user, that object can be shared across the CDB.

Here is an example of creating a common user called c##robert:

```
show con_name
CON_NAME
------------------------------
CDB$ROOT

create user c##robert identified by robert container=all;
```

Of course, we still live by the Oracle security rules, so when we try to log into the database using this newly created user, the following happens:

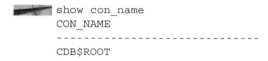

```
connect c##robert/ robert
ERROR:
ORA-01017: invalid username/password; logon denied
Warning: You are no longer connected to ORACLE.
```

As you might have guessed, we need to grant the **create session** privilege to the common user first, and then we can log in:

```
grant create session to c##robert;
connect c##robert/robert
```

In the previous example, we connected to the root container but not to a PDB. The procedure for connecting to a PDB is a bit different, as discussed later in this chapter.

Removing a Common User

Deleting a common user is quite simple: you connect to the root container as a user with privileges to drop other users and then you issue the **drop user** command, just as you always have. The following example drops the c##robert common user. The use of the **cascade** option causes a recursive removal of all objects that c##robert owns.

```
show con_name
CON_NAME
-------------------------------
CDB$ROOT

drop user c##robert cascade;
```

NOTE
*Did you notice that we use the **show con_name SQL*Plus** command a lot? With multiple PDBs it's even easier to find yourself in the wrong place within an Oracle database. Therefore, before you run a command, make sure you are in the right PDB.*

The Pluggable Database

A PDB is a logical collection of schema objects (tables, indexes, users, and so on). From the perspective of the application and local users, a PDB appears to be an independent database. This section discusses the following PDB topics:

- The PDB name
- Creating a PDB
- Connecting to a PDB
- The architecture of the pluggable database
- PDB performance
- PDB resource management

- Naming PDBs
- PDB local users
- Accessing PDBs

The PDB Name

Just as a CDB has a name (contdb, in our earlier example), each PDB has a unique name within the context of a CDB. The rules for naming PDBs are the same as the rules for naming services, which is important because local users can connect to an individual PDB only through a service name.

The rules for naming a PDB are as follows:

- The first character must be an alphabetical character.
- Subsequent characters can be alphanumeric or an underscore character.
- PDB names are case insensitive. Therefore, you cannot create a PDB called MYPDB and a PDB called mypdb—Oracle will not allow this.

Creating a PDB

We use the phrase "from scratch" to distinguish between two similar but different processes. In this case we are talking about the process of creating a PDB by using the **create pluggable database** command—specifically when the seed container is used to create the new PDB. This is, for all practical purposes, similar to the **create database** command in that you are creating a brand-new entity. Other methods of creating PDBs include cloning and plugging a database. We will talk about these options a little later in this section.

During your backup and recovery operations, you might need to create an empty PDB at some point in time. Sometimes RMAN will create the PDB for you during the operation, but sometimes you'll need to do it yourself. You have a great number of options you can use when issuing the **create pluggable database** command, and we leave it to you and the *Oracle SQL Reference Guide 12c* to work out those specific details.

To get you started, here is an example of using the **create pluggable database** command. In this case, we are logged into a running CDB as a user with SYSADMIN privileges. We have decided to call the new pluggable database newpdb, and we have decided on the admin user and the password for the admin user. In this case, the admin user is like the SYS user; however, because Oracle prefers you not to log in as SYS, you are provided with a way of defining an admin user for the PDB. This user is granted the role PDB_DBA.

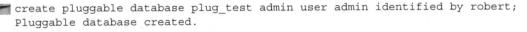
```
create pluggable database plug_test admin user admin identified by robert;
Pluggable database created.
```

PDB Users

As mentioned earlier, common users are created at the root level of the CDB and have the potential to roam across all attached PDBs. Within the PDB you find users, and their associated schemas, just like those in a non-CDB environment. The scope for a local user and that user's associated schema and schema objects is limited to the PDB that the user name is assigned to. That being said, if there is a need for a PDB user to traverse across the CDB landscape, this is actually quite easy, as long as the appropriate security privileges are granted. This is another benefit of a CDB environment: the cross-sharing of data across business units can be much easier and faster, and still remain as secure as it ever was (and, frankly, probably more secure).

The same local user name, the schema name, and any object names can be created in multiple PDBs within the same CDB. Each is created in its own separate and distinct user namespace. Here is an example of the creation of a local user in the PLUG_TEST PDB:

```
-- connect as a privileged user to the root container.
connect / as sysdba
 -- Change to the container we want to create the local user in.
alter session set container=plug_test;
 -- Create the local user in the container.
create user plug_test_local identified by robert;
-- allow the local user to connect to the PDB
 grant create session to plug_test_local;
Grant succeeded.
```

As you can see next, this local user is truly a *local* user because it cannot be used to log into the root container:

```
sqlplus plug_test_local/robert
ERROR: ORA-01017: invalid username/password; logon denied
```

Note that we got an error. This is because the method we are using to log in only allows us access to the root CDB. Each of the individual PDBs is isolated from the CDB, and the local users are specifically allocated to the PDB in which they are created. As a result of this isolation, connecting to a PDB directly is a bit different; you have to connect to it using the service that exists for that PDB, as shown here:

```
sqlplus plug_test_local/robert@plug_test
```

Let's look a little bit more at how to connect directly to a PDB then.

NOTE
If you get a connection error, make sure the PDB you are trying to connect to is listed in your tnsnames.ora. Although it will register with the listener when it's created or started, the PDB is not automatically added to your naming resolution method like tnsnames.ora.

Connecting to a PDB

Each PDB has a service name that is created when the PDB is created. If you want to connect directly to a specific PDB (which would be by far the most common access method for users of the PDB), you need to connect using the TNS service name for that PDB. This implies two major dependencies. First, the service name must be registered with the database listener. Issuing the **lsnrctl status** command will settle that question. The second requirement, if you are not using the EZConnect string, is that you need some form of client resolution. Of course, if you are using RAC, then this latter issue isn't a problem because you will simply be going to the SCAN listener to resolve the service name you are requesting.

The concept of service names should not be unfamiliar to you—you use them all the time to make network connections to databases. When you create a normal database, or even a CDB, a network service name for that database is created and registered with the listener. The same is true about PDBs. When the PDB is created, it is assigned the same service name as the PDB. That service name is then registered to the listener process. At that point, you can connect to the service just as you always would, using a tnsnames.ora entry, an EZConnect string, or whatever other method you use to connect to the database service. For example, in our database we have a PDB called robertpdb, which is open. When the PDB is open, it automatically registers with the listener, as you can see in this sample output (which has been cut for brevity):

```
lsnrctl status
Services Summary...
Service "contdb" has 1 instance(s).
  Instance "contdb", status READY, has 1 handler(s) for this service...
Service "contdbXDB" has 1 instance(s).
  Instance "contdb", status READY, has 1 handler(s) for this service...
Service "plug_test" has 1 instance(s).
  Instance "contdb", status READY, has 1 handler(s) for this service...
The command completed successfully
```

So, you can see from this output that both the CDB (contdb) and the service (plug_test) are registered with the service. Note that the listener will continue to provide the service for a PDB even if it's down. This allows an administrator to log into the service and open it, for example, with a minimum of fuss.

Let's look at some examples of logging into PDBs, because you may well need to do this as part of some backup or recovery exercise.

In this example we have a database called PLUG_TEST that we will connect to using its service name. When the PDB was created and we called it PLUG_TEST, Oracle created a service name called PLUG_TEST at the same time. Now that this is done, all we need to do is start SQL*Plus and log into the PDB through its service name, which we have done in the following example:

```
sqlplus joeuser/testing@plug_test
show con_name
CON_NAME
------------------------------
PLUG_TEST
```

You can also use the EZConnect naming method to connect to the PDB through SQL*Plus, as demonstrated here:

```
sqlplus plug_test_local/robert@bigdata:1521\/plug_test
```

Looking at the connect string, you can see that we are connecting to a service called PLUG_TEST. PLUG_TEST is a service for a PDB named PLUG_TEST. The PLUG_TEST PDB is attached to a CDB called CONTDB. PLUG_TEST lives on the database server called bigdata, and the listener port that the service is listening on is 1521.

To successfully connect to a PDB using a service, the following must be true:

- The main CDB is up and running.
- The PDB is open. The PDB might be open in migrate, read-write, read-only, or upgrade form. In some states, only users with restricted session privileges will be able to access the OM database PDBs. You can tell the status of a PDB by looking at the OPEN_MODE column of the V$PDBS view, as shown here:

```
select con_id, name, open_mode, restricted from v$pdbs order by 1;
    CON_ID NAME                                OPEN_MODE  RES
---------- ------------------------------ ---------- ---
         2 PDB$SEED                            READ ONLY  NO
         3 PLUG_TEST                           READ WRITE NO
```

   If the PDB is open, you can connect to it using the service assigned to that PDB. The service typically has the same name as the PDB. Therefore, in our example, the service is called PLUG_TEST. Through SQL*Plus, you can connect to the PDB through the PLUG_TEST service, as we did earlier using the EZConnect string.

   We showed you earlier that you can see the services registered with the listener. You can see a list of available services for a PDB from within the PDB by using the DBA_SERVICES view:

```
show con_name
CON_NAME
-------------------------------
PLUG_TEST

column name format a20
column network_name format a20
column global_service format a5
column pdb format a10
column enabled format a2
select service_id, name, network_name,global_service, pdb, enabled
from dba_services;
SERVICE_ID NAME                 NETWORK_NAME          GLO PDB         ENA
---------- -------------------- --------------------- --- ----------- ---
         6 plug_test            plug_test             NO  PLUG_TEST   NO
```

Note that if you issue this query from the root container, the results look different:

```
select service_id, name, network_name,global_service, pdb, enabled
from dba_services;
SERVICE_ID NAME                 NETWORK_NAME   GLO PDB         ENA
---------- -------------------- -------------- --- ----------- ---
         1 SYS$BACKGROUND                      NO  CDB$ROOT    NO
         2 SYS$USERS                           NO  CDB$ROOT    NO
         5 CONTDBXDB            CONTDBXDB       NO  CDB$ROOT    NO
         6 CONTDB               CONTDB          NO  CDB$ROOT    NO
```

   This is because the DBA* views (and USER and ALL views) only show data for the container you are currently in. We discuss this in more detail later, but there is a new set of views called the CDB* views that provide a CDB-wide view of things. Here we use the CDB_SERVICES view from the root container, and now we can see the service for plug_test:

```
select service_id, name, network_name,global_service, pdb, enabled
from cdb_services;
SERVICE_ID NAME                 NETWORK_NAME   GLO PDB         ENA
---------- -------------------- -------------- --- ----------- ---
         6 plug_test            plug_test       NO    PLUG_TEST  NO
         1 SYS$BACKGROUND                       NO  CDB$ROOT    NO
         2 SYS$USERS                            NO  CDB$ROOT    NO
         5 CONTDBXDB            CONTDBXDB        NO  CDB$ROOT    NO
         6 CONTDB               CONTDB           NO  CDB$ROOT    NO
```

   Note that we could also have used the view V$SERVICES (or GV$SERVICES in RAC) to see the service. The data in the V$ views is not localized to information for a specific PDB. Here is an example of using V$SERVICES to determine the service name. You might need to use V$SERVICES during certain recovery situations where the database can only be mounted:

```
SQL> select service_id, name, pdb from v$services;
SERVICE_ID NAME                 PDB
---------- -------------------- ----------
         6 plug_test            PLUG_TEST
         5 CONTDBXDB            CDB$ROOT
         6 CONTDB               CDB$ROOT
         1 SYS$BACKGROUND       CDB$ROOT
         2 SYS$USERS            CDB$ROOT
```

If you would rather not use the EZConnect string (which may well be the case), you can put the service information within a tnsnames.ora file and use that entry instead. Our tnsnames.ora entry for PLUG_TEST looks like this:

```
PLUG_TEST =
  (DESCRIPTION =
    (ADDRESS = (PROTOCOL = TCP)(HOST = bigdata)(PORT = 1521))
    (CONNECT_DATA =
      (SERVER = DEDICATED)
      (SERVICE_NAME = PLUG_TEST)
    )
  )
```

The service for the PDB should have been created when the PDB was created. If the service was not created, you will need to create the service manually, but this should be a rare occurrence. If you need to create a service for a PDB manually, this is documented in the *Oracle Database Administrator's Guide 12c* in the section "Creating, Modifying, or Removing a Service for a PDB."

Earlier we mentioned service name collision at the listener. Although this discussion is beyond the scope of this book, we did want to mention that there is a way around this problem. You can actually drop and re-create the service for a PDB with a different service name. This is done from within the CDB, and Oracle provides documentation on how to perform this activity should you need to do so. The other way around this problem is to create a second listener, but that listener would need to be listening on a different port, which could more administratively more complex.

Asking for Directions: Determining Which PDB You Are In

If you need to know which PDB you are in, you can use the **show con_name** SQL*Plus command, as you've seen frequently in this chapter. You can display the container ID by using the **show con_id** SQL*Plus command.

Oracle also provides functions that return the container's ID based on passing specific information to the function, including the container name, the container dbid, the container uid, and the container guid. For example, if you know the container name, you can get the container ID by using the **con_name_to_id** function, as shown here:

```
select con_name_to_id('PLUG_TEST') from dual;
```

There are four functions in total:

- **CON_NAME_TO_ID**   Returns the container ID based on the container name
- **CON_DBID_TO_ID**   Returns the container ID based on the container DBID (found by querying the DBID column of V$DATABASE)
- **CON_UID_TO_ID**   Returns the container ID based on the CONTAINER_UID
- **CON_GUID_TO_ID**   Returns the container ID based on the CONTAINER_GUID

You can find the DBID, UID, and GUID for a container in the V$CONTAINERS view.

Architecture of a Pluggable Database

We have already discussed what a PDB is, so now let's talk about how a PBD is physically manifested. In many ways, it's not unlike a regular database. When you create a normal database, you end up with physical datafiles that act as the persistent storage medium for that database. You also have physical online redo logs and control files that are created. We have already mentioned that these same types of physical files are created when you create the CDB. Let's look at how that physical file architecture looks.

Let's assume for the sake of this discussion that we have set the parameter DB_CREATE_FILE_DEST to a value of /u01/app/oracle/oradata. Further, let's say we allowed the Oracle Database Configuration Assistant to create our database using its default settings. Finally, let's assume that we allowed the DBCA to create one PDB for us called PLUG_TEST. Where would Oracle place the datafiles of the CDB and its PDB? Let's use the following query and its output to find out:

```
select a.name cont_name, c.name as tbs_name, b.name as file_name
from v$containers a, v$datafile b, v$tablespace c
where a.con_id=b.con_id
and b.con_id=c.con_id
and b.ts#=c.ts#
order by 1,2;
CONT_NAME   TBS_NAM FILE_NAME
----------  ------- ----------------------------------------
CDB$ROOT    SYSAUX
/u01/app/oracle/oradata/CONTDB/datafile/o1_mf_sysaux_b0847wy1_.dbf
CDB$ROOT    SYSTEM  /u01/app/oracle/oradata/CONTDB/datafile/o1_mf_system_b084olc8_.dbf
CDB$ROOT    UNDOTBS
/u01/app/oracle/oradata/CONTDB/datafile/o1_mf_undotbs1_b0855wy8_.dbf
CDB$ROOT    USERS
/u01/app/oracle/oradata/CONTDB/datafile/o1_mf_users_b0855r58_.dbf
PDB$SEED    SYSAUX
/u01/app/oracle/oradata/CONTDB/datafile/o1_mf_sysaux_b085f7sh_.dbf
PDB$SEED    SYSTEM
/u01/app/oracle/oradata/CONTDB/datafile/o1_mf_system_b085f7xl_.dbf
PLUG_TEST SYSAUX
/u01/app/oracle/oradata/CONTDB/01FCC6502
   01C027EE0530100007F8358/datafile/o1_mf_sysaux_b087dg82_.dbf
PLUG_TEST  SYSTEM
/u01/app/oracle/oradata/CONTDB/01FCC6502
   01C027EE0530100007F8358/datafile/o1_mf_system_b087dg3f_.dbf
PLUG_TEST USERS
/u01/app/oracle/oradata/CONTDB/01FCC6502
   01C027EE0530100007F8358/datafile/o1_mf_users_b087p8x0_.dbf
```

Note that this query will run on either a CDB or non-CDB database. This is because the CDB-related columns and views are also created when a non-CDB database is created. This makes it easier to write reusable SQL code for tasks such as viewing the data dictionary.

Do you recall earlier that we told you that the database considers CDB_ROOT to be a container but not a PDB? We have put this information to use here with the preceding query. Notice that we used the V$CONTAINERS view instead of the V$PDBS view. If we had used the V$PDBS view, we would have missed all of the datafiles for CDB$ROOT, which would have been a very bad thing!

Looking at the output you can see that we have three containers in this database: CDB$ROOT, PDB$SEED, and PLUG_TEST. Notice that the CDB$ROOT and PDB$SEED datafiles are all located in what is pretty much the expected location of database datafiles when using OFA (in this case, /u01/app/oracle/oradata/CONTDATA/datafile). The filenames follow the OFA naming convention that you are pretty much used to. You can also see the various tablespaces we used, such as SYSTEM and SYSAUX, and the datafiles assigned to them. So, nothing much different there—almost.

Note that the CDB$ROOT and CDB$SEED container files are maintained in the same directory; this is because they are part of the default container database install. The CDB$ROOT container is the root container we mentioned already. The CDB$SEED container is the seed container Oracle uses to create new PDBs. These two containers and the datafiles assigned to their tablespaces are created every time a CDB is created.

Then there is the PLUG_TEST PDB, which is quarantined into its own special directory. The reason these files (which we can see belong to the SYSTEM and SYSAUX tablespaces because of the filenames) are quarantined is to make the individual PDBs of a database easier to deal with. Because the datafiles of each PDB have their own unique location, this provides us additional flexibility with respect to the management of those PDBs. This also helps to protect the other PDBs during restore operations. If they are located in their own specific directory, you are less likely to overwrite the wrong datafile during a manual restore operation. Of course, RMAN reduces that risk considerably.

Let's look at where the files of the PLUG_TEST PDB are located. The initial file path looks right—/u01/app/oracle/oradata/PLUG_TEST—but then we see this crazy long number. What is that? It is the GUID of the individual PDB. GUID stands for *globally unique identifier,* and each PDB is assigned a GUID when it is created. This GUID keeps the PDB logically unique and is used for a variety of purposes. In our case, the GUID is used to create a unique directory structure that maintains the PDB datafiles. The directory structure ends with the familiar datafile directory and then the datafiles associated with the PDB in question.

If you want to know the GUID of a PDB, you can find it in the V$CONTAINERS and V$PDBS views in a column called GUID. Here is a sample query using V$CONTAINERS:

```
SQL> select name, guid from v$containers;
NAME               GUID
---------------    ---------------------------------
CDB$ROOT           FD9AC20F64D344D7E043B6A9E80A2F2F
PDB$SEED           01FC71C5C3567CD0E0530100007F929A
PLUG_TEST          01FCC650201C027EE0530100007F8358
```

You have a lot of control over where the datafiles are created. You can define them yourself when you create the PDBs, or you can move them later. There are also optional database parameters such as SEED_FILE_NAME_CONVERT and PDB_FILE_NAME_CONVERT that can be used to manage the file-creation locations of container-related datafiles.

Notice that each PDB has its own SYSTEM, SYSAUX, and USERS tablespace. The PDBs do not need an undo or temporary tablespace because these objects are shared with the CDB. You can create individual temporary tablespaces inside of a PDB if you wish, but you cannot create individual undo tablespaces. As with non-CDB databases, if you are running a RAC cluster, you would have an undo tablespace for each RAC database instance that is running.

PDB Constraints

Rules, rules, rules—we all live by rules. Well, the same is true with the Oracle CDB and PDB architecture. We thought it would be worthwhile to point out the rules that might come into play as a part of using RMAN with CDBs.

The first thing I want to say is that some of the "rules" are in flux as we write this book. Some features in the first release of Oracle Database 12*c* (12.1.0.1) were available in non-CDB databases but were not available in CDB-based databases. When release 12.1.0.2 came out, the list of unsupported features was reduced, and we expect to find that all of the features of Oracle Database 12*c* non-CDBs will be available in PDBs. That being said, we're not going to mention restrictions unless they have a specific impact on backup and recovery of your Oracle Database, should it be a multitenant or nonmultitenant database. These restrictions are only mentioned throughout the chapter when they become important. The *Oracle Database Readme Oracle Database 12c Release 1* provides a section on Oracle database features that are not yet supported by Oracle Multitenant. The list is fairly small as of the latest release of Oracle Database 12*c*.

The rules around movement of different versions of PDBs are something you should be aware of. Every CDB is running off of a specific Oracle software version. That means every PDB in that CDB must be running that version of Oracle. This can cause issues when plugging in new PDBs, of course.

All PDBs are owned by the parent CDB SYS user. A given CDB can have up to 252 PDBs plugged into it at any one time. Each PDB is an independent and isolated unit from any other PDB. Likewise, PDBs can be unplugged from a given CDB by the administrator. The PDB can be moved to a different CDB and then plugged into that CDB. PDBs can also be replicated within a given CDB.

You need to be careful naming a PDB. A given CDB cannot have two PDBs with the same name, and a given listener can't have two services with the same name. This means if two CDBs are using the same listener, the PDB names need to be unique across those listeners. Also, PDB names are not case sensitive.

PDB Performance

Using a CDB and consolidating existing databases into PDBs within the CDB offers a number of features—a major one being the sharing of system resources such as CPU and memory. You might think that adding more PDBs will incur a linear cost with respect to resources, but this is not the case. As shown in Figure 4-6, as additional PDBs are added, the total memory requirements of the CDB do not increase rapidly. In fact, in many cases, using a CDB can make much more efficient use of system resources than using individual databases, all with their own database instances.

PDB Resource Management

Now that we have a single database instance that contains many databases, sometimes concerns arise about possible performance impacts that might be caused by other database tenants within

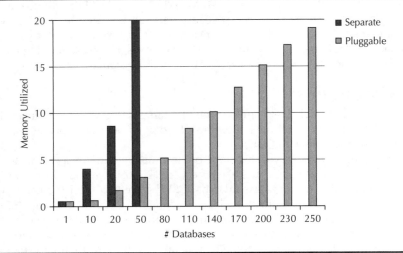

FIGURE 4-6. *Memory utilization as you add PDBs*

a given shared system. Oracle Database 12c has improved the Oracle Database Resource Manager, which can control various resources within a specific PDB, including the following:

- CPU
- Sessions
- Parallel server processes
- Disk I/O resources among the PDBs and the CDBs on the system (if you are running on Oracle Exadata)

With PDBs, you can divide the CPU into shares, with each share defining how much CPU a given resource is assured. This can be helpful in a consolidated environment where you want to be able to assure your customer that they will always have access to a minimum amount of CPU availability. Also, you can price your services based on a minimum guaranteed CPU allowance.

The guarantee of CPU is based on the distribution of shares across the CDB. The total number of shares divided by the individual shares that a PDB is assigned indicates the amount of guaranteed CPU that the PDB will have access to.

For example, assume you have the following three PDBs within a CDB and your resource plan defines that the PDBs have the indicated number of shares of CPU:

- MYPDB: two shares
- ORCL: one share
- YOURPDB: one share

In this case, a total of four shares are allocated within all the resource plans. As a result, MYPDB, with two shares, is assured access to 50 percent of the CPU. ORCL and YOURPDB are each assured access to 25 percent of the CPU because they have one share each.

The Database Resource Manager also provides the ability to define a CPU utilization limit for a given PDB. For example, if you define a utilization limit of 50 percent for the ORCL PDB, it still has a guaranteed 25 percent of the CPU (based on its one share), but it will never be able to use more than 50 percent of the CPU at any time.

The Oracle Database Resource Manager also makes it possible for you to define a default directive for shares and utilization that applies to PDBs by default. In that case, you can simply plug in the PDB, and the default directives of the resource plan will take effect.

Finally, if you own Exadata, you can use the IO Resource Manager (IORM) in concert with the Database Resource Manager to further manage the I/O impact of both CDB and PDB databases.

CDBs and PDBs and the Data Dictionary

Although the data dictionary is important to most DBAs, if you're involved in some restore exercise, it may well be all that stands between success and failure in a crisis. Knowing the data dictionary might also make the difference in meeting a recovery time objective (RTO) or recovery point objective (RPO).

Most DBAs have used the data dictionary views to some degree or another. Some are more comfortable with graphical interfaces such as Oracle Enterprise Manager, and as such they don't often traverse the universe of views, tables, and memory structures that make up the entirety of the data dictionary. Then there are those who know the data dictionary so well that we have to send them to the DBA asylum because they are just *that* scary.

Either way, the introduction of Oracle Multitenant has added quite a few new data dictionary views, as you might expect. These new data dictionary views generally come with the prefix of CDB_ or PDB_. As these prefixes might suggest, there are views that are specific to the CDBs and those specific to the PDBs. There are also a number of V$ (and GV$) views that provide information on the CDB and PDBs within it. So, let's look at the data dictionary views in a bit more detail.

This section covers the following topics:

- The multitenant database data dictionary
- The PDB data dictionary
- CDB/PDB administrative queries
- CDB/PDB object administration data dictionary queries

The Multitenant Database Data Dictionary

Both the CDB and each PDB contain data dictionary views. This includes both the standard DBA, USER, and ALL data dictionary views. Additionally there is now a set of views called the CDB views. Finally, there are new and changed V$ views available. Let's look at the CDB data dictionary and then the PDB data dictionary in a bit more detail.

The CDB Data Dictionary

The CDB data dictionary is stored in the CDB$ROOT container. It stores information about the CDB, such as the names of the data dictionary objects and the metadata related to data dictionary views and so on. The data dictionary in the CDB is owned by the SYS user, as has always been the case with Oracle databases. The CDB data dictionary data is stored in the SYSTEM tablespace, just as before.

The biggest difference between the data dictionary in a multitenant database and one that is not is that not all of the data dictionary information is actually stored in the data dictionary of the CDB. In fact, a great deal of the data dictionary information is stored in the PDB. This provides for a great deal of efficiency when dealing with PDBs, and Oracle manages all of the disparate data dictionary information for you automatically. We talk more about that next as we look at the PDB data dictionary.

The PDB Data Dictionary

Each PDB also has its own data dictionary. Shockingly, it's owned by the SYS user of the PDB and is stored in the SYSTEM tablespace of that PDB. Remember, the CDB and each PDB has its own SYSTEM tablespace, so each individual PDB has its own unique and secure data dictionary.

To help performance, Oracle stores CDB- and PDB-related data dictionary metadata in different places. Sometimes the data dictionary information is stored in the root of the CDB, and sometimes it's stored in the PDB itself. This is for a lot of reasons, including performance and making it easy to plug in or unplug individual PDBs. For example, if I don't have to bother exporting out all of the data dictionary views from the CDB and importing them into the PDB, this speeds up cloning and similar processes.

Generally the data dictionary within a PDB will be

- Contained within the PDB only.
- Metadata used in a PDB (like data dictionary view definitions) may actually be stored in the PDB as a metadata link to an object stored in the root container. Therefore, these commonly defined metadata objects do not need to be stored in more than one place.
- Object links in the PDB. Object links are links to actual data as opposed to metadata. For example, if you access the AWR repository from within a PDB, that data is actually stored in the root container. There is an object link from the PDB to the root container that facilitates access to those views from within the PDB.

We can see these different object types in the CDB_OBJECTS view column SHARING, as shown here:

```
SQL> select distinct sharing from dba_objects;
SHARING
-------------
METADATA LINK
NONE
OBJECT LINK
```

The various data dictionary views at both the CDB and PDB level know where to look for specific data dictionary information. If it's stored in the PDB, it will be collected from the PDB; otherwise, it's collected from the root container.

Multitenant Data Dictionary View Naming Conventions

At the CDB level we still have the standard set of data dictionary views (that is, the DBA_*, ALL_*, USER_*, and the V$ views) that Oracle Database has included for years. Also, each PDB has the same views in it. When queried, these views will always provide information specific to the PDB you are in. They do not show information for any other containers. Therefore, if you query USER_TABLES and don't find the information you are looking for, make sure you are in the right container.

Of course, administrators of the entire CDB (we call them CDB administrators) need to see data dictionary information for the entire CDB, including all of the PDBs. To help the CDB administrator, Oracle has added a set of new views called container data objects (CDOs). The CDO views provide this overall view of all CDB and PDB objects. Using these views from the root container enables you to see everything in all containers of the CDB.

The CDO views are similar to the regular DBA_* administrative views, but are prefixed with CDB_ instead of DBA_. So, now when you are in the root container you will have access to the DBA_TABLES view—which will only show you tables owned by the root container. You will also have a CDB_TABLES view that shows you all tables in the CDB plus all PDB tables.

The difference between the two views is starkly contrasted by a simple **select count(*)** query against them, as you can see here:

```
SQL> select count(*) from dba_objects;
  COUNT(*)
----------
     90756


SQL> select count(*) from cdb_objects;
  COUNT(*)
----------
    272228
```

The difference is that the DBA_OBJECT view is showing us objects for just the container we are in (in this case, the root container). The CDB_OBJECTS view is showing us the objects for the root container and any other PDB-related objects we might have the rights to see.

Additionally, many existing V$ (and the associated GV$) views have been adjusted to reflect the new CDB and PDB database architecture. New V$ views, such as V$CONTAINERS and V$PDBS, have been added to provide container-specific information. Keep this in mind because V$ views are often the only views available into the database (via memory structures or metadata in the control file) when the database instance is started or mounted. There are times, such as during a recovery, when we only have the V$ views to work with.

If you use AWR or ASH, you will be happy to know that AWR- and ASH-related views are now adjusted to reflect the new OM architecture. Most of these new and modified views include a new column called CON_ID that identifies the container in which the object resides. For example, the V$DATAFILE view now contains the CON_ID column so that you can know to which container the datafiles belong.

Figure 4-7 provides an example of how the various views all fit together between PDBs and the CDB. You will see many examples of the use of these views as you read this chapter.

PDB Administration

Now that you have become somewhat acquainted with Oracle Multitenant, you can probably imagine that some administration methods and commands have been changed or added. We have already discussed how to start and stop a CDB. In this section we show you how to start and stop individual PDBs. We then show you how to make sure that when the CDB is restarted that the individual PDBs return to the state they were in before the restart. We then briefly touch on controlling the storage allocation limits of a PDB, as well as the **alter system** commands that can be used to affect a PDB.

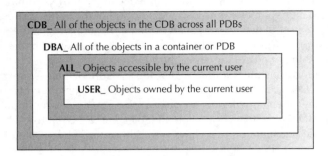

FIGURE 4-7. *Data dictionary view relationships*

Starting and Shutting Down the PDB

As mentioned in the previous section, shutting down the entire CDB is kind of a nuclear reaction to something that deserves a more tactical response. Let's use a small, laser-guided missile and cause as little collateral damage as we can rather than nuking the whole database. That being said, the DBA has a great deal of control over the state of the PDB. In this section we discuss that control, including starting the PDB and stopping the PDB.

It's always nice to know how to start something up and then how to shut it down again. In this section we cover those topics from the perspective of the PDB. First, we talk about starting up the PDB; then we will talk about shutting down the PDB. Then we will talk about how to get PDBs to start up for you automatically when you start up the CDB.

Starting the PDB   You may already know the name of the PDB you want to start. If you are like us, though, when you are dealing with tens of hundreds of PDBs in your organization, there are times when you just can't remember all of their names. Therefore, it's nice to know where to go to get a list of PDBs in your CDB database and to see their state so you can make sure you are opening the right PDB.

We can use the V$PDBS view for that information. Here is an example of a query against V$PDBS that lists the current PDBs in the database, their current open mode, and whether they are open in restricted session mode:

```
select con_id, name, open_mode, restricted from v$pdbs order by 1;
    CON_ID NAME                            OPEN_MODE  RES
---------- ------------------------------- ---------- ---
         2 PDB$SEED                        READ ONLY  NO
         3 PLUG_TEST                       MOUNTED
```

This query reports that the database currently has two PDBs: the PDB$SEED container and the PLUG_TEST container. The PLUG_TEST PDB is mounted and not open. As you might expect, there are several states a PDB can be in. These include the following:

- **Mounted**   This is essentially the state of a PDB when it is shut down.
- **Read Only**   Any PDB in read-only mode will be in this state.

■ **Read Write** Any PDB open for read-write operations will be in this state.

■ **Migrate** This status indicates that a PDB needs to be upgraded to the version of the current CDB. When the database is in migrate mode, it can only be accessed by users with restricted session privileges.

Opening a PDB is pretty easy: you simply need to connect to the database, switch over to the container you want to start, and then open the container. Optionally, you can connect to the PDB itself through its service and start it.

Let's look at an example. First, we log into the root container using the SYS account, including the SYSDBA privilege. We then use the **show con_name** SQL*PLUS command to double-check that we are currently logged into the CDB$ROOT container. Recall that in a CDB, the CDB$ROOT container is the main container:

```
[oracle@server12c ~]$ sqlplus / as sysdba

show con_name
CON_NAME
------------------------------
CDB$ROOT
```

We need to change to the container that we want to start, which is the PLUG_TEST container. We query the V$PDBS view to determine the status of our PDBs, and we find that PLUG_TEST is indeed mounted, as shown here:

```
select con_id, name, open_mode, restricted from v$pdbs order by 1;
     CON_ID NAME                           OPEN_MODE  RES
---------- ------------------------------ ---------- ---
         2 PDB$SEED                       READ ONLY  NO
         3 PLUG_TEST                      MOUNTED
```

Now, as SYS (or another privileged user), we need to change into the PLUG_TEST container to open it. Only then can we connect to that container as a regular user. We can change the currently working container from CDB$ROOT to PLUG_TEST by using the **alter session** command, as shown here:

```
alter session set container=PLUG_TEST;

show con_name
CON_NAME
------------------------------
PLUG_TEST
```

We then simply use the **startup** command to start the PDB:

```
SQL>startup
Pluggable Database opened.
connect / as sysdba
```

Consider here that the CDB of the OM database was already up and running, but that the PLUG_TEST PDB was not running. This is important to note—just starting the CDB does not automatically cause the PDBs associated with the CDB to open. You need to make sure you open those PDBs too. We will discuss automating PDB startup shortly.

Notice in the previous example that the output of the **startup** command is pretty basic. Because there is no SGA to allocate or control file to mount, all that's left is for the PDB to just open.

Once the PLUG_TEST database is up and running, we recheck the status of the databases using the V$PDBS view, ensuring that the PLUG_TEST PDB is indeed in read-write mode:

```
select con_id, name, open_mode, restricted from v$pdbs order by 1;
    CON_ID NAME                                OPEN_MODE  RES
---------- ------------------------------- ---------- ---
         2 PDB$SEED                            READ ONLY  NO
         3 PLUG_TEST                           READ WRITE NO
```

Note that when using the **startup** command on a PDB, you have a number of different options, including the following:

- **startup force**   Forces an inconsistent shutdown of the PDB and then reopens it in read/write mode.

- **startup restrict**   Starts the database and only allows users with **restricted session** system privileges to access the PDB.

- **Startup open [read write | read only]**   Indicates that the PDB should be open in **read write** or **read only** mode. The default on a normal database is **read write**. If the database is a Data Guard database, the default is **read only**.

For a user to open a PDB, that user must have one of the following privileges granted. The user can either be a common user and have the grant apply to that common user, or a local user in the PDB with the privilege granted to that local user. Here are the privileges:

- SYSDBA
- SYSOPER
- SYSBACKUP
- SYSDG

You can also connect to the PDB directly through its service name as a user with SYSDBA privileges (or the other privileges we list shortly) and then shut down the PDB from within the PDB. Note that the PDB does not have to be open to be registered with the listener. This happens automatically when the CDB is started. Here is an example of logging into the PDB using a TNS service name:

```
sqlplus sys/robert@plug_test as sysdba
```

Of course, it would be nice to be able to open all the pluggable databases at once. This can be accomplished using the command **alter pluggable database all open**. For this command to work, the CDB itself needs to be open, and you need to be logged into the root of the CDB.

You can then use the **alter pluggable database** command to open specific PDBs, as in this example:

```
alter pluggable database pdb_one open;
```

Shutting Down the PDB   Shutting down the PDB is not much different from starting it up. You have a couple of ways to do this. First, you can issue an **alter session** command to change to the correct PDB and then issue your **shutdown** command, as shown here:

```
alter session set container=PLUG_TEST;

SQL> show con_name
CON_NAME
------------------------------
PLUG_TEST
SQL> shutdown
```

Note that we issued the standard **shutdown** command. It is probably more common to shut down a PDB with the **shutdown immediate** command. If either the **shutdown** or **shutdown immediate** command completes, then that PDB will have been shut down in a consistent manner and the dirty blocks associated with that PDB will have been flushed to the database datafiles. Note that this does not ensure that any other part of the database is consistent in any way. You can also use the **shutdown abort** command for an immediate stop of the PDB that would leave it in an inconsistent state and require instance-level recovery when it's reopened, just as with any non-OM database.

Another option is to connect to the PDB through its service name as a user with SYSDBA privileges (or the other privileges we list shortly) and then shut down the PDB from within the PDB, as in this example:

```
sqlplus sys/robert@plug_test as sysdba

SQL> show con_name
CON_NAME
------------------------------
PLUG_TEST
SQL> shutdown
```

You can also close the PDB from within the PDB or from the root of the CDB by using the **alter pluggable database** command to close pluggable databases, as in this example:

```
alter pluggable database pdb_one close;
```

For a user to shut down a PDB, that user must have one of the following privileges granted. The user can either be a common user and have the grant apply to that common user, or a local user in the PDB with the privilege granted to that local user. Here are the privileges:

- SYSDBA
- SYSOPER
- SYSBACKUP
- SYSDG

Automating PDB Startup

Oracle Database 12c Release 12.1.0.2 provides the ability to preserve the open-mode PDB through CDB restarts. Thus, if a PDB was open when its parent CDB was shut down, the PDB will be reopened when the parent CDB is restarted. This is made possible through the use of the **alter**

pluggable database options **save state** and **discard state**. The individual states of instances are maintained across individual nodes in a RAC cluster.

Here is an example of using the **alter pluggable database** command to set the PDB PLUG_ TEST into the saved state. As a result of this command the PLUG_TEST PDB will return to the same state it was in before the CDB restart.

```
sqlplus sys/robert as sysdba

SQL> show con_name
CON_NAME
------------------------------
CDB$ROOT
SQL> alter pluggable database plug_test save state;
```

You can include more than one PDB in the command if you wish. Simply separate each PDB name by a comma. You can also save the state for all PDBs by using the **alter pluggable database all save state** command. If you want to discard the open mode of a PDB after a CDB restart, then simply use the **alter pluggable database discard state** command. You can use the DBA_PDB_ SAVED_STATES view to determine the current saved state for the PDBs in your CDB database.

This is great for normal HA operations. If a CDB is shut down for some maintenance activity, you don't need to worry about which mode the individual PDBs are in when you restart the CDB. However, this could be problematic in some kinds of backup and recovery situations, so be mindful that if you restart a CDB, it's possible that the PDB will not be in the state you expect unless you check to see if it's configured to return to the same state.

Setting Storage Limits for a PDB

You can set storage limits for a given PDB by using the **alter pluggable database** command from within the PDB when logged in as SYS or a common user with the appropriate privileges. In the following example, we set the default storage for the PDB to 2GB:

```
alter pluggable database storage(maxsize 2g);
```

You can also reset the storage limits to unlimited, as shown here:

```
alter pluggable database storage(maxsize unlimited);
```

Knowing that a PDB can be constrained by storage limits might help certain restore issues if they arise.

Using the alter system Command from Within a PDB

You can use the **alter system** command from within a PDB to perform many tasks. The following **alter system** commands are available from within a PDB:

alter system flush shared_pool	**alter system flush buffer_cache**
alter system enable restricted session	**alter system disable restricted session**
alter system set use_stored_outlines	**alter system suspend**
alter system resume	**alter system checkpoint**
alter system check datafiles	**alter system register**
alter system kill session	**alter system disconnect session**
alter system set *initialization_parameter*	

New Views Associated with PDBs

We have already mentioned the CDB views related to the entire CDB. There are also new V$ views that are specific to OM databases. You have seen many of them in use already in previous examples in this chapter. Here is a quick list of those we find the most important:

- The CDB_PDBS and DBA_PDBS views provide information on the PDBs in the database, such as their names and their status. This view is very useful because it provides detailed state information about the PDB, such as if it's new, unplugged, in the process of being converted, and a number of other states.

- The V$CONTAINERS view provides information on the PDBs, such as the open mode of the containers and other information.

- The V$PDBS view provides information about the individual PDBs, such as when they were opened, their current open mode, and whether they are open in restricted session mode.

- CDB_PDB_HISTORY provides information about the history of a PDB.

We discuss the question of developing an overall backup and recovery architecture in several different places throughout the book, including Chapter 15, which is dedicated to that topic.

Other CDB-Related Topics

In this section we cover other OM-related topics that might have popped into your head as you have read this chapter. In one case, we simply point you to the chapter where a particular topic is covered.

Here is what we address in this section:

- Dropping a CDB
- Dropping a PDB
- PDB cloning and plugging and unplugging PDBs

So, let's get to it!

Dropping a CDB

Dropping a CDB is as easy as using the SQL*Plus or RMAN **drop database** command. This command drops the CDB and all of its children PDBs. In most cases, all of the datafiles, control files, and online redo logs will be dropped. The archived redo logs are not removed.

Dropping a PDB

To drop a PDB, you use the command **drop pluggable database**. When the PDB is dropped, all references in the CDB control file are removed and all datafiles related to the PDB are removed. Archived redo logs are not removed. You can use the **keep datafiles** option of the command to preserve the datafiles of the PDB if you wish.

PDB Cloning and Plugging and Unplugging PDBs

Perhaps one of the nicest features of the Oracle Multitenant architecture is how easy it makes cloning PDBs within the parent CDB, or even to other CDBs. The ability to unplug a database from one CDB and plug it into another CDB is also fast and convenient. Because all these operations are very similar to the database-duplication operations that RMAN performs, we will cover these topics in Chapter 10, where we discuss database duplication.

Summary

In Oracle Database 12c, Oracle has come out with an amazing new feature in the form of CDBs and PDBs. This new feature certainly adds more complexity to the backup and recovery picture. In this chapter we introduced you to the concept of CDBs and PDBs in preparation for additional discussion about them throughout the rest of the book. The new CDB architecture is the way of the future, as Oracle has announced the removal of the old Oracle database architecture at some point in the future. Therefore, now is the time to get onboard and learn about this powerful new Oracle Database feature.

PART
II

RMAN Configuration, Backup, and Recovery Essentials

CHAPTER
5

RMAN Setup and Configuration

A s with previous versions of RMAN, RMAN in Oracle Database 12c provides a lot of functionality. Because of all of this functionality, many different options need to be considered when you are configuring RMAN for the first time. Also, as time goes on, these configuration options might change as your environment changes. For example, you might implement a stand-by database in your environment, which might require you to modify the database configurations related to RMAN.

Now, you can use RMAN right out of the box for the most part. RMAN will use a number of default settings in the course of executing the commands you give it. This is not the way to manage your backup and recovery architecture though, because it would be nice to have not only recoverable backups, but also to have everything backed up that you will need to recover your database.

Configurations are set based on requirements that are gathered. You can certainly guess at things such as retention, but this is not considered a good way to keep your job. So, regardless of whether you are using RMAN for the first time or are a long-time RMAN user, I'm going to call you out and say that this is probably a really good time to get up, take a deep breath, and actually go talk to someone about the important subject of backup and recovery. It's also a good time to review existing SLAs—and if they don't exist, it's a good time to create them. We will talk a lot more about these kinds of things in Chapter 25, where we discuss enterprise backup architectures and provide you with some guidance in the form of do's and don'ts when putting together your backup infrastructure.

When we talk about configuring RMAN, we are talking about how RMAN behaves. RMAN configurations typically come in two categories: the persistent preconfigured settings and the configuration settings you issue at run time that are related to a specific RMAN operation (and override the persistent settings). Run-time settings can be made in two different forms. The first form is to use them as a part of a run block, which is a set of RMAN commands run as a single unit. Second, you can set the run-time parameter as a part of an individual RMAN command that runs independently.

In this chapter we look at initial RMAN setup requirements and options. First, we dive into Oracle redo logs a little deeper than we did in Chapter 2. These are critical structures in the Oracle database for recovery. Building on that discussion, we look at putting the database in ARCHIVELOG mode, in case you want to do online backups. We then look at the basic RMAN interface, so that you can get into RMAN itself. Next, we discuss configuring RMAN for database backup operations. Finally, we discuss the RMAN recovery catalog, including why you might want to use it and how to configure it.

Configuring Your Database to Run in ARCHIVELOG Mode

Now that you have learned about ARCHIVELOG mode and NOARCHIVELOG mode in Chapter 2 and learned how important redo is to your database, you probably understand why many DBAs run their databases in ARCHIVELOG mode. If you are content with running in NOARCHIVELOG mode, then much of this section's discussion will not apply to you. If you are going to run in ARCHIVELOG mode, you will need to do some basic configuration, which is the topic of this section.

First, if you are running an Oracle Database 12c container database, everything we will be discussing with respect to putting the database in ARCHIVELOG mode will need to be done by an administrative user from the root of the CDB. PDBs within the CDB cannot run in their own ARCHIVELOG mode.

When running in ARCHIVELOG mode, you have two choices in configuring where the archived redo logs are copied. In fact, you can choose to use both choices. The first choice is to configure for ARCHIVELOG destination directories, and the second is to configure the Oracle Fast Recovery Area (FRA). We will discuss those two topics next. Afterward, we will discuss actually putting the database in ARCHIVELOG mode.

ARCHIVELOG Destination Directories

When configuring ARCHIVELOG mode, you need to decide where you want Oracle to create the archived redo logs. The option that has been available for the longest is to use archive log destination directories. To use archive log destination directories, you set some specific parameters in Oracle to configure this option. First, you use the LOG_ARCHIVE_DEST_n parameter (where n is a number in the range of 1 to 10) to define up to ten different archive log destinations. These destinations can be local directories, network directories (for example, NT folders), network-attached storage (NAS), or even a defined database service name if you are using standby database/Data Guard. Note that there is no default location defined for LOG_ARCHIVE_DEST_n.

If you are using SPFILES, you use the **alter system** command to set the LOG_ARCHIVE_DEST_n parameter, as shown here:

```
alter system set log_archive_dest_1='location=c:\oracle\oraarc\beta1';
```

NOTE
*Setting the LOG_ARCHIVE_DEST directory to a directory location that does not exist, or that Oracle cannot write to, is a common mistake. Just make sure that after you set the parameter and put the database in ARCHIVELOG mode, you issue an **alter system switch logfile** command to make sure that ARCH is writing the archived redo logs properly.*

Each LOG_ARCHIVE_DEST_n location can be defined as either a mandatory or optional location. By default, all LOG_ARCHIVE_DEST_n locations are optional in Oracle Database. Mandatory locations mean just that—the archived redo logs have to be written to that location. Failure of the ARCH process to write to mandatory locations will result in suspension of database activities fairly quickly (after you have cycled through all the online redo logs). Optional locations will have no impact on database operations.

```
alter system set log_archive_dest_1='location=c:\oracle\oraarc\beta1 mandatory';
```

Also, all LOG_ARCHIVE_DEST_n locations are optional by default (though one location must always succeed because the minimum setting of LOG_ARCHIVE_MIN_SUCCEED_DEST is 1). The parameter LOG_ARCHIVE_MIN_SUCCEED_DEST indicates how many archive log destination directories must have successful copies for an online redo log to be considered successfully archived. The default setting for LOG_ARCHIVE_MIN_SUCCEED_DEST is 1, and this is the minimum setting for this parameter. Here is an example of setting this parameter to a value of 2:

```
alter system set log_archive_min_succeed_dest=2;
```

Other parameters are related to archived redo logs, the ARCH process, and the LOG_ARCHIVE_DEST series of parameters:

- **LOG_ARCHIVE_STATE_*n*** Defines one of two different states for each archive log destination. If set to ENABLE, the ARCH process will consider the destination associated with this state as a valid archive log destination. If set to DEFER, the ARCH process will not archive logs to the related LOG_ARCHIVE_DEST_*n* location.

- **LOG_ARCHIVE_FORMAT** Provides a template for Oracle to use when naming archived redo logs. As Oracle creates the archived redo logs, it renames them in such a way that each of the archived redo logs has a unique name assigned to it. Using the LOG_ARCHIVE_FORMAT parameter, you can manipulate the default naming standard as you require. This parameter has no effect on archived redo logs being created in the FRA.

- **LOG_ARCHIVE_START** This parameter is obsolete in Oracle Database 10*g* and later versions. Oracle will now start the ARCH process for you automatically.

- **LOG_ARCHIVE_MAX_PROCESSES** This parameter defines the number of ARCH processes that Oracle initially starts when the database is started.

NOTE
If you are running Oracle Database 9i or earlier, you will need to make sure you set the LOG_ARCHIVE_START parameter to TRUE when configuring your database for ARCHIVELOG mode. This is no longer required in Oracle Database 10g and later.

Each of the different parameters mentioned thus far is defined in the *Oracle Database 12*c *Reference Manual* (which is part of the overall Oracle documentation), should you need further information on them.

In the following example, we have a database we want to put in ARCHIVELOG mode. We create three different archive log destination directories, including one to a service name that supports an Oracle standby database. We also enforce the requirements that at least two of these destinations must be written to in order for the movement of the archived redo log to be considered complete, and that the standby database must be one of those two locations. Here is an example of the use of the various database parameter file parameters related to ARCHIVELOG mode operations:

```
log_archive_dest_1='location=d:\oracle\oraarc\robt mandatory'
log_archive_dest_2='location=z:\oracle\oraarc\robt optional'
log_archive_dest_3='service=recover1 mandatory'
log_archive_min_succeed_dest=2
log_archive_format="robt_%s_%t.arc"
```

In this example, our first archive log destination goes to d:\oracle\oraarc\robt. The second archive log destination is to a secondary location on the Z: drive. We have made this an optional archiving location because it is a networking device (which may not be all that reliable). The third destination is to an Oracle Net service (probably a standby database) called recover1. This will cause Oracle to send the archived redo logs through Oracle Net as they are generated.

Proceeding through the example, by using the LOG_ARCHIVE_MIN_SUCCEED_DEST parameter, we have indicated that the archived redo logs must be successfully copied to at least two different locations. The format of the archived redo log is defined with the LOG_ARCHIVE_FORMAT parameter.

The Fast Recovery Area

In this section we want to quickly introduce you to the Fast Recovery Area (FRA). We will be discussing the FRA throughout the chapter, so we wanted to give you some higher-level information about the FRA at this point, and later in the chapter we will revisit the FRA to talk about it in a bit more detail. First, we introduce you to the FRA. We then address some configuration- and monitoring-related topics. In doing so, we will probably answer some of the preliminary questions that might come up as you read further in this book.

The FRA allows you to centralize storage of all recovery-related files. The FRA can use locally attached storage, the Oracle Cluster File System (OCFS), or Automatic Storage Management (ASM) features. Table 5-1 lists the file types that can be contained within the FRA. The FRA helps with the management of overall disk space allocation and provides a centralized storage area for all recovery-related files.

One of the unique things about the FRA is that Oracle will manage the retention of backups (both database and archivelog backups) within the FRA for you automatically. This means you don't need to perform any maintenance operations on backups within the FRA (such as **delete obsolete** to remove old backup files). Retention of files in the FRA is determined by the RMAN retention policy, which you define. The retention policy for the FRA is set via the RMAN **configure retention policy** command. We will discuss the RMAN retention policy in much more detail later in this chapter.

Monitoring of the FRA

As you can imagine, this whole running out of logical space and not physical space can be a troubling thing at times. If you have not allocated enough disk space to the FRA (logically or

File Type	Notes
Archived redo logs	Archived redo logs will be stored in the FRA.
Control file	One copy of the control file is created in the FRA when the database is created.
Control file autobackups	The default location for the RMAN control file autobackups will be the FRA, if it is defined.
Flashback logs	Flashback logs (discussed later in this chapter) will be stored in the FRA, if it is defined.
Redo log	One copy of each redo log group member can be stored in the FRA.
RMAN datafile copies	The default location for the RMAN datafile copies will be the FRA, if it is defined.
RMAN backup and other related files	The default location for the RMAN files in general (backup set pieces and such) will be the FRA, if it is defined.

TABLE 5-1.   *File Types Found in the Fast Recovery Area*

physically), then when you start the Oracle database, a message is included in the alert log that indicates how much of the FRA is currently in use. The message will look something like this:

```
db_recovery_file_dest_size of 51200 MB is 0.29% used. This is a
user-specified limit on the amount of space that will be used by this
database for recovery-related files, and does not reflect the amount of|
space available in the underlying filesystem or ASM diskgroup.
```

When things go bad and you run out of space in the FRA, you will get all sorts of messages from both the backup and the alert log. Here is an example of where a backup died due to lack of space. First, the alert log clearly tells us that we have a problem with the FRA:

```
Errors in file C:\APP\ORACLE\diag\rdbms\orcl12c\orcl12c\trace\orcl12c_
arc2_5140.trc:
ORA-19815: WARNING: db_recovery_file_dest_size of 157286400 bytes is 100.00%
used, and has 0 remaining bytes available.
```

Also, our backup failed with this message:

```
ORA-19809: limit exceeded for recovery files
ORA-19804: cannot reclaim 10338304 bytes disk space from 157286400 limit
```

Note that the total size of the FRA is the later number in this error message. The message also indicates another fact about the FRA—before RMAN just gives up on a backup and fails from space exhaustion, it will try to free up space from the FRA.

Oracle monitors the space available in the FRA used by the database, and once the amount of available space in the FRA starts to diminish to an unsafe level, Oracle generates a warning in the alert log and also on the OEM console.

The warning threshold is hit when the FRA space is less than 15 percent of the DB_RECOVERY_FILE_DEST_SIZE value. The critical threshold is signaled when the FRA free space is less than 3 percent of reclaimable space. These alerts appear in the OEM console and in the alert log, or you can review the DBA_OUTSTANDING_ALERTS view, as shown in this example:

```
SQL> select reason, message_type, metric_value from dba_outstanding_alerts;
REASON
-------------------------------------------------------------------
MESSAGE_TYPE METRIC_VALUE
------------ ------------
db_recovery_file_dest_size of 230686720 bytes is 89.63% used and has
 23920640 remaining bytes available.
Warning                 89
```

In this case, the FRA is 89 percent full and a warning has been generated. This warning will be propagated to Oracle Cloud control, and you can manage any notification from there.

There are a number of views available to reference to monitor and manage the Fast Recovery Area. One of the best views, besides the DBA_OUTSTANDING_ALERTS view is the V$RECOVERY_FILE_DEST view. This view provides a quick way to look at how much space is allocated to the FRA, how much space has been used, and if any space is able to be reclaimed

by Oracle should the need arise. Here is an example of a query against the V$RECOVERY_FILE_
DEST view:

```
select name, space_limit, space_used, space_reclaimable
from v$recovery_file_dest;
NAME                              SPACE_LIMIT      SPACE_USED   SPACE_RECLAIMABLE
--------------------------------  --------------   ----------   -----------------
C:\app\oracle\fast_recovery_area  10,737,418,240   249,298,944                  0
```

In this case, we have an FRA that has plenty of space. There is over 10GB available for use,
and we have only used some 229MB of that space. That's not even 1 percent of the available
space. There are other views that you can use to look at the FRA- and RMAN-related operations.
We will introduce those throughout this book.

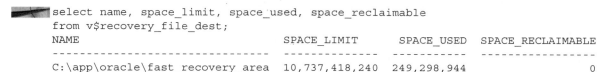

NOTE
*Running out of space in the FRA can be troublesome if that
area is your only archive log destination, as this can cause your
database to eventually halt. If the FRA is going to be your only
archive log destination, monitor space availability carefully. We feel
like a minimum of two archive log destination directories (one on
a different set of disks or even on a different server) is a best
practice. An Oracle Data Guard server would easily satisfy
this requirement.*

Sizing the FRA

Figuring out how much space to allocate to the FRA can be a bit challenging. To really produce a
good estimate, you will need to ask yourself the following:

- How much space will my backups take? (This implies that you have decided on what
  kind of backup strategy you will be using.)
- How many archived redo logs am I generating?
- What is my FRA retention period going to be?
- Do I need to store backup-related files in some place other than the FRA?
- Will I be storing control files and online redo logs in the FRA and, if so, how much
  additional space will they need?

For an existing database that you are moving over to use RMAN, it's probably not too hard to
determine the answers to these questions. When you have a new database, it can be difficult to
impossible to determine the answers to these questions. So many factors come into play with
database backups that will impact how much space they require now—and how much they might
require a year from now. Let's look at some ways you can make educated guesses with a new
database and how you can look at existing data from older databases to determine how you
should size the FRA.

Educated FRA Sizing Guesses for New Systems So, you start with some educated guesses. Sometimes all you can do is guess. In creating your best guess, you will want to consider a number of factors:

Question No.	Question	Answer	FRA Space Required
1	What is the approximate size of the database in data (not the actual allocated size)?	20GB	
	Full Backup Calculation		
2	How many days' worth of backups do you wish to store?	14	
3	How many full backups will occur in this time? If this is an incremental backup strategy, add one to this number.	2+1=3	
4	Multiply the number in question 1 by the number in question 2 and put the answer in the FRA Space Required column.		60GB
5	Will you use compression? If, Yes, then multiply the number in the FRA Space Required column in Step 4 by the amount of expected compression (we use 40% here).	40%	36GB
	Incremental Backup Additional Calculation		
6	How many incremental backups will occur? Divide that number by the number of full backups and add the result. For example, 12 total incremental + (12/2 full backups) = 18 incremental. This is because you will always have an additional set of full/incremental backups if you base your retention on a recovery window. See more on retention criteria later in this chapter.	18	
7	What percentage of the full backup size do you expect the incremental backup will be? (This represents the amount of daily change.)	10	
8	Multiply the backup size in question 1 by the percentage listed in question 7.	2GB	
9	Multiply the value in Step 8 by the expected compression percentage in Step 5.	1.2GB	
10	Multiply the value in Step 9 by the number in Step 6.	21.6GB	
11	Add the number in Step 10 to the number in the FRA Space Required column in Step 5.	21.6+36GB	57.6GB
12	What percentage of change do you expect in the database per day (insert/update/delete)?	2	

Question No.	Question	Answer	FRA Space Required
13	Multiply the value in question 1 by the value in question 12.	400MB	
14	Multiply the value in Step 13 by the number in Step 6. Add this number to the FRA Space Required value in Step 11.	4.8GB	62.4GB
	Other Database Files		
15	What is the size of one member of the online redo log groups?	25M	
16	How many online redo log groups will you have?	4	
17	Multiply the number in question 15 by the number in question 16. Add this to the number in Step 14.	100m	62.5GB
18	Multiply Step 17's FRA Space Required value by 1.10 percent and round it up to the nearest GB. Put this value in the FRA Space Required column of this step. This is because Oracle recommends that you add 10% overhead to the space you allocate to the Fast Recovery Area.		69GB
19	What is the total FRA space required for this database?		69GB

Note that this table does not factor in items such as flashback logs, and we didn't include sizes for the control files since they tend to be quite small (and you will have only one in there). If you plan on doing additional "one-off" backups (for example, at the end of the month), you would need to factor in that information. In our case, based on this analysis, our database will require around 69GB of FRA space for a two-week incremental backup strategy.

After you initially allocate the FRA space to the database, you should monitor the space usage and adjust the size of the FRA as required. We will discuss monitoring the utilization of the FRA later in this chapter.

Educated FRA Sizing Guesses for Existing Systems   If your database is already running and you are converting to use the FRA, then you probably already have the information you need to determine the size of the FRA. The view V$RMAN_BACKUP_JOB_DETAILS will give you pretty much all the information you need to make your estimate of how much space you need to allocate. This view gives you a summary of all RMAN backups that have been taken. It does not reset itself when the database is restarted, like many V$ views do, because its information sources from the metadata in the database control file. This view is an abstracted view of a given backup. When the view is queried, the statistics of one RMAN backup "job" execution is presented.

So, for example, say that we issued one RMAN command to back up the database and all of the archived redo logs:

```
backup database plus archivelog;
```

All of the backup operations that occur because of the execution of that one command will be considered one backup job. A backup job may have one or more backup operations associated with it.

In our case, the command we executed had three separate backup operations. The first was a full backup, then the backup of the archived redo logs, and, finally, the automated backup of the control file and database parameter file. After the backup, we would then query the V$RMAN_JOB_DETAILS_VIEW with this query:

```
select start_time, end_time, status, input_type, output_bytes_display
from v$rman_backup_job_details
where start_time > sysdate-1/24
order by 1,2;
```

Here we are just looking for backups that started less than 24 hours ago. Here is the result of the query:

```
START_TIME            END_TIME             STATUS      INPUT_TYPE    OUTPUT
                                                                     _BYTES
-------------------   -------------------  ----------  ----------    ----------
10/01/2014 13:05:24 10/01/2014 13:07:13 COMPLETED   DB INCR         435.74M
10/01/2014 23:08:33 10/01/2014 23:09:35 COMPLETED   DB INCR         629.00K
```

In this output we see that two backups have happened. Both were incremental backups. Although we don't know if they were level 0 or level 1 backups from this view, the OUTPUT_ BYTES_DISPLAY gives us a pretty good idea. Still, for our purposes, we don't really need that degree of detail; we just need sizing information. This view will also include any archived redo log backup jobs and any other kinds of jobs. So, let's look at how we calculate the total backup space required for a 14-day retention period. Let's assume that we are already using an incremental backup strategy and that these numbers are representative of that strategy in use. So, it's just a matter of summing up the total bytes backed up to get a good estimate of how much space we need. In this case, we will use the column OUTPUT_BYTES instead of OUTPUT_BYTES_DISPLAY because that column is a true number column (so we can do a sum of the values). So, here is our query:

```
Column total_fra_for_backups format 9,999,999,999,999
select sum(output_bytes) total_fra_for_backups
from v$rman_backup_job_details
where start_time >= sysdate-21;
```

```
TOTAL_FRA_FOR_BACKUPS
---------------------
       26,913,161,216
```

In this case, we're going to need about 26GB of space to store all the backups. You might have noticed that instead of picking 14 days, we picked 21 days. This is because of the nature of recovery windows, which we will discuss later in this chapter. For now, just know that you will need to actually store 21 days' worth of backup pieces in order to achieve a true 14-day recovery window.

Now, this does not cover all the files we will be storing in the FRA and that we need to accommodate space for. First and foremost are the archived redo logs. These are usually stored in the FRA, and we want to make sure we have plenty of room to store those. The query to determine the size of the archived redo logs is pretty simple. We just use the view DBA_HIST_LOG and summarize the size of the archived redo logs in bytes over a period of three days. We can assume that within three days the archived redo logs will have been backed up and then deleted from the FRA. We have figured the size of those archived redo log backups previously (when we calculated the size of all backups in the last 21 days earlier).

So, here is the query we are interested in:

```
Column bytes format 9,999,999,999
Select sum(bytes) bytes
from dba_hist_log
where archived='YES'
and first_time >= sysdate-21;

        BYTES
-------------
   524,288,000
```

In this case, we have some 524MB of redo logs backed up in the last 21 days. So, now we just add up the roughly 27GB of backups and 524MB of archived redo logs, and we have a pretty close estimate of how big to make the FRA. We might want to proceed to calculate the size of the online redo log group members that we would need to store in the FRA. This query will do that trick for us:

```
select sum(bytes) bytes
from v$log;
        BYTES
-------------
   157,286,400
```

And, if we really wanted to get fancy, we could do something like this:

```
Set numf 9,999,999,999,999
Select sum(bytes) * 1.10 total_bytes
from
(
select sum(output_bytes) bytes
from v$rman_backup_job_details
where start_time >= sysdate-21
union all
Select sum(bytes) bytes
from dba_hist_log
where archived='YES'
and first_time >= sysdate-21
Union all
select sum(bytes) bytes
from v$log
);

        TOTAL_BYTES
------------------
   30,354,209,178
```

So, there is our estimate of FRA space needed for a 21-day retention, considering the current backup pattern and the storage of archived redo logs and online redo logs. Oracle recommends that you add 10 percent to this number, which has been done in this calculation.

Note that this method of sizing applies to both Oracle CDB databases and non-CDB databases. In the case of the CDB, you should log into the root of the CDB when running these queries.

Playing Nicely in the FRA   Many large database servers run more than one Oracle database. Each of these databases will have its own backups, archive logs, and so on that will be stored either in the FRA or some other storage location. These all consume storage space, of course. On occasion, a single rogue database can consume all the space on that storage device. This can impact all databases using that storage device because they will no longer be able to create archived redo logs. In cases like these, phones start ringing, threats are made, cars are keyed, and in general the repercussions are not pleasant.

To manage this problem, the FRA provides the ability to allocate a specific space quota to each database. Thus, with an FRA, you can reduce the risk that one database will consume all archive log space and negatively impact other databases. As a result, you can freely exit the building at night without having to watch your back for users who might be silently waiting for you to leave so they can discuss how badly you manage databases.

We mentioned earlier how to monitor the FRA for space availability. If you find that the FRA has run out of space, you can respond to the problem as follows:

1. If the problem is one of insufficient space allocation via the parameter DB_RECOVERY_FILE_DEST_SIZE and sufficient physical disk space exists to increase the space allocated to the FRA, increase the size of the parameter. This will immediately add space to the FRA. Of course, you cannot increase this parameter to a value that is greater than the amount of space that is physically available on the file system.

2. If you need more physical space, allocate additional physical space to the file system and then increase the size of the DB_RECOVERY_FILE_DEST_SIZE parameter. This parameter is dynamic, so it can be set while the database is running.

3. If additional space is not available, you can move the FRA to another file system where more space is available.

4. You can also make room in the FRA by using the RMAN **backup recovery area** command to move the contents of the FRA to another location. We will cover the **backup recovery area** command and its limitations during discussions on performing RMAN backups.

5. As a last-ditch effort, physically remove older backup set pieces and/or archived redo logs from the FRA, and then use the RMAN **crosscheck** command to get the database to recognize that the files have been removed. You can later copy the files back to the FRA and use the RMAN **catalog** command to make them available to the database again. As an alternative, you can also move the files to a new location and then catalog them so their new location will be stored in the database control file and the recovery catalog. Note that if you do this, these backup files will not benefit from the features of the FRA such as retention.

NOTE
If you find yourself queasy at the idea of removing physical files from the FRA, your gut instincts are good. Essentially this means either that your retention policy is not correct or that you have not allocated enough space to support the retention policy established for your database. Also, removing files potentially compromises the recoverability of your database, so exercise extreme caution when removing files.

Setting Up the Fast Recovery Area

Two parameters are used to define the FRA. The first defines where the FRA is created. The DB_RECOVERY_FILE_DEST is used to define the base of the FRA location. From this base location, RMAN will create additional directories that standardize the internal structure of the FRA. In other words, you should never need to manage the directories in the FRA; Oracle does it for you. The FRA destination location can be a file system or an ASM volume. It cannot be any location that is an SBT location.

You define the quota of space allocated to the database's FRA by using the parameter DB_RECOVERY_FILE_DEST_SIZE. The DB_RECOVERY_FILE_DEST_SIZE parameter can be a bit confusing at times. This parameter simply places a logical cap on how much physical space a database may consume in the FRA at any given time. Thus, the amount of space defined by this parameter is a logical limit and not a physical limit.

For example, you may have a file system called something like /fra that has a terabyte of space available to it. You might also have a consolidated database environment where you charge users for how much backup disk space they use and all of these databases have /fra set as their FRA location. To control how much space any one of these databases can consume in the FRA, you would use the DB_FILE_RECOVERY_DEST_SIZE parameter So, if you set the parameter to 100GB, that database can only use 100GB of the 1TB file system at any time.

If the FRA exceeds the space allocated to it, Oracle will try to free space automatically. It will delete any backup-related files that are no longer needed by Oracle based on the retention criteria you have defined. These file deletions will be recorded in the database alert log. Note that we didn't say that RMAN deleted these files; rather, this is a somewhat combined responsibility of RMAN and Oracle. If the space becomes exhausted during a backup, RMAN will trigger the file cleanup. If it's triggered by Oracle trying to copy over an archived redo log, for example, then the database will trigger the space cleanup.

Eventually, you will reach a point where you are out of FRA space (usually logically, but sometimes it can be physically too). In this case the following happens:

- Any database backup will fail, indicating you are out of space in the FRA.
- An error message will appear in the alert log indicating that the FRA is out of space.

Also note that when you start the database, Oracle reports the amount of free space available in the FRA in the alert log. But don't forget, these out-of-space conditions are all logical conditions—which are a result of exceeding the amount of space allocated to the FRA through the parameter DB_RECOVERY_FILE_DEST_SIZE. It is entirely possible that you have more than enough physical space available on the underlying storage device(s).

To set up the FRA, you will want to configure the following parameters:

Parameter	Example	Purpose
DB_RECOVERY_ FILE_DEST_SIZE	`Alter system set db_recovery_file_ dest_size=20G scope=both;`	Sets the allocated size of the FRA, in bytes, and must be defined in order to enable the FRA. This allows you to control how much disk space is allocated to the FRA. You should not set this value to a size greater than the total amount of available disk space.
DB_RECOVERY_ FILE_DEST	`Alter system set db_recovery_file_ dest='/u01/oracle/ flash_recovery' scope=both;`	Specifies the location of the FRA. This can be a file system, an ASM disk location, or an OMF location.

Note that you must specify the DB_RECOVERY_FILE_DEST_SIZE parameter before you specify the DB_RECOVERY_FILE_DEST parameter. Failure to do so will result in an ORA-32001 error message. In a similar fashion, you must disable the DB_RECOVERY_FILE_DEST parameter before you reset the DB_RECOVERY_FILE_DEST_SIZE parameter. Leaving DB_RECOVERY_FILE_DEST empty will disable the FRA. Here is an example of disabling the FRA by resetting the DB_ RECOVERY_FILE_DEST parameter:

```
alter system set db_recovery_file_dest=' ' scope=both;
```

If you are running an Oracle CDB, you would configure the FRA when logged in as an administrative user of the CDB.

Oracle allows you to archive to both the FRA and to one or more additional locations through the use of the LOG_ARCHIVE_DEST_*n* parameters. One case when you would want to do this is if you were configuring standby databases and you still wanted to take advantage of the features of the FRA.

To configure both FRA and archive log destination directories, you set the standard FRA parameter DB_RECOVERY_FILE_DEST, defining the location of the FRA. You will also define the various LOG_ARCHIVE_DEST_*n* parameters that are required. By default, when a LOG_ ARCHIVE_DEST_*n* parameter is defined, that location will be used instead of the FRA. To get Oracle to use the FRA when a LOG_ARCHIVE_DEST_*n* parameter is set, you need to define an additional LOG_ARCHIVE_DEST_*n* parameter for the FRA. Typically, this will be LOG_ARCHIVE_ DEST_10, and you will use the Oracle-supplied constant USE_DB_RECOVERY_FILE_DEST to indicate that this destination is the FRA. Here is an example where we configure Oracle to use the FRA and a regular archive log destination directory:

```
alter system set log_archive_dest_10='LOCATION=USE_DB_RECOVERY_FILE_DEST';
alter system set log_archive_dest_1='location=c:\oracle\oraarc\beta1 mandatory';
```

Note that in some cases, Oracle will not set this default value when using the FRA.

In this example, the ARCH process will now create archived redo logs in both LOG_ARCHIVE_DEST_1 and LOG_ARCHIVE_DEST_10, which is the FRA.

Fast Recovery Area Views

We have seen most of the views that are available to help you manage the FRA. These views include the following:

- DBA_OUTSTANDING_ALERTS
- V$RECOVERY_FILE_DEST
- V$ RECOVERY_AREA_USAGE (Note that this changed from V$FLASH_RECOVERY_AREA_USAGE in Oracle Database 12c.)

Also, columns are available in several other views that help you to manage the FRA. Let's look at each of these views and columns in more detail.

The DBA_OUTSTANDING_ALERTS View   As files are added to or removed from the FRA, records of these events are logged in the database alert log. You can check the new DBA view, DBA_OUTSTANDING_ALERTS, for information on outstanding issues with the FRA. Note that there is somewhat of a lag between the time a space-related issue occurs and when the warning appears in the DBA_OUTSTANDING_ALERTS view.

The following is an example where the FRA has run out of space and is posting an alert to the DBA_OUTSTANDING_ALERTS view. You would need to deal with this situation quickly or risk the database coming to a complete halt. In this case, we used the **alter system** command to increase the amount of space allocated to the FRA.

```
SQL> select reason from dba_outstanding_alerts;
REASON
---------------------------------------------------------------
db_recovery_file_dest_size of 524288000 bytes is 100.00% used
and has 0 remaining bytes available.

SQL> alter system set db_recovery_file_dest_size=800m;
```

The V$RECOVERY_FILE_DEST View   The V$RECOVERY_FILE_DEST view provides an overview of the FRA that is defined in your database. It provides the size that the FRA is configured for, the amount of space used, how much space can be reclaimed, and the number of files in the FRA. In the following example, we can see that the increase in space to the FRA to 800MB has been recorded (SPACE_LIMIT). However, we still have used too much space (SPACE_USED), and the FRA is still full.

```
SQL> select * from v$recovery_file_dest;
NAME
-----------------------------------------------------------------
    SPACE_LIMIT             SPACE_USED  SPACE_RECLAIMABLE NUMBER_OF_FILES
--------------- ---------------------- ------------------ ---------------
c:\oracle\product\10.2.0\flash_recovery_area
    838,860,800          1,057,116,672        338,081,280              11
```

One nice thing about Oracle is that it manages the FRA space for us as much as it can, and if there is reclaimable space available, it will free it as required. Note that in the previous query, Oracle indicated we were out of FRA space. Did you notice the SPACE_RECLAIMABLE column, though? This column indicates that there is reclaimable space available. This is space that is taken up by archived redo logs or backup set pieces that are no longer needed by virtue of whatever retention criteria we have selected (we will discuss retention criteria and setting those criteria later in this chapter). When Oracle needs space in the FRA (say, for example, we force a log switch), it will remove any files that are reclaimable and free up space. In the next query, we can see that this has occurred. After we ran the previous query, which indicated we were out of FRA space, we forced a log switch. This caused Oracle to reclaim space from the FRA for reuse, and it then was able to write out the archived redo log. We can query the V$RECOVERY_FILE_DEST view and see that this has indeed occurred:

```
SQL> alter system switch logfile;
System altered.
SQL> select * from v$recovery_file_dest;
NAME
------------------------------------------------------------------------
    SPACE_LIMIT           SPACE_USED  SPACE_RECLAIMABLE NUMBER_OF_FILES
------------- ---------------------- ------------------ ---------------
c:\oracle\product\10.2.0\flash_recovery_area
    838,860,800           719,412,736             64,000               7
```

The V$RECOVERY_AREA_USAGE View The V$RECOVERY_AREA_USAGE view provides more detailed information on which types of files are occupying space in the FRA. This view groups the file types and then provides the percentage of space that is used by each file type, the percentage of the total FRA reclaimable space that comes from that group, and the number of files in the FRA that come from that group. Here is a query of the V$RECOVERY_AREA_USAGE view:

```
SQL> SELECT * FROM V$RECOVERY_AREA_USAGE;
```

FILE_TYPE	PERCENT_SPACE_USED	PERCENT_SPACE_RECLAIMABLE	NUMBER_OF_FILES
CONTROLFILE	0	0	0
ONLINELOG	0	0	0
ARCHIVELOG	17.14	17.09	7
BACKUPPIECE	108.88	23.22	4
IMAGECOPY	0	0	0
FLASHBACKLOG	0	0	0

In this example, we notice a few things:

■ We are over our defined space allocation (the PERCENT_SPACE_USED of all the rows exceeds 100 percent). This is probably because the size of the FRA was recently changed and Oracle has not yet reclaimed enough space to bring the total used below 100 percent.

■ The backup set pieces are consuming most of that space, and 23.22 percent of that space is reclaimable.

■ The archived redo logs consume only 17 percent of the space allocated to the FRA, and even if we were to remove all of the archived redo logs, we would not free up enough space to bring the FRA under the amount of space allocated to it.

Other Views with FRA Columns   The column IS_RECOVERY_DEST_FILE can be found in a number of Oracle Database V$ views, such as V$CONTROLFILE, V$LOGFILE, V$ARCHIVED_LOG, V$DATAFILE_COPY, V$DATAFILE, and V$BACKUP_PIECE. This column is a Boolean that indicates whether the file is in the FRA.

Another column, BYTES, can be found in the V$BACKUP_PIECE and RC_BACKUP_PIECE (an RMAN recovery catalog view) views. This column indicates the size of the backup set piece in bytes.

NOTE
*Manually removing fixed files from the FRA can have unexpected consequences. Oracle does not immediately detect the removal of these files, and thus the space is not reclaimed. If you end up manually removing files (or lose a disk perhaps), use the RMAN **crosscheck** command along with the **delete** command to cause Oracle to update the current control file information on the FRA. The folks at Oracle recommend that you not manually remove files managed by Oracle if at all possible.*

Other Fast Recovery Area Features
The **alter database add logfile** and **alter database add standby logfile** commands create an online redo log member in the FRA if the OMF-related parameter DB_CREATE_ONLINE_LOG_DEST_*n* is not set. The **alter database drop logfile** and **alter database rename file** commands also support files in the FRA. The nice thing about using these OMF-related features is that Oracle will manage the physical files for you. Therefore, if you drop an online redo log group, and the physical files of that group were created by Oracle based on the setting of DB_CREATE_ONLINE_LOG_DEST_*n*, Oracle will remove those physical files for you.

During database creation, Oracle can use the FRA to store the database control file and online redo logs. If the OMF-related parameter DB_CREATE_ONLINE_LOG_DEST_*n* is defined, the control file and redo logs will be created in those locations but will not be created in the FRA, even if the FRA is defined. If DB_CREATE_ONLINE_LOG_DEST_*n* is not defined but DB_CREATE_FILE_DEST is defined, the control file and online redo logs will be created in the location defined by DB_CREATE_FILE_DEST. If DB_RECOVERY_FILE_DEST is also defined, a copy of the control file and online redo logs will get created there as well. The result is a multiplexed online redo log. Finally, if only DB_RECOVERY_FILE_DEST is defined, the control file will get created in that location. If none of these parameters is defined, the control file and online redo logs will be created in a default location, which is OS specific.

An additional use of the FRA has to do with Flashback Database–related features. We discuss Oracle's Flashback Database features in more detail in Chapter 16.

The FRA and ASM
RMAN supports the use of Automatic Storage Management (ASM) for the storage of RMAN backups. What is ASM? ASM is a disk management tool that eliminates the need for the DBA to manage the physical files associated with a given database. ASM is somewhat like the logical volume groups you might be used to in Unix. ASM uses *ASM disk groups,* which are logical units of storage. Physical disks are assigned to an ASM disk group, providing the overall storage capability of that ASM disk group. ASM disk groups can exist on previously allocated file systems or on raw disks. Combined with OCFS, clustered servers can share ASM disks in RAC configurations. Having configured ASM and having defined the various disk groups, you can

then assign datafiles, control files, online redo logs, and various RMAN backup files to the ASM disk groups.

ASM offers a number of features, including load balancing, data redundancy, and easy addition and removal of new disks to the ASM disk groups. It is beyond the scope of this book to discuss configuration of ASM in general. However, be aware that RMAN does support ASM disk groups should you wish to use them. Additionally, features of ASM since 11.2 provide extra tuning of the input and output buffers that RMAN uses.

If you are using ASM, you can configure the FRA such that it will be created in the ASM file system, as shown in this example:

```
alter system set db_recovery_file_dest='+ASMV01';
```

In this case, Oracle will use the ASM disk volume ASMV01 for the FRA. We can then use RMAN to back up to the FRA. We discuss backups in Chapter 7.

Should You Use the FRA?

We think the idea behind the FRA is a good one. We also like to copy those backups to some other media, such as tape, so we can send them offsite for disaster-recovery purposes (nothing like a good flood, bomb, or tornado to make your disaster-recovery planning seem really important).

We also like the FRA for the archived redo logs, but we also like the idea of copying archived redo logs to more than one location (and more specifically, to more than one disk). Keep in mind that the archived redo logs are critical to database recovery, and if you lose one, all the others after that one are pretty much worthless. Therefore, we tend to configure our databases using FRA and at least one other archive log destination that is on a different disk. This means that we use the LOG_ARCHIVE_DEST_*n* parameters to configure the database to use both the FRA and another, separate file system to store our archived redo logs.

Another benefit of the FRA we like is the implementation of space quotas. Consolidation is one of the big things we have seen happening in the last few years, and it does not seem to be slowing down. As a result, more databases are sharing the same server. This causes situations where one database has consumed all of the physical disk space with archived redo logs. This causes problems not only for the database that filled up the archived redo log destination directory, but also for all the other databases on the system. By using a quota system, you can limit one database's ability to impact others.

Therefore, we strongly recommend that you use the FRA, as does Oracle. Using the FRA is part of the Oracle MAA–recommended architecture.

Switching Between ARCHIVELOG Modes

Once you have configured the database to run in ARCHIVELOG mode, you can switch it between NOARCHIVELOG and ARCHIVELOG mode quite easily. To put the database in ARCHIVELOG mode, you must first shut down the database in a consistent state using one of these commands: **shutdown**, **shutdown immediate**, or **shutdown transactional**. Once the database has been cleanly shut down, mount the database by issuing the **startup mount** command. Once the database is mounted, issue the command **alter database archivelog** to put the database in ARCHIVELOG mode. You can then open the database with the **alter database open** command.

If you wish to take the database out of ARCHIVELOG mode, reverse the process. First shut down the database. Once the database has been shut down, mount the database by issuing the **startup mount** command. Once the database is mounted, issue the command **alter database**

noarchivelog to put the database in NOARCHIVELOG mode. You can then open the database with the **alter database open** command.

If You Created Your Database with the Oracle Database Configuration Assistant

If you created your database with the Oracle Database Configuration Assistant (ODBCA), it is likely that Oracle has configured much of RMAN for you. ODBCA will configure the database in ARCHIVELOG mode, configure the FRA, and even offer you the chance to schedule RMAN backups. For smaller installations, this may well be all that is needed, and you will not need to worry about any other basic RMAN configuration issues. Still, it's a good idea to be aware of all the options that RMAN offers. For example, encryption of backups is not enabled when you create a database with the ODBCA, and you might want to enable that feature.

RMAN Workshop: *Put the Database in ARCHIVELOG Mode*

Workshop Notes

As with all the workshops, please do *not* run this workshop in a production environment. Some of the steps could be, at the very least, disruptive in a production environment, if not downright destructive.

For this workshop, you need an installation of the Oracle software, as well as a database that is up and running in NOARCHIVELOG mode. To make sure the database is in NOARCHIVELOG mode, log in as SYS and issue the following command:

```
sqlplus robert/password as sysdba
SQL> select log_mode from v$database;
LOG_MODE
------------
NOARCHIVELOG
```

If the response to the previous query is ARCHIVELOG, the database is in ARCHIVELOG mode. If you wish to take it out of ARCHIVELOG mode, we provide instructions on how to do that just after the end of this workshop.

Before you start the workshop, determine where you want the Fast Recovery Area to reside. You will also need to decide where a second archive log destination directory will be because this workshop will have you archiving to two locations.

Step 1. Configure both the FRA and a separate archive log destination for the archived redo logs. First, set your environment for your Oracle 12c database and then log in as a user with SYSDBA or SYSBACKUP privileges. Then, set the FRA parameters DB_RECOVERY_FILE_DEST_ SIZE and DB_RECOVERY_FILE_DEST:

```
sqlplus robert/password as sysdba
SQL> alter system set db_recovery_file_dest_size=2G;
System altered.
```

```
SQL> alter system set
db_recovery_file_dest='c:\oracle\product\10.2.0\flash_recovery_area';
System altered.
```

Step 2. Now, define two archive log destination directories, one of which will be the FRA. Set the database parameter file, and set the LOG_ARCHIVE_DEST_1 parameter so that it is pointing to a predefined file system that will be our first archive log directory. Since we are configuring LOG_ARCHIVE_DEST_1 and we want to use the FRA, we need to set the LOG_ARCHIVE_DEST_10 parameter to point to the FRA by using the parameter USE_DB_RECOVERY_FILE_DEST. Use the **show parameter** command to verify that the settings are correct:

```
SQL> alter system set log_archive_dest_1='location=d:\archive\rob10R2';
System altered.
SQL> alter system set
log_archive_dest_10='LOCATION=USE_DB_RECOVERY_FILE_DEST';
SQL> show parameter log_archive_dest
NAME                    TYPE         VALUE
--------------------- ----------- --------
log_archive_dest_1      string
location=d:\archive\rob10R2
log_archive_dest_10     string
LOCATION=USE_DB_RECOVERY_FILE_DEST
```

Step 3. Shut down the database:

```
SQL> shutdown immediate
Database closed.
Database dismounted.
ORACLE instance shut down.
```

Step 4. Mount the database:

```
SQL> startup mount
ORACLE instance started.
Total System Global Area   84700976 bytes
Fixed Size                   282416 bytes
Variable Size              71303168 bytes
Database Buffers           12582912 bytes
Redo Buffers                 532480 bytes
Database mounted.
```

Step 5. Put the database in ARCHIVELOG mode:

```
SQL> alter database archivelog ;
Database altered.
```

Step 6. Open the database:

```
SQL> alter database open;
Database altered.
```

Although it is not part of the workshop, the process of taking the database out of ARCHIVELOG mode is as simple as reversing the process described in the workshop. Shut down the database, restart the database instance by issuing the **startup mount** command, and put the database in NOARCHIVELOG mode by issuing the command **alter database noarchivelog**. Note that you are not required to shut down the database in a consistent manner when moving from ARCHIVELOG mode to NOARCHIVELOG mode. Here is an example of switching back into NOARCHIVELOG mode:

```
SQL> shutdown
ORACLE instance shut down.
SQL> startup mount
ORACLE instance started.
Total System Global Area     84700976 bytes
Fixed Size                     282416 bytes
Variable Size                71303168 bytes
Database Buffers             12582912 bytes
Redo Buffers                   532480 bytes
Database mounted.
SQL> alter database noarchivelog;
Database altered.
SQL> alter database open;
Database altered.
```

Finally, you should do a backup of the database once you have completed either task. You can look at Chapter 2 for a quick-and-dirty way of doing a backup at this point. Starting in Chapter 7, we really give RMAN backups some detailed treatment.

The Oracle Database Fault Diagnosability Infrastructure

Oracle Database 11*g* introduced the Fault Diagnosability Infrastructure. We cover the various features associated with the new Fault Diagnosability Infrastructure throughout this book. This infrastructure is designed to help prevent, detect, diagnose, and resolve problems such as database bugs and various forms of corruption. With respect to backup and recovery operations, with or without RMAN, the information contained within the infrastructure can be very helpful in determining what has failed and how to correct for that failure.

What are the purposes of the Fault Diagnosability Infrastructure? The purposes are several-fold:

- The ability to quickly diagnose a problem (first-failure diagnosis)
- Providing means of preventing problems before they occur
- Limiting the impact and damage of problems that have been detected
- Reducing the time it takes to diagnose and resolve a problem
- Improving the interaction experience you have with Oracle Support

The ADR and Related Fault Diagnosability Infrastructure Components

The Fault Diagnosability Infrastructure is made up of a number of different components. Many of these have been around for a while, and others are brand new. These components include the following:

- The Automatic Diagnostic Repository (ADR) and the content contained within it
- The Incident Packaging Service
- The SQL Test Case Builder
- Various views used to support the Fault Diagnosability Infrastructure
- The alert log
- Trace files, dump files, and core files
- DDL and debug logs
- Enterprise Manager Support Workbench
- The ADRCI command-line utility

In this section we address the main components in more detail, and we discuss how to configure the ADR.

The Automatic Diagnostic Repository (ADR)

This Fault Diagnosability Infrastructure centers around a file-based repository called the Automatic Diagnostic Repository, or ADR. Within the ADR the new diagnostic infrastructure stores various files related to the status, health, and well being of the database.

The Fault Diagnosability Infrastructure really kicks into high gear when certain critical kinds of database issues occur (such as an ORA-0600 error). The issues that trigger a response are those that have a high probability of causing an interruption in service. By trapping them on their first occurrence, the DBA can begin root-cause analysis much sooner than was previously possible. Thus, the DBA has an opportunity to get ahead of the problem before it can really cause a much broader set of systematic issues. When a problem occurs, a record of that event, along with diagnostic data (such as trace files), is maintained in the ADR. Since this information is stored outside of the database, it is not a problem collecting it should the database be down.

You can find a number of logs and files in the ADR that may come in handy when trying to diagnose your database problem. These include the following:

- **The database alert log**   This log maintains a record of major events that occur in the database such as startup and shutdown, critical failure events, and informational records that can be used to diagnose database problems. The database alert log is maintained in both text and XML format in the ADR.
- **The DDL log**   This log is new in Oracle Database 12c. It provides a record of all DDL events that occur in the database. You need to enable DDL logging before this log file will be populated. To do so, set the ENABLE_DDL_LOGGING parameter to TRUE. The default for this parameter is FALSE.

- **The debug log** This log is new in Oracle Database 12*c* and it provides a log file of events that occur in the database that were unusual but did not impact the state of the database itself. Many of these events were originally recorded to the database alert log and now are recorded in the debug log.

- **Trace files** These files are stored in the ADR infrastructure. Trace files are important tools that you, and Oracle Support, can use to review and see what a given Oracle Database process is doing, or was doing. They are very helpful when you're trying to troubleshoot a database failure. They are also useful during database performance tuning.

The files listed here are the ones that are most commonly used by the DBA. There are many other types of files in the ADR, such as core files, dump files, a health check result file, and the like. We will discuss configuring the ADR repository in the Oracle database later in this chapter.

The Incident Packaging Service

When problems are detected (as with the ORA-0600 incident suggested earlier), a service called the Incident Packaging Service (IPS) gathers the diagnostic information stored in the ADR and also determines which files are needed by Oracle for diagnosis of the problem. ADR will then package those files into a single .zip file (called an incident package or just package) that can be sent to Support. This process simplifies the support process significantly.

These packages are also stored in the ADR. You can easily add, remove, and change the files in these packages before you send them to Oracle if you wish (for example, you might want to scrub some of the data contained in these files). Once you are ready, the file can be sent to Support to help them in their problem diagnosis (thus saving you lots of time chasing down these files in disparate directory structures filled with hundreds of different files, as you had to do in the past).

The Database Support Workbench

Using a related tool, the Database Support Workbench, you can proceed to open Oracle Database service requests (SRs) with Oracle Support, sending them the diagnostic information that was collected and packaged to provide them with significant information as to the nature of the problem. This can reduce the time it takes for you and Support to request and send diagnostic information, thus reducing the time it takes to resolve a problem. The easiest method of accessing the Database Support Workbench is through Oracle Cloud Control—but you can also access it though the **adrcli** command-line interface.

The SQL Test Case Builder

Another tool in the Fault Diagnosability Infrastructure is the SQL Test Case Builder. This tool provides a way to build a reproducible test case for a given problem. The SQL Test Case Builder gathers the information needed about a given problem and provides Oracle with the significant information it needs to be able to reproduce the problem. Since it is sometimes difficult to reconstruct the exact conditions of a problem, the SQL Test Case Builder can be a significant aid when trying to reproduce a problem.

Fault Diagnosability Infrastructure–Related Data Dictionary Views

The Fault Diagnosability Infrastructure collects and provides a great deal of information. This information typically is accessed and acted upon from Oracle Cloud Control. However, the infrastructure also provides a number of data dictionary views that allow you to look at the current state reported by the Fault Diagnosability Infrastructure.

Here are some of the available views that tie into the Fault Diagnosability Infrastructure:

- **DBA_OUTSTANDING_ALERTS**   This view provides the ability to see any alerts that are currently active within the Fault Diagnosability Infrastructure. For example, earlier when we wanted to see if the FRA was running out of space, we used this view. It was the Fault Diagnosability Infrastructure that provided the information we were seeing.

- **V$DIAG_INFO**   This view provides various information about the ADR. This is a denormalized view that contains individual records for various pieces of reportable information from the ADR and then the data related to that piece. As of Oracle Database 12c this view provides 11 specific pieces of information, including the active problem and incident count, the various diagnostic directory locations for different ADR components, the location of the ADR base, and whether the ADR is enabled (which it is by default).

- **V$DIAG_CRITICAL_ERROR**   This view simply presents the various ORA errors that are considered critical and creates an automated incident package.

- **V$DATABASE_BLOCK_CORRUPTION**   This view can be populated by the Oracle health checkers or by an RMAN backup or validation. In either case, corrupted database blocks are displayed in this view. This can be quite helpful to the DBA when trying to perform block-level media recovery, which is discussed in Chapter 9.

- **V$CORRUPT_XID_LIST**   Provides information on corrupted undo segments, which often is a result of a corrupted transaction. Oracle tries to recover these corrupted transactions automatically. If it cannot correct the corruption, the V$CORRUPT_XID_LIST view is populated with the transaction information. The response to the corruption is dependent on the nature of the corruption and is beyond the scope of this book. If you see records in this view, you should open a support ticket with Oracle.

- **V$HM_RUN**   Provides a list of health checks that have run in the past and the status of that run.

- **Various V$HM_* views**   These views provide information on the health checks that are run by Oracle. The types of health checks, the parameters used when the individual health checks are executed, and the findings and recommendations of the health check runs are all listed in various V$HM views.

- For example, you can find the specific execution of a health check using the V$HM_RUN view. Once you find the health check run you wish to report on, you can run the PL/SQL program DBMS_HM.GET_RUN_REPORT to generate a detailed report on that specific health check run. Here is an example of doing just this:

```
select name, check_name, start_time from v$hm_run;
NAME          CHECK_NAME                    START_TIME
------------  ----------------------------  ----------------------------
HM_RUN_1      DB Structure Integrity Check  06-MAR-14 09.31.16.833000 AM

set long 1000000
-- Note some output removed and reformatted for brevity.
select dbms_hm.get_run_report('HM_RUN_1') from dual;
DBMS_HM.GET_RUN_REPORT('HM_RUN_1')
------------------------------------------------------------------------
```

```
Basic Run Information
  Run Name                    : HM_RUN_1
  Run Id                      : 1
  Check Name                  : DB Structure Integrity Check
  Mode                        : REACTIVE
  Status                      : COMPLETED
  Start Time                  : 2014-03-06 09:31:16.833000 -08:00
  End Time                    : 2014-03-06 09:31:19.547000 -08:00
  Error Encountered           : 0
  Source Incident Id          : 0
  Number of Incidents Created : 0
Input Parameters for the Run
Run Findings And Recommendations
  Finding
  Finding Name  : Control File needs recovery
  Finding ID    : 2
  Type          : FAILURE
  Status        : CLOSED
  Priority      : CRITICAL
  Message       : Control file needs media recovery
  Message       : Database cannot be opened
Finding
  Finding Name  : Missing System datafile
  Finding ID    : 5
  Type          : FAILURE
  Status        : CLOSED
  Priority      : CRITICAL
  Message       : System datafile 1:
                  'C:\ADE\AIME_V\ORACLE\ORADATA\SEEDDATA\SYSTEM01.DBF' is
                  missing
  Message       : Database cannot be opened
  Finding
  Finding Name  : Missing Data Files
Finding ID      : 8
  Type          : FAILURE
  Status        : CLOSED
  Priority      : HIGH
  Message       : One or more non-system datafiles are missing
  Message       : See impact for individual child failures
  Finding
  Finding Name  : Missing datafile
```

You can see in this output that the database was suffering from some major datafile losses. Since the health checks run on a scheduled basis, it's very possible that the health checks will pick up on a missing datafile before your users will experience the results of that missing datafile—especially if the data file is not frequently accessed. Similar health checkers exist for various types of database corruptions, both logical and physical.

In Oracle Database 12c (and earlier versions) the ADR contains many different file areas you will be interested in with respect to backup and recovery. The database alert log is contained in this directory structure, as are all database-related trace files and trace files from other Oracle components, such as the listeners that will be running.

NOTE
Oracle seems to be moving more log files and diagnostic information to the ADR as time goes on. For example, in 12.1.0.2 Oracle moved some Oracle Clusterware–related files to the ADR. The bottom line is that if your Oracle-related log files, or other diagnostic-related data, does not seem to be getting created in the previously normal places, check to see if that information has moved to a directory in the ADR.

Other Oracle Database tools are associated with this framework. This includes tools such as the Database Support Workbench mentioned earlier. There are also a number of health checkers that attempt to be proactive about database health. The health checks run on a regular basis, trying to actively find certain things like corruption of the data dictionary, undo and redo corruption, data block corruption, and other database-related problems that tend not to surface without causing a failure. Also, when a problem is detected and an incident created, certain health checkers may run automatically as part of building an incident package so that the root cause might be more easily detected.

Finally, within this diagnostic framework is the Database Recovery Advisor. This tool uses the ADR data to help determine what kind of failure the database is experiencing, and then based on that information it will analyze the problem, suggest a resolution, and then optionally execute the resolution for you. We discuss these various components throughout the chapters of this book—so keep an eye out for them!

Configuring the Fault Diagnosability Infrastructure

For the purposes of setting up the Fault Diagnosability Infrastructure for an Oracle database, what we are concerned with in this chapter is the setting of the new parameter DIAGNOSTIC_DEST, which defines the root of the ADR and deprecates several other parameters, including USER_DUMP_DEST, CORE_DUMP_DEST, and BACKGROUND_DUMP_DEST. As a result, if you create a new Oracle database with the DBCA, you will not find the alert log or user trace files where you previously would have expected them.

Before we discuss configuring the ADR, you should know that the process of configuring does not change if you are running Oracle Multitenant in Oracle Database 12c. The ADR structure remains the same because it stores information at the grain of the CDB, not at the grain of the PDB. That being said, if a session connected to a PDB raises an error that the ADR records, it will still be recorded in the ADR—it simply won't be recorded in a directory that is specific to that PDB. Rather it will be created in the directories that are at the level of the CDB itself. Even trace files are listed at the CDB level, so if you enable SQL tracing in a PDB, the resulting trace file will have the name of the CDB in the filename, not the name of the PDB.

By default, the DIAGNOSTIC_DEST parameter is set to $ORACLE_BASE. If $ORACLE_BASE is not set, the parameter is set to the value of $ORACLE_HOME. The root directory of the ADR directory structure starts with a directory called diag, under which is a subdirectory that references the product type. For example, for the database, the product is called rdbms. Under rdbms is a directory for each database, followed by a directory for each individual instance.

For example, if $ORACLE_BASE is **/u01/oracle**, the database name is **mydb**, and the database instance is **mydb1**, then the structure of the ADR directory for that database will be /u01/oracle/diag/rdbms/mydb/mydb1. This directory structure is called the ADR home, and each instance has its own ADR home. If you are using RAC, you can either use shared storage for ADR or individual storage

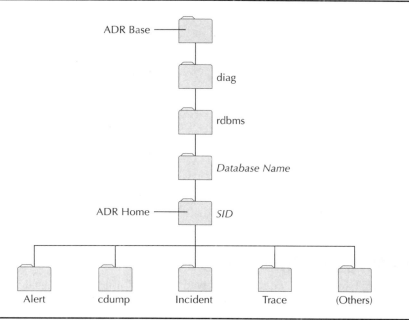

FIGURE 5-1. *ADR base structure*

on each node. We would recommend shared storage in a RAC environment because you can see the aggregate diagnostic data from any node. Also, a shared ADR allows for more robust recovery options for the Data Recovery Advisor. However, the truth is that we usually see ADRs stored on local, nonshared storage most of the time.

Under this directory structure will be a number of other directories. Here are some of the most common ones:

- **Alert**   This is the location of the XML-formatted alert log.
- **cdump**   This is the location of the core dumps for the database.
- **Trace**   This directory contains trace files generated by the system, as well as a text copy of the alert log.
- **Incident**   This directory contains multiple subdirectories, one for each incident.

Figure 5-1 provides a diagram of the ADR Base structure.

The view, V$DIAG_INFO, provides information on the various ADR locations, as well as information related to ADR, such as active incidents. Here is an example of a query against the V$DIAG_INFO view:

```
SQL> select * from v$diag_info;
    INST_ID NAME                         VALUE
---------- ------------------------ ------------------------------------
         1 Diag Enabled                 TRUE
         1 ADR Base                     C:\ORACLE\PRODUCT
```

```
      1 ADR Home                C:\ORACLE\PRODUCT\diag\rdbms\rob12\
                                rob12
      1 Diag Trace              C:\ORACLE\PRODUCT\diag\rdbms\rob12\
                                rob12\trace
      1 Diag Alert              C:\ORACLE\PRODUCT\diag\rdbms\rob12\
                                rob12\alert
      1 Diag Incident           C:\ORACLE\PRODUCT\diag\rdbms\rob12\
                                rob12\incident
      1 Diag Cdump              C:\ORACLE\PRODUCT\diag\rdbms\rob12\
                                rob12\cdump
      1 Health Monitor          C:\ORACLE\PRODUCT\diag\rdbms\rob12\
                                rob12\hm
      1 Default Trace File      C:\ORACLE\PRODUCT\diag\rdbms\rob12\
                                rob12\trace\rob12_ora_7832.trc
      1 Active Problem Count    1
      1 Active Incident Count   1
11 rows selected.
```

The RMAN Command Line

The first step in using RMAN is learning how to start the RMAN client. The client is used to configure RMAN and to perform both online and offline backup and restore operations. Because using the RMAN command line is fundamental to almost everything we will be doing in this book, we need to spend some time learning how to use it.

Connecting via the RMAN Command Line

There are two different ways to get to RMAN. The first is from the command line, and the second is by using OEM (Oracle Enterprise Manager). We will deal with the OEM interface in more detail in Chapter 14. Most of the examples you will see in this book, however, will be done using the command-line interface. We figure that if you can do something from the command line, you can do it from anywhere. In this section, we look at how to connect to databases with the RMAN command line and also how to use the **connect** command.

The RMAN Command-Line Parameters

You can start RMAN from the OS prompt simply by typing the command **rman**. Once you have started the RMAN command interpreter, you can perform whatever operations you might need to perform. Often, it's much easier to get some of the preliminary work done by using command-line parameters. Therefore, when we start RMAN, we can pass several command-line parameters. You can use the command-line parameters to connect RMAN to the database you are going to back up (known as the *target database*), to the recovery catalog, or for a number of other tasks. Table 5-2 provides a list of the command-line parameters, the data type for the argument of the parameter (if there is one), and the purpose of the parameter.

Starting RMAN and Connecting to the Target Database

Probably the most common way to start RMAN is to indicate what target database you wish to connect to. For example, if we wanted to connect to the orcl database as our target, we would

RMAN Command-Line Parameter	Parameter Argument Type	Purpose
target	Character string	Defines the username, password, and service name of the target database to connect to.
catalog	Character string	Defines the username, password, and service name of the recovery catalog.
nocatalog	No arguments	Indicates that no recovery catalog is going to be used by this session. This parameter is the default parameter in Oracle8*i* and Oracle9*i*.
cmdfile	Character string	Indicates the name of a command file script to execute.
log	Character string	Indicates that the RMAN session should be logged. The log file will take the name of the argument to this parameter. It also causes all RMAN messages to the screen to be suppressed (except the RMAN prompt).
trace	Character string	Indicates that the RMAN session should be traced. The trace file will take the name of the argument to this parameter.
append	No arguments	Indicates that the log file (defined by the log parameter) should be appended to.
debug	Various arguments	Indicates that RMAN should be started in debug mode.
msgno	No arguments	Indicates that the RMAN- prefix should be shown with each error message. If this option is not selected, then certain nonerror messages will not include a message number with them.
send	Character string	Sends the character string message to the media management layer.
pipe	String	Invokes the RMAN pipe interface.
timeout	Integer	Indicates the number of seconds to wait for pipe input.
auxiliary	Character string	Defines the username, password, and service name of the auxiliary database to connect to.
checksyntax	None	Checks the command file listed for syntax errors.
slaxdebug	None	Checks for command-line and RMAN prompt parsing errors.
Script	Character string	Name of a catalog script to run.
Using	List of arguments	Provides the arguments for RMAN variables.

TABLE 5-2.   *RMAN Command-Line Parameters*

set the Oracle environment to point to the orcl instance (using .oraenv, for example, or setting ORACLE_SID correctly). Once that is done, starting RMAN is as easy as this:

```
export ORACLE_SID=orcl
rman target=backup/manager
```

In this case, the orcl database will need to have a user called backup that has either SYSDBA or SYSBACKUP privileges, as we discussed earlier. If you prefer to use an Oracle Net service name, you would modify the connection string to look like this:

```
rman target=backup/manager@orcl
```

Of course, in this case the database listener needs to be up and running for you to connect using an Oracle service.

You will see many examples of the use of RMAN command-line parameters throughout the chapters of this book.

NOTE
The = sign between the command-line parameter and the value of that parameter is optional. Also, if you are running Oracle Database Real Application Clusters, you can connect to only one instance of that cluster. However, you can easily spread your backups across multiple nodes of your RAC cluster, which we demonstrate in Chapter 18.

If you are running Oracle Multitenant databases, you may want to be able to connect directly to a PDB. In this case, you will need to use the service name for that PDB in the RMAN connect string, as shown here:

```
rman target=system/manager@mypdb
```

Note that you cannot connect directly to a container database when using RMAN, and you cannot use the **alter session set container** command from the RMAN client to change to a given PDB. If you try, you will get the following error:

```
rman target=sys/password
RMAN> alter session set container=mypdb;
RMAN-00571: ===========================================================
RMAN-00569: =============== ERROR MESSAGE STACK FOLLOWS ===========
RMAN-00571: ===========================================================
RMAN-03002: failure of sql statement command at 10/03/2014 19:40:20
RMAN-06815: cannot change the container in RMAN session.
```

RMAN Connection Privileges

In versions prior to Oracle Database 12*c*, RMAN would always connect as SYSDBA to the target database. Thus, the user you used to log into the database needed to have SYSDBA privileges. You can still follow this model, but SYSDBA privileges are very powerful and should not be assigned without serious consideration to the security requirements of your database.

Because SYSDBA is so powerful, there is now a new administrative privilege, starting in Oracle Database 12*c*, called SYSBACKUP. This privilege can be assigned to any common user (users created using c##) or to any user within a given PDB. Because common users can be assigned privileges based on specific containers, they need to have SYSBACKUP privileges on the root container for full database backup privileges. If they only have SYSBACKUP privileges on a PDB, they can only back up that PDB (which can be problematic because they can back up a PDB but can't perform archived redo log backups from a PDB).

The SYSBACKUP privilege provides specific administrative privileges needed to back up and recover the database, while restricting privileges that are not needed. For example, if you log into the database as a user with SYSBACKUP privileges, that user will not have the ability to create other user accounts, because that privilege is not required to perform backup and restore operations. For example, the SYSBACKUP privilege does not provide the ability to create users within the database.

RMAN Command-Line Help

If you forget the command-line arguments to RMAN (and somehow manage to leave this book and your documentation at home), there is a way to get RMAN to display the valid command-line parameters. Simply start RMAN with an invalid parameter. As you can see in the following example, RMAN will return an error, but will also provide you with a list of valid command-line parameters (we removed some of the errors at the bottom of the listing for brevity):

```
rman help
Argument        Value          Description
-------------------------------------------------------------------
target          quoted-string  connect-string for target database
catalog         quoted-string  connect-string for recovery catalog
auxiliary       quoted-string  connect-string for auxiliary database
nocatalog       none           if specified, then no recovery catalog
cmdfile         quoted-string  name of input command file
log             quoted-string  name of output message log file
trace           quoted-string  name of output debugging message log file
append          none           if specified, log is opened in append mode
debug           optional-args  activate debugging
msgno           none           show RMAN-nnnn prefix for all messages
send            quoted-string  send a command to the media manager
pipe            string         building block for pipe names
script          string         name of catalog script to execute
using           list of args   arguments for rman variables
timeout         integer        number of seconds to wait for pipe input
checksyntax     none           check the command file for syntax errors
-------------------------------------------------------------------
Both single and double quotes (' or ") are accepted for a quoted-string.
Quotes are not required unless the string contains embedded white-space.
-------------------------------------------------------------------
```

RMAN also offers the **checksyntax** parameter, which provides the ability to check the RMAN commands you want to issue for errors. Here is an example of the use of the **checksyntax** parameter:

```
rman checksyntax
Recovery Manager: Release 12.1.0.1.0 -
Production on Fri Oct 3 20:15:02 2014
Copyright (c) 1982, 2013, Oracle and/or its affiliates.  All rights reserved.
RMAN> backup database pls archivelog;
RMAN-00571: ===========================================================
RMAN-00569: =============== ERROR MESSAGE STACK FOLLOWS ===============
RMAN-00571: ===========================================================
```

```
RMAN-00558: error encountered while parsing input commands
RMAN-01009: syntax error: found "identifier": expecting one of: "archivelog,
auxiliary, backupset, backup, channel, controlfilecopy, copy, current,
database, datafilecopy, datafile, db_recovery_file_dest, delete, diskratio,
filesperset, force, format, from, include, keep, maxsetsize, noexclude,
nokeep, not, plus, pool, recovery, reuse, section, skip readonly, skip,
spfile, tablespace, tag, to, (, ;"
RMAN-01008: the bad identifier was: pls
RMAN-01007: at line 1 column 17 file: standard input

RMAN> backup database plus archivelog;
The command has no syntax errors
```

Note that a lot can be divined from RMAN error messages. Often, within the message, you can see that RMAN is expecting a particular keyword or phrase.

NOTE
*There is a bug in some versions of Oracle Database 12c where the **checksyntax** option does not work correctly for all RMAN commands issued.*

RMAN Client Compatibility

When using the RMAN client, you will want to consider the compatibility of that client with the target database to which you are connecting. You will also need to consider the compatibility of the recovery catalog, which we will discuss in more detail in Chapter 9.

Table 5-3 provides guidelines on RMAN compatibility between the target and auxiliary databases and the RMAN client.

Note in Table 5-3 that the rules somewhat changed in Oracle Database 12c. It used to be that you could use older RMAN client versions with more recent target and auxiliary database versions. This has changed in Oracle Database 12c—you must use the same version of the RMAN executable as the version of the target or auxiliary database. There is no indication at the time of the writing of this book as to whether Oracle will allow you to use an older version of the 12.1 RMAN executable with newer versions of the 12.1 database, as has previously been allowed.

Target/Auxiliary Database Version	Client Version Requirement
8.0.6	8.0.6 only
8.1.7	8.0.6.1 or 8.1.7 only
8.1.7.4	8.1.7.4 only
9.0.1	9.0.1 only
9.2.0	>= 9.0.1.3 and <= target database executable version
10.1.0.5	>= 10.1.0.5 and <= target database executable version
10.2.0	>= 10.1.0.5 and <= target database executable version
11.1.0	>= 10.1.0.5 and <= target database executable version
11.2.0	>= 10.1.0.5 and <= target database executable version
12.1.0.x	=12.1.0.x

TABLE 5-3. *RMAN Client and Database Version Compatibility Matrix*

RMAN is stored in the $ORACLE_HOME/bin directory, and this directory should be in the PATH on which the OS Oracle is running. If you have several ORACLE_HOME directories, you will want to be cautious. Make sure that the OS PATH is pointing to the correct ORACLE_HOME before you start RMAN. If you do not set the PATH correctly, you could be using the wrong ORACLE_HOME directory. Also, be cautious that there is not some other **rman** executable in the path before the RMAN executable. For example, an **rman** command in some versions of Unix sometimes ends up running instead of RMAN because it comes first in the path. In cases like this, you will need to adjust the path, or you may need to change to the $ORACLE_HOME/bin directory and run **rman** directly from that location.

Typically, RMAN will generate an error if you are using an incompatible client version. You can use OS-level utilities (such as export|grep ORACLE_HOME on Linux) to determine whether you are using the correct ORACLE_HOME, or you can check the banner of the RMAN client when you execute it.

Using the RMAN connect Command

If you start RMAN and realize that you either have not connected to the correct database or wish to connect to a different database (target, catalog, or auxiliary), you can use the **connect** command to change which database RMAN is connected to. To change to another target database, use the **connect target** command. To change to a different recovery catalog, use the **connect catalog** command. To connect to a different auxiliary database, use the **connect auxiliary** command. To connect to a PDB in a multitenant database, you would connect using the service name of the PDB. Here are some examples of the use of the **connect** command:

```
connect target sys/password@testdb;
connect catalog rcat_user/password@robdb;
```

Executing Oracle SQL Commands from the RMAN Client

In versions of RMAN before Oracle Database 12c you could run SQL commands from the RMAN prompt by using the **sql** keyword, as seen in this example:

```
RMAN> sql 'select * from dual';
```

The problem with this was that you would not see the resulting output of the SQL command, nor could you be sure if it actually worked.

In Oracle Database 12c you can now run most SQL commands from the RMAN prompt natively—without the RMAN SQL parameter being required. Here is an example:

```
RMAN> select file_name from dba_data_files;
FILE_NAME
-----------------------------------------------------------------
C:\APP\ORACLE\ORADATA\MYCDB\DATAFILE\O1_MF_SYSTEM_9KKD9YCT_.DBF
C:\APP\ORACLE\ORADATA\MYCDB\DATAFILE\O1_MF_SYSAUX_9KKD78L1_.DBF
C:\APP\ORACLE\ORADATA\MYCDB\DATAFILE\O1_MF_UNDOTBS1_9KKDF1SW_.DBF
C:\APP\ORACLE\ORADATA\MYCDB\DATAFILE\O1_MF_USERS_9KKDDYCX_.DBF
```

So, now we can actually see the results of our SQL statements when we execute them from the RMAN command line. This means we can issue queries against the data dictionary views like V$DATAFILE without having to switch back and forth between SQL*Plus and RMAN. This is very convenient indeed!

Note that Oracle Database 12c provides a backup privilege called the SYSBACKUP privilege. You grant and use the SYSBACKUP privilege just like you do the SYSDBA privilege. When granted this privilege, a backup administrator can log into the database to perform backup and recovery operations. However, the SYSBACKUP privilege is limited in its abilities to do other things, such as query the database. This provides an added level of security you can use to protect your database.

Exiting the RMAN Client

When you are done with RMAN, it's time to get out of the client. RMAN offers two commands: **quit** and **exit**. These commands will return you to the OS prompt. RMAN also allows you to shell out to the OS with the **host** command. Here are some examples:

```
RMAN> host;
-- shells out to your host. Exit the host shell to return to RMAN
RMAN> exit
Recovery Manager complete.
```

Configuring the Database for RMAN Operations

Now that you know how to start RMAN, we need to deal with some configuration issues. While it is possible to just fire up RMAN and do a backup, it's a better idea to deal with some configuration questions before you do so. First, you need to set up the database user RMAN will be using. Next, you can configure RMAN to use several settings by default, so we will look at those settings as well.

Setting Up the Database User

We mentioned security earlier, and it's important. In the past, it wasn't uncommon for DBAs to just use the SYS account to perform RMAN backups. This is a bad idea from a security point of view—and if you are doing that, please stop.

If you are using versions of Oracle previous to Oracle Database 12c, you will simply need to create some user account that is dedicated to backup operations and assign the SYSDBA privilege to that account. We strongly recommend that you lock down this account as much as possible.

You could use login triggers that check the user context settings with the **sys_context** function. For example, the **sys_context('USERENV', 'HOST')** output would identify the host from which the RMAN client is connecting. We could then build a logon trigger that checks the environment and validates it against approved hosts. A very basic logon trigger might look like this:

```
-- Yes, I know this is basic and inelegant.
Create or replace trigger  check_host_valid_ctx_proc
after logon on c##backup.schema
Begin
If sys_context('USERENV','HOST')='WORKGROUP\MININT-2HGBGQCD'
then
     -- valid workstation
     NULL;
else
     -- Invalid workstations are the default
     raise_application_error(-20000,'Illegal Login from Host');
end if;
end;
/
```

So, if we try to logon from an invalid host, we get the following error:

```
SQL> connect c##backup/robert
ERROR:
ORA-00604: error occurred at recursive SQL level 1
ORA-20000: Illegal Login from Host
ORA-06512: at line 6
```

If you want to lock down your database using logon triggers and more complex context checking, you should look at the Oracle Database Security Guide. In it, you will find a wealth of information that can help you create logon triggers for locking down your database.

So, we have made it clear that you really should create a special account from which to run backups. In the following workshop, we walk you through that process. Note that the workshop will provide steps relevant to both multitenant and nonmultitenant databases.

RMAN Workshop: *Create the Target Database RMAN Backup Account*

Workshop Notes

For this workshop, you need an installation of the Oracle software and a database that is up and running. You also need administrative privileges on this database.

Step 1. Determine the user account name that you want to use, and create it with the database **create user** command. In the case of nonmultitenant databases, the command would look like this:

```
CREATE USER backup_admin IDENTIFIED BY backupuserpassword
DEFAULT TABLESPACE users;
```

In the case of multitenant databases, you would need to use a common account (prefixed with c##), as shown in this example:

```
CREATE USER c##backup_admin IDENTIFIED BY backupuserpassword
DEFAULT TABLESPACE users;
```

Step 2. Grant the sysdba privilege to the BACKUP_ADMIN user. We will use the SYSBACKUP privilege in these examples. If you are running a version of the database earlier than Oracle Database 12c, you will need to replace the SYSBACKUP privilege with the SYSDBA privilege. Here is an example of granting the SYSBACKUP privilege to the BACKUP_ADMIN account within the nonmultitenant database:

```
GRANT sysbackup TO backup_admin;
```

And here is an example of doing so when dealing with a multitenant database:

```
GRANT sysbackup TO c##backup_admin;
```

NOTE
*If you created your database with the **dbca**, you were offered an option to set up automated daily backups. If you selected this option, Oracle will do some initial RMAN configuration for you (it will configure the FRA, for example). Although this RMAN configuration is sufficient for databases that are not of consequence, if you are managing databases that are mission critical, you should still follow the steps outlined in this chapter and ensure that your database is properly configured for RMAN operations.*

So, what happens if you try to connect RMAN to an account that is not properly created? The following error will occur:

```
D:\oracle\oradata\robt>RMAN target=backup/backup@robt
RMAN-00571: ===========================================================
RMAN-00569: =============== ERROR MESSAGE STACK FOLLOWS ===============
RMAN-00571: ===========================================================
RMAN-00554: initialization of internal recovery manager package failed
RMAN-04005: error from target database:
ORA-01031: insufficient privileges
```

Now that we have created the user and granted that user the required privileges, we are a step closer to being ready to use RMAN. Still, we have some RMAN default settings we need to configure, so let's look at those next.

Setting Up Database Security

We need to discuss briefly the differences between connecting to RMAN on the local server and connecting to it via Oracle Net. Security has changed a little over the various versions of Oracle Database, but the basics are still pretty much the same. When you connect to an Oracle database to perform backups, you will use one of four main ways of connecting:

- Via an OS-authenticated account
- Via a username and password if OS authentication is not permitted
- To a database or the root of a CDB via Oracle Net
- To a PDB of a CDB via Oracle Net

Using a local connection via OS authentication is probably the least secure of all the connection methods. Anyone logged onto the database server could directly connect to the database without any credentials required. In this case, you simply log into an account that is set up for Oracle operations and then log into RMAN directly, as seen here:

```
Rman target /
```

In this case, if you are logged on using a privileged OS user account, you do not need to do anything beyond the two steps in the preceding RMAN Workshop. How do you know whether your user account is a privileged one? It depends on the OS you are using. If you are using Unix, there is generally a Unix group called dba (though it may be called something else). This group is created before the Oracle Database software is installed, and the Oracle software is associated with this group when it's installed. If your Unix user account is assigned to this group, you will be able to connect to a target database without any additional work, unless the database is configured to not allow OS authenticated connections. Other operating systems have other ways of providing OS authentication.

Databases can be configured not to allow user authentication. In this case, you can still do RMAN local connections simply by authenticating into the database using the username and password, as shown here:

```
Rman target sys_backup/password
```

In this case the password is clear text of course, which is a problem. This is why using OEM to schedule backups is a much better solution than using CRON jobs, which can have clear-text passwords in them if OS authentication is required. There are ways to encrypt these clear-text passwords in Linux and other forms of Unix. OS utilities such as aesutil (aes) and base64 encoding are examples.

If you are using Oracle Enterprise Manager or are connecting to databases with RMAN over Oracle Net, you will need to use a Net service name for the database to which you will be connecting. You can use this method if you are connecting to a regular database and the root container of a multitenant database. You must use this method to connect to a PDB of a multitenant database. Here is an example of using RMAN when connecting to a network service:

```
Rman target=backup/password@database_service
```

If you are using this connection method, you need to make sure that the database listener (and the SCAN listeners if you are using Clusterware) are up and running.

Create the Password File

If you are going to use the remote authentication method via a service, you will need to create a database password file. This password file provides the ability for remote users connecting to the database to authenticate when using Oracle Net services. To create the Oracle password file, you use the Oracle utility **orapwd**. This command takes three parameters:

- **file**   The password filename
- **password**   The password for the sys user
- **entries**   Any number of entries to reserve for additional privileged Oracle user accounts

The password file-naming standard is determined by the OS platform. For example, in Unix or Linux, it's orapw*sid,* where *sid* is the database name. In Windows, the password file takes the naming standard of PWD*sid*.ora, where *sid* is your database name.

Here is an example of the creation of a password file; in this case, we are creating a password file for a Windows database called robt:

```
orapwd file=PWDrobt.ora password=robert entries=20
```

So, now that we have created the password file, we need to configure the database to use it, which will allow us to do remote backups via Oracle Net.

Configure the Database to Use the Password File

By default, an Oracle database is not configured to use the password file (unless you have used the ODBCA to create your database). To configure the database, edit the parameter file (init.ora) in your favorite editor, or follow the upcoming instructions if you are using an SPFILE. The parameter we are interested in is REMOTE_LOGIN_PASSWORDFILE. This parameter can be set to one of three values in an Oracle database:

- **none** The default value. In this case, Oracle will ignore the password file, and only local privileged logins will be recognized for sysdba access.

- **shared** This parameter indicates that multiple databases can use the same password file. When in this mode, only the SYS user account password can be stored.

- **exclusive** This parameter indicates that the password file is used by only one database. In this mode, the password file can contain passwords for several privileged Oracle accounts. This is the recommend mode of operation, particularly when running RMAN. If you wish to connect RMAN to your database from a remote client, you must use this parameter setting.

If you are using an SPFILE instead of a text-based parameter file, use the **alter system** command to modify this parameter setting:

```
alter system set REMOTE_LOGIN_PASSWORDFILE=EXCLUSIVE scope=spfile;
```

Finally, the REMOTE_LOGIN_PASSWORDFILE parameter is not dynamic, so you cannot change it with the database up and running. Instead, you will have to change the SPFILE (using the **scope=spfile** parameter of the **alter system** command) and then shut down the database and restart it.

Setting the CONTROL_FILE_RECORD_KEEP_TIME Parameter

When configuring your database for RMAN, you should consider how long you wish backup records to be stored in the control file. This includes records of full database backups and of specific datafile, control file, parameter file, and archive log backups. The database parameter CONTROL_FILE_RECORD_KEEP_TIME is defined in days (the default setting is **7**). Therefore, by default, Oracle will maintain RMAN backup and recovery records for seven days. You can set this parameter to any value between **0** and **365** (days).

This parameter can have a number of operational database impacts. First, it directly impacts the size of the database control file, because as RMAN backups occur, records relating to these backups are stored in the control file. As records are saved in the control file, the control file might well run out of space. In this case, Oracle will expand the control file to accommodate the storage of the required number of backup records. Setting this parameter to **0** will disallow any control file growth, but has the negative effect of making the RMAN backup history retention period uncertain.

We suggest that you set CONTROL_FILE_RECORD_KEEP_TIME to a value no less than your selected database backup retention period. Otherwise, you risk having database backups available on your backup media without related backup records available in the control file. This can cause serious complications if you need to recover these older backups for some reason!

One important thing to keep in mind is that the more records you keep in the control file, the more impact that RMAN operations on the control file can have on the database. If you are going to do a large number of backups (including archived redo logs), we strongly suggest that you use a recovery catalog and keep the number of records being stored in the control file to a reasonable number (say, 30 to 60 days).

CAUTION
There are a number of places where incorrectly set file retention can cause your backup's retention strategy to fail. These include incorrectly setting CONTROL_FILE_RECORD_KEEP_TIME, RMAN retention policies, and retention policies on your tape vendor products. Make sure all retention policies are aligned so you don't wake up someday and find you are unable to restore your backups.

Configuring RMAN Default Settings

RMAN allows you to perform automated database backup and recovery, as you will see in later chapters. To support this feature, RMAN allows you to define default values for a number of settings, such as channel configuration. In this section, we look at the configuration of default RMAN settings. Of course, if you can configure something, you will want to be able to change that configuration, and even to remove it completely if required. We will look at that, too. So, what will be the benefit of all of this configuration work? It will make the process of actually doing backups much easier in the end. First, we quickly examine the **configure** command in RMAN and all that it provides us. Then, we look at several of the different defaults you might want to configure by using the **configure** command.

Setting and using the default parameters is important. It's a way to standardize RMAN configurations and ensure that they are consistently used. This reduces the possibility of error when more than one person is performing RMAN backups.

Throughout this section, we use a number of terms that you might not yet be familiar with because they are covered in later chapters. Many of the terms were introduced in Chapter 2, though others may not be quite clear to you yet. That's okay, because to use RMAN, none of the default configuration options are really required. We suggest that you skim this section to get a feel for the various default values you can set, and then, after you have read later chapters, return here and reread this section. At that point, you will be ready to decide what defaults you want to apply to your Oracle database.

When you configure a default setting in RMAN, you will need to connect to the database just as you would when doing a backup. If you are connecting to a multitenant database, you will need to connect to the root container of the database and not a PDB. You cannot configure default values when connected to a PDB.

Introducing the configure Command

RMAN provides the **configure** command, which allows you to define default values to be applied when executing backup and recovery sessions. Using the **configure** command, you can make changes to the default values of the various parameters that are persistent until cleared or changed again. The ability to customize default configuration settings allows you to execute automated RMAN operations. The following are several of the different settings you can configure:

- A default device type, such as disk or SBT (system backup tape), to use for RMAN jobs.

- The number of channels that are automatically allocated when performing automated backup and restore jobs.

- A tablespace exclusion policy to configure specific tablespaces to be excluded during full database backup operations.

■ The maximum size for any given backup piece and the size of any backup set when doing an automated backup.

■ You can set backup optimization to default to ON or OFF. Backup optimization eliminates duplicate backups of identical datafiles (for example, those associated with read-only tablespaces) and archived redo logs.

■ The default filename for the snapshot control file (refer to Chapter 3 for more details on the snapshot control file).

■ The default setting for automated backups of the control file can be configured either ON or OFF.

■ You can configure the default format for the control file, backup output files, and the default device on which to create these backups.

■ The default filenames for files of an auxiliary database.

■ A default retention policy, which determines which backups and copies are eligible for deletion because they are no longer needed.

■ The default encryption value and the associated encryption algorithm.

■ The default compression algorithm to use if compression is to be used.

■ A deletion policy for archived redo logs.

Each configurable setting has a default value assigned to it. The defaults are stored in the database control file (as are any configured values). This is true even if you are connecting to a recovery catalog. You can see the currently configured values for the various RMAN parameters by using the **show** command. Any nondefault RMAN-configured settings are also listed in the V$RMAN_CONFIGURATION database view. Here are some examples of the **show** command's use:

```
show default device type;
show maxsetsize;
show retention policy;
show all;
```

Configuring Various RMAN Default Settings

This section looks at setting RMAN defaults. First, let's look at configuration of channel default settings. You can configure channels in different ways. You can configure defaults for all channels with the **configure channel device type** command, or configure defaults for specific default channels with the **configure channel _n_ device type** command.

You can clear channel defaults for all channels with the **configure channel device type clear** command, and clear channel defaults for specific default channels with the **configure channel _n_ device type clear** command. Note that you can only clear the entire configured setting; you cannot clear a parameter within a setting. Therefore, a command like

```
CONFIGURE DEVICE TYPE disk clear;
```

(which we will go into more detail on shortly) is legal because it clears the whole configuration and resets it to the default. On the other hand, a command like

```
CONFIGURE DEVICE TYPE DISK BACKUP TYPE clear;
```

is not valid because you are trying to clear a parameter (**backup type**) of the device type configuration rather than the entire configuration.

When you issue the **configure** command, Oracle displays the previous configuration settings, followed by the new configuration setting. Now, let's look at some of the ways you can use the **configure** command to automate the backup and restore process with RMAN.

Examples of Using the configure Command

This section presents some examples of using the **configure** command to define default values. In this section, we cover a number of topics revolving around the **configure** command, including the following:

- Configuring channel default settings
- Configuring backup set–related settings
- Configuring RMAN logging
- Using the format string
- Configuring default automated backups of the control file and the SPFILE
- Configuring default retention policies
- Configuring default levels of encryption
- Configuring archive log deletion policies

Configuring Channel Default Settings

When you allocate a channel with the **allocate channel** command, you can specify the assigned names to the channels you allocate. For example, the **allocate channel d1 device type disk** command will create a channel called d1. When automated channels are allocated, Oracle assigns default names to these channels. These default names depend on the type of default device used. The following table provides an example of the default name format that will be used:

Device Type	Default Name Format	Example
Disk	ORA_DISK_n	ORA_DISK_1 ORA_DISK_2
Tape	ORA_SBT_TAPE_n	ORA_SBT_TAPE_1 ORA_SBT_TAPE_2

The number of channels that are automatically allocated depends on the default level of parallelism defined (which we will discuss later in this chapter).

The nice thing about configuring things in RMAN is that we can tell RMAN what to do by default when we issue a command. For example, we can configure RMAN to always do a backup to disk or to do a backup to an SBT device. This seems like a pretty basic configuration setup, and it is. In this case, we use the **configure** command to cause the channels that will be allocated during a RMAN backup to be allocated to disk:

```
CONFIGURE DEFAULT DEVICE TYPE TO DISK;
```

Keep in mind that we are setting defaults here. When default device types are configured, Oracle will use that default channel unless you override the default using the **backup** command with the **device type** parameter, or if you use the **allocate channel** command within a **run** block (run blocks are discussed in Chapter 7). Maintenance channels for **delete** commands and auxiliary channels for **duplicate** operations will also be automatically allocated.

Once we have configured a default device type, we can configure defaults for the specific type of backup that should occur when that device is used. For example, when doing backups to disk, we have two principal options on how the backups are created. We can opt to have Oracle back up the database by default using the standard Oracle backup set/backup set piece methodology (see Chapter 3), or we can have it default to using image copies, also called mirrored copies (see Chapter 3). You can also indicate that backup sets should be compressed by default and indicate the degree of parallelism (which represents the number of channels that will be allocated for that backup). Here are examples of configuring for these different options:

```
CONFIGURE DEVICE TYPE DISK BACKUP TYPE TO BACKUPSET;
CONFIGURE DEVICE TYPE DISK BACKUP TYPE TO COMPRESSED BACKUPSET;
CONFIGURE DEVICE TYPE DISK BACKUP TYPE TO COPY;
CONFIGURE DEVICE TYPE DISK PARALLELISM 2;
```

If we wanted to reset these device configurations to the default, we would use the **configure device type** command with the **clear** option, as shown here:

```
CONFIGURE DEVICE TYPE DISK BACKUP TYPE clear;
```

Note that individual parameters of a given **configure** command cannot be changed using the **clear** command. For example, this command will fail:

```
CONFIGURE DEVICE TYPE DISK BACKUP TYPE clear;
```

One word about compression, which was a new feature of RMAN in Oracle Database 10g: Compression provides real compression of your Oracle backup sets, not unlike ZIP compression. This can make your backup sets much smaller. Of course, the compression itself consumes resources and will make the backups take longer to complete or restore.

Now, let's look at an example of configuring the number of channels to be allocated during an automated backup or recovery operation. Also, in this example we have set the default level of parallelism for disk operations to two. Thus, if you start an automated backup, two channels will be allocated to perform the backup in parallel.

```
CONFIGURE CHANNEL 1 DEVICE TYPE DISK FORMAT 'd:\backup\robt\backup_%U';
CONFIGURE CHANNEL 2 DEVICE TYPE DISK FORMAT 'e:\backup\robt\backup_%U';
```

NOTE
Generally, you should set the default level of parallelism to the number of tape drives you will be backing up to. When using disks, some trial and error might be called for. Because disks have multiple heads and may be stripped, it may be that multiple channels will result in better throughput. Test parallelism to your disks and act accordingly on the results.

Several options are available when configuring channels. With the **maxpiecesize** parameter, you can control the size of a backup set piece. You can control the maximum number of files that RMAN can open at one time with the **maxopenfiles** parameter. The **rate** parameter allows you to throttle RMAN and to control the rate at which a backup occurs in bytes, kilobytes, megabytes, or gigabytes per second.

In this example, we put all these options to use. We limit channel 1 to creating each individual backup piece at a maximum size of 100MB, and we limit RMAN to opening a maximum of eight files on this channel. Finally, we have constrained the channel such that it cannot have a throughput of more than 100MB.

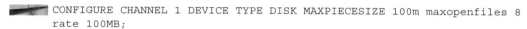

```
CONFIGURE CHANNEL 1 DEVICE TYPE DISK MAXPIECESIZE 100m maxopenfiles 8
rate 100MB;
```

NOTE
Don't get confused about the difference between the **maxpiecesize**
parameter and the **maxsetsize** *parameter:* **maxpiecesize** *limits the size
of the individual backup set pieces and has no impact on the overall
cumulative size of the backup. The* **maxsetsize** *parameter, on the
other hand, can and will limit the overall size of your backup,
so use it carefully!*

If we had wished to limit all channels, we could have issued the command slightly differently:

```
CONFIGURE CHANNEL DEVICE TYPE DISK MAXPIECESIZE 100m;
```

So, why might we want to change the maximum size that a given backup set piece can be? First, we might have some specific file size limitations that we have to deal with. Tapes can only handle so much data, and some disk file systems have limits on how large a given datafile can be.

We might also want to set a tape device as the default device for all channels, along with some specific parameter settings. In this case, our **configure** command might look like this:

```
-- Note that we could have used the = sign after the PARMS clause if
-- we preferred like this:
-- PARMS='ENV=(NB_ORA_CLASS=RMAN_rs100_tape).
-- This is true with many parameters.
CONFIGURE CHANNEL DEVICE TYPE sbt MAXPIECESIZE 100m
PARMS 'ENV=(NB_ORA_CLASS=RMAN_rs100_tape)';
```

When using the **configure** command, you may find that you need to clear a given configuration so that you can use the default. To do this, use the **configure** command with the **clear** option. In this example, we are clearing out the default options set for default channel 1:

```
CONFIGURE CHANNEL 1 DEVICE TYPE DISK CLEAR;
```

Configuring Backup Set–Related Settings

You may wish to configure a default maximum size for an entire backup set, in which case you would use this slightly modified syntax (it is followed by an example of resetting this value back to the default, which is unlimited):

```
CONFIGURE MAXSETSIZE TO 7500K;
CONFIGURE MAXSETSIZE CLEAR;
```

CAUTION
Be careful when using **maxsetsize** *to limit the size of the entire backup
that is being created. While your database might be smaller than
the* **maxsetsize** *defined initially, it could quickly grow beyond the*
maxsetsize*, causing your database backups to fail.*

As you will see in later chapters, you can configure the backup process to create duplexed backups; in other words, multiple copies of the backup can be created at different locations. You can also configure database default settings such that automatic backups will be duplexed using the **configure** command. Here is an example where we have defined that all backups to disk by default will be duplexed, with two copies:

```
configure datafile backup copies for device type disk to 2;
```

You may wish to exclude specific tablespaces during an automated backup, which Oracle allows you to do with the **configure** command. Here is an example of excluding a tablespace by default:

```
configure exclude for tablespace old_data;
```

The **configure** command allows you to enable or disable backup optimization. When enabled, *backup optimization* will cause Oracle to skip backups of files that already have identical backups on the device being backed up to. Here is an example of configuring backup optimization:

```
configure backup optimization on;
```

Note that for optimization to occur, you must have enabled it. In addition, you must issue the **backup database** or **backup archivelog** command with the **like** or **all** option. Alternatively, you can use the **backup backupset all** command (more information on these types of backups is provided in later chapters). Finally, you can disable the setting for backup optimization by using the **force** parameter of the **backup** command.

Configuring RMAN Logging

The output from an RMAN operations is stored in two views: V$RMAN_OUTPUT, which is sourced from the control file of the database, and RC_RMAN_OUTPUT, which is available in the RMAN recovery catalog. The default logging period is seven days.

In Oracle Database 12c, you can indicate how long you wish to maintain the output from a given RMAN session by using the **configure rman output to keep for *n* days** command. In this case, *n* represents in integer that indicates how many days you wish to keep the output. You can disable RMAN logging by using a 0, in which case no logging will occur by default. You can use the **configure rman output clear** command to reset RMAN logging to the configured default.

The records in the RMAN V$ logging view won't disappear immediately when you reset the logging—even beyond the default seven-day retention period. This is because Oracle does not clear out the V$ view until it reaches the end of the space allocated in the control file for those records (the RC view is cleared immediately). Only then are the records deleted. Therefore, you cannot really use the **configure rman output clear** to "scrub" the data from the V$RMAN_OUTPUT view. If you need to do that for some reason, you would need to re-create the control file. That seems like an awful lot of work.

Perhaps a better option to clearing the circular reuse section of the control file is to use the **dbms_backup_restore.resetcfilesection** procedure. For example, the command **exec sys.dbms_backup_restore.resetcfileSection(28)** will remove all job-related entries from the control file. The result is that the V$RMAN_BACKUP_JOB_DETAILS view will be emptied until the next RMAN backup is executed.

Configuring Snapshot Control File Settings

We discussed the snapshot control file in Chapter 2. This file is a point-in-time copy of the database control file that is taken during RMAN backup operations. The snapshot control file ensures that the backup is consistent to a given point in time. Thus, if you add a tablespace or datafile to a database after the backup has started (assuming an online backup, of course), that tablespace or datafile will not be included in the backup. Sometimes it is desirable to have RMAN create the backup control file in a location other than the default location. In this event, you can use the **configure** command to define a new default location for the snapshot control file:

```
configure snapshot controlfile name to 'd:\oracle\backup\scontrolf_mydb';
```

Note that Oracle does not create the snapshot control file in the FRA even if the FRA is configured. Also note in this example that we include the name of the database (or database instance if running RAC) to ensure the snapshot control filenames are unique.

Using the Format String

Note in previous examples that in several places we defined one or more disk locations and filename formats. This is known as the *format string specification*. You will see the format string specification used a great deal in this book, and you will often use it when working with RMAN unless you are using the FRA. The FRA uses Oracle's own file-naming conventions, so using a format string when backing up to the FRA is not recommended or required (and can cause problems with file maintenance). Because the FRA is the default location for backups, there is no need to configure a backup device to point to the FRA. You may need to configure channels for other reasons, but do not configure them such that they have a format string pointing to the FRA.

The format string is platform independent (though directory structures will be platform specific). A format string on Windows will look pretty much the same on Unix or on any other platform. For example, if we were using a Unix system, our format string might look like this:

```
CONFIGURE CHANNEL 1 DEVICE TYPE DISK FORMAT
'/u01/opt/oracle/backup/robt/backup_%U';
CONFIGURE CHANNEL 2 DEVICE TYPE DISK FORMAT
'/u01/opt/oracle/backup/robt/backup_%U';
```

NOTE
Oracle will not manage your backup files if you use the FORMAT parameter, even if you are backing up to the FRA, because the backup is not managed by Oracle. If the FORMAT parameter is used, the retention policy will not apply to those backups. If FORMAT is not used, OMF names are used, and the files are created in the FRA. Do not use the FORMAT option when backing up to the FRA.

The format string is used a lot in the **configure** command. You will also see it in other RMAN commands such as the **backup**, **restore**, and **allocate channel** commands. RMAN offers several *syntax elements* associated with the format string specification. These elements are placeholders that will cause RMAN to replace the format string with the associated defined values. For example, the **%U** syntax element in the previous example tells RMAN to substitute a system-generated unique identifier for the filename. **%U** then keeps each backup filename unique. Table 5-4 lists the valid syntax elements and gives a quick description of their use.

Element	Description
%a	Indicates that the activation ID of the database should be substituted.
%b	Specifies the filename without any directory paths. This can only be used with the **set newname** command or for creating a backup using image copies.
%c	Specifies that the copy number of the backup piece within a set of duplexed backup pieces, with a maximum value of 256, should be substituted. This number will be 1 for nonduplexed backup sets and 0 for proxy copies.
%d	Indicates that the name of the database should be substituted.
%D	Indicates that the current day of the month from the Gregorian calendar in the format DD should be substituted.
%e	Indicates that the archived log sequence number should be substituted.
%f	Indicates that the absolute file number should be substituted.
%F	Provides a unique and repeatable name that combines the database ID (DBID), day, month, year, and sequence.
%h	Indicates that the archived redo log thread number should be substituted.
%I	Indicates that the DBID should be substituted.
%M	Indicates that the month in the Gregorian calendar in the format MM should be substituted.
%N	Indicates that the tablespace name should be substituted.
%n	Indicates that the name of the database, padded on the right with x characters to a total length of eight characters, should be substituted. For example, if ROBDB is the database name, then the padded name is ROBDBxxx.
%p	Indicates that the piece number within the backup set should be substituted. This value starts at 1 for each backup set and is incremented by 1 as each backup piece is created.
%s	Indicates that the backup set number should be substituted. This number is a counter in the control file that is incremented for each backup set. The counter value starts at 1. This number will be unique for the lifetime of the control file (thus, it is reset at RESETLOGS or when the control file is restored or re-created).
%t	Indicates that the backup set timestamp, which is a 4-byte value derived as the number of seconds elapsed since a fixed reference time, should be substituted. **%s** and **%t** combined can be used to form a unique name for the backup set.
%T	Indicates that the year, month, and day from the Gregorian calendar in the format YYYYMMDD should be substituted.
%u	Indicates that an eight-character name, consisting of compressed representations of the backup set or image copy number and the time the backup set or image copy was created, should be substituted.

TABLE 5-4. *Format String Specification Descriptions*

Element	Description

%U	This is the default file-naming pattern and provides a system-generated unique filename for RMAN-related files. The meaning of this substitution string differs when dealing with image copies or backup pieces.
	When using backup set pieces, **%U** specifies a convenient shorthand for **%u_%p_%c** that guarantees uniqueness in generated backup filenames. The meaning differs when using image copies, and depending on the type of image copy.
	Meaning when used with an image copy of datafiles:
	`data-D-%d_id-%I_TS-%N_FNO-%f_%u`
	Meaning when used with an image copy of an archived redo log:
	`arch-D_%d-id-%I_S-%e_T-%h_A-%a_%u`
	Meaning when used with an image copy of a control file:
	`cf-D_%d-id-%I_%u`

%Y	Indicates that the year in the format YYYY should be substituted.
%%	Indicates that you wish to actually use the % character (for example, **%%Y**).

TABLE 5-4. *Format String Specification Descriptions (Continued)*

Configuring Default Automated Backups of the Control File and the SPFILE

RMAN in Oracle Database 10*g* and later offers the ability to back up the control file and the database parameter file, and you can configure these backups to take place by default. You should always configure control file autobackups if you are not using a recovery catalog (and really even if you are using one). In fact, this configuration is considered so important that in Oracle Database 12*c* control file backups are enabled by default when backing up a CDB database. Control file backups are not enabled when backing up a non-CDB database.

Again, you can use the **configure** command to configure this automated backup process to happen automatically during a backup. Here is an example of configuring automated backups of these important database files and an example of turning off the default configuration:

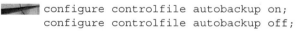
```
configure controlfile autobackup on;
configure controlfile autobackup off;
```

In Oracle Database 12*c*, when autobackup of the control and parameter files is configured, the following rules apply:

- The control file and SPFILE will be automatically backed up with each RMAN **backup** or **copy** command issued.

- If a run block is used, then the control files and SPFILE will be backed up at the end of the run block unless the last command in the run block is a **backup** command or a **copy** command.

- If the database is in ARCHIVELOG mode, a control file autobackup will occur after any structural change occurs. This backup will always be to disk. You can use the command

configure controlfile autobackup for device type disk to indicate a nondefault disk location for the control file autobackup. Here is an example of the use of this specific command:

```
RMAN> configure controlfile autobackup format for device type
disk to 'd:\backup\contf\robt_%F'
```

Control file autobackups deserve a bit more mention. Control file autobackups will back up the database control file and the server parameter file each time. During a backup operation, the first channel that was allocated will be the one that writes the control file autobackup during a backup. Also, the Oracle RDBMS will automatically back up the control file during database structure changes that impact the control file. These changes might include adding a new tablespace, altering the state of a tablespace or datafile (for example, bringing it online), adding a new online redo log, renaming a file, adding a new redo thread, and so forth.

Control file autobackups (those related to the automatic backup of the control file after database changes are made—not control file autobackups as a part of an RMAN operation) can only be to disk, because tape is not supported. These backups can get a bit large (since the control file contains a history of many of the past backups), so make sure you allocate enough disk space to the backup directory. In spite of the additional space that will be required, these backups can be incredibly handy to have for recovery. Finally, be aware that if the backup fails for any reason, the database operation itself will not fail.

Note that starting in Oracle Database 11gR2 that the write of the automatic control file backups does not occur immediately. Since it's likely that more than one structural change could happen within a given period of time (for example, the creation of three tablespaces within just a few moments to accommodate new partitions), Oracle does not write a backup control file for each atomic operation. Rather, it will write the control file autobackup after a few minutes, writing just one control file autobackup rather than several, which can consume a large amount of disk space.

Also, in previous versions of the database, messages related to control file autobackups would be stored in the alert log of the database. In Oracle Database 12c, control file autobackup messages are now stored in the trace file of one of the MMON background slave processes (Mmmm processes).

NOTE
You need to know the DBID of the database. You should, as a part of your initial setup and configuration of RMAN, note the DBIDs of the databases you will be backing up and save that list somewhere safe. The DBID of the database is available from the V$DATABASE view in the DBID column. The DBID of the database is also displayed when you start RMAN and connect to a target database. It's possible to figure out the DBID of a database by looking at the backup set piece filename, though. We will discuss that in more detail in Chapter 8.

Configuring Default Retention Policies

So, how long do you want to keep your database backups? RMAN enables you to configure a backup retention policy by using the **configure retention policy** command. If you configure a retention policy and are using the FRA, then RMAN and Oracle will automatically remove backups when they become obsolete. If you are not using the FRA, configuring a retention policy will not cause backups to be deleted automatically, but will cause expired backup sets to appear when the **report obsolete** command is executed. See Chapter 12 for more on **report obsolete**.

There are really three kinds of retention policies in Oracle: recovery window based, redundancy based, and none. Let's look at each of these in more detail next.

Recovery Window–Based Retention Policies   The recovery window–based retention policy is designed to ensure that your database can be recovered to a specific point in time. For example, if you wanted to make sure you can recover your database back to any point in time up to three days ago (assuming you were running in ARCHIVELOG mode, of course), you would set a recovery window–based retention policy of three days. The command to configure such a retention policy would be as follows:

```
RMAN> configure retention policy to recovery window of 3 days;
old RMAN configuration parameters:
CONFIGURE RETENTION POLICY TO RECOVERY WINDOW OF 7 DAYS;
new RMAN configuration parameters:
CONFIGURE RETENTION POLICY TO RECOVERY WINDOW OF 3 DAYS;
new RMAN configuration parameters are successfully stored
```

Note that the recovery window–based retention criteria can result in backups actually being maintained longer than the stated recovery window. For example, if your recovery window is three days, but your last full backup was five days ago, then that backup will remain valid until it is no longer needed to restore your database. Even if you back up your database today, five days later, the backup that is five days ago is still needed because it is the only source of recovery back to day 3. Figure 5-2 provides a graphical demonstration of this.

Now that we have configured our retention policy, let's see which previous backups are reported to be obsolete:

```
RMAN> report obsolete;
RMAN retention policy will be applied to the command
RMAN retention policy is set to recovery window of 3 days
Report of obsolete backups and copies
Type                 Key    Completion Time    Filename/Handle
-------------------- ------ ------------------ --------------------
Archive Log          12     08-SEP-14
/oracle/app/oracle/flash_recovery_area/ROB1/archivelog/2014_09_08/
o1_mf_1_9_5bd8qv45_.arc
Backup Set           24     08-SEP-14
  Backup Piece       34     08-SEP-14
/oracle/app/oracle/flash_recovery_area/ROB1/backupset/2014_09_08/
o1_mf_annnn_TAG20140908T202600_5bg4kr90_.bkp
Backup Set           25     08-SEP-14
  Backup Piece       35     08-SEP-14
/oracle/app/oracle/flash_recovery_area/ROB1/backupset/2014_09_08/
o1_mf_nnnd0_TAG20140908T202601_5bg4ktk1_.bkp
```

In this example, we have two backup sets and two related backup pieces that are obsolete based on our backup retention policy. Additionally, we have an archived redo log that is ready to be removed as well. If these backups are in a defined FRA (which these are), Oracle will remove them as required. If you are not using an FRA, or if these backups were created before you converted to using an FRA, you will need to use the **delete obsolete** command to remove them.

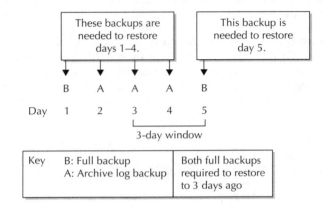

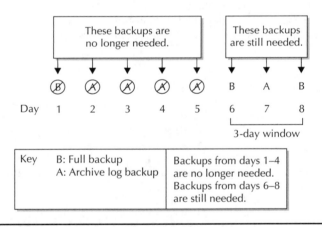

FIGURE 5-2. *Recovery window maintaining older backups*

More information on the **delete obsolete** command can be found in Chapter 12, and an example is provided here, too:

```
RMAN> delete obsolete;
RMAN retention policy will be applied to the command
RMAN retention policy is set to recovery window of 3 days
using channel ORA_DISK_1
using channel ORA_DISK_2
Deleting the following obsolete backups and copies:
```

```
Type                      Key    Completion Time    Filename/Handle
------------------------- ------ ------------------ --------------------
Archive Log               12     08-SEP-14
/oracle/app/oracle/flash_recovery_area/ROB1/archivelog/2014_09_08/
o1_mf_1_9_5bd8qv45_.arc
Backup Set                24     08-SEP-14
  Backup Piece            34     08-SEP-14
/oracle/app/oracle/flash_recovery_area/ROB1/backupset/2014_09_08/
o1_mf_annnn_TAG20140908T202600_5bg4kr90_.bkp
Backup Set                25     08-SEP-14
  Backup Piece            35     08-SEP-14
/oracle/app/oracle/flash_recovery_area/ROB1/backupset/2014_09_08/
o1_mf_nnnd0_TAG20140908T202601_5bg4ktk1_.bkp
Do you really want to delete the above objects (enter YES or NO)? yes
```

Note in the preceding example that the system will ask you to confirm that you really want to remove the objects that are slated to be removed. If any of the listed objects are not available to be removed, you will need to run the **crosscheck** command (discussed in Chapter 11). Otherwise, each item listed as deleted in the **delete obsolete** output will be deleted by Oracle.

Redundancy-Based Retention Policies   This kind of retention policy is based on the total number of backups maintained by RMAN and is more typically used if you are backing up your database infrequently. This is the default retention policy, with a default value of 1. If you were to set this value to 3, Oracle would consider the last three backups as current, and any other backups would be considered obsolete. Here is an example of configuring a redundancy retention policy of 3:

```
RMAN> configure retention policy to redundancy 3;
old RMAN configuration parameters:
CONFIGURE RETENTION POLICY TO REDUNDANCY 3;
new RMAN configuration parameters:
CONFIGURE RETENTION POLICY TO REDUNDANCY 3;
new RMAN configuration parameters are successfully stored
```

Note in the output that RMAN displays both the old and new settings for the retention policy.

No Retention Policy   If you want to disable the retention policy, you use the command **configure retention policy to none**, and no retention policy will be applicable. Use the **configure retention policy clear** command to reset the retention policy to the default value, which is a redundancy of 1.

NOTE
If you are using a tape management system, it may have its own retention policy. If the tape management system's retention policy conflicts with the backup retention policy you have defined in RMAN, the tape management system's retention policy will take precedence, and your ability to recover a backup will be in jeopardy.

Configuring Default Levels of Encryption
RMAN can create encrypted backups starting with Oracle Database 10*g* Release 2. During the backup, the backup sets are encrypted as they are created. When the backups are restored, Oracle will decrypt the backup sets. In this section, we discuss the different modes of encryption

that are available when doing RMAN backups. Then we will look at how to configure RMAN so that it can use encryption.

Modes of Encryption   Oracle offers three different encryption modes:

- **Transparent mode**   Transparent mode encryption (TDE) requires no DBA interaction. To use this mode, you must have configured the Oracle Encryption Wallet.

- **Password mode**   Password mode encryption requires that a password be supplied when creating backups to be encrypted or when restoring backups that were encrypted when they were created. The password is supplied by using the command **set encryption on identified by password only** in your RMAN backup scripts. This is the encryption mode we will use in this text.

- **Dual mode**   Dual mode backups can be restored either by password or by the presence of the Oracle Encryption Wallet. This makes offsite restores of backups easier because the install of the Oracle Encryption Wallet is not required. To create a dual mode encrypted backup, you use the **set encryption on identified by password** command (note that the **only** keyword is missing).

Oracle Database 12c supports encryption for either an entire nonmultitenant database or individual PDBs. Additionally, you can choose to encrypt specific tablespaces at the database, CDB, or PDB level. Note that as of Oracle 12.1.0.2, there is no way to encrypt a specific PDB except at the tablespace level of that PDB. If you are using a later version of RMAN and you are using CDB/PDBs, you might want to check whether anything with respect to support for encryption has been added.

Use the **configure** command to configure various persistent settings related to RMAN encryption of backups. You can use the RMAN **configure** command to indicate the following:

- Whether all database files should be encrypted
- Whether specific tablespaces should be encrypted
- Which of the available encryption algorithms should be used to encrypt your backups

If you are using Oracle Encryption Wallet–based security, you only need to set the persistent RMAN settings required by the **configure** command. If you wish to use password mode encryption or dual mode encryption, you need to configure the persistent security defaults with the configure **command**, and then use the **set** command when starting your backups to set the correct password for the backup. RMAN does not persistently set the backup password, so it must be entered for each RMAN backup or recovery session. The **set** command, and how to use it during backups, is covered in much more detail in Chapter 9. In the following command, we configure and enable backup encryption for the entire database. Notice that if we have not configured the Oracle Encryption Wallet, any subsequent backups will fail unless we use the **set** command to establish an encryption password for the session (we are jumping the gun just a bit, but we provide an example of using the **set** command to set the backup password in the appropriate context).

```
-- Configures default encryption.
-- Uses transparent mode encryption by default.
RMAN> CONFIGURE ENCRYPTION FOR DATABASE ON;
-- For this session, we want password mode encryption,
```

```
-- so we have to set the
-- password. This is good only for this session, until we exit RMAN or
-- issue another connect command.
RMAN> SET ENCRYPTION ON IDENTIFIED BY robert ONLY;
-- Way ahead of ourselves, but this backs up the database!
RMAN> BACKUP DATABASE PLUS ARCHIVELOG;
```

Archived redo log backups are backed up using encryption if the following are true:

- The **set encryption on** command is in effect at the time that the backup of the archived redo logs is occurring.
- Encryption has been configured for the entire database, or for at least one tablespace of the database.

The **configure** command also provides the ability to determine the encryption algorithm you wish to use. The available algorithms can be seen in the V$RMAN_ENCRYPTION_ALGORITHMS view, as shown in this example:

```
SQL> select algorithm_name from V$RMAN_ENCRYPTION_ALGORITHMS;
ALGORITHM_NAME
------------------------------------------------------------
AES128
AES192
AES256
```

Knowing the algorithms available, we can now configure the default encryption algorithm we want to use, as shown here:

```
RMAN> Configure encryption algorithm 'AES128';
using target database control file instead of recovery catalog
new RMAN configuration parameters:
CONFIGURE ENCRYPTION ALGORITHM 'AES128';
new RMAN configuration parameters are successfully stored
```

You can also configure encryption for the database as a whole (including any PDBs if you are using Oracle Multitenant) or specific tablespaces within the backup by using the **configure** command with the **encrypt for tablespace** option. You can encrypt tablespaces in a non-CDB or a tablespace in the root container in a CDB using this method. Here is an example of configuring encryption for the entire database and then turning encryption off:

```
RMAN> Configure encryption for database on;
CONFIGURE ENCRYPTION FOR DATABASE ON;
new RMAN configuration parameters are successfully stored
-- to disable encryption
CONFIGURE ENCRYPTION FOR DATABASE OFF
```

If you wish to configure a specific tablespace, use the following:

```
RMAN> Configure encryption for tablespace users on;
```

If you are using Oracle Multitenant, you can configure encryption for a tablespace in a PDB. In this example, we encrypt the tablespace users in the PDB **plug_test**:

```
RMAN> Configure encryption for tablespace plug_test:users on;
```

Simply repeat these commands using the **off** keyword instead of **on** to turn off encryption. You can also use the **clear** keyword to reset the configuration to its default.

NOTE
RMAN does not back up any of the keystores (such as the auto-open wallet or the encryption keystores). You will need to back these up with your OS-based backup, which should be used to back up the OS, all ORACLE_HOME directories, and any other critical directories that contain configuration files.

If you are using TDE, you will have to ensure that the wallet is open before executing your backups; otherwise, the backup will fail. Oracle Database 12*c* provides for auto-login wallets, which eliminate the requirement of opening the wallet when opening the database or backing it up. If you are using an auto-login wallet, you do not need to worry about opening the wallet before doing a backup or a restore. The wallet should already be opened, and the backup or recovery should be normal.

We are often asked how RMAN treats encrypted data during a backup. The following table provides you with information on the different possibilities:

Application Data	Backup with RMAN Compression Enabled	Backup with RMAN Encryption Enabled	Backup with RMAN Compression and Encryption Enabled
Not encrypted.	Data compressed.	Data encrypted.	Data compressed first, then encrypted.
Encrypted with TDE column encryption.	Data compressed; encrypted columns are treated as if they were not encrypted.	Data encrypted; double encryption of encrypted columns.	Data compressed first, then encrypted; encrypted columns are treated as if they were not encrypted; double encryption of encrypted columns.
Encrypted with TDE tablespace encryption.	Encrypted tablespaces are decrypted, compressed, and re-encrypted.	Encrypted tablespaces are passed through to the backup unchanged.	Encrypted tablespaces are decrypted, compressed, and re-encrypted.

Configuring Archive Log Deletion Policies

You can configure RMAN to manage your archived redo log deletion policy for you. By default, Oracle applies the configured backup retention policy to the archived redo logs. In Oracle Database, you can also configure a separate deletion policy for archived redo logs. This policy will get applied to archived redo logs in both the FRA and in those stored outside the FRA. Only those in the FRA will be removed by Oracle, however. If logs are in the FRA, Oracle will try to keep them as long as possible, only removing them when additional space is required. If you are using a non-FRA location, you will need to use the **delete obsolete** or **delete archivelog** command to remove archived redo logs marked as obsolete. In this example, we use the **configure** command to configure an archive log deletion policy. In this case, all archived redo logs that are backed up three times will be eligible for removal:

```
RMAN> Configure archivelog deletion policy to backed up 3 times
to device type disk;
new RMAN configuration parameters:
CONFIGURE ARCHIVELOG DELETION POLICY TO BACKED UP 3 TIMES TO DISK;
new RMAN configuration parameters are successfully stored
```

In versions of Oracle before Oracle Database 11*g*, the archived redo log deletion policy applied only to archived redo logs being applied on a standby database. In these versions, you could configure RMAN to mark archived redo logs as eligible for removal after they have been applied to a mandatory standby database by using the **configure archivelog deletion policy to applied on standby** command. In this case, once the archived redo log has been successfully applied to a mandatory standby database location, it is eligible for removal from the FRA by Oracle. This functionality remains in Oracle Database 11*g* and later.

One thing to mention about archived redo logs and container databases: RMAN-archived redo log operations on a CDB database need to be done in the root container. If you try to back up archived redo logs from within a PDB, for example, that backup job will fail.

If You Are Using Shared Servers

If you are using Oracle's Shared Servers option (known as Multi-Threaded Server, or MTS, in previous Oracle versions), you have to configure a dedicated server for use with RMAN because RMAN cannot use a Shared Servers session to connect to the database. If you are using a Shared Servers architecture, refer to Chapter 5 of the *Oracle Database Backup and Recovery Advanced Users Guide (11g Release 2)* for more information on how to configure RMAN for use with the Oracle Database Shared Servers option.

Essentially, you must configure a dedicated connection in Oracle Net for your server by using the **SERVER=dedicated** syntax, as shown in this example (note that Oracle Net configurations vary greatly, so what may be required of you might differ):

```
Rob1_ded =
  (DESCRIPTION=
    (ADDRESS=(PROTOCOL=tcp)(HOST=robpc)(port1521))
    (CONNECT_DATA=(SERVICE_NAME=rob1_ded)(SERVER=dedicated)))
```

Summary of RMAN Configuration Tasks

We have thrown a great deal of information at you in this chapter. With the introduction of Oracle Multitenant, the RMAN picture can get even more murky at times.

To try to help you filter through all we have discussed in this chapter, we thought it would be good to summarize the main tasks you will need to perform to get set up to do database backups with RMAN. We also provide a few suggestions along the way. Each of the steps listed here has detailed instructions included earlier in this chapter:

1. Determine whether you wish to run the database in ARCHIVELOG mode or NOARCHIVELOG mode. Configure the database accordingly. In most cases, we would recommend ARCHIVELOG mode because it provides a large number of recovery options.

2. Create a recovery catalog (see Chapter 6).

3. Configure and use the FRA.

4. Set up a separate database user account (not sys) for use with RMAN. Assign this account SYSBACKUP privileges if you are running Oracle Database 12c; otherwise, you will need to provide the account with SYSDBA privileges.

5. In the database parameter file, set the CONTROL_FILE_RECORD_KEEP_TIME parameter to a number of days equivalent to or greater than the number of days you wish to ensure that RMAN-related backup metadata is stored in the database control file.

6. Configure the retention criteria for your FRA.

7. If you are backing up to tape, make sure you coordinate your backup-retention criteria with your tape administrators.

8. If you are using shared servers, set up a dedicated server address for RMAN to connect to.

9. Using RMAN, connect to the target database to ensure that the database is set up correctly (error messages will appear if your RMAN account is not correctly set up).

10. Use the **configure** command to establish your default RMAN values. In particular, consider configuring the following:

    ■ Configure the default degree of parallelism for tape or disk backups. Set it to a default value equivalent to the number of disks or tape drives you will be backing up to. If you are backing up to a SAN with many disk drives, consider using parallel channels to back up to those disk devices.

    ■ If you are using Oracle Real Application Clusters, make sure you configure channels in a way that you can take advantage of the CPUs on the database nodes of the clusters. See Chapter 18 for more detailed information on using RMAN with RAC.

    ■ Configure automatic channels and device types. The number of channels you configure should equal the degree of parallelism you have configured. Configure as many channels as you have individual devices, and configure the same number of channels as you have.

    ■ Configure automated control file/database parameter file autobackups if they are not already configured by default (for the CDB of a multitenant database).

    ■ If you own ASO (Advanced Security Option, which is the license required to use encryption), configure an auto-open wallet to make RMAN backups on encrypted tablespaces easier to perform.

11. Configure the retention policy as required. Make sure this retention policy is in sync with any other retention policies, such as those associated with tape management systems. Also, if required, consider retention criteria for your archived redo logs.

12. Configure RMAN for control file and SPFILE automatic backups.

13. Before you use it for production database backups, test your RMAN configuration by doing a backup and recovery, as demonstrated in later chapters.

Other Backup and Recovery Setup and Configuration Considerations

Finally, let's consider the other backup and recovery implications of your database. RMAN will not back up certain things that you need to consider as a part of your overall backup and recovery strategy planning. These include such things as the base Oracle RDBMS software and the parameter files (tnsnames.ora, names.ora, sqlnet.ora, and so on). You need to make plans to back up and recover these files as a part of your overall backup and recovery planning.

You also need to consider your disaster planning with regard to RMAN and non-RMAN backups. How will you protect these backups from flood, fire, and earthquake? In advance is a very good time to consider these questions, not when the fire is burning two flights below!

Finally, Chapter 15 provides a good overall architectural discussion on implementing RMAN backup and recovery in the enterprise. This chapter provided guidance, best practices, and recommendations that you will want to consider when architecting your enterprise backup solution. Remember that the best solutions are the ones that scale easily. In Chapter 15 we try to help you pull your backup and recovery architecture together into a single, scalable, backup and recovery solution that requires minimal care and feeding.

Summary

Whew! We have covered a great deal of ground in this chapter, and, indeed, there are several things you need to do before you start using RMAN. First, we described how to set up the database in ARCHIVELOG mode, if that is what you wish to do. Next, we looked at the RMAN command line and at how to configure your database for use with RMAN, including setting up the password file and configuring a user account for use with RMAN. We also looked at configuring RMAN default settings. We strongly suggest you take advantage of this feature in RMAN, because it can make your life much easier. Finally, we provided you with a summary of RMAN configuration tasks and talked about other backup and recovery considerations.

CHAPTER
6

The RMAN
Recovery Catalog

O racle maintains all the metadata related to RMAN operations in the *RMAN repository*. The RMAN repository is *always* stored in the control file of the target databases. However, in most cases we will also want to store this metadata in a database. The name of the database where we store RMAN-related metadata is called the RMAN *recovery catalog*.

RMAN does not require the recovery catalog for most operations. There are a few operations that the recovery catalog makes easier, and there are very few things that require a recovery catalog (such as cases where you want to store backups for more than a year). Because the recovery catalog serves as a central repository for all RMAN metadata, it is an enterprise-based solution, as opposed to you having to access each individual control file for each database in your environment.

In this section, first we look at what the recovery catalog is and when you need to use it. Then, we look at how you create a recovery catalog both in a nonmultitenant environment and an Oracle Multitenant environment. We discuss various administrative activities related to the recovery catalog such as registering databases, upgrading catalogs, and merging catalogs. We also look at the RMAN virtual recovery catalog, stored scripts, and other recovery catalog–related features. So, let's get going!

What Is the Recovery Catalog?

The *recovery catalog* is an optional component of RMAN that stores historical backup information from RMAN backups. Unlike the database control file's RMAN information, the recovery catalog data is not purged on a regular basis. Therefore, the RMAN metadata in the recovery catalog tends to be more comprehensive and to date further back than the historical information in the control file. Using a recovery catalog does have a few additional benefits over just using the database control file:

- You must use a recovery catalog if you want to use stored RMAN scripts.
- You want to use the **keep forever** option when performing an RMAN backup.
- You must use a recovery catalog if you are using one or more standby databases.
- You must use a recovery catalog if you are using a split-mirror backup model.
- A recovery catalog offers a single, enterprise-wide repository of RMAN information. This provides an easier and more flexible central repository of enterprise backup information.
- A recovery catalog allows more flexibility when you are doing reporting because you can report on the target database at a time other than the current time.
- With a recovery catalog, certain default database RMAN channel configuration information will still be maintained without you needing to manually recover it in the event of a control file failure.

If you are an old hand at RMAN, you may have noticed some bulleted items missing here. First, since version 10g, Oracle Database has easily supported recovery through **resetlogs** without a recovery catalog. Also, if you are using control file autobackups (which we strongly suggest), the need for a recovery catalog for control file recoveries is pretty much removed.

NOTE
If you are not going to use a recovery catalog, keep a record of your database DBIDs. Although this is not required and you can work around it, having the DBIDs for your databases will make recovery operations much easier.

Should you use a recovery catalog? What are the best practices revolving around a recovery catalog? Let me answer the first question with a resounding *yes*. Unless you are only managing one or two databases, never have to do any database cloning, and are a master of the RMAN command line, it would be considered a best practice to use a recovery catalog. After you read this chapter, it should be pretty obvious why that is, but in short it provides an easy way to maintain all of your RMAN backup metadata. It adds functionality to RMAN that is not normally available. A recovery catalog also eases some restore operations (like control files) and other operations. Although RMAN does not depend on a recovery catalog, the benefits of having one make it a best practice.

Of course, adding a recovery catalog means adding another moving part to the whole infrastructure. Therefore, it does add a certain amount of risk of failure. If you try to connect to a recovery catalog and the network is down, or if the recovery catalog is not listed in whichever Oracle Net naming resolution you use (such as tnsnames.ora), then the attempt to connect to the recovery catalog will fail, and RMAN will generate an error like this one:

```
[oracle@bigdatalite admin]$ rman target=/ catalog=robert/robert@rcatpdb
Recovery Manager: Release 12.1.0.2.0 - Production on Thu Oct 9 13:22:29 2014
Copyright (c) 1982, 2014, Oracle and/or its affiliates.  All rights reserved.
connected to target database: CONTDB (DBID=1247424844)
RMAN-00571: ===========================================================
RMAN-00569: =============== ERROR MESSAGE STACK FOLLOWS ===============
RMAN-00571: ===========================================================
RMAN-00554: initialization of internal recovery manager package failed
RMAN-04004: error from recovery catalog database: ORA-12154: TNS:could not
resolve the connect identifier specified
```

If you create the recovery catalog user (as we will demonstrate later in this chapter) and do not proceed to create the recovery catalog schema or register the database with the recovery catalog, then an interesting thing happens. In this case, RMAN will connect to the recovery catalog just fine, but when you try to start the backup, the backup will fail, indicating that the recovery catalog schema does not exist, as shown in this example:

```
[oracle@bigdatalite admin]$ rman target=/ catalog=robert/robert@rcatpdb
Recovery Manager: Release 12.1.0.2.0 -
Production on Thu Oct 9 13:25:16 2014
Copyright (c) 1982, 2014, Oracle and/or its affiliates.
All rights reserved.
connected to target database: CONTDB (DBID=1247424844)
connected to recovery catalog database
RMAN> backup as compressed backupset database;
Starting backup at 09-OCT-14
RMAN-00571: =================================================
RMAN-00569: ======= ERROR MESSAGE STACK FOLLOWS ==========
RMAN-00571: =================================================
RMAN-03002: failure of backup command at 10/09/2014 13:29:14
RMAN-03014: implicit resync of recovery catalog failed
RMAN-06428: recovery catalog is not installed
```

So in this case, the login is successful and the failure does not occur until you attempt an RMAN operation. All of this really boils down to another best practice, and that is monitoring your backups and making sure they are successful. In light of that best practice, we recommend that you use Oracle Enterprise Manager Cloud Control to schedule and monitor all of your backup jobs.

Additionally, a recovery catalog is an essential part of a Data Guard backup environment and split-mirror backups. In these configurations, when you back up the database from the backup host, the recovery catalog is considered the most current information, so it is the brains behind the strategy and becomes a single point of failure if not maintained properly. The bottom line is that you need to decide for yourself whether your environment calls for a recovery catalog.

When connecting to RMAN, you must use the **catalog** command-line parameter to indicate that you want RMAN to connect to a recovery catalog. By default, RMAN uses the **nocatalog** option, which indicates that a recovery catalog will not be used. After using the **catalog** parameter, indicate the user ID and password of the recovery catalog schema that contains the recovery catalog objects. Here is an example of connecting to the recovery catalog by using the RMAN command line:

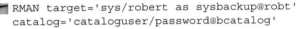

```
RMAN target='sys/robert as sysbackup@robt'
catalog='cataloguser/password@bcatalog'
```

This method works when connecting to a recovery catalog in a regular Oracle database or if the recovery catalog is in a PDB of a multitenant database. Obviously, we need a recovery catalog user to which we can connect, so let's address that next.

Creating the Recovery Catalog Owning Schema in a Nonmultitenant Database

As you might expect, some setup is required before we can actually connect to the recovery catalog. First, we need to create the recovery catalog user and grant it the appropriate privileges. Then, we need to connect to it and create the recovery catalog schema objects. Let's look at each of these steps next.

Configuring the Database for the Recovery Catalog

The recovery catalog database should, if possible, exist on its own database. However, in our experience, many sites use an active database as the recovery catalog database, which is fine as long as you take precautions when backing up that database.

Oracle makes the following suggestions with regard to space allocations for a recovery catalog database that would maintain recovery catalog records for one year:

Tablespace Name	Size Requirement
SYSTEM	90MB
TEMP	5MB
UNDO	5MB
RECOVERY CATALOG SCHEMA	15MB per registered database
ONLINE REDO LOGS	1MB per online redo log file

Creating the Recovery Catalog User

Generally, the recovery catalog should reside in its own database, because the recovery catalog is pretty useless if it is in the same database you are trying to recover.

When you connect to a recovery catalog from RMAN, you will not use the SYSDBA or SYSBACKUP privilege during that connection. Therefore, the recovery catalog schema does not need such privileges. Nor does it need the sweeping privileges available from the DBA group. The only privilege that is really needed is the RECOVERY_CATALOG_OWNER privilege.

The following RMAN Workshop provides a set of detailed instructions on creating the recovery catalog user account.

RMAN Workshop: *Create the Recovery Catalog User Account*

Workshop Notes

For this workshop, you need an installation of the Oracle software. You also need to identify a database in which to create the recovery catalog schema. You need administrative privileges in this database to create the recovery catalog user account. Finally, determine the name and password you will assign to the recovery catalog user account. You will need a tablespace for the recovery catalog schema objects. We suggest that you size the tablespace at about 30MB to start. In this lab we use a tablespace called catalog.

Also, we use an account called dbadmin to create the recovery catalog owning account. Here is what we did to create the dbadmin account:

```
# set the environment to the correct database
[oracle@bigdatalite tmp]$ . oraenv
ORACLE_SID = [rcdb] ? rcdb
sqlplus sys/password as sysdba
create user dbadmin identified by password
default tablespace users;
grant create session to dbadmin;
grant create user to dbadmin;
grant recovery_catalog_owner to dbadmin with admin option;
```

And here is how we created the catalog tablespace:

```
create tablespace catalog
datafile '/u01/app/oracle/oradata/orcl/catalog_01.dbf' size 30m;
```

Step 1.   Create the recovery catalog user. In this step we log into the database using the dbadmin account. This account has the privileges we need to create the recovery catalog owner. We will create the recovery catalog owner, making sure to assign it to the tablespace CATALOG that we created earlier.

You need to log into the database with a user that has the ability to create other users and has the ability to grant the role RECOVERY_CATALOG_OWNER to the schema you will create. When creating the recovery catalog user, make sure you do not use the SYSTEM tablespace as the default tablespace for that user. Hopefully, you have already identified a default tablespace for your database. If not, now would be a good time to do so.

Assign the recovery catalog tablespace that you have created (as suggested in "Workshop Notes") to this schema as its default tablespace. Also, assign the recovery catalog user to an *unlimited quota* on the recovery catalog tablespace. Here is an example of this operation creating a catalog-owning user called rcat_user. We logged into an account called admin after setting our Oracle environment properly. We assume that the admin account has **create session** and **create user** privileges. Additionally, it needs to have been granted the role RECOVERY_CATALOG_OWNER with admin privileges. Note that because the admin account has been granted these specific privileges, we don't need to use SYSDBA to connect to the database:

```
# set the environment to the correct database
[oracle@bigdatalite tmp]$ . oraenv
ORACLE_SID = [rcdb] ? rcdb
sqlplus dbadmin/password
CREATE USER rcat_user IDENTIFIED BY rcat_password
DEFAULT TABLESPACE catalog;
```

Step 2. Grant the **recovery_catalog_owner** role to the recovery catalog user, as shown in this example, where we grant **recovery_catalog_owner** to the RCAT_USER user:

```
GRANT recovery_catalog_owner TO rcat_user;
```

NOTE
The recovery catalog user account is somewhat of a privileged database account. Therefore, secure it as you would sys or system.

Creating the Recovery Catalog–Owning Schema in a Multitenant Database

With Oracle Database 12c and a multitenant database, you will need to create the catalog-owning schema differently than you did with a nonmultitenant database. The differences are not that great, but you should make sure you are comfortable with the basics of how Oracle Multitenant works. Chapter 4 provides a good primer on Oracle Multitenant databases, so if you are not comfortable with the concepts associated with Oracle Multitenant, you might want to review Chapter 4 before you proceed through this next section.

Creating the Recovery Catalog PDB

Before we can create the RMAN recovery catalog user, we need to create the PDB that will own the recovery catalog. In a multitenant database we create a PDB specifically for the recovery catalog. Just as having a database in a nonmultitenant environment dedicated to the recovery catalog is important and considered a best practice, so too is having a PDB dedicated to the recovery catalog.

In this example we are creating a recovery catalog PDB. The CDB is called contdb, and we will create a PDB within that CDB called rcatpdb. Note that we are not using SYS again or connecting as SYSDBA. This is in keeping with best practices. In this case we have created an administrative account called superman, and it has the privileges needed to create a PDB:

```
# set the environment to the correct database
[oracle@bigdatalite tmp]$ . oraenv
ORACLE_SID = [contdb] ? contdb
```

```
The Oracle base remains unchanged with value /u01/app/oracle
[oracle@bigdatalite tmp]$ sqlplus superman/lanexyz
create pluggable database rcatpdb
admin user robertadm identified by mypassword
-- roles = (dba)
default tablespace rcat datafile size 100m;
-- We need to open the PDB after it's created...
alter pluggable database rcatpdb online;
```

Exciting! We have created our recovery catalog PDB along with the tablespace we need to create our recovery catalog schema. Note that we could have granted the robertadm user the DBA role if we wanted to. The syntax is included here but commented out, in keeping with best practices. We want the robertadm to only have the privileges it needs to administer this PDB. We will talk more about that in a moment.

Let's discuss the **create pluggable database** statement for a moment. Note that we have defined an admin user called robertadm. (Yes, the password is a simple one; I do that just so you don't see my real uber-complex passwords. You should always use complex passwords when creating user accounts, of course!) Note the **roles=(dba)** syntax, which grants the DBA role to the robertadm user account. If we didn't grant him that role, the admin user would not be able to do anything in the PDB. So, don't let the keyword **admin user** fool you—all it's really doing is creating a user account. Unless you grant the admin user a role, such as DBA, you won't be able to connect using that admin user. That being said, you will still be able to connect to the PDB using SYS, and then you can grant privileges and roles to the admin user that way.

It's a best practice to not grant the admin user any roles, and instead log in after creating the PDB and grant the admin user only the specific privileges it needs. Because it's also a best practice to not log into a PDB or a CDB using sys, you should grant the admin user sufficient privileges to perform the administrative functions you think that user will need to perform. Functions such as the creation of a user, a tablespace, and the like are privileges that would be needed. From a security perspective, the best practice is to assign the user the least number of privileges needed. That might take some trial and error, but it beats being hacked into and having a highly privileged user account being abused.

Notice that when we created the PDB we also created a tablespace in the PDB called rcat. This is the tablespace into which we will be putting our recovery catalog objects. It's just kind of nice to go ahead and create it, and assign it as the default tablespace, when you create the PDB.

NOTE
We could also have connected to the CDB using a TNS connection string like this:

```
-- Connect to the CDB (called CONTDB)
[oracle@bigdatalite tmp]$ sqlplus Connect superman/lanexyz0@contdb
```

When the PDB was created, a service was created for that PDB, and it should have registered with the listener. You will still need to configure whatever naming resolution method you are using (for example, tnsnames.ora) so that the new service will be reflected in it and you can connect to it.

Now that we created the PDB, we should go ahead and grant the admin user the roles it will need to assign to the recovery catalog user we will create shortly. The admin user will need the following grants at a minimum:

- Create user.
- Create session. (Technically the RECOVERY_CATALOG_OWNER role will give you create session privileges, but I like to explicitly grant it anyway in the case of admin users.)
- A grant to the RECOVERY_CATALOG_OWNER role with admin privileges.

Here is an example of granting those privileges to the robertadm account in the newly created rcatpdb PDB:

```
Connect superman/lanexyz0@contdb
alter session set container=rcatpdb;
grant create session, create user to robertadm;
grant recovery_catalog_owner to robertadm with admin option;
```

Notice in this example that we start out logged into the root of the CDB. We then use the **alter session** command to make the rcatpdb the current container. The reason we did this was to be able to use an account with sufficient privileges to issue the grants that we need to issue to the admin user of the PDB. We could have also connected directly to the rcatpdb PDB as the sys user using the SYSDBA privilege, but we already know that we don't log in as SYSDBA unless we need to do so. We then grant the privileges that the robertadm account will need in the rcatpdb to create the recovery catalog owner.

NOTE
When we connected to the database to create the PDB, we did not use the SYSDBA privilege. This is because, in accordance with best practices, we have limited the rights of the superman user to only the specific administrative privileges that we need it to have in order to perform most normal administrative activities. We did not grant that user the SYSDBA role. In fact, it was not even granted the DBA role. This is the application of least privilege in action.

Creating the Recovery Catalog in a PDB with a Local User
Now that we have created the PDB that we will use to store the recovery catalog and configured the admin user for that PDB, we need to create a user that will own the recovery catalog schema. We can choose from two options here:

- Creation of a common user
- Creation of a local user

If you are not sure what the difference between the two user types is, go brush up on the topic in Chapter 4 real quick and then come back. We will wait for you.

The best practice is to create a local user for the recovery catalog owner in the PDB. In general we think that using local users to own any schema in a PDB is a best practice. We also think that the proliferation of common users is a bad practice and should be avoided. Here is an example of the creation of a local user and granting that user the role that it needs to create the recovery catalog called RECOVERY_CATALOG_OWNER:

```
create user rcat_user identified by catalog;
grant recovery_catalog_owner to rcat_user;
```

That being said, there may be a case for the use of a common user when dealing with the recovery catalog. If you have more than one recovery catalog PDB, it might make sense to create a common user and give that common user privileges in both PDBs. Of course, you can also create the same local user name in both PDBs and kind of meet the same goal. The benefit you get with the common user is that you only need to remember one password, rather than two, three, or more—depending on how many recovery catalogs you want to have.

The creation of the local user is pretty straightforward. We simply log into the PDB using an administrative account that has the privileges to create users and grant them the RECOVERY_ CATALOG_OWNER role. Then we use the **create user** command to create the user and the **grant** command to grant the user the RECOVERY_CATALOG_OWNER role. The RECOVERY_CATALOG_ OWNER role includes the **create session** privilege, so we don't need to grant that here.

Finally, we will need to grant our user unlimited quota (or some quota) on the rcat tablespace so that it can create objects in that tablespace. Here is an example of doing just that, where the PDB is called rcat:

```
-- The adminuser user will need these system grants:
-- create session, create user
-- Also the role RECOVERY_CATALOG_OWNER needs to be granted to the
-- adminuser with the admin option so it can grant that role to the
-- new user.
Connect robertadm/mypassword@rcatpdb
create user backup_user identified by backup;
grant recovery_catalog_owner to backup_user;
alter user backup_user quota unlimited on rcat;
```

We have now created a local user in the recovery catalog PDB that we will use when we create the recovery catalog schema, which we will do later in this chapter.

Creating the Recovery Catalog in a PDB with a Common User

Creating the recovery catalog with a common user is almost the same as creating one with a local user. In this case, we will assume the rcatpdb PDB has already been created, as demonstrated earlier in this chapter. Once the PDB is created, we would create the common user that we want to own our recovery catalog schema. To do this, we need to log into the root of the CDB, as shown here:

```
[oracle@bigdatalite tmp]$ . oraenv
ORACLE_SID = [contdb] ? contdb
The Oracle base remains unchanged with value /u01/app/oracle
[oracle@bigdatalite tmp]$ sqlplus superman/lanexyz
```

Once we are logged in, we will create the common user c##backup_user, as shown in this example:

```
create user c##backup_user identified by backup;
```

This creates the c##backup_user in the root of the CDB and in all of the connected PDBs, and in any PDB that will be connected to the CDB later. Even though this common user is present in all of the PDBs, it does not have any privileges in any of those PDBs, or the root PDB for that matter. We need to give this common user the privileges required to be the owner of the recovery catalog schema in the rcatpdb PDB. To do this, we will connect to the CDB with a user that has administrative privileges. We will then use the **alter system** command to connect to the rcatpdb PDB and then issue the grants required. Finally, we will alter the common user so that it has an unlimited quota on the rcat tablespace where we will be creating the objects:

```
[oracle@bigdatalite tmp]$ . oraenv
ORACLE_SID = [contdb] ? contdb
The Oracle base remains unchanged with value /u01/app/oracle
[oracle@bigdatalite tmp]$ sqlplus superman/lanexyz
alter session set container=rcatpdb;
grant create session, create user to c##backup_user container=current;
grant recovery_catalog_owner to c##backup_user with admin option
container=current;
alter user c##backup_user quota unlimited on rcat;
```

Note that the use of the **container=current** clause is pretty much optional because it's the default setting, and in fact the only valid option when connected to a PDB. Still, it's a good practice to put it in there.

Creating the Recovery Catalog Schema Objects

Now that you have created the recovery catalog database (or PDB) and user, it's time to actually create the recovery catalog. This is a pretty simple process. All you need to do is use RMAN and the **catalog** parameter to connect to the recovery catalog database schema using the username and password you just created to manage the recovery catalog. If you are using a catalog in a PDB, you would need to connect to that database using the database service name.

Once you have connected to the recovery catalog, you then issue the **create catalog** command. Optionally, you can use the **tablespace** parameter to define a tablespace in which to create the RMAN schema objects. The next RMAN Workshop provides an example of using the **create catalog** command to create the recovery catalog schema.

RMAN Workshop: *Create the Recovery Catalog*

Workshop Notes
For this workshop, you should have completed the previous RMAN Workshop ("Create the Recovery Catalog User Account"). Also, we assume that you have created a tablespace called RCAT. We will be creating the RMAN schema objects in that tablespace.

Step 1. Connect to the recovery catalog with RMAN. If you are using a nonmultitenant database (we called ours rcdb), you would set the environment for that database and then log in with RMAN to create the catalog schema:

```
[oracle@bigdatalite tmp]$ . oraenv
ORACLE_SID = [rcdb] ? rcdb
[oracle@bigdatalite tmp]$RMAN catalog=backup_user/backup
```

You can also use a service name to connect to a nonmultitenant database. If you are using a PDB in a multitenant database, you must connect using a service name. Here is an example where we are connecting to a PDB with a service name of rcatpdb:

```
[oracle@bigdatalite tmp]$RMAN catalog=backup_user/backup@rcatpdb
```

Step 2.   Issue the **create catalog** command from the RMAN prompt:

```
create catalog tablespace rcat;
```

NOTE
If you were to connect to a catalog in a PDB, the RMAN connection syntax would look like this:

```
RMAN catalog=backup_user/backup@rcatpdb
```

*The **create catalog** command would be the same. If you were using a common user, the connection string would be*

```
RMAN catalog=c##backup_user/backup@rcatpdb
```

Register the Database with the Recovery Catalog

Now that you have prepared the recovery catalog for use, you need to register databases with it. This is required before you can perform an RMAN backup of a database by using the recovery catalog. This is a rather simple process, as you can see in the associated RMAN Workshop.

RMAN Workshop: *Register Your Database in the Recovery Catalog*

Workshop Notes

For this workshop, you should have completed the previous RMAN Workshop ("Create the Recovery Catalog").

Step 1.   If you are using a nonmultitenant database, set your Oracle environment and then use the RMAN client to sign into the database and the recovery catalog at the same time:

```
[oracle@bigdatalite tmp]$ . oraenv
ORACLE_SID = [contdb] ? orcl
RMAN target=backup_admin/backupuserpassword
CATALOG=rcat_user/rcat_password@rcdb
```

If you are using a recovery catalog in a PDB, the connection would look like this:

```
[oracle@bigdatalite tmp]$ . oraenv
ORACLE_SID = [contdb] ? newdb
RMAN target=backup_admin/backupuserpassword
CATALOG=rcat_user/rcat_password@rcatpdb
```

If a common user owns the recovery catalog, your login looks like this:

```
[oracle@bigdatalite tmp]$ . oraenv
ORACLE_SID = [contdb] ? newdb
RMAN target=backup_admin/backupuserpassword
CATALOG=c##backup/password@rcatpdb
```

Step 2. Register the database with the recovery catalog:

```
RMAN> Register database;
```

Note that if you are using an Oracle Multitenant database, you will only connect to and register the CDB. Oracle will not permit you to register any PDBs in the database, so there is no need to connect to them when registering a database in the recovery catalog. When you register the CDB, all of the PDBs will be registered at the same time.

(Optional) Step 3. Verify that the registration of the database was successful by issuing the **report schema** command from the RMAN prompt when connected to the target database:

```
RMAN> Report Schema;
```

Dropping the Recovery Catalog
Just as you can create the recovery catalog schema, you may wish to drop it. Use the **drop catalog** command to drop the recovery catalog schema. Of course, you should understand that all the information contained in the schema is going to be lost, so you should consider backing up the recovery catalog database before you drop the catalog schema.

Adding RMAN Backups to the Recovery Catalog
If you have already executed RMAN backups without a recovery catalog and you want to add them to the recovery catalog later, you can use the **catalog** command. You can catalog datafile copies, back up set pieces, archive log backups, and even archive whole directories of backups, as shown in the following examples:

```
RMAN> CATALOG DATAFILECOPY 'D:\ORACLE\ORA102\DATABASE\system01.dbf';
RMAN> CATALOG ARCHIVELOG 'D:\ORACLE\ORA102\DATABASE\arch_988.arc',
      'D:\ORACLE\ORA102\DATABASE\arch_988.arc';
RMAN> CATALOG BACKUPPIECE 'D:\ORACLE\ORA102\DATABASE\backup_820.bkp';
RMAN> CATALOG START WITH 'D:\ORACLE\ORA102\DATABASE\';
```

NOTE
*Beware of the **catalog start with** command. You must have the trailing backslash at the end of the directory path. If you were to use D:\ORACLE\ORA102\DATABASE instead, Oracle would traverse all possible directory combinations of DATABASE that are available in C:\ORACLE\ORA102. This might include directories such as C:\ORACLE\ORA102\DATABASE, C:\ORACLE\ORA102\ DATABASE-123, and C:\ORACLE\ORA102\DATABASE-OLD. Use the trailing backslash to indicate that you just want C:\ORACLE\ORA102\ DATABASE\.*

Unregistering a Database from the Recovery Catalog

You can use the **unregister database** command in RMAN to unregister a database. If you want to unregister an existing database (or CDB), simply connect to that database (or CDB) and to the recovery catalog—then issue the **unregister database** command:

```
RMAN>unregister database;
```

If the database (or CDB) has been removed and you want to remove it from the recovery catalog, you simply need to know the name of the database (or CDB) you want to unregister, in most cases. If you want to unregister the OLDROB database (or CDB), you would issue this command after connecting to the recovery catalog:

```
RMAN>unregister database OLDROB;
```

In cases where multiple databases with the same name are registered in the recovery catalog, you need to know the DBID for the database that you want to unregister. You then need to run the **unregister database** command in a **run** block while also using the **set dbid** command, as shown in this example:

```
rman CATALOG rman/rman@catdb
RMAN> RUN
{   SET DBID 2414555533;    # specifies the database by DBID
    UNREGISTER DATABASE ROBOLD NOPROMPT;
}
```

Utilizing an RMAN Virtual Private Catalog

The RMAN Virtual Private Catalog provides the ability to control access to the recovery catalog data by specific users. Using the Virtual Private Catalog features of the RMAN recovery catalog, you can use a single recovery catalog but provide effective administrative separation of catalog metadata among users of that recovery catalog. As a result, you can assign users to be able to look at specific catalog records on a "need-to-know" basis. This tightens security on the catalog and the databases it serves.

The Virtual Private Catalog for RMAN has been around for a while. As of the time we were updating this book, there were two different ways of creating the Virtual Private Catalog in the Oracle database. The first way is for versions of the Oracle database at 12.1.0.1 and below. The second way is for an Oracle database at version 12.1.0.2. In this section, we cover both methods of creating the Virtual Private Catalog.

Creating an RMAN Virtual Private Catalog in Oracle Database Version 12.1.0.1 and Earlier

Building an RMAN Virtual Private Catalog requires performing actions in SQL*Plus on the recovery catalog database, as well as actions while connected to the catalog with the RMAN client. These actions are as follows:

1. Create the new user in the recovery catalog database to which you will be granting restricted access via the RMAN Virtual Private Catalog.

2. Grant that user the role RECOVERY_CATALOG_OWNER.

3. As the recovery catalog owner, log into RMAN and use the **grant catalog for database** command to assign specific databases to the user you created in step 1. These are the RMAN Recovery Catalog records the user will be able to see when they log in.

4. From the RMAN prompt, grant the **register database** privilege to the user created in step 1. This will provide the user rights so that they may register other databases in the recovery catalog.

5. Log into RMAN as the user created in step 1. Execute the RMAN **create virtual catalog** command to create the virtual catalog.

6. Finally, if you intend on using a version of RMAN that is Oracle Database release 10.2 or earlier, you will need to log into SQL*Plus as the recovery catalog owner and run the package **rcat_user.DBMS_RCVCAT.create_virtual_catalog** to support these older versions of the database.

You must repeat these steps for each Virtual Private Catalog user you want to create. Thus, you might have a Virtual Private Catalog user called VPROD that can see only production database RMAN records, and you might have one called VDEV that can only see development database RMAN records.

RMAN also provides steps to drop a Virtual Private Catalog. These steps are pretty simple:

1. Log in as the Virtual Private Catalog owner and not the base catalog owner.

2. Issue the **drop catalog** command if you are running Oracle Database 11g or later.

3. Use the **dbms_rcvcat.delete_virtual_catalog** procedure to drop the catalog if you are using a version of Oracle Database previous to version 11g.

You can use the **revoke catalog for database** RMAN command to revoke the ability of a user to see records of a specific database. Also, you can use the **revoke register database** RMAN commands to remove the register database privilege from a catalog user.

RMAN Workshop: *Create a Virtual Private Catalog for Oracle 12.1.0.1 and Earlier Databases*

Workshop Notes
In this workshop, we create a VPC for user ebank in the recovery catalog, which is housed in a database called rcdb. The recovery catalog is owned by the user backup_user.

Step 1. Grant access to the catalog from within the database:

```
[oracle@bigdatalite tmp]$ . oraenv
ORACLE_SID = [rcdb] ? rcdb
sqlplus backup_user/backup

Create user ebank identified by missing
Default tablespace rcat
Quota unlimited on rcat;
Grant recovery_catalog_owner to ebank;
```

Step 2. Log into RMAN and grant access to the database PROD, as well as the ability to register any new databases:

```
Rman CATALOG=backup_user/backup
RMAN> Grant catalog for database PROD to ebank;
RMAN> Grant register database to ebank;
```

Step 3. Exit RMAN, log back in as ebank, and create the VPC:

```
Rman CATALOG=ebank/lost
RMAN> create virtual catalog;
```

Step 4. Log back into the database and use the **rcat_user.dbms_rcvcat.create_virtual_catalog** procedure to create the virtual catalog:

```
Sqlplus rcat_user/rcat_password
SQL> execute rcat_user.DBMS_RCVCAT.create_virtual_catalog;
```

Now, the user ebank will only be able to see RMAN records for the database called PROD and any other databases that that user registers.

Creating an RMAN Virtual Private Catalog in Oracle Database Version 12.1.0.2

The process of creating an RMAN Virtual Private Catalog in Oracle Database 12.1.0.2 has changed, as mentioned earlier. The basic steps now are as follows:

1. Using SQL*Plus, create the new user in the recovery catalog database to which you will be granting restricted access via the RMAN Virtual Private Catalog.

2. Grant the user created in step 1 the **create session** role. This allows the user to log into the database.

3. As the base recovery catalog owner (not the user created in step 1), log into catalog database with RMAN (using the catalog connect string format) and use the **grant catalog for database** command to assign specific databases to the user you created in step 1. These are the RMAN Recovery Catalog records the user will be able to see when they log in.

   The first time you issue a **grant catalog for database** command is when the RMAN Virtual Recovery Catalog will be created. This is now done by RMAN in the background, and you no longer need to do anything to start that process. The catalog will be deleted when all the databases granted with the **grant catalog for database** command have subsequently been revoked with the **revoke catalog** command.

4. From the RMAN prompt, grant the **register database** privilege to the user created in step 1. This will provide the user rights so that they may register other databases in the recovery catalog.

Note that the main differences in this procedure and the former is that there is no longer a need to run the **create virtual catalog** command at all. Also, the recovery catalog users that will be created don't need the **recovery_catalog_owner** role anymore. The new users only need the create session privilege. This is because RMAN is now using the Virtual Private Database (VPD) features of Oracle. This does not mean that you have to use the Virtual Recovery Catalog features, however. It just simplifies the process of using these features.

Note that the **revoke catalog** RMAN command is still used to revoke catalog permissions from users.

Upgrading a Virtual Private Catalog to Version 12.1.0.2

If you are upgrading to Oracle Database 12.1.0.2 from an earlier version, you will need to upgrade any existing Virtual Private Catalogs. The steps to do this are as follows:

1. Connect to the recovery catalog database as the SYS user using the SYSDBA privileges.

2. Run the script $ORACLE_HOME/rdbms/admin/dbmsrmansys.sql.

3. Using RMAN, connect to the recovery catalog as the base recovery catalog schema owner.

4. Run the **upgrade catalog** command twice. Running this command twice is required to confirm that you truly want to execute the command.

5. Connect to the recovery catalog database using the SYS user with the SYSDBA privileges.

6. Run the script $ORACLE_HOME/rdbms/admin/dbmsrmanvpc.sql {catalog_schema_ owner} to upgrade the virtual private catalog schemas. It is required to pass in the name of the owning schema of the recovery catalog as a parameter when you run this command.

Once you have completed these steps, all previous Virtual Private Catalog schemas of the base catalog will be updated.

NOTE
Yes, we know that we said you should almost never log in as SYS using the SYSDBA privilege. This is one of those exceptions because that's what Oracle tells you to do. When Oracle tells you to use SYS as SYSDBA, then do so. You won't get any argument from us!

Merging Multiple Recovery Catalogs

The other primary headache, once we overcome the inability to adequately share the recovery catalog via Virtual Private Catalogs, is to vanquish catalog sprawl. For whatever reason, sometimes you end up with multiple catalogs, and there has historically been no way to import records from one catalog to the next in a way that didn't make matters worse.

The **import catalog** command is used to easily import catalog metadata from one recovery catalog into another. This import can include all databases in the source catalog, or only a subset that you specify at the time of import. This functionality provides the mechanism of sorting through the records and ensuring the correct records are brought in without creating dependency issues or duplicate rows.

The **import catalog** command in RMAN can merge two catalogs; it cannot be used as an upgrade mechanism. Before you can import a lower version of the catalog into a newer version, you will have to use the **upgrade** command first against the source catalog to upgrade it to the same level as the destination catalog. Then you can import that catalog schema. While we are on the matter of versions, it should be noted that the source catalog, destination catalog, and RMAN executable version must all be the same version for the import to work.

The **import catalog** command can also be used to move an existing catalog to a new database or to a new schema. In such a case, you would create the new catalog in the new location, then use that new catalog as the destination catalog in an **import catalog** operation.

RMAN Workshop: *Merge Two Recovery Catalogs*

Workshop Notes

In this workshop, we will import a subset of databases from the catalog RCAT1 into the destination catalog RCAT2.

Step 1. Connect to the destination catalog in RMAN:

```
Rman catalog=rcvcat_user/password@RCAT2
```

Step 2. Run the **import** command by specifying a connect string to the source catalog:

```
RMAN> import catalog rcvcat_user@RCAT1 DB_NAME=TEST, DEV, PROD;
```

Step 3. Confirm that the metadata for the databases was imported:

```
RMAN> CONNECT TARGET SYS/PASSWORD@TEST
RMAN>list backup of database;
```

RMAN Stored Scripts

We honestly don't find much use for RMAN stored scripts because we prefer to use Oracle Enterprise Manager to maintain our backup scripts and other kinds of jobs. However, stored scripts are available with RMAN if you are using the recovery catalog, so we will cover them here quickly.

Stored scripts provide the ability to save a set of RMAN commands in the form of a script in the recovery catalog. Later you can take that script and re-execute it on the same or another database. Scripts are considered either local or global—depending on how you created them.

There are other ways of storing scripts with RMAN commands. You could create a command file, which is just a text file physically located on disk somewhere, with the RMAN commands, and then execute the command file from the RMAN command-line interface using the **cmdfile** parameter, as shown in this example:

```
rman target robert/password cmdfile=run_backup.cmd
```

Alternatively, you can run a command file from within RMAN itself using the @ command:

```
@run_backup.cmd
```

Then, as we mentioned, there is our favorite—using Oracle Enterprise Manager Cloud Control.

In this section we are interested in the creation, use, and administration of stored scripts in the RMAN catalog. We look at creating stored scripts, finding stored scripts in the recovery catalog, and changing and deleting a stored script. We then look at how to start a stored script and how to print out the stored script for documentation purposes.

Creating Stored Scripts

To store a script in the recovery catalog, you use the **create script** RMAN command. Each stored script is assigned a name when you create it. You can create scripts that do backups, recoveries, and maintenance of your databases. To create a script, you must be connected to the recovery catalog. Here is an example of using the **create script** command to create a backup script. RMAN also allows you to store comments related to your stored scripts by using the **comment** parameter:

```
create script my_backup_script
comment 'This script backs up the database'
{ backup database plus archivelog;}
```

Starting with Oracle Database 11g, RMAN supports the use of substitution variables. Each substitution variable is denoted with an ampersand and a number that makes each variable unique. For example, you could rewrite this script as follows:

```
create global script my_backup_script
comment 'This script backs up the database'
{ backup database tag '&1' plus archivelog;}
```

This is a global script, so we only need to be connected to the recovery catalog (instead to a specific target database) to create the script. When you create the script, RMAN will prompt you for a value for the substitution variable. This is okay, and whatever you select for the variable is not stored as a default value. If you want to avoid being prompted for the value, you can start RMAN and define the argument value on the command prompt, as shown here:

```
rman target=/ catalog=rcat_user/robert@mypdb using 'test'
```

In this case we have defined the default value for the **&1** parameter as **test**. We will show you how to run a stored script with parameters later in this chapter when we discuss running stored scripts.

Querying the Recovery Catalog for Stored Script Information

You can use the recovery catalog views to determine the name of scripts stored in the recovery catalog by querying the RC_STORED_SCRIPT view. You can see the contents of a given script by querying the RC_STORED_SCRIPT_LINE view. Let's look at an example of using the RC_STORED_SCRIPT view. Here we are displaying information on the stored script we created earlier in this section called my_backup_script:

```
SQL> select * from rc_stored_script;
    DB_KEY DB_NAME  SCRIPT_NAME          SCRIPT_COMMENT
---------- -------- -------------------- ----------------------------------
           GLOBAL   my_backup_script     This script backs up the database
```

Changing Stored Scripts

You use the **replace script** command to replace stored scripts in the recovery catalog. Here is an example of using the **replace script** command. Note that we also add a comment to the script.

```
replace script my_backup_script
comment 'This script backs up the database'
{ backup database plus archivelog delete input;}
```

Deleting Stored Scripts

To drop a script, you use the **delete script** command. You must be connected to the recovery catalog to successfully drop a stored script. Here is an example of using the **delete script** command:

```
delete script my_backup_script;
```

Using Stored Scripts

Now that you have created some stored scripts, you probably want to use them. This is what the **execute script** command is for. Simply connect to the recovery catalog and use the **execute script** command within the confines of a **run** block, as shown in this example:

```
run {execute script my_backup_script;}
```

If you are using substitution variables, you can use the **using** parameter to include the values of those parameters in the **execute script** command, as shown in this example:

```
Run {execute script my_backup_script using TEST_BACKUP;}
```

Also, when you start RMAN, you can use the **using** parameter at the command line to indicate what command-line parameters are to be used, as shown here:

```
rman target=backup_user/backup catalog=rcat_user/robert@mypdb
script=my_backup_script using 'tag_custom'
```

Note that when you execute the **create script** command, which we showed you earlier, if you are using a substitution variable in that script, RMAN will prompt you for a value for that substitution variable. This is just part of the process of creating the script, and the variable value has no actual use. Thus, when creating scripts with substitution variables, it is common to start RMAN with the **user** parameter and add variables so you will not be prompted for them when saving the scripts.

Printing Stored Scripts

If you want to print a copy of your stored script, you can use the **print script** command. Connect to the recovery catalog and run the **print script** command, as shown in this example:

```
RMAN> print script my_backup_script;
printing stored script: my_backup_script
{ backup database plus archivelog;}
```

You can also use the RC_STORED_SCRIPT_LINE recovery catalog view to display the contents of a stored script, as shown in this example:

```
select script_name, text from rc_stored_script_line
order by script_name, line;
SCRIPT_NAME      TEXT
---------------  ---------------------------------------
my_backup_script { backup database plus archivelog;}
```

RMAN Workshop: *Using RMAN Stored Scripts*

Workshop Notes

This workshop expects that you have an operational Oracle database (called recover) and that you are also using a separate Oracle database in which to store the recovery catalog (called catalog).

Step 1. Connect to the target database and to the recovery catalog:

```
rman target rman_account/rman_password catalog rcat_user/rcat_password@catalog
```

Step 2. Create a stored script to back up the target database:

```
RMAN> create script my_backup_script
2> {backup database plus archivelog;}
created script my_backup_script
```

Step 3. Print the stored script:

```
RMAN> print script my_backup_script;
printing stored script: my_backup_script
{backup database plus archivelog;}
```

Step 4. Execute the stored script to back up your database:

```
RMAN> run {execute script my_backup_script;}
```

Step 5. Delete the stored script:

```
RMAN> delete script my_backup_script;
```

Recovery Catalog Maintenance

Use of the recovery catalog involves some additional maintenance activities, which include upgrading the catalog during a database upgrade or migration, manually resetting the database incarnation, and resynchronizing the recovery catalog after certain database operations. This section describes those activities, as well as other maintenance considerations, including removing a database from the recovery catalog and using the Oracle EXP/IMP utilities to back up the recovery catalog. Finally, this section reviews the different recovery catalog views and what they are used for.

Unregistering a Database in RMAN

Prior to Oracle Database 10g, unregistering a database from the recovery catalog was a manual process. Now, Oracle makes removing a database from the recovery catalog as easy as issuing the command **unregister database**. Here is an example:

```
RMAN> Unregister database mydb;
```

When this command is executed, the metadata for the database in the recovery catalog is removed completely. Also, any metadata older than CONTROL_FILE_RECORD_KEEP time is removed from the control file. All local scripts for that database will also be removed from the recovery catalog.

Database Migration/Upgrade Issues

As you upgrade your Oracle databases, you need to upgrade your recovery catalog as well. As you will see in Chapter 9, some strict rules apply with regard to the version of the database you are using, the version of RMAN, and the version of the recovery catalog.

You can determine the version of your recovery catalog by querying the VERSION column of the RCVER view in the recovery catalog schema:

```
% sqlplus rman/rman @catdb
SQL > SELECT * FROM rcver;
VERSION
------------
11.01.00
```

If the table displays multiple rows, the highest version in the RCVER table is the current catalog schema version. For example, assume that the RCVER table displays the following rows:

```
VERSION
------------
08.01.07
09.02.00
10.02.00
```

As long as the version of the recovery catalog is at the same level or higher than your database, you will be in good shape. Therefore, if you are storing multiple databases in the same recovery catalog, it's okay to upgrade the catalog to a higher version, even if only one of the databases stored in the recovery catalog is being upgraded.

To upgrade your recovery catalog, simply issue the command **upgrade catalog** from RMAN. RMAN will prompt you to enter the **upgrade catalog** command again. RMAN will then upgrade the recovery catalog for you. Make sure you check all documentation on the version of the Oracle database to which you are upgrading in order to ensure that you are using the proper upgrade method for that version of the Oracle database.

Manually Resetting the Database Incarnation (reset catalog)

Sometimes when you restore an Oracle database you will need to use the **resetlogs** command to complete the restore (we discuss this in Chapter 9 quite a bit). When the **resetlogs** command is used, one of the things that happens is a new incarnation of the database is created.

An *incarnation* of a database is a point in time when the redo log stream diverged into a different temporal version. When you first create an Oracle database, that is the first incarnation of the database. If you ever recover the database to the point of a failure, then the temporal state of the database is consistent. If you recover the database to some point in time when some of the records that had previously processed were not processed, then the database will have been opened with the **resetlogs** command, and this would create a new incarnation of the database. Each subsequent recovery action that ends in a **resetlogs** command will create a new incarnation of a database. We discuss the **resetlogs** command in much more detail in Chapter 9.

If you are not connected to the recovery catalog when a **resetlogs** operation occurs, then the recovery catalog will be resynchronized the next time the target database is connected to the recovery catalog and an RMAN operation occurs or when a resynchronize operation on the recovery catalog database occurs.

If this is done during an RMAN operation, the recovery catalog will be correctly updated. However, if you manually issue a **resetlogs** command (through SQL*Plus, for example), you need to reset the database incarnation in the recovery catalog. This is done with the **reset database** command:

```
reset database to incarnation 5;
```

Manually Resynchronizing the Recovery Catalog (resync catalog)

When RMAN uses a recovery catalog, it uses a resynchronization process to ensure that the recovery catalog is consistent with the target database control file. Generally, Oracle performs database resynchronization itself after RMAN operations such as backups and recoveries, so you really don't need to resync the recovery catalog often. One example of the need to resync the recovery catalog is if you are running backups sometimes with and sometimes without a recovery catalog. To manually get Oracle to resync the recovery catalog, use the **resync catalog** command:

```
resync catalog;
```

When Oracle synchronizes the recovery catalog, it first creates a snapshot control file and compares it with the recovery catalog. Once that comparison is complete, Oracle will update the recovery catalog so it is in sync with the database control file.

Purging Recovery Catalog Records

In earlier versions of RMAN (think 9*i* and earlier), the recovery catalog records were not purged at all and as a result the recovery catalog would get quite large. Even in later versions of the Oracle Database there were cases where the recovery catalog would get out of sync with the database control file and certain records would not be deleted. Also, there have been bugs in the past that would cause certain tables in the recovery catalog not to have deleted records removed from them.

These problems have largely been solved for some time, and in most cases there should be no reason to manually need to purge recovery catalog records at all. If you find that the recovery catalog is growing uncontrollably, you probably need to make sure that you are managing your retention correctly. If you are only using an FRA, then RMAN should manage the retention for you quite well and you should not see any divergence in the recovery catalog. If you do, you may well have hit a bug and you should report this to Oracle Support.

In cases where your backups are being moved to a second or third tier that is not on the FRA, you will need to manually manage the retention of these RMAN files and the metadata associated with them. This requires the use of the **delete obsolete** command to remove obsolete backups and also the use of the **crosscheck** command to ensure that nothing has removed the physical files from the backup media, leaving orphan metadata records in the recovery catalog. We discuss the **delete obsolete** and **crosscheck** commands later in this book in Chapter 11. We also cover how to report on recovery catalog records using RMAN in Chapter 17, as well as provide some information about the internal tables of the recovery catalog in this chapter, should you want to traverse the views of the recovery catalog.

Do keep an eye on the growth of the recovery catalog because performance of the catalog can be impacted by uncontrolled growth.

The recovery catalog will maintain old incarnation records forever. These records can be found in the RC_DATABASE_INCARNATION view, which is based on the underlying recovery catalog table DBINC. It is rare to need to remove old incarnation records from the recovery catalog. However, you can use the **delete** SQL command to remove incarnation information from the DBINC table if you need to. We would strongly suggest you open a support ticket with Oracle before you do this, however.

Backing Up the Recovery Catalog

The procedure for using RMAN to back up a database can be found in Chapter 7, and it just so happens that it is perfectly okay to use RMAN to back up your recovery catalog database. Just make sure you have a sound recovery strategy so you can restore your recovery catalog as quickly as possible. Also, remember that losing the recovery catalog is not the end of the world. Even if you are using a recovery catalog, you can still recover your databases later without it. All you really need is a backup of the database control file—or, in a really bad situation, some fancy work with DBMS_BACKUP_RESTORE! The really important thing to note is that you need to test your entire recovery strategy. Only then can you know, and be comfortable with, your ability to recover your databases.

Recovery Catalog Views

The recovery catalog provides a series of views that can be used to explore the metadata being produced by your RMAN backup strategy. These views have base tables that are populated when you register your database and then populated, updated, or removed on any subsequent **resync** command from the catalog. Additionally the recovery catalog records will be modified and removed by retention criteria established for the RMAN FRA.

In this section we review what the RMAN recovery catalog base table's views are for. We then list the different recovery catalog base tables and views. Finally, we provide some examples of querying the data dictionary views.

The Purpose of the Recovery Catalog Views and the Database Data Dictionary Views

Just like the Oracle database data dictionary tables, there are a number of recovery catalog views that are created when the recovery catalog is created. The naming convention for these views follows the convention of RC_*. For example, there are views called RC_BACKUP_SET and RC_BACKUP_REDOLOG, along with many more.

Keep in mind that almost every RMAN operation is independent of the recovery catalog. Therefore, a number of V$ views in the database provide RMAN metadata similar to what's stored in the database control file.

The big difference between the database recovery catalog base tables and views and the related V$ views is the fact that the recovery catalog views will contain information on all the databases contained in the recovery catalog. This can be a security issue, which is addressed by the Virtual Private Catalog features we discussed earlier in this chapter.

You will find slight differences in the V$ views and recovery catalog views. For example, the primary keys for the records in the V$ views are going to be different from the primary key values in the recovery catalog. Again, this is because there are likely to be many more databases in the recovery catalog. Also, you will find that there may well be more records in the recovery catalog than in the V$ views for a given database. This is because some records in the recovery catalog may have a retention requirement that is longer than the control file is able to maintain a record for. The database control file can only hold a year's worth of RMAN backup metadata, whereas the recovery catalog can hold this metadata forever. Therefore, it's quite likely that the recovery catalog records will be much larger than those within the control file.

The Recovery Catalog Base Tables, Views, and Database Data Dictionary Views

So, what are the base tables of the recovery catalog, and what are they for? The following table provides this information for you:

Name	Description
AL	Contains archived logs. Archived logs are uniquely identified by dbinc_key, recid, and stamp.
BCB	Contains corrupt block ranges in datafile backups.
BCF	Contains control file backups (in backup sets).
BDF	Contains all datafile backups (in backup sets).
BP	Contains all backup pieces of backup sets.
BRL	Contains backup redo logs (in backup sets).
BS	Contains all backup sets for all database incarnations.
CCB	Contains corrupt block ranges in datafile copies.
CCF	Contains control file copies.
CDF	Contains all datafile copies.
CKP	Records all recovery catalog checkpoints.
DB	Contains all target databases that have been registered in this recovery catalog.
DBINC	Contains all incarnations of the target databases registered in this recovery catalog.
DF	Contains all datafiles of all database incarnations.
DFATT	Datafile attributes that change over time.
OFFR	Stores datafile offline ranges.
ORL	Contains all redo log files for all database incarnations.
RCVER	Recovery catalog version.
RLH	Records all redo log history for all threads.
RR	Contains redo ranges for all database incarnations.
RT	Redo threads for all database incarnations.
SCR	Contains one row for each stored script.
SCRL	Contains one row for each line of each stored script.
TS	Contains all tablespaces of all database incarnations.
TSATT	Tablespace attributes that change over time.

A number of views are built on top of the base tables. The following table lists these views and what is contained in them:

Name	Associated V$ View	Description
RC_ARCHIVED_LOG	V$ARCHIVED_LOG	Information about all archive logs. This view does not include information on backups of archived redo logs.
RC_BACKUP_CONTROLFILE	V$BACKUP_DATAFILE	Backup control files in backup sets.
RC_BACKUP_CORRUPTION	V$BACKUP_CORRUPTION	Corrupt blocks in datafile backups and copies.
RC_BACKUP_DATAFILE	V$BACKUP_DATAFILE	Datafile backups (in backup sets).
RC_BACKUP_PIECE	V$BACKUP_PIECE	Backup pieces.
RC_BACKUP_REDOLOG	V$BACKUP_REDOLOG	Redo log backups (in backup sets).
RC_BACKUP_SET	V$BACKUP_SET	Backup sets.
RC_CHECKPOINT	V$CHECKPOINT	RC_CHECKPOINT is replaced by RC_RESYNC, but is still used by some tests.
RC_CONTROLFILE_COPY	V$DATAFILE_COPY	Controlfile copies.
RC_COPY_CORRUPTION	V$COPY_CORRUPTION	Corrupt block ranges in datafile copies for all database incarnations.
RC_DATABASE	V$DATABASE	Information about databases and their current incarnations.
RC_DATABASE_INCARNATION	V$DATABASE_INCARNATION	Information about all incarnations registered in the recovery catalog.
RC_DATAFILE	V$DATAFILE	Information about all datafiles registered in the recovery catalog.
RC_DATAFILE_COPY	V$DATAFILE_COPY	Datafile copies (on disk).
RC_LOG_HISTORY	V$LOG_HISTORY	Information about redo log history.
RC_OFFLINE_RANGE	V$OFFLINE_RANGE	Offline ranges for datafiles.
RC_REDO_LOG	V$REDO_LOG	Information about online redo logs.
RC_REDO_THREAD	V$REDO_THREAD	Information about redo threads.

Name	Associated V$ View	Description
RC_RESYNC	None	Information about recovery catalog resyncs (checkpoints).
RC_STORED_SCRIPT	None	Stored scripts.
RC_STORED_SCRIPT_LINE	None	Each line of each stored script.
RC_TABLESPACE	V$TABLESPACE	Information about all tablespaces registered in the recovery catalog.

Examples of Using the Recovery Catalog Base Tables and Views

Here are some examples of querying the RC_* views.

Looking at Archived Redo Logs

First, here is a query against the RC_ARCHIVED_LOG that provides information on the archived redo logs that exist on disk.

```
column name format a50
column completion_time format a25
alter session set nls_date_format= 'DD-MON-YYYY:HH24:MI:SS';
select name, sequence#, status, completion_time
from rc_archived_log;
NAME                                                SEQUENCE# S COMPLETION_TIME
-------------------------------------------------- ---------- - --------------------------C:\APP\
ORACLE\FAST_RECOVERY_AREA\MYCDB\ARCHIVELOG\             58 A 05-OCT-2014:22:35:08
2014_10_05\O1_MF_1_58_B34BJ8MP_.ARC
C:\APP\ORACLE\FAST_RECOVERY_AREA\MYCDB\ARCHIVELOG\      59 A 06-OCT-2014:01:00:48
2014_10_06\O1_MF_1_59_B34M1F2G_.ARC
C:\APP\ORACLE\FAST_RECOVERY_AREA\MYCDB\ARCHIVELOG\      60 A 06-OCT-2014:10:35:00
2014_10_06\O1_MF_1_60_B35NP0MO_.ARC
C:\APP\ORACLE\FAST_RECOVERY_AREA\MYCDB\ARCHIVELOG\      61 A 06-OCT-2014:20:00:23
2014_10_06\O1_MF_1_61_B36OT5KD_.ARC
```

Note that once we back up these archived redo logs and then delete them after the backup (and we are connected to the recovery catalog during the backup), this view will no longer contain any records, which you can see here:

```
rman target rman_account/rman_password catalog rcat_user/rcat_password@catalog
RMAN> backup archivelog all delete input;

sqlplus rcat_user/rcat_password@catalog
SQL> select name, sequence#, status, completion_time
  2  from rc_archived_log;
no rows selected
```

Looking at Databases Registered in the Recovery Catalog

You can find out which databases are registered in the recovery catalog by using the RC_DATABASE view, as shown here:

```
SQL> SELECT * FROM RC_DATABASE;
    DB_KEY  DBINC_KEY       DBID NAME     RESETLOGS_CHANGE# RESETLOGS
---------- ---------- ---------- -------- ----------------- ---------
         1          2 2186698322 MYCDB             2255672 06-MAR-14
```

Looking at Tablespaces Registered in the Recovery Catalog

We can now see which tablespaces are stored in the recovery catalog by querying the RC_TABLESPACE view, as shown here:

```
SELECT DB_KEY, DBINC_KEY, con_id,db_name, NAME, CREATION_CHANGE#,
CREATION_TIME FROM RC_TABLESPACE
order by 1,2,3,5;
DB_KEY DBINC_KEY  CON_ID DB_NAME  NAME      CREATION_CHANGE# CREATION
------ --------- ------- -------- --------- ---------------- ---------
     1         2       1 MYCDB    SYSAUX                4337 28-JUN-13
     1         2       1 MYCDB    SYSTEM                   7 28-JUN-13
     1         2       1 MYCDB    TEMP               2255793 06-MAR-14
     1         2       1 MYCDB    UNDOTBS1              5729 28-JUN-13
     1         2       1 MYCDB    USERS                23341 28-JUN-13
     1         2       2 MYCDB    SYSAUX             2256046 06-MAR-14
     1         2       2 MYCDB    SYSTEM             2256043 06-MAR-14
     1         2       2 MYCDB    TEMP               2256044 06-MAR-14
     1         2       3 MYCDB    SYSAUX             2268790 06-MAR-14
     1         2       3 MYCDB    SYSTEM             2268787 06-MAR-14
     1         2       3 MYCDB    TEMP               2268788 06-MAR-14
     1         2       3 MYCDB    USERS              2269682 06-MAR-14
     1         2       4 MYCDB    SYSAUX             2272472 06-MAR-14
     1         2       4 MYCDB    SYSTEM             2272469 06-MAR-14
     1         2       4 MYCDB    TEMP               2272470 06-MAR-14
     1         2       4 MYCDB    USERS              2272475 06-MAR-14
```

Looking at Database Incarnations

This listing highlights the increased information presented in data dictionary views with the addition of the Oracle Multitenant database. Now, we have to consider the contained ID along with the additional information to determine what information applies to what container in the database.

We can also see the history of the incarnations of the databases in the recovery catalog by querying the RC_DATABASE_INCARNATION view:

```
SQL> select db_key, dbid, dbinc_key, name, current_incarnation, status, par-
ent_dbinc_key from rc_database_incarnation;

    DB_KEY       DBID DBINC_KEY NAME     CUR STATUS   PARENT_DBINC_KEY
---------- ---------- ---------- -------- --- -------- ----------------
         1 2186698322          2 MYCDB    YES CURRENT                10
         1 2186698322         10 UNKNOWN  NO  PARENT
```

In this case, we can see that there are two records for the database identified by the DBID column. The incarnation that has the status of PARENT is the initial incarnation of the database with the DBID 2186698322. The incarnation with a status of CURRENT is the current incarnation of that database. You can tell that both are the same database (or in rare cases, copies of the same database that were not copied correctly) because the DBID is the primary identifier of any database. When a database is created, it is assigned a DBID, which is considered a GUID—a numbering scheme designed to provide a unique number at all times. This GUID is then assigned to each database and uniquely identifies that database. So, in the recovery catalog it's the DBID that really uniquely identifies a database and not the name of the database. This helps avoid naming conflicts that might otherwise occur.

Datafile Backup Block Corruption

The RC_BACKUP_CORRUPTION view lists the corruption that exists in datafile backups. To tolerate corruption, the value of MAXCORRUPT must be set to a non zero value, which indicates how many corrupt blocks RMAN will back up before it throws an error and aborts. The corrupt blocks are not discarded, but rather are backed up as is.

A similar view, RC_DATABASE_BLOCK_CORRUPTION, lists blocks that are corrupt in the database based on the last backup operation (or **backup validate**). The difference between these two views is that RC_BACKUP_CORRUPTION lists blocks that are corrupt in the backup, not in the database itself.

The following code provides a list of corrupt blocks, with block number, file number, the backup piece in which the corruption exists, and the type of corruption for the database V102:

```
select db_name, piece#, file#, block#, blocks, corruption_type
from rc_backup_corruption where db_name='V102';
```

Returning to the RC_BACKUP_CORRUPTION view we find that it provides the corruption list that is populated when a **backup** or **backup validate** operation discovers corrupt blocks. Remember that these are the actual corrupt blocks in the database, and not in the backups or copies themselves. This view is refreshed on each backup operation to reflect current corruption (if any). V$DATABASE_BLOCK_CORRUPTION is the view used during block media recovery when you specify **blockrecover corruption list** and is therefore the one you will most often be referencing. The following code is a sample **select** statement against this view:

```
select file#, block#, corruption_type
from v$database_block_corruption;
```

Backup Files in the Recovery Catalog

The RC_BACKUP_FILES view provides a list of the backup files (backup set copies or image copies, for example) created by the **backup database** command. This view provides details about all backup files known to the recovery catalog, regardless of whether the file is a backup set, datafile copy, or proxy copy.

One thing that is different in this view than other views is that before you can query the view, you must first call DBMS_RCVMAN.SETDATABASE to indicate which database you are looking for. You pass the DBID of the database from which you want to collect information to the procedure. Then you can query the RC_BACKUP_FILES view, as shown in this example:

```
CALL DBMS_RCVMAN.SETDATABASE(null,null,null,2283997583,null);
select backup_type, file_type, status, bytes from rc_backup_files;
```

RMAN Configuration Information

The RC_RMAN_CONFIGURATION view is equivalent to a **show all** command, giving the name and value for each configuration parameter that is set for each of your target databases. It is worth noting that three configuration parameters are not stored here: **configure exclude** information is found in RC_TABLESPACE (V$TABLESPACE), **configure auxname** information is found in RC_DATAFILE (V$DATAFILE), and **configure snapshot controlfile** information is found only in the target database control file (there is no catalog equivalent).

It is also important to point out that RC_RMAN_CONFIGURATION does not have a DB_NAME column, so you have to use the primary key DB_KEY value from RC_DATABASE to get the values for the appropriate database registered in your catalog.

Furthermore, no values are listed in either V$RMAN_CONFIGURATION or RC_RMAN_CONFIGURATION for default values. Only values that have been manually changed will appear in this list. The following code is a sample **select** statement against this view:

```
select name, value from rc_rman_configuration where db_key=1;
```

Catalog Views Intended for Use by Oracle Enterprise Manager

A series of new views in the recovery catalog were created specifically to provide performance and functionality enhancements to the OEM Console. Many of these views can be very interesting when performing diagnostic information on RMAN backup or restore problems. For example, the RC_RMAN_OUTPUT view is very helpful because it stores all the output for an RMAN run. There is a V$RMAN_OUTPUT view that provides like information from the Oracle control file.

V$RMAN_OUTPUT excepted, most of these views do not have corresponding V$ views in the target database control file. It is worth taking a look at these views and identifying their parts to avoid any misunderstanding. If you are looking for a way to leverage the information in these views, you can find the same information in them in OEM's backup and recovery functionality. The following table lists and briefly describes the RC_* views that are built primarily for use by the OEM.

RC_* View	Notes
RC_BACKUP_ARCHIVELOG_DETAILS	Detailed information about backed-up archive logs.
RC_BACKUP_ARCHIVELOG_SUMMARY	Summarized archive log backup information.
RC_BACKUP_CONTROLFILE_DETAILS	Detailed control file backup information.
RC_BACKUP_CONTROLFILE_SUMMARY	Summarized information about all control file backups known to RMAN.
RC_BACKUP_COPY_DETAILS	Detailed information regarding all control file and datafile copies.
RC_BACKUP_COPY_SUMMARY	Summarized control file and datafile copy information.
RC_BACKUP_DATAFILE_DETAILS	Detailed information about all datafile backups—in backup sets as well as image copies.

RC_* View	Notes
RC_BACKUP_DATAFILE_SUMMARY	Summary information about datafile backups.
RC_BACKUP_PIECE_DETAILS	Detailed information about available backup pieces in the catalog.
RC_BACKUP_SET_DETAILS	Detailed information regarding available backup sets in the catalog. This includes backups created with the **backup backupset** command.
RC_BACKUP_SET_SUMMARY	Aggregated information about available backup sets.
RC_BACKUP_SPFILE_DETAILS	Detailed information about available SPFILE backups.
RC_BACKUP_SPFILE_SUMMARY	Summarized information about available SPFILE backups.
RC_RMAN_OUTPUT	Assists OEM with job status tracking. The corresponding V$ view is V$RMAN_OUTPUT.
RC_RMAN_BACKUP_JOB_DETAILS	Detailed information on individual backup job sessions, combining all operations in the same session.
RC_RMAN_BACKUP_SUBJOB_DETAILS	Details concerning groups of similar operations within an RMAN session.
RC_RMAN_STATUS	A historical view of RMAN sessions for all databases in the recovery catalog. It does not contain current session information, as does its corresponding V$ view, V$RMAN_STATUS.
RC_UNUSABLE_BACKUPFILE_DETAILS	A list of all backup files of any type that have been marked as UNAVAILABLE or EXPIRED.
RC_RMAN_BACKUP_TYPE	Provides filtering information to OEM during its report building.

Summary

In this chapter, we detailed what a recovery catalog is and how it can help you to manage your backups—and save you during a recovery. We discussed how to build the catalog, how to add managed databases to it, and how to drop it. RMAN provides the option for generating virtual private catalogs to maintain privacy and security. In addition, RMAN offers the capability to merge multiple catalogs as you work to centralize and simplify your ecosystem management. Finally, we provided an overview of the critical recovery catalog views that can be utilized to understand the metadata surrounding your backups and to help guide your backup maintenance and recovery operation planning.

CHAPTER
7

RMAN Backups

This chapter is all about backing up your Oracle database with RMAN. This chapter is largely tactical and not strategic. Therefore, we show you the various options available when using the RMAN **backup** command. We also show you the different types of backups you can perform when using the RMAN **backup** command.

Continuing the chapter preview the next thing we will do is show you how to do backups (and provide best practices revolving around the **backup** command where it makes sense), but we save the more strategic topics for Chapter 15, including where you should put your backups and designing a multitiered backup strategy.

In this chapter we cover the following:

- Using the RMAN **backup** command
- Using the RMAN **set** command
- RMAN **backup** command options
- Configuring RMAN default settings
- Offline backups with RMAN
- Online backups with RMAN
- Incremental backups with RMAN
- Image copies
- Incrementally updated backups
- A review of RMAN backup best practices

That's a lot of material to cover, so let's get to it!

Using the RMAN Backup Command

As you might have guessed, backing up your database with RMAN is the main point of this chapter. The main command we will use to perform a backup in RMAN is called, oddly enough, **backup**. I'll wait a moment while you recover from the shock of this knowledge.

Up to this point, we have gotten the prerequisites to using the **backup** command out of the way. We have discussed channels, what they are, how they work, and how to allocate them manually. We then built on that knowledge by discussing the configuration of persistent configurable default settings in RMAN using the **set** command. Let's look at the backup command in a bit more detail next. Then we will be ready to use it to do some RMAN backups!

The Backup Command

The **backup** command, by default, will back up the entire database into backup sets and backup set pieces, as we discussed in Chapter 3. The **backup** command comes with a number of options we will introduce you to in this chapter. The main options with respect to backups involve the type of backup you will be performing. Here are the types of backups RMAN supports:

- Full offline backups in both NOARCHIVELOG and ARCHIVELOG modes
- Full online backups in ARCHIVELOG mode
- Incremental backups with an option to perform cumulative or differential backup strategies

- Exact mirror (image) copies of the individual database datafiles
- A combination of a mirrored copy, regular application of historical incremental copies, and the generation of new incremental copies

As you can see, the **backup** command offers a deep set of backup-related features. Here is an example of a common use of the **backup** command that backs up the database and its associated archived redo logs:

```
backup database plus archivelogs;
```

If that looks pretty easy to you, that's because it is. Notice that we started with the **backup** command. Then we indicated what we wanted to back up—in this case, the whole database. There are a whole host of other options we will address throughout this chapter, including backup of tablespaces and datafiles. What this does demonstrate is that the process of backing up the database with RMAN is pretty straightforward. All you need to do is configure the specific persistent configuration settings, as discussed in Chapter 5, and then issue the **backup** command with any parameters that might be needed.

The Backup Command, Channels, and Performance

We mentioned RMAN channels in Chapter 5. The use of the **backup** command requires that at least one channel be allocated. As a result, a channel must be configured prior to the backup using the **configure** command, as described in Chapter 5, or a channel must be allocated using the **allocate channel** command, as described in Chapters 3 and 5.

Parallelism is key to performance with the **backup** command. The number of channels that are allocated determine the degree of parallelism (DOP) used when the backup is executed. Allocate too few channels, and the backup will go slower than it needs to. Allocate too many channels, and the backup will bog down as system resources become strained. Finding the proper DOP takes time and patience.

The DOP is determined based on how you configure channels. If you manually allocate channels, then the number of channels manually allocated will be the DOP—configured defaults will not apply or override allocated channels. Lacking manually allocated channels, the configured RMAN defaults for that database will determine the DOP.

If you are running Oracle Real Application Clusters, make sure you read Chapter 18, where we discuss DOP and performance of RMAN backups on a RAC cluster. If you wish to use RMAN for duplication or cloning, including cloning across platforms, make sure you take a look at Chapter 10 for lots of information on those operations.

RMAN Backup Command Options

Now that we have introduced you to the **backup** command, let's look at the number of different options you can use with it. First, the **backup** command is used to create the following types of backups (the associated **backup** command is shown in parentheses):

- Database (**backup database, backup database root, backup pluggable database**)
- Tablespace (**backup tablespace**)
- Datafile (**backup datafile**)

- Archive log (**backup archivelog**)
- Control files (**backup controlfilecopy, backup current controlfile**)
- Backup sets and backup set pieces to other locations (**backup backupset, backup backuppiece**)
- The Fast Recovery Area (**backup recovery area**)
- Recovery files (**backup recovery files**)
- Image copies (**backup copy of database, backup copy of database root, backup copy of datafile**, and so on)
- SPFILE (**backup spfile**)

A number of different options available for use with the **backup** command allow you to do such things as provide a tag to identify the specific backup, define the naming format and location for the individual backup pieces (overriding the defaults or allocated channels), limit the size of backup set pieces, and many other tasks. A number of options are available. In the next sections we look at the most commonly used **backup** command options, including the following:

- Backing up to specific device types
- Controlling the makeup of the backup sets and backup set pieces
- Creating multisection backups
- Compressing RMAN backups
- Tags
- Restore points
- Backup duration and I/O consumption
- Retention policies
- Override exclusion policies
- Skipping offline, inaccessible, or read-only datafiles
- Overriding backup optimization
- Backing up datafiles based on the last time they were backed up, or datafiles that have had unrecoverable operations occur on them
- Checking corruption during an RMAN backup
- Creating more than one copy of your backup
- Including control file backups in backup sets where they don't automatically occur

Typically any setting included in the **backup** command will override any RMAN persistent configuration setting or manually allocated setting.

There are other options related to advanced features such as platform migration that we won't cover now, but have their own chapters dedicated to them. For example, if you are interested in cross-platform migration, see Chapter 21 for information on the options available for this feature.

Backing Up to a Specific Device Type

Perhaps you have configured different default channels, one to disk and one to tape. You can use the **device type** parameter to define which automatic channel device you wish to use when the backup begins. Here is an example:

```
backup database device type disk;
backup database device type sbt;
```

Controlling Attributes of Backup Sets and Backup Set Pieces

You can control a number of attributes related to backup sets and backup set pieces using options available when you issue the **backup** command at the RMAN command line. Here are some of the attributes you can modify (the name of the option is listed in parentheses):

- Backup set size (**maxsetsize**). Limit the size of any backup set.

- Maximum files per backup set (**filesperset**). Limit the total number of backup files per backup set. The default is the number of files to be backed up divided by the number of channels. If the result is less than 64, that becomes the default value for the **filesperset** parameter. Otherwise, the default value is 64.

- Include datafiles from at least *n* disks for each backup set (**diskratio**).

- Name and location of backup set pieces (**format**).

- Ignore backup optimization and force a backup of all files specified in the backup set (**force**).

- Overwrite existing backup set pieces or image copies (**reuse**).

These options will help you deal with the cases where you need to limit or modify the default behaviors of RMAN. It should be fairly rare to need to use these options, however. If you find you are using these settings on a regular basis, be sure to review them and determine whether you really need to be using them still.

Multisection Backups

Backups of databases with a few large datafiles can take longer than they need. By default, each datafile can only be backed up on an individual channel. This is a point of serialization with respect to backups and can have a serious performance impact. Multisection backups are the solution to this problem. Multisection backups provide the ability to take large datafiles and subdivide them into smaller-sized units that RMAN can treat individually for backup and restore purposes. This allows for processing of a large datafile by multiple channels, significantly improving throughput and reducing the execution time of the backup.

NOTE
Multisection backups are probably the single most overlooked performance option available to the DBA when trying to performance-tune a database RMAN backup (perhaps second only to channel parallelization management, but it's close).

Multisection backups are enabled through the use of the **section size** parameter of the **backup** command. This option provides the ability to parallelize the backup of large database datafiles, which can improve the performance of a backup of a database with a few small datafiles and several large ones quite a bit. As the backup progresses, each datafile will be backed up in a chunk that is of the size defined by the **section size** parameter. With the section size designated, these datafile chunks can be backed up individually over different channels, thus parallelizing the backup of a large datafile. This provides the way to parallelize the backups of bigfile tablespaces and use all of the bandwidth at your disposal when backing up normal tablespaces with large database datafiles.

Here is an example of backing up a bigfile tablespace called USER_DATA, chunking the backup into 1GB sections. If the datafile housing the USER_DATA data is 5GB in size, then the result will be five backup set pieces, spread across however many channels are allocated.

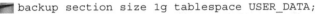
```
backup section size 1g tablespace USER_DATA;
```

RMAN Compression

As you saw in previous examples, you can actually compress backup sets (but not image copies). RMAN offers the following kinds of compression:

- Unused block compression (supported during RMAN backups to disk and using Oracle Secure Backup to tape)
- Null block compression (supported by any RMAN backup type)
- Traditional compression of backup sets

Let's look at each of these types of compression next.

Unused Block Compression

During a backup, RMAN will skip reading any block that is not currently allocated to an object in use by the database. This compression is available regardless of whether or not the space in the datafile was once used. The following conditions must exist in order for RMAN to use this feature:

- The COMPATIBLE parameter must be set greater than or equal to 10.2.
- Guaranteed restore points cannot be configured.
- The datafiles must be locally managed.
- The backup is a full or level 0 incremental backup. Image copies cannot use unused block compression.
- The backup is created to disk, or Oracle Secure Backup is the media management software in use.

Null Block Compression

With this form of compression, Oracle does not back up any blocks in a database datafile that were never used. This kind of compression is always available for RMAN full backups and level 0 incremental backups without restriction. Image copies cannot use null block compression.

RMAN Backup Compression

We provided an example earlier in this chapter of a database backup using RMAN compression. RMAN has the ability to apply compression algorithms to your backup sets. The end result is that backup sets are often much smaller. RMAN compression can significantly reduce the size of backup sets. Compression can be significant; for example, in one of our test databases, we saw a 70 percent difference in the size of the backup set images when using compression. If you don't have the database configured to automatically compress backup sets, you can use the **as compressed backupset** parameter to create the backup set as a compressed backup set. If you have compression configured and you do not wish to use it in a given **backup** command, simply use the **as backupset** parameter (without the **compressed** keyword) of the **backup** command.

RMAN offers several different compression options to choose from:

- None (the default)
- BASIC (the default type of compression, if compression is used)
- LOW
- MEDIUM
- HIGH

You can see all of the available compression methods by querying the Oracle Database view V$RMAN_COMPRESSION_ALGORITHM. This view also includes algorithms that are no longer supported by RMAN.

By default, RMAN does not use compression during backups. If you choose to use compression, then the default type of compression that will be used is BASIC. BASIC compression does quite a good job of compressing a backup. Compression ratios of 50 to 60 percent are not unusual with BASIC compression. The nice thing about BASIC compression is that no additional licensing is required, so you are free to use BASIC compression any time!

The remaining compression methods (LOW, MEDIUM, and HIGH) require that you license the Oracle Advanced Compression option. These levels of compression offer you the ability to control the overall impact of compression on the system. LOW offers some compression with minimal CPU impact, whereas MEDIUM and HIGH offer incrementally better compression with incrementally higher performance impacts.

To use a specific compression algorithm other than the default, you will need to use the **configure** command's **compression algorithm** parameter followed by the type of compression you want to use. Here are the commands you can use to configure the compression algorithm default:

```
Configure compression algorithm 'BASIC';
Configure compression algorithm 'HIGH';
Configure compression algorithm 'MEDIUM';
Configure compression algorithm 'LOW';
Configure compression algorithm clear;
```

Configuring the compression algorithm will not cause backups to use compression by default. To enable compression of backup sets by default, you need to use the RMAN **configure** command to set the default device type, where the backup type is **compressed backupset**, or you can indicate that you want to use compression on the **backup** command line itself.

Here is an example of configuring the default device type to use compression:

```
Configure device type disk backup type to compressed backupset;
```

In this case, each time you issue the RMAN **backup** command, the backup will be compressed automatically using the configured compression algorithm. All backup sets created by that backup will be encrypted. Therefore, if you include the **plus archivelog** command (discussed later in this chapter in more detail), which will create archived redo log backup sets, then those backup sets will also be compressed.

You can reset the default to a noncompressed backupset using the **configure** command, as shown here:

```
Configure device type disk backup type to backupset;
```

You can clear these settings and reenable the defaults using the **configure** command with the **clear** option, as shown here:

```
Configure device type disk clear;
```

You can override the configured defaults for the compression algorithm or if compression is used. To override the default compression algorithm of RMAN for a backup without changing the default, you use the **set** command before executing that backup. In this example, we are modifying the compression algorithm to LOW before we execute our compressed backup. Here we are setting the compression algorithm to LOW:

```
Set compression algorithm 'LOW';
```

This configuration setting will apply to the current RMAN session. It will only apply until we exit our session or if we use the **set** command to change the compression algorithm again.

You can also enable compression from the **backup** command directly (or use a type of compression that is different from the default value you configured). To do so, you simply use the **backup** command with the **as compressed backupset** option.

If you wish to override the default compression algorithm of RMAN for a backup without changing the default, you use the **set** command before executing that backup. In this example, we are modifying the compression algorithm to LOW before we execute our compressed backup:

```
Set compression algorithm 'LOW';
backup as compressed backupset database;
```

Here is an example of enabling compression from the **backup** command. In this example, we are going to back up the database using the default configured compression algorithm:

```
Backup as compressed backupset database;
```

In this next example, we enable compression from the **backup** command using a specific type of compression algorithm. In this case, we are going to back up the database using the LOW compression algorithm:

```
Backup as compressed backupset database;
```

Compression can make a substantial impact on the size of your backups. For example, we backed up a database that had datafiles that totaled 3.1GB in size. (This does not include the size of any database tempfiles, which are not included in an RMAN backup anyway.) We ran a backup without any compression, as well as backups using BASIC and LOW compression. We also ran the backups using only one channel to ensure that we got consistent results.

The uncompressed backup consumed 2.5GB of disk space and took five and a half minutes. Remember that we ran this backup in serial, so we were not looking to optimize the backup time in this example. So, here we see the effects of default compression features such as reduced undo backup, null block compression, and the like.

When we backed up the database using BASIC compression, that backup consumed only 625GB of disk space. The time it took to compress the backup was longer than the uncompressed backup (in this case, 14 minutes). This should not be considered a typical benchmark test with respect to time-based performance, as this was not our goal. Our experience is that run times of compressed and uncompressed backup sets can vary considerably by system, depending on a number of factors. We have often seen compressed backups run much faster than their uncompressed cousins. So, the bottom line is to test compression on your system to figure out what benefit it might give you, and at what cost.

With compression, finding the correct degree of parallelization of the backup is critical. Depending on the device you are writing to, CPU availability, and other factors, it may be that you will see better compressed backup performance by allocating additional channels as opposed to an uncompressed backup. This will distribute the compression process across more CPUs (assuming you have the capacity) and reduce the overall I/O footprint. There is no easy way to determine the correct degree of parallelization, so experimentation will be required.

When we enabled parallelization across three CPUs on our four-CPU system, we found that the compressed backup set time was reduced to eight minutes. The uncompressed backup set time took about five and a half minutes. So, at the cost of two and a half minutes (over the original five-and-a-half-minute backup earlier) we received a savings of roughly 73 percent of the used disk space. This can be a significant savings in environments where disk space is critical.

Other considerations for the use of compression beyond the CPU might include things such as the connection between the database server and the device you are backing up to. For example, an RMAN backup going across a 1Gb Ethernet channel might well be much faster if you enable compression. Enabling compression trades an increase in CPU utilization for a decrease in I/O. This can result in a significant reduction in the throughput required on a network to write the backup set. However, if you are CPU constrained, you might not see any improvement. Again, testing is the key, and finding the right combination of parallelization and compression (or lack thereof) will just take testing time.

RMAN backup to tape devices or other devices that utilize their own compression technologies (or de-duplication) are of special interest. Often we are asked, should we compress the backup with RMAN or allow the device to compress the backup, or both? The answer is, as usual, it depends. We discuss this subject in quite a bit more depth in Chapter 15 when we look at designing an overall backup and recovery architecture.

RMAN Precompression Block Processing

When you execute a compressed backup, by default, Oracle will compress the blocks when they are moved to the output buffer from the input buffer of the channel. This offers a reasonable compression ratio without major CPU impact. If you wish to achieve better compression ratios, but at some cost in CPU, you can enable precompression block processing.

RMAN precompression block processing consolidates all of the free space in a block and optimizes the free space for compression. As you might expect, this consolidation process usually results in more CPU overhead. However, it can also improve the compression ratios of your database backups.

Using precompression block processing has the best effect when you have a database with high DML transaction rates (lots of insert and delete activity in particular). This can often leave blocks in a "Swiss cheese" state, where the block is fragmented with empty space and used space. This kind of database is a perfect candidate for precompression block processing. If your database has low DML **update** or **delete** activity, you will find little benefit from this option because the blocks in databases with little or no **delete** or **update** DML activity tend not to have a great deal of wasted space.

NOTE
*Although Oracle does coalesce fragmented space within a free block, this is done on an irregular basis (during subsequent **insert** and **update** statements that need space available in a block, but the block is fragmented) to reduce the performance impact on the database. As a result, a great deal of block fragmentation may be present in a database, especially when it is heavily used.*

To enable precompression block processing, use the **configure** command along with the compression **algorithm optimize for load false** parameter. Use the parameter **optimize for load true** to disable precompression block processing. Here is an example of enabling precompression block processing:

```
Configure compression algorithm 'BASIC' optimize for load false;
```

Note that you must also indicate the compression algorithm (BASIC in our case) in the same **configure** command that you use to enable precompression block processing.

NOTE
RMAN does not need to back up most of the undo within the database. This is because most undo is not really needed to recover the database. This can reduce the time to complete backups, as well as reduce the overall size of a database backup!

Tags

Each backup (except control file autobackups) in Oracle is assigned either a default tag or a user-defined tag. A tag is a name of no more than 30 characters that is associated with a specific backup and can be referenced during restore operations to indicate a specific backup to be used.

Tags are not required to be unique, so you can reuse the same tag for similar types of backups—say, for example, a "DAILY_LEVEL_1" tag. Tags are stored in all uppercase, regardless of the case used when the tag was defined. When the same tag is used for multiple RMAN backup operations, RMAN will restore the most current version of that tagged backup, subject to any other constraints issued within the **restore** command (see Chapter 8 for more on the RMAN **restore** and **recover** commands).

Tags can be used with RMAN full backups, tablespace backups, datafile backups, incremental backups, and even backup copies (all of which will be discussed in this chapter). Here is an example of assigning a tag to a full backup:

```
backup database tag='test backup';
```

In this example, we used the **tag** parameter to identify this backup. Each tag should be unique, and RMAN will allocate a tag to each backup set by using a default naming convention if one is not assigned. The same tag can be applied to multiple backups, and the latest backup will be restored by default.

We strongly support the use of tags to identify specific RMAN backup operations. For example, FULL_INCREMENTAL and INCREMENTAL_CUM tags might be used for your incremental backups and ARCHIVELOG_BACKUP_HOURLY might be used for automated hourly archive log backups.

Restore Points

Whereas a tag is associated with a specific backup, a restore point is associated with a specific point in time. You can create a restore point from the RMAN prompt easily using the SQL **create restore point** command, as shown here (you will need to use the SQL command if you are trying to execute this in RMAN versions prior to Oracle Database 12c):

```
RMAN>Create restore point Charlie_one;
```

You can also create a restore point from the SQL*Plus point with the **create restore point** command, as shown in this example:

```
SQL>Create restore point Charlie_one;
```

Normal restore points are subject to being removed after a period of time. The primary constraint is the availability of undo, which Oracle will try to retain for a period of time, as designated by the parameter DB_FLASHBACK_RETENTION_TARGET. However, this retention period is not guaranteed, and it's possible that you will lose the undo required to perform the flashback operation.

If you need to ensure that you can effectively use a restore point at all times, you can create a guaranteed restore point as shown here:

```
RMAN>Create restore point Charlie_one guarantee flashback database;
```

In this case, Oracle will preserve the information needed to flash back the database to the restore point identified by the name Charlie_one. Guaranteed restore points require that the FRA be configured, and they can consume a lot of space in the FRA. Also, guaranteed restore points only guarantee that the entire database can be restored to the point in time defined by the guaranteed restore point. This same guarantee does not apply to the flashback of tables or other kinds of flashback operations.

If you create backups using the **keep** option, you can also create a normal restore point during that backup. See the section on the **keep** option later in this chapter for more information on creating restore points when using the **keep** option. This restore point will be maintained for the life of the backup.

Restore points can be referenced during RMAN restores in lieu of other point-in-time restore methods (such as time-based restores). We will discuss using restore points for recovery in more detail in Chapter 16.

The duration Command: Putting Limits on Backups

To assist you in reducing the overall I/O impact of an RMAN backup on other processes, RMAN offers the **duration** parameter of the **backup** command. The **duration** parameter is like an alarm clock; if the backup runs longer than the duration specified, RMAN will cancel the backup. Here is an example of using the **backup duration** command:

```
backup duration 00:30 database;
```

When using the **duration** parameter, you can indicate how RMAN should treat backups that fail the **backup duration** time restriction. When you use the **partial** parameter, if the backup is terminated because it has exceeded the **duration** parameter, RMAN will not treat it as a failed backup. Thus, remaining commands in any **run** block will continue to be executed. This is handy if you have subsequent **backup** commands such as archived redo log backups. Regardless of the setting of **partial**, Oracle will consider any backup set that has been completed successfully to be usable even if the entire backup process did not complete.

One thing that makes the **duration** parameter a bit less usable is that you cannot use the **backup database plus archivelog** command. However, you can separate the two backups and use the **duration** parameter for each, as shown here:

```
backup duration 00:30 partial database;
backup duration 00:30 partial archivelog all delete input;
```

The **duration** parameter also helps you to throttle your backups. When defining a duration, you can indicate that RMAN should try to minimize either of the following:

- The time that the backup takes to run
- The I/O load that the backup consumes

If you try to minimize the time the backup runs, RMAN will back up at full speed. This is the default setting. Another feature when you use the default **minimize time** parameter is that RMAN will prioritize the datafiles that are backed up. Those that were backed up recently will have a lower priority than those that have not been backed up recently.

You can also tell RMAN to try to spread out the backup I/O over the duration window that you have established, thus eliminating the overall impact that the backup has on the system:

```
backup duration 00:30 minimize time database;
backup duration 00:30 minimize load database;
```

Archival Backups

The **keep** parameter of the RMAN **backup** command is used to override default retention criteria. When a backup is created with the **keep** option, the backup is called an archival backup. This archival backup is a completely self-contained backup (meaning it includes the archived redo logs needed to perform a consistent recovery).

NOTE
*How backups using the **keep** parameter worked in earlier versions of RMAN is different than described here. Please reference the Oracle RMAN Backup and Recovery Reference for your version of RMAN and the Oracle Database to make sure you properly understand how the **keep** parameter works in your version of the database.*

You cannot store archival backups in the FRA. Any attempt to do so will cause an error to occur during the backup.

You can use the keep parameter when performing incremental backups. In such cases the full backup needs to use the **keep** parameter and must have a tag. The subsequent incremental backups must also use the **keep** parameter and must have the same tag as the parent backup. These backups would be considered completely different from incremental backups that do not use the **keep** parameter, such as your normal daily backups.

The **keep** parameter has the following options:

- **forever** Indicates that the archival backup should be maintained until it is manually removed. Using the **keep forever** option requires the use of a recovery catalog since control file records can be aged out. Here is an example of the use of the **keep forever** parameter during a backup:

```
backup database keep forever;
```

- **until time string** This option defines an alternative retention criterion for the backup. Note that if the time exceeds 365 days, it is possible that the records will be aged out of the control file. Regardless, RMAN does not require that you use a recovery catalog as it does when you use the **keep forever** parameter.

```
backup database format 'c:\oracle\backup\%U' keep until time='sysdate+180' tag
Keep_backup;
```

The use of the tag in this case is to be able to easily identify the backup for restore purposes. We can also associate a restore point with a given archival backup, as shown here:

```
backup database format 'c:\oracle\backup\%U'
keep until time='sysdate+180'
restore point gold_copy;
```

If you want information on your archival backup, you can use the **list backup of database** command to provide this information. We discuss the **list** command in more detail in Chapter 12, but here is an example of the output you might expect to see. Note in the output that there is a line that says "Keep: LOGS," followed by "Until" and a date. This indicates that this backup is an archival backup and that it will be kept up to the date listed in the Until section of the report.

```
BP Key: 36    Status: AVAILABLE  Compressed: NO  Tag: KEEP_FULL
        Piece Name: C:\ORACLE\BACKUP\1FKJVSSA_1_1
Keep: LOGS                  Until: 08-JAN-14
  List of Datafiles in backup set 36
  File LV Type Ckp SCN    Ckp Time   Name
  ---- -- ---- ---------- --------- ----
   1      Full 4358741    12-JUL-14
C:\ORACLE\ORADATA\MY\SYSTEM01.DBF
   2      Full 4358741    12-JUL-14
C:\ORACLE\ORADATA\MY\SYSAUX01.DBF
   3      Full 4358741    12-JUL-14 C:\ORACLE\ORADATA\MY\UNDOTBS01.DBF
   4      Full 4358741    12-JUL-14
C:\ORACLE\ORADATA\MY\USERS01.DBF
   5      Full 4358741    12-JUL-14 C:\ORACLE\ORADATA\MY\EXAMPLE01.DBF
   6      Full 4358741    12-JUL-14 C:\ORACLE\ORADATA\MY\UNDO_NEW_01.DBF
   7      Full 4358741    12-JUL-14
```

```
C:\ORACLE\ORADATA\MY\SMALL01.DBF
   8       Full 4358741     12-JUL-14
C:\ORACLE\ORADATA\MY\SMALLTWO.DBF
   9       Full 4358741     12-JUL-14 C:\ORACLE\ORADATA\MY\SMALL_THREE01.DBF
```

Also, you can query the V$BACKUP_SET and V$BACKUP_PIECE views, as shown in the sample query that follows. You can also substitute the RC* views to retrieve this same information from the recovery catalog schema.

```
select a.set_stamp, a.set_count, a.backup_type, a.pieces, b.piece#, a.keep_until,
a.keep_options
from v$backup_set a, v$backup_piece b
where a.set_stamp=b.set_stamp
and a.set_count=b.set_count
and a.keep='YES';
SET_STAMP   SET_COUNT B    PIECES      PIECE# KEEP_UNTIL              KEEP_OPTION
---------- ---------- -  ---------- ---------- -------------------- -----------
 691981428         26 D           1          1 01/08/2014 01:03:48 BACKUP_LOGS
 691982114         27 D           1          1 01/08/2014 01:15:13 BACKUP_LOGS
 691982117         28 L           1          1 01/08/2014 01:15:17 BACKUP_LOGS
 691982121         29 D           1          1 01/08/2014 01:15:20 BACKUP_LOGS
 691982247         30 D           1          1 01/08/2014 01:17:26 BACKUP_LOGS
 691983183         31 D           1          1 01/08/2014 01:33:02 BACKUP_LOGS
 691983206         32 L           1          1 01/08/2014 01:33:25 BACKUP_LOGS
 691983252         33 D           1          1 01/08/2014 01:34:11 BACKUP_LOGS
 692023212         36 D           1          1 10/20/2009 12:40:12 LOGS
 692024018         37 D           1          1 10/20/2009 12:40:12 LOGS
 692056970         47 D           1          1 01/08/2014 22:02:50 LOGS
 692057685         48 D           1          1 01/08/2014 22:02:50 LOGS
```

Overriding the Configure Exclude Command

You can configure RMAN to exclude from your backups any datafiles that have not changed since the last backup by issuing the **configure exclude** command (discussed in Chapter 5). If you want to ensure that RMAN backs up these datafiles, you can include the **noexclude** parameter in the **backup** command. In this example, we are creating an archive backup using the **keep** parameter. It makes since that we would want to back up all of the excluded datafiles in that backup, which we do in this example:

```
backup database noexclude keep forever tag='test_backup';
```

Skipping Offline, Inaccessible, or Read-Only Datafiles

Sometimes, you will have a datafile in your database that has a status other than ONLINE. In the case of read-only datafiles, you may not want to back them up every time you do a backup of the database. In the case of offline or inaccessible datafiles, RMAN backups will fail if you don't do something to indicate to RMAN to skip the missing datafiles. This is what the **skip** parameter is used for. You can skip offline, read-only, or inaccessible datafiles (or all three) as required. Here are some examples of how to do this:

```
backup database skip readonly;
backup database skip offline;
backup database skip inaccessible;
backup database skip readonly skip offline skip inaccessible;
```

The **inaccessible** parameter causes Oracle to skip files that cannot be read at all. These files are not physically on the disk (for example, if the datafiles have been deleted from the disk or moved to another location). Datafiles that are offline but physically still in place are skipped using the **offline** parameter. Finally, the **skip readonly** parameter is used to cause Oracle to skip backing up a read-only datafile. Of course, you can use the **configure** command to enable backup optimization, indicating that Oracle should not back up read-only tablespaces at all, which leads us to our next section.

Override Backup Optimization

In the preceding section, we showed you how to cause a backup to skip read-only datafiles, but this can be a bit tedious. Oracle offers backup optimization to make life a bit easier. We talked about backup optimization in Chapter 3 in association with the **configure** command. Backup optimization causes RMAN to not back up unchanged tablespaces (for example, read-only tablespaces) by default. If you want a specific backup to be forced to ignore that configuration setting, you can use the **force** parameter to ensure that all datafiles are backed up. Here is an example:

```
backup database force;
```

Backing Up Datafiles Based on Their Last Backup Time

Oracle allows you to indicate in your backup process if you prefer to only back up database datafiles that have not been backed up since a given time. This is handy if you have added new datafiles (as we discuss first in this section), or if you only want to back up datafiles that have changed in a given number of days. Let's look at each of these choices in a bit more detail.

Backing Up Only Newly Added Datafiles

Here is a neat option you can use. Suppose you have just added four or five new datafiles to the database, and you want to back them up without having to back up the entire database. You could just back up the individual datafiles (as we will show you later in this chapter), but there is an easier way. You can use the **not backed up** option of the **backup** command, and RMAN will only back up datafiles that have not been backed up. Here is an example:

```
backup database not backed up;
```

Backing Up Files Not Backed Up in a Specific Time Period

Perhaps you have a backup strategy in which you back up only specific datafiles on specific nights. The **since time** option is also really handy if you need to restart a failed backup. If the backup fails, you can use this option, after you have corrected the cause of the failure, to restart the backup. For example, let's assume that your tape system died two days ago in the middle of a backup. You finally got the tape system fixed, so how would you restart the backup? Simply issue this command:

```
backup database not backed up since time='sysdate - 2';
```

In this case, RMAN only backs up those datafiles that have not been backed up within the last two days. Note that you can express the time in the database NLS_DATE format, or you can use a SQL date expression such as the one in our example. An additional parameter to the **since time** option applies to archive log backups to ensure that each archive log is backed up a certain number of times before it is removed. We cover that option later in this chapter.

Some backup strategies include backing up the archived redo logs once, every so often on a regular basis, and then later during the nightly backup. In some cases, configured retention policies can manage the strategy you wish to use, especially if you are creating archived redo logs in the FRA.

Sometimes the configured retention defaults don't always provide the exact flexibility you need, or if you are backing up archived redo logs in a non-FRA, those retention criteria won't be applied at all. In these cases, we need to perform backups in such a way that we manage the preservation of archived redo logs and remove them at the appropriate time.

You can manage the removal of source archived redo logs after they are backed up by using a number of options to the **backup archivelog** command. For example, we may want to make sure that all archived redo logs are backed up twice and then deleted. The command to perform this operation would be as follows:

```
-- This command backs up archived redo logs not already backed up.
Backup archivelog all not backed up 2 times delete input;
```

In this case, this command will back up all archived redo logs that have not been backed up at least two times. The **delete input** parameter will cause all of the archived redo logs that have been backed up at least twice (including this backup) to be deleted:

```
backup as compressed backupset database plus archivelog
not backed up 2 times delete input;
```

Checking for Logical Corruption during a Backup

By default, RMAN checks for physical corruption of database blocks. If any corruption is discovered, the backup will fail. If you want even more error checking, you can configure a backup to check for logical corruption by using the **check logical** option of the **backup** command. Here are a couple of examples of the use of this option:

```
backup check logical database;
backup validate check logical database;
```

NOTE
If you are using Oracle Active Data Guard, did you know that it offers the ability to automatically repair corrupt blocks on the primary database, in the background, without an outage? See Chapter 17 for more information on this feature!

The first example physically backs up the database as it is checking for logical corruption. The second example just validates the database blocks performing a logical database verification without performing an actual physical backup of the database. If you want the backup to continue through a given number of errors, you need to set the **maxcorrupt** parameter first. Interestingly, the **set maxcorrupt** command is one of the few RMAN commands left that still requires using a **run** block, as shown in this example:

```
run {
set maxcorrupt for datafile 1,2,3,4,5,6,7 to 10;
backup validate check logical database;
}
```

NOTE
*Even though some of the text generated during an RMAN **validate** run
will make it look like a backup set is being created, this is not the case.
No RMAN backup file pieces will be generated during the **validate** run.*

Making Copies of Backups on Your RMAN Copier

Perhaps you wish to create multiple copies of the backup pieces of a backup set. Although this
can be configured by default, you can also use the **copies** parameter to configure a specific
backup to create multiple copies of the backup pieces. (You could also use the **set backup copies**
parameter.) Here is an example of this option in use:

```
backup database copies=2;
```

Capturing the Elusive Control File

We have already discussed control file autobackups in Chapter 5. Other methods of backing up
the control file with RMAN include the following:

- Using the **include current controlfile** option during a backup. This creates a snapshot
  of the current control file and places it into each backup set produced by the **backup**
  command. Here is an example of the use of this command:

  ```
  backup database device type disk include current controlfile;
  ```

  If you do a backup of datafile 1, the control file will get backed up anyway. So this
  parameter comes in much more handy if you are doing tablespace or datafile backups.
  Furthermore, if automated backup of control files is configured, this command can
  cause the current control file to be stored in the backup set also (so you have two copies
  of the control file, even though they might be slightly different if you are running in
  ARCHIVELOG mode).

- Issuing the **backup as copy current controlfile** will create a backup of the current
  control file.

Using the RMAN Set Command

Now that we have discussed the RMAN **backup** command, we should take a quick detour and
look at the RMAN **set** command. The **set** command is used to define settings that apply only to
the current RMAN session. In other words, the **set** command is a lot like the **configure** command
(refer to Chapter 3), but the settings are not persistent. You can use the **set** command in one of
two ways, depending on the **set** command you need to use. You can use it outside a **run** block for
these operations:

- To display RMAN commands in the message log, use the **set echo** command.
- To specify a database's database identifier (DBID), use the **set dbid** command.

Certain **set** commands can only be used within the confines of a **run** block. The most
common are the following:

- The **set newname** command is useful if you are performing tablespace point-in-time
  recovery (TSPITR) or database duplication. The **set newname** command allows you
  to specify new database datafile names. This is useful if you are moving the database

to a new system and the file system names are different. You need to use the **switch** command in combination with the **set newname** command. You will see examples of this in later chapters.

■ Using the **set maxcorrupt for datafile** command enables you to define the maximum number of data block corruptions allowed on a given datafile before the RMAN operation will fail. This setting applies to a specific datafile setting. All corrupted blocks will be transferred to the V$DATABASE_BLOCK_CORRUPTION view.

■ Using the **set archivelog destination** command allows you to modify the archive_log_dest_1 destination for archived redo logs. This is most useful during restore operation because it allows you to not overwrite any existing files in the FRA.

■ Using **set** with the **until** clause enables you to define a specific point in time, an SCN, or a log sequence number to be used during database point-in-time recovery.

■ Using the **set backup copies** command enables you to define how many copies of the backup files should be created for each backup piece in the backup set.

■ Using the **set command id** setting enables you to associate a given server session to a given channel.

■ Using the **set controlfile autobackup format for device type** command enables you to modify the default format for control file autobackups.

■ The **set incarnation** command is used to reset the database incarnation. We cover this particular setting in more detail in Chapter 9.

When doing backups, you may well need to use some of these commands. For example, if you want to perform a backup that creates two copies of each backup piece that is created and you want to allow for ten corruptions in datafile 3, you would craft a backup script that looks like this:

```
run
{
set maxcorrupt for datafile 3 to 10;
set backup copies = 2;
backup database;
}
```

Offline RMAN Database Backups

The first kind of RMAN backup we want to discuss is called an offline (or cold) backup. An offline backup simply means that the database is mounted and not open when the backup occurs. In this chapter we discuss performing offline database backups with RMAN where you have configured default settings (as discussed in Chapter 5). Then, we discuss offline backups where you need to define settings that are different from the configured default settings (or you have not configured default settings).

Offline Backups Using Configured Settings

In this section we discuss offline backups of databases where you have already configured default settings via the RMAN **configure** command. We consider configuring database default settings via the RMAN **configure** command to be a best practice, but there will be cases when you will want to use something other than the configured defaults. If you are feeling a bit unsure about the **configure** command, go have a peek at Chapter 5, where we discuss it quite a bit. It's important (in fact, we consider it a best practice), so go ahead and we will wait for you to read the chapter and then come back and join us—for everyone else, go grab a doughnut.

Now that you understand the **configure** command and have configured the default settings as appropriate, we are ready to perform the first backup in this chapter—the offline backup using configured RMAN settings.

Keep in mind that we are discussing offline backups. Specifically, this means that the database is not running when the backups are being done. Offline backups are independent of the logging mode of the database. However, keep in mind that what you can restore (and, more particularly, where you can restore to) is not independent of the logging mode. Knowing this might inform your backup strategy.

In this section we first consider backing up a nonmultitenant database and an Oracle Multitenant database at the CDB level. This is because both methods of backing up an Oracle database at that level are the same. Then we look at offline backups of PDBs within an Oracle Multitenant database.

Complete Offline Backups of Multitenant and Nonmultitenant Databases

Offline backups in Oracle Database 12c may come in two forms. One form is a backup of the entire database. The other form can occur when you are using Multitenant Oracle, and this would be to back up a PDB offline. We will show you examples of each of these in a moment, but we want to strongly suggest to you that the best practice is to put your database in ARCHIVELOG mode and do online backups. This is less disruptive, and it allows you to standardize on one backup process. Some DBAs feel like putting development or test databases in ARCHIVELOG mode is a waste of disk space because they will be generating archived redo logs. The truth is that if your space availability is so low that you can't store a few archived redo logs, you have a much bigger problem than running in ARCHIVELOG mode and generating those logs.

Offline Backups of Nonmultitenant Databases or CDBs in NOARCHIVELOG Mode   The process of performing an offline backup of a database that is not a multitenant database and the one for performing a backup of a multitenant database that includes all PDBs of the multitenant database are exactly the same.

To start the backup, sign into RMAN (in the example we provide for this backup, we are not using a recovery catalog). Next, use the RMAN commands **shutdown** and **startup mount** to mount the database, which is the condition that the database must be in to perform an offline backup. You should not use the **shutdown abort** command to shut down the database at this time. This is because RMAN will detect that the database was shut down in an inconsistent manner and refuse to back up the database (it is pretty particular about things). You can use the **shutdown immediate** and **shutdown transactional** RMAN commands because these will provide for consistent shutdowns of the database. You can also issue these commands from SQL*Plus, if you prefer, and then return to RMAN.

Once the database has been successfully mounted, simply issue a **backup database** command, and the backup will occur. Here is an example of the commands you would issue to perform an offline backup via RMAN:

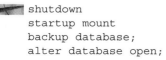

```
shutdown
startup mount
backup database;
alter database open;
```

If you prefer, you could do this as a compressed backup set:

```
shutdown
startup mount
backup as compressed backupset database;
alter database open;
```

Offline Backups of Nonmultitenant Databases or CDBs in ARCHIVELOG Mode   Now, sometimes there is confusion about offline backups and when the database is in ARCHIVELOG mode. If you perform an RMAN offline backup when the database is in ARCHIVELOG mode, should you back up the archived redo logs? Our answer is, "Yes, of course." While the database itself will be consistent during the backup, and no redo logs would be required to recover it, the presence of the redo logs will provide the ability to restore the database to some previous point in time (assuming you have a previous backup that would support the restore). So, if your database is in ARCHIVELOG mode, the **backup** command would look like this:

```
shutdown
startup mount
backup as compressed backupset database plus archivelog
delete input;
alter database open;
```

We have added a couple of things to this command. First, notice the **as compressed backup set** clause. This enables compression on the backup. We discuss compression later in this chapter as well as in other chapters, but we thought we would give you a preview of how to use it. Note that you can use the default compression, as we are here, without needing any special license. Oracle offers other compression options for RMAN, and for the database, that require a separate license called Advanced Compression be purchased.

In this case, we are also using the command **plus archivelog delete input** in this example. This backs up all the archived redo logs produced before the database was shut down and then deletes them after they have been backed up. So you will see an archive log backup before the database backup begins. Because the database is down, there is no log switch that occurs at the end of the backup (and indeed, none is needed). As a result, no archivelog backup is needed at the end of the backup (you will see this is different with online backups later in this chapter).

As you will see later, this is the same way you do online backups. Frankly, doing an offline backup when your database is in ARCHIVELOG mode does seem a bit silly.

Offline Backups of Specific PDBs within an Oracle Multitenant Database
Backing up specific PDBs requires that the database be in ARCHIVELOG mode. If the database is in NOARCHIVELOG mode, individual backups of PDBs are not supported by RMAN. When a database is in ARCHIVELOG mode, RMAN will permit you to perform offline backups of individual PDBs.

The only way to perform a truly offline backup of a PDB is to use the **startup mount** command to mount the CDB. You can then use the **backup pluggable database** command to back up specific PDBs. Here is an example of performing this kind of operation:

```
Rman target=/
Startup force mount;
backup pluggable database mypdb plus archivelog delete input;
alter database open;
```

In this case, we use the **backup** command to back up the mypdb pluggable database. We also use the **plus archivelog delete input** command to back up and delete the archived redo logs. This will cause all the archived redo logs for the entire CDB to be backed up. Keep in mind that although the PDBs are separate logical entities in their own right, they share the redo stream with the entire CDB database. As a result, we need to back up the archived redo logs so that the PDB we are backing up (and indeed, the entire CDB) can be restored.

The truth of the matter is that because backing up an individual PDB requires the database to be in ARCHIVELOG mode, it does not make much sense to do these kinds of backups. In cases where the database is in ARCHIVELOG mode, the best practice is to perform online backups and not offline backups.

One final point: you might ask if you can connect to an open CDB that is in NOARCHIVELOG mode and back up a PDB that is not open. The answer is no, and in fact Oracle will not let you do such a thing. If you try, you will get this error message:

```
RMAN-00571: ===========================================================
RMAN-00569: =============== ERROR MESSAGE STACK FOLLOWS ===============
RMAN-00571: ===========================================================
RMAN-03002: failure of backup command at 10/21/2014 20:33:16
RMAN-06817: Pluggable Database MYPDB cannot be backed up in NOARCHIVELOG mode.
```

RMAN Workshop: *Perform an Offline Backup*

Workshop Notes

This workshop assumes the following:

- That the database is in NOARCHIVELOG mode.
- That the database has been configured with automatic channels, as shown in Chapter 5.
- You have configured a database account called backup_admin for backups (as described in Chapter 5).
- You are backing up to a disk device.
- That the database is an Oracle Database 12c multitenant database that has one PDB in it called MYPDB.

Note that this workshop will work just fine if you run it on a database that is a nonmultitenant database. The only difference is that the output will be slightly different, in that it will not contain any PDB backup output. You would also log into a CDB using a common user account (c## account).

Let's do this workshop then.

Step 1. Set your environment and start RMAN:

```
C:\>set ORACLE_SID=mycdb
C:\>rman target=backup_admin/robert
```

Step 2. Shut down the database with the **shutdown immediate** command:

```
RMAN> shutdown immediate
```

Step 3. Mount the database with the **startup mount** command:

```
RMAN> startup mount
```

Step 4. Back up the database with the **backup database** command. In this case, to save disk space, we will compress our backup set (because we have not configured compression as a default setting):

```
RMAN> backup as compressed backupset database;
```

Step 5. Use the **alter database open** command to open the database:

```
RMAN> alter database open;
```

Here is an example of a complete offline RMAN backup following these steps:

```
C:\>rman target=backup_admin/Robert
Recovery Manager: Release 12.1.0.2.0 - Production on Thu Oct 23 15:45:29 2014
Copyright (c) 1982, 2013, Oracle and/or its affiliates.
All rights reserved.
connected to target database (not started)
RMAN> shutdown
using target database control file instead of recovery catalog
database closed
database dismounted
Oracle instance shut down
RMAN> startup mount
connected to target database (not started)
Oracle instance started
database mounted
Total System Global Area      272629760 bytes
Fixed Size                      1248504 bytes
Variable Size                  83886856 bytes
Database Buffers              184549376 bytes
Redo Buffers                    2945024 bytes
RMAN> backup as compressed backupset database;
Starting backup at 23-OCT-14
allocated channel: ORA_DISK_1
channel ORA_DISK_1: SID=5 device type=DISK
channel ORA_DISK_1: starting compressed full datafile backup set
channel ORA_DISK_1: specifying datafile(s) in backup set
input datafile file number=00001
name=C:\APP\ORACLE\ORADATA\MYCDB\DATAFILE\O1_MF_SYSTEM_
B4GG5PTF_.DBF
input datafile file number=00003
name=C:\APP\ORACLE\ORADATA\MYCDB\DATAFILE\O1_MF_SYSAUX_
B4GG2F4H_.DBF
input datafile file number=00005 |
name=C:\APP\ORACLE\ORADATA\MYCDB\DATAFILE\O1_MF_UNDOTBS1_
B4GG9TBL_.DBF
input datafile file number=00006
```

```
name=C:\APP\ORACLE\ORADATA\MYCDB\DATAFILE\O1_MF_USERS_
B4GG9PGZ_.DBF
channel ORA_DISK_1: starting piece 1 at 23-OCT-14
channel ORA_DISK_1: finished piece 1 at 23-OCT-14
piece handle=C:\APP\ORACLE\FAST_RECOVERY_AREA\MYCDB\BACKUPSET
\2014_10_23\
O1_MF_NNNDF_TAG20141023T154746_B4M1DM1F_.BKP
tag=TAG20141023T154746 comment=NONE
channel ORA_DISK_1: backup set complete, elapsed time: 00:01:16
channel ORA_DISK_1: starting compressed full datafile backup set
channel ORA_DISK_1: specifying datafile(s) in backup set
input datafile file number=00008
name=C:\APP\ORACLE\ORADATA\MYCDB\
E57174E6384646F1BAECA9C7CE13D85E\DATAFILE\
O1_MF_SYSAUX_B4GJ1YVW_.DBF
input datafile file number=00007
name=C:\APP\ORACLE\ORADATA\MYCDB
\E57174E6384646F1BAECA9C7CE13D85E\DATAFILE\
O1_MF_SYSTEM_B4GJ1YVT_.DBF
input datafile file number=00009
name=C:\APP\ORACLE\ORADATA\MYCDB\
E57174E6384646F1BAECA9C7CE13D85E\DATAFILE\
O1_MF_USERS_B4GJ42C3_.DBF
channel ORA_DISK_1: starting piece 1 at 23-OCT-14
channel ORA_DISK_1: finished piece 1 at 23-OCT-14
piece handle=C:\APP\ORACLE\FAST_RECOVERY_AREA\MYCDB\
E57174E6384646F1BAECA9C7CE13D85E\BACKUPSET\2014_10_23\
O1_MF_NNNDF_TAG20141023T154746_B4M1GYP4_.BKP
tag=TAG20141023T154746 comment=NONE
channel ORA_DISK_1: backup set complete, elapsed time: 00:00:45
channel ORA_DISK_1: starting compressed full datafile backup set
channel ORA_DISK_1: specifying datafile(s) in backup set
input datafile file number=00004 name=C:\APP\ORACLE\ORADATA\MYCDB\DATAFILE\
O1_MF_SYSAUX_B4GGMQC0_.DBF
input datafile file number=00002 name=C:\APP\ORACLE\ORADATA\MYCDB\DATAFILE\
O1_MF_SYSTEM_B4GGMQJZ_.DBF
channel ORA_DISK_1: starting piece 1 at 23-OCT-14
channel ORA_DISK_1: finished piece 1 at 23-OCT-14
piece handle=C:\APP\ORACLE\FAST_RECOVERY_AREA\MYCDB\
A1B392142CBC43A1939B97E6E087A74C\BACKUPSET\2014_10_23\
O1_MF_NNNDF_TAG20141023T154746_B4M1JD3P_.BKP
tag=TAG20141023T154746 comment=NONE
channel ORA_DISK_1: backup set complete, elapsed time: 00:00:45
Finished backup at 23-OCT-14
Starting Control File and SPFILE Autobackup at 23-OCT-14
piece handle=C:\APP\ORACLE\FAST_RECOVERY_AREA\MYCDB\AUTOBACKUP\
2014_10_23\O1_MF_S_861723875_B4M1KV64_.BKP comment=NONE
Finished Control File and SPFILE Autobackup at 23-OCT-14
RMAN> alter database open;
```

Breaking Down the Workshop Output

A lot of output is created when an RMAN backup is executed. The previous workshop pretty well demonstrated that, didn't it? In the workshop we had configured some default settings, which reduced the number of commands we needed to use significantly. If you need to review the configuration of default RMAN settings, you will want to review Chapter 5.

We logged into the database using RMAN and issued all the commands from the RMAN prompt. We really didn't have to do a lot of work. We issued the **shutdown** and **startup mount** commands to shut down and then restart the database. Next, we then issued the **backup as compressed backupset database** command and sat back to watch our backup take off. Pretty easy, huh? RMAN has backed up our database datafiles, our control file, and our SPFILE (assuming we have configured it to do so). Once it's done, all we have to do is issue the **alter database open** command to open the database, and our backup is complete.

In the workshop, the CDB we backed up has a PDB in it called MYPDB. In our case, we have the PDB configured to auto-open when the CDB starts. If we did not have the PDB configured to open automatically, we would need to open the PDB with the **alter pluggable database** command, as shown here:

```
Alter pluggable database mypdb open;
```

What we want to do now is to look at the output in a bit more detail. This is important because we want to be able to interpret what RMAN is telling us during the backup process. The ability to interpret the RMAN output is critical to successful troubleshooting if you are having RMAN issues during backups or restores. In the following sections we will discuss the output from top to bottom, in this order:

- Backup of the CDB root container or non-CDB database
- Backup of the PDB
- Backup of the seed container
- Controlfile automatic backup

Note that if you are backing up a non-CDB database, the middle two components—backup of the seed container and backup of the PDB—will not occur because they only exist in a multitenant environment.

Also, the backup we did in the exercise and are discussing in this section was limited to a single channel. If we parallelized the backup, it would still back up the datafiles in this order, but it would take full advantage of running in parallel. Thus, the backup of the PDBs will not be restricted to waiting until the backup of the CDB is complete. We just ran this exercise in serial mode so we could break down the individual components and talk about them in a bit more depth.

Let's look at the output for each of these parts of the backup in more detail. Also, let's address how we might have connected to and used the recovery catalog during this backup in a bit more detail.

NOTE
You might have noticed that we switch back and forth between the use of the terms container *and* PDB. *Technically, all PDBs are considered containers, including the seed container/PDB. The root*

*of the CDB is also a container, but it's not a PDB. We tend to revolve
around the use of both of those words often. Usually people call them
PDBs, but use of the word* container *is perfectly acceptable. Referring
to the root container as a PDB would not be correct, however.*

Backup of the CDB Root Container or Non-CDB Database

In the workshop, the first thing RMAN does is back up the datafiles related to the root component
of the CDB. If the database were a nonmultitenant database, this would have been a backup of
the entire database. Both are, for all practical purposes, the same.

This is a backup of what is called the root container in a multitenant database. Recall that in
the multitenant architecture, the root container is the central storage for all metadata related to
the entire CDB. With a non-CDB, the whole database would be backed up. Let's look at the
RMAN output specific to this part of the backup:

```
RMAN> backup as compressed backupset database;
Starting backup at 23-OCT-14
allocated channel: ORA_DISK_1
channel ORA_DISK_1: SID=5 device type=DISK
channel ORA_DISK_1: starting compressed full datafile backup set
channel ORA_DISK_1: specifying datafile(s) in backup set
input datafile file number=00001
name=C:\APP\ORACLE\ORADATA\MYCDB\DATAFILE\O1_MF_SYSTEM_B4GG5PTF_.DBF
input datafile file number=00003
name=C:\APP\ORACLE\ORADATA\MYCDB\DATAFILE\O1_MF_SYSAUX_B4GG2F4H_.DBF
input datafile file number=00005 |
name=C:\APP\ORACLE\ORADATA\MYCDB\DATAFILE\O1_MF_UNDOTBS1_B4GG9TBL_.DBF
input datafile file number=00006
name=C:\APP\ORACLE\ORADATA\MYCDB\DATAFILE\O1_MF_USERS_B4GG9PGZ_.DBF
channel ORA_DISK_1: starting piece 1 at 23-OCT-14
channel ORA_DISK_1: finished piece 1 at 23-OCT-14
piece handle=C:\APP\ORACLE\FAST_RECOVERY_AREA\MYCDB\BACKUPSET\2014_10_23\
O1_MF_NNNDF_TAG20141023T154746_B4M1DM1F_.BKP tag=TAG20141023T154746
comment=NONE
channel ORA_DISK_1: backup set complete, elapsed time: 00:01:16
```

Let's break this output down a bit. First, there is this part of the output:

```
Starting backup at 23-OCT-14
allocated channel: ORA_DISK_1
channel ORA_DISK_1: SID=5 device type=DISK
channel ORA_DISK_1: starting compressed full datafile backup set
```

Here, we see a line that indicates that the backup is starting. We see the allocation of
a single channel. The configuration of that channel was done with the **configure** command,
as demonstrated in Chapter 5 of this book. We then see that the channel is allocated to disk.

Notice the SID=5 part of the output. That is the Oracle Database session identifier (SID) that
channel ORA_DISK_1 is associated with. Each channel represents a unique connection between
either the RMAN client and the database, the target database and the recovery catalog, or the
target database and the media where the backup is being moved to. In this case, SID 5 is being

used to manage the channel that is actually writing the database backup out to disk. The use of Oracle sessions is what provides the ability to parallelize an RMAN backup. In our case, we just had a single channel. In a later workshop we will enable more than one channel for the backup. Finally, we see the output that tells us the backup is beginning. Notice it is telling us that the backup is a compressed full datafile backup set—this makes it clear to us what kind of backup is occurring here. It's possible that there will be other kinds of backups reported here, which you will see later in this chapter.

Next, we see the actual backup of the datafiles of the CDB listed in the backup output:

```
channel ORA_DISK_1: specifying datafile(s) in backup set
input datafile file number=00001
name=C:\APP\ORACLE\ORADATA\MYCDB\DATAFILE\
O1_MF_SYSTEM_B4GG5PTF_.DBF
input datafile file number=00003
name=C:\APP\ORACLE\ORADATA\MYCDB\DATAFILE\
O1_MF_SYSAUX_B4GG2F4H_.DBF
input datafile file number=00005 |
name=C:\APP\ORACLE\ORADATA\MYCDB\DATAFILE\
O1_MF_UNDOTBS1_B4GG9TBL_.DBF
input datafile file number=00006
name=C:\APP\ORACLE\ORADATA\MYCDB\DATAFILE\
O1_MF_USERS_B4GG9PGZ_.DBF
channel ORA_DISK_1: starting piece 1 at 23-OCT-14
channel ORA_DISK_1: finished piece 1 at 23-OCT-14
piece handle=C:\APP\ORACLE\FAST_RECOVERY_AREA\MYCDB\BACKUPSET\
2014_10_23\
O1_MF_NNNDF_TAG20141023T154746_B4M1DM1F_.BKP
tag=TAG20141023T154746 comment=NONE
channel ORA_DISK_1: backup set complete, elapsed time: 00:01:16
```

In this example we backed up all four datafiles that belong to the root container of the MYCDB database. We can see these same four datafiles in this query when we are logged into the root container of the database:

```
SQL> select file_id, file_name from dba_data_files;
    FILE_ID FILE_NAME
---------- -------------------------------------------------------
          6 C:\APP\ORACLE\ORADATA\MYCDB\DATAFILE\O1_MF_USERS_B4GG9PGZ_.DBF
          5 C:\APP\ORACLE\ORADATA\MYCDB\DATAFILE\O1_MF_UNDOTBS1_B4GG9TBL_.DBF
          3 C:\APP\ORACLE\ORADATA\MYCDB\DATAFILE\O1_MF_SYSAUX_B4GG2F4H_.DBF
          1 C:\APP\ORACLE\ORADATA\MYCDB\DATAFILE\O1_MF_SYSTEM_B4GG5PTF_.DBF
```

Note the association with the file number listed in the RMAN output and the FILE_ID column value for the datafiles listed in the preceding query. This relationship can help you during specific recovery situations where you just need to recover one or a few datafiles. In those cases you can opt to restore the datafile by number, which can make things much easier.

Also, looking at this output we can confirm that RMAN did, in fact, back up all of the datafiles related to the root container of the database. Each of the individual database datafiles were contained into one single backup set piece, which is listed here:

```
piece handle=C:\APP\ORACLE\FAST_RECOVERY_AREA\MYCDB\BACKUPSET\
2014_10_23\O1_MF_NNNDF_TAG20141023T154746_B4M1DM1F_.BKP
tag=TAG20141023T154746 comment=NONE
```

The notion of RMAN backup sets and backup set pieces is critical to understand with respect to backups. We discuss these fundamental elements of RMAN in Chapter 3. In this case, the four datafiles were all backed up into a single backup set piece with the huge name of O1_MF_NNNDF_TAG20141023T154746_B4M1DM1F_.BKP. I guess it's a good thing that the old filename size limitation of the DOS days are not still with us!

Note that this backup set piece is created in the Fast Recovery Area (FRA). This is the default location where backup set pieces will be created, and using the Fast Recovery Area is considered a best practice. Note that the directories in the FRA are created by RMAN for you, so you don't need to worry about them. Also, note that the directory structures are very logical, including the database name (MYCDB), the type of file contained in the directory (BACKUPSET), and the date of the backup. This is the general format you will find used throughout the FRA when you use it with RMAN. Finally, note that the backup set piece is given a tag. We will discuss tags shortly, but for now just know that they are shorthand identifiers of backup sets.

Backup of the PDBs

If you are not backing up a multitenant database, RMAN will proceed to the automatic backup of the control file, discussed later in this section. If you are backing up a multitenant database, then the next items RMAN will back up are the various PDBs in the database. You can see this PDB, and all of the other PDBs in the database, along with their status, by querying the V$PDBS view, as shown here:

```
SQL> select name from v$pdbs;
NAME
------------------------------
PDB$SEED
MYPDB
```

In this output we can see that our CDB has two PDBs in it. The first is the seed PDB called PDB$SEED (see Chapter 4 for more information on the seed PDB/container). Next is the PDB MYPDB. When performing a single-channel full backup of a CDB, RMAN will always back up the root CDB first, then all of the PDBs, and then finally RMAN will back up the seed container. If you are using parallel channels, you will find the CDB and a mix of PDBs being backed up in parallel.

RMAN will always back up the root CDB into its own individual backup set (or backup sets). RMAN will also back up each individual PDB and the seed container into their own backup sets. The net effect of this is that each container is localized to its own unique backup set, which makes it easier to restore a specific container.

It's possible that this division of PDBs into separate backup sets could have some performance impacts if the DOP is not set correctly. This would not be unlike the situation where you have a database with one or two large datafiles that cause the backup to take longer than it needs to.

One very large PDB could consume all of the channels of the backup and hold up the backup of smaller or medium-sized PDBs. In some extreme cases this could lead to longer backup times. The usual solutions, more DOP and using the **section size** parameter, can be used to deal with these rare situations.

Let's look at the details of the backup of the MYPDB that occurred as a part of the workshop we just did:

```
channel ORA_DISK_1: starting compressed full datafile backup set
channel ORA_DISK_1: specifying datafile(s) in backup set
input datafile file number=00008
name=C:\APP\ORACLE\ORADATA\MYCDB\
E57174E6384646F1BAECA9C7CE13D85E\DATAFILE\
O1_MF_SYSAUX_B4GJ1YVW_.DBF
input datafile file number=00007
name=C:\APP\ORACLE\ORADATA\MYCDB\
E57174E6384646F1BAECA9C7CE13D85E\DATAFILE\
O1_MF_SYSTEM_B4GJ1YVT_.DBF
input datafile file number=00009
name=C:\APP\ORACLE\ORADATA\MYCDB\
E57174E6384646F1BAECA9C7CE13D85E\DATAFILE\
O1_MF_USERS_B4GJ42C3_.DBF
channel ORA_DISK_1: starting piece 1 at 23-OCT-14
channel ORA_DISK_1: finished piece 1 at 23-OCT-14
piece handle=C:\APP\ORACLE\FAST_RECOVERY_AREA\MYCDB\
E57174E6384646F1BAECA9C7CE13D85E\BACKUPSET\2014_10_23\
O1_MF_NNNDF_TAG20141023T154746_B4M1GYP4_.BKP
tag=TAG20141023T154746 comment=NONE
channel ORA_DISK_1: backup set complete, elapsed time: 00:00:45
```

The first thing to note is that the PDB has its own unique backup set. It is possible for a given PDB to be in more than one backup set, depending on how you parallelize the backup or other configuration parameters that might restrict some attribute of a backup set or backup set piece. However, the PDB datafiles will always be wholly self-contained within those individual backup sets and there will not be datafiles related to other containers within those backup sets. Keeping the PDBs self-contained makes sense, because if you need to restore a specific PDB, RMAN will only need to access a few backup set pieces, rather than all of the backup sets related to the backup itself. This will speed up a PDB-level restore quite a bit.

In the preceding output snippet, we can see the indication that RMAN is creating a new backup set, as we would expect. We see that this is a full compressed backup set and we are backing up the files for the MYPDB PDB. All of the PDBs will be backed up at this point.

Look at the location of the database datafiles being backed up. Do you see the difference in how the PDBs are stored by default by Oracle when they are created? Here is one of the datafiles being backed up:

```
name=C:\APP\ORACLE\ORADATA\MYCDB\
E57174E6384646F1BAECA9C7CE13D85E\DATAFILE\
O1_MF_SYSAUX_B4GJ1YVW_.DBF
```

There is an additional directory level (the big long name that ends in 85E). The name of this directory is also the GUID of the PDB that owns these datafiles. We discussed the GUID in detail in Chapter 4. To quickly refresh your memory, the GUID is a unique identifier that is assigned to each PDB. The purpose of the GUID is to be unique across the entire database infrastructure. This uniqueness prevents naming collisions that might occur otherwise (such as datafiles with the same name that might occur during a duplication process).

NOTE
You might be wondering why the data dictionary and V$ views are important if you're using RMAN and Cloud Control. If you are going to be truly proficient in backup and recovery, you need to understand how things work. There may come a point in your career that you will need to do something during a recovery where Cloud Control is not available, or where RMAN isn't working like you expect. For example, knowing that the V$ views are available when the database is mounted but the CDB views are not could be very helpful when diagnosing a problem.

So, how can you tell what the GUID of a given PDB is? I'm glad you asked! It's actually very simple. The GUID is contained in the V$CONTAINERS (and V$PDBS) view, as shown in this example:

```
SQL> Select name, guid from v$containers;
NAME             GUID
---------------  --------------------------------
CDB$ROOT         615F41223B2E4E08A704DD1EBBD46056
PDB$SEED         A1B392142CBC43A1939B97E6E087A74C
MYPDB            E57174E6384646F1BAECA9C7CE13D85E
```

Knowing the GUID, we can tell which PDB datafiles are being backed up by RMAN since the PDB name is not listed in the RMAN output. To get the name of the PDB, we join V$CONTAINERS to either the V$DATAFILE view or DBA_DATA_FILES view, using the GUID as the predicate, as shown in this example:

```
SQL> select a.name con_name, b.name
from v$pdbs a, v$datafile b
where a.con_id=b.con_id
and guid='E57174E6384646F1BAECA9C7CE13D85E';

CON_NAME    NAME
----------  -------------------------------------------------
MYPDB       C:\APP\ORACLE\ORADATA\MYCDB\E57174E6384646F1BAECA9
            C7CE13D85E\DATAFILE\O1_MF_SYSTEM_B4GJ1YVT_.DBF
MYPDB       C:\APP\ORACLE\ORADATA\MYCDB\E57174E6384646F1BAECA9
            C7CE13D85E\DATAFILE\O1_MF_SYSAUX_B4GJ1YVW_.DBF
MYPDB       C:\APP\ORACLE\ORADATA\MYCDB\E57174E6384646F1BAECA9
            C7CE13D85E\DATAFILE\O1_MF_USERS_B4GJ42C3_.DBF
```

Backup of the Seed Container
Finally, RMAN will back up the seed container (internally called PDB$SEED) into its own backup set. We discussed the seed container earlier in this book when we introduced you to the concept of container databases. There really isn't much different about this backup, except to note that the

datafiles for the seed are once again stored in the directory where the datafiles for the CDB are stored. This makes sense given that they really are a unit. Because the backup of the seed is pretty much the same and requires no real additional explanation, we won't bother reprinting the RMAN output for that part of the backup here.

Control File Automatic Backup

We mentioned in the workshop that we had enabled control file automated backups. In the last section, we see that backup occurring. This backup will occur at the end of any backup of the database or of the database archived redo logs. The control file and the database SPFILE are both backed up at this time. As you will see in Chapter 8, this backup can later be used to restore these files, making for much easier recoveries than might otherwise be possible.

One thing to be aware of is that if we had not configured automated backups of our control file, RMAN would still back up the control file as long as we are backing up datafile 1. The control file would be backed up into the backup set that contains datafile 1. We would also want to do a separate control file backup after our database backup is complete, so we would have the most current control file backed up (because the control file backed up with the backup set will not have the complete information on the current backup in it). Note that this control file is a bit more complicated to recover if you do not configure control file autobackups. Because of this, we strongly suggest that you configure control file autobackups on your system.

Once this backup is complete, the channel is released and you can go home.

NOTE
Oracle only supports backups of SPFILEs into a control file automated backup. You cannot back up your database's text-based init.ora parameter file with RMAN.

Using the Recovery Catalog

If we had created a recovery catalog, as mentioned in Chapter 6, we could have connected to that catalog when we did the previous workshop exercise. Nothing in the exercise would need to be different except for one change on how we connected to RMAN. In the workshop we connected to RMAN using this connection string:

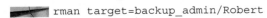

```
rman target=backup_admin/Robert
```

Because we didn't use the **catalog** parameter, we will be using the control file as the repository for our backup metadata. If we had created a recovery catalog, we could have easily used it when running the workshop. All you would need to do is modify the RMAN command line to have it also connect to the recovery catalog, as you can see here:

```
C:\>rman target=backup_admin/Robert
catalog=rcat_owner/password@robt
```

Notice that we connected to our recovery catalog using Oracle Net. This is because the ORACLE_SID identifier was set to point to the database we were backing up. Because the recovery catalog is in a different database, we had to use an Oracle Net service name to connect to the recovery catalog. We could have done things the other way around, setting the ORACLE_SID to point to the catalog database and then connecting to the target database through the Net service name—unless the catalog database was in a PDB, of course, in which case we would have to use a network service name.

Controlling Chatty RMAN Output

RMAN is chatty, isn't it? Sometimes we just want the backup to run and for it to either not produce output or to redirect output somewhere other than the display. RMAN output can be suppressed by using the **log** RMAN command-line parameter. Using **log**, you can redirect RMAN logging to a file, or you can redirect logging to /dev/null on Linux to totally suppress logging. Using the **log** parameter will stop all logging to the screen.

Because you can suppress RMAN logging, it makes sense that there is a view that maintains the output you would have otherwise seen from RMAN. This information is available in the V$RMAN_OUTPUT view. This view can support a maximum of 32,768 rows of the last RMAN client output. This information is stored in the database control file, and it is not reset when the database is shut down, as is the case with many V$ views. There is also the RC_RMAN_OUTPUT view, which is the RMAN recovery catalog equivalent of the V$RMAN_OUTPUT view.

Here is an example of how to query the V$RMAN_OUTPUT view:

```
select output from v$rman_output order by stamp;
```

Offline Backups without Using Configured Defaults

What if we had not configured the default settings mentioned earlier in this chapter? Or what if the defaults were not what we wanted to use? Sometimes we can override the defaults within the given RMAN command itself. For example, if we wanted to back up to a different disk device than the FRA (or defined default), we can easily override this using the **format** option of the **backup** command, as shown here:

```
backup as compressed backupset database
format 'c:\Users\Robert\backup\%u'
plus archivelog format 'c:\Users\Robert\backup\%u';
```

Sometimes we can't override a preconfigured or unconfigured setting on the **backup** command line. In these cases, a **run** block is required. For example, in this case we assume that the default degree of parallelism is 3 and the default is to write to the FRA. If we want to change the degree of parallelism to 2 for one time only and write to a different location, we can use a **run** block to perform this activity. Also, a **run** block provides the ability to coordinate several actions into one operation.

A **run** block consists of the use of the keyword **run**, followed by an open bracket ({). You then enter the command that you want to have executed within the context of the **run** block and then terminate the **run** block with a close bracket (}).

In this example, we want to use a **run** block to perform several operations all at one time. First, we use the **shutdown** command to shut down the database and then mount it with the **startup mount** command. Then we run our backup using the **backup** command. We then back up the current control file, and finally the database is restarted:

```
run
{
shutdown
startup mount
backup as compressed backupset database;
backup current controlfile;
alter database open;
}
```

When you create the **run** block, Oracle waits until all of the statements in the block have been entered and you have closed out the **run** block with the close bracket. All of the statements within that **run** block will then run as a single unit. If one statement fails, the rest of the statements will not be executed inside the block. You can see how this might be a problem in the preceding example should one of the backups fail for some reason. The **alter database open** command would not be used and we would return the next morning to a database that is not open. As a result, the use of the **run** block is less and less frequent. Instead, now we see RMAN scripts being run, either from OEM Cloud Control, from a shared common directory, or those stored in the recovery catalog (my preference is OEM Cloud Control).

Online RMAN Database Backups

We have spent the first half of this chapter on offline backups and the **set** command. If you are interested in online backups, then this section (and the following one) is for you. Still, don't skip the previous sections, because they present a great deal of foundational information that won't be repeated here. If you are jumping into the chapter at this point, first go back and read the previous sections. If you have read the first half of the chapter already and you find that you are a bit punchy, then take a short break before you forge on.

In this section, we first discuss several different kinds of online backups: backups of the entire database, tablespace backups, and datafile backups. We then look at archive log file backups and, finally, backups of the control file and parameter files.

Online Database Backups

As described in Chapters 2 and 3 in detail, to perform online backups with RMAN, our database must be in ARCHIVELOG mode. If your database is not in ARCHIVELOG mode, RMAN will generate an error if you try to perform an online backup. You can determine whether your database is in ARCHIVELOG mode by querying the V$DATABASE view, as shown here:

```
SQL> select log_mode from v$database;
LOG_MODE
------------
ARCHIVELOG
```

There is one key difference in online backups (other than the fact that the database must be in ARCHIVELOG mode) that you will want to be aware of. You must back up not only the database, but also the archived redo logs of that database. This is also recommended for offline backups of ARCHIVELOG database, as we mentioned previously. The main difference is that with an offline backup of a database in NOARCHIVELOG mode, the database will be in a consistent state during the backup; therefore, you can restore and recover that database to the point of the backup without needing the archived redo logs. With an online backup, you always need to apply redo logs. There is no exception or magic available to avoid this. If you try to avoid applying archived redo logs and, in reading the Internet, assume that it's okay to try to force your database open, we will send in the black helicopters, the Oracle shock troops will silently make their way in, and we will take your databases away from you. You will then be required to go through a very rigorous retraining program before you get your databases back in such situations.

Sometimes people are confused by this need for archived redo logs, so let us explain. When you start an online backup, the database is still running. The backup itself is going to be wholly inconsistent. If the backup takes 30 minutes to run, then a number of blocks will have changed in those 30 minutes. The database does not stop writing to the datafiles, it does not cache changes, it does not pass Go, nor does it collect $200. It just goes about its merry way with DBWR writing to the datafiles.

The result of this is that when the backup is done, the database will have changed during the course of that backup in some way. It may be a small way, it might be a big way, but it will have changed. As a result, the only way to restore this backup is to have all of the redo stream generated during the entire backup, from beginning to end, available to RMAN. To ensure this, we need to make sure we back up all the redo generated during the backup, after the backup has been completed.

So, having ensured that we are in ARCHIVELOG mode, we are ready to do our first RMAN online backup.

NOTE
*From this point on in this chapter, we will assume that you have configured default channels, as discussed earlier in this chapter, unless we need to point out something specifically. This saves you typing and allows us to leave out commands such as **allocate channel**, thus giving us more space to give you important information.*

You will find that online backups are not all that different from offline backups. In fact, they are a bit simpler because you don't have to mess with shutting down and then mounting the database. When you have your defaults configured (refer to Chapter 5), an online backup is as simple as this:

```
backup database plus archivelog;
```

This command does it all. First, the process does a log switch (using the **alter system archivelog current** command). Next, it backs up any existing archived redo logs. Then, the actual database backup occurs. At this point, another log switch occurs (using the **alter system archivelog current** command), and RMAN backs up the remaining archived redo logs (using the **backup archivelog all** command). Finally, the autobackup of the control file and SPFILE occurs.

RMAN Workshop: *Perform an Online Backup*

This workshop walks you through an online backup of your Oracle database. It works for both nonmultitenant and multitenant databases, just as the workshop on offline backups did earlier. First, we will review a few notes about the workshop and then we will back up our database.

Workshop Notes

This workshop assumes that your database has been configured with automatic channels (as shown in Chapter 5). If you are running a nonmultitenant database, you will use the database account called backup_admin that we described in Chapter 5. If you are running a CDB database, you will want to modify the backup_admin account to be a common user account (c##backup_admin), which we also described in Chapter 5.

In addition, it assumes that the MML layer has been configured (if you are using it). Finally, your database must be configured for and operating in ARCHIVELOG mode.

Step 1. Start up RMAN:

```
C:\>rman target=backup_admin/robert
```

Step 2. Start the backup:

```
RMAN> backup database plus archivelog;
```

Here is an example of a complete online RMAN backup following these steps:

```
C:\>rman target=backup_admin/robert
RMAN> backup database plus archivelog;
Starting backup at 15-JUN-02
current log archived
using target database controlfile instead of recovery catalog
configuration for DISK channel 3 is ignored
allocated channel: ORA_DISK_1
channel ORA_DISK_1: sid=13 devtype=DISK
channel ORA_DISK_1: starting archive log backupset
channel ORA_DISK_1: specifying archive log(s) in backup set
input archive log thread=1 sequence=351 recid=13 stamp=464457020
channel ORA_DISK_1: starting piece 1 at 15-JUN-02
input archive log thread=1 sequence=352 recid=14 stamp=464609012
input archive log thread=1 sequence=353 recid=15 stamp=464609115
channel ORA_DISK_1: finished piece 1 at 15-JUN-02
piece handle=D:\BACKUP\ROBT\BACKUP_20DR2QJ8_1_1 comment=NONE
channel ORA_DISK_1: backup set complete, elapsed time: 00:00:11
channel ORA_DISK_1: starting archive log backupset
channel ORA_DISK_1: specifying archive log(s) in backup set
input archive log thread=1 sequence=357 recid=19 stamp=464610450
input archive log thread=1 sequence=358 recid=20 stamp=464611007
input archive log thread=1 sequence=359 recid=21 stamp=464611921
channel ORA_DISK_1: starting piece 1 at 15-JUN-02
channel ORA_DISK_1: finished piece 1 at 15-JUN-02
piece handle=D:\BACKUP\ROBT\BACKUP_22DR2QJK_1_1 comment=NONE
channel ORA_DISK_1: backup set complete, elapsed time: 00:00:03
Finished backup at 15-JUN-02
Starting backup at 15-JUN-02
using channel ORA_DISK_1
channel ORA_DISK_1: starting full datafile backupset
input datafile fno=00001 name=D:\ORACLE\ORADATA\ROBT\SYSTEM01.DBF
input datafile fno=00005 name=D:\ORACLE\ORADATA\ROBT\USERS01.DBF
input datafile fno=00004 name=D:\ORACLE\ORADATA\ROBT\TOOLS01.DBF
input datafile fno=00003 name=D:\ORACLE\ORADATA\ROBT\INDX01.DBF
input datafile fno=00002
name=D:\ORACLE\ORADATA\ROBT\ROBT_TEST_RECOVER_02.DBF
input datafile fno=00010
name=D:\ORACLE\ORADATA\ROBT\ROBT_RBS_01.DBF
input datafile fno=00011
name=D:\ORACLE\ORADATA\ROBT\ROBT_TEST_TBS_01.DBF
```

```
input datafile fno=00007
name=D:\ORACLE\ORADATA\ROBT\ROBT_TEST_RECOVER_01.DBF
input datafile fno=00006
name=D:\ORACLE\ORADATA\ROBT\ROBT_TEST_RECOVER_03.DBF
channel ORA_DISK_1: starting piece 1 at 15-JUN-02
channel ORA_DISK_1: finished piece 1 at 15-JUN-02
piece handle=D:\BACKUP\ROBT\BACKUP_23DR2QJU_1_1 comment=NONE
channel ORA_DISK_1: backup set complete, elapsed time: 00:04:56
Finished backup at 15-JUN-02
Starting backup at 15-JUN-02
current log archived
using channel ORA_DISK_1
channel ORA_DISK_1: starting archive log backupset
channel ORA_DISK_1: specifying archive log(s) in backup set
input archive log thread=1 sequence=360 recid=22 stamp=464612416
channel ORA_DISK_1: starting piece 1 at 15-JUN-02
channel ORA_DISK_1: finished piece 1 at 15-JUN-02
piece handle=D:\BACKUP\ROBT\BACKUP_25DR2R2K_1_1 comment=NONE
channel ORA_DISK_1: backup set complete, elapsed time: 00:00:04
Finished backup at 15-JUN-02
Starting Control File and spfile Autobackup at 15-JUN-02
piece handle=D:\BACKUP\ROBT_C-3395799962-20020615-02 comment=NONE
Finished Control File and spfile Autobackup at 15-JUN-02
```

We have now completed an entire online database backup! Next, we will look at tablespace backups.

NOTE
As we will discuss later in this chapter, a full database backup cannot be used as a base backup for application of incremental backups. They are two similar but different things.

Variations on a Theme: Other Types of RMAN Online Backups

We have discussed full database backups, which are the most common kinds of backups. However, there are other kinds of backups that you might want to create for various reasons. In this section we introduce you to these backups and give you some idea as to why you might want to perform them.

Tablespace Backups

Occasionally, you will want to do tablespace-level backups instead of backups of the entire database. This might be before you drop a partition that is specific to that tablespace, or perhaps just after you have made the tablespace read-only. To do a tablespace-level backup, simply use the **backup** command with the **tablespace** parameter:

```
backup tablespace users;
```

If you want to back up any archived redo logs at the same time, you could issue the command like this:

```
backup tablespace users plus archivelog;
```

Or perhaps you want to also make sure your current control file is backed up:

```
backup tablespace users
include current controlfile plus archivelog;
```

Of course, you are not really backing up a tablespace but rather the datafiles associated with that tablespace. Oracle just converts the tablespace name into a list of datafiles that are associated with that tablespace. Normally, a control file backup will not occur during these backups unless you have configured automatic control file backups (refer to Chapter 5) to occur (and you are not backing up datafile 1). If you use the **include current controlfile** parameter, the control file will be backed up.

If you are running Oracle Multitenant, then backing up a tablespace is a bit different because you could have the same named tablespace in many different PDBs. The solution to PDB backups is to log directly into the PDB and back up the tablespace from there.

Here is an example of logging a PBD directly and backing up the users tablespace:

```
Export ORACLE_SID=mycdb
rman target=backup_id/password@mypdb
RMAN>backup tablespace users;
```

Note in this example that we do not back up the archived redo logs. This is because any backup from within a given PDB is not able to back up archived redo logs. Backups of archived redo logs must occur from the root container (at the time this book was written). Thus, after this backup you should switch back to the root container and back up the archived redo logs, as shown here:

```
RMAN>target c##backup_admin/password
RMAN>backup archivelog all delete input;
```

Datafile Backups

You might want to back up specific database datafiles. Perhaps you are getting ready to move them to a new device and you wish to back them up before you move them. RMAN allows you to back up a datafile by using the **backup** command with the **datafile** parameter, followed by the filename or number of the datafiles you want to back up. The following are examples of some **backup datafile** commands:

```
backup datafile 2;
backup datafile 'd:\oracle\oradata\robt\users01.dbf';
backup datafile 'd:\oracle\oradata\robt\users01.dbf'
plus archivelog;
```

Again, the control file and the SPFILE will get backed up if datafile 1 is backed up or if automated control file backups are configured. In the last example, the archived redo logs will get backed up as well.

Backing up individual datafiles for CDBs can be done from the root by using the same method that we showed you earlier. You simply get the datafile number or filename from V$DATAFILE and issue the **backup** command for that datafile or set of datafiles.

Archived Redo Log Backups

For a number of reasons, you might well want to back up your archived redo logs but not the database. In this event, you use the **backup archivelog** command. To back up all of the archived redo logs, simply issue the command **backup archivelog all**. Optionally, you might want to back up a specific range of archived redo logs, for which you have several options available, including time, SCN, and redo log sequence number (or a selected range of those values). Specific options are **from SCN**, **from sequence**, and **from time**. Keep in mind that using the **from** option may result in some archived redo logs being left on disk and not being backed up. Here are some examples of backing up the archived redo logs:

```
backup archivelog all;
backup archivelog from time 'sysdate - 1';
backup archivelog from sequence 353;
```

A couple of notes about the previous examples. When the **backup archivelog all** command is run, a log switch will occur and all of the archived redo logs, including the current redo log, will be backed up. When you use the **from** clause of the **backup archivelog** command, the current redo log will not be backed up. This is important if you are very short on space, because if you archive the current redo log file, this might fill up your FRA and the database might hang.

> **NOTE**
> *If an archived redo log in the FRA is corrupted, Oracle will "fail over" to any other defined archived redo log destination. If the archived redo log is in that destination directory and it is not corrupted, RMAN will back up the archived redo log from that source destination.*

Once you have backed up archived redo logs, you may want to have RMAN remove them for you. The **delete input** option allows you to perform this operation. The **delete input** option can also be used with datafile copies (which we will discuss later in this chapter) or with backup set copies. Here are a couple of examples of using the **delete input** parameter on an archived redo log backup:

```
backup archivelog all delete input;
backup archivelog from sequence 353 delete input;
```

You can also instruct RMAN to make redundant copies of your archived redo logs. In the following example, we use the **not backed up *n* times** parameter of the **backup** command to make sure that we have backed up our archived redo logs at least three times. Any archived redo logs that have already been backed up three times will not be backed up again.

```
backup archivelog not backed up 3 times;
```

Also, you can use the **until time** parameter with the **backup** command to ensure that a certain number of days' worth of archived redo logs remain on disk:

```
backup archivelog until time 'sysdate - 2' delete all input;
```

NOTE
*Use of the **not backed up** parameter and use of the **delete input** parameter are somewhat mutually exclusive. The **delete input** parameter will remove the archived redo log regardless of how many times it has been backed up.*

One last note about archived redo log backups. As of the time we wrote this book, archived redo log backups could only occur when you were logged into the root of the CDB. Attempts to start archived redo log backups from a PDB would fail with an error.

Control File and Parameter File Backups

Just as with archived redo logs, sometimes you may just want to back up the control file or the server parameter files. RMAN provides specific commands for these functions as well. Use the **backup spfile** command to back up the server parameter file. This is handy if you have made a configuration change to the database, for example. To back up the control file, you can use the **current controlfile** parameter of the **backup** command to generate a copy of the current control file. The **current controlfile** parameter also comes with a **for standby** clause that will create a backup control file for use with a standby database.

You can use the **controlfilecopy** parameter of the **backup** command to create a backup set that contains an externally created backup of the control file. This control file backup might be the result of the **alter database backup controlfile to 'file_name'** SQL command or the use of the RMAN **copy** command (covered later in this chapter) to create a control file backup. Also, you can back up a standby database control file that was created with the **alter database create standby controlfile** command. The benefit of this feature is that you can take external control file backup files and register them with RMAN and create a backup set that contains the control file backup. Here are some examples of the use of this parameter:

```
backup current controlfile;
sql "alter database backup controlfile
to ''d:\backup\robt\contf_back.ctl''";
backup controlfilecopy 'd:\backup\robt\contf_back.ctl';
```

Backup Set Backups

Perhaps you like to back up to disk first and then to back up your backup sets to tape. RMAN supports this operation through the use of the **backup** command. For example, suppose we issued a **backup database** command, and the entire backup set went to disk because that is our configured default device. Now, we wish to move that backup set to tape. We could issue the **backup** command with the **backupset** parameter, and Oracle would back up all of our backup sets to the channel that is allocated for the backup.

You can choose to back up all backup sets with the **backup backupset** command, or you can choose to back up specific backup sets. Further, you can only back up from disk to disk or from disk to tape. There is no support for tape-to-tape or tape-to-disk backups. The **delete input** option, which we previously discussed in regard to archive log backups, is also available with backup set backups. When used, the **delete input** option will cause the files of the source backup set to get deleted after a successful backup. Here are some examples of this command:

```
backup backupset all;
backup backupset all
format='d:\backup\newbackups\backup_%U.bak'
```

```
tag='Backup of backupsets on 6/15'  channel 'ORA_DISK_1';
backup backupset completed before 'sysdate - 2';
backup backupset completed before 'sysdate - 2' delete input;
backup backupset completed after 'sysdate - 2' delete input;
```

An example of a backup strategy here might be to perform RMAN backups to disk and then to back up the backup sets to tape with the **backup backupset** command. Perhaps you want to keep two days' worth of your backup sets on disk. You could then issue two commands. First, issue the **backup backupset completed before 'sysdate - 2'** command to back up the last two days of backups. Next, to back up and then remove any backup sets older than two days, issue the **backup backupset completed after 'sysdate - 2' delete input** command, which would cause one final backup of the old backup sets and then remove them.

Note that in designing a strategy, it would be preferable to use the Fast Recovery Area (FRA) and the **backup recovery area** command, which we will discuss next. Check out Chapter 15 for more information on architecture and best practices.

NOTE
Backup set backups are very handy if you want to back up your control file automated backups elsewhere and still have the catalog track the location of the backup set.

Fast Recovery Area Backups

More and more people are seeing the benefits of the Fast Recovery Area (FRA). As you will see in Chapter 15, one of the most common architectures is to do your initial backup to the FRA and then back up the FRA to a secondary form of storage. RMAN makes the movement of backup sets from the FRA to secondary storage very easy by providing the **backup recovery area** command.

Backup optimization is enabled by default when you are using the **backup recovery area** command and is not impacted by the **configure backup optimization** setting. You can override this behavior by using the **force** parameter of the **backup recovery area** command. Thus, once you have issued the **backup recovery area** command and copied the current contents of the FRA to another location, those files will not be copied to that same location again. However, if you back up the FRA to a different location later, then any files not backed up to that location will be backed up at that time.

When the **backup recovery area** command is issued, the following files will be backed up from the FRA:

- Full and incremental backup sets
- Control file autobackups
- Datafile copies
- Archived redo log files

When the command attempts to back up the archived redo log files, it may find that one is missing or corrupted. If so, RMAN will look outside the FRA and see if it can find a copy of that archived redo log in another location.

It is important to note, with respect to the FRA, that files contained in the FRA can have one of two attributes. They are either managed by the FRA or not managed by the FRA. If a given file (such as an archived redo log) is not considered managed by the FRA, it will not participate in the various commands, space management, or retention controls associated with the FRA. One thing that can cause a backup file to not be managed by the FRA is the use of the **format** clause to define the location of the backup file. Even if you define the **format** clause to use the correct location in the FRA, the file that is created will not be considered managed by the FRA. Thus, if you try to back up the FRA to another location using the **backup recovery area** command, you will find that those files created when you used the **format** clause will not be moved over. In essence, you have out-thought yourself. See Chapter 5 for more on the FRA and how to properly configure it.

NOTE
*Most of the time when we see FRA-related issues, it tends to be because either the FRA is not configured correctly or the **backup** command or configured default is disabling FRA feature use. If you find something isn't working right when working with the FRA (for example, if FRA files don't move over when you issue the **backup recovery area** command), ensure that the FRA is configured correctly and that you have not inadvertently created files in the FRA that cannot be managed by the FRA.*

In Chapter 15 we will discuss how to manage different retention criteria that will be present in a multitiered backup architecture.

Copies

Okay, all this newfangled talk of backup sets and pieces is just blowing your mind. You ask, "Can't I just make a copy of these database datafiles?" We're here to make you feel better. With RMAN, you can just make copies of your different database structures, and that's what we are going to talk about in this section. First, we will review the upside, and downside, to creating copies instead of backup sets. Then, we will look at how we create datafile copies, control file copies, and archived redo log file copies.

Image Copies

RMAN can create an exact duplicate of your database datafiles, archived redo logs, or control file. An RMAN image copy is just that—it is simply a copy of the file with the name and/or location changed. There are no backup pieces or anything else to worry about. Image copies can only be made to disk, and you cannot make incremental copies. The database must be either mounted or open to make image copies. A history of the copies made is kept in the database control file, so you can track when copies have been made and where they reside.

You can make image copies of the entire database, tablespaces, or datafiles, just like a regular backup (this is very different from earlier versions of RMAN). The RMAN copy process provides some of the same protections as normal RMAN backup sets, such as checking for corrupted blocks and, optionally, logical corruption. Also, image copies can be combined with normal backup sets such as incremental backups and archived redo log backups to facilitate a complete database recovery.

Database, Tablespace, and Datafile Image Copies

The **backup** command supports the creation of database image copies. Simply use the **backup as copy** command to do image copies, and the process is much like performing backup sets. Here is an example of making a database image copy with RMAN:

```
RMAN> backup as copy database;
```

RMAN will use the FRA to store backup copies, if it is configured. If you are using the FRA, the datafile images will be stored in a directory called datafile, as shown in this partial sample output from a datafile image copy:

```
RMAN> backup as copy database;
Starting backup at 12-NOV-05
using channel ORA_DISK_1
using channel ORA_DISK_2
channel ORA_DISK_1: starting datafile copyinput datafile fno=00001
name=C:\ORACLE\PRODUCT\10.2.0\ORADATA\ROB10R2\SYSTEM01.DBF
channel ORA_DISK_2: starting datafile copy
input datafile fno=00003
name=C:\ORACLE\PRODUCT\10.2.0\ORADATA\ROB10R2\SYSAUX01.DBF
output Filename=C:\ORACLE\PRODUCT\10.2.0\FLASH_RECOVERY_AREA\
ROB10R2\DATAFILE\O1_MF_SYSAUX_1QFBPPON_.DBF
tag=TAG20151112T205403 recid=
2stamp=574203351
channel ORA_DISK_2: datafile copy complete,
elapsed time: 00:01:55
channel ORA_DISK_2: starting datafile copy
```

Image copies of tablespaces work pretty much the same way; just use the **backup as copy** command and the **tablespace** keyword, like so:

```
backup as copy tablespace users;
```

Finally, you can create image copies of datafiles:

```
backup as copy datafile 1;
backup as copy datafile
'C:\ORACLE\PRODUCT\10.2.0\ORADATA\ROB10R2\SYSTEM01.DBF';
```

NOTE
An image copy can be made with the database mounted or, if the database is in ARCHIVELOG mode, with the database open.

Control File Copies

Control file copies can also be made with the **backup controlfile** command. These backups can occur with the database either mounted or open. Generally, it is a best practice to enable control file autobackups and allow RMAN to back up the control file automatically after a backup.

If you need to manually create an RMAN backup set that contains a control file, here is an example of such a backup:

```
backup current controlfile;
```

Note that this is not the same as a control file autobackup, and an attempt to restore from a control file autobackup will not result in the recovery of a control file backed up using this method.

You can also create control file copies. These copies are just like backup control files created with the **alter database backup controlfile to trace** command; thus, they are usable for recovery purposes. Here is an example of the creation of a control file copy from RMAN:

```
backup as copy current controlfile
format 'c:\controlback\control01.ctl' reuse;
```

Note that the **backup as copy** command will not overwrite an existing backup control file unless you use the **reuse** keyword as we did in our example. Also note that the **backup as copy** command does not create an RMAN backup set, only a physical file that is a backup control file.

If you wish to create a control file for use with a standby database that you are creating, you use the **for standby** clause. Again, this will create an RMAN backup set:

```
backup as copy standby controlfile;
```

As you did with regular backup control files, you can indicate a specific filename/location when you create a control file backup, which would result in the physical file being created in that location and not in the creation of an RMAN backup set:

```
backup as copy current controlfile format 'c:\oracle\controlfilecopy.ctl';
```

ARCHIVELOG Image Copies

Having copies of archived redo logs can be helpful. It's certainly easier to mine a copy of an archived redo log with Oracle's LogMiner product than to have to first extract that archived redo log from a backup set. The **copy** command allows you to create copies of archived redo logs by using the **archivelog** parameter of the **copy** command. Unfortunately, as we mentioned earlier, the use of **copy archivelog** requires us to list each archived redo log by name, rather than to specify some temporal range when we make copies of the archived redo logs. Here is an example of making an ARCHIVELOG file copy:

```
backup as copy archivelog all;
```

Incremental RMAN Backups

We hope you have made it this far through the book without much difficulty and have been able to get at least one good backup of your database done. Now, we are going to move on to incremental backups in RMAN. Through incremental backups, RMAN allows you to back up just the data blocks that have changed since the last incremental backup. The following are the benefits of incremental backups:

- Less overall tape or disk usage
- Less network bandwidth required
- Quicker backup times

You can do incremental backups either online or offline and in either ARCHIVELOG mode or NOARCHIVELOG mode, which is pretty handy. Keep in mind that if you choose an incremental backup strategy, a give and take exists in terms of the benefits. While you are deriving a benefit in the reduction of overall backup times (and this may be significant), the cost comes on the recovery side. Because Oracle will need to use several backup sets to recover the database if an incremental strategy is used, the time required to recover your database can significantly increase.

NOTE
If you choose to do incremental backups on a NOARCHIVELOG mode database, make sure you shut down the database in a consistent manner each time you back up the database.

The Block Change Tracking File

By default, when you're doing an incremental backup, any datafile that has changed in any way will be backed up. This can make incremental backups take longer and will make them larger. RMAN offers the ability to just back up changed database blocks. This can make your incremental database backups much smaller and shorter. To enable block change tracking, issue the command **alter database enable block change tracking**. The result of this command will be the creation of a file called the block change tracking file (BCTF).

When enabling block change tracking, you can choose to allow Oracle to name the related block change tracking file for you. Oracle will use the Oracle Managed Files (OMF) naming standard when naming the BCTF. You can also choose to define the location and name of the block change tracking file yourself, as shown in this example:

```
alter database enable block change tracking using file
'/u01/app/oracle/block_change/rob10gr2_block_change.fil';
```

If a previous block change tracking file already exists, you need to use the **reuse** parameter:

```
alter database enable block change tracking using file
'/u01/app/oracle/block_change/rob10gr2_block_change.fil' reuse;
```

You disable block change tracking by using the **alter database disable block change tracking** command. The block change tracking file size is preallocated and is related to the size of the database and the number of redo log threads. The typical size of the block change tracking file is quite small and is proportional to the size of the database. Its size is roughly 1/250,000 the size of the database.

If you are running an Oracle Real Application Clusters (RAC) database configuration, each node will need to have access to the BCTF. In these configurations, you may want to consider storing the BCTF in ASM for ease of file sharing.

The BCTF size also depends on the number of incremental backups that occur between each level 0 backup. The more incremental backups, the more changed block-related metadata has to be stored in the BCTF.

The BCTF can hold a maximum of eight backups' worth of information (for example, one base and seven level-1 incremental backups). After this, the next backup will remove the information of a previous backup, making the BCTF useless. The BCTF file will grow automatically in 10MB increments. A minimum of 320KB of space is allocated to each datafile in the BCTF regardless of the size of the datafile.

The Oracle Database defaults to not using block change tracking, and you can determine if block change tracking is enabled by checking the V$BLOCK_CHANGE_TRACKING view. The

STATUS column indicates if block change tracking is enabled, and the FILENAME column contains the filename of the block change tracking file. You can move the block change tracking file by using the **alter database rename file** command just as you would any other database file.

```
SQL> select status from v$block_change_tracking;

STATUS
----------
DISABLED
```

The Base Backup

When doing an incremental backup, the first thing you need is an *incremental base backup*. This backup is the backup that all future incremental backups will be based on. Each time you perform a backup of the database, you assign that backup an incremental level identifier through the use of the **incremental** parameter of the **backup** command. Incremental backups have levels assigned to them. A *base* backup will always have a level value of 0, and you must have a base backup to be able to perform any type of incremental backup. An incremental backup will always have a level value of 1 (more on level 1 incrementals in a moment). If you do not have a base backup and you try to perform an incremental backup (using a backup level 1), then RMAN will perform a base backup for you automatically. Here is an example of performing a base incremental backup:

```
backup incremental level=0 database;
```

> **NOTE**
> *Earlier versions of RMAN used to support more than level 0 and level 1 backups. Starting in Oracle Database 10g Release 1, any incremental level backup other than 0 or 1 was deprecated by Oracle.*

Differential vs. Cumulative Incremental Backups

Now, we need to decide how we want to perform our incremental backups. We can use one of two methods:

- Differential
- Cumulative

Each is a different method of performing an incremental backup. Let's look at these two different types of incremental backup in a bit more detail.

Differential Backups

This is the default type of incremental backup that RMAN generates. With a differential backup, RMAN backs up all blocks that have changed since the last level 1 backup or since the last level 0 backup if the differential backup is the first incremental backup after a level 0 backup. Understanding how this all works can get a bit confusing. Figure 7-1 should help you better understand the impacts of using different levels.

In this example, we have a level 0 differential backup being taken on Sunday. This backup will back up the entire database. Following the level 0 backup, we perform a level 1 differential

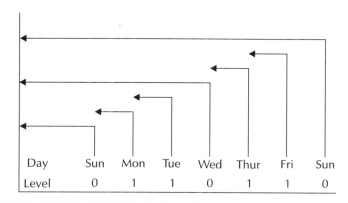

FIGURE 7-1. *Differential backups*

backup on Monday. This backup will back up all changed blocks since the level 0 backup on Sunday. On Tuesday, the level 1 incremental backup will back up all blocks changed since the level 1 backup on Monday. On Wednesday, another level 0 backup is performed, which backs up all database blocks. On Thursday and Friday, we have level 1 backups again, which back up only the changed blocks, just as the Monday and Tuesday backups did. Finally, on Sunday, we start all over again with a level 0 backup.

Here is an example of a level 1 differential backup being executed. Remember, if a level 0 has not already occurred, this will result in a level 0 backup instead of a level 1 backup.

```
backup incremental level=1 database;
```

Cumulative Backups

RMAN provides another incremental backup option: the cumulative backup. Using this option causes backup sets to back up changed blocks since the last level 0 backup, ignoring any previous level 1 backups. This is an optional backup method and requires the use of the **cumulative** keyword in the **backup** command. Again, this can all be somewhat confusing, so let's look at an example. Figure 7-2 is an example of the impacts of cumulative backups using different levels.

In Figure 7-2, just as in Figure 7-1, we start with a level 0 differential backup being taken on Sunday. This backup backs up the entire database. Following that, on Monday, we perform a level 1 backup. This backup is not unlike the differential backup. Now things change a little bit. On Tuesday, we perform another level 1 differential backup. This time, the backup will contain not only changed blocks since Monday's backup, but also the blocks that were contained in Monday's backup. Thus, a cumulative backup accumulates all changed blocks for any backup level equal to or less than the level of the backup. As a result, for recovery purposes, we need only Tuesday's backup along with Sunday's base backup. We continue to take level 0 and level 1 backups over the remainder of the week to complete our backup strategy.

Here is an example of the creation of a level 1 cumulative backup:

```
backup incremental level=1 cumulative database;
```

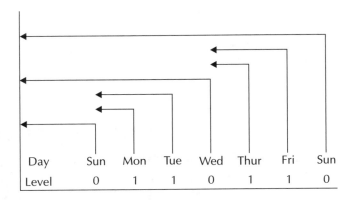

Day	Sun	Mon	Tue	Wed	Thur	Fri	Sun
Level	0	1	1	0	1	1	0

FIGURE 7-2. *Incremental backups*

Incremental Backup Options

Oracle allows you to perform incremental backups of not only the database, but also tablespaces, datafiles, and datafile copies. Control files, archived redo logs, and backup sets cannot be made as incremental backups. Additionally, you can choose to back up the archived redo logs at the same time. Here are some examples:

```
backup incremental level=0 tablespace users;
backup incremental level=1 tablespace users;
backup incremental level=0 datafile 4;
backup incremental level=1 datafile 4;
backup incremental level=1 database plus archivelog;
```

Metalink note 7457989.1 provides some insight into the block change tracking file and an inherent limit in that file. By default, Oracle's block change tracking file can only track bitmap changes of up to eight days between **recover** commands. If you need a recovery window of more than seven days or if you want to perform additional level 1 incrementals, you will need to modify the parameter **_bct_bitmaps_per_file** to allow for additional bitmaps.

Incrementally Updated Backups

RMAN offers incrementally updated backups (also called merged incremental backups), which let you avoid the overhead of taking full image copy backups of datafiles, yet provide the same recovery advantages as image copy backups.

Merged incremental backups are cumulative incremental backups by default. Older versions of Oracle will generate an error if you try to do them as differential incremental backups. With a merged incremental backup, you create a level 0 (full) backup. Subsequent backups will be level 1 incremental backups. As these incremental backups are made, they are merged into the previous level 0 backup. Thus, there is no need to re-create the level 0 backup, which can save time. Use a block change tracking file in combination with a merged incremental backup to further reduce the time it takes to back up a database.

Let's look at an example of a merged incremental backup:

```
RUN {
RECOVER COPY OF DATABASE WITH TAG 'incr_update';
BACKUP INCREMENTAL LEVEL 1 FOR RECOVER OF COPY WITH TAG 'incr_update'
DATABASE;
}
```

The **recover copy of database** command does not actually recover your database, but it causes RMAN to apply any incremental backups to the datafile copies associated with the tag listed (incr_update). The previous commands will create the backup in three stages:

1. The first backup using these commands will result in the creation of a level 0 backup (assuming a level 0 incremental backup does not already exist). Note that some errors will appear during this backup, starting with "no copy of datafile 1 found to recover." This is expected, since there is no level 1 incremental backup.

2. The second time you run this set of commands, a level 1 incremental backup will occur. Nothing else will occur during this run. Again, you will see the same error as seen on execution number 1.

3. On the third and subsequent iterations of this backup, the previous level 1 incremental backup will be applied to the level 0 backup. As a result, the level 0 backup will be up to date as of the applied level 1 incremental backup. A new level 1 incremental backup will then occur. This means that any recovery/restore effort only requires the recovery of the level 0 backup, followed by only one level 1 incremental backup (and any required archived redo logs). This can significantly reduce the time required to restore your database.

Note that we use tags for these backups. It is important that the tags are named the same in both the **recover** and **backup** commands.

You can also change the order of the command, performing the **backup incremental** first and then the **recover copy of database** command second, as shown in this example:

```
RUN {
BACKUP INCREMENTAL LEVEL 1 FOR RECOVER OF COPY WITH TAG 'incr_update'
DATABASE;
RECOVER COPY OF DATABASE WITH TAG 'incr_update';
}
```

Changing the order in this way will result in the incremental level 1 backups being applied to the level 0 base backups immediately; thus, there is no delay in the application of the incrementals to the base backup. This keeps the base backup as current as possible.

Note that this strategy assumes a retention policy of redundancy 1. If you need a more complex retention policy, you will need to use the **until** clause to ensure that you can meet your recovery window. For example, if your retention policy is seven days, you will set your retention policy to a redundancy of 1, and you will adjust your script to use the **until** clause, as shown here:

```
RUN {
BACKUP INCREMENTAL LEVEL 1 FOR RECOVER OF COPY WITH TAG 'incr_update'
DATABASE;
RECOVER COPY OF DATABASE WITH TAG 'incr_update' until time "sysdate-8";
}
```

Metalink note 351455.1 provides a more detailed discussion on the issue of retention and incrementally updated backups. When you use this method of guaranteeing a recovery window, it is important that you still configure the FRA to a redundancy of 1, and that you use the **until** clause to properly ensure your recovery window. Using a recovery window or a redundancy greater than 1 will result in files never being removed from the FRA, and thus you will quickly run out of space.

RMAN Workshop: *Perform an Incremental Backup*

Workshop Notes

This workshop assumes that your database has been configured with automatic channels (as shown in Chapter 5). It also assumes that you have configured a database account called backup_admin for backups (as described in Chapter 5). In addition, it assumes that if you are using the MML layer, it has been configured. Finally, your database must be configured for and operating in ARCHIVELOG mode.

Note that this workshop can be successfully used with either a multitenant database or a nonmultitenant database. If this database is a CDB, then the user you would log into would be a common user (C##), as was the case in the previous workshops.

Step 1.   Start up RMAN:

```
C:\>rman target=backup_admin/robert
```

Step 2.   Perform a level 0 incremental backup. Include the archived redo logs in the backup set, and then remove them after the backup:

```
backup incremental level=0 database plus archivelog delete input;
```

Step 3.   The next day, perform a level 1 incremental backup. Again, include the archived redo logs in the backup, and remove them after they are backed up:

```
backup incremental level=1 database plus archivelog delete input;
```

That about covers RMAN backups. The next chapter will be even more fun, because in it we discuss how to restore these backups and recover our databases.

Getting Started

We have covered a number of different backup options, and you may be left wondering where you should start. Let us make a suggestion or two. We recommend that you start with a test database, one that is very unimportant (better yet, one you have created for just this process). Here is an RMAN Workshop to get you started!

RMAN Workshop: *Get Your Database Backed Up!*

Workshop Notes

This workshop is more of an overall list of things you need to accomplish to get your database backed up. We have covered a great deal of ground in the last few chapters, and we felt it would be a good idea to summarize everything important up to this point. Note that if this database is a CDB, the user that you would log into would be a common user (C##), as was the case in the previous workshops.

Step 1. Set up a special account in your test database that will be responsible for backup operations. Configure the account as described in Chapter 5. Note that you can opt to use the SYS account, but we prefer to use a separate account.

Step 2. Set up your MML layer, and be clear on what it requires you to do when performing backup and recovery commands.

Step 3. As we describe in Chapter 5, use the **configure** command to configure a separate default channel for each device that you are backing up to, unless your specific device supports multiple channels (as some do). Set the default degree of parallelism, as shown in Chapter 5, such that each of the channels will be used during the backup. If you need to configure maximum set sizes, do so; otherwise, don't bother with that now.

Step 4. Use the **configure** command to configure automated backups of your control file and SPFILE (if you are using one). For now, let them be created in the default location. You will want to change this later, but for now, just leave it there.

Step 5. Make sure your operating system backup backs up your Oracle RDBMS software. (This also makes sure your control file backups will be backed up!)

Step 6. At first, we suggest that you not use a recovery catalog. Once you have the RMAN basics down pat and are ready to deploy RMAN to the enterprise, you can consider a recovery catalog.

Step 7. For the first few trials, run your database in NOARCHIVELOG mode if you can. Shut down and mount your database, and execute a few **backup database** commands. Make sure the backup sets are getting created where you expect them to.

Step 8. Go to Chapter 8 and recover the database. We suggest you make cold backups of the entire database, control file, and online redo logs (using the **cp** or **copy** command) first, just in case you run into some learning curves.

Step 9. Once you are good at recovering databases in NOARCHIVELOG mode, put the database in ARCHIVELOG mode, and do the same thing again. Back up the database using the **backup database plus archivelog** command.

Step 10. Go to Chapter 8 and Chapter 9 and do some recoveries. Become an RMAN recovery expert before you go any further.

Step 11. Play around with the **crosscheck** command, the **list** command, and the **report** commands (see Chapters 11 and 12 for more details on these commands). Become really comfortable with these commands and their purpose.

Step 12. If you have a large enterprise environment (say, more than ten databases), go ahead and add a recovery catalog to the mix, and connect to it and back up your database with it. We strongly encourage you to use a separate recovery catalog for development/test and production databases. Again, we suggest that you run through the gamut of backup and restore situations while using a recovery catalog before you move on.

Although Step 13 suggests the use of OS scripts to manage the RMAN backup, this is not considered a best practice. We are suggesting the solution here because we have not yet talked about Oracle Cloud Control, which we will cover in Chapter 14. Scheduling your backups through Oracle Database Cloud Control is the recommended best practice and will also be discussed in that context within Chapter 14.

Step 13. Once you are very comfortable with RMAN, create scripts to automate and schedule the process. For example, if you are running on Unix, a script such as the following could be scheduled through **cron** (we include an offline and online script here):

```
# For offline backups, use this script
#!/bin/ksh
# for offline backups, avoid shutdown aborts at all costs!
rman target rman_backup/password<<EOF
shutdown immediate
startup mount
backup database;
alter database open;
quit
EOF
```

If you are doing online backups, use this script:

```
#!/bin/ksh
rman target rman_backup/password<<EOF
backup database plus archivelog;
quit
EOF
```

These are korn shell scripts, which is one of the more commonly used shell scripting languages in Unix. Of course, RMAN works on a number of different platforms, so you can use the scripting language you are most comfortable with. In this script, we use what is known as a *here* document. That's what the EOF is in the fourth line of the first script and in the second line of the second script. A here document acts like the user is "here" and typing the input that you see listed from the EOF on the top line, until the closing EOF several lines later. Optionally, you could just use a command script created by a text editor and then call it from the RMAN command line, like this:

```
rman target rman_backup/password @backup.cmd
```

In this case, your backup.cmd script would look like this for an offline backup:

```
shutdown immediate
startup mount
backup database;
alter database open;
quit
```

For a hot backup, it would look like this:

```
backup database plus archivelog;
quit
```

You can also store scripts in RMAN by using the RMAN **create script** command. We will discuss stored RMAN scripts in Chapter 6, since storing scripts in RMAN requires a recovery catalog.

Step 14.   Before you move your backups into production, test restores of the backups you have set up in your test environments. Make sure you are comfortable that everything works as it should. We suggest that you keep using your old backup strategy in tandem until you have successfully tested several restores.

Step 15.   Move your RMAN backup strategy into production carefully. Do it one system at a time. Choose your least "visible" systems to convert first. We suggest that you do several test recoveries as you move out into production, and continue (if possible) to do dual backups on each database until you have recovered that production database on a test box with an RMAN backup successfully. Also, you might want to consider separate archived redo log backups, if that is required.

Step 16.   Perform disaster recovery and test backups often. We also suggest that, at least once a week, you execute a **restore database validate check logical** command on each database to make sure that the database is recoverable.

You will note that with each of these steps, we err on the side of caution. We leave it up to you to decide when you feel comfortable with your RMAN setup. There is just nothing more disheartening than trying to restore your database and getting a message that indicates an error in your attempted restore has occurred.

RMAN Best Practices Introduced in This Chapter

We have introduced you to several RMAN best practices in this chapter. Let's review them:

- When appropriate, use the RMAN configure command to set default settings for backups and use those settings to make your RMAN commands as basic as possible.
- For an OLTP database, the best backup strategy is typically an incremental backup strategy.
- Make sure you use a block change tracking file when performing incremental backups.

- For a data warehouse, use the Oracle Incrementally Updated backup strategy, including the appropriate recovery window.

- Use a RMAN recovery catalog.

- Use Oracle Cloud Control 12c to manage your backups. Store all of your backup scripts in Cloud Control and not on a variety of different servers or even a common shared script location.

Summary

In this chapter, we have covered RMAN backups galore. We looked at how to do offline backups and online backups using RMAN. We also looked at RMAN incremental backups. We discussed the impact of configured defaults on backups and how much easier they make the backup process. We also introduced the numerous options you can use with backups, such as using tags, overriding the default retention policy and forcing backups of read-only datafiles. We looked at methods of detecting database corruption with RMAN. All in all, it has been a full chapter, but we hope you have found it to be a worthwhile one. You are now a step closer to being an RMAN expert, but the real fun is yet to come, and that's recovery. Hang on, because that's coming up next.

CHAPTER
8

RMAN Restore
and Recovery

We have talked about backing up your database. Now, it's time to talk about how we are going to restore and recover your database from those backups. First, unless there is a specific reason not to do so, we will treat nonmultitenant databases and the entirety of a multitenant database CDB pretty much the same. In most respects, the operations you do on one are the same as on the other. We, of course, cover all aspects of PDB restore and recovery in this chapter as well.

In this chapter we cover the following topics:

- RMAN restore and recovery basics
- The RMAN restore and recovery commands
- Preparing for an RMAN restore
- Restoring the database SPFILE
- Restoring the database control file
- Complete restore and recovery of a database in NOARCHIVELOG mode
- Complete restore and recovery of a database in ARCHIVELOG mode
- Complete restore and recovery of a PDB
- Recovering from the loss of online redo logs
- Using the Data Recovery Advisor

This chapter covers basic point-of-failure restore and recovery in RMAN. Chapter 9 will build on this chapter, covering database incarnations as well as incomplete database restores of CDBs and PDBs. Chapter 9 will also cover other RMAN restore topics such as the restore of archived redo logs, recovery of corrupt database blocks, tablespace point-in-time recovery, and other RMAN-related topics.

RMAN Restore and Recovery Basics

In this chapter we discuss database restores and recoveries using RMAN. First, when we talk about a database restore or a database recovery, we mean the actual process of taking a database that has somehow become corrupted and restoring it to use. In this context, the terms are interchangeable. When we talk about the RMAN commands **restore** and **recover**, these are very specific individual and unique commands that are used to perform a database restore.

Database restores usually occur because something has happened to a database that has caused it to become corrupted in some way. Because of this corruption, the database must be restored. This corruption can be as simple as a user accidently truncating a table, to the actual loss of the database physical files on its operating media. In any event, there are a great number of reasons we will find ourselves facing a database restore.

When we are using Oracle, we use RMAN to perform a database recovery. In this effort you will use two commands. First, you will use the RMAN **restore** command and then you will use the RMAN **recover** command. Therefore, the two commands are frequently used together when performing RMAN database recovery operations.

When we talk about an RMAN restore, we mean using the RMAN **restore** command to start a restore of a database. In this case, the **restore** command extracts the needed backup files from the appropriate backup sets, copying those files to some physical location.

In most cases the RMAN **restore** command will be followed by the RMAN **recover** command to complete an RMAN Oracle database recovery. The RMAN **recover** command will extract any needed archived redo logs, apply them to the restore database datafiles, and complete the recovery process. All that is left to you as the DBA, then, is to open the database.

NOTE
Probably the main point here to understand is that in most cases, when you are using RMAN to recover a database from some failure, you will almost always use the restore command first, and then the recover command second.

There are other uses of the **restore** and **recover** commands beyond those described here. For example, the **restore** command can be used to validate existing RMAN backup files that have been created by previous backups. The **restore** command can also be used to restore old archived redo logs, or it can be used to ensure that the files that are required to restore an Oracle database are available on media and that those files are not corrupt. We discuss these uses of the **restore** and **recover** commands throughout the chapters in this book.

Types of Oracle Database Recoveries

One other huge consideration with respect to Oracle Database is what logging mode the database was in when it was backed up. We discussed the ARCHIVELOG and NOARCHIVELOG modes in Chapter 2. How you perform RMAN-based database recoveries, and the options you can use with the RMAN **restore** and **recover** commands, will depend very much on which database logging mode you are using.

Three main kinds of database recovery are supported by RMAN. These are point-of-backup, point-of-failure (or complete), and point-in-time restores. Point-of-backup restores are the only kind of restore supported when the database is in NOARCHIVELOG mode. It is really its own special kind of point-in-time restore because the database can only be restored to the time when the database was actually backed up.

When the database is in ARCHIVELOG mode, you have an option to perform either a point-of-failure restore or a point-in-time restore. A point-of-failure database recovery allows for the complete restore of the database without any loss of data. There are some requirements to be able to do a point-in-time restore that we will cover in more detail later in this chapter. A point-in-time restore is a database restore to any point in time that is covered by available RMAN database backups and archived redo logs.

Of course, the time to decide what kind of restore you wish to be able to perform is before you actually need to restore the database. Thinking ahead is very important when it comes to backup and recovery of an Oracle database.

About Restoring Multitenant Databases

Oracle Database 12c introduced the multitenant database feature, which we introduced you to in Chapter 4. In this chapter we cover full database restores of nonmultitenant databases. These same procedures will also apply to full database restores of Oracle Multitenant databases exactly as written. In Chapter 9, we discuss other topics related to the recovery of Oracle PDBs and any other issues unique to restores of Oracle Multitenant databases. Within this chapter, the restores that are demonstrated are applicable to both Oracle Multitenant databases and those that are not using the Oracle Multitenant feature. In the case where any distinction is required, we will point it out.

Preparing for an RMAN Restore

Before RMAN can do its thing, you need to do a few things first. Preparation is the mother of success, someone once said, and this is so true when it comes to restoring your database. You need to work with your system administrator to make sure the following tasks are done before you attempt your restore/recovery:

- The OS parameters are configured for Oracle.
- Your disks are configured correctly and are the correct sizes.
- The tape drives are installed, and the tape software is installed and configured.
- Your network is operational.
- The Oracle RDBMS software is installed.
- The MML is configured.
- Ancillary items are recovered from backups that RMAN does not back up, including
    - The database networking files (for example, sqlnet.ora and listener.ora)
    - The oratab file, if one is used
    - The database parameter files, if they are not SPFILEs and are not backed up by RMAN
- Ensure that the appropriate RMAN backup set pieces are in place, including the backup set pieces for automated control file backups.

Once these items have been restored, you are ready to begin restoring your Oracle database. If you are using a recovery catalog, you will want to recover it first, of course. Then, you can recover the remaining databases.

If you are not using the recovery catalog, and if you do not have a good backup of the control file, you will need to manually create the database control file using the **create control file** SQL command (this can be run from the RMAN prompt or from SQL*Plus). Once you have manually created the control file, you will want to use the RMAN **catalog** command to catalog the backup set pieces that need to be used for the database recovery. We discuss the use of the **catalog** command in more detail later in this chapter.

When you start recovering databases, you need to start by recovering the SPFILE (if you are using one and it was backed up), followed by the control file. The next two sections cover those topics for you.

NOTE
In this chapter we generally assume that you are not using a recovery catalog when doing your database recoveries. In most cases, nothing will be different if you are using a recovery catalog. If there are important distinctions to make with respect to the use of a recovery catalog, we indicate these in the chapter, as appropriate.

Staging RMAN Backup Set Pieces for Restores

Real database restores are rarely convenient things. First of all, just the fact that something has happened to make you have to restore your database is enough to ruin your day. Often, whatever the cause of your failure is, there are often ancillary ramifications. One of these might be that all of the backup files in the Fast Recovery Area (FRA) you backed up to have been deleted.

In Chapter 15, we help you build an architecture where we eliminate the FRA as a single point of failure. In the architecture that we recommend, RMAN will always know where the various backup set pieces are so that restores will be easy and quick.

Your backup architecture may be different though. We often find that legacy backup architectures will back up the RMAN backup set pieces to some other location, not using RMAN. In these cases, RMAN loses "touch" of where these backup set pieces are. In these cases, the first thing you need to do is recover the backup set pieces from the backup media and restore them to the directory where RMAN will be expecting them to reside. This might be the FRA or some other external directory. It may be that you cannot restore the backup set pieces to the original directory structure. In this case, you should restore the backup set pieces to some directory that is accessible to RMAN. Recover the database control file if that is required, and then use the **catalog** command (discussed later in this chapter) to catalog these backup set pieces in the database control file and/or recovery catalog.

The main points here are that the RMAN backup set pieces need to reside somewhere that RMAN can access them and that RMAN needs to know where those backup set pieces are. For many kinds of restores, you probably won't have to do anything, but for more critical database restore operations, you may have to stage the backup files before you can even start an RMAN database recovery.

Restoring the SPFILE

Now that you have staged your RMAN backup set pieces (or ensured that they are where you expected them to be already), we are ready to restore whatever part of the database has gone missing or that needs to be replaced. Let's begin at the beginning, which is the restore of database SPFILEs.

You really should be using SPFILEs. Although Oracle still supports the text-based parameter file, and probably always will, we'll still say it—use the SPFILE. That being said, RMAN has the ability to back up database SPFILEs and control files automatically. We have discussed configuring control file automatic backups in previous chapters in this book. Now we will put them to good use!

As we discuss restoring the SPFILE in this chapter, we will assume that you have in fact lost the SPFILE. Thus, any configuration required because of the loss of that file will be covered. It's pretty easy to tell if the SPFILE has been lost. When you try to start the database you will get an error that looks something like this:

```
C:\Users\Robert>sqlplus / as sysdba
SQL*Plus: Release 12.1.0.1.0 Production on
Tue Dec 2 09:34:24 2014
Copyright (c) 1982, 2013, Oracle.  All rights reserved.
Connected to an idle instance.
SQL> startup
ORA-01078: failure in processing system parameters
LRM-00109: could not open parameter file 'C:\APP\ORACLE\PRODUCT\12.1.0
\DBHOME_1\DATABASE\INITORCL12C.ORA'
```

It really does not matter what your operating system is, the message will look pretty much the same, except the path of the missing SPFILE will look like the type of path common to your operating system.

If you want to see a list of SPFILE backups, you can issue the **list backup of spfile** command when the database is mounted or when you are connected to a recovery catalog. As with many other types of restores, SPFILE restores can occur with different kinds of permutations. For example, you may or may not be using a recovery catalog, or you may or may not be using a Fast Recovery Area (FRA). In the following sections we will look at recovering the SPFILE from an RMAN control file autobackup where the FRA was not in use. Then we will look at recovering an SPFILE when the database FRA is in use.

Recovering the SPFILE from Memory on a Running Database

If you have mistakenly deleted the database SPFILE and the database is still running, the easiest way to re-create the SPFILE is to use the SQL command **create spfile from memory**. Note that this is a SQL command and not an RMAN command (though the command can be run from the RMAN prompt). In most cases, you will need to create an SPFILE to a location other than one where the old SPFILE previously existed. You should then use the temporary file to create a new copy of the database SPFILE. Let's look at an example. First, let's find the location of the SPFILE by looking at the SPFILE parameter (the SPFILE parameter might not be used, in which case the SPFILE would be contained in the default directory of the database—for example, $ORACLE_HOME/dbs in Linux). In this case, we find the SPFILE parameter is in use:

```
SQL> show parameter spfile
NAME                              TYPE          VALUE
--------------------------------  -----------   ----------------
spfile                            string        C:\APP\ORACLE\PRODUCT\12.1.0\D
                                                BHOME_1\DATABASE\SPFILEORCL12C
                                                .ORA
```

However, when we look at the directory where the SPFILE is supposed to be located, we find that the SPFILE is missing:

```
C:>Dir C:\APP\ORACLE\PRODUCT\12.1.0\DBHOME_1\DATABASE\SPFILEORCL12C.ORA
Volume in drive C is OSDisk
Volume Serial Number is 8885-2E99
Directory of C:\APP\ORACLE\PRODUCT\12.1.0\DBHOME_1\DATABASE
File Not Found
```

The database is still running, fortunately. So, we will just use the **create spfile from memory** SQL command. We will create an SPFILE that is named differently than the one the database was started with. This is because Oracle will not let you override the current SPFILE—even if that file has been accidently deleted. Once we create the temporary SPFILE, we will use the OS **copy** command to copy it into place. Here is an example of this operation:

```
Rman target=/
RMAN> create spfile='c:\robert\newspfile.ora' from memory;
File created.
RMAN>exit
c:>copy c:\robert\newspfile.ora
C:\APP\ORACLE\PRODUCT\12.1.0\DBHOME_1\DATABASE\ SPFILEORCL12C.ORA
        1 file(s) copied.
```

As you can see, in the previous example we don't even need an RMAN backup of the SPFILE to correct the problem. However, this solution isn't available if the database is not running.

NOTE
If you are using SPFILEs and you did not configure autobackups and didn't manually back up the SPFILE with RMAN (or some other way), you won't be able to restore the SPFILE. In this case, you will need to manually re-create a text-based parameter file and then use the SQL*Plus command **create spfile from pfile** *to re-create the SPFILE.*

Recovering the SPFILE when Using RMAN Controlfile Autobackups and an FRA

If the database is not running, then re-creation of the SPFILE from memory is not possible. In this section we assume you have enabled SPFILE autobackups. To restore the SPFILE, we need a way to get the database instance started so we can perform the RMAN recovery of that file.

To prepare for a restore of the SPFILE, you will need to first configure the Oracle database environment on the OS. For example, on a Linux system you would set parameters such as ORACLE_HOME, ORACLE_SID, and the PATH required by the database you want to restore.

Start the database instance (**startup nomount**) through the RMAN interface. When you issue the **startup nomount** command from the RMAN prompt and no SPFILE or database parameter file is available, then the database instance will be started with a temporary parameter file to allow RMAN to restore the database SPFILE from backup. Note that only RMAN will be able to start the database instance this way; this function is not available through SQL*Plus.

Now that the instance is started, you will want to make sure you know the name of the database and the location where the RMAN files are located.

NOTE
If you are using ASM for the FRA, the ASM instance will need to be running before you can configure the DB_RECOVERY_FILE_DEST properly.

Now that you have collected all the information you need, we are ready to restore the backup of the database SPFILE. To perform this restore we use the RMAN **restore spfile** command. In our case the recovery area is defined as "/u01/app/oracle/fast_recovery_area" and the database name is called ROB. In the following example, we have done the following:

1. Set the database environment.
2. Started RMAN.
3. Started the database instance with the **startup nomount** command from the RMAN prompt. The output from RMAN indicates that the parameter file could not be opened and that it's opening the database without a parameter file so we can restore the SPFILE.
4. The Oracle instance is started.
5. The database SPFILE was extracted using the **restore spfile from autobackup** command. Note that we have included the location of the recovery area and the name of the database as parameters to the **restore spfile** command.

6. Once the SPFILE was restored, we restarted the database with the **startup force** command.

```
[oracle@bigdatalite ~]$ . oraenv
ORACLE_SID = [rob] ?
The Oracle base remains unchanged with value /u01/app/oracle
[oracle@bigdatalite ~]$ rman target=/
Recovery Manager: Release 12.1.0.2.0 - Production on Wed Dec 3 14:33:13 2014
Copyright (c) 1982, 2014, Oracle and/or its affiliates.
All rights reserved.
connected to target database (not started)
RMAN> startup nomount
startup failed: ORA-01078: failure in processing system parameters
LRM-00109: could not open parameter file '/u01/app/oracle/product/12.1.0.2/
dbhome_1/dbs/initrob.ora'
starting Oracle instance without parameter file for retrieval of spfile
Oracle instance started
Total System Global Area    1073741824 bytes
Fixed Size                     2932632 bytes
Variable Size                293601384 bytes
Database Buffers             771751936 bytes
Redo Buffers                   5455872 bytes
RMAN> restore spfile from autobackup
recovery area='/u01/app/oracle/fast_recovery_area' db_name='ROB';
Starting restore at 03-DEC-14
using target database control file instead of recovery catalog
allocated channel: ORA_DISK_1
channel ORA_DISK_1: SID=6 device type=DISK
recovery area destination: /u01/app/oracle/fast_recovery_area
database name (or database unique name) used for search: ROB
channel ORA_DISK_1: AUTOBACKUP
/u01/app/oracle/fast_recovery_area/ROB/autobackup/
2014_12_03/o1_mf_s_865347235_b7yr7nw4_.bkp found in the
recovery area AUTOBACKUP search with format "%F" not attempted
because DBID was not set
channel ORA_DISK_1: restoring spfile from AUTOBACKUP
/u01/app/oracle/fast_recovery_area/ROB/autobackup/
2014_12_03/o1_mf_s_865347235_b7yr7nw4_.bkp
channel ORA_DISK_1: SPFILE restore from AUTOBACKUP complete
Finished restore at 03-DEC-14
RMAN> startup force;
```

A few things to note about the restore of an SPFILE. First, RMAN will search for backups of SPFILES, restoring the most current one that is available. If you wish to find a different SPFILE, you can reference a specific tag name or use the **until** clause (or the **set until** clause if you prefer) to indicate the day on which you want to start your search. RMAN will check back in time for a default value of seven days for backups of the SPFILE. You can use the **maxdays** parameter to change the number of days you want to have RMAN check. RMAN can check back for a maximum of 366 days for a control file autobackup to restore. Here is an example where we have RMAN check for backups that are at least seven days old, and then checking for backups ten days from that point in time. You can also use the **maxseq** parameter (not shown here) to control how many sequence numbers to traverse. Finally, note in the example that we are restoring the SPFILE to a different directory:

```
Restore spfile to '/tmp/spfilecopy' from autobackup
maxdays 10 until time 'sysdate -7';
```

NOTE
Control file RMAN autobackups are stored in their own specific backup location in the FRA. Under the root of the FRA you will find them in a directory structure that looks like the following: <instance_ name>/autobackup/<date>. The backup files are named, by default, using OFA. Although this naming convention can be changed, we recommend against it.

Recovering the SPFILE when Using RMAN Controlfile Autobackups and No FRA

If you are using RMAN controlfile autobackups but you are not backing up to the FRA, then you will need to slightly adjust your restore procedure. The most common reason why the controlfile autobackups are being located in a place different from the FRA is because the RMAN **configure controlfile autobackup** command has been used to indicate that a different location for the controlfile autobackup backup set pieces should be used.

We should take a second to talk about what defines the filename of the RMAN control file autobackup backup set pieces and the location in which they are stored. The location and name of these backup set pieces are controlled by the **configure controlfile autobackup format** RMAN command. When this command is used to define the location of the controlfile backup set pieces, the format must always contain the %F parameter. The use of the %F parameter is required and provides a standardized format for the name of the resulting backup set pieces.

When the controlfile autobackups are not stored in the FRA, RMAN needs different information to be able to locate them. This is because the standardized format of the FRA was not used. In this case, the information we need is the location where the controlfile autobackups will be stored and the DBID of the database.

Each Oracle database is assigned a DBID when it's created. The DBID for any given database is supposed to be unique (though there are ways, such as a manual database duplication, that can result in a DBID being duplicated). You can find the DBID for a given database by querying the DBID column of the V$DATABASE view, as shown here:

```
RMAN> select dbid from v$database;
     DBID
----------
1146089261
```

The DBID is used by RMAN when naming the control file autobackup backup set pieces. Since the database DBID is used, all of the backup set pieces for a specific database are guaranteed to be uniquely named from any other database.

If you don't know the DBID of the database you need to restore the SPFILE for, don't panic—there are a couple of ways of going about finding it. First, if the location where the controlfile autobackup backup set pieces are stored is unique to the database, then finding the DBID of the database is simple because you can find the DBID of the database in the filename of the controlfile autobackup backup set pieces.

If there is more than one database using the same directory to store its control file autobackup backup set pieces, then you can use a command similar to the Linux **strings** command to search the various control file automatic backup set pieces for the name of your database. For example, in this case, we've used strings to search for the DB_NAME parameter within the backup set piece that belongs to a controlfile autobackup. The DB_NAME parameter will tell us the name of the database contained in the autobackup:

```
[oracle@bigdatalite ~]$ ls -al /u02/backup
total 405208
drwxr-xr-x. 2 oracle oinstall      4096 Dec  3 15:43 .
drwxr-xr-x. 6 oracle oinstall      4096 Dec  3 15:24 ..
-rw-r-----. 1 oracle oinstall  18055168 Dec  3 15:43
c-1146089261-20141203-03
[oracle@bigdatalite backup]$ strings c-1146089261-20141203-03|
grep db_name
*.db_name='rob'
```

Now that we know the name of the backup set piece, we know the DBID for the database called rob. It's in the name of that backup set piece. Notice that the backup set piece starts with a c-, which indicates that it's a controlfile autobackup backup set piece. The next number (1145089261) is the DBID for the database. (See, we found it!) The next number is the date of the backup (12/03/2014), which is followed by a sequence number assigned to that backup (03). For each given day, when a controlfile autobackup occurs, it will be assigned its own unique sequence number. The sequence numbers reset each day. Up to 256 sequences (starting with the number 1) are allowed each day.

Now that we have collected all the information we need, it's time to restore the SPFILE using the RMAN **restore spfile** command. In the following example, we have done the following:

1. Set the database environment.

2. Started RMAN.

3. Set the DBID of the database that is the owner of the SPFILE we need to restore.

4. Started the database instance with the **startup nomount** command from the RMAN prompt. The output from RMAN indicates that the parameter file could not be opened and that it's opening the database without a parameter file so we can restore the SPFILE.

5. Used the **set controlfile autobackup format** RMAN command to define the location and filenaming format of the control file autobackups.

6. Allocated a channel for the restore to use with the **allocate channel** RMAN command. Note that we do not need to define a location when this channel is allocated because we set the controlfile autobackup location and format earlier.

7. Extracted the database SPFILE using the **restore spfile from autobackup** command.

8. Once the SPFILE was restored, we restarted the database with the **startup force** command.

```
[oracle@bigdatalite ~]$ . oraenv
ORACLE_SID = [rob] ?
rman target sys/robert
set DBID = 1145089261;
startup nomount;
run
```

```
{
set controlfile autobackup format for device type disk
to '/u02/backup/%F';
allocate channel c1 device type disk;
restore spfile from autobackup;
}
startup force;
```

We have issued a **startup force** after this example and several others. After any SPFILE restore, you will need to restart the instance to have the correct parameters take effect. If all that is missing is the SPFILE, the database will start up normally. If you need to perform other recovery activities, you will now be able to do so. You can perform any additional recovery activities that might be required.

As earlier, we can also use the **maxdays** and **maxseq** parameters to control how many days' worth of backups to search for and how many sequences we want to process for each day. Also, the **until time** parameter is perfectly valid. What's more, as we showed you earlier, you can use this technique to restore an SPFILE to a different location, as you can see in this example:

```
[oracle@bigdatalite ~]$ . oraenv
ORACLE_SID = [rob] ?
rman target sys/robert
set DBID = 1145089261;
startup nomount;
run
{
set controlfile autobackup format for device type disk
to '/u02/backup/%F';
allocate channel c1 device type disk;
Restore spfile to '/tmp/spfilecopy' from autobackup
maxdays 10 until time 'sysdate -7';
}
startup force;
```

If you know the specific backup set piece from which you want to extract the SPFILE, you can reference it in the **restore** command by including the **from backup** clause, as shown in this example:

```
[oracle@bigdatalite ~]$ . oraenv
ORACLE_SID = [rob] ?
rman target=/
set DBID = 1145089261;
startup nomount;
run
{
set controlfile autobackup format for device type disk
to '/u02/backup/%F';
allocate channel c1 device type disk;
Restore spfile
from 'd:\backup\recover\C-2539725638-20060629-00';
}
startup force;
```

This allows you to simply indicate the backup set piece that contains the SPFILE backup in it. You can save a great deal of time if you know which backup set piece you want to use to restore the SPFILE.

Recovering the SPFILE when Using a Recovery Catalog

If you are using a recovery catalog, restoring the most current SPFILE is as simple as setting the environment correctly, connecting to the database instance, and starting it (**nomount**). Then you would issue the **restore spfile** command. RMAN will use the recovery catalog to locate the most current control file backup and will extract that backup for your use. Therefore, there is no need to use the **autobackup** parameter. Here is an example:

```
[oracle@bigdatalite ~]$ . oraenv
ORACLE_SID = [rob] ?
rman target sys/robert catalog rcat_manager/password@robt
startup nomount;
restore spfile;
startup force;
```

Extracting a Copy of the SPFILE and Converting to a PFILE

Extracting a copy of your SPFILE from a database backup with the database up is really easy regardless of whether you are using a control file or a recovery catalog. You should note that this operation will result in a text parameter file, and not an SPFILE, so you will need to convert it if you want it to be an SPFILE. Here is an example where we create a PFILE from an SPFILE backup:

```
RMAN> restore spfile to pfile 'd:\backup\test.ora'
from autobackup;
```

Note that you would need to include the additional steps we already demonstrated depending on whether you are using the FRA or a non-FRA location. If you are using a recovery catalog, you can remove the **autobackup** parameter.

RMAN Workshop: *Recover Your SPFILE*

Workshop Notes

For this workshop, you need an installation of the Oracle software and an operational test Oracle database. We also assume the following:

- The archivelog mode of the database can be either ARCHIVELOG mode or NOARCHIVELOG mode.

- That you are using the FRA when doing backups.

- That the location of the FRA is /u02/fast_recovery_area. Replace all instances of this directory structure with the FRA path for your database. You can determine this location from SQL*Plus by issuing the command **show parameter db_recovery_file_dest**.

- That the name of your database is rob. Replace this with the correct name of the database that you are using.

Step 1.   Ensure that you have configured automated backups of your control files:

```
configure controlfile autobackup on;
```

In this case, we are accepting that the control file backup set pieces will be created in the default location.

Step 2.   Complete a backup of your system (in this case, we assume this is a hot backup):

```
set oracle_sid=recover
rman target rman_backup/password
backup database plus archivelog;
```

In this workshop, we assume that the backup is to a configured default device.

Step 3.   Shut down your database by using the **shutdown immediate** command (from either SQL*Plus or RMAN):

```
shutdown immediate;
```

Do not use the **shutdown abort** command in this workshop.

Step 4.   Rename your database SPFILE. Do not remove it, just in case your backups cannot be recovered. You can generally find the name of your SPFILE by using the **show parameter spfile** command in SQL*Plus. The SPFILE may also be contained in the OS-specific default directory defined for parameter files. In Linux this would be $ORACLE_HOME/dbs. The name of the SPFILE is generally spfile<dbname>.ora, though it may be named differently.

Step 5.   From RMAN, attempt to start the database using the **startup** command:

```
startup;
```

RMAN will indicate that the SPFILE and parameter file cannot be found, and it will start the instance with a temporary parameter file. RMAN then will return an error indicating that it could not find the control file.

Step 6.   Recover your control file with RMAN by using your autobackup of the control file:

```
restore spfile from autobackup
recovery area='/u02/fast_recovery_area' db_name='ROB';
```

Step 7.   We will test the SPFILE restore by issuing the **startup force nomount** command. The database instance should start normally now:

```
Startup force nomount;
```

Restoring the Control File

Restoring the control file is essentially the same process as restoring the database parameter file. As with the parameter files, the main distinctions are

- Restoring when you have used an FRA
- Restoring when you have not used the FRA
- Restoring when you have used a recovery catalog

In the first section we discuss restoring the control file given the conditions shown in the preceding list. Then we will discuss restoring RMAN-related records to the control file.

Restoring the Control File with RMAN

Before you can restore the control file, you need to have started the database instance with the correct SPFILE. This is because only the correct SPFILE will have the metadata required to know where the control files are supposed to be located. We discussed restoring the database SPFILE in the previous section, so you should be aware of how to restore the database SPFILE.

The RMAN methods used to restore an SPFILE are exactly the same as those used to restore a control file, with a few differences. First, you use the **controlfile** keyword instead of the **spfile** keyword. Either you will be using the FRA, a user-defined backup location for control file autobackups, or a recovery catalog. One difference is if you are using the FRA, you will not need to define the FRA location or define the name of the database as you did with an SPFILE restore.

First, here is an example of the recovery of a control file when you are using an FRA:

```
[oracle@bigdatalite ~]$ . oraenv
ORACLE_SID = [rob] ?
rman target=/
startup nomount
restore controlfile from autobackup;
recover database;
alter database open resetlogs;
startup force;
```

Note that this looks almost identical to the method used to restore the SPFILE, with a few differences:

- We used the keyword **restore controlfile**.
- After restoring the control file, we need to issue the RMAN **recover database** command. This indicates to RMAN to prepare the Oracle database to be opened with the recovered control file. The **recover database** command prepares the database to be opened with the **alter database resetlogs** command. If you need to restore datafiles, you would perform that function before issuing the **recover database** command. You will see this demonstrated later in this chapter.
- The database is then opened with the **alter database open resetlogs** command.

Note that if your database is in NOARCHIVELOG mode, the **recover database** command might need to look slightly different. If you have lost the online redo logs, you will need to add the **noredo** parameter to the **recover database** command. If the online redo logs are intact, the **noredo** parameter is not required. Here is an example of using the **noredo** parameter when restoring a control file if the online redo logs were lost as well:

```
[oracle@bigdatalite ~]$ . oraenv
ORACLE_SID = [rob] ?
rman target=/
startup nomount
restore controlfile from autobackup;
recover database noredo;
alter database open resetlogs;
startup force;
```

This indicates to RMAN that the online redo logs have been lost. Obviously, if you need to perform a recovery of database datafiles, you would not yet use the **recover database** or **alter database open resetlogs** command. Instead, you would begin the recovery of your database, after which you would open it.

The next example is if you are restoring the control file and you are not using the FRA for control file autobackups. Again, this procedure looks similar to the one used to restore the SPFILE that you saw earlier in this chapter. This includes setting the database DBID before the restore and setting the backup location of the control file autobackups with the **set controlfile autobackup format** RMAN command.

As with the previous control file restore, we also needed to execute the **recover database** command and the **alter database open resetlogs** command to open the database after the restore:

```
[oracle@bigdatalite ~]$ . oraenv
ORACLE_SID = [rob] ?
rman target sys/robert
set DBID = 1145089261;
startup nomount;
run
{
set controlfile autobackup format for device type disk
to '/u02/backup/%F';
allocate channel c1 device type disk;
restore controlfile from autobackup;
}
recover database;
alter database open resetlogs;
startup force;
```

Restoring RMAN-Related Records to the Control File

Once you have restored the control file, you need to consider the distinct possibility that you have lost RMAN-related data. If you are using an RMAN recovery catalog, all of your backup records will be contained in there, so you really have lost nothing. If you are only using the control file, then because RMAN stores all of its data in the control file, there is a good possibility you have at least lost some records that relate to archived redo logs (which Oracle needs for a full recovery).

RMAN makes this problem pretty easy to deal with, because you can register various RMAN-related backup files after the restore of a control file, just to ensure that you have everything you need for a recovery in the control file. To re-create RMAN-related archived redo log records, you can use the RMAN **catalog** command to register archived redo logs in your control file. The **catalog** command can be used to register a specific backup set piece, as shown in this example:

```
RMAN>Catalog backuppiece 'c:\oracle\product\10.2.0\flash_recovery_area
\testoem\backupset\2005_12_09\O1_MF_ANNNN_TAG20051209T041150_
1SLP386H_.BKP';
```

You can also catalog archived redo logs, as in this example:

```
RMAN>Catalog archivelog
'c:\oracle\product\10.2.0\flash_recovery_area\testoem\archivelog\
2005_12_15\O1_MF_1_2_1T3SVF05_.ARC';
```

Now, if you are thinking ahead, you might sigh and say to yourself, "Who wants to manually catalog the 1,000 archived redo logs that were generated throughout the day?" Fortunately, the RMAN developers had the same thought! With RMAN, you can catalog a whole directory without having to list individual files. Simply use the **catalog** command again, but use one of the following keywords:

- **recovery area** or **db_recovery_file_dest**
- **start with**

The **recovery area** and **db_recovery_file_dest** keywords have the same function: they cause the entire FRA to be cataloged by RMAN. If RMAN finds files that are already cataloged, it simply skips over them and continues to catalog any remaining files that are not found in the control file. Here is an example of cataloging all files in the FRA:

```
RMAN> catalog recovery area;
```

If you are not using the FRA, you will want to use the **start with** syntax instead. The **start with** syntax allows you to traverse a non-FRA backup directory and to catalog any RMAN-related files contained in that directory and any subdirectories under that directory. Here is an example of the use of the **catalog start with** command:

```
catalog start with 'c:\oracle\backups\testoem';
```

NOTE
RMAN automatically catalogs the FRA for you if you perform a restore operation with a backup control file.

RMAN Workshop: *Recover Your Control File*

Workshop Notes

For this workshop, you need an installation of the Oracle software and an operational test Oracle database. Also, we assume the following:

- That the database is in NOARCHIVELOG mode.
- That you are using the FRA when doing backups.

■   That the location of the FRA is /u02/fast_recovery_area. Replace all instances of this directory structure with the FRA path for your database. You can determine this location from SQL*Plus by issuing the command **show parameter db_recovery_file_dest**.

■   That the name of your database is rob. Replace this with the correct name of the database you are using.

NOTE
For this workshop, the database is in ARCHIVELOG mode.

Step 1.   Ensure that you have configured automated backups of your control files:

```
configure controlfile autobackup on;
```

In this case, we are accepting that the control file backup set pieces will be created in the default location.

Step 2.   Complete a backup of your system (in this case, we assume this is a hot backup):

```
set oracle_sid=recover
rman target rman_backup/password
backup database plus archivelog;
```

In this workshop, we assume that the backup is to a configured default device.

Step 3.   Shut down your database by using the **shutdown immediate** command:

```
shutdown immediate;
```

Do not use the **shutdown abort** command in this workshop.

Step 4.   Rename all copies of your database control file. Do not remove them, just in case your backups cannot be recovered.

Step 5.   Start your database:

```
startup;
```

It should complain that the control file cannot be found and it will not open.

Step 6.   Recover your control file with RMAN by using the RMAN **restore controlfile** command:

```
restore controlfile from autobackup;
```

Step 7.   Mount the database and then simulate incomplete recovery to complete the recovery process:

```
Alter database mount;
recover database;
alter database open resetlogs;
```

Restore and Recover the Database in NOARCHIVELOG Mode

If your database is in NOARCHIVELOG mode, you will be recovering from a full, offline backup, and point-in-time recovery won't be possible. If your database is in ARCHIVELOG mode, read the "Database Recoveries in ARCHIVELOG Mode" section later in this chapter. If you are doing incremental backups of your NOARCHIVELOG database, you will also want to read the "What If I Use Incremental Backups?" section, also later in this chapter.

Preparing for the Restore

If you are running in NOARCHIVELOG mode, and assuming you actually have a backup of your database, performing a full recovery of your database is very easy. First, it's a good idea to clean everything out. You don't have to do this, but we have found that in cases of NOARCHIVELOG recoveries, cleaning out old datafiles, online redo logs, and control files is a good idea. You don't want any of those files lying around. Because you are in NOARCHIVELOG mode, you will want to start afresh. (Of course, it's also a very good idea to make sure that those files are backed up somewhere just in case you need to get them back!)

Having cleaned out your datafiles, control files, and redo logs, you are ready to start the recovery process. First, recover the control file from your last backup, as demonstrated earlier in this chapter. Alternatively, you can use a backup control file that you created at some point after the backup from which you want to restore. If you use the **create control file** command, you need to catalog the RMAN backup-related files before you can restore the database.

For this example, we assume that you are not using a recovery catalog. We also assume you want to recover from the most current backup, which is the default setting for RMAN. If you want to recover from an older backup, you need to use the **set time** command, which we will discuss later in this section.

The differences in recovery with and without a recovery catalog are pretty much negligible once you are past the recovery of the SPFILE and the control file. Therefore, we will only demonstrate recoveries without a recovery catalog. Also, at this point, there is little difference in how you perform a recovery regardless of whether you are using the FRA or not. In the upcoming examples, we use the FRA and highlight any issues that arise from this fact in the text.

First, let's look at the RMAN commands you use to perform this recovery:

```
startup mount;
restore database;
recover database;
alter database open resetlogs;
```

Looks pretty simple. Of course, these steps assume that you have recovered your SPFILE and your database control files. The first command, **startup mount**, mounts the database. So, Oracle reads the control file in preparation for the database restore. The **restore database** command causes RMAN to actually start the database datafile restores. Following this command, **recover database** instructs RMAN to perform final recovery operations in preparation for opening the database. Finally, we open the database with the **alter database open resetlogs** command. Because we have restored the control file and we need the online redo logs rebuilt, we need to use the **resetlogs** command. In fact, you will probably use **resetlogs** with about every NOARCHIVELOG recovery you do.

So, let's look at a NOARCHIVELOG database recovery in action. In this case, we assume that the database SPFILE and control file are already recovered or are intact:

```
-- SPFILE and Control files already restored.
RMAN> alter database mount;
Statement processed
released channel: ORA_DISK_1
RMAN> select log_mode from v$database;
LOG_MODE
------------
NOARCHIVELOG
RMAN> restore database;
Starting restore at 05-DEC-14
Starting implicit crosscheck backup at 05-DEC-14
allocated channel: ORA_DISK_1
channel ORA_DISK_1: SID=243 device type=DISK
allocated channel: ORA_DISK_2
channel ORA_DISK_2: SID=355 device type=DISK
Crosschecked 6 objects
Finished implicit crosscheck backup at 05-DEC-14
Starting implicit crosscheck copy at 05-DEC-14
using channel ORA_DISK_1
using channel ORA_DISK_2
Finished implicit crosscheck copy at 05-DEC-14
searching for all files in the recovery area
cataloging files...
cataloging done
List of Cataloged Files
=======================
File Name: /u01/app/oracle/fast_recovery_area/MYCDB/autobackup/
2014_12_05/o1_mf_s_865551026_b84zxbqo_.bkp
using channel ORA_DISK_1
using channel ORA_DISK_2
channel ORA_DISK_1: starting datafile backup set restore
channel ORA_DISK_1: specifying datafile(s) to restore
from backup set
channel ORA_DISK_1: restoring datafile 00003 to /u01/app/oracle/oradata/MYCDB/
datafile/
o1_mf_sysaux_b84vocw8_.dbf
channel ORA_DISK_1: restoring datafile 00004 to /u01/app/oracle/oradata/MYCDB/
datafile/
o1_mf_undotbs1_b84wk1v1_.dbf
channel ORA_DISK_1: reading from backup piece /u01/app/oracle/fast_recovery_area/
MYCDB/backupset/
2014_12_05/o1_mf_nnndf_TAG20141205T225129_b84zb6mx_.bkp
channel ORA_DISK_2: starting datafile backup set restore
channel ORA_DISK_2: specifying datafile(s) to restore from
backup set
channel ORA_DISK_2: restoring datafile 00001 to /u01/app/oracle/oradata/MYCDB/
datafile/o1_mf_system_b84w0k8q_.dbf
channel ORA_DISK_2: restoring datafile 00006 to /u01/app/oracle/oradata/MYCDB/
datafile/o1_mf_users_b84wjr0j_.dbf
channel ORA_DISK_2: reading from backup piece /u01/app/oracle/fast_recovery_area/
MYCDB/backupset/2014_12_05/
o1_mf_nnndf_TAG20141205T225129_b84zb62w_.bkp
channel ORA_DISK_1: piece handle=/u01/app/oracle/fast_recovery_area/MYCDB/backupset
```

```
/2014_12_05/o1_mf_nnndf_TAG20141205T225129_b84zb6mx_.bkp
tag=TAG20141205T225129
channel ORA_DISK_1: restored backup piece 1
channel ORA_DISK_1: restore complete, elapsed time: 00:04:37
channel ORA_DISK_1: starting datafile backup set restore
channel ORA_DISK_1: specifying datafile(s) to restore from backup
set
channel ORA_DISK_1: restoring datafile 00007 to
/u01/app/oracle/oradata/MYCDB/datafile/o1_mf_sysaux_b84wrzq0_.dbf
channel ORA_DISK_1: reading from backup piece
/u01/app/oracle/fast_recovery_area/MYCDB
/0984942EDFD02640E0530100007F6315/backupset/2014_12_05/
o1_mf_nnndf_TAG20141205T225129_b84zkyjk_.bkp
channel ORA_DISK_2: piece handle=/u01/app/oracle/fast_recovery_area/MYCDB/backupset/
2014_12_05/o1_mf_nnndf_TAG20141205T225129_b84zb62w_.bkp
tag=TAG20141205T225129
channel ORA_DISK_2: restored backup piece 1
channel ORA_DISK_2: restore complete, elapsed time: 00:07:33
channel ORA_DISK_2: starting datafile backup set restore
channel ORA_DISK_2: specifying datafile(s) to restore from backup
set
channel ORA_DISK_2: restoring datafile 00008 to /u01/app/oracle/oradata/MYCDB/0984F46A
4A902B83E0530100007F7A04
/datafile/o1_mf_system_b84ysl80_.dbf
channel ORA_DISK_2: restoring datafile 00010 to /u01/app/oracle/oradata/MYCDB/0984F46A
4A902B83E0530100007F7A04/
datafile/o1_mf_users_b84yxb74_.dbf
channel ORA_DISK_2: reading from backup piece /u01/app/oracle/fast_recovery_area/
MYCDB/
0984F46A4A902B83E0530100007F7A04/
backupset/2014_12_05/o1_mf_nnndf_TAG20141205T225129_b84zq3bw_.bkp
channel ORA_DISK_1: piece handle=/u01/app/oracle/fast_recovery_area/MYCDB/
0984942EDFD02640E0530100007F6315/backupset/2014_12_05/
o1_mf_nnndf_TAG20141205T225129_b84zkyjk_.bkp
tag=TAG20141205T225129
channel ORA_DISK_1: restored backup piece 1
channel ORA_DISK_1: restore complete, elapsed time: 00:03:53
channel ORA_DISK_1: starting datafile backup set restore
channel ORA_DISK_1: specifying datafile(s) to restore from backup
set
channel ORA_DISK_1: restoring datafile 00009 to /u01/app/oracle/oradata/MYCDB/0984F46A
4A902B83E0530100007F7A04/
datafile/o1_mf_sysaux_b84yslfn_.dbf
channel ORA_DISK_1: reading from backup piece /u01/app/oracle/fast_recovery_area/
MYCDB/
0984F46A4A902B83E0530100007F7A04/backupset/2014_12_05/
o1_mf_nnndf_TAG20141205T225129_b84zon32_.bkp
channel ORA_DISK_2: piece handle=/u01/app/oracle/fast_recovery_area/MYCDB/
0984F46A4A902B83E0530100007F7A04/backupset/2014_12_05/
o1_mf_nnndf_TAG20141205T225129_b84zq3bw_.bkp
tag=TAG20141205T225129
channel ORA_DISK_2: restored backup piece 1
channel ORA_DISK_2: restore complete, elapsed time: 00:02:02
channel ORA_DISK_2: starting datafile backup set restore
channel ORA_DISK_2: specifying datafile(s) to restore from backup
set
```

```
channel ORA_DISK_2: restoring datafile 00005 to /u01/app/oracle/oradata/MYCDB/
datafile/
o1_mf_system_b84wrzsj_.dbfchannel
ORA_DISK_2: reading from backup piece
/u01/app/oracle/fast_recovery_area/MYCDB/
0984942EDFD02640E0530100007F6315/backupset/2014_12_05/
o1_mf_nnndf_TAG20141205T225129_b84ztgrz_.bkp
channel ORA_DISK_2: piece handle=/u01/app/oracle/fast_recovery_area/MYCDB/
0984942EDFD02640E0530100007F6315/backupset/2014_12_05/
o1_mf_nnndf_TAG20141205T225129_b84ztgrz_.bkp
tag=TAG20141205T225129
channel ORA_DISK_2: restored backup piece 1
channel ORA_DISK_2: restore complete, elapsed time: 00:02:06
channel ORA_DISK_1: piece handle=/u01/app/oracle/fast_recovery_area/MYCDB/
0984F46A4A902B83E0530100007F7A04/backupset/2014_12_05/
o1_mf_nnndf_TAG20141205T225129_b84zon32_.bkp
tag=TAG20141205T225129
channel ORA_DISK_1: restored backup piece 1
channel ORA_DISK_1: restore complete, elapsed time: 00:03:44
Finished restore at 05-DEC-14
RMAN> recover database;
Starting recover at 05-DEC-14
using channel ORA_DISK_1
using channel ORA_DISK_2
starting media recovery
RMAN-08187: WARNING: media recovery until SCN 1607446 complete
Finished recover at 05-DEC-14
RMAN> alter database open resetlogs;
Statement processed
RMAN>
```

Note that this particular restore was done using an Oracle database that had Oracle Multitenant (OM) enabled. Also, in this case we are using the FRA. The output would look similar to a non-OM database, except fewer datafiles would have been restored. Also, if you are not using the FRA, the output would pretty much look the same. The commands used to restore the database would be exactly the same, although in some cases you may need to allocate a channel or two. Let's look at parts of this output in a bit more detail.

First, notice that after we issued the **restore database** command that RMAN performed an implicit crosscheck between the control file and the files within the FRA itself. Then, RMAN proceeded to catalog the files in the FRA. These two operations are occurring because we restored the control file of this database. RMAN knows that this has occurred and, as such, during the **restore database** process it will automatically crosscheck the FRA and also catalog the contents of the FRA.

The crosscheck occurs because it is possible that records will have already been added to the control file after it's restored, and RMAN must make sure that those records are valid. The catalog process ensures that the control file has all of the backup records it needs when processing the restore operation. Note that if we had not restored the control file, the crosscheck and the catalog operation would not have occurred unless we executed those commands explicitly.

Next, RMAN will start the database restore process. It extracts the datafiles from the various backup set pieces, reassembles them, and then moves them to the location where the database expects them to be. During this restore operation, two disk channels were allocated (automatically), so two different processes were running the restore tasks in parallel.

Parallelism is probably one of the main ways you can speed up restores (and backups) with RMAN. However, parallelism is also a good way to slow things down. Therefore, be careful that you balance the degree of parallelism with the available system resources. Once the restore is complete, we then proceed to issue the **recover database** command. Because this database is in NOARCHIVELOG mode, this command does not have a great deal to do, so it completes quickly.

Finally, we issue the **alter database open resetlogs** command to open the database. The reason we included the **resetlogs** option is because we renamed the online redo logs, simulating their loss. The **resetlogs** option will cause Oracle to re-create the online redo logs when it opens the database. This also creates a new incarnation of our database from RMAN's point of view.

We discuss the notion and impact of database incarnations in the next chapter. At this point, however, it's not really important to know much about them. For now, just know that an incarnation represents a logical lifespan of a database from either the time the database was created or the last time the **resetlogs** command was used to the execution of another **resetlogs** operation. Some more complex RMAN restores require you to identify the incarnation from which you want to restore. We discuss that topic in the next chapter.

Restoring to a Different Location

Of course, we don't always have the luxury of restoring back to the original file system names where the Oracle files resided. For example, during a disaster recovery drill, you might have one big file system to recover to rather than six smaller-sized file systems. That can be a bit of a problem, because, by default, RMAN is going to try to restore your datafiles to the same location they came from when they were backed up. So, how do we fix this problem?

Enter the **set newname for datafile** and **switch** commands. These commands, when used in concert with **restore** and **recover** commands, allow you to tell RMAN where the datafiles need to be placed.

The **set newname** command offers several options with respect to relocation of database datafiles. The **set newname** command provides the ability to either set the new filename for individual datafiles, or you can change the location for all datafiles in a tablespace or in the entire database.

In our first example, we have datafiles originally backed up to d:\oracle\data\recover, and we want to recover them to a different directory: e:\oracle\data\recover. To do this, we first issue the **set newname for datafile** command for each datafile, indicating its old location and its new location. Here is an example of this command's use:

```
set newname for datafile 'd:\oracle\data\recover\system01.dbf'
to 'e:\oracle\data\recover\system01.dbf';
```

This example would work for all versions of the Oracle Database when using RMAN. Note that we define both the original location of the file and the new location that RMAN should copy the file to. Once we have issued **set newname for datafile** commands for all of the datafiles that we want to restore to a different location, we proceed as before with the **restore database** and **recover database** commands. Finally, before we actually open the database, we need to indicate to Oracle that we really want to have it use the relocated datafiles that we have restored. We do this by using the **switch** command.

The **switch** command causes the datafile locations in the database control file to be changed so that they reflect the new location of the Oracle database datafiles. Typically, you use the **switch datafile all** command to indicate to Oracle that you wish to switch all datafile locations in the control file. Alternatively, you can use the **switch datafile** command to switch only specific datafiles.

If you use the **set newname for datafile** command and do not switch all restored datafiles, then any nonswitched datafile will be considered a datafile copy by RMAN, and RMAN will not try to use that nonswitched datafile when recovering the database. Here is an example of the commands you might use for a restore using the **set newname for datafile** command:

```
startup nomount
restore controlfile from autobackup;
alter database mount;
run
{
set newname for datafile 'd:\oracle\oradata\recover\system01.dbf'
to 'e:\oracle\oradata\recover\system01.dbf';
set newname for datafile
'd:\oracle\oradata\recover\recover_undotbs_01.dbf' to
'e:\oracle\oradata\recover\recover_undotbs_01.dbf';
set newname for datafile 'd:\oracle\oradata\recover\users01.dbf'
to 'e:\oracle\oradata\recover\users01.dbf';
set newname for datafile 'd:\oracle\oradata\recover\tools01.dbf' to
'e:\oracle\oradata\recover\tools01.dbf';
set newname for datafile 'd:\oracle\oradata\recover\indx01.dbf' to
'e:\oracle\oradata\recover\indx01.dbf';
restore database;
recover database;
switch datafile all;
alter database open resetlogs;
}
```

Note that if the recovery is not successful but the files were restored successfully, the datafiles restored will become datafile copies and will not be removed.

Of course, all of the individual **set newname** commands involve a lot of typing for a large number of database files. We can reset the names of all the restored database files by using the **set newname for database** command. If we want to rename all the database files at a less granular level, we can reset the filenames at the tablespace level with the **set newname for tablespace** command. The **set newname for tempfile** command provides the same service for tempfiles.

With the advent of CDBs, new options for the **set newname** command are available. You can now use the **set newname for database root** and **set newname for pluggable database** commands to set the new default datafile and tempfile names for the root CDB and any individual PDB.

In conjunction with the **set newname for database** command, you must use substitution variables to avoid any collisions with filenames that might occur during the movement of the datafiles. The substitution variables are available for use with the other **set newname** commands, too. The substitution variables are detailed in Table 8-1.

Here is an example of using the **set newname for database** command that will result in the renaming of all datafiles of that database:

```
RUN
{
shutdown abort;
startup mount;
SET NEWNAME FOR DATABASE TO 'C:\oradata1\%b';
Restore database;
Recover database;
switch datafile all;
Alter database open;
}
```

Variable	Meaning
%b	This will result in the full filename without any directory path information.
%f	This will result in the absolute file number for the datafile.
%U	This will result in a system-generated filename guaranteed to be unique.
%I	This will result in the DBID of the database.
%N	This will result in the tablespace name.

TABLE 8-1. *The set newname Substitution Variables*

If you just wanted to rename the files for a specific tablespace, you would change the **set newname** command slightly, as seen in this example:

```
RUN
{
shutdown immediate;
startup mount;
SET NEWNAME FOR TABLESPACE user_data TO 'c:\oradatanew\users\user_data%b.dbf';
Restore database;
switch datafile all;
Recover database;
Alter database open;
}
```

RMAN Workshop: *Recover Your NOARCHIVELOG Mode Database*

Workshop Notes

For this workshop, you need an installation of the Oracle software and an operational test Oracle database. Also, in this workshop we assume the following:

- That the database is either a CDB or non-CDB database
- That the database is in NOARCHIVELOG mode
- That you are using the FRA when doing backups

Step 1. Set the ORACLE_SID and then log into RMAN. Ensure that you have configured automated backups of your control files. Because this is an offline backup, you need to shut down and mount the database, as shown here:

```
set oracle_sid=recover
rman target rman_backup/password
configure controlfile autobackup on;
shutdown immediate;
startup mount;
```

Note that in this case, we are accepting that the control file backup set pieces will be created in the default location.

Step 2.   Complete a cold backup of your system:

```
backup database;
```

In this workshop, we assume that the backup is to a configured default device.

Step 3.   Shut down your database:

```
shutdown immediate;
```

Step 4.   Rename all database datafiles. Also rename the online redo logs and control files. (Optionally, you can remove these files if you don't have the space to rename them and if you really can afford to lose your database should something go wrong.) You can find the names of the files you need to rename in the following data dictionary views:

- **Database datafiles**   v$datafile (column name)
- **Control files**   v$controlfile (column name)
- **Online redo logs**   v$logfile (column member)

> **NOTE**
> *We are not restoring the SPFILE during this workshop because we are not removing or renaming it.*

Step 5.   From RMAN, issue the **startup nomount** command to start your database. Then, use the **restore controlfile** command to restore your control file. Finally, after the control file has been restored, mount the database with the **alter database mount** command:

```
Startup nomount;
restore controlfile from autobackup;
alter database mount;
```

Step 6.   Restore your database datafiles with RMAN using the **restore database** command. This will restore the database with the backup you took in Step 2. You will notice that when you issue the **restore database** command, RMAN will catalog all of the datafiles in the FRA. This is because we restored the control file in Step 5. After it has done so, it can then restore those datafiles.

After the datafiles have been restored, complete the recovery by issuing the **recover database** command and then open the database with the **alter database open command**, all from the RMAN prompt:

```
restore database;
recover database;
alter database open resetlogs;
```

Step 7.   Complete the recovery by backing up the database again:

```
shutdown immediate;
startup mount;
backup database;
```

Note that although this is not absolutely required, it is considered a best practice.

Database Recoveries in ARCHIVELOG Mode

Typically, you will find production databases in ARCHIVELOG mode because of one or more requirements, such as the following:

- Point-in-time recovery
- Minimal recovery time service-level agreements (SLAs) with customers
- The ability to do online database backups
- The ability to recover specific datafiles while the database is available to users

When the database is in ARCHIVELOG mode, you have a number of recovery options from which you can choose:

- Full database recovery
- Tablespace recoveries
- Datafile recoveries
- Incomplete database recovery
- Online block media recovery

We cover the first three items in this section. Later in this chapter, we look at incomplete database recoveries. In Chapter 9, we look at online block media recovery in more detail. With each of these types of recoveries, you will find that the biggest difference compared with NOARCHIVELOG mode recovery is the application of the archived redo logs, as well as some issues with regard to defining when (meaning to what point in time) you want to recover to if you are doing an incomplete recovery. For now, let's start by looking at a full database recovery in ARCHIVELOG mode.

NOTE
Recoveries of SPFILEs and control files are the same regardless of whether you are running in NOARCHIVELOG or ARCHIVELOG mode.

Point-of-Failure Database Recoveries

With a point-of-failure database recovery (also known as a full database recovery), you hope that you have your online redo logs intact; in fact, any unarchived online redo log must be intact. If you lose your online redo logs, you are looking at an incomplete recovery of your database. Reference Chapter 9 for more information on incomplete recoveries. Finally, we are going to assume that at least one control file is intact. If no control file is intact, you need to recover a control file backup, and again you are looking at an incomplete recovery (unless your online redo logs are intact).

In this first example, we have lost all of our database datafiles. We have also lost the control files. Fortunately, the online redo logs remain intact. This requires a full recovery of the database, of course. Therefore, we will restore our control file and then restore and recover the database. Finally, we will open the database. Here are the commands used to perform this restore operation:

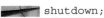
```
shutdown;
startup mount;
restore controlfile from autobackup;
```

```
restore database;
recover database;
alter database open resetlogs;
```

You will find the output from this restore next. Note that we interrupt the output a few times to make a few comments.

```
[oracle@bigdatalite oracle]$ . oraenv
ORACLE_SID = [MYCDB] ? mycdb
The Oracle base remains unchanged with value /u01/app/oracle
[oracle@bigdatalite oracle]$ rman target=/
Recovery Manager: Release 12.1.0.2.0 - Production on Sat Dec 6 12:59:32 2014
Copyright (c) 1982, 2014, Oracle and/or its affiliates.
All rights reserved.
connected to target database (not started)
RMAN> startup mount
Oracle instance started
RMAN-00571: ===========================================================
RMAN-00569: =============== ERROR MESSAGE STACK FOLLOWS ===============
RMAN-00571: ===========================================================
RMAN-03002: failure of startup command at 12/06/2014 13:54:12
ORA-00205: error in identifying control file, check alert log for more info
RMAN> restore controlfile from autobackup;
Starting restore at 06-DEC-14
using target database control file instead of recovery catalog
allocated channel: ORA_DISK_1
channel ORA_DISK_1: SID=355 device type=DISK
recovery area destination: /u01/app/oracle/fast_recovery_area
database name (or database unique name) used for search: MYCDB
channel ORA_DISK_1: AUTOBACKUP
/u01/app/oracle/fast_recovery_area/MYCDB/autobackup/2014_12_06/
o1_mf_s_865556951_b8551j5d_.bkp found in the recovery area
AUTOBACKUP search with format "%F" not attempted because
DBID was not set
channel ORA_DISK_1: restoring control file from AUTOBACKUP
/u01/app/oracle/fast_recovery_area/MYCDB/autobackup/2014_12_06/
o1_mf_s_865556951_b8551j5d_.bkp
channel ORA_DISK_1: control file restore from AUTOBACKUP complete
output file name=/u01/app/oracle/oradata/MYCDB/controlfile/
o1_mf_b84wnwc1_.ctl
output file name=/u01/app/oracle/fast_recovery_area/MYCDB/
controlfile/o1_mf_b84wnycy_.ctl
Finished restore at 06-DEC-14
RMAN> alter database mount;
Statement processed
```

Here we tried to start the database only to discover that the control file was missing. We proceeded to restore the control file. There are some implications to this. First, when we start the database restore, the control file will be crosschecked and then the FRA will be cataloged. Also, because we are restoring the control file, we need to use the **resetlogs** command when opening the database. Once the database control file is restored, we can mount the database and prepare to restore the database datafiles.

Continuing our example, because we restored the control files, we may want to make sure the RMAN persistent configurations are set correctly. For example, we might want to make sure we have the degree of parallelism set properly for a quick restore. To do this, we use the **show all** RMAN command, as you can see here:

```
RMAN>show all;
RMAN configuration parameters for database with db_unique_name
are:
CONFIGURE RETENTION POLICY TO REDUNDANCY 1; # default
CONFIGURE BACKUP OPTIMIZATION OFF; # default
CONFIGURE DEFAULT DEVICE TYPE TO DISK; # default
CONFIGURE CONTROLFILE AUTOBACKUP ON; # default
CONFIGURE CONTROLFILE AUTOBACKUP FORMAT FOR DEVICE TYPE DISK TO '%F'; # default
CONFIGURE DEVICE TYPE DISK PARALLELISM 2 BACKUP TYPE TO
COMPRESSED BACKUPSET;
CONFIGURE DATAFILE BACKUP COPIES FOR DEVICE TYPE DISK TO 1;
# default
CONFIGURE ARCHIVELOG BACKUP COPIES FOR DEVICE TYPE DISK TO 1;
# default
CONFIGURE MAXSETSIZE TO UNLIMITED; # default
CONFIGURE ENCRYPTION FOR DATABASE OFF; # default
CONFIGURE ENCRYPTION ALGORITHM 'AES128'; # default
CONFIGURE COMPRESSION ALGORITHM 'BASIC' AS OF RELEASE 'DEFAULT'
OPTIMIZE FOR LOAD TRUE ; # default
CONFIGURE RMAN OUTPUT TO KEEP FOR 7 DAYS; # default
CONFIGURE ARCHIVELOG DELETION POLICY TO NONE; # default
CONFIGURE SNAPSHOT CONTROLFILE NAME TO
'/u01/app/oracle/product/12.1.0.2/dbhome_1/dbs/snapcf_mycdb.f';
# default
```

We have determined that a parallelism of 2 is sufficient for our needs. In this case, there are no other settings we need to configure (we address some of the cases where you might need to change configuration settings in the next chapter). Now, let's restore the database:

```
RMAN> restore database;
Starting restore at 06-DEC-14
Starting implicit crosscheck backup at 06-DEC-14
allocated channel: ORA_DISK_1
channel ORA_DISK_1: SID=357 device type=DISK
allocated channel: ORA_DISK_2
channel ORA_DISK_2: SID=355 device type=DISK
Crosschecked 15 objects
Finished implicit crosscheck backup at 06-DEC-14
Starting implicit crosscheck copy at 06-DEC-14
using channel ORA_DISK_1
using channel ORA_DISK_2
Finished implicit crosscheck copy at 06-DEC-14
searching for all files in the recovery area
cataloging files...
cataloging done
List of Cataloged Files
=======================
File Name:
```

```
/u01/app/oracle/fast_recovery_area/MYCDB/archivelog/2014_12_06/
o1_mf_1_3_b85w0sfs_.arc
File Name: /u01/app/oracle/fast_recovery_area/MYCDB/archivelog/2014_12_06/
o1_mf_1_5_b86b26cw_.arc
File Name:
/u01/app/oracle/fast_recovery_area/MYCDB/archivelog/2014_12_06/
o1_mf_1_4_b8623dcv_.arc
File Name:
/u01/app/oracle/fast_recovery_area/MYCDB/autobackup/2014_12_06/
o1_mf_s_865556951_b8551j5d_.bkp
using channel ORA_DISK_1
using channel ORA_DISK_2
```

Here we see the automatic crosscheck and cataloging in process. This has happened because we restored the control file. RMAN knows that the control file is newly created and automatically performs the crosscheck and cataloging. This would not have occurred if we had not restored the control file.

In the next example, the first channel will be allocated. We can see the backup set it is restoring and the datafiles that are going to be restored from that backup set.

```
channel ORA_DISK_1: starting datafile backup set restore
channel ORA_DISK_1: specifying datafile(s) to restore from
backup set
channel ORA_DISK_1: restoring datafile 00003 to
/u01/app/oracle/oradata/MYCDB/datafile/o1_mf_sysaux_b850jvcm_.dbf
channel ORA_DISK_1: restoring datafile 00004 to
/u01/app/oracle/oradata/MYCDB/datafile/
o1_mf_undotbs1_b850jvon_.dbf
channel ORA_DISK_1: reading from backup piece
/u01/app/oracle/fast_recovery_area/MYCDB/backupset/2014_12_06/
o1_mf_nnndf_TAG20141206T000514_b853npvx_.bkp
```

Now the second channel will be allocated. Remember that both of these channels will be restoring database datafiles in parallel.

```
channel ORA_DISK_2: starting datafile backup set restore
channel ORA_DISK_2: specifying datafile(s) to restore from
 backup set
channel ORA_DISK_2: restoring datafile 00001 to
/u01/app/oracle/oradata/MYCDB/datafile/o1_mf_system_b850jvl9_.dbf
channel ORA_DISK_2: restoring datafile 00006 to
/u01/app/oracle/oradata/MYCDB/datafile/o1_mf_users_b850jw11_.dbf
channel ORA_DISK_2: reading from backup piece /u01/app/oracle/fast_recovery_
area/MYCDB/backupset/2014_12_06/
o1_mf_nnndf_TAG20141206T000514_b853nmqz_.bkp
channel ORA_DISK_1: piece
handle=/u01/app/oracle/fast_recovery_area/MYCDB/backupset/
2014_12_06/o1_mf_nnndf_TAG20141206T000514_b853npvx_.bkp
tag=TAG20141206T000514
```

After a while, we see that the first channel, called ORA_DISK_1, has completed its restore. We can also see how long the restore took:

```
channel ORA_DISK_1: restored backup piece 1
channel ORA_DISK_1: restore complete, elapsed time: 00:04:47
```

The backup is not complete at this point—there are more files to restore. Since the first channel completed its initial work, it's reallocated to restore another backup set. Thus, the channels will continue to be reused until all of the backup set pieces are restored. You will also see in this next example that the second channel has completed its work, and it also starts to work on another backup set restore:

```
channel ORA_DISK_1: starting datafile backup set restore
channel ORA_DISK_1: specifying datafile(s) to restore from
backup set
channel ORA_DISK_1: restoring datafile 00007 to /u01/app/oracle/oradata/MYCDB/
datafile/o1_mf_sysaux_b850sjp6_.dbf
channel ORA_DISK_1: reading from backup piece
/u01/app/oracle/fast_recovery_area/MYCDB/
0984942EDFD02640E0530100007F6315/backupset/2014_12_06/
o1_mf_nnndf_TAG20141206T000514_b8549lq9_.bkp
channel ORA_DISK_2: piece
handle=/u01/app/oracle/fast_recovery_area/MYCDB/backupset/
2014_12_06/o1_mf_nnndf_TAG20141206T000514_b853nmqz_.bkp
tag=TAG20141206T000514
channel ORA_DISK_2: restored backup piece 1
channel ORA_DISK_2: restore complete, elapsed time: 00:07:33
channel ORA_DISK_2: starting datafile backup set restore
channel ORA_DISK_2: specifying datafile(s) to restore from
backup set
channel ORA_DISK_2: restoring datafile 00008 to
/u01/app/oracle/oradata/MYCDB/datafile/o1_mf_system_b850z29j_.dbf
channel ORA_DISK_2: restoring datafile 00010 to
/u01/app/oracle/oradata/MYCDB/datafile/o1_mf_users_b850z2ls_.dbf
channel ORA_DISK_2: reading from backup piece
```

We wanted to point out that these next few lines are the restore of the PDB of the multitenant database. Note that the directory in which the PDB datafiles are stored has an additional directory name. This directory name is the GUID of the PDB that owns the datafiles stored in that directory. We discuss GUIDs and their use in multitenant databases in Chapter 4. This next section completes all of the datafile restores across the two different channels:

```
/u01/app/oracle/fast_recovery_area/MYCDB/
0984F46A4A902B83E0530100007F7A04/backupset/2014_12_06/
o1_mf_nnndf_TAG20141206T000514_b854ppkm_.bkp
channel ORA_DISK_1: piece
handle=/u01/app/oracle/fast_recovery_area/MYCDB/
0984942EDFD02640E0530100007F6315/backupset/2014_12_06/
o1_mf_nnndf_TAG20141206T000514_b8549lq9_.bkp
tag=TAG20141206T000514
channel ORA_DISK_1: restored backup piece 1
```

```
channel ORA_DISK_1: restore complete, elapsed time: 00:03:43
channel ORA_DISK_1: starting datafile backup set restore
channel ORA_DISK_1: specifying datafile(s) to restore from
backup set
channel ORA_DISK_1: restoring datafile 00009 to
/u01/app/oracle/oradata/MYCDB/datafile/o1_mf_sysaux_b8510t70_.dbf
channel ORA_DISK_1: reading from backup piece
/u01/app/oracle/fast_recovery_area/MYCDB/
0984F46A4A902B83E0530100007F7A04/backupset/2014_12_06/
o1_mf_nnndf_TAG20141206T000514_b854jrn7_.bkp
channel ORA_DISK_2: piece handle=/u01/app/oracle/fast_recovery_area/MYCDB/
0984F46A4A902B83E0530100007F7A04/backupset/2014_12_06/
o1_mf_nnndf_TAG20141206T000514_b854ppkm_.bkp
tag=TAG20141206T000514
channel ORA_DISK_2: restored backup piece 1
channel ORA_DISK_2: restore complete, elapsed time: 00:02:02
channel ORA_DISK_2: starting datafile backup set restore
channel ORA_DISK_2: specifying datafile(s) to restore from
backup set
channel ORA_DISK_2: restoring datafile 00005 to
/u01/app/oracle/oradata/MYCDB/datafile/o1_mf_system_b8512y4s_.dbf
channel ORA_DISK_2: reading from backup piece
/u01/app/oracle/fast_recovery_area/MYCDB/
0984942EDFD02640E0530100007F6315/backupset/2014_12_06/
o1_mf_nnndf_TAG20141206T000514_b854w99c_.bkp
channel ORA_DISK_2: piece handle=/u01/app/oracle/fast_recovery_area/MYCDB/
0984942EDFD02640E0530100007F6315/backupset/2014_12_06/
o1_mf_nnndf_TAG20141206T000514_b854w99c_.bkp
tag=TAG20141206T000514
channel ORA_DISK_2: restored backup piece 1
channel ORA_DISK_2: restore complete, elapsed time: 00:02:06
channel ORA_DISK_1: piece
handle=/u01/app/oracle/fast_recovery_area/MYCDB/
0984F46A4A902B83E0530100007F7A04/backupset/2014_12_06/
o1_mf_nnndf_TAG20141206T000514_b854jrn7_.bkp
tag=TAG20141206T000514
channel ORA_DISK_1: restored backup piece 1
channel ORA_DISK_1: restore complete, elapsed time: 00:03:42
Finished restore at 06-DEC-14
```

Now that the restore is complete, we need to issue the recover database command to cause the archived redo logs to be applied to the restored datafiles. At first in this output, RMAN finds that the archived redo logs are on disk and that they have not been backed up. RMAN will always use the archived redo logs that are on disk first. If it can't find them on disk, it will try to restore them.

```
RMAN> recover database;
Starting recover at 06-DEC-14
using channel ORA_DISK_1
using channel ORA_DISK_2
starting media recovery
archived log for thread 1 with sequence 3 is already on disk
```

```
as file /u01/app/oracle/fast_recovery_area/MYCDB/archivelog/2014_12_06/
o1_mf_1_3_b85w0sfs_.arc
archived log for thread 1 with sequence 4 is already on disk
as file /u01/app/oracle/fast_recovery_area/MYCDB/archivelog/2014_12_06/
o1_mf_1_4_b8623dcv_.arc
archived log for thread 1 with sequence 5 is already on disk as file /u01/app/
oracle/fast_recovery_area/MYCDB/archivelog/2014_12_06/
o1_mf_1_5_b86b26cw_.arc
```

Now, RMAN will start to restore archived redo log sequences 1 and 2 from an RMAN backup set because these archived redo logs are not available on disk:

```
channel ORA_DISK_1: starting archived log restore to default destination
channel ORA_DISK_1: restoring archived log
archived log thread=1 sequence=2
channel ORA_DISK_1: reading from backup piece
/u01/app/oracle/fast_recovery_area/MYCDB/backupset/2014_12_06/
o1_mf_annnn_TAG20141206T002903_b855118t_.bkp
channel ORA_DISK_1: piece
handle=/u01/app/oracle/fast_recovery_area/MYCDB/backupset/
2014_12_06/o1_mf_annnn_TAG20141206T002903_b855118t_.bkp
tag=TAG20141206T002903
channel ORA_DISK_1: restored backup piece 1
channel ORA_DISK_1: restore complete, elapsed time: 00:00:03
archived log file name=/u01/app/oracle/fast_recovery_area/MYCDB/archivelog/
2014_12_06/o1_mf_1_2_b86oqkoq_.arc thread=1 sequence=2
channel default: deleting archived log(s)
archived log file
name=/u01/app/oracle/fast_recovery_area/MYCDB/archivelog/
2014_12_06/o1_mf_1_2_b86oqkoq_.arc RECID=6 STAMP=865606819
archived log file name=/u01/app/oracle/fast_recovery_area/MYCDB/archivelog/
2014_12_06/o1_mf_1_3_b85w0sfs_.arc thread=1 sequence=3
archived log file name=/u01/app/oracle/fast_recovery_area/MYCDB/archivelog/
2014_12_06/o1_mf_1_4_b8623dcv_.arc thread=1 sequence=4
archived log file name=/u01/app/oracle/fast_recovery_area/MYCDB/archivelog/
2014_12_06/o1_mf_1_5_b86b26cw_.arc thread=1 sequence=5
media recovery complete, elapsed time: 00:00:04
Finished recover at 06-DEC-14
```

At this point, RMAN has applied all of the redo. If it can't find the redo in the archived redo logs, it will try to apply it from the online redo logs. If neither is available, RMAN will apply all of the redo it can and then generate an error.

Once the **recover** command is complete, the database is in a consistent state and can be opened. In this case, we used the **alter database open resetlogs** command to open the database. The **resetlogs** command is required because we restored the control file earlier. Here is an example in which we opened the database with the **alter database open resetlogs** command:

```
RMAN> alter database open resetlogs;
Statement processed
```

There are a few things to realize about restore operations like this. First, if the datafile already exists, then Oracle determines whether the file it's going to restore already exists. If so, and the file that exists is the same as the file it's preparing to restore, RMAN will not restore that file again. If the file on the backup image is different in any respect from the existing datafile, RMAN will recover that file. So, if you lose a datafile or two, you will want to perform a datafile or tablespace recovery instead of a full database recovery (because a datafile recovery will be faster), which we will talk about shortly. You can indicate to RMAN that you want it to overwrite all of the files by using the **force** option of the **restore database** command.

NOTE
If you attempt a full database restore and it fails, all recovered datafiles will be removed. This can be most frustrating if the restore has taken a very long time to complete. We suggest that you test different recovery strategies, such as recovering tablespaces (say, four to five tablespaces at a time), and see which works best for you and which method best meets your recovery SLA and disaster recovery needs.

RMAN Workshop: *Complete Recovery of Your ARCHIVELOG Mode Database*

Workshop Notes
For this workshop, you need an installation of the Oracle software and an operational test Oracle database. Also, in this workshop we will assume the following:

- That the database is either a CDB or non-CDB database
- That the database is in ARCHIVELOG mode
- That you are using the FRA when doing backups

> **NOTE**
> *For this workshop, the database must be configured for and running in ARCHIVELOG mode.*

Step 1. Ensure that you have configured automated backups of your control files:

```
set oracle_sid=recover
rman target rman_backup/password
configure controlfile autobackup on;
```

Note that in this case, we are accepting that the control file backup set pieces will be created in the default location.

Step 2. Because this is an online backup, there is no need to shut down and then mount the database. Complete an online backup of your system:

```
backup database plus archivelog delete input;
```

Note that in this case, we will back up the database and the archived redo logs. Once the archived redo logs are backed up, we will remove them. In this workshop, we assume that the backup is to a configured default device.

Step 3. Shut down your database:

```
shutdown immediate;
```

Step 4. Rename all database datafiles. Also rename the control files. Do not rename your online redo logs for this exercise. (Optionally, you can remove the database datafile and control file if you don't have the space to rename them and if you really can afford to lose your database should something go wrong.)

Step 5. Issue the **startup nomount** command and then restore your control file:

```
Startup nomount;
restore controlfile from autobackup;
alter database mount;
```

Step 6. Recover your database with RMAN using the backup you took in Step 2:

```
restore database;
recover database;
alter database open resetlogs;
```

Step 7. Complete the recovery by backing up the database again:

```
shutdown immediate;
startup mount;
backup database;
```

Note that although it is not strictly required to back up your database again, it is a best practice.

Tablespace Recoveries

Perhaps you have just lost datafiles specific to a given tablespace. In this event, you can opt to recover just a tablespace rather than the entire database. One nice thing about tablespace recoveries is that they can occur while the rest of the database is humming along. For example, suppose you lose your accounts payable tablespace, but your accounts receivable tablespace is just fine. As long as your application doesn't need to access the accounts payable tablespace, you can be recovering that tablespace while the accounts receivable tablespace remains accessible. Here is an example of the code required to recover a tablespace:

```
alter tablespace users offline;
restore tablespace users;
recover tablespace users;
alter tablespace users online;
```

As you can see, the recovery process is pretty simple. First, we need to take the tablespace offline. Note that as of Oracle Database 12*c* we no longer need to use the **sql** command to execute the SQL DDL commands. Now RMAN just interprets the SQL commands for what they are without any fancy syntax. The **sql** command is still available for backward-compatibility purposes.

In the previous example we took the USERS tablespace offline with the command **alter tablespace users offline** command, which is a SQL DDL command. Next, we issued the **restore tablespace** command to restore the datafiles associated with the USERS tablespace. Then we used the **recover tablespace** command to apply the redo logs to the tablespace. Finally, we used the **alter tablespace users online** command to bring the tablespace online. This completed the recovery of the USERS tablespace.

NOTE
You cannot use this method to recover an individual tablespace to a point in time different from that of the rest of the database. You will need to use the RMAN feature called tablespace point-in-time recovery to perform this operation.

You can also recover multiple tablespaces in the same command set, as shown in this code snippet:

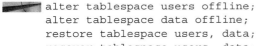

```
alter tablespace users offline;
alter tablespace data offline;
restore tablespace users, data;
recover tablespace users, data;
alter tablespace users online;
alter tablespace data online;
```

Datafile Recoveries

Second cousin to a tablespace recovery is a datafile recovery, which is a very granular approach to database recovery. Here, we can replace lost database datafiles individually, while the rest of the tablespace remains online. Datafile recovery allows the DBA to recover specific datafiles while allowing the rest of the tablespace to remain online for users to access. This feature is particularly nice if the datafile was empty or sparsely populated, as opposed to recovering the entire tablespace. Here is some sample code required to recover a datafile:

```
alter database datafile 6 offline;
alter database datafile '/u01/app/oracle/oradata/ROB/datafile/
o1_mf_users_b86k20gc_.dbf' offline;
restore datafile 6;
restore datafile '/u01/app/oracle/oradata/ROB/datafile/
o1_mf_users_b86k20gc_.dbf';
recover datafile 6;
recover datafile '/u01/app/oracle/oradata/ROB/datafile/
o1_mf_users_b86k20gc_.dbf';
alter database datafile 6 online;
alter database datafile '/u01/app/oracle/oradata/ROB/datafile/
o1_mf_users_b86k20gc_.dbf' online;
```

We recovered a couple of datafiles in this example by using two methods of defining which datafile we were recovering. First, we took the offending datafiles offline with an **alter database datafile offline** command (they may be already offline in some cases, but we want to make sure).

We then restore the datafiles with the **restore datafile** command. The first command restores the datafile by number, and the second restores the datafile by name.

Next, we recover the datafiles. Again, we recover the first datafile by number and then we recover the datafile by name. Finally, we use the **alter database datafile** SQL command to bring the datafiles back online. Again, we used the datafile number in the first SQL command, and the datafile name in the second.

Before we move on, let's look more closely at one component of the **alter database** command: how we reference datafiles. There are two different ways to reference datafiles. The first is to reference the datafile by number, and that's what we did with datafile 3 in the preceding example. The second is to reference a datafile by name, '/u01/app/oracle/oradata/ROB/datafile/o1_mf_users_b86k20gc_.dbf'. Either method is acceptable, but we often find using the datafile number is easier. Generally, when a datafile is missing or corrupt, Oracle gives you both the datafile name and number in the associated error message, as shown in this example:

```
ORA-01157: cannot identify/lock data file 4 - see DBWR trace file
ORA-01110: data file 4: 'D:\ORACLE\ORADATA\RECOVER\TOOLS01.DBF'
```

Notice in this listing that datafile 4 is associated with the tools01.dbf datafile. Often, it's much easier to just indicate that you want to restore datafile 4 than to indicate you want to restore d:\oracle\oradata\recover\tools01.dbf.

Once we have taken our datafiles offline, we will restore them (again, using either the file number or the filename) and then recover them. Finally, we bring the datafiles online again, which will complete the recovery process.

What If I Use Incremental Backups?

Oracle will determine automatically if you are using an incremental backup strategy when you restore your datafiles and will automatically apply the required incremental backup sets as required. You do not need to do anything different to recover in these cases.

During a restore using an incremental backup, the **restore** command restores only the base backup. Once that restore is complete, you issue the **recover** command, which causes the incremental backups to be applied to the database, and then the archived redo logs will be applied. Once that is complete, you can open the database as usual. In all cases, Oracle attempts to restore the base backup and incremental backup that is the most recent. This reduces the amount of redo that has to be applied to fully recover the database and thus reduces the overall restore time.

Note that because the database will likely be applying multiple backup sets during the recover process, your recovery will likely take longer than you might expect. However, depending on a number of factors (data change velocity being a large factor), applying incremental backup sets can be faster than the application of a generous amount of redo, and thus the incremental backup solution can be a faster one. Therefore, the ultimate benefit of incremental backups is a quicker backup strategy (and a smaller overall space requirement for the backup set pieces) at the expense of a potentially slower recovery timeline.

Recovering from Online Redo Log Loss

One recovery situation you might experience is the loss of the database online redo logs. You will need to contend with four different situations if you lose the online redo logs:

- Loss of a redo log file group member
- Loss of an inactive online redo log group

- Loss of an active but not current online redo log group
- Loss of the current online redo log group

The first two types of online redo log loss are an annoyance at best. The last two categories can be catastrophic with respect to data loss.

Recall that the redo logs are written to as soon as there is a commit or as soon as the online redo log buffer is filled to a certain size (and other events can cause writes, too). As a result, uncommitted undo, along with committed changes, can be written to the online redo logs. Because the database datafiles are written to later, sometimes much later, the database datafiles are often way out of synchronization with the actual current state of the database. Due to this lack of synchronization between the actual state of the database data and the data contained in the database datafiles, Oracle will have to apply redo from the online redo logs during database recoveries.

Because database datafiles are often out of synch with the actual state of the database, loss of an *active online redo log* can result in loss of data. Loss of the current online redo log can also result in data loss. Obviously, redo logs are quite important. The current, active, and inactive redo logs differ as follows:

- **Active** This is an online redo log that is not currently in use. However, it contains redo that still needs to be written to the datafiles, and the group may (or may not) still need to be archived.
- **Current** This is the current online redo log group. Oracle is actively writing to this online redo log group.
- **Inactive** This online redo log is not currently in use, and redo has been written to datafiles by DBWR.

You can see the status of an online redo log group by querying the STATUS column of the V$LOG view. Let's look at what to do when it comes to recovering from loss of our redo log groups.

Loss of an Inactive Online Redo Log Group Member

To recover from the loss of one or more members of an online redo log group (but not the entire group), the response is pretty easy. You can simply re-create the member by using the **alter database add logfile member** command. You might discover that you have lost a member via an alert in OEM or in the alert log, which might look something like this:

```
ORA-00313: open failed for members of log group 2 of thread 1
ORA-00312: online log 2 thread 1: 'C:\ORACLE\ORADATA\DANCE\REDO01a.LOG'
```

As a best practice, we'd recommend that if the database has not shut down and the member is part of an active or current redo log group, you immediately attempt to checkpoint the database by using the **alter system checkpoint** command. The **alter system checkpoint** command will force the database to write any dirty blocks from the database buffer cache to the database datafiles in an urgent manner. This can help protect your database against data loss should the database crash because of this missing online redo log.

Once the checkpoint has completed, we would issue the **alter database add logfile** command to re-create the redo log group member redo02a.log:

```
Alter database add logfile
'C:\ORACLE\ORADATA\DANCE\REDO02a.LOG' reuse to group 2;
```

If the database happened to crash before you could add the logfile, you would mount the database and then issue the **alter database add logfile** command. You should then be able to open the database.

Another available option is that you shut down the database in a consistent manner (**shutdown normal**) and then copy another member of the redo log group to the missing member. You can then restart the database normally.

> **NOTE**
> *We strongly advise against using a **shutdown abort** any time you are dealing with the loss of an online redo log group or a member of such a group. This is to eliminate the risk that database changes are not flushed to the database datafiles, which can lead to the loss of data.*

Loss of an Inactive Online Redo Log Group

Loss of an *inactive online redo log group* is a very survivable event and is easy to recover from. You will need to understand two different situations that might occur. First is loss of an inactive online redo log group during database startup. Second is loss of an inactive online redo log group during database operations. In the next two sections, we address these situations.

Loss of an Inactive Online Redo Log Group on Startup

If you start up the database and the inactive online redo log group cannot be opened, you will get the following error message:

```
ORA-00313: open failed for members of log group 2 of thread 1
ORA-00312: online log 2 thread 1: 'C:\ORACLE\ORADATA\DANCE\REDO02a.LOG'
```

First, determine if one of the online redo log group members has survived. If so, follow the steps listed in the previous section on recovering from the loss of an online redo log member. If none of the members survived, you will need to drop the logfile group by using the **alter database** command, as shown here:

```
alter database drop logfile group 2;
```

Once the online redo log group is dropped, you simply re-create the online redo log group by using the **alter database add logfile** command:

```
Alter database add logfile
group 2 'c:\oracle\oradata\dance\redo02a.log' size 50m;
```

Loss of an Inactive Online Redo Log Group when the Database Is Running

If you have lost an inactive online redo log group (or it becomes corrupted) while the database is running, it is possible that the database will continue to operate. Oracle Database will sometimes skip the online redo log group that went missing and continue to operate normally. If this occurs, you can issue an **alter system checkpoint** command and then clear the logfile group with the **alter database clear logfile group** command, as shown here:

```
alter system checkpoint;
alter database clear logfile group 1;
```

If the logfile you are trying to clear has not been archived, you may get the following error:

```
SQL> alter database clear logfile group 1;
alter database clear logfile group 1
*
ERROR at line 1:
ORA-00350: log 1 of instance orcl (thread 1) needs to be archived
ORA-00312: online log 1 thread 1: '/oracle01/oradata/dance/redo01.log'
```

Of course, because the logfile is not there, it cannot be archived. In this case, we use the **alter database clear unarchived logfile** command to clear the unarchived log file and rebuild the log file in its current location, as shown here:

```
alter database clear unarchived logfile '/oracle01/oradata/dance/redo01.log';
```

You will need to back up your database in this case because an archived redo log will have been lost.

In some cases, the database will not crash, but will freeze. If this occurs, open another SQL*Plus session and connect to the database. Then issue the **alter database checkpoint** command followed by either the **alter database clear logfile** or the **alter database clear unarchived logfile** command, depending on the type of recovery required. After you issue these commands, the database should operate as usual.

Loss of an Active but Not Current Online Redo Log Group

If you suffer the loss of an *active online redo log group,* you will need to use the **alter database clear unarchived logfile** command, as shown in the previous section. This is because the active online redo log will not have been archived, and you need to indicate to Oracle that this is okay. This command rebuilds the online redo log and allows Oracle to proceed with normal operations. You should always back up the database after this operation.

Loss of the Current Online Redo Log Group

If you want to have a bad day, losing the *current online redo log group* probably would do it for you. If you have lost the current online redo log group, you probably will experience some loss of data. When you lose the current online redo log group, you can expect that the database will shut down, and not in the normal, pleasant kind of way that you would like.

If you are lucky and the database has not yet shut down, you should immediately attempt to reduce the overall loss of data by checkpointing the database using the **alter system checkpoint** command and then shut down the database afterward as soon as practical. The **alter system checkpoint** command forces the database to write any dirty blocks from the database buffer cache to the database datafiles.

You may be able to open the database without any recovery being required. To try to restart the database, follow these steps:

1. Issue the **startup mount** command.
2. Issue the **alter database clear unarchived logfile** command for the redo log group that was lost. Examples of this command can be seen in earlier sections of this chapter.
3. Issue the **alter database open** command.

If the database opens successfully, you are in luck and a celebration is warranted.

If the database fails to open, you are in a bad way. You will need to perform incomplete recovery of the database. Incomplete recovery with RMAN is covered in Chapter 9 of this book.

The Data Recovery Advisor

In Oracle Database 11*g*, Oracle introduced a new feature called Automatic Diagnostic Repository (ADR). The ADR provides a great deal of new information and many new tools that ease database administration. In this section we discuss one of these new tools: the Data Recovery Advisor (DRA).

The Data Recovery Advisor has both an OEM interface and a command-line interface. In this section, we cover the command-line interface. If you wish to use the OEM interface, refer to Chapter 14, which contains much more information about using OEM and RMAN.

Using the Data Recovery Advisor Through RMAN

To use the manual interface into the Data Recovery Advisor, you simply use the RMAN command-line interface. Oracle has added these new RMAN commands to allow you to execute the Data Recovery Advisor from the command line:

- list failure
- advise failure
- repair failure
- change failure

All of the DRA commands will work when the database instance is started. If the failure is new and the database has been shut down, you will often not get any results until you have tried to open the database and a failure has been detected. Once a failure has been detected, though, the DRA will remember the failure, and you can access it with the **advise failure** command with the database in the nomount, mount, or open state.

The state that the database needs to be in when you are repairing failures depends on the nature of the failure. For example, for a control file recovery, the database must be in NOMOUNT state. If you are repairing missing data files, the **repair failure** command will require the database to be mounted or open.

Typically, when you are dealing with a data corruption error, the workflow is to use the **list failure** command, then the **advise failure** command, and, finally, the **repair failure** command, in that order.

There are cases where the **repair failure** command does not quite complete the job the first time around. The most common case seems to be where control file recoveries occur. In cases like this, all you usually need to do is to run through the list, advise, and the repair failure flow two times. The first time will cause it to restore the control file. Once the control file is restored, the second run of the Data Recovery Advisor will determine how to complete the database recovery, usually finishing with a **recover database** RMAN command.

We've mentioned the Data Recovery Advisor commands you would use: that is, the **list failure**, **advise failure**, and **repair failure** commands. Let's look at the use of these commands in a bit more detail.

The list failure Command   The RMAN **list** command (discussed in detail in Chapter 12) is used with the **failure** keyword to list detected failures, their priorities (Critical, High, or Low), status (Open or Closed), when they occurred, and a summary of the failures. In this context, a failure is any persistent data corruption that currently exists on your system. Here is an example of the **list failure** command:

```
RMAN> list failure;
using target database control file instead of recovery catalog
List of Database Failures
=========================
Failure ID Priority Status    Time Detected Summary
---------- -------- --------- ------------- -------
187        HIGH     OPEN      05-DEC-14     One or more non-system
                                            datafiles are missing
```

Note that in the preceding sample output, the datafiles that are missing are not listed. You can use the **list failure detail** command to generate additional details on the failure. Additionally, the **list failure exclude failure *n*** command allows you to exclude specific failure numbers from the report output. Other options include listing only closed failures, only critical failures, only failures with high or low priorities, and listing or excluding failures by failure ID. Here are some examples of the use of these options:

```
RMAN> list failure detail;
List of Database Failures
=========================
Failure ID Priority Status    Time Detected Summary
---------- -------- --------- ------------- -------
187        HIGH     OPEN      05-DEC-14     One or more non-system
                                            datafiles are missing
  List of child failures for parent failure ID 187
  Failure ID Priority Status    Time Detected Summary
  ---------- -------- --------- ------------- -------
  2075       HIGH     OPEN      05-DEC-14     Datafile 6:
'C:\ORACLE\ORADATA\ROB\ROB\BOOGLE01.DBF' is missing
     Impact: Some objects in tablespace BOOGLE might be unavailable

-- Let's exclude failure_id 187 - note that it excludes the child
-- failure too
RMAN> list failure exclude failure 187;
no failures found that match specification
```

The following table gives a complete list of all the options available on the **list failure** command:

Option	Description
ALL	List all failures.
CRITICAL	List only failures with a priority of critical.
HIGH	List only failures with a priority of high.
LOW	List only failures with a priority of low.
CLOSED	List only failures that are closed.
EXCLUDE FAILURE	From the list, remove the failure numbers listed. This option is followed by a comma-delimited list of failure IDs that you want to exclude.

Option	Description
DETAIL	Provide additional detail for the failure listed.
#	This is the actual failure number to be listed.
UNKNOWN	List failures where the priority is unknown.

Here are some additional examples (note that some unimportant output was removed for brevity's sake. We do like trees, after all!):

```
RMAN> list failure closed 254;
List of Database Failures
=========================
Failure ID Priority Status     Time Detected Summary
---------- -------- ---------  ------------- -------
254        HIGH     CLOSED     05-DEC-14     Redo log file
C:\ORACLE\ORADATA\DOODLE\REDO03.LOG is corrupt

RMAN> list failure closed exclude failure 242,248;
List of Database Failures
=========================
Failure ID Priority Status     Time Detected Summary
---------- -------- ---------  ------------- -------
8298       CRITICAL CLOSED     05-DEC-14     System datafile 1:
'C:\ORACLE\ORADATA\DOODLE\SYSTEM01.DBF' needs media recovery
8295       CRITICAL CLOSED     05-DEC-14     Control file needs media recovery
8104       CRITICAL CLOSED     05-DEC-14     Control file
C:\ORACLE\ORADATA\DOODLE\CONTROL03.CTL is missing
8101       CRITICAL CLOSED     05-DEC-14     Control file
C:\ORACLE\ORADATA\DOODLE\CONTROL02.CTL is missing
8098       CRITICAL CLOSED     05-DEC-14     Control file
C:\ORACLE\ORADATA\DOODLE\CONTROL01.CTL is missing
```

NOTE
*The **list failure** command can only be run on a single-instance database (thus, the RAC cluster must now be brought to single-instance mode). You also cannot use this command with a physical standby database.*

The **list failure** command does not check for database errors itself. The database is constantly checking for corruption issues, and those issues regularly are recorded in the data dictionary (and in the physical ADR repository, which is on disk and not in the database).

If the failure occurred while the database was shut down, a failure will not be detected until that missing component is needed. For example, if the control file is missing, that will not be detected until an attempt to mount the database occurs. If a datafile is missing, then that event will not be detected until you try to open the database. If the database was open when the event occurred, it is likely that the event will be detected while the database is open.

If a failure with an OPEN status appears in the list, this means you have a current problem that you will need to deal with. This problem will be linked to one or more repair actions that you can view via the new **advise failure** command. These options will help you to determine what repair options are available to correct the situation. Let's look at that command next.

NOTE
If you just have a datafile offline, then that datafile will not be reported as a failure. If the offline datafile is physically missing, it will be reported as a failure.

The advise failure Command   Once the **list failure** command displays an open failure, the **advise failure** command can be used to provide recommended actions that you can take to correct the failure. Here is an example of the use of the **advise failure** command:

```
RMAN> advise failure;
List of Database Failures
=========================
Failure ID Priority Status     Time Detected Summary
---------- -------- ---------- ------------- -------
187        HIGH     OPEN       05-DEC-14     One or more
non-system datafiles are missing
analyzing automatic repair options; this may take some time
allocated channel: ORA_DISK_1
channel ORA_DISK_1: SID=129 device type=DISK
analyzing automatic repair options complete

Manual Checklist
================
1. If file C:\ORACLE\ORADATA\ROB11GR4\ROB11GR4\DOOGLE01.DBF was
unintentionally renamed or moved, restore it

Automated Repair Options
========================
Option Repair Description
------ ------------------
1      Restore and recover datafile 6
  Strategy: The repair includes complete media recovery with
            no data loss
Repair script:
C:\ORACLE\PRODUCT\diag\rdbms\rob11gr4\rob11gr4\
hm\reco_1214740950.hm
```

NOTE
*As with the **list failure** command, the **advise failure** command can only be run on a single-instance database (thus, the RAC cluster must be open with just a single instance in single-instance mode). You also cannot use this command with a physical standby database.*

You will notice from the output that RMAN provides both manual and automated repair options. The automated repair option contains RMAN commands that can be used to correct the problem. These automated repair options may differ based on the state the database is in (say, NOMOUNT versus MOUNT). We recommend then that you get as close to opening the database as possible before you use the Data Recovery Advisor. For example, if you can successfully mount the database, do so rather than leave it in NOMOUNT mode.

Also note that repair options may involve data loss, and that the Data Recovery Advisor will indicate if data loss will occur if a given recovery option is used. These commands are contained in a file within the ADR structure. Here is an example of the recovery file:

```
# restore and recover datafile
restore datafile 6;
recover datafile 6;
sql 'alter database datafile 6 online';
```

You can choose to run the recovery file manually, or you can use the **repair failure** command, which is our next topic.

The repair failure Command   Now that we have detected a failure and determined the recovery actions recommended by Oracle, we can manually repair the failure, or allow Oracle to repair the failure automatically with the **repair failure** command. To run the **repair failure** command, the target database instance must be started. If multiple repairs are required, Oracle will try to consolidate them into one repair operation. Also, RMAN will double-check that the failures still exist and will not perform a recovery operation if the failure has been corrected. Here is an example of using the **repair failure** command from RMAN (we have removed some RMAN output for brevity's sake):

```
RMAN> repair failure;
Strategy: The repair includes complete media recovery
with no data loss
Repair script:
C:\ORACLE\PRODUCT\diag\rdbms\rob11gr4\rob11gr4\
hm\reco_110341808.hm
contents of repair script:
   # restore and recover datafile
   restore datafile 6;
   recover datafile 6;
   sql 'alter database datafile 6 online';
Do you really want to execute the above repair
(enter YES or NO)? yes
executing repair script
Starting restore at 05-JUN-09
using channel ORA_DISK_1
... Typical RMAN restore output is removed for brevity...
Starting recover at 05-JUN-00
using channel ORA_DISK_1
... Typical RMAN recover output is removed for brevity...
media recovery complete, elapsed time: 00:00:03
Finished recover at 05-JUN-09
sql statement: alter database datafile 6 online
repair failure complete
```

NOTE
*Again, the **repair failure** command can only be run on a single-instance database (thus, the RAC cluster must be open with just a single instance in single-instance mode). Note that this command will not repair failures such as datafiles that cannot be accessed by a specific node in a RAC cluster.*

If you wish to preview a failure action, you can use the **repair failure preview** command. This command will display the repair actions to be applied, but not execute the repair itself.

The change failure Command   The RMAN **change** command now provides the **failure** keyword, which allows you to change the status of failures detected by the Oracle Database. For example, you can change the priority of a specific failure, or change all failures from high to low. You can also opt to close one or more failures. By default, RMAN will prompt you to ensure that you want to make the change. You can use the **noprompt** clause of the **change** command to force the change to occur without prompting. Here is an example where we change the priority of failure 187 to LOW:

```
RMAN> Change failure 187 priority low;
List of Database Failures
=========================
Failure ID Priority Status    Time Detected Summary
---------- -------- --------- ------------- -------
187        HIGH     OPEN      09-JUN-09     One or more non-system
                                            datafiles are missing
Do you really want to change the above failures (enter YES or NO)? yes
changed 1 failures to LOW priority
```

NOTE
You cannot switch the status of a CLOSED failure to OPEN.

Data Recovery Advisor Data Dictionary Views

Several new views have been added to Oracle Database 12c to support the Data Recovery Advisor. These views all start with V$IR, as shown in the following table:

View Name	Description
V$IR_FAILURE	Provides information on the failure. Note that records in this view can have parent records within this view.
V$IR_FAILURE_SET	This table provides a list of the various advice records associated with the failure. This allows you to join the view V$IR_FAILURE to the V$IR_MANUAL_CHECKLIST view.
V$IR_ MANUAL_CHECKLIST	This view provides detailed informational messages related to the failure. These messages provide information on how to manually correct the problem.
V$IR_REPAIR	This view, when joined with V$IR_FAILURE and V$IR_FAILURE_SET, provides a pointer to the physical file created by Oracle that contains the repair steps required to correct a detected error.

Here is an example of a query against the DRA views:

```
-- Do we have an open error reported?
select failure_id, time_detected, description from v$ir_failure
Where status='OPEN';

FAILURE_ID TIME_DETE DESCRIPTION
---------- --------- -------------------------------------
       242 19-SEP-07 One or more non-system datafiles are missing
       605 19-SEP-07 Datafile 4: '/oracle01/oradata/orcl/user
                      s01.dbf' is missing
```

Summary

In this chapter, we looked at the basics of recovering your database with RMAN. We looked at the many different ways you can recover your control files and SPFILEs. We also looked at restoring and recovering your databases from RMAN backups with the **restore** and **recover** commands. We discussed the different recovery options available, from full database recovery to recovery of specific tablespaces or datafiles. Finally, we provided some workshops for you to practice your newly learned recovery skills.

We want to leave you with one big piece of advice at the end of this chapter. Practice recoveries, over and over and over. Know how RMAN works and how to recover your database without having to use this book. Become the RMAN expert in your place of work. Then you are poised to be the hero!

CHAPTER
9

Advanced RMAN
Recovery Topics

his chapter introduces you to additional RMAN recovery topics. In the previous chapter we introduced you to full database restore and recovery. This included both the traditional Oracle database and databases using the new multitenant option. We will start this chapter by focusing a bit more on multitenant database restores by looking at how to restore an individual pluggable database (PDB). This includes restoring the root container, the seed container, and one or more PDBs.

After we have discussed full recovery of PDBs, we then move on to a somewhat more complex topic: incomplete (or point-in-time) restores and recoveries. In our experience, it's these kinds of recoveries (and the failures that lead to having to do them) that can cause the most trouble. We will look at incomplete recoveries of an entire database (CDB and non-CDB) and we will also look at point-in-time recoveries of PDBs.

Following that discussion, we move on to tablespace point-in-time recovery. We close out this chapter by discussing how you can check the integrity of your backups on a regular basis.

Recovery of Pluggable Databases

A full recovery of a pluggable database within a CDB is quite similar to the recovery of an entire Oracle database—the commands only differ slightly. The nice thing about being able to restore and recover individual PDBs is that the other PDBs can continue to be used while the recovery operation is running.

In this section we look at the three kinds of PDB recoveries you might face: a recovery of the root container, the seed container, and one or more PDBs within your Oracle Database.

Before we get into the specifics of the CDB recovery, we want to take a moment and point out how important failure analysis is before you begin your recovery process. Way too often we have seen people just blindly restore a whole database, when all that was needed was to simply restore four or five datafiles. With a non-PDB database, the proper analysis of what has failed and what kind of recovery is needed is important and can make a huge difference in how long the recovery takes and how many people are impacted by that recovery.

This concern gets taken to a whole new level when we start talking about Oracle CDBs and their pluggable databases. Instead of having just one database assigned to a given application, as you usually have with a non-CDB, now you potentially have many different databases all running within the same instance. That being said, take great care in analyzing what has failed and then determine what kind of recovery is the best for your particular situation. The Data Recovery Advisor (DRA), mentioned elsewhere in this book, can be helpful in guiding you to a recovery solution, but it's no substitute for actual failure analysis for an experienced DBA.

Recovering the Root Container

Recall from previous chapters that the root container is the owner of the data dictionary for the entire CDB. It is much like the SYS schema in a non-CDB database, so you can imagine that it's quite important. If you should happen to lose one or more datafiles associated with the root container, it's highly unlikely that your database will stay up. As a result, your root container recoveries will be done with the database down.

The process of restoring the root container involves mounting the database and then using the **restore database root** RMAN command, followed by the **recover database root** command. After you have recovered the root container, assuming there are no other container databases that need to be recovered, you can then use the **alter database open** command to open the CDB. Note that all of this is done from an account with SYSDBA or SYSBACKUP privileges.

Let's look at an example of the recovery of the root container of an Oracle CDB database. First, we try to open the database, and we receive the following error:

```
ORA-01157: cannot identify/lock data file 1 - see
DBWR trace file
ORA-01110: data file 1:
'C:\APP\ROBERT\ORADATA\ROBERTCDB\DATAFILE\
O1_MF_SYSTEM_B9YFM006_.DBF'
```

Note the error message and the files that are being reported as missing. After careful review of the missing files (and going out to the file system and making sure that there have not been more files lost that we are not yet aware of), we decide that restoring the root container is the proper course of action. We use the **restore database root** command, followed by the **recover database root** command, to perform this recovery, as shown here:

```
Startup force mount
Restore database root;
Recover database root;
alter database open;
```

Notice that this recovery requires the database to be down. We could also have performed a datafile recovery if we preferred (because only one datafile was lost). We discussed datafile restores in the previous chapters.

That there are different options to consider here is an important point. In this case, only one datafile associated with the root database is missing. Also, the restore of just that single datafile might be much faster than restoring the entire set of root datafiles as we are doing in this example. In the end, analyzing the damage that needs to be repaired and choosing the most efficient method to use to repair it is the expertise you will need to bring to a database-recovery situation.

NOTE
The recovery of the ROOT container does not include recovering the SEED PDB.

Recovering the Seed Container

Recall that the seed container (or seed database) is the default set of database files used when a new PDB is created during the operation of the **create pluggable database** command. This SEED container is created when the CDB itself is created.

Should the seed container be missing, the database will still open successfully and no error message will appear on the console. Additionally, no error will appear in the database alert log. You can discover that the datafile is missing by querying the V$RECOVER_FILE view, as shown in this query example (note that due to page constraints we've modified the output slightly):

```
select a.file#, a.name,b.error
from v$datafile a, v$recover_file b
where a.file#=b.file#;
     FILE#
       NAME
       ERROR
```

```
---------- ---------------------------------------------------
2
C:\APP\ROBERT\ORADATA\ROBERTCDB\DATAFILE\O1_MF_SYS TEM_B9YFVM6W_.DBF
FILE NOT FOUND
```

You might also notice there is a problem because the seed container will be in the wrong mode. Normally, the seed container (called PDB$SEED in the data dictionary) will be open in READ ONLY mode, like this:

```
SQL> select name, open_mode from v$pdbs;
NAME                            OPEN_MODE
------------------------------- ----------
PDB$SEED                        READ ONLY
ROBERTPDB                       MOUNTED
```

However, if there is a problem with the seed container, it will only show up in MOUNT mode, as shown in this example:

```
SQL> select name, open_mode from v$pdbs;
NAME                            OPEN_MODE
------------------------------- ----------
PDB$SEED                        READ ONLY
ROBERTPDB                       MOUNTED
```

Oracle Cloud Control will also generate an alert when it detects the missing file. However, it's possible that you won't actually notice the file is missing until you try to create a pluggable database, as shown here:

```
SQL> create pluggable database tplug admin user robert identified by robert;
create pluggable database tplug admin user robert
identified by robert
*
ERROR at line 1:
ORA-65036: pluggable database PDB$SEED not open in required mode
```

The bottom line of this is that the loss of the seed database will not impact your ability to start up the CDB or open any of the other PDBs. Therefore, there is no outage (except for processes that require the seed PDB). This also means that a restore of the seed PDB can be done as an online restore, as opposed to an offline restore.

The process of the restore is pretty basic. First, we know that the name of the seed container is PDB$SEED (we learned this from the earlier query). We can use the **restore pluggable database** command to restore the seed container, followed by the **recover pluggable database** command to recover the seed container. After that, to be able to use the seed container, we will have to shut down and restart the database. Here is an example of the commands used to restore the seed PDB:

```
Restore pluggable database "pdb$seed";
Recover pluggable database "pdb$seed";
-- these next commands can be run later.
shutdown immediate
startup
```

Note that it's important to use the double quotes on the name of the seed database (PDB$SEED). This is because of the $ symbol that is used in the name of this database.

While in most cases you would not need to technically recover the seed container since it's typically in a READ ONLY mode, it's still a best practice to do so. There are some specific conditions that would require this, such as recovering your database to a point after the upgrade with a database backup taken before the upgrade started.

You can also opt to restore the seed container at the tablespace or datafile level (we will discuss these kinds of restores later in this chapter), if that makes more sense.

Recovering PDBs

RMAN supports recovery of one or more PDBs at one time. The recovery of a PDB in the CDB does not require an outage with any other PDB. In this section, we first look at recovery of one or more complete PDBs. Then we look at how to restore tablespaces and datafiles of specific PDBs. Point-in-time restores of PDBs are also possible. We cover that topic later in this chapter as we discuss point-in-time restore in more detail.

Full PDB Recovery

To restore a complete PDB, that PDB must first be closed. You then use the RMAN **restore pluggable database** and **recover pluggable database** commands to restore and recover a given PDB. Once the recovery is complete, you can then open the PDB for access. Note that in the case of a complete PDB recovery, we must first shut down the PDB. This is not required for tablespace or datafile recoveries of PDBs, which we discuss in the next section.

Let's look at two examples of the restore and recovery of PDBs in an Oracle database. In this first example, we restore and recover a single PDB called ROBERTPDB:

```
Alter pluggable database robertpdb close;
Restore pluggable database robertpdb;
recover pluggable database robertpdb;
Alter pluggable database robertpdb open;
```

In the second example, we restore and recover two PDBs (called ROBERTPDB and TPLUG) at once. Here is the next example:

```
Alter pluggable database robertpdb,tplug close;
Restore pluggable database robertpdb, tplug;
recover pluggable database robertpdb. tplug;
Alter pluggable database robertpdb, tplug open;
```

PDB Tablespace Recoveries

It might be that the fastest way to recover a PDB is to just restore a given tablespace (or set of tablespaces). Such might be the case if only datafiles of a specific tablespace have been lost. A tablespace-level recovery also allows you to keep the rest of the database open, only restricting access to the tablespaces being restored.

To restore the tablespace of a specific PDB, you must first be logged into that PDB. Once you are logged into that PDB, you can then use the **restore tablespace** and **recover tablespace** commands to restore and recover any set of tablespaces in that PDB. Finally, you will open those tablespaces once they have been restored.

In the following example, we are connecting to a PDB called TPLUG. Once we have connected to that PDB, we take the tablespace that we are going to recover offline. Then we restore and recover the tablespace called TESTING. After the recovery, we bring the tablespace TESTING back online again:

```
rman target robert/robert@minint-2hgbgqc:1522/tplug
alter tablespace testing offline;
restore tablespace testing;
recover tablespace testing;
alter tablespace testing online;
```

If you want to restore a set of tablespaces, simply separate the names of the tablespaces to be recovered by commas in both the **restore** and **recover tablespace** commands. Here is an example:

```
rman target robert/robert@minint-2hgbgqc:1522/tplug
alter tablespace testing offline;
alter tablespace testing2 offline;
restore tablespace testing, testing2;
recover tablespace testing, testing2;
alter tablespace testing online;
alter tablespace testing2 online;
```

NOTE
If you get into a real situation where you need to recover a tablespace, it is likely that the tablespace is already offline. You can determine this by querying the STATUS column of the DBA_TABLESPACES view or the ERROR column of the V$RECOVER_FILE view.

PDB Datafile Recoveries

As with tablespaces before, it might be that the fastest way to recover a PDB is to just restore a given datafile instead. Such might be the case if only a few datafiles have been lost or corrupted. This allows you to just take those datafiles offline, leaving the remaining datafiles in the database available for use. This reduces the impact of any outage.

To restore datafiles of a specific PDB, you must first be logged into that PDB. Once you are logged into that PDB, you would take offline the datafiles you want to restore, assuming they are not already in an offline state. You then use the **restore datafile** and **recover datafile** commands to restore and recover the set of datafiles in that PDB. Finally, you bring the datafiles online after the recovery.

In the following example, we are connecting to a PDB called TPLUG. Once we have connected to that PDB, we take the datafile that we are going to recover offline. Then we restore and recover the datafile (datafile 12). After the recovery, we bring the datafile back online again:

```
rman target robert/robert@minint-2hgbgqc:1522/tplug
alter database datafile 12 offline;
restore datafile 12;
recover datafile 12;
alter database datafile 12 online;
```

NOTE
*As with tablespaces, if you get into a situation where a datafile
recovery is needed, it may well already be offline.*

If you try to open a PDB and find a datafile associated with that PDB is missing, you will not
be able to open that PDB without taking the datafile offline. Here is an example where we try to
open the PDB TPLUG and get an ORA-01157 error, as shown here:

```
Sqlplus / as sysdba
SQL> alter pluggable database tplug open;
alter pluggable database tplug open
*
ERROR at line 1:
ORA-01157: cannot identify/lock data file 12 -
see DBWR trace file
ORA-01110: data file 12:
'C:\APP\ROBERT\ORADATA\ROBERTCDB\DATAFILE\
O1_MF_TESTING_BB1BOOGK_.DBF'
```

The end result of this is that the PDB will not open. The first thing you might think to do in this
case is to take the offending datafile offline using the **alter database datafile offline** SQL command
(assuming that the application associated with the database would still continue to function) and
then get the PDB open. After that, you would restore the datafile with RMAN. Unfortunately when
you try to offline a datafile for a PDB that has a status of MOUNTED with the **alter database offline**
command, you get the following error:

```
RMAN> alter database datafile 12 offline;
RMAN-00571: ===========================================================
RMAN-00569: =============== ERROR MESSAGE STACK FOLLOWS ===============
RMAN-00571: ===========================================================
RMAN-03002: failure of sql statement command at 12/28/2014 17:44:17
ORA-01516: nonexistent log file, data file,
or temporary file "12"
```

The **alter pluggable database** command has an option to offline datafiles; however, that
command only works from within the PDB itself, and the PDB in this case cannot be opened.
This provides us with a problem: How can we take the datafile offline so we can open the PDB
and then work on restoring the datafile?

The way to fix this problem is to log directly into the root container of the CDB and then
use the **alter session set container** command, connecting to the container in which you need to
take the datafile offline.

So, in our case, to get the TPLUG PDB open, we would first log into the root container as
sysdba and then use the **alter session set container** command to change to the TPLUG container
(the terms *container* and *PDB* are largely synonymous). Once we are connected, we can then
take datafile 12 offline. After taking datafile 12 offline, we would go ahead and use the **alter
pluggable database** command (still in the TPLUG container) to open the database.

Now that we have the database open, we can deal with the missing or corrupted datafile
while other users are doing business. At this point, the restore is a normal datafile restore,

performed from RMAN while connected to the TPLUG PDB. All of that is a lot to take in, but the commands to execute the restore are pretty simple, as you can see here:

```
Sqlplus / as sysdba
alter session set container=tplug;
alter database datafile 12 offline;
alter pluggable database tplug open;
rman target robert/robert@minint-2hgbgqc:1522/tplug
restore datafile 12;
recover datafile 12;
alter database datafile 12 online;
```

Incomplete Database Recoveries on Non-CDB and Entire CDB Databases

Now, we will move on to the topic of incomplete database recoveries. An incomplete database recovery involves restoring the database to a point in time other than the current point in time. It is similar to a complete recovery in many respects; the basic command set is the same, but with a few added wrinkles. The possible reasons for an incomplete recovery are numerous, such as the loss of online or archived redo logs or a major user error that has seriously compromised the database. You might want to "reset" a testing database to a specific point in time where the data is at a known state so that you can test with that known data set.

In this section we discuss what incomplete recoveries are. We then discuss how RMAN performs an incomplete recovery. Finally, we cover the different types of incomplete database recoveries.

What Is an Incomplete Recovery?

Incomplete recoveries (also known as point-in-time recoveries, or PITRs) impact the entire database; in other words, you cannot perform an incomplete recovery on just one part of the database because it would result in that part of the database having a different System Change Number (SCN, or point in time if you prefer) than the remainder of the database. Incomplete recoveries come in four different flavors:

- Point-in-time recoveries
- SCN-based recoveries
- Change-based recoveries
- Point-in-time recoveries based on a restore point

We cover each of these different types of recoveries in this section.

Before we proceed, we want to review the important impact incomplete recovery has on the entire database. Oracle demands that a database be in a consistent state at startup, and if it is not consistent, Oracle will complain bitterly. To illustrate this point, consider an example in which a user who has his own tablespace has just mistakenly truncated a table in that tablespace for which he has no backup. He calls a junior DBA in a panic and asks her to recover just that tablespace to the point in time before he issued the truncate operation.

At first thought, the junior DBA might think that she can just restore the datafiles of the offending tablespace and recover them to a time before the truncate operation was executed. Seems somewhat logical, doesn't it? (In fact, that's what a logical backup is for.) So, the junior DBA restores the datafiles and recovers the tablespace to a point in time before the truncate operation. Now, she's feeling pretty good about herself. Unfortunately, her euphoria is short lived, because when she tries to open the database, RMAN slaps her with this message:

```
ERROR at line 1:
ORA-01113: file 3 needs media recovery
ORA-01110: data file 3: 'D:\ORACLE\ORADATA\RECOVER\
INDX01.DBF'
```

In this case, Oracle is basically saying, "You recovered the datafile all right, but you didn't do enough recovery on it, and it's not consistent with the rest of the database!" The point is that with database PITR, you have to restore the entire database to the same point in time.

If this is not the type of restore you want to perform, you have other options to consider. First, there are all the options associated with Flashback Database. The second option, which is especially useful if you want to only restore tablespaces to a specific point in time without restoring the entire database, is called tablespace point-in-time recovery. We discuss tablespace point-in-time recoveries in more detail later in this chapter.

Incomplete Recovery: How Does It Work?

When you perform incomplete recovery with RMAN, what happens? During the restore process, you issue a **restore database** command, indicating the point in time (by virtue of defining the time, SCN, log change number, or restore point) to which you want to restore. Then you issue a **recover database** command, again indicating the point in time to which you want to recover. Finally, you open the database with the **alter database open resetlogs** command.

When you issue the **restore database** command, RMAN will restore the database backup that was completed nearest to the point in time to which you want to restore. Next, when you issue the **recover database** command, RMAN will apply any incremental backups and archived redo logs that are needed to restore the database to the point in time desired.

To open the database after the recovery is complete, you use the **alter database open resetlogs** command. When performing an incomplete recovery, you always use the **resetlogs** command when opening the database. When you use the **resetlogs** command, you indicate to Oracle that you are knowingly deviating from an already established stream of redo. As a result, Oracle will need to clear out the online redo logs and prepare the database to support the new incarnation of the database that will be created. An incarnation represents the logical life of a given database. The first incarnation starts when the database is created and ends when you open the database with the **resetlogs** command. The next incarnation, and each subsequent incarnation, spans the time between the use of the **resetlogs** commands. Each **resetlog** command starts a new incarnation. You can see each incarnation by querying the V$DATABASE_INCARNATION view. In this example, our database is in its second incarnation:

```
select incarnation#, resetlogs_time, status
from v$database_incarnation;
INCARNATION# RESETLOGS_TIME     STATUS
------------ ------------------ -------
           1 09/11/2014 08:40:48 PARENT
           2 12/27/2014 14:48:48 CURRENT
```

Note that with each use of the **resetlogs** command, the SCN counter is not reset. However, Oracle does reset other counters, such as the log sequence number, and resets (and re-creates if required) the contents of the online redo logs. It is possible to travel back and forth between incarnations during recovery, if that is required. We discuss this later in this chapter.

In older versions of Oracle, you were required to perform backups after you opened the database with the **resetlogs** command. This is no longer required, and has not been for some time. Oracle will now recover a database using backups taken before you issued the **resetlogs** command and will perform a full recovery without any intervention required. Still, it's probably a good practice to back up your database as soon as reasonably possible after performing a database point-in-time recovery.

Establishing a Point to Recover To

One of the things you need to do when performing incomplete recovery with RMAN is to establish a recovery target. The recovery target is the point at which you want to terminate the recovery process and can be identified based on a point in time, a specific SCN, a log sequence number, or a restore point.

The recovery target can be established in a number of different ways. First, you can use the **set** command along with the **until time**, **until SCN**, **until sequence**, or **until restore point** parameter within a **run** block. In the following example, we are choosing to perform a time-based recovery using a **run** block. In this case, we are using the **set until time** command to establish the recovery target as 3 P.M. on July 1, 2014:

```
run
{
set until time "to_date('07/01/14 15:00:00','mm/dd/yy hh24:mi:ss')";
restore database;
recover database
alter database open resetlogs;
}
```

When this command is issued, RMAN looks for the backup set closest to, but not including or after, this period and restores the database from that backup set. If the database is in NOARCHIVELOG mode, then recovery will stop at that point; otherwise, during the execution of the **recover** command, Oracle will apply the archived redo logs (and any incremental backups that need to be applied) up to, but not including, the defined recovery target.

NOTE
*If you are trying to recover to the point of completion of a specific backup, you must recover to the CKP SCN or CKP TIME of the files in the backup set as listed in the RMAN **list** command for the different backup sets (for example, **list backup set**). Using the CKP TIME of the backup is not sufficient and can lead to ORA-1152 errors.*

You can also opt to use the **until time**, **until SCN**, **until sequence**, or **until restore point** command directly in the **restore** and **recover** commands, which eliminates the need for the **run** block entirely (which we prefer). Here is an example of the use of the **until time** command directly within the **restore** and **recover** commands during an RMAN restore. We will also reference this example in the next section on time-based database recoveries:

```
-- We assume that your control file is intact
startup mount;
restore database UNTIL TIME
"TO_DATE('06/28/06 13:00:00','MM/DD/YY HH24:MI:SS')";
recover database UNTIL TIME
"TO_DATE('06/28/06 13:00:00','MM/DD/YY HH24:MI:SS')";
alter database open resetlogs;
```

In this chapter (and the book) we generally use this method, and not **run** blocks.

Time-Based Recoveries

We already demonstrated a time-based recovery earlier in this chapter. With a time-based recovery, we use the **until time** clause to determine what point in time to restore the database to, as shown in the previous example. One thing to be aware of is that the time you indicate to restore to is an approximation—the actual point in time that any database is restored to is based on an SCN. In the case of a time-based restore, the time requested is translated into an approximate SCN value. Therefore, the resulting restore, if done based on time, will not likely be done to the exact point in time you request. In its documentation, Oracle suggests that this time variation may be as much as three minutes.

SCN-Based Recoveries

If you want to ensure the database is restored to a specific point in time, you need to use an SCN-based restore. The SCN of the database can be determined in various ways. For example, there is a column in the V$DATABASE view called CURRENT_SCN. You can find the SCN range associated with an online or archived redo log group by using the V$LOG_HISTORY view and its FIRST_CHANGE# and NEXT_CHANGE# columns. You might even use the ORA_ROWSCN pseudo-column to determine the SCN when a specific record changed and then base your restore on that value.

Here is an example of an SCN-based database restore:

```
-- We assume that your control file is intact
startup mount;
restore database UNTIL SCN 10000;
recover database UNTIL SCN 10000;
alter database open resetlogs;
```

Change-Based Recoveries

RMAN allows you to perform a recovery up to a specific archived redo log sequence number. This is handy if there is a gap in your archived redo logs, which generally means that you can recover only up to the point where the gap begins. Here is the command to perform this recovery in RMAN:

```
-- We assume that your control file is intact
startup mount;
restore database UNTIL SEQUENCE 100 thread 1;
recover database UNTIL SEQUENCE 100 thread 1;
alter database open resetlogs;
```

In this case, we restore up to, but not including, log sequence 100 of thread 1.

Restore Point–Based Recoveries

You can use restore points to define the point in time to which you want to restore your database. First, you would create a restore point using the **create restore point** command. Here's an example of creating a restore point called REST_001:

```
create restore point rest_001;
```

A restore point is not guaranteed to be maintained by the database. It will eventually be aged out of the control file (up to 2,048 restore points will be maintained). If you are concerned that your restore point might age out over time, you can use a guaranteed restore point, as shown here:

```
create restore point rest_001 guarantee flashback database;
```

Restore points can be identified by querying the V$RESTORE_POINT view, as shown in this example:

```
SQL> select name, database_incarnation# DI, time, scn from
v$restore_point;
NAME        DI#  TIME                                       SCN
----------  --   ---------------------------------   ----------
TANGO_ONE   2    30-DEC-14 04.04.06.000000000 PM     3312444
ROBERT1     2    30-DEC-14 02.27.57.000000000 AM     3278140
SUCKS1      2    30-DEC-14 03.20.19.000000000 AM     3283034
```

To restore a database based on a restore point, simply include the **to restore point** clause of the **restore** and **recover** commands, as shown in this example:

```
Startup mount;
Restore database until restore point TANGO_ONE;
Recover database until restore point TANGO_ONE;
Alter database open resetlogs;
```

You can also use a **run** block and use the **set until restore point** command to establish the target restore point. Here's an example:

```
Startup mount;
run {
set restore point TANGO_ONE;
Restore database TANGO_ONE;
Recover database TANGO_ONE;  }
Alter database open resetlogs;
```

Performing Incomplete Recoveries of Pluggable Databases (PDB)

Oracle offers the ability to perform point-in-time recoveries (PITRs) on PDBs as well. This makes the multitenant architecture very flexible because it allows for a finer grain of control with respect to the restore and recovery of PDBs within that architecture. For example, you may have a CDB that is assigned to store a number of PDBs used for testing. This CDB may have many tenants in it, and there may be a need to refresh these tenant PDBs to different points in time. Oracle's ability to perform point-in-time recovery within a PDB makes this possible.

In this section we look at the details of how a PDB point-in-time restore is done. We then look at restrictions and requirements of a PDB point-in-time recovery. Next, we look at the different kinds of point-in-time recoveries available: time based, SCN based, change based, and recoveries to a given restore point.

About PDB Point-in-Time Recoveries

With a non-CDB database, a point-in-time restore is simply a matter of restoring the database datafiles over the existing datafiles and applying recovery to whatever point in time you are interested in restoring the database to. Point-in-time restore of a PDB is more akin to what happens during a tablespace point-in time restore.

First, RMAN needs to create an auxiliary database. To do this, RMAN restores the datafiles needed to start and open the auxiliary instance. The datafiles associated with these tablespaces are stored in the FRA by default. If the FRA is not defined, you must define the location for the files to be created when you execute the **restore** and **recovery** commands.

When the tablespaces are restored, they will include the SYSTEM, SYSAUX, and UNDO tablespaces. These are the basic tablespaces required to start the auxiliary instance. Additionally, the tablespaces associated with the PDB(s) involved are restored. Once the datafiles are restored, it's then time for the execution of the recovery process via the recovery command.

During the recovery, the auxiliary instance is started and then mounted. It is then rolled forward to the point in time to which you want to restore the PDB. The cloning process then moves the recovered tablespace datafiles over to the PDB and brings them online. At that point the PDB is restored to the point in time. All that remains is to open the PDB using the **alter pluggable database open resetlogs** command. At that point, the PDB will be open and usable.

One difference between normal database point-in-time restores and point-in-time restores of PDBs is the amount of space required to perform the point-in-time restores of the PDB. When you restore a non-CDB database (or the entire CDB database), the only space that is required is that of the restored database datafiles and for the archived redo logs required to perform the restore. With a PDB PITR, you need all the space consumed by the database datafiles plus all the space required to create the auxiliary database. This can mean that a significant amount of space might well be required for a PITR of a PDB.

Restrictions and Requirements Associated with PDB Point-in-time Recoveries

When RMAN does a PDB point-in-time recovery, an auxiliary instance is created. This auxiliary instance uses the Fast Recovery Area (or the location defined by the auxiliary destination parameter) for storage of the datafiles that will be created to perform the recovery. If you do not use a FRA, you must use the auxiliary destination parameter when issuing both the **restore** and **recover** commands.

Because you will be using the FRA, you need to make sure enough physical space is allocated to the directory where the FRA is located. Additionally, on a Windows platform, you may have issues with the creation of the auxiliary instance if you do not use the **auxiliary destination** parameter.

Restoring a PDB to a different point in time also impacts your ability to use Flashback Database on the entire CDB. When you restore a PDB to a different point in time, you will only be able to flash back the database from the current point in time to the point in time to which you restored the PDB. There are some ways to work around this restriction, which we will cover when we discuss RMAN and Flashback Database later in this book.

It might seem obvious, but another requirement is to have a backup of all the datafiles from a backup completed before the point in time to which you wish to restore the PDB. You also need all the archived redo logs from the time that backup started until the point in time to which you wish to restore the database. The **recover database** command will take care of extracting the archived redo logs, as it always does, but if it can't find the backup set pieces, it can't restore them.

One nice thing about PDB PITR is that it only requires that the PDB being recovered be closed. The remainder of the CDB can continue to run normally. Some other things to be aware of: You will want to ensure you have sufficient disk space. You will also want to ensure that the OS directory you want to use to create the files for the automatic instance has the appropriate OS-level privileges required.

If the restore or recover operation does fail, you need to make sure that the automatic instance is completely cleaned up after the failure. This may mean any number of tasks, including the following:

- Connecting to the automatic instance and using the **drop database** command to remove it from the system.
- Executing the following package to clear certain metadata settings related to the automatic instance:

```
dbms_backup_restore.manageAuxInstance('{automatic_instance_name}',1)
```

One of the requirements of any PDB PITR is that we have a backup available of the PDB. This backup should have completed at some point in time before the point in time to which we want to restore the PDB. There are several ways to validate that we have such a backup. First, we can use the **list** command (which we discuss later in this book when we talk about administration of RMAN) to list all the backups available. We would then need to manually check off that we have the backup we need.

An easier solution is to use the **restore pluggable database validate** command to make sure the required backup is available. This will simulate a restore of the database without actually doing it. Thus, we know right away if we have a valid backup, and we also know if some of the backup pieces are missing and might need to be restored from some other media. In our example, let's say we want to restore our PDB called TPLUG to a point in time of 12/28/2014 at 5 P.M. We would then run the following command to validate that we can actually restore to that point in time:

```
Restore pluggable database tplug
until time "to_date('12/28/2014 17:00:00','mm/dd/yyyy hh24:mi:ss')"
validate;
```

RMAN will proceed to simulate the restore. If no errors occur, we can proceed with the next step, which is to actually do the PITR restore. This step does not guarantee us success, but it is a good check that can help reduce the possibility of errors. We can also simulate restores based on an SCN, change, or restore point.

Something else that's helpful is to make sure the current redo log file is archived before you start your PITR restore—especially if you are testing. In many cases, the redo needed in the online redo log file will be required by the recovery process. If that redo is not archived, it's possible that the PITR will fail. Therefore, if you are having problems with the PITR failing, issue an **alter system switch logfile** command followed by an **alter system archive log all** command to ensure that all the redo you need is archived.

Finally, suppose you start a PDB PITR and get an error similar to the following:

```
Restore pluggable database tplug
until time "to_date('12/28/2014 17:00:00','mm/dd/yyyy hh24:mi:ss')"
validate;
RMAN-00571: ===========================================================
RMAN-00569: =============== ERROR MESSAGE STACK FOLLOWS ===============
RMAN-00571: ===========================================================
RMAN-03002: failure of sql statement command at 12/30/2014 03:33:18
ORA-01113: file 14 needs media recovery
ORA-01110: data file 14: 'C:\APP\ROBERT\ORADATA\ROBERTCDB\
0EA6466993554DD393A7DE69001594A1\DATAFILE\
O1_MF_USERS_BB4CMB1G_.DBF'
```

In this case, it's likely that when you tried to open the PDB with the **alter pluggable database open** statement, you forgot to include the **resetlogs** parameter. Using the **resetlogs** parameter is required any time you perform a PITR on a PDB.

PDB Time-Based Recovery

Now that we have discussed the basic requirements around PDB point-in-time recoveries, we can proceed to actually performing them. First, let's look at a time-based PITR of a PDB within a CDB. Time-based recovery is probably the most common method of restoring a particular PDB to a different point in time.

NOTE
Even though time-based recovery is the most common, it is not the most accurate way of ensuring a given database is restored to the point in time you desire. When a time value is defined, it is converted to an approximate SCN number. According to the Oracle documentation, the variance in the relationship between time and SCN can be as great as three minutes. Therefore, if you need to restore at a specific, fine-grained point in time, you should consider a PDB PITR based on using the SCN rather than time. Also, there are times when the lack of specificity with respect to time can actually cause the restore to report inadvertent errors. If you are experimenting with this feature, make sure you give yourself three to five minutes between the time you perform your backup and the time you actually perform your restore.

In this case, we will take the PDB (called TPLUG) for which we want to do the PITR offline. We will then perform the PDB PITR using the **restore pluggable database until time** and **recover pluggable database until time** commands. After a successful restore, we will open the pluggable database with the **alter pluggable database open** command, including the **resetlogs** parameter. Here is an example of these commands in use:

```
Rman target=/
alter pluggable database tplug close;
Restore pluggable database tplug
until time "to_date('12/29/2014 15:00:00','mm/dd/yyyy hh24:mi:ss')" ;
```

```
recover pluggable database tplug
until time "to_date('12/29/2014 15:00:00','mm/dd/yyyy hh24:mi:ss')"
auxiliary destination 'c:\robert\robert';
alter pluggable database tplug open resetlogs;
```

When these commands are executed, the **restore** command extracts the database files that are required, and the **recover command** proceeds to create the automatic instance and complete the PITR for the PDB.

> **NOTE**
> *A lot of things can go wrong with a PDB PITR operation because of its complexity. It's a really good idea to educate yourself and try a number of PDB PITRs before you go into the big leagues.*

Note that we could have used a **run** block and the **set until time** RMAN command to perform this restore, too. This is true for any of the PDB PITR restores we discuss in this section. In fact, the Oracle documentation recommends that you use a **run** block. This seems to mostly be to ensure that if the restore operation fails, the recovery operation will not begin. If you are going to automate the PITR, then you should use a **run** block. If you are going to be doing the PITR manually, you should include the **until time** parameter in the **restore** and **recover** commands. Either way works, so use whichever way works best for you. Here is what such a **run** block would look like:

```
Rman target=/
run
{
alter pluggable database tplug close;
set until time "to_date('12/29/2014 17:48:00','mm/dd/yyyy hh24:mi:ss')" ;
Restore pluggable database tplug ;
recover pluggable database tplug ;
alter pluggable database tplug open resetlogs;
}
```

PDB SCN-Based Recovery

As with a tablespace PITR, you can restore a PDB to a point in time based on a specific SCN number. The SCN of the database can be determined in various ways. For example, there is a column in the V$DATABASE view called CURRENT_SCN. You can find the SCN range associated with an online or archived redo log group by using the V$LOG_HISTORY view and its FIRST_CHANGE# and NEXT_CHANGE# columns. You might even use the ORA_ROWSCN pseudo-column to determine the SCN when a specific record changed and base your restore on that value.

For example, let's say we created a table called INPUT_DATA in TPLUG PDB. We will include the **rowdependencies** clause in our **create table** DDL to ensure that the SCN recorded for each row is unique to that row (by default it's unique to the block):

```
Create table input_data (id number, the_date varchar2(300) )
rowdependencies
tablespace users;
```

We then proceed to enter data into that table using some PL/SQL:

```
Begin
      for tt in 1..500
      Loop
           Insert into input_data values (tt, 'This is data first run');
      End loop;
      commit;
      Dbms_lock.sleep(300);
      for tt in 1..500
      Loop
           Insert into input_data values (tt, 'This is data second run');
      End loop;
      commit;
end;
/
```

Note that we committed the first batch, waited 300 seconds, and then loaded the second batch. This is to simulate two discrete points in time where we loaded two batches of data. All of the records associated with the two different points in time will share the same ORA_ROWSCN value. Therefore, the 500 records loaded before the first commit will have one common ORA_ROWSCN value, and the second set of 500 records will have a second unique SCN to identify them. In this query, we can plainly see this fact:

```
SQL> select distinct ora_rowscn from input_data;
ORA_ROWSCN
----------
   3250835
   3250815
```

Now we are ready to perform a PDB SCN-based PITR. Here are the RMAN commands we would use to perform a restore to SCN 3250816—the SCN from the earlier set of inserts plus 1. We have to increase the SCN value by 1 because the **until SCN** parameter restores up to but not including the SCN listed in the parameter. When this restore is complete, we should see the records with SCN 3250835 disappear! Here is the set of commands we would use to perform this PDB PITR:

```
Rman target=/
alter pluggable database tplug close;
Restore pluggable database tplug until SCN 3250816;
recover pluggable database tplug until SCN 3250816;
alter pluggable database tplug open resetlogs;
```

After the recovery, we query the INPUT_DATA table again and, as expected, we now only see the first set of records and their associated SCN—but the result is a bit odd:

```
SQL> select distinct ora_rowscn from input_data;
ORA_ROWSCN
----------
   3251709
```

Notice how the SCN has changed? We have correctly just restored the first set of 500 records, but one result of the PDB PITR is that the ORA_ROWSCN of all of the rows of that table have now changed. This is because even though you can have many PDBs, they all still share one common SCN scheme. Even though you are rolling back one PDB, the single SCN counter is still ticking away in the CDB and all of the other PDBs. Therefore, when you perform a PITR of a PDB, the SCNs for the records that are restored will always be different (higher) than they were in the previous incarnation of that PDB. Don't confuse this with the ROWID of the unique rows—these will remain the same. Therefore, the indexes of a table are not impacted by the restore and don't need to be rebuilt.

PDB Change-Based Recovery

A PDB change-based PITR follows the same concept as a database change-based PITR in that the recovery is bounded by a specific archived redo log sequence number. This log sequence number can be found in views such as V$LOG_HISTORY and V$ARCHIVED_LOG. The column called SEQUENCE# provides the log sequence number you are interested in. Once you have determined the change number you wish to apply, the commands to perform the restore include the **restore pluggable database** and **recover pluggable database** commands, along with the **until change** parameter, as shown in this example:

```
Rman target=/
alter pluggable database tplug close;
Restore pluggable database tplug until change 325;
recover pluggable database tplug until SCN 325;
alter pluggable database tplug open resetlogs;
```

Recovering Based on a Restore Point

Restore points provide a way to define the point in time to which you want to recover based on an already defined—and named—point in time called a *restore point*. You create a restore point using the **create restore point** command. We discuss restore points in much more detail later in this book when we discuss Flashback Database and RMAN.

You can find the list of restore points in the database by querying the view V$RESTORE_POINT. Once you have found the restore point to which you want to recover your PDB, the set of commands to use looks familiar. In this case, we will restore the TPLUG PDB back to the point in time defined by the restore point ROBERT1:

```
Rman target=/
alter pluggable database tplug close;
Restore pluggable database tplug to restore point robert1;
recover pluggable database tplug to restore point robert1;
alter pluggable database tplug open resetlogs;
```

Other RMAN Recovery Topics

We need to cover a few more things before we finish this chapter. First, we need to discuss some issues with read-only tablespaces. Then we'll talk about archived redo log restores, datafile copy restores, and recovering corrupted datafile blocks. Then we'll turn to a discussion about recovering to a previous incarnation. More riveting RMAN stuff coming your way!

Read-Only Tablespace Recovery Considerations

By default, RMAN will not restore read-only datafiles when you do a full database restore, even if the read-only datafile is not there. To restore a read-only datafile during a full recovery, you need to include the **check readonly** or **force** parameter in the **restore** command, as shown in these examples:

```
restore database check readonly;
restore database force;
```

Note that the RMAN behavior is different if you issue a **recover tablespace** or **recover datafile** command. When you use either of these two **recover** commands, recovery occurs regardless of the read-only nature of the tablespace.

Archived Redo Log Restores

During the normal course of recovery with RMAN, there is no real need to recover the archived redo logs. However, restoring one or more archived redo logs may be required occasionally. For example, you might want to use LogMiner to mine some information from the archived redo log files stored in your backups. In this event, RMAN allows you to restore specific archived redo logs by using the **restore archivelog** command, as shown in these examples:

```
restore archivelog all;
restore archivelog from logseq=20 thread=1;
restore archivelog from logseq=20 until logseq=30 thread=1;
```

You might want to have Oracle restore the archived redo logs to a location other than the default location. To do this, use the **set** command with the **archivelog destination to** parameter:

```
run
{
set archivelog destination to "d:\oracle\newarch";
restore archivelog all;
}
```

Note that there is no alternative to the **set** command, so a **run** block is required. Finally, be aware that RMAN will not restore an archived redo log to disk if it determines that the archived redo log already exists. Even if you change the destination to a destination other than the default archive log destination, Oracle will not recover an archived redo log to that new destination.

Datafile Copy Restores

You can restore your database datafiles from a datafile copy (as opposed to a backup set). To do this, use the **restore from datafilecopy** command and then use the **recover** command as you normally would to recover the database (or tablespace or datafile), as shown in this example:

```
restore (datafile 5) from datafilecopy;
recover datafile 5;
sql "alter database datafile 5 online;"
```

Note that when you issue a **restore** command, it will identify the most current copy of the datafiles that need to be restored and then restore those datafiles from that copy. The most current copy of a datafile might be within a datafile copy rather than a backup set. In that case, Oracle will recover the datafile copy. Also note that the use of parentheses is important; if they are not used, this command will fail.

Recovering Corrupted Data Blocks

RMAN offers block media recovery (BMR), which allows you to do block-level recoveries to repair logically or physically corrupted blocks in your Oracle database, even while the associated datafile is online and churning away the whole time.

So, just how do you perform a block media recovery? It's easy, as demonstrated in the following example. Suppose you receive the following error message when querying an Oracle table:

```
ORA-01578: ORACLE data block corrupted
(file # 19, block # 44)
ORA-01110: data file 19: 'd:\oracle\oradata\data\mydb_maintbs_01.dbf'
```

This message is telling you that a block in the MAINTBS tablespace is corrupted. Of course, you need to do something about that. Without BMR, you would have had to recover the datafile from a backup. During this recovery, all data within that datafile would be unavailable to the users.

Instead, you can use BMR to recover just the corrupted blocks. BMR is implemented via the **recover** command using the **datafile** and **block** options, as shown in this example:

```
Recover datafile 19 block 44;
```

You can recover multiple blocks in multiple datafiles at the same time, as shown in this example:

```
Recover
datafile 19 block 44
datafile 19 block 43
datafile 18 block 44,66,150;
```

Of course, Oracle tracks block corruption that occurs during backups and copies. If a backup or copy operation has detected corruption, the operation will fail by default because Oracle will allow zero corruption in a backup. You can configure RMAN to allow a set amount of corruption, but this is not a recommended practice.

If you want to see all database corruption that might be detected by RMAN, you can use the **backup validate database** command, which populates the views V$BACKUP_CORRUPTION and V$DATABASE_BLOCK_CORRUPTION with the results of all corrupted blocks. The backup validate database will check all the database blocks for corruption and report on any corruption that has been discovered.

If corruption appears in the V$DATABASE_BLOCK_CORRUPTION view, you can use the **recovery corruption list** RMAN command to repair those blocks online, as shown here:

```
RECOVER CORRUPTION LIST;
```

Once you have corrected the database block corruption, rerun the **backup validate database** command and then query V$DATABASE_BLOCK_CORRUPTION to ensure that no further corruption exists.

A few closing comments on some of the corruption views: If corruption occurs during a copy operation, the V$COPY_CORRUPTION view will indicate which backup sets contain corruption. There is also a view called V$BACKUP_CORRUPTION that is a historical view of past corruption. The view previously mentioned, V$DATABASE_BLOCK_CORRUPTION, provides a view of only current block corruption. Any corrupted blocks that have already been repaired will be removed from V$DATABASE_BLOCK_CORRUPTION. However, these blocks will remain in the V$BACKUP_CORRUPTION view.

Recovering to a Previous Incarnation

Recall from our earlier discussion about the **resetlogs** command that an incarnation of a database is a representation of a specific logical lifetime for that database. As a hotshot DBA, you may find yourself in an odd restore situation where you need to restore your database using a backup that took place from before the last time you opened the database using the **resetlogs** command and/or you may want to restore to a point in time before you issued the last **resetlogs** command.

Preparing for the Restore

To do a restore to a previous incarnation, you need to know to which incarnation you want to restore. To find out which incarnations are available, RMAN provides the **list incarnation** command:

```
RMAN> list incarnation of database;
List of Database Incarnations
DB Key  Inc Key DB Name  DB ID        STATUS   Reset SCN
------- ------- -------- -----------  ---      ----------
1       1       ROBERTCD 2645377104   PARENT   2233668    12/27/2014 14:48:48
2       2       ROBERTCD 2645377104   PARENT   3315564    12/30/2014 20:47:55
3       3       ROBERTCD 2645377104   CURRENT  3318384    12/30/2014 21:28:26
```

In this list we see that we have three incarnations we have to work with. Depending on whether you are using a control file or recovery catalog, the number of records that appear in this list may well be different. This is because the recovery catalog records are not subject to be removed as control file records are. Also, if you re-create the control file, some incarnation records will be lost.

The Reset SCN and Reset Time columns indicate the SCN and time that the incarnation was created. This can be helpful when you are trying to figure out which incarnation you will need to use to perform your restore.

In this list our database incarnation keys are 1, 2, and 3 (where 3 is the oldest incarnation). Assume that you did a PITR of a database and created incarnation 3 as a result of that restore. You did the PITR restore of the database because tables were mistakenly dropped (and purged). After the recovery was complete, you opened the database with the **resetlogs** command. However, after opening the database you discover that your tables are still not there—so you obviously restored too much redo during your first restore attempt, and the tables were still dropped.

After some research, you determine the correct SCN to which you should restore. You start the restore and get the following error:

```
RMAN-03002: failure of restore command at
12/30/2014 21:42:30
RMAN-20208: UNTIL CHANGE is before RESETLOGS change
```

This message indicates that you are trying to restore to a point in time before that of the current incarnation of the database. In order to perform this restore, we need to indicate to RMAN which incarnation you actually want to recover back to. To do that, you use the **reset database to incarnation** command. In this case, you will reset to incarnation 2, because you know that's where the backup taken nearest to the point you want to restore to resides.

Executing the Restore

Now that you know which incarnation you want to recover, you can proceed to do the recovery. The basic process is the same regardless of whether or not you are using a recovery catalog. You will do the following:

1. Shut down the database and then mount it.

2. Restore the control file associated with the incarnation you want to restore.

3. Reset the database incarnation.

4. Execute the restore and recovery based on the time you wish to restore to.

5. Open the database.

As we suggested, there are two different cases here you need to consider. The first is a recovery when you have a recovery catalog. In this case, you would connect to the recovery catalog and run the following commands:

```
Startup force nomount
reset database to incarnation 2;
run {
set until time "to_date('12/30/2014 21:27:00','mm/dd/yyyy hh24:mi:ss')";
restore controlfile;
restore database;
recover database;
}
alter database open resetlogs;
```

Notice that the first thing you need to do is reset the database incarnation. Then you restore the control file. You need a copy of the control file from the time period within the incarnation to which you are restoring. Note that when you are connected to a recovery catalog, you can set the incarnation you are working with before the database is mounted. Once you have restored the control file, you proceed to restore and recover the database to the point in time you have identified.

If you are not using a recovery catalog, then the process you will follow changes just a bit. Here are the commands you would run if you are not using a recovery catalog:

```
startup force nomount;
run {
set until time "to_date('12/30/2014 21:27:00','mm/dd/yyyy hh24:mi:ss')" ;
restore controlfile from autobackup;
}
alter database mount;
```

```
reset database to incarnation 2;
run {
set until scn 3318383;
restore database force;
recover database;
}
alter database open resetlogs;
```

As you can see, the steps required if you are not using a recovery catalog are ordered differently. Also, you will reset the database incarnation at a different place in the workflow. Still, it's a pretty easy process. Something else that's thrown in here is a mix of restoring the control file based on a date and the database based on an SCN. When restoring your control file with an autobackup, you can only limit the restore by date. However, when you do the database restore afterward, you can use SCN, time, change, and even restore points, as discussed earlier in this chapter.

Table and Partition Point-in-Time Recovery

There are many scenarios in which tables (partitioned and nonpartitioned) may need to be restored. For example, a data load failure might impact only certain tables. Or perhaps your database is subdivided into many schemas and you need to restore only the objects in one specific schema. These kinds of restores could be problematic because a physical database restore requires that you restore the entire database and then roll it forward in its entirety.

A second option is to use Oracle Data Pump to restore individual tables and/or schemas. The problem with this option is that it is not possible to roll the data backed up in the Data Pump export forward in time after it has been restored. Thus, if your export was taken three days ago at 4 P.M., then that is the image of the data you're going to see when you restore the export file to the database.

Yet another method sometimes used is to create a second database (often called a *stub* database) using the backup of the first database. In this situation, you restore the SYSTEM, SYSAUX, and UNDO tablespaces. Additionally, you restore the individual tablespaces that contain the data you want to restore. After the restore is complete, you alter any tablespaces that you did not restore offline. You then apply the archived redo logs to the point in time to which you want to restore the individual objects. Having restored the database to the appropriate point in time, you then use Oracle Data Pump to export the objects, and then you import them into the original database, again using Oracle Data Pump. As you can probably tell, the problem with this option is that it is a fairly convoluted process to do manually. Fortunately, Oracle Database 12c introduces new functionality in RMAN that supports point-in-time restore of individual database tables and individual table partitions.

In this section we discuss the following topics:

- ■ Prerequisites for restoring and recovering tables and partitions
- ■ Restrictions on restoring and recovering database tables and partitions
- ■ Options to consider when restoring tables and table partitions
- ■ How RMAN implements the restore and recovery of tables and partitions
- ■ An example of using RMAN to restore and recover a database table

Prerequisites for Restoring and Recovering Database Tables and Partitions

If you want to take advantage of RMAN's ability to restore tables and table partitions, you need to follow a few rules. The following are the prerequisites to be able to restore tables or table partitions:

- The database was in ARCHIVELOG mode when it was backed up, and it remained in ARCHIVELOG mode up until the point in time to which you want to restore the database.
- If you want to recover individual partitions, the COMPATIBLE parameter must be set to 11.1.0 or later.
- An RMAN backup of the SYSTEM, SYSAUX, and UNDO tablespaces must be available, and this backup must have been completed before the point in time to which you want to restore the object(s).
- One or more backups of the tablespace (or tablespaces) that contains the objects you want to restore must be available. This backup (or backups) must have been completed before the time to which you want to restore the objects.
- All tablespaces in the restore set must be restored to the same point in time.
- You must have all the archived redo logs generated from the point of the start of the backup that is being used to recover the objects until the point in time to which you are trying to restore the object(s).
- The database you are restoring the table or partitions to (the target database) must be open in read-write mode.
- The target database must also be in ARCHIVELOG mode.

A table or partition restore is like any other RMAN point-in-time recovery in that you will need to know the time, log sequence number, or SCN to which you want to restore the table or partitions. Having met these prerequisites, you are ready to perform a restore of tables or table partitions using RMAN. First, though, let's take a look at some of the restrictions related to restoring and recovering database tables and table partitions.

Restrictions on Restoring and Recovering Database Tables and Partitions

As always, there are a few restrictions you need to be aware of. First, you cannot restore tables that belong to the SYS schema. Also, you can't restore tables that are stored in the SYSTEM and SYSAUX tablespaces, and you can't restore tables and table partitions in standby databases.

You cannot perform these restores on stand-by databases.

Also, Oracle provides a remap option for the **recover table** command (discussed in the next section) that allows you to restore tables to a different name. If the table has a NOT NULL constraint, you can't use the remap option.

Options to Consider when Restoring Tables and Partitions

When you're recovering tables and table partitions, you have a number of options you can take advantage of. The following table provides a list of these parameters and describes the purpose of each.

Parameter Name	Purpose
AUXILIARY DESTINATION	The location that the **recover** command will use to create the auxiliary instance–related files. If you do not use this parameter, you will need to define each file manually; otherwise, the process will fail.
	If this parameter is not used, the export dump file created by the process is created in the directory $ORACLE_HOME/dbs. Because of this default, it's critical to use the **auxiliary destination** parameter or use the **datapump destination** parameter.
DUMP FILE	The name of the Data Pump export file.
DATAPUMP DESTINATION	The location where the Data Pump export file should be created.
NOTABLEIMPORT	Indicates that the export file should be created but that the contents should not be imported into the target database. This is helpful if you want to complete the restore into another schema or another database.
REMAP TABLE	Provides the ability to rename the table in the target database when it's created.
REMAP TABLESPACE	Provides the ability to create the tables in a different tablespace of the target database.

How RMAN Implements the Restore and Recovery of Tables and Partitions

The process of restoring individual tables and partitions with RMAN is started with the execution of the RMAN **restore** command. RMAN first creates an auxiliary database and then restores to that database all the tablespaces it needs from the physical backups that were previously taken. RMAN restores only the SYSTEM, SYSAUX, UNDO, and SYSEXT (if it exists) tablespaces, as well as the tablespaces that contain the specific objects being restored. RMAN does not restore other tablespaces and associated datafiles.

After RMAN restores the auxiliary database, it rolls that database forward to the point in time you indicated in the **restore** command. RMAN then creates an Oracle Data Pump export of the objects to be restored. After it has created that export, RMAN will then, optionally, import the objects into the target database. You can instruct RMAN to not import the objects into the target database, leaving this task to complete yourself. RMAN will clean up the auxiliary database once the operation is completed.

Restoring Tables and Partitions from PDBs

The process of restoring a table or partition from a PDB is generally the same as it is when you are restoring from a non-CDB. Differences include the following:

- You must use the **auxiliary destination** clause.
- Use the **recover table** command along with the **of pluggable database** option.

Using RMAN to Restore and Recover a Database Table: An Example

This example uses a database called ORCL, which includes a schema named SCOTT. This example assumes that an RMAN backup of the database exists and that all of the database's archived redo logs are either backed up by RMAN or available on disk. You are going to restore the tables owned by the SCOTT schema by using the RMAN **restore file** command, after making some changes to those tables. First, take a look at the current time before any changes were made:

```
SQL> alter session set
nls_date_format='mm/dd/yyyy hh24:mi:ss';

Session altered.
SQL> select sysdate, current_scn from v$database;

SYSDATE               CURRENT_SCN
------------------- -----------
09/08/2013 19:15:09     2074999
```

The SCOTT schema has four tables, as shown in this query:

```
SQL> select table_name from dba_tables where owner='SCOTT';
TABLE_NAME
-------------------------------------------
DEPT
EMP
BONUS
SALGRADE
```

The row counts in the table are shown here:

```
SQL> select count(*) from DEPT;
  COUNT(*)
----------
        4

SQL> select count(*) from EMP;
  COUNT(*)
----------
       14

SQL> select count(*) from BONUS;
  COUNT(*)
----------
        0

SQL> select count(*) from SALGRADE;
  COUNT(*)
----------
        5
```

For the purposes of this example, assume that something terribly bad happened when developers were testing. Instead of deleting individual rows, the new bulk update application, lacking an appropriate **where** clause in the **delete** statement, managed to remove all the records in all the tables instead of removing unique ones. After the run of the application, this is what the row counts looked like:

```
SQL> select count(*) from DEPT;
  COUNT(*)
----------
         0
SQL> select count(*) from EMP;
  COUNT(*)
----------
         0
SQL> select count(*) from BONUS;
  COUNT(*)
----------
         0
SQL> select count(*) from SALGRADE;
  COUNT(*)
----------
         0
```

It's a shame, but the developers also forgot to do an export of their test schema before the test. It's not a good day for the developers: not only did they lose their data, but they also know that the whole database will probably have to be restored instead of just the SCOTT schema (and lots of good and important data exists in the other schemas).

The developers call you, their brilliant DBA, and ask how they can get their data restored. Fortunately for you, the database is running Oracle Database 12c. You tell them to hang tight and you will take care of the problem for them. After asking them what time they started their testing, you tell them you will restore SCOTT to the second before testing, and that you'll get back to them when you are done. One important bit of information that the developers were able to give you is the specific point in time to which you need to recover the table objects. Assume that it's the same time and date for the query against V$DATABASE provided earlier in this section.

Sitting down at your laptop, you set your Oracle environment for the correct database and you start RMAN. Next, you use the RMAN **recover** command to recover the tables in the SCOTT schema. Knowing that you can't recover a specific schema, but only the tables in it, you specify in your **recover** command the schema and names of the tables you need to restore.

NOTE
Recovery of any object with RMAN implies that you have completed a successful backup of the tablespace the object is in and have all of the archived redo logs and online redo logs generated since the beginning of that backup.

Before you start the restore, you need to decide where you want the auxiliary database–related files to be stored. For this example, assume you have chosen to use the directory /u01/app/oracle/aux. So, you first make sure the directory exists.

Additionally, you will want to decide if you want to use the same object names as before, or if you want to remap the newly restored objects to different names. Once you decide these things, you log into RMAN and enter the following:

```
recover table scott.emp, scott.dept, scott.bonus, scott.salgrade
until time "to_date('09/08/2013 19:15:09','mm/dd/yyyy hh24:mi:ss')"
auxiliary destination '/u01/app/oracle/aux'
remap table scott.emp:rest_emp, scott.dept:rest_dept,
scott.bonus:rest_bonus, scott.salgrade:rest_salgrade;
```

If this restore had been from a PDB, the command would be slightly different in that you would add the **of pluggable database** option, including the name of the pluggable database, as shown here:

```
recover table scott.emp, scott.dept, scott.bonus, scott.salgrade
of pluggable database dbplug1
until time "to_date('09/08/2013 19:15:09','mm/dd/yyyy hh24:mi:ss')"
auxiliary destination '/u01/app/oracle/aux'
remap table scott.emp:rest_emp, scott.dept:rest_dept,
scott.bonus:rest_bonus, scott.salgrade:rest_salgrade;
```

Once you press ENTER, RMAN will start the restore. The output of the restore is quite lengthy, so we've decided not to waste trees by printing it here. In summary, you will see the following in the output:

- Allocation of channels
- Creation of the auxiliary instance
- Restore of the control file for the auxiliary instance
- A list of datafiles that will be restored, followed by their restore and recovery in the auxiliary instance
- Export of tables from the auxiliary instance via Oracle Data Pump
- Import of tables, constraints, indexes, and other dependent objects into the target database from the Data Pump export file
- Cleanup of the auxiliary instance

NOTE
If the tables you are trying to move are already in the schema, you will get an error. You need to rename or drop those tables before you restore them via RMAN.

Tablespace Point-in-Time Recovery

RMAN provides the ability to perform a tablespace point-in-time-recovery. This functionality enables the DBA to restore tablespaces within the database at a point in time that is different from the rest of the database. In a way, this potentially results in the database data being logically inconsistent. However, as far as Oracle is concerned, it will consider the database to be totally consistent after the restore.

Tablespace point-in-time recovery provides a great deal of flexibility to deal with the needs a database might have. Perhaps you want to have a set of tablespaces that always contain the same data every morning. Tablespace point-in-time recovery makes this easy. Perhaps a set of tables contained in a tablespace have been accidently changed or dropped. Tablespace point-in-time makes it easy to correct these kinds of problems. The nice thing is that if you have properly configured your relationships, all the various objects that might span tablespaces will be restored together. This ensures that at least these objects will be restored in a consistent way.

A tablespace point-in-time recovery (TSPITR) uses an Oracle auxiliary instance to create a temporary work area. A long time ago, DBAs used to have to do all sorts of things to set up the environment for the auxiliary instance. Now, it's all pretty much automatic. The only thing you might have to worry about is where you want to put the files for the auxiliary instance if you are not using a Fast Recovery Area.

There are a few things you will need to do to prepare for a TSPITR. Let's look at these items next.

Preparing for the TSPITR

Before you can begin the TSPITR, you need to complete the following steps:

- Determine what point in time to restore to.
- Make sure the objects are fully contained within the tablespace(s) you want to restore.
- Preserve objects or data that will otherwise be lost.

Determine the Point in Time to Restore To

The most critical factor here is to determine what point in time you want to restore your tablespace to. Be cautious here, because recovery of the tablespace is a one-shot deal if you are not using a recovery catalog. If you misidentify the point in time to recover to, you will not be able to retry the recovery. On the other hand, if you are using a recovery catalog, this restriction does not exist.

Make Sure the Objects in the Transport Set Are Self-Contained

You should also use the TS_PITR_CHECK view to make sure your recovery set is complete, and identify any other tablespaces that might need to be included. For example, assume that you have a tablespace called TEST_RECOVER and need to restore it using TSPITR. You first need to check the TS_PITR_CHECK view to make sure there are no other dependent tablespaces. Here is an example of a query to check whether the TEST_RECOVER tablespace can be transported alone:

```
Set lines 132
Column obj1_owner format a20
column obj1_name format a20
column obj1_type format a20
column reason format a60
SELECT obj1_owner, obj1_name, obj1_type, reason
FROM SYS.TS_PITR_CHECK
WHERE ( TS1_NAME IN ('TEST_RECOVER')
```

```
                AND TS2_NAME NOT IN ('TEST_RECOVER') )
OR      ( TS1_NAME NOT IN ('TEST_RECOVER')
            AND TS2_NAME IN ('TEST_RECOVER') );
```

This would return no rows if there were no conflicts. If there were conflicts, you would see
a row describing each conflict, as shown here:

```
OBJ1_OWNER    OBJ1_NAME          OBJ1_TYPE      REASON
-----------   ----------------   -----------    ---------------------------
SCOTT         TEST_TSPITR        TABLE          Tables and associated indexes
                                                not fully contained in the
                                                recovery set
```

In this case, we have an index that appears to be created in another tablespace. This index is
associated with the TEST_TSPITR object. We need to find out what tablespace that index is in and
restore that tablespace too.

Preserve Objects or Data that Might Be Lost in the Recovery

Obviously, if you are going to restore the TEST tablespace to 2 P.M., any changes to that tablespace
(new objects or update, insert, or delete operations) will be lost after that point. Losing those
objects may be fine, but suppose that you need to preserve that data. If this is the case, you need
to export the data to be preserved (or, alternatively, copy it to somewhere else in the database).
Oracle provides a view, TS_PITR_OBJECTS_TO_BE_DROPPED, that lists all objects that will be
lost during the recovery operation. Use this view to determine what the status of the objects in the
tablespace will be after the recovery.

For example, if you were going to restore the TEST_TSPITR tablespace to a point in time
of 02/20/2015 at 23:40:00, you would lose the TEST_TSPITR_TWO object, as shown in this
sample output:

```
SQL>select * from TS_PITR_OBJECTS_TO_BE_DROPPED where
tablespace_name='TEST_RECOVER';

OWNER        NAME                 CREATION_TIME        TABLESPACE_NAME
----------   --------------------  -------------------  ---------------
SCOTT        TEST_TSPITR_TWO      02/20/2015 23:42:46  TEST_RECOVER
SCOTT        TEST_TSPITR          02/20/2015 23:26:26  TEST_RECOVER
SCOTT        TEST_TSPITR_THREE    02/21/2015 00:18:29  TEST_RECOVER
```

Performing the Actual TSPITR

RMAN will perform automated TSPITR for you, which means that it will create the auxiliary
instance for you. In this case, all you need to do is connect to the target database and the optional
recovery catalog (if you use one) and issue the **recover tablespace** command. RMAN will do the
rest of the work for you.

In the following code snippet, we provide an example of using the **recover tablespace**
command to recover the TEST_RECOVER tablespace. In this example, we use the optional
parameter **auxiliary destination** to indicate where RMAN and Oracle should create the files
associated with the auxiliary database. Using this parameter makes this recovery a *customized
TSPITR with an automatic instance*. If you do not use this parameter, the TSPITR is known as a
fully automated TSPITR recovery.

Note that if you use the **auxiliary destination** parameter, the destination directory should already be created, and Oracle must be able to write to that destination. Also note that there is no trailing slash (either \ or /, depending on your OS) in the destination pathname. Including a slash will cause TSPITR to fail (and the message you get isn't exactly all that descriptive). Here is an example of the **recover tablespace** command that we used to successfully perform TSPITR:

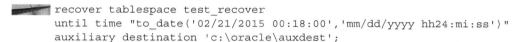

```
recover tablespace test_recover
until time "to_date('02/21/2015 00:18:00','mm/dd/yyyy hh24:mi:ss')"
auxiliary destination 'c:\oracle\auxdest';
```

NOTE
To do automatic TSPITR, you must have configured channels on the target. That way, channels used in the auxiliary instance will be the same as those on the target.

Once the TSPITR has been completed, you should be able to look at the objects in the recovered tablespace and find that they have been recovered to the point in time you requested. You need to bring the tablespaces recovered back online to use them. From RMAN, you can issue the command

```
Sql 'alter tablespace test_recover online';
```

If an error occurs, Oracle leaves the auxiliary instance and its related datafiles intact. You can try to correct the problem and restart the recovery. In this case, you would restart RMAN using the **auxiliary** parameter, connecting to the auxiliary instance.

If the auxiliary instance creation is not entirely successful, it may be easier to just remove the auxiliary instance and its service than to restart the recovery using the manual TSPITR process. First, figure out what failed, and then remove the auxiliary instance/service and restart the automated TSPITR process. You can remove the auxiliary instance/service by issuing the following command from SQL*Plus when logged in as SYSDBA:

```
exec dbms_backup_restore.manageauxinstance
('auxiliary_sid_name',1);
```

Note that you need to put the SID that Oracle assigned to the auxiliary instance in the place of the **auxiliary_sid_name** placeholder. The name of the SID will be listed in the RMAN output. This will clean up any old auxiliary instances before you start your TSPITR recovery. You will want to go to the auxiliary destination directory after you execute this command and remove any files that are in that directory.

Customized Automated TSPITR with an Automatic Instance

We already mentioned that you can customize some aspects of the automatic instance creation when performing TSPITR. We demonstrated the use of the **auxiliary destination** parameter to indicate where the recovery set should be created. Other ways of customizing the creation of the TSPITR, while still allowing Oracle to create the instance for you, include the following:

- Using the **set newname** command to indicate the location of the individual datafiles of the recovery set.
- Using the **configure auxname** command to define the name of the auxiliary instance.

■ Creating your own parameter file for the auxiliary instance and supplying parameters such as **db_file_name_convert** in that parameter file. This can be done by creating a file called parms_auxint.ora in $ORACLE_HOME/rdbms/admin (this filename and location are OS dependent). Optionally, you can use the RMAN command **set auxiliary instance parameter file** to indicate the path on the client where the auxiliary instance parameter file resides.

Once you have customized your auxiliary instance, you can have RMAN create it for you by issuing the **recover tablespace** command.

Summary

We have covered a lot of ground in this chapter. Everything from restoring CDBs and PDBs to incomplete recoveries of non-CDB databases and CDB databases. We covered other database restore topics such as the recovery of read-only tablespaces, archived redo logs, and datafile copies. We discussed recovery of corrupted database blocks, recovery of database tables, and tablespace point-in-time recoveries. There are still many more topics to discuss, such as cloning databases, as well as maintaining and monitoring database backups. Those topics are coming up!

CHAPTER
10

Duplication: Cloning the Target Database

W e've hinted at this chapter's content since the earliest part of the book: RMAN will help you leverage your backups beyond disaster recovery. We covered using RMAN for corruption, but one of the most highly leveraged ways to use backups is to make copies of the production database for testing and development purposes. In the database world, we refer to this as *cloning*.

Database cloning can provide an excellent way to test version upgrades, new application rollouts, and even bug patches. Cloning can also be used to prepare reporting databases that are kept separate from transaction processing databases, and finally the backups are tested to ensure they are valid. In these ways, database backups can be put to work. They can be used to restore the database to another system, or even just to another disk on the same system. We can then do load testing for performance reasons, or try out a new hardware configuration. With clone databases at our disposal, we can leave little to chance and have an almost perfect grasp of what will happen if we change our production environment. RMAN can be also be used to create a standby database that can be kept up to date for disaster recovery—but we are getting ahead of ourselves.

RMAN helps you create clones via the **duplicate** command. This simple little command hides many levels of complexity that are worth knowing about before you begin to use it. In addition, there is a fair amount of prep work required so that duplication goes smoothly. But once understood, and after you've had a little time to practice, you'll find that database duplication is one of the real "killer apps" within the backup and recovery world. Or perhaps you already know this. Regardless, leveraging the RMAN interface will save you hours of scripting pain.

RMAN Duplication: A Primer

The RMAN **duplicate** command is a simple command that hides a high level of complexity. If you've ever been through the process of restoring image copy backups of your database to another system, you know the amount of information that you have to keep track of: filenames, file locations, backup locations, archive log information, ftp processes, moving tapes around… there's plenty to keep track of. RMAN, on the other hand, has a straightforward command:

```
duplicate target database to aux1;
```

This will perform the entire process of cloning your target database to another database. Granted, you have to do a little legwork first, but once you become familiar with the architecture, you'll see that the legwork is not too bad a trade-off.

Why Use RMAN Duplication?

Why is duplication necessary? Why can't we just copy the control file to a new location and run a restore and recovery? The answer is, you can! There is no reason that this won't work. The only problem is, you will have an exact copy—not just of the data in the database (the part you want to be the same), but also of the metadata about the database (this will cause headaches). If you use a recovery catalog, you will run into problems if you clone your database without using duplication. You see, RMAN registers databases in the catalog based on the database ID (DBID), which is a number that identifies your database as unique, even if it has the same DB_NAME as another database. If you don't use the **duplicate** command, you will have two databases with the same DBID. If you try to register your clone in the same catalog as your production system, you will get an error:

```
rman-20002: target database already registered in recovery catalog
```

This error can be a little misleading: you haven't registered the database! If you shrug your shoulders at this and go ahead and try to back up your database, it will give you an even stranger error:

```
rman-20011: target database incarnation is not current in
recovery catalog
```

"Whoa," you say, "what does that mean?" So you go ahead and issue a **reset database**, as you think you should, and this works. You can now back up your database. Sweet. However, you have caused bigger problems. Now, you connect RMAN to your original production server and try to back it up. But when you do, you get a hauntingly similar error:

```
rman-20011: target database incarnation is not current in
recovery catalog
```

The reason for this error is that RMAN considers your clone no more than a restored version of your production system, so it now thinks the clone is the current incarnation of your production server, and it has no idea what your production server is. You can reset the incarnation back to the one that actually matches your production database, but you've essentially corrupted your catalog and should unregister your database and reregister it in the catalog (see Chapter 6). It should be noted, of course, that the Oracle documentation clearly states in each release that you should never connect RMAN to a test database and the recovery catalog because of this very problem.

If you don't use a catalog, nonduplicated clones can wreak havoc as well. Let's lay it out in an example. You clone your database to the same system as your primary database. You are using RMAN to back up both databases to tape, and because you aren't using a catalog, you have automatic control file backups turned on for both instances. One day, you lose a disk array, and your entire system goes belly up. Both databases, and all of their control files, are lost. "No problem," you think, "I've got control file autobackup turned on. I'll just use one of those to restore my systems."

But here's the stickler: the command **restore controlfile from autobackup** uses the DB_ID to track down the control file autobackup. Because both of your databases back up to the same tape, it may try to restore the control file from the wrong database, giving you the wrong files with the wrong data.

A third reason, new to environments where you are using Oracle Enterprise Manager Grid Control, also comes to the surface. Grid Control needs to understand all of its managed targets as unique snowflakes. If you clone a database, and you leave the metadata the same for both databases, and then try to use Grid Control to manage both databases, you give Grid Control brain damage. It will either refuse to discover one of the databases, or make you go through some gyrations to rectify how the new clone registers itself with the listener (note: this problem can occur even if your clone database is on a different server).

Obviously, any of these scenarios can be fixed, and they don't cause a loss of data. But they cause a loss of time. They can potentially extend your downtime past your agreement levels. In addition to these problems, using duplication in RMAN provides the power of the RMAN interface to keep things as simple as possible. And simple is good. Simple is wise.

Different Types of RMAN Duplication

Oracle 12c offers multiple ways to perform database cloning using RMAN. In the past, you always needed a few critical things to perform duplication: access to the target database (the one you want to copy) and access to existing backups. In different situations, both of these dependencies have been stripped, allowing for more flexibility in how you plan and execute a clone operation with RMAN.

Duplicate Using RMAN Backups and with Access to the Target Database

This is the "traditional" RMAN duplication from versions 9i and 10g: we leverage our existing RMAN backups to create a copy of an existing target database to a new location. To understand how far, and what, to duplicate, RMAN connects to the existing database's control file throughout the duplication operation.

Duplicate Using RMAN Backups and No Access to the Target

Starting with 11g, now you have the option of performing a duplication when the target is not available. This is useful in situations where the target database is in a different incarnation, is in an inaccessible network location, or is simply not at your disposal for the duplication. In this case, RMAN can pull most of what it needs from the recovery catalog. There are only a few additional parameters you will pass to the **duplicate** command. We cover this near the end of the chapter, in the section "Targetless Duplication in 12c."

Duplicate an Active Database Without Using Backups

Duplicating an active database sounds new, but this operation was actually introduced in Enterprise Manager in the 10g timeframe. At that time, Enterprise Manager would clone a database by calling the package **dbms_backup_restore** directly, instead of using the RMAN client command syntax, and it would make a live copy of each datafile in the database in real time and then would move each datafile to the new location.

In 11g, this was codified in the RMAN command syntax, but it's the same operation. Instead of relying on an existing RMAN backup, RMAN simply connects to the target database, runs a backup operation directly against the database in real time, and writes the file to the specified location. So, nothing all that special, other than a syntactic difference in what you call the operation.

All three of these duplication types rely on the same underlying architecture. We will walk through the operations for the backup-based, target database–connected duplication so that the underlying principles can be observed.

The Duplication Architecture

Here's how duplication works: RMAN connects to your target database or to the catalog, if you use one. This connection is necessary to gain access to the target database control file for details about where to locate backups. After you connect to the target or catalog, you must connect to your auxiliary instance (the instance that will house your cloned database). Before duplication starts, you must have already built an init.ora file for the auxiliary instance and have started it in NOMOUNT mode. This way, the memory segment has been initialized, and therefore RMAN can make a SYSDBA connection to it. The auxiliary instance does not have a control file yet (duplication will take care of that), so you cannot mount the auxiliary instance, even if you want to.

With these connections made, you can issue your **duplicate** command. It can look as simple as this:

```
duplicate target database to aux1;
```

Or it can be complicated, depending on where the auxiliary instance is, as shown here:

```
run {
set until time = '08-DEC-2014:11:30:00';
duplicate target database to aux1 pfile=/u02/oracle/admin/aux1/pfile/init.ora
nofilenamecheck
device type sbt parms "env=(nb_ora_serv=rmsrv)"
logfile
'/u04/oracle/oradata/aux1/redo01.log' size 100m,
'/u05/oracle/oradata/aux1/redo02.log' size 100m,
'/u06/oracle/oradata/aux1/redo03.log' size 100m;}
```

The duplication process can be broken down into its distinct phases:

1. RMAN determines the nature and location of the backups.
2. RMAN allocates an auxiliary channel at the auxiliary instance.
3. RMAN restores the datafiles to the auxiliary instance.
4. RMAN builds a new auxiliary control file.
5. RMAN restores archive logs from backup (if necessary) and performs any necessary recovery.
6. RMAN resets the DBID for the auxiliary instance and opens the auxiliary database with **open resetlogs**.

First, RMAN sets any run-time parameters, such as an **until time** clause on the **duplicate** command. Then, based on these parameters, it checks the target database control file (or recovery catalog) for the appropriate backups. It then builds the RPCs for how to access the backups, and which ones to access, but it does not execute the code at the target. Instead, RMAN creates a channel process at the auxiliary instance, referred to as the *auxiliary channel,* and to this channel RMAN passes the call to DBMS_BACKUP_RESTORE. The auxiliary instance, then, accesses the backups and restores all necessary datafiles. Figure 10-1 illustrates how this takes place for both disk backups and tape backups.

Auxiliary Channel Configuration

For duplication to work, RMAN must allocate one or more channel processes at the auxiliary instance. From Oracle9*i* onward, you do not need to manually allocate an auxiliary channel at the time of duplication, because one will automatically be created using permanent configuration parameters stored in the target control file. The makeup of the auxiliary channel mainly comes from parameters you established for target channels: the default device type and the degree of parallelism both get set using the same persistent parameters that set the target channels. Therefore, if you are duplicating using backups taken to disk, you need not do anything to configure your auxiliary channels. However, if you are duplicating your database using backups taken to tape, you need to configure your auxiliary channels to contain any media manager environment parameters your target channels have. For example, the following code sets the

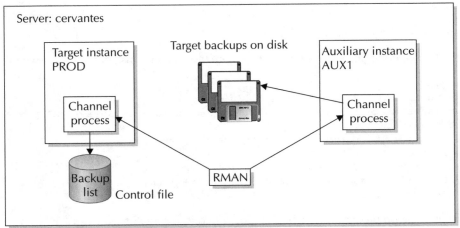

Duplication from Disk (same server)

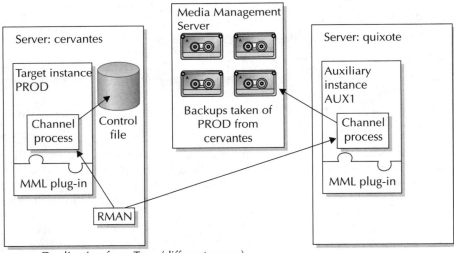

Duplication from Tape (different server)

FIGURE 10-1. *A bird's-eye view of duplication*

default device type to tape, sets the default level of parallelism to 2, and then configures two auxiliary channels with the correct parameters:

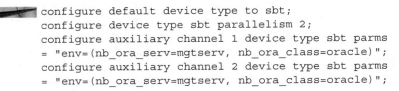

```
configure default device type to sbt;
configure device type sbt parallelism 2;
configure auxiliary channel 1 device type sbt parms
= "env=(nb_ora_serv=mgtserv, nb_ora_class=oracle)";
configure auxiliary channel 2 device type sbt parms
= "env=(nb_ora_serv=mgtserv, nb_ora_class=oracle)";
```

Restoring Datafiles to a Different File Location

After mounting the new control file, RMAN moves forward with the datafile restore. If you are duplicating your database to the same server on which your target resides, it is obviously necessary to change the location to which the files will be restored.

Even when you're restoring to a different server, differences in mount points and directory structures can require a new file location. The datafile restore step of the duplication process can be modified to point to a new file location in three ways.

First, you can use the **configure** command to configure the auxname for any (or all) datafiles that need a new location. These configurations are stored in the target database control file.

```
configure auxname for datafile 1 to
'/u04/oradata/aux1/system01.dbf';
configure auxname for datafile 2 to
'/u04/oradata/aux1/undo01.dbf';
...
```

Second, you can specify the new datafile names in a **run** command the same as you would in previous versions, as shown here:

```
run {allocate channel c1 type 'sbt_tape';
set newname for datafile 1 to '/u04/oradata/aux1/system01.dbf';
set newname for datafile 2 to '/u04/oradata/aux1/undo01.dbf';
duplicate target database to aux1;}
```

Finally, you can use a parameter in your auxiliary database's init.ora file to set a new location for the files. The parameter is DB_FILE_NAME_CONVERT, and you pass two strings to it: first, the old location of the file on the target; second, the new location for the file in your auxiliary instance. You can do this in matched file pairs, like this:

```
db_file_name_convert=(
'/u02/oradata/prod/system01.dbf',
'/u02/oradata/aux1/system01.dbf',
'/u03/oradata/prod/prd_data_01.dbf', '/u03/oradata/aux1/prd_data_01.dbf')
```

NOTE
In 11gR2, the SET NEWNAME function was significantly improved to make scripting even simpler. Now you can do a SET NEWNAME for an entire tablespace, or even for the entire database. Here's an example:

```
SET NEWNAME for tablespace USERS01 to '/u01/%U';
```

This will rename all datafiles to the new location, with unique naming as defined by the variable %U. This greatly simplifies the duplication scripting in situations where the new location will have a different, but consistent, file location.

In addition, there is a Metalink note for those with Oracle Support access that provides methods for dynamic SQL to generate the SET NEWNAME commands for user-managed files, or for converting files to Oracle's Automatic Storage Manager (ASM) and Oracle Managed Files (OMF) infrastructure. This is Note 549972.1, "RMAN: SET NEWNAME Command SQL."

This is a simple string conversion parameter, so you can simply pass a single directory name to be changed. For instance, let's say you have your files spread over four mount points, but they all have prod in the directory structure, so that a **select** from V$DATAFILE looks like this:

```
Select name from v$datafile;
--------------------------------------------------------
/u02/oradata/prod/system01.dbf
/u03/oradata/prod/prd_data_01.dbf
/u04/oradata/prod/indx_prd01.dbf
/u05/oradata/prod/temp01.dbf
```

Instead of pairing up each file, you can simply do the following:

```
db_file_name_convert=('prod' , 'aux1')
```

This works, so long as everything else about the file location is the same for your auxiliary database, such as the mount point.

Creating the New Control File

The new control file is created for the auxiliary instance after all the files have been restored. RMAN just issues a **create controlfile** command at the auxiliary instance, using the parameters you outlined in your **duplicate** command. After creating the control file, the auxiliary database is mounted. Now, RMAN performs a switch operation to switch to the new files. The switch is the means by which RMAN modifies the new control file at the auxiliary site to point to the new location of the datafiles.

Recovery and Archive Logs

After the files are restored and switched, it is time to perform recovery on the database, either to bring it to the current point in time or to bring it to the time specified in the **until time** clause. To perform recovery, RMAN needs access to the archive logs. If they have been backed up by RMAN, then RMAN can simply restore them from the backup location to the LOG_ARCHIVE_ DEST specified in the init.ora file of the auxiliary database. You can also manually move archive logs to the location required by the new instance so that they are found on disk by RMAN and no restore is required. If you are duplicating to the same server as the one on which the target currently resides, RMAN can find the archive logs in the LOG_ARCHIVE_DEST of the target.

Once the archive logs are restored, RMAN performs the required amount of recovery. If you did not specify a point in time to end the recovery, RMAN restores up to the last available archive log (as found in the view V$ARCHIVED_LOG) and then stops. During duplication, RMAN cannot check the online redo log files for further recovery information. After it hits the end of the archive logs, it stops recovery. After recovery has completed, if RMAN restored any archive logs from backup, they are deleted.

Changing the Database ID (DBID)

After media recovery is complete, the database is in a consistent state, and it is time for RMAN to change the database ID of the new clone. RMAN has to wait until all other activity in the database has completed, as all operations to this point required the clone database to have the same DBID as the target. The archive logs would not apply to the clone during media recovery if the control file had a different DBID.

The process of changing the DBID is simple. RMAN has at its disposal a little procedure called **dbms_backup_restore.zerodbid()**. With the database in a mounted state (not open), this package goes into the file headers and zeros out the DBID in each file header. Then, RMAN shuts down the database and re-creates the auxiliary control file again. When the control file is rebuilt,

Oracle checks the file headers for the DBID. When it does not find one, Oracle generates a new one and broadcasts it to every file header.

Log File Creation at the Auxiliary Site

When RMAN issues the final **open resetlogs** command at the completion of the duplication process, it must build brand-new log files for the auxiliary database. This always happens when you issue a **resetlogs** command, but with a **duplicate** command, you need to take into consideration what you want the new redo log files to look like. If you are duplicating to the same system as your target, at a minimum you will have to rename your log files.

The zerodbid Procedure: Warning! Achtung!

As you can imagine, the following is a very vulnerable state for a database to be in: shut down without a DBID in the file headers and with a control file that is being rebuilt. In the RMAN duplication process, however, elements that could go wrong are tightly controlled, so you don't have to worry too much. We point this out because it is possible to execute this package against any database to generate a new DBID. You just mount the database and run the following code:

```
execute sys.dbms_backup_restore.zerodbid(0);
```

Then, you shut down the database and rebuild the control file using the **set** parameter:

```
create controlfile SET database <db_name> resetlogs...
```

And, voilà, you have a new DBID. Seems simple enough, doesn't it?

However, a lot can go wrong if you are trying to do this without the complete control over the environment that RMAN has during duplication. For instance, if you did not get a clean shutdown and you need to perform media recovery before you can open reset logs, you are out of luck. The archive logs have a different DBID. There is no way you will be able to open the database—it is stuck in an inconsistent state, and you cannot fix it. The same thing can happen if a file was accidentally left offline—it won't get the new DBID when you do an **open resetlogs** command, and therefore you will not be able to bring it online. Ever. Instead, you will get the following error:

```
ORA-01190: control file or datafile <name> is from before
the last RESETLOGS
```

The moral of the story is to be very careful if you decide to use this procedure manually. There is a better way. As of Oracle9*i* Release 2, Oracle has a utility called DBNEWID, which provides a safe and secure way of generating a new ID for a database without making a manual call to the DBMS_BACKUP_RESTORE package. We talk about DBNEWID at the end of this chapter in the section "Incomplete Duplication: Using the DBNEWID Utility."

You can specify completely new redo log file definitions when you issue the **duplicate** command. Do this if you want to change the size, number, and/or location of the redo logs for the new database. This would look something like the following:

```
duplicate target database to aux1
pfile=/u02/oracle/admin/aux1/init.ora
logfile
'/u04/oracle/oradata/aux1/redo01.log' size 100m,
```

```
'/u05/oracle/oradata/aux1/redo02.log' size 100m,
'/u06/oracle/oradata/aux1/redo03.log' size 100m;
```

Alternatively, you can use the existing log file definitions from your target and simply move them to a new location using the init.ora parameter LOG_FILE_NAME_CONVERT. This parameter acts exactly like DB_FILE_NAME_CONVERT, so you can convert the log files in coupled pairs, or you can simply use string conversion to change a single directory name:

```
log_file_name_convert=('/u02/oracle/oradata/redo01a.dbf',
'/u03/auxiliary/redo01a.dbf',...)
```

Duplication: Location Considerations

So far, we've completely glossed over one of the biggest stumbling blocks to understanding duplication. You must account for the location of your auxiliary instance in relation to the location of your target instance. Duplicating to the same server is very different from duplicating to a remote server. There are elements unique to each that you must understand before you proceed with duplication.

Duplication to the Same Server: An Overview

You must tread lightly when duplicating to the same server, so that you don't walk all over your existing target database. Suppose you were to simply make a copy of your target init.ora file and then run the following code:

```
duplicate target database to aux1;
```

In this case, you would run into a series of problems and errors. These errors would be related to the fact that you already have an instance running with the same name and have the same file locations for two databases.

Memory Considerations

The first memory consideration is the database name. Oracle references memory segments on the server based on the value of the init.ora parameter DB_NAME. Therefore, Oracle cannot allow two instances with the same DB_NAME to run on the same system. If you try to startup mount a second instance with the same name, you will get the following error:

```
ORA-01102: cannot mount database in EXCLUSIVE mode
```

Therefore, when duplicating to the same system, you need to change the DB_NAME parameter in the auxiliary init.ora file to be different from the database name of your target:

```
db_name='aux1'
instance_name='aux1'
```

File Location Considerations

Okay, you've squared away your memory problems, but you still have two databases that are trying to write to the same file locations. In fact, you have three different types of files that are all competing for the same name. If you don't account for file locations, duplication will fail at the step of trying to rebuild the control file:

```
RMAN-00571: ===========================================================
RMAN-00569: =============== ERROR MESSAGE STACK FOLLOWS =========
RMAN-00571: ===========================================================
```

```
RMAN-03002: failure of Duplicate Db command 12/02/2014 13:52:14
RMAN-06136: ORACLE error from auxiliary database:
    ORA-01503: CREATE CONTROLFILE failed
ORA-00200: controlfile could not be created
ORA-00202: controlfile:
'/space/oracle_user/OraHome1/oradata/sun92/control01.ctl'
ORA-27086: skgfglk: unable to lock file - already in use
SVR4 Error: 11: Resource temporarily unavailable
```

This is good news for you, because otherwise you would have overwritten your production control file. You must change the auxiliary init.ora parameter CONTROL_FILES to point to a new location on disk, as this is the means by which RMAN determines where to restore the control files to.

After we change the location of the control files, we must change the location of the datafiles. We talked about this previously: your three choices are to use the **configure** command, use the DB_FILE_NAME_CONVERT parameter, or use a **run** block, Oracle8*i* style. If you fail to change the datafile locations when duplicating to the same server, you will get an error very similar to the preceding control file error, telling you that the files are currently in use and cannot be overwritten.

Finally, you must change the redo log file location. We talked about this previously, when we discussed the different steps that duplication walks through. You can use the **logfile** keyword as part of the **duplicate** command to build completely different redo files, with different sizes, number of groups, and number of members. This option essentially rewrites the similar **logfile** parameter of the **create controlfile** stage of duplication. Alternatively, you can simply use the LOG_FILE_NAME_CONVERT parameter in the auxiliary init.ora file.

Duplication to the Same Server, Different ORACLE_HOME

It is common practice to clone the production database from its location to a different location on the same server but to have it be hosted by a different Oracle software installation. When you have a different ORACLE_HOME for the auxiliary instance, slightly different rules apply. All the rules about hosting on the same system apply as outlined previously. However, you must also consider the location of the backup pieces. If you are duplicating from disk backups, this won't be a problem—just make sure you have your OS permissions worked out ahead of time. If you are duplicating from tape backups, however, you need to make sure you have your MML file appropriately linked with the auxiliary ORACLE_HOME in the same way as it is linked in your target's ORACLE_HOME. Otherwise, your tape backups will be inaccessible by the auxiliary instance, and duplication will fail because the media manager will be inaccessible.

Duplication to a Remote Server: An Overview

A successful duplication to an auxiliary instance on a different server from the target is no more or less complicated than duplication to the same server. It's just complicated in different ways.

Memory Considerations

Unlike duplication to the same server, you do not have to worry about the DB_NAME parameter in the init.ora file. Because you are on a different server, Oracle has no hang-ups about the LOCK_NAME used for memory.

Of course, it is good operational procedure to always be mindful of the DB_NAME parameter during a duplication process and crosscheck all other instances running on the same server before beginning the duplication. That way, you have no unexpected errors down the road. In addition, from a management perspective, it makes the most sense to always have every database in your ecosystem with a unique name.

File Location Considerations

Again, because we are on a new server, there is not quite the urgency to change any of the file location specifications for your auxiliary instance. No database already is running with the same files, so we can leave all file specifications the same as for the target instance, and thus avoid any possible errors in the configuration. Again, we can simplify much of this process when we are on a different system. If you do not change the location of the files, you must specify **nofilenamecheck** in the **duplicate** command. This tells duplication not to confirm that the filenames are different before performing the restore. If this is not specified, RMAN will give you an error.

The one caveat to this simplicity is if the auxiliary host does not have the same file structure and mount point setup that the target host has. If you have different mount points or drive configurations, you still need to change your file specifications for the auxiliary instance so that RMAN can restore to a location that actually exists.

The Backup Location: Disk

The complicating factor for restoring to a different server comes from providing the auxiliary channel process access to backups that were taken at a different server. You must account for whether you backed up to disk or to tape.

If you are duplicating from disk backups, your choices are limited. Remember that RMAN passes the calls to DBMS_BACKUP_RESTORE to a channel process at the auxiliary instance, but it cannot take into account any file system differences. It must look for the backup pieces in the exact location and format recorded in the target database control file. For example, suppose you took a full database backup at your target system using the following command:

```
backup database format= '/u04/backup/prod/%U.full.PROD';
```

This creates your backup piece as a file called 01DSGVLT_1_1 in the directory /u04/backup/prod. This is recorded in the target control file. Then, during duplication, RMAN passes the **file restore** command to the auxiliary instance and tells it to restore from /u04/backup/prod/01DSGVLT_1_1. That means your auxiliary instance must have a mount point named /u04, and there must be a directory named backup/prod in which a file called 01DSGVLT_1_1 resides. If not, the duplication will fail with an error:

```
RMAN-03002: failure of Duplicate Db command 12/02/2014 14:49:55
RMAN-03015: error occurred in stored script Memory Script
ORA-19505: failed to identify "/u04/backup/prod/01dsgvlt_1_1"
ORA-27037: unable to obtain file status
SVR4 Error: 2: No such file or directory
Additional information: 3
```

You can make duplication from disk work in three ways. The first, and most straightforward, is to simply copy the backups from your target host to the auxiliary host and place them in the same location. Obviously, this involves a huge transfer of files across your network.

The second way to proceed is to NFS mount the backup location on the target host from the auxiliary host. This works only if you can mount the target location with the same mount point name as RMAN will use (in the preceding example, you would have to NFS mount /u04/backup/prod as /u04/backup/prod). For example, you would need to do the following from your auxiliary instance:

```
mount cervantes:/u04/backup/prod /u04/backup/prod
```

That way, from your auxiliary node, you should be able to do the following:

```
cd /u04/backup/prod
ls -l
touch testfile
ls -l
```

If you get an error when you try to change directories, or when you try to touch a file, you need to sort out your NFS and permissions issues before you proceed with duplication. Figure 10-2 illustrates the mounted file system approach to duplicating to a different server using disk backups.

If you are on a Windows platform instead of NFS, you will be mounting a network drive. The same rule applies: the drive specification must be the same on the auxiliary as it is on the target. So if the backup was written to F:\backup, you must be able to use F: as a network drive; otherwise, duplication will fail. In addition, you will have to set up your auxiliary service (oracleserviceaux1) and your listener service (oracleOraHome92tnslistener) to log on as a domain

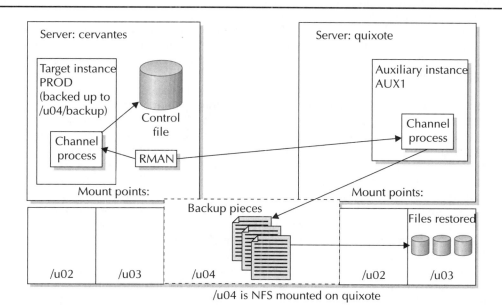

FIGURE 10-2. *Duplication to a different server using disk backups*

administrator that has read/write privileges at both the auxiliary host and the target host. Otherwise, you will not be able to access the backups over the networked drive.

As you may have already noticed, it could be difficult to make a network file system operation be successful. If you have the same file systems on both the target and the auxiliary servers, you would not be able to use a straight NFS mount from the auxiliary node to the target location of the backups on disk. Therefore, your only option would be to copy the backup pieces from one node to the other.

The source of these types of headaches, of course, is the fact that RMAN hard-codes the backup location when we back up to disk, and this location cannot be changed. RMAN provides a solution with two options for us to change the backup location: the **backup backupset** command and the **catalog backupset** command.

With the **backup backupset** command, we can back up a previous backup set that was on disk and move it to a different disk location. This gives us considerable flexibility. Now, we can move the backup pieces from /u04/backup/prod to, say, /u06/backup/prod, which could then be NFS mounted from our auxiliary system. Alternatively, from the target host, we could NFS mount a drive at the auxiliary host and then use the **backup backupset** command to move the backups to the auxiliary host. For more information on this command, see Chapter 9.

The **catalog backupset** (and **catalog datafilecopy**) command offers another, simpler means of relocating backup sets on a new server. To make RMAN aware that a backup set exists in any location, you need only tell RMAN to catalog a certain file (or a certain directory), and it will look for any valid backups in that location and generate metadata for them. For more details on the **catalog** command, see Chapter 6.

The Backup Location: Tape

By all estimations, duplicating to a remote server using tape backups is far less complicated or demanding than using disk backups, because a tape backup does not have a location, per se, just a file handle. This file handle is all that RMAN knows or cares about; how that file handle relates to a location on a specific tape is completely controlled by the media manager. Therefore, all configuration steps that occur for duplication from tape come from the media management layer.

First, you must configure your MML file at the auxiliary site in the same way as at the target site. Because an auxiliary channel is doing the restore operations, it must be able to initialize the MML, as outlined in Chapter 21. So, make sure you've linked your MML at the auxiliary site.

Next, you need to make sure that your media management server is configured correctly. This means that your auxiliary node must be registered as a client in the same media management server that your target node is registered in, and it must have the necessary privileges to access the tapes for restore purposes. In particular, you must enable the auxiliary node to restore backups that were taken from a different server. This functionality is usually disabled by default in most media management software, because allowing files to be restored from one client to another is a potential security hole. The steps for enabling clients to restore files from a different client are outlined in each of our five media management chapters (Chapters 22, 23, 24, 25, and 26), depending on your software vendor.

After configuring your media management server, your final configuration step is to set up your auxiliary channels. As mentioned earlier, RMAN allocates one or more channels at the auxiliary instance to perform the restore and recovery steps of duplication. You configure these channels via the **configure** command when you are connected to your target database from RMAN. The **parms** parameter for the auxiliary channels must contain the usual media management environment control variables. In particular, it needs to specify the client from which the backups were taken. For instance, let's say your target node is named cervantes, and your auxiliary node is named quixote. Because you have been backing up from cervantes, this client name is encoded with your RMAN backups at the media management server. So, to be able to access these backups from the client quixote, you must specify from within RMAN that the client name is cervantes. In other words, where the backup database is RAC and all the nodes have participated in the backup, a channel must be allocated with the client name of all the participating nodes. Your auxiliary channel configuration command, then, would look something like this (given a NetBackup media management system):

```
RMAN> configure auxiliary channel 1 device type sbt parms
2> = "env=(nb_ora_serv=mgtserv, nb_ora_client=cervantes)";
new RMAN configuration parameters:
CONFIGURE AUXILIARY CHANNEL 1 DEVICE TYPE 'SBT_TAPE' PARMS
"env=(nb_ora_serv=mgtserv, nb_ora_client=cervantes)";
new RMAN configuration parameters are successfully stored
```

Then, when the auxiliary channel makes its **sbt()** calls to the MML, it is telling the media management server to access backups that were taken using the client cervantes, instead of checking for backups made by quixote.

Duplication and the Network

Take a deep breath; we're almost through explaining all the intricacies of duplication and are about to walk you through the steps themselves. There's one more area you need to prepare prior to running a **duplicate** command from RMAN: the network. By *network,* we mostly mean configuring your Oracle Net files—tnsnames.ora and listener.ora. However, take this opportunity to consider your overall network as well. Make sure that the target node, auxiliary node, and media management server can all access each other okay and that you have plenty of bandwidth.

From an Oracle perspective, we have to configure the Oracle Net files. As discussed in Chapter 2, RMAN must make a SYSDBA connection to the target database. If you are connecting remotely, you have to configure a password file for the target node. In addition, you need a TNS alias that uses a dedicated server process instead of a shared server process. For duplication, this still holds true, but you must also be able to connect to the auxiliary instance as SYSDBA using only dedicated servers.

This means that, no matter what, you have to create a password file for either your target or your auxiliary machine. You may have been forgoing this step until now by always making a local connection to the target database. However, you cannot simultaneously make a local connection to both the target and the auxiliary instance. So now, if you haven't done so already, it's time to build a password file.

After your password file has been created for your auxiliary instance, you need to configure the listener to route incoming connections to the auxiliary instance. As you may have already noticed, there is no need starting with 10*g* for a listener.ora file if you will be connecting only to open databases. This is because the database PMON process automatically registers the database

RMAN Workshop: *Build a Password File*

Workshop Notes

On Unix platforms, the name of the password file must be orapw<sid>, where <sid> is the value of the ORACLE_SID to which the password is giving access. In this workshop, the ORACLE_SID is prod. On Windows, the filename must be in the format pwd<sid>.ora. The locations given in this workshop must be used; the password file cannot be created anywhere else, or it will be unusable.

Step 1. Edit the init.ora file and add the following parameter:

```
remote_login_passwordfile=exclusive
```

If you are using an SPFILE, you need to execute the following:

```
alter system set remote_login_passwordfile=exclusive scope=spfile;
```

Both operations require a database restart to take effect.

Step 2. Decide what your password will be, and then navigate to your ORACLE_HOME/dbs directory (ORACLE_HOME/database on Windows) and type the following:

```
orapwd file=orapwprod password=<OraclE4ever>
```

Step 3. Check that the file was created successfully, and then test it by making a remote connection as SYSDBA.

with a running listener daemon on the system if the listener is using the default port of 1521. So, you will often see that after a default 12c installation, a listener is running, and it is listening for your database, even though you've done no configuration.

While this is excellent news, it does nothing for us in a duplication environment, because we must be able to make a remote connection to an auxiliary instance that is started (in NOMOUNT mode) but not open. Because it is not open, there is no PMON process to register the auxiliary instance with the listener, so the listener has no idea the auxiliary instance exists. To get past this, you must set up an old-fashioned listener.ora file, with a manual entry for the auxiliary database. We recommend using the Oracle Net Manager utility, shown here, to build this entry:

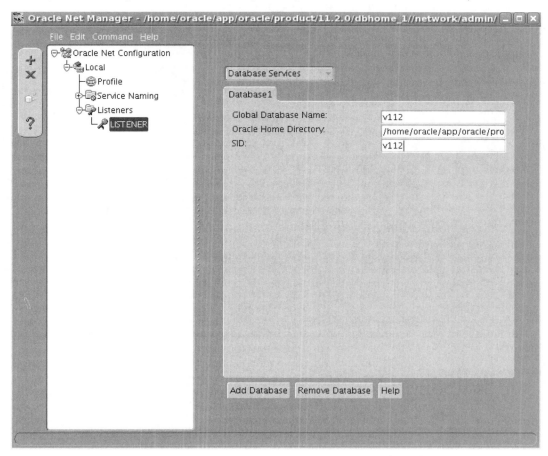

After you have configured the listener.ora at your auxiliary instance location, you must also build a tnsnames.ora entry at the site from which you will be running RMAN. This is the same as almost any other entry, except that when you build it, you must specify the auxiliary SID_NAME instead of the SERVICE_NAME. From the Net Manager, you fire up the Net Service Name Wizard by clicking Service Naming and then going to the menu and choosing Edit | Create. After you give the Net Service name (Step 1), then provide the protocol (Step 2), provide the hostname and port number (Step 3), and finish with specifying the service name.

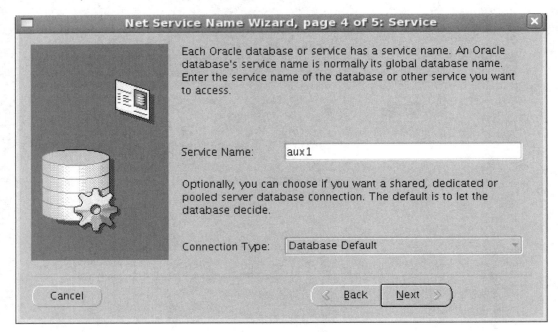

Duplication to the Same Server

Okay, so enough of the explanations, it's time to run through the duplication itself. First, we give a detailed step-by-step workshop for duplicating to the same server on which the target resides, using disk backups. Then, we briefly explain what you would need to do the same thing with tape backups.

Setting an until Clause when Duplicating
When performing duplication, you sometimes will encounter a situation that requires you to specify an **until** clause. If you have ever used RMAN to restore your database using a backup control file, and you are now attempting to duplicate that database, you will be required to set an **until** clause. Starting with 10g, if you omit the **until** clause, RMAN will use the last archive log in the backup to set the **until** value.

```
run { set until sequence n thread 1;
duplicate target database... }
```

Or, as a fix-all, you can set the SCN to an impossibly high value:

```
set until scn 281474976710655;
```

RMAN Workshop: *Duplication to the Same Server Using Disk Backups*

Workshop Notes

Make sure that your OS has been configured to handle another Oracle instance and that adequate memory and disk space exist. In the following example, our target database, v121, has all of its datafiles, control files, and redo log files located at /u01/app/oracle/product/oradata/v121. All backups have been going to the local FRA at /u01/app/oracle/product/flash_recovery_area. We will set the ORACLE_SID for the auxiliary instance to be aux1.

Step 1. Build your auxiliary database directory structures:

```
$ pwd
/u01/app/oracle/product/oradata
$ mkdir aux1
$ mkdir aux1/arch
$ cd ../admin
$ mkdir aux1
$ cd aux1
$ mkdir pfile
$ ls
 pfile
```

Step 2. Copy the target init.ora file to the auxiliary location. If your target database uses an SPFILE, you need to create a PFILE from the SPFILE to capture parameters to move over.
    If you use an SPFILE at your target, enter the following:

```
SQL> connect / as sysdba
Connected.
SQL> create pfile=
'/u01/app/oracle/product/admin/aux1/pfile/init.ora'
  from spfile;
```

    If you use an init.ora file at your target, enter the following:

```
cp u01/app/oracle/product/admin/v121/pfile/init.ora
   u01/app/oracle/product/admin/aux1/pfile/init.ora
```

Step 3. Make all necessary changes to your aux1 init.ora file:

```
audit_file_dest='/u01/app/oracle/product/admin/aux1/adump'
compatible='12.1.0.1.0'
control_files=
'/u01/app/oracle/product/oradata/aux1/control01.ctl',
    '/u01/app/oracle/product/oradata/aux1/control02.ctl',
    '/u01/app/oracle/product/oradata/aux1/control03.ctl'
db_block_size=8192
db_name='aux1'
db_recovery_file_dest='/u01/app/oracle/product/flash_recovery_area'
```

```
db_recovery_file_dest_size=4294967296
dispatchers='(PROTOCOL=TCP) (SERVICE=aux1XDB)'
job_queue_processes=10
open_cursors=300
pga_aggregate_target=93323264
processes=150
remote_login_passwordfile='EXCLUSIVE'
sga_target=279969792
undo_management='AUTO'
undo_tablespace='UNDOTBS1'
db_file_name_convert=('v121','aux1')
instance_name='aux1'
```

Step 4.   Build your aux1 password file. See the "Build a Password File" RMAN Workshop earlier in this chapter.

Step 5.   Start up the aux1 instance in NOMOUNT mode:

```
ORACLE_SID=aux1
export ORACLE_SID
sqlplus /nolog
sql>connect / as sysdba
SQL> startup nomount
pfile=/u01/app/oracle/product/admin/aux1/pfile/init.ora
```

Step 6.   Configure your network files for connection to aux1. After making any changes to your listener.ora file, be sure that you bounce your listener; otherwise, the change will not take effect.

```
$ lsnrctl reload
```

The tnsnames.ora file should have an entry like this:

```
AUX1 =
  (DESCRIPTION =
    (ADDRESS_LIST =
(ADDRESS = (PROTOCOL = TCP)(HOST = horatio)(PORT = 1521))
    )
    (CONNECT_DATA =
      (SID = aux1)
      (SERVER = DEDICATED)
    )
  )
```

The listener.ora file should have an entry like this:

```
SID_LIST_LISTENER =
  (SID_LIST =
    (SID_DESC =
      (GLOBAL_DBNAME = aux1)
      (ORACLE_HOME = /u01/app/oracle/product/12.1.0/dbhome_1)
```

```
        (SID_NAME = aux1)
    )
)
```

Step 7. From RMAN, connect to the target and auxiliary instance and run the **duplicate** command:

```
$ ORACLE_SID=aux1;export ORACLE_SID
$ rman target /
RMAN> connect auxiliary sys/ora12g@aux1
RMAN> duplicate target database to aux1
 pfile=/u01/app/oracle/product/admin/aux1/pfile/init.ora
 logfile
 '/u01/app/oracle/product/oradata/aux1/redo01.dbf' size 100m,
 '/u01/app/oracle/product/oradata/aux1/redo02.dbf' size 100m,
 '/u01/app/oracle/product/oradata/aux1/redo03.dbf' size 100m;
```

Using Tape Backups

If you were to perform the preceding exercises but with your backups on tape, little would change. In fact, none of the code itself would change; you would simply insert an additional step prior to running the **duplicate** command itself. That step would be to configure your auxiliary channel(s) to resemble the channels with which the backups were taken. In other words, do a **show** command:

```
RMAN> show channel;
RMAN configuration parameters are:
CONFIGURE CHANNEL 1 DEVICE TYPE 'SBT_TAPE' PARMS
"env=(nb_ora_serv=mgtserv)";
CONFIGURE CHANNEL 2 DEVICE TYPE 'SBT_TAPE' PARMS
"env=(nb_ora_serv=mgtserv)";
```

Then, simply create the auxiliary channels to match:

```
CONFIGURE AUXILIARY CHANNEL 1 DEVICE TYPE 'SBT_TAPE' PARMS
"env=(nb_ora_serv=mgtserv)";
CONFIGURE AUXILIARY CHANNEL 2 DEVICE TYPE 'SBT_TAPE' PARMS
"env=(nb_ora_serv=mgtserv)";
```

Duplication to a Remote Server

Duplication to a remote server has many of the same configuration steps as duplication to the same server. In particular, if you are duplicating remotely but will use disk backups, the steps would be identical, although you could forgo all file-renaming steps. In addition, you would have to either copy your backups to the remote server or use NFS to mount the backups at the remote site. Covering NFS is outside the scope of this book, so we assume in the following RMAN Workshop that you have the same file systems on both the target and auxiliary servers and have copied the backups to the auxiliary system.

RMAN Workshop: *Duplication to a Remote Server Using Disk Backups*

Workshop Notes

This workshop assumes the use of two servers: dex (the target) and horatio (the auxiliary). It assumes that you have the same file system on both nodes and have copied your backups from dex to horatio. The most important thing to note here is that we maintain the v121 database SID throughout the process (instead of changing it to aux1, which we do when duplicating to the same server).

Step 1.   At horatio (the auxiliary server), build your auxiliary database directory structures:

```
$> pwd
/u01/app/oracle/oradata
$> mkdir v121
$> cd ../admin
$> pwd
/u01/app/oracle/admin
$> mkdir v121
$> cd v121
$> mkdir adump
$> ls
adump
```

Step 2.   At dex (the source server), make a copy of the target init.ora file so that it can be moved to the auxiliary server. If your target database uses an SPFILE, you need to create a PFILE from the SPFILE in order to capture parameters to move over.

  If you use an SPFILE at your target, enter the following:

```
SQL> connect / as sysdba
Connected.
SQL> create pfile='/home/oracle/scratchpad/init.ora'
  from spfile;
```

  If you use an init.ora file at your target, enter the following:

```
cp /u01/app/oracle/admin/v121/pfile/init.ora*
   /home/oracle/scratchpad/init.ora
```

Step 3.   Move the target init.ora file to the auxiliary site:

```
cd /home/oracle/scratchpad/
ftp horatio.hadba.com
username: oracle
password:
cd /u01/app/oracle/admin/v121/pfile
put init.ora
exit
```

You also need a local copy of the init.ora file at the target server dex for reference by RMAN in the **duplicate** command itself. We will reference the copy that we left in /home/oracle/scratchpad/init.ora when we run the **duplicate** command in Step 9.

Step 4.   Start the auxiliary instance in NOMOUNT mode at quixote:

```
ORACLE_SID=v121; export ORACLE_SID
sqlplus /nolog
SQL>connect / as sysdba
SQL>startup nomount
pfile=/u01/app/oracle/admin/v121/pfile/init.ora
```

Step 5.   Configure the listener.ora at the auxiliary site (proto):

```
SID_LIST_LISTENER =
  (SID_LIST =
    (SID_DESC =
      (GLOBAL_DBNAME = v121)
(ORACLE_HOME = /u01/app/oracle/product/12.1.0/dbhome_1)
      (SID_NAME = v121)
    )
  )
```

Step 6.   Configure the tnsnames.ora file at the target site (dex):

```
V121_HORATIO =
  (DESCRIPTION =
    (ADDRESS_LIST =
      (ADDRESS = (PROTOCOL = TCP)(HOST = horatio)(PORT = 1522))
    )
    (CONNECT_DATA =
      (SERVICE_NAME = v121)
    )
```

Step 7.   Create a password file at the remote server (proto). Follow the instructions from the earlier RMAN Workshop titled "Build a Password File."

Step 8.   Move the FRA files from dex to horatio.

Step 9.   From the target system (dex), run your duplicate command:

```
ORACLE_SID=v121; export ORACLE_SID
rman target /
RMAN> connect auxiliary sys/password@v121_horatio
duplicate target database to v121
pfile=/home/oracle/scratchpad/init.ora
logfile
'/u01/app/oracle/12.1.0/oradata/v102/redo01.dbf' size 100m,
'/u01/app/oracle/12.1.0/oradata/v102/redo02.dbf' size 100m,
'/u01/app/oracle/12.1.0/oradata/v102/redo03.dbf' size 100m;
```

Using Tape Backups for Remote Server Duplication

All the steps in the preceding RMAN Workshop apply if you are using tape backups instead of disk backups; again, the only difference is that you would also have to configure your auxiliary channels to reflect the needs of your media manager. In addition to specifying the media management server, and any classes or pools that you have for your regular channels, you also need to specify the target client name:

```
RMAN> configure auxiliary channel 1 device type sbt parms
2> = "env=(nb_ora_serv=mgtserv, nb_ora_client=dex)";
```

Targetless Duplication in 12c

Starting in 11gR2, RMAN was innovated to break some of the dependencies that made the duplication process complex in previous versions. Then, it became possible to duplicate a database from RMAN backups, without making a connection to the actual target database the backup was created on. Although providing this made some aspects of duplication simpler, it still sometimes wasn't possible. Perhaps Oracle heard our cries of anguish. Now, we can truly perform targetless database duplication.

To duplicate without a target, the next best thing is a connection to your recovery catalog, where the requisite target database metadata can be extracted with little effort. The primary element to be concerned with in this situation is to care for the database ID (DBID) when performing the duplication. When you are connected to the target database, RMAN has no difficulty understanding what "prod" means. But if you have multiple "prod" databases in your catalog, you may run into ambiguity issues. Therefore, you should dig into the recovery catalog and get your DBID:

```
SQL> select dbid, name, resetlogs_time from rc_database;

      DBID NAME     RESETLOGS
---------- -------- ---------

2203908660 V121     08-DEC-14
```

Once the DBID is known, you can kick off your nontarget duplication in much the same way as our previous workshops:

```
RMAN> connect auxiliary sys/password@v121_horatio
Connect catalog rman2/rman2@rcv_cat
duplicate database v121 to aux1
dbid 2203908660
until time "to_date('2014-12-08', 'YYYY-MM-DD')"
pfile=/home/oracle/scratchpad/init.ora
logfile
'/u01/app/oracle/12.1.0/oradata/v102/redo01.dbf' size 100m,
'/u01/app/oracle/12.1.0/oradata/v102/redo02.dbf' size 100m,
'/u01/app/oracle/12.1.0/oradata/v102/redo03.dbf' size 100m;
```

Incomplete Duplication: Using the DBNEWID Utility

One of the most frustrating elements of performing duplication is that there is no "restartable duplication." What we mean by this is that if you make it through the step that restores all your files—arguably the longest step of the process—but a failure occurs, say, during the recovery, you must restart the duplication process from scratch and restore all the files again. There is no way to correct the recovery process (by making missing archive logs available, for instance) and then pick up where you left off.

With RESTORE OPTIMIZATION turned ON, RMAN will not restore files again that already exist in the restore location with the same datafile header SCN information. This applies to duplication as well: if duplication restores a file and then duplication restarts, RMAN will not restore the file again. However, if you have applied even one archive log to the file, it will be restored again.

Starting in version 9*i* Release 2, Oracle Database includes the DBNEWID utility, which gives your clone database a new DBID in a safe and controlled manner. This allows you to do manual recovery against a duplicated database, prepare all the elements, and then run DBNEWID, which will complete the process started by duplication. This allows you to at least manually complete a duplication.

DBNEWID usage is simple. First, you must make sure you have a good backup taken prior to using DBNEWID. Although it has a verification process, DBNEWID can still encounter unrecoverable errors during the changing of the DBID. After confirming a good backup, you need to get the database shut down in a consistent state and then brought back up to a mounted state:

```
shutdown immediate;
startup mount
```

Then, run the DBNEWID utility from the command line:

```
nid target=/
DBNEWID: Release 12.1.0.2.0 - Production on
Sat Dec 13 16:29:44 2014
Copyright (c) 1982, 2014, Oracle and/or its affiliates.
All rights reserved.
Connected to database UPG (DBID=896149210)
Connected to server version 12.1.0
Control Files in database:
    +DATA/upg/controlfile/current.643.865699999
    /u01/app/oracle/fast_recovery_area/UPG/controlfile/
o1_mf_b89jqkm4_.ctl

Change database ID of database UPG? (Y/[N]) => Y

Proceeding with operation
Changing database ID from 896149210 to 896654008
    Control File +DATA/upg/controlfile/current.643.865699999 - modified
    Control File /u01/app/oracle/fast_recovery_area/UPG/controlfile
/o1_mf_b89jqkm4_.ctl - modified
 Datafile +DATA/upg/datafile/system.747.86570003 - dbid changed
 Datafile +DATA/upg/datafile/sysaux.749.86570011 - dbid changed
 Datafile +DATA/upg/datafile/undotbs1.751.86570017 - dbid changed
    Datafile +DATA/upg/datafile/users.488.86570024 - dbid changed
```

```
      Datafile +DATA/upg/tempfile/temp.553.86570020 - dbid changed
    Control File +DATA/upg/controlfile/current.643.865699999 -
dbid changed
      Control File /u01/app/oracle/fast_recovery_area/UPG/controlfile/
o1_mf_b89jqkm4_.ctl - dbid changed
      Instance shut down

Database ID for database UPG changed to 896654008.
All previous backups and archived redo logs for this database are unusable.
Database is not aware of previous backups and archived logs in Recovery Area.
Database has been shutdown, open database with RESETLOGS option.
Successfully changed database ID.
DBNEWID - Completed successfully.

[oracle@dex oracle]$ sqlplus "/ as sysdba"

SQL> startup mount
ORACLE instance started.
Total System Global Area 1048576000 bytes
Fixed Size                   2932336 bytes
Variable Size              385876368 bytes
Database Buffers           654311424 bytes
Redo Buffers                 5455872 bytes
Database mounted.
SQL> alter database open resetlogs;
```

New RMAN Cloning Features for 12*c*

As previously discussed, 11*g*R2 added a feature that allowed cloning by streaming the data files directly from the target database, with no backup required. Streaming the data files from the target does provide advantages, but there are tradeoffs compared to using a backup set as the source for copying the data files. In this section we review the tradeoffs and how 12*c* is an improvement.

Using Compression

When you're backing up a database using RMAN, it is possible to compress the backup as it's written to disk or tape. You may be wondering what benefit there is to compressing the backup set files when the FROM ACTIVE clause doesn't use backup sets. The answer lies in where the compression takes place when backing up. Many file systems and tape libraries offer the ability to compress files when they are written to the file system. RMAN is, of course, not a file system, so RMAN compresses the data before it is sent to the file system or tape library. Having RMAN compress the data has two benefits: reduced file size and reduced network traffic. The first benefit is not realized because backup sets are not used, but the network compression can be a major benefit. It's no secret that databases are only getting bigger, and it's no surprise that it takes less time to copy a smaller file than a larger file. So if the duplicate process is network bound, then compressing the data on the wire could provide a significant duplicate performance increase. Having RMAN compress the data before it is sent is easily done using a single clause:

```
DUPLICATE TARGET DATABASE TO dev_db
FROM ACTIVE DATABASE
```

```
PASSWORD FILE
USING COMPRESSED BACKUPSET;
```

The USING COMPRESSED BACKUPSET clause instructs RMAN to compress the data before sending it to the target. Be aware that compression happens on the source side, which is usually production, and that compressing data does require resources. Therefore, you should ensure there is adequate CPU resources to compress the data without impacting source-side workloads.

Duplicating Large Tablespaces

The fact that databases continue to grow ever larger has had the effect of tablespaces also growing larger. An Oracle database using 8K block size limits the size of a single data file to 32GB. For example, a nonpartitioned 750GB table would require 24 data files. Although a single table and 24 data files may not seem like much of a issue, once you compound the problem with other very large tables that are growing rapidly, you quickly have a database with hundreds of data files. Those data files have to be created, so it could become almost a weekly or even daily routine to add data files to your tablespaces.

In 11*g*R1, Oracle addressed this issue with BIGFILE tablespaces. BIGFILE tablespaces are tablespaces that only allow a single data file. With an 8K block size, the file can be up to 32TB in size. The major benefit is that when you create a BIGFILE tablespace, you never have to worry about adding data files again. One downside with only having a single very large data file is backups. Suppose a regular tablespace is 320GB in size and contains ten data files; the same tablespace created as a BIGFILE tablespace would only have a single data file. The regular tablespace could use ten RMAN processes to back up the data files in parallel, whereas the BIGFILE tablespace would be limited to a single backup process and would likely take far longer to complete. In 11*g*R2, a feature was added that allowed a single data file to be broken up into sections during a backup. Each section of a data file can be backed up with a different RMAN process, allowing a parallel backup of a single data file. With 12*c*, this feature is now available when performing a duplicate. Using the SECTION SIZE parameter specifies how large each section of a data file should be, as demonstrated in the following sample command:

```
DUPLICATE TARGET DATABASE TO dev_db
    FROM ACTIVE DATABASE
    PASSWORD FILE
    SECTION SIZE 500M;
```

In this example, the dev_db database will be duplicated by streaming the data files directly from the target database, and data files over 500MB in size will be divided into 500MB sections.

Summary

In this chapter, we discussed the architecture behind the RMAN duplication process. Using duplication, we can produce clone databases from our RMAN backups to either the local system or a remote server. There are different configuration steps, depending on whether you will be duplicating locally or remotely. In addition, you have specific guidelines to follow, depending on whether your backups are on disk or on tape. We offered RMAN Workshops that gave step-by-step instructions for duplication. We wrapped everything up with a brief discussion of some of the new RMAN 12*c* features that can greatly help in cloning your databases.

PART
III

RMAN Maintenance
and Administration

CHAPTER
11

Maintaining RMAN

E ntropy is a nasty result of the second law of thermodynamics. Basically, *entropy* describes the tendency of an ordered system to become disordered, the result of which is the requirement to maintain that system. RMAN is no different. When using RMAN, you have to maintain a number of things to keep it running smoothly.

In this chapter, we talk all about maintaining RMAN. From the **crosscheck** command to retention policies to redundancy policies, everything you need to know about keeping RMAN from falling apart is provided here. After we have talked about RMAN maintenance issues, we discuss some issues specific to the recovery catalog, including an introduction to the recovery catalog schema itself.

RMAN Maintenance

You didn't think you could just continue using RMAN without having to maintain it, did you? The truth is, RMAN is fairly maintenance free, but you need to be aware of a few maintenance-related things, which we address in this section. First, we are going to talk about the **crosscheck** command, followed by a discussion of retention policies. Next, we discuss the **change** command, and then the **delete** command. Finally, we end this section with a discussion of cataloging your existing database backups in RMAN.

Crosschecking RMAN Backups

You may encounter situations in which backup set pieces or copies are listed in the control file or recovery catalog but do not physically exist on the backup media (disk or tape). The physical files constituting the backup or copy might have been deleted, either by some process (for example, a separate retention policy for the tape management system that you are using or a damaged tape) or perhaps by the loss of a physical device that had backup set pieces on it.

In cases where the RMAN catalog and the physical backup destinations are out of synchronization, the **crosscheck** command is used to validate the contents of the RMAN information in the control file or in the recovery catalog against the actual physical backup set pieces that are on the backup media.

When using the **crosscheck** command, we are interested in the status of each backup set or copy. Each backup set or copy has status codes that are listed in the STATUS column of the views: V$BACKUP_SET for backup set pieces and V$DATAFILE_COPY for copies if you are using a control file, and RC_BACKUP_SET for backup set pieces and RC_DATAFILE_COPY for copies if you want to look in the recovery catalog. There are several different backup status codes, but for now we are interested primarily in two:

- **A** AVAILABLE; RMAN assumes the item is available on the backup media.
- **X** EXPIRED; the backup set piece or the copy is stored in the RMAN catalog (meaning the control file or the recovery catalog), but is not physically on the backup media.

When the **crosscheck** command is executed, RMAN checks each backup set or copy listed in the catalog and determines if it is on the backup media. If it is not, that piece will be marked as EXPIRED and will not be a candidate for any restore operation. If the piece exists, it will maintain its AVAILABLE status. If a backup piece or copy was previously marked EXPIRED and it becomes available again (for example, after the recovery of a failed disk drive), then the **crosscheck** command will return that piece's status to AVAILABLE.

If the backup set piece is on disk, RMAN simply makes sure that the piece is there, but does no checks for physical or logical corruption. If the backup set piece is on tape, RMAN will query the media management software to ensure the backup set piece is present. It is up to the media management software to determine how it will service the request. It's possible it will just check the command against its own metadata, or it may actually go out and verify the backup set piece is physically present.

You must be connected to a target database to run the **crosscheck** command. There is no requirement to be connected to a recovery catalog. If your backups are on disk, you will not need to allocate a channel before issuing the **crosscheck** command. If you are backing up to a tape device (via MML, for example), you will need to either have a preconfigured channel defined for that device or use the **allocate channel for maintenance** command before you can issue the **crosscheck** command. This is not required if you have configured predefined channels. If you use mixed channels (some to disk and some to SBT, for example), then the **crosscheck** command will only check the backups that were made with the channel used during the backup.

In the following example of the execution of the **crosscheck** command, we are checking the status of all backup sets and determining whether they exist on the backup medium:

```
RMAN> crosscheck backup;
using channel ORA_DISK_1
crosschecked backup piece: found to be 'AVAILABLE'
backup piece
handle=/oracle/app/oracle/flash_recovery_area/ROB1/backupset/2015_09_08
/o1_mf_annnn_TAG20150908T025101_5bd6qydw_.bkp RECID=2 STAMP=696999070
crosschecked backup piece: found to be 'AVAILABLE'
backup piece
handle=/oracle/app/oracle/flash_recovery_area/ROB1/backupset/2015_09_08
/o1_mf_nnndf_TAG20150908T025112_5bd6r0mz_.bkp RECID=3 STAMP=696999072
crosschecked backup piece: found to be 'EXPIRED'
backup piece
handle=/oracle/app/oracle/flash_recovery_area/ROB1/backupset/2015_09_08
/o1_mf_annnn_TAG20150908T031112_5bd7xjo7_.bkp RECID=9 STAMP=697000272
Crosschecked 3 objects
```

In this example, we have crosschecked a total of three backup set pieces. Notice that the **crosscheck** command lists all the backup set pieces that were found to be available. It also lists those backup set pieces that were not found on the backup media, shows them to be EXPIRED, and sets their status to EXPIRED at the same time. Note that the **crosscheck** command will not change a backup set piece with a status of DELETE to AVAILABLE. Any backup marked with a status of DELETE cannot be changed.

You can also crosscheck datafile backups, tablespace backups, control file backups, and SPFILE backups. Additionally, you can be selective in the specific backup you want to crosscheck by identifying the tag associated with that backup. You can even crosscheck all backups taken based on the device used or based on a time period. The following are several examples of crosschecking backups:

```
crosscheck backup of datafile 1;
crosscheck backup of tablespace users;
crosscheck backup of controlfile;
crosscheck backup of spfile;
```

```
crosscheck backup tag='SAT_BACKUP';
crosscheck backup completed after 'sysdate - 2';
crosscheck backup completed between 'sysdate - 5' and 'sysdate - 2';
crosscheck backup device type sbt;
```

You can crosscheck archived redo log backups based on a number of criteria, including time, SCN (specific or high/low range), or log sequence number. You can even use the **like** parameter, along with wildcards, to crosscheck specific archive log backups. Here are some variations in the **crosscheck** command:

```
crosscheck archivelog like 'ARC001.log';
crosscheck archivelog 'D:\ORACLE\ADMIN\RECOVER\ARCH\ARC00012.001';
crosscheck archivelog like '%ARC00012.001';
crosscheck archivelog from time "to_date('01-10-2006', 'mm-dd-yyyy')";
crosscheck archivelog until time "to_date('01-10-2006', 'mm-dd-yyyy')";
crosscheck archivelog from sequence 12;
crosscheck archivelog until sequence 522;
```

To crosscheck copies, use the **crosscheck copy** command. You can crosscheck datafile copies, control file copies, archived redo log copies, and archived redo logs (on disk). Here are two examples of crosschecking these kinds of objects:

```
crosscheck copy of datafile 5;
crosscheck datafilecopy 'd:\oracle\oradata\recover\recover_users_01.dbf';
```

RMAN Workshop: *Using the Crosscheck Command*

Workshop Notes

This workshop assumes that you have a functional Oracle database running in ARCHIVELOG mode. Additionally, this workshop assumes that you are backing up your database to disk, that you have a tablespace called USERS in your database, and that one datafile is associated with the USERS tablespace. Note that our sample output might look different than your output does.

Step 1. Using RMAN, back up the USERS tablespace (your output will look different, of course):

```
RMAN> backup tablespace users;
Starting backup at 08-SEP-15
using channel ORA_DISK_1
channel ORA_DISK_1: starting full datafile backup set
channel ORA_DISK_1: specifying datafile(s) in backup set
input datafile file number=00004 name=/ora01/oracle/rob1/rob1/users01.dbf
channel ORA_DISK_1: starting piece 1 at 08-SEP-15
channel ORA_DISK_1: finished piece 1 at 08-SEP-15
piece handle=/oracle/app/oracle/flash_recovery_area/ROB1/backupset/2015_09_08
/o1_mf_nnndf_TAG20150908T032848_5bd8yjmq_.bkp tag=TAG20090908T032848
comment=NONE
channel ORA_DISK_1: backup set complete, elapsed time: 00:00:01
Finished backup at 08-SEP-15
```

```
Starting Control File and SPFILE Autobackup at 08-SEP-15
piece handle=/oracle/app/oracle/flash_recovery_area/ROB1/autobackup/2015_09_08
/o1_mf_s_697001330_5bd8ylgv_.bkp comment=NONE
Finished Control File and SPFILE Autobackup at 08-SEP-09
```

Step 2.   Look at the output of the backup and determine the backup set piece that has just been created. The backup set piece is highlighted in the output in Step 1. Note that we are not removing the control file autobackup set piece.

Step 3.   Remove the backup piece from the disk.

Step 4.   Issue the **crosscheck** command to determine the status of the backup set piece. RMAN will detect that the backup set piece has been removed and mark it EXPIRED. Note that the control file autobackup piece is still available.

```
RMAN> crosscheck backup;
using channel ORA_DISK_1
crosschecked backup piece: found to be 'AVAILABLE'
backup piece
handle=/oracle/app/oracle/flash_recovery_area/ROB1/backupset/2015_09_08
/o1_mf_annnn_TAG20015908T025101_5bd6qydw_.bkp RECID=2 STAMP=696999070
crosschecked backup piece: found to be 'AVAILABLE'
backup piece
handle=/oracle/app/oracle/flash_recovery_area/ROB1/backupset/2015_09_08
/o1_mf_nnndf_TAG20150908T025112_5bd6r0mz_.bkp RECID=3 STAMP=696999072
crosschecked backup piece: found to be 'EXPIRED'
backup piece
handle=/oracle/app/oracle/flash_recovery_area/ROB1/backupset/2015_09_08
/o1_mf_annnn_TAG20150908T031112_5bd7xjo7_.bkp RECID=9 STAMP=697000272
crosschecked backup piece: found to be 'EXPIRED'
backup piece
handle=/oracle/app/oracle/flash_recovery_area/ROB1/backupset/2015_09_08
/o1_mf_nnndf_TAG20150908T032848_5bd8yjmq_.bkp RECID=14 STAMP=697001328
crosschecked backup piece: found to be 'AVAILABLE'
backup piece
handle=/oracle/app/oracle/flash_recovery_area/ROB1/autobackup/2015_09_08
/o1_mf_s_697001330_5bd8ylgv_.bkp RECID=15 STAMP=697001330
Crosschecked 5 objects
```

Verifying Your Backups

Perhaps the worst feeling in the world is the moment when you have a real database recovery going on, and you find out that the media storing the backups is corrupted. This happens, and probably more frequently than anyone would like to believe. The second worst feeling is the frustration involved when you are starting a restore, and you realize that you are not sure which RMAN backup set pieces you need to restore.

There are solutions to these problems, and we discuss them in this section. First, we discuss the **restore database preview** command, which will help you figure out what datafiles you need to restore your database and if, in fact, your database can be recovered to a consistent point in time. Then there is the **restore database validate** command, along with the **check logical** RMAN command, which can be used to check the RMAN backup images on your backup media.

The Restore...Preview Command

The **restore...preview** command is used to check that various kinds of RMAN backups can be restored. As with regular restores, you can use various restore criteria (such as the use of the **until time** option) successfully. One main reason to use this command is that it can be used to generate a list of all of the backup files that will be needed to facilitate some type of recovery. The files listed will be the RMAN backup set pieces needed to restore whatever objects you are restoring. If you are previewing a database restore (**restore database preview**), then both the database and those backup set pieces that contain the archived redo logs will be needed. If any piece is missing, RMAN will generate an error, indicating what needs to be done to correct the situation.

The **restore...preview** command is especially helpful if you are using some method other than RMAN to manage the backup set pieces created by RMAN. For example, suppose you back up to the FRA with RMAN and then subsequently move those backup set pieces to some other disk location. In this case, RMAN will not be aware that the piece has been moved, and any effort to use that piece in a database restore or recovery will fail. Running the **restore database preview** command will provide a list of the backup set pieces you will need to recover from the non-RMAN-aware backup set piece storage. This can ease your recovery significantly. The **restore...preview** command requires minimal I/O, and it does not check to ensure that the backup set pieces actually exist on disk or if they are not corrupt. The command only reports based on the backup set pieces that are contained in either the control file or the recovery catalog.

Note that the **restore...preview** command can also be used to perform these functions for backups of datafiles, tablespaces, archived redo logs, control files, and SPFILE backups. Also, you can run a preview of an entire database restore, which will check the database backup files and the archived redo log files that need to be restored. Here are some examples of the use of the **restore...preview** command:

```
restore database preview;
restore tablespace user preview;
restore datafile 1 preview;
restore archivelog all preview;
restore controlfile preview;
```

Using the Restore...Validate and Check Logical Commands

Media becomes corrupted for many reasons, and we want to avoid corruption at all costs. RMAN provides a way of checking the backup set images on media for corruption both physically and logically on a regular basis. Through the use of the **restore...validate check logical** command set, you can check the backup set pieces on media to ensure that they are physically and logically sound on a regular basis. You can validate database backups, tablespace backups, backups of specific datafiles, and backups of archive logs. Here are some examples of the command set's use for different object types:

```
restore database validate check logical;
restore datafile 1 validate check logical;
restore tablespace users validate check logical;
restore archivelog all validate check logical;
restore controlfile validate check logical;
```

This command set reads the backup set pieces and checks them for corruption. Therefore, it requires a considerable amount of I/O on the part of the backup media itself. It also requires CPU to read and process the backup set pieces. Additionally, it will consume network bandwidth, just as would be the case with a regular restore. All that being said, it can be a significant consumer of resources. This fact needs to be balanced against the benefits it provides and the availability of resources in order to determine how often to run the command and when to run it. We typically run the **restore database validate check logical** command frequently (say, daily) in a newly created database infrastructure environment. Once we are satisfied that the environment is stable, we reduce the executions of this command (say, once a week).

Using the validate Command

The little sister to the **restore database validate** command is the RMAN **validate** command. The **validate** command checks the headers of the backups, whereas the **restore database validate** command does a block-by-block check of the backups. Here are some examples of the use of the **validate** command:

```
Validate datafile 3;
Validate tablespace users;
Validate corruption list;
Validate database include current controlfile plus archivelog;
Validate backupset 50;
validate recovery area;
```

Note that the **validate** command is similar to the **backup validate** command, with a few extra bells and whistles. With this command, you can choose which backup sets to verify, whereas the **validate** parameter of the **backup** or **restore** command allows RMAN to determine which backup set to validate. Typically, in a production environment, you would use the **backup validate check logical** command after you have completed a backup to perform database validation. Thus, the **validate** command is most often used for specific occasions where you want to check specific backup sets, or perhaps you want to check all backup sets in the Fast Recovery Area.

The **validate** command does not check all database blocks. Those blocks that have never been used will not be checked. If you are running with compatibility set to 10.2 or greater, then blocks contained in locally managed tablespaces that were once used but are now unused will not be checked.

The **validate** command, by default, will only check for physical corruption, and logical corruption is not considered. If you want to also check for logical corruption of the block, use the **check logical** option of the **validate** command. When the **validate** command has completed its checks, it will populate the V$DATABASE_BLOCK_CORRUPTION view. It might be a good idea, if you have configured monitoring of your databases, to include the count of the number of rows in this view in that monitoring. This way, you can tell if you have corruption issues you need to deal with.

The **validate** command will not discover certain types of corruption. Therefore, it's possible to run this command and still experience problems with your database. These situations are rare, but they do happen. One example of this is interblock corruption. This is corruption that occurs between two blocks, as might be the case in a block-chaining situation. The **validate** command will not detect interblock corruption.

Backup Retention Policies

We have already mentioned that you can configure a retention policy for RMAN backups and copies. A *retention policy* is a method of managing backups and copies and specifying how long you want to keep them on your backup media. You can define two basic types of retention policies: the *recovery window backup retention policy* and the *backup redundancy backup retention policy*. We will talk more about those shortly.

Each redundancy policy is persistent until changed or removed (or until the control file is rebuilt using the **create controlfile** command). Additionally, the two redundancy policies are mutually exclusive. Finally, even with a redundancy policy, physical backup pieces are not removed until you use the **delete** command with the **obsolete** parameter to remove them.

Retention policies are based on backup sets, not individual copies of a given backup. So a single backup set of a tablespace with two copies will just count as just one backup toward the retention policy.

Now, let's look at each of these retention policies in more detail. After that, we will look at how we manage RMAN backups and copies that are made obsolete as a result of the retention policies.

Recovery Window Backup Retention Policy

The use of this type of retention policy is based on the latest possible date to which you want to be able to recover your database. With a recovery window backup retention policy, you can direct Oracle to make sure that if you want to be able to recover your database to a point in time two weeks ago, you will be able to do so.

For example, assume that today is Monday and you have three backups. The first backup was taken the day before, on Sunday; the second backup was taken on the previous Thursday; and the last backup was taken ten days ago, last Saturday. If the recovery window is set to seven days, then the first two backups (Sunday's and Thursday's) would be considered current. However, the backup taken ten days ago, on the previous Saturday, would be considered obsolete. If we wanted to establish this seven-day redundancy policy for RMAN, we would use the **configure** command with the **retention policy to recovery window** parameter:

```
configure retention policy to recovery window of 7 days;
```

Backup Redundancy Backup Retention Policy

When the backup redundancy backup retention policy is used, RMAN will maintain *x* number of database backups, starting with the most current backup. For example, suppose you have configured a backup redundancy of 3 and you did backups on Monday, Tuesday, Wednesday, and Thursday. Because the retention policy is set to 3, Oracle will obsolete the Monday backup as soon as the Thursday backup is successfully completed.

The backup window backup retention policy is enabled using the **configure** command with the **retention policy to redundancy** parameter. If you wanted to set the backup window backup retention policy to 3, you would use the following command:

```
configure retention policy to redundancy 3;
```

Archive Log Retention Policies

Archive log retention policies are supported by RMAN. Archive log deletion policies can be complicated by the presence of standby databases and multiple archive log destinations. Archive log deletion policies are automatically applied to archive logs that are copied to the FRA. If you are not using the FRA, you can run the **list obsolete** command to list files that are eligible for deletion based on the deletion policies. The **delete obsolete** command is used to apply the retention policies to archived redo logs present in non-FRA destinations. We discuss the **list** command later in this book when we discuss reporting on RMAN.

Default Archive Log Retention Policies
When you are using an FRA, there is a default archive log deletion policy that will be followed. In this case archived redo logs will be deleted when

■ The archived redo logs have been backed up to the remote destination defined by LOG_ARCHIVE_DEST_*n*.

And one of the two following conditions is met:

■ The archived redo logs have been backed up at least once to a disk or SBT device.

Or

■ The log files are obsolete as a result of the backup retention policy established for the FRA.

If an archived redo log is needed for Flashback Database operations or if a guaranteed restore point has been created, then those archived redo logs will not be eligible for removal regardless of the deletion policy. Oracle will attempt to keep logs in the FRA beyond the retention period, and will only delete those eligible for the retention policy when space requires it.

Defining Archive Log Retention Policies
You can modify the default archive log deletion policy when you are using the FRA. This is done with the RMAN **configure archivelog deletion policy** command. You can configure the following retention policies:

■ Application of redo logs has occurred on standby databases.

■ Archived redo logs have been backed up *n* times on a specific device.

Let's look at each of these in more detail, including how to remove the deletion criteria.

Application or Shipped Redo Logs to Standby Databases You issue the command **configure archivelog deletion policy to [applied | | shipped] on [all] standby** to configure a retention policy. This policy is specific to the application of the archived redo logs on configured standby databases. When the applied option is used, the retention criteria will apply to archived redo logs that are applied on the standby databases based on the following criteria:

■ If the **all** parameter is included, the criteria applies to all standby database sites.

■ If the **all** parameter is not included, the archived redo log must have been applied to all mandatory archive log destinations.

■ The archived redo log meets the requirements of the **applied n times archived** redo log policy, if one is set. This policy is discussed in the next section.

The **shipped** option applies the same criteria, but only requires that the archived redo logs be shipped to the standby databases, and not applied. You cannot configure both the **shipped** and **applied** policies at the same time. Here is an example of configuring these archive log deletion policies:

```
Configure archivelog deletion policy to applied on standby;
Configure archivelog deletion policy to shipped on standby;
```

If an appropriate archive log destination to a standby database does not exist, then an error will be returned by RMAN.

Archived Redo Logs Have Been Applied n Times   You can configure an archived redo log retention policy that is specific to the number of times that the archived redo log has been backed up to a specific device type. In this case, the policy will be applied with the following criteria:

- The specific number of archive log backups exist on the device.
- The requirements of any configured **policy to [applied||shipped] on standby** have been met.

The setting of this policy will also impact the backup of an archived redo log. Once the archived redo log has been backed up the number of times defined in the policy, it will no longer be backed up by RMAN, unless you use the **force** option of the **backup** command. Here is an example of the use of **configure archivelog deletion policy to backed up n times to device type**:

```
Configure archivelog deletion policy to backed up 2 times to device type disk;
```

Clearing Archive Log Deletion Policies   If you have configured an archive log deletion policy by using the **configure archivelog deletion policy to none** command. When you do this, the default retention policy for archived redo logs will apply in the FRA and will also be applied when you run the **list obsolete archivelog** command.

Retention Policy Maintenance

When a given backup or copy meets the criteria of a backup retention policy and becomes obsolete, what happens depends on whether you are using the FRA or a manual backup location. You may also want to change a backup so that its retention policy is different from the default retention policy. Let's look at these options next.

Retention Policy Maintenance When Using the FRA   If you are using the FRA, RMAN will eventually remove the backup set pieces, image copies, or archived redo logs (we will just call these backups for now) from the FRA based on space demands. This means that the backups will remain in place potentially for some time, until the space is needed by another backup or archive log. As a result, you might look at FRA space utilization and be concerned because it's growing when you feel it should be steady state. You can determine the amount of FRA space that is consumed by obsolete backups by querying the V$RECOVER_FILE_DEST view column SPACE_RECLAIMABLE. By using this view, you can determine if you have allocated sufficient space to the FRA. Here is an example of a query against V$RECOVER_FILE_DEST:

```
SQL> select * from v$recovery_file_dest;
NAME                            SPACE SPACE   SPACE NUM   LIMIT USED RECLAIMABLE FILES
------------------------------- ------------- ----------- ------------- -----------------
c:\oracle\flash_recovery_area 3,221,225,472 934,699,008   23,445,504                17
```

In this case, we find that about 23MB of space is reclaimable. RMAN will clear these files once there is a need for the free space. If we were to find that the amount of used space is quite high and the amount of reclaimable space is low, we may have underallocated the amount of space to the FRA. If you find the amount of reclaimable space is quite high, then you might want to review your retention criteria and make sure they are set correctly. You will also want to make sure you have not overallocated space to the FRA.

If you see that you have space being allocated to obsolete backup sets, you can use the RMAN **report obsolete** command to see details of the obsolete backups, as seen here:

```
RMAN> report obsolete;
using target database control file instead of recovery catalog
RMAN retention policy will be applied to the command
RMAN retention policy is set to redundancy 2
Report of obsolete backups and copies
Type                     Key     Completion Time     Filename/Handle
-------------------- ------ ------------------ --------------------
Backup Set               61      08-SEP-12
  Backup Piece           71      08-SEP-12
/oracle/app/oracle/flash_recovery_area/ROB1/autobackup/2012_09_08
/o1_mf_s_697001330_5bd8ylgv_.bkp
```

Retention Policy Maintenance When Using a Manual Backup Location   If you are not using the FRA, you are backing up to a manual backup location. In this case, you will need to manage the expired backups a little differently. As with the FRA, once a backup is no longer needed, RMAN will mark the backup or copy as OBSOLETE. You can determine which backups RMAN has marked as OBSOLETE with the **report obsolete** command (we will look at the **report** command in the next chapter):

```
report obsolete;
```

In the case of a manual backup area, you will need to perform one more step to get RMAN to remove the obsolete backups. This extra step is the execution of the **delete obsolete** command. This command tells RMAN to physically delete the backup on physical disk. It will also mark the metadata related to the backup in the control file as deleted, and it will remove all records associated with the backup in the recovery catalog.

Retention Policy Maintenance When Using the FRA   Of course, you might take a backup and decide that you want to change its retention policy. In this event, you would use the RMAN **change** command to change the retention policy of the backup you want to retain. When you use this command, the backups or copies impacted are considered to be *long-term backups* and are not subject to the defined retention policy.

You can create an archival backup by using the **change…keep** command. An archival backup contains all of the datafiles and archived redo logs required to restore a database at a given point in time. It is a wholly self-contained backup that allows you to restore the database to the point in time that the backup was completed. You must be using a recovery catalog in order to create an archival backup.

The **change…nokeep** command allows you to remove the retention policy defined by the **change…keep** command. Once this command is issued, the archived redo logs will be subject to the configured retention policy.

You can also use the **change** command to define a new date when the archival backup should be considered obsolete. If the retention date is greater than 365 days from now, you will need a recovery catalog.

You can reference backups in the **change** command by using the backup set key identifier or a tag associated with the backup. Both of these identifiers are available when you run the **list backup {summary}** command. You can also get the backup set key by querying the V$BACKUP_SET column RECID. Tags can be found in the TAG column of the V$BACKUP_FILES data dictionary view. Once you get the ID of the backup set you want to change, you can then issue commands to alter the retention criteria, as shown in these examples:

```
change backupset 267 keep forever;
change backupset 267 nokeep;
change backupset 267 keep until time 'sysdate + 7' logs;
change backup tag 'my_backup_endofyear2014' keep forever;
```

NOTE
*If you are using an FRA, you cannot use the **keep forever** clause of the **keep** command.*

The Change Command

We have just mentioned the **change** command and explained how it can be used to modify the retention window assigned to a specific backup. The **change** command allows you to change the status of a backup. You might have a case where one of your backup media devices becomes unavailable for a period of time (perhaps someone spilled a drink down the power supply). In this event, you can use the **change** command to indicate that the backups on that device are unavailable.

Once you have properly scolded the employee for fiddling around in your hardware area with a drink and have fixed the device, you can change the status of that backup set with the **change** command again so that it will take on an AVAILABLE status. You can also change a backup status to UNAVAILABLE, indicating that the backup is not currently available. This effectively disqualifies the backup from consideration during restore and recovery operations, but protects the backup record from being removed during the execution of the **delete expired** command. Some **change** commands, such as the **change…unavailable** command, are not valid when the backup set pieces are stored in the FRA. Here are some examples of the use of the **change** command:

```
change backup of database tag = 'GOLD'  unavailable;
change backup of database like '%GOLD%' unavailable;
change backupset 33 unavailable;
change backupset 33 available;
change archivelog 'd:\oracle\mydb\arch\arch_001.arc' unavailable;
```

Using the **change** command, you can modify the status of archived redo log backups. For example, you can modify the status to UNAVAILABLE for all archived redo logs that have been backed up at least a given number of times. You can also change the status of all backups that occurred using a given device. Examples of these operations are shown next:

```
change archivelog all backed up 5 times to device type disk unavailable;
change backup of database device type disk unavailable;
```

You can also use the **change** command to delete backup sets (physically on the backup media and from the control file and recovery catalog). The **delete** parameter is used for this operation. First, you need to identify the RMAN backup IDs of the backups that you want to remove, or the tags that are associated with a given backup. You can use the **list backup** or **list copy** command (each of which is covered in detail in the next chapter) to perform this operation. You can also get the backup set (BS) key by querying the V$BACKUP_SET column RECID. Tags can be found in the TAG column of the V$BACKUP_FILES data dictionary view.

Using the BS key or tag, we can then remove either the entire backup set or individual backup set pieces. Let's assume we want to remove both backup sets. For example, if the backup set IDs for a given backup are 117 and 118, we can use the **change** command with the **delete** parameter, and our backup will be gone. If you are not using the FRA, the physical piece will be removed. If you are using an FRA, the physical file will be removed as any other file in the FRA is removed. Here is what we would do to remove these backup sets:

```
RMAN> change noprompt backupset 56, 57, 58, 59 delete;
```

Note that the backups assigned to these IDs will be displayed, and, by default, you will be asked to confirm whether you want to remove the backup. If you do not want to be prompted to confirm the action, simply use the **noprompt** option.

Here are some additional examples of other options for the **change** command that will result in the removal of backup set pieces:

```
change backuppiece 1304 delete;
change archivelog until logseq = 544 delete;
```

Finally, you can use the **change backuppiece uncatalog** command to remove backup set pieces from the catalog. If the **change backuppiece uncatalog** command removes the last remaining backup set piece, it will also remove the backup set record. Here is an example of using the **change backuppiece uncatalog** command:

```
RMAN> Change backuppiece
'/u01/oracle/RMAN/mydb/mydb_user01_01.bak' uncatalog;
```

RMAN Workshop: *Using the Change Command*

Workshop Notes

This workshop assumes that you have a functional Oracle database running in ARCHIVELOG mode, that you are backing up your database to disk, that you have a tablespace called USERS in your database, and that one datafile is associated with the USERS tablespace.

Step 1. Using RMAN, back up the USERS tablespace:

```
RMAN> backup tablespace users;
Starting backup at 08-SEP-14
using channel ORA_DISK_1
channel ORA_DISK_1: starting full datafile backup set
channel ORA_DISK_1: specifying datafile(s) in backup set
input datafile file number=00004 name=/ora01/oracle/rob1/rob1/users01.dbf
```

```
channel ORA_DISK_1: starting piece 1 at 08-SEP-14
channel ORA_DISK_1: finished piece 1 at 08-SEP-14
piece handle=/oracle/app/oracle/flash_recovery_area/ROB1/backupset/2014_09_08
/o1_mf_nnndf_TAG20140908T051140_5bdgzfc9_.bkp tag=TAG20140908T051140
comment=NONE
channel ORA_DISK_1: backup set complete, elapsed time: 00:00:01
Finished backup at 08-SEP-09
```

Step 2.   Look at the output of the backup and determine the backup set piece that has just been created. The backup set piece is highlighted in the output in Step 1. Note that the name of your backup set piece will be different than that listed in Step 1.

Step 3.   Use the **list backup of tablespace users** command to determine the backup key of the backup set piece that you need to mark as DELETED in the control file or recovery catalog. Note in the following output that we have highlighted the backup set key and the related backup set piece:

```
RMAN> list backup of tablespace users;
List of Backup Sets
===================
BS Key  Type LV Size
------- ---- -- ----------
68      Full    1.03M
  List of Datafiles in backup set 68
  File LV Type Ckp SCN    Ckp Time   Name
  ---- -- ---- ---------- --------- ----
  4       Full 637442     08-SEP-09 /ora01/oracle/rob1/rob1/users01.dbf

  Backup Set Copy #2 of backup set 68
  Device Type Elapsed Time Completion Time Compressed Tag
  ----------- ------------ --------------- ---------- ---
  DISK        00:00:01     08-SEP-14       NO         TAG20140908T032815

    List of Backup Pieces for backup set 68 Copy #2
    BP Key  Pc# Status      Piece Name
    ------- --- ----------- ----------
    96      1   AVAILABLE
/oracle/app/oracle/flash_recovery_area/ROB1/backupset/2014_09_08
/o1_mf_nnndf_TAG20140908T032815_5bd9pon1_.bkp

  Backup Set Copy #1 of backup set 68
  Device Type Elapsed Time Completion Time Compressed Tag
  ----------- ------------ --------------- ---------- ---
  DISK        00:00:01     08-SEP-09       NO         TAG20140908T032815

    List of Backup Pieces for backup set 68 Copy #1
    BP Key  Pc# Status      Piece Name
    ------- --- ----------- ----------
    84      1   AVAILABLE
/oracle/app/oracle/flash_recovery_area/ROB1/backupset/2014_09_08
/o1_mf_nnndf_TAG20140908T032815_5bd8xhxm_.bkp
```

```
BS Key   Type LV Size        Device Type Elapsed Time Completion Time
-------  ---- -- ----------  ----------- ------------ ---------------
176      Full   5.07M        DISK         00:00:01    08-SEP-14
      BP Key: 179   Status: AVAILABLE  Compressed: NO  Tag: TAG20140908T040309
      Piece Name: /oracle/backup/0hkomrbt_1_1
  List of Datafiles in backup set 176
  File LV Type Ckp SCN    Ckp Time  Name
  ---- -- ---- ---------- --------- ----
   4      Full 642222     08-SEP-09 /ora01/oracle/rob1/rob1/users01.dbf

BS Key   Type LV Size        Device Type Elapsed Time Completion Time
-------  ---- -- ----------  ----------- ------------ ---------------
421      Full   5.52M        DISK         00:00:00    08-SEP-14
      BP Key: 424   Status: AVAILABLE  Compressed: NO  Tag: TAG20140908T051140
      Piece Name:
oracle/app/oracle/flash_recovery_area/ROB1/backupset/2014_09_08
/o1_mf_nnndf_TAG20140908T051140_5bdgzfc9_.bkp
  List of Datafiles in backup set 421
  File LV Type Ckp SCN    Ckp Time  Name
  ---- -- ---- ---------- --------- ----
   4      Full 644956     08-SEP-14 /ora01/oracle/rob1/rob1/users01.dbf
```

Step 4. Exit to the operating system, and do a directory listing on the backup set piece. You should see it.

Step 5. Use the **change backuppiece** command to change the status flag of this backup set piece from AVAILABLE to DELETED:

```
RMAN> change backuppiece 96 delete;
using channel ORA_DISK_1
List of Backup Pieces
BP Key  BS Key  Pc# Cp# Status       Device Type Piece Name
-------  ------- --- --- ----------- ----------- ----------
96       68      1   2   AVAILABLE   DISK
/oracle/app/oracle/flash_recovery_area/ROB1/backupset/2014_09_08
/o1_mf_nnndf_TAG20140908T032815_5bd9pon1_.bkp
Do you really want to delete the above objects (enter YES or NO)? yes
deleted backup piece
backup piece
handle=/oracle/app/oracle/flash_recovery_area/ROB1/backupset/2014_09_08
/o1_mf_nnndf_TAG20140908T032815_5bd9pon1_.bkp RECID=25 STAMP=697002101
Deleted 1 objects
```

Step 6. Use the **list backup of tablespace users** command to determine that the backup set piece is no longer available for use during a recovery:

```
RMAN> list backup of tablespace users;
```

Step 7. Exit to the operating system, and do a directory listing on the backup set piece. You should no longer see the backup set piece. Oracle removed it, if it existed.

The Delete Command

All good things must come to an end, and the same is true about the life of a given backup set. With a retention policy, we can mark backups whose usefulness and lifetime are at an end. As we mentioned already, enforcement of a redundancy policy does not remove the backups from the catalog, but rather just marks the backups with a status of OBSOLETE. The same is true with the **crosscheck** command, which we discussed earlier in this chapter. The **crosscheck** command marks obsolete backups and copies as EXPIRED, but does not remove them. Marking expired records as deleted will help keep the timing to resync RMAN at a minimum.

Enter the **delete** command, the grim reaper of RMAN. It is the raven that swoops down and puts the kibosh on your backups and copies. With the **delete** command, you can remove any backups that have been made obsolete based on a retention criterion, and you can change the status of any expired backups in the recovery catalog or control file to a status of DELETED. Here are a couple of examples of the **delete** command in use:

```
delete expired;
delete obsolete;
```

When you issue a **delete** command, the associated RMAN backup records will be removed from the recovery catalog. You can see this by looking at the recovery catalog view RC_BACKUP_PIECE. Records contained in the database control file will be kept in the control file until overwritten. These records will appear in the V$BACKUP_PIECE view with a status of D. These deleted records will not appear in RMAN command output, such as **list backup of database summary**.

When you issue a **delete** command, RMAN will request that you confirm your instructions. Once you have confirmed your instructions, RMAN will complete the **delete** operation. You can use the **noprompt** option of the **delete** command to avoid the requirement to verify the execution of the **delete** command. This is handy if you are writing scripts to work with RMAN. Here is an example of using the **delete** command with the **noprompt** option:

```
delete noprompt obsolete;
```

If you are not using an FRA and you want to physically remove the files associated with the backup, you will need to use the **force** parameter. Note that **force** will ignore any I/O errors (such as the case when the physical file is not there). You can see the use of the **force** parameter in this example:

```
delete noprompt obsolete force;
```

NOTE
*Once a backup has been marked with a DELETED status, you cannot get it back. You can still recover the backup, if it's physically available, by using the **catalog** command to register the backup sets in the control file/recovery catalog.*

RMAN Workshop: *Using the Delete Command*

Workshop Notes

This workshop builds on the previous RMAN Workshop, "Using the change Command," which deals with using the **crosscheck** command.

Step 1. Having determined that the backup set piece is missing, we want to mark it as permanently missing. From the RMAN prompt, issue the **delete expired backup** command:

```
RMAN> delete expired backup;
using channel ORA_DISK_1
using channel ORA_DISK_2
List of Backup Pieces
BP Key  BS Key  Pc# Cp# Status       Device Type Piece Name
------- ------- --- --- -----------  ----------- ----------
53      53      1   1   EXPIRED      DISK
D:\BACKUP\RECOVER\BACKUP_1VE25VC0_1_1
Do you really want to delete the above objects (enter YES or NO)?
```

Step 2. Review the objects listed to be marked with a DELETED status. If they can all be marked as DELETED, reply to the prompt with a YES and press ENTER. Review the output for a successful operation:

```
deleted backup piece
backup piece handle=D:\BACKUP\RECOVER\BACKUP_1VE25VC0_1_1 recid=53
stamp=472055171
Deleted 1 EXPIRED objects
```

Cataloging Other Backups in RMAN

The **catalog** command enables you to record datafile backups, archive log backups, and control file backups in RMAN, and these backups can later be used to restore and recover the database. Oracle Database allows you to also use the **catalog** command to catalog existing backup set pieces in the control file. This is a nice feature if you have to restore the database with an old backup control file that might not have the most current RMAN information in it.

Here are some examples of the use of the **catalog** command to catalog old datafile backups:

```
-- first, backup the users tablespace
sqlplus sys/robert as sysdba
alter tablespace users begin backup;
host copy d:\oracle\oradata\recover\users01.dbf
d:\backup\recover\users01.dbf.backup
alter tablespace users end backup;
alter system archive log current;
host copy d:\oracle\admin\recover\arch\*.* d:\backup\recover
-- get a list of archivelog files that were created
host dir d:\backup\recover
```

```
alter database backup control file to 'd:\backup\recover.ctl'
quit
-- Now, catalog the backup in rman
rman target sys/robert
catalog datafilecopy 'd:\backup\recover\users01.dbf.backup';
-- Replace arc001.log with the list of archive logs you generated earlier
catalog archivelog 'd:\backup\recover\arc001.log';
-- Now catalog the control file.
catalog controlfilecopy 'd:\backup\recover.ctl';
```

The **catalog** command allows you to enter new backup set–related information into the control file or recovery catalog. RMAN overwrites any preexisting catalog information that conflicts with the information being cataloged. This command can be handy if you need to move the location of your backup set pieces. In this example, we have moved all our backup set pieces to a new directory. We use the **catalog** command to load the correct directory location for each of the moved pieces in the control file:

```
RMAN> catalog backuppiece '/opt/oracle/oracle-12.0.0/dbs/backup';
```

You can also use the **catalog** command with the **start with** option, which allows you to define the directory that contains the RMAN backup set pieces to be cataloged. RMAN will then catalog all backup set pieces in that directory. Here is an example of using the **catalog** command in this way:

```
RMAN> catalog start with '/u01/oracle/RMAN/mydb';
```

Once you press ENTER, this command prompts you with a list of files to catalog and asks if you wish to catalog the files listed. If you respond in the affirmative, RMAN catalogs all the backup set pieces listed (which will be contained in the /u01/oracle/RMAN/mydb directory). This command also allows you to catalog several like-named backup set pieces. For example, if you want to catalog several backup set pieces that start with the name "backup" (for example, backupset01, backupset02, and so forth), then you could issue the following command:

```
RMAN> catalog start with '/u01/oracle/RMAN/mydb/backup';
```

When you use the **catalog start with** command, it is indiscriminate about which files it tries to catalog; it will try to catalog everything that matches the argument list. However, as the **catalog** process proceeds, files that are not backup set pieces will fail the catalog process and an error will occur. Files that are backup set pieces will be cataloged successfully, in spite of other errors.

RMAN Stored Scripts

If you find that you are often doing the same RMAN operations over and over, you would probably like to be able to store those operations somewhere and execute them when needed. Of course, you could create a command file, which is just a text file physically located on disk somewhere, with the RMAN commands, and then execute the command file from the RMAN command-line interface using the **cmdfile** parameter, as shown in this example:

```
rman target robert/password cmdfile=run_backup.cmd
```

Alternatively, you can run a command file from within RMAN itself, using the @ command:

```
@@run_backup.cmd
```

RMAN offers another option, which is to store scripts in the recovery catalog. As you might guess, this requires that you use a recovery catalog, so if you are not using one, you will not be able to store RMAN scripts. This section shows you how to store scripts in the recovery catalog and how to manage those scripts.

Creating Stored Scripts

To store a script in the recovery catalog, you use the **create script** RMAN command. Each stored script is assigned a name when you create it. You can create scripts that do backups, recoveries, and maintenance of your databases. To create a script, you must be connected to the recovery catalog. Here is an example of using the **create script** command to create a backup script. RMAN also allows you to store comments related to your stored scripts by using the **comment** parameter:

```
create script my_backup_script
comment 'This script backs up the database'
{ backup database plus archivelog;}
```

Oracle Database supports the use of substitution variables. Each substitution variable is denoted with an ampersand and a number that makes each variable unique. For example, you could rewrite this script as follows:

```
create script my_backup_script
comment 'This script backs up the database'
{ backup database tag '&1' plus archivelog;}
```

When you execute this command, RMAN will prompt you for initial values for the substitution variables.

Querying the Recovery Catalog for Stored Script Information

You can use the recovery catalog views to determine the name of scripts stored in the recovery catalog by querying the RC_STORED_SCRIPT view. You can see the contents of a given script by querying the RC_STORED_SCRIPT_LINE view.

Changing Stored Scripts

You use the **replace script** command to replace stored scripts in the recovery catalog. Here is an example of using the **replace script** command. Note that we also add a comment to the script.

```
replace script my_backup_script
comment 'This script backs up the database'
{ backup database plus archivelog delete input;}
```

Deleting Stored Scripts

To drop a script, you use the **delete script** command. You must be connected to the recovery catalog to successfully drop a stored script. Here is an example of using the **delete script** command:

```
delete script my_backup_script;
```

Using Stored Scripts

Now that you have created some stored scripts, you probably want to use them. This is what the **execute script** command is for. Simply connect to the recovery catalog and use the **execute script** command within the confines of a **run** block, as shown in this example:

```
run {execute script my_backup_script;}
```

If you are using substitution variables, you can use the **using** parameter to include the values of those parameters in the **execute script** command, as shown in this example:

```
Run {execute script my_backup_script using TEST_BACKUP;}
```

Printing Stored Scripts

If you want to print a copy of your stored script, you can use the **print script** command. Connect to the recovery catalog and then run the **print script** command, as shown in this example:

```
RMAN> print script my_backup_script;

printing stored script: my_backup_script
{ backup database plus archivelog;}
```

You can also use the RC_STORED_SCRIPT_LINE recovery catalog view to display the contents of a stored script, as shown in this example:

```
select script_name, text from rc_stored_script_line
order by script_name, line;
SCRIPT_NAME       TEXT
---------------- -----------------------------------------
my_backup_script { backup database plus archivelog;}
```

RMAN Workshop: *Using RMAN Stored Scripts*

Workshop Notes
This workshop expects that you have an operational Oracle database (called recover) and that you are also using a separate Oracle database to store the recovery catalog in (called catalog).

Step 1. Connect to the target database and to the recovery catalog:

```
rman target rman_account/rman_password catalog rcat_user/rcat_password@catalog
```

Step 2. Create a stored script to back up the target database:

```
RMAN> create script my_backup_script
2> {backup database plus archivelog;}
created script my_backup_script
```

Step 3. Print the stored script:

```
RMAN> print script my_backup_script;
printing stored script: my_backup_script
{backup database plus archivelog;}
```

Step 4. Execute the stored script to back up your database:

```
RMAN> run {execute script my_backup_script;}
```

Step 5. Delete the stored script:

```
RMAN> delete script my_backup_script;
```

When You Just Can't Take It Anymore

If you are sick and tired of your database and you just can't take it anymore, RMAN offers the perfect response: the **drop database** command. If only terrorists were as easy to get rid of. Simply put the database in restricted session mode, connect to the target database with RMAN, issue the **drop database** command, and watch your database quietly go away. You can add the **including backups** parameter, and all RMAN-related backups will be removed, too. When you issue this command, RMAN will confirm the action first and then proceed to remove the database. If you wish to not be prompted, you can use the **noprompt** parameter. Here is an example of the use of the **drop database** command:

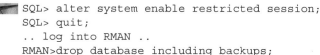

```
SQL> alter system enable restricted session;
SQL> quit;
.. log into RMAN ..
RMAN>drop database including backups;
```

Summary

In this chapter, we discussed the various maintenance operations that RMAN may require. We discussed the **crosscheck** command and validating RMAN backups, both very important operations. We also talked about retention policies and how RMAN uses them to control how long your backups will remain available to you for recovery purposes.

We also talked about the **change** and **delete** commands and how they can be used to modify the status of RMAN records in the control file or recovery catalog. We also covered adding backups to the control file or recovery catalog. Finally, we discussed maintenance of the recovery catalog and the use of stored scripts for RMAN operations.

CHAPTER
12

Monitoring and
Reporting in RMAN

B ecause everyone wants to know for sure that their databases have been backed up and are currently recoverable, RMAN comes with some good reporting tools. This chapter covers RMAN reporting in some depth. First, we look at the RMAN **list** command, followed by the RMAN **report** command. Each of these commands provides facilities for in-depth analysis of the database that you are using RMAN to back up and its backups. These commands are the primary ways of extracting information from RMAN. You will find that lists and reports come in handy not only during recovery, but also when you want to see how RMAN is configured and when you need to perform other administrative tasks (such as determining if a tablespace has been backed up).

The RMAN List Command

The RMAN **list** command is a method of querying either the database control file or the recovery catalog for historical information on backups. Lists provide an array of information, from lists of database incarnations, to lists of backup sets and archive log backups. The bottom line is that if you want to know whether the database was backed up and when, then you want to generate a list. The format of lists initially tends to appear not very reader friendly. Once you have looked at a few lists, though, they seem a little easier to read. So, let's look at the **list** commands and how they can be interpreted.

Listing Incarnations

The **list incarnation** command provides you with a list of each database incarnation for the target database. This list can be used to recover your database to a point in time before your last **resetlogs** command was issued. Here is an example of the **list incarnation** command output:

```
RMAN> list incarnation of database;
using target database control file instead of recovery catalog
List of Database Incarnations
DB Key  Inc Key DB Name  DB ID             STATUS  Reset SCN  Reset Time
-------  ------- --------  ----------------  ------- ---------- ----------
2       2       ROBERTCD 2645377104        PARENT  3315564    30-DEC-14
4       4       ROBERTCD 2645377104        ORPHAN  3318384    30-DEC-14
5       5       ROBERTCD 2645377104        PARENT  3318384    30-DEC-14
6       6       ROBERTCD 2645377104        PARENT  3348216    02-JAN-15
7       7       ROBERTCD 2645377104        CURRENT 3349333    02-JAN-15
```

In this listing, we find that our database has had several different incarnations, with each incarnation represented in each row of the report. Each individual incarnation has its own key (Inc Key), which we would use if we wanted to reset the database incarnation (refer to Chapter 9). We also get our database name and ID in this report.

The STATUS column displays the status of the incarnation listed. It indicates whether the incarnation is an older incarnation (PARENT), the current incarnation (CURRENT), or, if a recovery past **resetlogs** has occurred, an ORPHAN incarnation. Finally, the Reset SCN and Reset Time columns basically indicate when the database incarnation was created (which is why the Reset SCN for the first entry is 1). This column helps support recovery through **resetlogs** and also helps support easier recovery to a previous incarnation.

An important point to note is that output generated with a recovery catalog and output generated without a recovery catalog generally look somewhat different. For example, this is the output of the **list incarnation** command while attached to a recovery catalog:

```
RMAN> list incarnation of database;
List of Database Incarnations
DB Key  Inc Key DB Name  DB ID            STATUS   Reset SCN  Reset Time
-------  ------- --------  ----------------  -------  ---------  ----------
2        18      ROB1     1854903786       PARENT   1          07-SEP-12
2        4       ROB1     1854903786       CURRENT  635384     08-SEP-12
```

Note in this example that both the DB keys and the incarnation keys are different from those reported when using the control file. This leads to an important point: many reports have keys that identify specific items in the reports, and you will use these keys in other RMAN commands (such as in the **reset database** command). Because the values of the keys change depending on whether you are connected to the recovery catalog, you need to be careful about determining which keys you need.

Listing Backups

The **list** command comes with a number of different options that allow you to report on the status of database backups and copies. In this section, we are going to look at several of these reports.

Summarizing Available Backups

Let's first look at a few ways of getting summary backup information. The **list** command provides a couple of options. The first option is the **list backup summary** report:

```
RMAN> list backup summary;
List of Backups
===============
Key   TY LV S Device Type Completion Time #Pieces #Copies Compressed Tag
----- -- -- - ----------- --------------- ------- ------- ---------- ---
60    B  A  A DISK        08-SEP-14       1       2       YES
TAG20140908T025311
61    B  A  A DISK        08-SEP-14       1       2       NO
TAG20140908T025326
421   B  F  A DISK        08-SEP-14       1       1       NO
TAG20140908T051140
430   B  0  A DISK        08-SEP-14       1       1       NO
TAG20140908T051190
460   B  1  A DISK        08-SEP-14       1       1       NO
TAG20140908T051332
```

This report provides us with some nice summary information on backups. The backup set key is listed in the Key column. The TY (type) and the LV (level) columns indicate the type of backup listed (B = backup, F = full, A = archive log, and 0 and 1 = incremental backups). The S column indicates the status of the backup (AVAILABLE, UNAVAILABLE, or EXPIRED). The Device Type column lets us know whether the backup is a tape or disk backup. We also have columns for the date of the backup (Completion Time), the number of pieces (#Pieces) or copies (#Copies) that the backup set consists of, whether the backup was compressed, and any tag that was assigned to the backup set (Tag).

Most of the list commands will accept the summary parameter at the end. Here's an example:

```
list backup of database summary;
list expired backup of archivelog all summary;
list backup of tablespace users summary;
```

Listing Backups by Datafile

Another way to summarize backups is to use the **list backup by file** command to list each backup set and backup set piece. Here is an example of this report (we have removed some output to save a few trees):

```
RMAN> list backup by file;
List of Datafile Backups
========================
File Key    TY LV S Ckp SCN  Ckp Time    #Pieces #Copies Compressed Tag
---- -----  -  -- - --------  ----------  ------- ------- ---------- ---
4    421    B  F  A 644956    08-SEP-14 1        1       NO
TAG20140908T051140
     176    B  F  A 642222    08-SEP-14 1        1       NO
TAG20140908T040309
     68     B  F  A 637442    08-SEP-14 1        1       NO
TAG20140908T032815
List of Archived Log Backups
============================
Thrd Seq    Low SCN  Low Time   BS Key  S #Pieces #Copies Compressed Tag
---- -----  -------- ---------  ------- - ------- ------- ---------- ---
1    8      637317   08-SEP-14 67       A 1       2       NO
TAG20140908T032531
1    9      637320   08-SEP-14 67       A 1       2       NO
TAG20140908T032531
1    10     637324   08-SEP-14 67       A 1       2       NO
TAG20140908T032531
List of Control File Backups
============================
CF Ckp SCN Ckp Time  BS Key  S #Pieces #Copies Compressed Tag
--------- --------   ------- - ------- ------- ---------- ---
642268    08-SEP-14 207      A 1       1       NO         TAG20140908T040315
637490    08-SEP-14 70       A 1       1       NO         TAG20140908T032850
List of SPFILE Backups
======================
Modification Time BS Key  S #Pieces #Copies Compressed Tag
----------------- ------- - ------- ------- ---------- ---
08-SEP-14         207     A 1       1       NO         TAG20140908T040315
08-SEP-14         70      A 1       1       NO         TAG20140908T032850
```

This report summarizes each backup file that has been created by the type of backup (datafile backup, archived log backup, control file backup, and SPFILE backup) and then by datafile for the datafile backups. In this report, we get the date of the backup and the specific keys associated with the backup file. Depending on the type of backup, we get information that pertains to that type of backup.

Additional Backup Information

If you want as much information reported on your RMAN backups as you can get, then the **list backup** command is for you. It provides detailed information on the backups you have taken, including backup sets, archived redo log backups, and control file/SPFILE backups. Let's look at an example of the results of the execution of the **list backup** command:

```
RMAN> list backup;
BS Key   Size        Device Type Elapsed Time Completion Time
-------  ----------  ----------- ------------ ---------------
509      12.43M      DISK        00:00:04     08-SEP-14
BP Key: 513    Status: AVAILABLE   Compressed: YES   Tag: TAG20140908T192844
Piece Name: /oracle/app/oracle/flash_recovery_area/ROB1/
backupset/2014_09_08/o1_mf_annnn_TAG20140908T192844_5bg16fk5_.bkp

  List of Archived Logs in backup set 509
  Thrd Seq     Low SCN    Low Time  Next SCN   Next Time
  ---- ------- ---------- --------- ---------- ---------
  1    7       636872     08-SEP-14 637317     08-SEP-14
  1    8       637317     08-SEP-14 637320     08-SEP-14
  1    10      637324     08-SEP-14 637349     08-SEP-14
  1    11      637349     08-SEP-14 675660     08-SEP-14
  1    12      675660     08-SEP-14 676291     08-SEP-14
```

This first listing is an archive log backup. The backup set key (BS Key) is 509. The size of the backup is listed, and we see that it went to disk instead of to SBT. The elapsed time of the backup is pretty short, at four seconds, and we see that it was completed on September 8. Later in the report, we see that the backup is available and that it is a compressed backup. We also find the backup set piece name, which tells us where the backup is physically located. Finally, a list of archived redo logs appears. These are the archived redo logs contained in this backup set. Here is an example of the listing of the rest of this backup:

```
BS Key   Type LV Size        Device Type Elapsed Time Completion Time
-------  ---- -- ----------  ----------- ------------ ---------------
510      Full    243.36M     DISK        00:01:16     08-SEP-14
BP Key: 514    Status: AVAILABLE   Compressed: YES   Tag: TAG20140908T192853
Piece Name: /oracle/app/oracle/flash_recovery_area/ROB1
/backupset/2014_09_08/o1_mf_nnndf_TAG20140908T192853_5bg16pwv_.bkp

  List of Datafiles in backup set 510
  File LV Type Ckp SCN    Ckp Time  Name
  ---- -- ---- ---------- --------- ----
  1       Full 676334     08-SEP-14 /ora01/oracle/rob1/rob1/system01.dbf
  2       Full 676334     08-SEP-14 /ora01/oracle/rob1/rob1/sysaux01.dbf
  3       Full 676334     08-SEP-14 /ora01/oracle/rob1/rob1/undotbs01.dbf
  4       Full 676334     08-SEP-14 /ora01/oracle/rob1/rob1/users01.dbf
```

```
BS Key   Size         Device Type Elapsed Time Completion Time
-------  ----------   ----------- ------------ ---------------
536      783.00K      DISK            00:00:01     08-SEP-14
BP Key: 541    Status: AVAILABLE   Compressed: YES   Tag: TAG20140908T193014
Piece Name: /oracle/app/oracle/flash_recovery_area/ROB1/
backupset/2014_09_08/o1_mf_annnn_TAG20140908T193014_5bg196xr_.bkp

  List of Archived Logs in backup set 536
  Thrd Seq     Low SCN    Low Time  Next SCN   Next Time
  ---- ------- ---------- --------- ---------- ---------
  1    13      676291     08-SEP-14 676364     08-SEP-14

BS Key   Type LV Size         Device Type Elapsed Time Completion Time
-------  ---- -- ----------   ----------- ------------ ---------------
555      Full    9.67M        DISK            00:00:01     08-SEP-14
BP Key: 557    Status: AVAILABLE   Compressed: NO   Tag: TAG20140908T193017
Piece Name: /oracle/app/oracle/flash_recovery_area/ROB1/
autobackup/2014_09_08/o1_mf_s_697059017_5bg19b6p_.bkp
  SPFILE Included: Modification time: 08-SEP-14
  SPFILE db_unique_name: ROB1
  Control File Included: Ckp SCN: 676443       Ckp time: 08-SEP-14
```

This is an actual database backup. The output looks much like the previous output, except that now we get a full list of all the datafiles contained in the backup. We see that the datafile backup consists of one backup set piece (BS Key 510). Of course, when we perform a recovery, RMAN will look for the most current backup. Once it knows that, it will pick the best backups to use to perform the recovery. Perhaps this is a small point, but it's an important one.

Also in this listing, we find that there is an archive log backup (backup set key 536) with a single archive log in it. On the final section of the report, we find an autobackup of the control file/SPFILE (backup set 555). We know this is an autobackup by virtue of the "SPFILE Included" and "Control File Included" wording in the output.

Let's look at the archive log backup output a bit more closely:

```
BS Key   Size         Device Type Elapsed Time Completion Time
-------  ----------   ----------- ------------ ---------------
536      783.00K      DISK            00:00:01     08-SEP-14
BP Key: 541    Status: AVAILABLE   Compressed: YES   Tag: TAG20140908T193014
Piece Name: /oracle/app/oracle/flash_recovery_area/ROB1/
backupset/2014_09_08/o1_mf_annnn_TAG20140908T193014_5bg196xr_.bkp

  List of Archived Logs in backup set 536
  Thrd Seq     Low SCN    Low Time  Next SCN   Next Time
  ---- ------- ---------- --------- ---------- ---------
  1    13      676291     08-SEP-14 676364     08-SEP-14
```

This backup set has a backup set key of 536. The header information looks the same as in the previous backup set. However, this backup is an archive log backup, so in subsequent lines, RMAN provides a list of the archived redo logs backed up in the backup set. The thread and sequence number of the archive log are listed, along with the low SCN and time, and the next SCN and time. The low time/SCN and high (or Next SCN as listed in the report) time/SCN ranges allow you to determine when the archive log was created.

Let's look at an incremental backup set report:

```
BS Key   Type LV Size       Device Type Elapsed Time Completion Time
-------  ---- -- ---------- ----------- ------------ ---------------
857      Incr 1  1000.00K   DISK          00:00:27    08-SEP-14
BP Key: 861   Status: AVAILABLE  Compressed: YES  Tag: TAG20140908T202840
Piece Name: /oracle/app/oracle/flash_recovery_area/ROB1/
backupset/2014_09_08/o1_mf_nnnd1_TAG20140908T202840_5bg4psxw_.bkp
  List of Datafiles in backup set 857
  File LV Type Ckp SCN    Ckp Time  Name
  ---- -- ---- ---------- --------- ----
  1    1  Incr 679212     08-SEP-14 /ora01/oracle/rob1/rob1/system01.dbf
  2    1  Incr 679212     08-SEP-14 /ora01/oracle/rob1/rob1/sysaux01.dbf
  3    1  Incr 679212     08-SEP-14 /ora01/oracle/rob1/rob1/undotbs01.dbf
  4    1  Incr 679212     08-SEP-14 /ora01/oracle/rob1/rob1/users01.dbf
```

Again, this report is very similar to the other reports. The only differences are that Incr is used in the Type field to indicate that the backup is an incremental backup, and the LV (level) column shows the level of the incremental backup. If the incremental backup were a level 0 backup, then the LV column would show the number 0, which corresponds to a level 0 base backup.

Listing Backups Eligible for Recovery

If you want to see all datafile backups or copies that are able to be used to restore and recover your database, then use the **list recoverable** command. This **list** command provides a list of all backups with a status of AVAILABLE that can be used to restore your database (this is only for the current incarnation). Backups, image copies, and incremental backups will all be included. If an incremental backup does not have a valid parent, it will not be included in this backup.

```
RMAN> list recoverable backup of database;
List of Backup Sets
===================
BS Key   Type LV Size       Device Type Elapsed Time Completion Time
-------  ---- -- ---------- ----------- ------------ ---------------
713      Incr 0  243.27M    DISK          00:01:10    08-SEP-14
BP Key: 715   Status: AVAILABLE  Compressed: YES  Tag: TAG20140908T202601
Piece Name: /oracle/app/oracle/flash_recovery_area/ROB1/
backupset/2014_09_08/o1_mf_nnnd0_TAG20140908T202601_5bg4ktk1_.bkp

  List of Datafiles in backup set 713
  File LV Type Ckp SCN    Ckp Time  Name
  ---- -- ---- ---------- --------- ----
  1    0  Incr 678900     08-SEP-14 /ora01/oracle/rob1/rob1/system01.dbf
  2    0  Incr 678900     08-SEP-14 /ora01/oracle/rob1/rob1/sysaux01.dbf
  3    0  Incr 678900     08-SEP-14 /ora01/oracle/rob1/rob1/undotbs01.dbf
  4    0  Incr 678900     08-SEP-14 /ora01/oracle/rob1/rob1/users01.dbf

BS Key   Type LV Size       Device Type Elapsed Time Completion Time
-------  ---- -- ---------- ----------- ------------ ---------------
857      Incr 1  1000.00K   DISK          00:00:27    08-SEP-14
BP Key: 861   Status: AVAILABLE  Compressed: YES  Tag: TAG20140908T202840
```

```
Piece Name: /oracle/app/oracle/flash_recovery_area/ROB1/
backupset/2014_09_08/o1_mf_nnnd1_TAG20140908T202840_5bg4psxw_.bkp

   List of Datafiles in backup set 857
   File LV Type Ckp SCN    Ckp Time   Name
   ---- -- ---- ---------- ---------- ----
    1    1  Incr 679212     08-SEP-14  /ora01/oracle/rob1/rob1/system01.dbf
    2    1  Incr 679212     08-SEP-14  /ora01/oracle/rob1/rob1/sysaux01.dbf
    3    1  Incr 679212     08-SEP-14  /ora01/oracle/rob1/rob1/undotbs01.dbf
    4    1  Incr 679212     08-SEP-14  /ora01/oracle/rob1/rob1/users01.dbf
```

Listing Expired Backups

Using the **list backup** command shows you both available and expired backup sets. If you want to see only expired backups, you can use the **expired** keyword, as shown in this example:

```
RMAN> list expired backup;
List of Backup Sets
===================
BS Key  Size        Device Type Elapsed Time Completion Time
------- ----------  ----------- ------------ ---------------
1025    489.00K     DISK          00:00:01     08-SEP-14
BP Key: 1028    Status: EXPIRED  Compressed: NO  Tag: TAG20140908T203418
Piece Name: /oracle/app/oracle/flash_recovery_area/ROB1/
backupset/2014_09_08/o1_mf_annnn_TAG20140908T203418_5bg51c2c_.bkp
List of Archived Logs in backup set 1025
   Thrd Seq     Low SCN    Low Time   Next SCN   Next Time
   ---- ------- ---------- ---------- ---------- ---------
    1    18      679230     08-SEP-14  679716     08-SEP-14
```

This command will display all expired backup sets. With the **list expired backup** command, you can also get a list of expired tablespace and datafile backups and lists of expired archive log backups and control file/SPFILE autobackups by inserting the correct keyword, such as **list expired backup of datafile 3** or **list expired backup of archivelog all**.

Listing Backups by Tablespace Name and Datafile Number

The output of the **list backup of tablespace** or **list backup of datafile** command is very similar to the **list backup** output. These two **list backup** commands allow you to list output specific for a tablespace or a datafile, as shown in this example:

```
RMAN> list backup of tablespace users;
List of Backup Sets
===================
BS Key  Type LV Size        Device Type Elapsed Time Completion Time
------- ---- -- ----------  ----------- ------------ ---------------
713     Incr 0  243.27M     DISK          00:01:10     08-SEP-14
BP Key: 715    Status: AVAILABLE  Compressed: YES  Tag: TAG20140908T202601
Piece Name: oracle/app/oracle/flash_recovery_area/ROB1/
backupset/2014_09_08/o1_mf_nnnd0_TAG20140908T202601_5bg4ktk1_.bkp

   List of Datafiles in backup set 713
```

```
 File LV Type Ckp SCN    Ckp Time  Name
 ---- -- ---- ---------- --------- ----
  4    0  Incr 678900     08-SEP-14 /ora01/oracle/rob1/rob1/users01.dbf


BS Key  Type LV Size       Device Type Elapsed Time Completion Time
------- ---- -- ---------- ----------- ------------ ---------------
857      Incr 1 1000.00K   DISK         00:00:27     08-SEP-14
BP Key: 861   Status: AVAILABLE  Compressed: YES  Tag: TAG20140908T202840
Piece Name: /oracle/app/oracle/flash_recovery_area/ROB1/
backupset/2014_09_08/o1_mf_nnnd1_TAG20140908T202840_5bg4psxw_.bkp
  List of Datafiles in backup set 857
  File LV Type Ckp SCN    Ckp Time  Name
  ---- -- ---- ---------- --------- ----
   4    1  Incr 679212     08-SEP-14 /ora01/oracle/rob1/rob1/users01.dbf
```

Note in this example that this backup has expired, which might be of particular interest to us, especially if this were the only backup of the USERS tablespace available! Again, you can use the **expired** keyword to only list expired backups (**list expired backup of tablespace**).

In much the same way, you can list the backups of a specific datafile with the **list backup of datafile** command:

```
RMAN> list backup of datafile 3;
List of Backup Sets
===================


BS Key  Type LV Size       Device Type Elapsed Time Completion Time
------- ---- -- ---------- ----------- ------------ ---------------
713      Incr 0 243.27M    DISK         00:01:10     08-SEP-14
BP Key: 715    Status: AVAILABLE  Compressed: YES  Tag: TAG20140908T202601
Piece Name: /oracle/app/oracle/flash_recovery_area/ROB1/
backupset/2014_09_08/o1_mf_nnnd0_TAG20140908T202601_5bg4ktk1_.bkp

  List of Datafiles in backup set 713
  File LV Type Ckp SCN    Ckp Time  Name
  ---- -- ---- ---------- --------- ----
   3    0  Incr 678900     08-SEP-14 /ora01/oracle/rob1/rob1/undotbs01.dbf
```

One place where the **list** command can be helpful is if you are trying to do a point-in-time restore and you are getting errors that indicate no backup or copy is found. In this case, try a **list** command, using the same **until** clause to see if it lists any available backups. Doing this can help reveal any problems with your **until** clause, and you can adjust the **until** clause to determine from what point-in-time recovery is truly available.

Listing Archive Log Backups

Several options exist for listing archive log backups in RMAN. To obtain a complete summary of archive logs currently on disk (this does not mean that they have been backed up), the **list archivelog all** command is perfect, as shown here:

```
RMAN> list archivelog all;
List of Archived Log Copies for database with db_unique_name ROB1
```

```
=======================================================================
Key      Thrd Seq     S Low Time
-------  ---- ------- - ---------
54       1    9        X 08-SEP-14
Name: /oracle/app/oracle/flash_recovery_area/ROB1/
archivelog/2014_09_08/o1_mf_1_9_5bd8qv45_.arc

1170     1    19       A 08-SEP-14
Name: /oracle/app/oracle/flash_recovery_area/ROB1/
archivelog/2014_09_08/o1_mf_1_19_5bg6114l_.arc
```

Here, we find a list of each archived redo log that Oracle has created that is waiting to be backed up, along with the thread number and the sequence number of that archived redo log.

To get a report of those archive logs that we have backed up, we use the **list backup of archivelog all** report, as shown here:

```
RMAN> list backup of archivelog all;

List of Backup Sets
===================
BS Key   Size       Device Type Elapsed Time Completion Time
-------  ---------- ----------- ------------ ---------------
894      63.00K     DISK        00:00:01     08-SEP-14
BP Key: 899   Status: AVAILABLE  Compressed: YES  Tag: TAG20140908T202920
Piece Name: /oracle/app/oracle/flash_recovery_area/ROB1/
backupset/2014_09_08/o1_mf_annnn_TAG20140908T202920_5bg4r0y0_.bkp

  List of Archived Logs in backup set 894
  Thrd Seq     Low SCN    Low Time   Next SCN   Next Time
  ---- ------- ---------- ---------- ---------- ---------
  1    17      679163     08-SEP-14 679230      08-SEP-14

BS Key   Size       Device Type Elapsed Time Completion Time
-------  ---------- ----------- ------------ ---------------
1025     489.00K    DISK        00:00:01     08-SEP-14
BP Key: 1028   Status: EXPIRED  Compressed: NO  Tag: TAG20140908T203418
Piece Name: /oracle/app/oracle/flash_recovery_area/ROB1/
backupset/2014_09_08/o1_mf_annnn_TAG20140908T203418_5bg51c2c_.bkp

  List of Archived Logs in backup set 1025
  Thrd Seq     Low SCN    Low Time   Next SCN   Next Time
  ---- ------- ---------- ---------- ---------- ---------
  1    18      679230     08-SEP-14 679716      08-SEP-14
```

Note that the last archive log backup set in this report has an EXPIRED status, whereas the others have an AVAILABLE status. Thus, all the archived redo log backup sets are available for RMAN recoveries, whereas the last is not. If you want to look at expired backup sets only, add the **expired** keyword, as in **list expired backup of archivelog all**.

Listing Control File and SPFILE Backups

As you might expect, you can also list control file and SPFILE backups. The **list backup of controlfile** command provides you with a list of control file backups, and the **list backup of spfile** command provides output for SPFILE backups. Here is an example of each command and its results:

```
RMAN> list backup of controlfile;
List of Backup Sets
===================
BS Key  Type LV Size       Device Type Elapsed Time Completion Time
------- ---- -- ---------- ----------- ------------ ---------------
928     Full    9.67M      DISK          00:00:01     08-SEP-14
BP Key: 930   Status: AVAILABLE  Compressed: NO  Tag: TAG20140908T202923
Piece Name: /oracle/app/oracle/flash_recovery_area/ROB1/
autobackup/2014_09_08/o1_mf_s_697062563_5bg4r47m_.bkp
  Control File Included: Ckp SCN: 679329      Ckp time: 08-SEP-14

BS Key  Type LV Size       Device Type Elapsed Time Completion Time
------- ---- -- ---------- ----------- ------------ ---------------
1062    Full    9.67M      DISK          00:00:01     08-SEP-14
BP Key: 1064   Status: AVAILABLE  Compressed: NO  Tag: TAG20140908T203421
Piece Name: /oracle/app/oracle/flash_recovery_area/ROB1/
autobackup/2014_09_08/o1_mf_s_697062861_5bg51g1m_.bkp
  Control File Included: Ckp SCN: 679822      Ckp time: 08-SEP-14

RMAN> list backup of spfile;
List of Backup Sets
===================
BS Key  Type LV Size       Device Type Elapsed Time Completion Time
------- ---- -- ---------- ----------- ------------ ---------------
928     Full    9.67M      DISK          00:00:01     08-SEP-14
BP Key: 930   Status: AVAILABLE  Compressed: NO  Tag: TAG20140908T202923
Piece Name: /oracle/app/oracle/flash_recovery_area/ROB1/autobackup/
2014_09_08/o1_mf_s_697062563_5bg4r47m_.bkp
  SPFILE Included: Modification time: 08-SEP-14
  SPFILE db_unique_name: ROB1

BS Key  Type LV Size       Device Type Elapsed Time Completion Time
------- ---- -- ---------- ----------- ------------ ---------------
1062    Full    9.67M      DISK          00:00:01     08-SEP-14
BP Key: 1064   Status: AVAILABLE  Compressed: NO  Tag: TAG20140908T203421
Piece Name: /oracle/app/oracle/flash_recovery_area/ROB1/
autobackup/2014_09_08/o1_mf_s_697062861_5bg51g1m_.bkp
  SPFILE Included: Modification time: 08-SEP-14
  SPFILE db_unique_name: ROB1
```

We'll bet you have already guessed that you can use the **list expired backup of archivelog all** command here, too. Also, you can limit the report by time or log sequence number. For example, to list expired archive log backups until a given sequence, you could use the command **list expired backup of archivelog until sequence**.

Listing Image Copies

Just as you can use the **list** command to determine the status of backup sets, you can also use the **list** command to determine the status of database image copies. In this section we discuss producing reports on image copies with the **list copy** command. We discuss listing all copies within the RMAN catalog. Then we look at listing datafile copies and archived redo log copies. Finally, we will look at listing control file copies.

Listing RMAN Copies

You can generate a list of all copies with the **list copy** command:

```
RMAN> list copy;
starting full resync of recovery catalog
full resync complete
specification does not match any control file copy in the repository
List of Datafile Copies
=======================
Key     File S Completion Time Ckp SCN    Ckp Time
------- ---- - --------------- ---------- ---------------
1215    3    A 08-SEP-14         681024     08-SEP-14
Name: /oracle/app/oracle/flash_recovery_area/ROB1/datafile
/o1_mf_undotbs1_5bg6sw1s_.dbf  Tag: TAG20140908T210427

List of Archived Log Copies for database with db_unique_name ROB1
=====================================================================
Key     Thrd Seq     S Low Time
------- ---- ------- - ---------
54      1    9       X 08-SEP-14
Name: /oracle/app/oracle/flash_recovery_area/ROB1/
archivelog/2014_09_08/o1_mf_1_9_5bd8qv45_.arc

1170    1    19      A 08-SEP-14
Name: /oracle/app/oracle/flash_recovery_area/ROB1/
archivelog/2014_09_08/o1_mf_1_19_5bg6l14l_.arc
```

Listing Datafile Copies

Oracle allows you to generate a summary list of all database datafile copies with the **list copy of database** command:

```
RMAN> list copy of database;

List of Datafile Copies
=======================
Key     File S Completion Time Ckp SCN    Ckp Time
------- ---- - --------------- ---------- ---------------
1215    3    A 08-SEP-14         681024     08-SEP-14
Name: /oracle/app/oracle/flash_recovery_area/ROB1/datafile
/o1_mf_undotbs1_5bg6sw1s_.dbf Tag: TAG20140908T210427
```

In this output, we have two copies of datafiles that belong to our database: datafile2.copy and datafile3.dbf. While the actual name of the datafile or its assigned tablespace name is not listed, the file number is listed in the second column of the report. We could relate this file number to the associated tablespace by running the **report schema** command, which we discuss later in this chapter.

If you want to know whether you have a datafile copy of a tablespace or a datafile, you can use the **list copy of tablespace** or **list copy of datafile** command, as shown here:

```
RMAN> list copy of tablespace undotbs1;
List of Datafile Copies
=======================
Key     File S Completion Time Ckp SCN    Ckp Time
------- ---- - --------------- ---------- ---------------
1215    3    A 08-SEP-14         681024     08-SEP-14
Name: /oracle/app/oracle/flash_recovery_area/ROB1/datafile
/o1_mf_undotbs1_5bg6sw1s_.dbf  Tag: TAG20140908T210427
```

Listing Archived Redo Log Copies

If you want a list of archived redo log copies, you can use the **list copy of archivelog all** command:

```
RMAN> list copy of archivelog all;
List of Archived Log Copies for database with db_unique_name ROB1
=====================================================================
Key     Thrd Seq    S Low Time
------- ---- ------- - ---------
54      1    9       X 08-SEP-14
Name: /oracle/app/oracle/flash_recovery_area/ROB1/
archivelog/2014_09_08/o1_mf_1_9_5bd8qv45_.arc

1170    1    19      A 08-SEP-14
Name: /oracle/app/oracle/flash_recovery_area/ROB1/
archivelog/2014_09_08/o1_mf_1_19_5bg6114l_.arc
```

You can also list copies of specific archived redo logs by time, sequence, or database SCN. Here are some examples of listing archived redo logs based on differing criteria:

```
RMAN> list copy of archivelog from sequence 9;

List of Archived Log Copies for database with db_unique_name ROB1
=====================================================================
Key     Thrd Seq    S Low Time
------- ---- ------- - ---------
54      1    9       X 08-SEP-14
Name: /oracle/app/oracle/flash_recovery_area/ROB1/
archivelog/2014_09_08/o1_mf_1_9_5bd8qv45_.arc

1170    1    19      A 08-SEP-14
Name: /oracle/app/oracle/flash_recovery_area/ROB1/
archivelog/2014_09_08/o1_mf_1_19_5bg6114l_.arc
```

```
RMAN> list copy of archivelog from sequence 9 until sequence 19;
List of Archived Log Copies for database with db_unique_name ROB1
======================================================================
Key      Thrd Seq     S Low Time
-------- ---- ------- - ---------
54        1    9       X 08-SEP-14
Name: /oracle/app/oracle/flash_recovery_area/ROB1/
archivelog/2014_09_08/o1_mf_1_9_5bd8qv45_.arc

1170      1    19      A 08-SEP-14
Name: /oracle/app/oracle/flash_recovery_area/ROB1/
archivelog/2014_09_08/o1_mf_1_19_5bg6114l_.arc
```

Listing Control File Copies

Finally, RMAN can report on control file copies with the **list copy of controlfile** command:

```
RMAN> list copy of controlfile;
List of Control File Copies
===========================
Key      S Completion Time Ckp SCN    Ckp Time
-------- - --------------- ---------- ---------------
1795      A 08-SEP-14       682922     08-SEP-14
Name: /oracle/app/oracle/flash_recovery_area/ROB1/
controlfile/o1_mf_TAG20140908T213230_5bg8gh41_.ctl
Tag: TAG20140908T213230
```

Listing Restore Points

The **list** command also provides the ability to generate a list of all restore points in the database. In this example we create two restore points. We create a normal restore point called rsp_1, and we create a second guaranteed restore point called gur_1. We then use the **list restore point all** command to list these restore points:

```
create restore point rsp_1;
create restore point rsp_1 preserve;
create restore point gur_1 guarantee flashback database;
RMAN> list restore point all;

SCN               RSP Time  Type        Time       Name
----------------- --------- ----------- ---------- ----
3700477                                  08-JAN-15  RSP_1
3700552                      GUARANTEED  08-JAN-15  GUR_1
3700689                      PRESERVED   08-JAN-15  RSP_2
```

We can also list an individual restore point as seen here:

```
RMAN> list restore point rsp_1;
SCN               RSP Time  Type        Time       Name
----------------- --------- ----------- ---------- ----
3700477                                  08-JAN-15  RSP_1
```

Listing the DB_UNIQUE_NAME

There are times where the setting of the database's DB_UNIQUE_NAME is critical, such as with standby databases. In cases where you need to know the DB_UNIQUE_NAME of a database, the RMAN **list db_unique_name** command will help, as shown here:

```
RMAN> list db_unique_name all;
List of Databases
DB Key  DB Name  DB ID             Database Role    Db_unique_name
-------  -------  ----------------  ---------------  ------------------
7          ROBERTCD 2645377104        PRIMARY          ROBERTCDB
```

The RMAN Report Command

The RMAN **report** command is used to determine the current recoverable state of your database and to provide certain information on database backups. In this section, we look at reports that tell you which datafiles have not been backed up in a specified period. We also look at reports that tell you when specific tablespaces need to be backed up because of UNRECOVERABLE operations on datafiles. Finally, we look at the use of the **report** command to report on database schemas and obsolete database backups.

Reporting on Datafiles that Have Not Been Backed Up Recently

A question DBAs frequently ask themselves is, "When was the last time I backed up this tablespace?" RMAN provides some answers to that question with the **report need backup** command. For example, if you want to know what tablespaces have not been backed up in the last three days, you could issue the **report need backup days=3** command and find out. Here is an example of the output of just such a report:

```
RMAN> report need backup days=3;
Report of files whose recovery needs more than 3 days of archived logs
File Days  Name
----  -----  -------------------------------------------------------
4     2      D:\ORACLE\ORADATA\RECOVER\TOOLS01.DBF
5     2      D:\ORACLE\ORADATA\RECOVER\USERS01.DBF
```

From this report, it appears that two datafiles require application of more than three days' worth of archived redo to be able to recover them (which implies that these datafiles have not been backed up in the last three days). In this event, we might well want to back up the datafiles or their associated tablespaces.

We can also generate reports based on a given number of incrementals that would need to be applied, as shown in this example:

```
RMAN> report need backup incremental = 3;

Report of files that need more than 3 incrementals during recovery
File Incrementals Name
----  ------------  -------------------------------------------------
```

```
1    4              D:\ORACLE\ORADATA\RECOVER\SYSTEM01.DBF
2    4              D:\ORACLE\ORADATA\RECOVER\RECOVER_UNDOTBS_01.DBF
3    4              D:\ORACLE\ORADATA\RECOVER\INDX01.DBF
4    4              D:\ORACLE\ORADATA\RECOVER\TOOLS01.DBF
5    4              D:\ORACLE\ORADATA\RECOVER\USERS01.DBF
```

In this example, several database datafiles require four RMAN incremental backups to be applied. This may well indicate that we need to perform a new backup on these datafiles at a higher incremental level, or even perform a new incremental base backup.

Reporting on Backup Redundancy or Recovery Window

We can use the **report need backup redundancy** command to determine which, if any, datafiles need to be backed up to meet our established backup redundancy policy. The following is an example of the use of this report. In this case, we want a list of all datafiles that do not have at least two different backups that can be used for recovery. These may be backup set backups or datafile copies.

```
RMAN> report need backup redundancy = 2;

Report of files with less than 2 redundant backups
File #bkps Name
---- ----- -----------------------------------------------
1    1     D:\ORACLE\ORADATA\RECOVER\SYSTEM01.DBF
4    1     D:\ORACLE\ORADATA\RECOVER\TOOLS01.DBF
5    1     D:\ORACLE\ORADATA\RECOVER\USERS01.DBF
```

Likewise, we can establish a minimum recovery window for our backups and report on any datafiles whose backups are older than that recovery window. This is done with the **report need backup recovery window days** command:

```
RMAN> report need backup recovery window of 2 days;

Report of files whose recovery needs more than 2 days of archived logs
File Days  Name
---- ----- -----------------------------------------------
1    4     D:\ORACLE\ORADATA\RECOVER\SYSTEM01.DBF
2    4     D:\ORACLE\ORADATA\RECOVER\RECOVER_UNDOTBS_01.DBF
3    4     D:\ORACLE\ORADATA\RECOVER\INDX01.DBF
4    4     D:\ORACLE\ORADATA\RECOVER\TOOLS01.DBF
5    4     D:\ORACLE\ORADATA\RECOVER\USERS01.DBF
```

In this case, several of our datafiles require application of more than two days' worth of archived redo. So, if our recovery policy says we want backups where we only need to apply one day of redo, then we need to back up these datafiles.

Reporting on Unrecoverable Operations on Datafiles

Unrecoverable operations on objects within tablespaces, and the datafiles that make up those tablespaces, lead to certain recoverability issues. For example, if a table is created using the **Unrecoverable** option and is subsequently loaded using the direct load path, then the tablespace needs to be backed up, or else the data that was loaded will not be recoverable. It is for these circumstances that the **report unrecoverable** command is used, as shown here:

```
RMAN> report unrecoverable;
Report of files that need backup due to unrecoverable operations

File Type of Backup Required Name
---- ---------------------- -------------------------------------
5    full or incremental     D:\ORACLE\ORADATA\RECOVER\USERS01.DBF
```

Reporting on the Database Schema

We are using the word "schema" here to mean the physical structure of the database. The schema includes the datafile name and number, the tablespaces they are assigned to, the size of the datafiles, and whether the datafiles contain rollback segments. This can be the current schema, or you can generate a report on the database schema at some past point in time. Here is an example of the execution of the **report schema** command:

```
RMAN> report schema;

Report of database schema for database with db_unique_name ROB1
List of Permanent Datafiles
===========================
File Size(MB) Tablespace       RB segs Datafile Name
---- -------- ---------------- ------- ------------------------
1    700      SYSTEM           YES     /ora01/oracle/rob1/rob1/system01.dbf
2    600      SYSAUX           NO      /ora01/oracle/rob1/rob1/sysaux01.dbf
3    280      UNDOTBS1         YES     /ora01/oracle/rob1/rob1/undotbs01.dbf
4    8        USERS            NO      /ora01/oracle/rob1/rob1/users01.dbf
```

Reporting on Obsolete Backups

Backups are marked with an OBSOLETE status if you are using a retention policy (which we discussed in Chapter 9). Here is an example of the execution of **report obsolete** with a retention policy set to **redundancy 1**:

```
RMAN> report obsolete;
RMAN retention policy will be applied to the command
RMAN retention policy is set to redundancy 1
Report of obsolete backups and copies
Type                 Key    Completion Time     Filename/Handle
-------------------- ------ ------------------- --------------------
Archive Log          54     08-SEP-14
/oracle/app/oracle/flash_recovery_area/ROB1/archivelog/2014_09_08
/o1_mf_1_9_5bd8qv45_.arc
Backup Set           712    08-SEP-14
  Backup Piece       714    08-SEP-14
/oracle/app/oracle/flash_recovery_area/ROB1/backupset/2014_09_08
/o1_mf_annnn_TAG20140908T202600_5bg4kr90_.bkp
Backup Set           774    08-SEP-14
  Backup Piece       776    08-SEP-14
```

```
/oracle/app/oracle/flash_recovery_area/ROB1/autobackup/2014_09_08
/o1_mf_s_697062444_5bg4ndym_.bkp
Backup Set            928    08-SEP-14
  Backup Piece        930    08-SEP-14
/oracle/app/oracle/flash_recovery_area/ROB1/autobackup/2014_09_08
/o1_mf_s_697062563_5bg4r47m_.bkp
Backup Set           1062    08-SEP-14
  Backup Piece       1064    08-SEP-14
/oracle/app/oracle/flash_recovery_area/ROB1/autobackup/2014_09_08
/o1_mf_s_697062861_5bg51g1m_.bkp
Backup Set           1259    08-SEP-14
  Backup Piece       1262    08-SEP-14              /oracle/app/oracle/flash_
recovery_area/ROB1/
autobackup/2014_09_08/o1_mf_s_697064685_5bg6tfxj_.bkp
Backup Set           1413    08-SEP-14
  Backup Piece       1416    08-SEP-14              /oracle/app/oracle/flash_
recovery_area/ROB1/backupset/2014_09_08
/o1_mf_ncnnf_TAG20140908T212707_5bg84dxo_.bkp
Backup Set           1475    08-SEP-14
  Backup Piece       1477    08-SEP-14
/oracle/app/oracle/flash_recovery_area/ROB1/autobackup/2014_09_08
/o1_mf_s_697066032_5bg84jf9_.bkp
Backup Set           1598    08-SEP-14
  Backup Piece       1601    08-SEP-14
/oracle/app/oracle/flash_recovery_area/ROB1/backupset/2014_09_08
/o1_mf_ncnnf_TAG20140908T213150_5bg8f7q1_.bkp
Control File Copy    1795    08-SEP-14
/oracle/app/oracle/flash_recovery_area/ROB1/controlfile
/o1_mf_TAG20140908T213230_5bg8gh41_.ctl
Backup Set           1664    08-SEP-14
  Backup Piece       1666    08-SEP-14
/oracle/app/oracle/flash_recovery_area/ROB1/autobackup/2014_09_08
/o1_mf_s_697066314_5bg8fbx9_.bkp
```

This report has several different backup sets, datafile copies, control file copies, and archive log copies that have been marked OBSOLETE by Oracle. If you want to mark these backups as DELETED, run the **delete obsolete** command, as shown in Chapter 9.

Data Dictionary Views for Reporting

Oracle provides a number of RMAN-related data dictionary views (V$views) that you can use to perform reporting from the SQL prompt. You can use these views to produce customized reports. You can then use these reports for a number of purposes, such as notifications when databases have not been backed up, or of databases that are not registered with the recovery catalog (you would use some form of configuration control that is reliable to compare against). All of the Oracle views related to RMAN are available in the Oracle Reference Guide, along with the purpose of the view and description of the columns. Many of the RMAN views begin with V$BACKUP*, V$RECOVERY*, and V$RMAN. Some of the more useful views are seen in the following table:

View Name	Description
V$BACKUP_ARCHIVELOG_DETAILS	Contains information about all restorable archive logs
V$BACKUP_ASYNC_IO	Provides performance information about ongoing and recently completed RMAN backups and restores
V$BACKUP_CONTROLFILE_DETAILS	Provides information about restorable control files
V$BACKUP_COPY_DETAILS	Provides information about all available control file and datafile copies
V$BACKUP_CORRUPTION	Provides information about corrupt block ranges in datafile backups from the control file
V$BACKUP_DATAFILE	Provides information about control files and datafiles in backup sets from the control file
V$BACKUP_DATAFILE_DETAILS	Provides information about restorable datafiles
V$BACKUP_FILES	Provides information about all RMAN backups (both image copies and backup sets) and archived logs
V$BACKUP_PIECE	Provides information about backup pieces from the control file
V$BACKUP_PIECE_DETAILS	Provides information about all available backup pieces
V$BACKUP_REDOLOG	Provides information about archived logs in backup sets from the control file
V$BACKUP_SET	Provides information about backup sets from the control file
V$BACKUP_SET_DETAILS	Provides detailed information on backup sets from the control file
V$BACKUP_SPFILE	Provides information from the control file on SPFILEs contained in backup sets
V$BACKUP_SPFILE_DETAILS	Provides information from the control file on SPFILEs contained in backup sets
V$BACKUP_SYNC_IO	Provides performance information about ongoing and recently completed RMAN backups and restores
V$DATABASE_BLOCK_CORRUPTION	Provides information about database blocks that were corrupted after the last backup
V$RECOVER_FILE	Contains the status of files needing media recovery
V$RECOVERY_FILE_DEST	Provides information about the Fast Recovery Area (FRA)
V$RMAN_BACKUP_JOB_DETAILS	Provides details about backup jobs
V$RMAN_BACKUP_TYPE	Provides information about RMAN backup types
V$RMAN_CONFIGURATION	Provides information about RMAN persistent configuration settings
V$RMAN_OUTPUT	Displays messages reported by RMAN
V$RMAN_STATUS	Contains information on the finished and ongoing RMAN jobs

Many of the RMAN control file views also have recovery catalog equivalents. Each of these views starts with an RC_ instead of a V$ prefix. The names are generally very similar. For example, V$ARCHIVED_LOG shows the archived redo logs listed in the control file. The RC_ARCHIVED_ LOG provides the same view sourced from the recovery catalog. Finally, you will find that many of the performance-related views in Oracle can be used to help performance-tune RMAN operations. We will discuss the use of those views in more detail next in Chapter 13.

Summary

Information! We want information! This chapter provides you with the commands you can use to extract information from RMAN. The **list** and **report** commands provide a wealth of information that you can use to administer RMAN and make sure that you are getting good backups of your database. We think it's a good idea to sit down and determine what kinds of reporting you want to do for your databases, and to automate that reporting so that you always know the backup and recovery state of your database.

CHAPTER
13

Performance Tuning RMAN Backup and Recovery Operations

RMAN actually works pretty well right out of the box, and you generally will find that it requires very little tuning. However, a number of other pieces fit into the RMAN architectural puzzle, and when all those pieces come together, you sometimes need to tweak a setting here or there to get the best performance out of your backup processes. Generally, then, the RMAN tuning you end up having to do involves dealing with inefficiencies in the logical or physical database design, tuning of the Media Management Library (MML), or tuning RMAN and the MML layer to coexist better with the physical device to which you are backing up.

In this chapter, we look at what you need to tune before you begin to tune RMAN itself. We then provide some tuning options for RMAN.

Before You Tune RMAN

If your RMAN backups take hours and hours to run, it's probably not RMAN's fault. More likely, it's some issue with your database or with your MML. The last time you drove in rush-hour traffic, did you think the slow movement was a problem with your car? Of course not. The problem was one of too many cars trying to move on a highway that lacked enough lanes. This is an example of a bandwidth problem, or a bottleneck. Cities attempt to solve their rush-hour problem by expanding the highway system or perhaps by adding a subway, buses, or light rail.

The same kind of problem exists when it comes to tuning RMAN and your backup and recovery process. It's often not the fault of RMAN, although RMAN often gets blamed. More likely, the problem is insufficient bandwidth of the system as a whole or some component in the infrastructure that is not configured correctly. RMAN often gets the initial blame, but in the end, it is just a victim.

You can use a number of tools to test the throughput of the media to which you are backing up to help you determine the baseline throughput you can expect from RMAN. For example, if you are backing up to the disk-based FRA, you might use the Oracle Orion tool to test the file system that the FRA will be using. You can use Orion to test disks that are part of a file system or a prepared set of disks to which ASM would attach. The nice thing about Orion is that it has the ability to simulate concurrent load, so you can get an idea of how many parallel processes can be streaming data before you start to see performance being impacted.

Most MML vendors provide some method of measuring throughput, though this might be as simple as copying a file through their interface and timing how long that file takes to copy. You will want to make sure your performance tests take concurrency into consideration. So, if you're going to be using four RMAN channels for your backups, you need to make sure you test four concurrent read/write processes when measuring throughput.

These tests provide a baseline for performance and can also clearly show you if your infrastructure has performance issues that might impact RMAN. Trying to tune RMAN when you don't really know what your goal is, is futile. First of all, it might be that your throughput will never be able to give you the performance you want, no matter what you do with RMAN. In that case, you will need to be looking at fixing the architecture, not RMAN. Second, if the testing does prove that the infrastructure can handle the throughput, you will know an approximate value of how much throughput you should be trying to tune toward. It provides you a goal, of sorts, to shoot for.

Once you have the architecture working correctly, and you understand how much performance you can get out of your architecture, much of RMAN tuning really turns out to be an exercise in tuning your Oracle database. The better your database performs, the better your RMAN backups will perform. Very large books have already been written on the subject of tuning your Oracle database, so we will just give a quick look at these issues. There are a number of good titles out there if you need more detailed information on Oracle database performance tuning.

> **NOTE**
> *We make some tuning recommendations in this chapter and in other places in this book. Make sure you test our recommendations on your system before you decide to "fire and forget" (meaning to make a change without checking that the change was positive). While certain configurations may work for us in our environments, you may find that they do not work as well for you.*

RMAN Performance: What Can Be Achieved?

What level of RMAN performance can be achieved? The answer is, it depends on the technology. If you are stuck on a 1GB network connection, then the best you will see is 100MB/sec to 125MB/sec. A 10GB network connection will provide significantly more throughput, from between 1GB/sec and 1.25GB/sec. If you are using Oracle Exadata and taking advantage of its Infiniband fabric, you might well see throughput rates of greater than 2.5GB/sec at its 40Gb/sec rate. Later versions of Exadata provide even faster potential Infiniband throughput.

If you are directly connected to your media devices via Fiber Channel, then the speeds of these connections might vary between 200MB/sec for 2GB/sec FC up to 800MB/sec for 8GB/sec FC. This throughput can be increased with additional channels, of course. All of these throughput rates have a direct impact on the performance of your backups. If you have a 1TB database that you are backing up over a 10GB network connection, then 1.25GB/sec is the best throughput you are going to get. That would mean that you can back up a terabyte of data in about 14–15 minutes.

Also, keep in mind that your performance is limited by the slowest part of the stack. So, it does not matter how blazingly fast your disks are if your infrastructure can only handle 200MB/sec—that is the best throughput you will get in that environment.

So the answer to the question of what can be achieved is simply, "It depends." It depends on everything from the server you are on, the network, the network adapters, the speed of the media you are backing up to, and even configuration of things such as buffer sizes. With an Exadata full rack, Oracle whitepapers document backup rates to local disk of from 20TB/hr for image copies to 50TB/hr for incremental backups (that is, using incrementally updated backups). Documented restore rates of 20TB/hr are also reported. When you include database compression into the backup picture, you can easily double the throughput with respect to TB of actual records. For example, if you have on average of 2× compression in your database, then the 20TB/hr of data movement actually turns into 40TB/hr. The same is true with restores. This means that it is possible to back up and restore huge amounts of data in a period of time that even a few years ago seemed dizzying.

You can find an excellent Oracle whitepaper on the backup and recovery performance that can be gained on an Exadata Database Machine at http://www.oracle.com/technetwork/database/features/availability/maa-tech-wp-sundbm-backup-11202-183503.pdf.

Have the Right Hardware in Place

If you want high backup performance, the first thing to look at is the backup hardware at your disposal. This consists of items such as tape drives, as well as the associated infrastructure such as cabling, robotic tape interfaces, and any MML-layer software that you might choose to employ.

Backup media hardware will provide you with a given speed at which the device will read and write. Of course, the faster the device writes, the faster your backups. Also, the more devices you can back up to, the better your backup timing tests will be. This was clearly pointed out in Oracle's RMAN performance whitepaper mentioned in the preceding section. The doubling of the number of drives that RMAN could write to causes an almost linear improvement in performance of both backup and restore operations. The ability to parallelize your backups across multiple channels (or backup devices) is critical to quickly backing up a large Oracle database.

RMAN will benefit from parallel CPU resources, but the return diminishes much quicker with the addition of CPUs, as opposed to the addition of physical backup devices. The bottom line, then, is that in most cases, having multiple backup devices will have a much greater positive impact on your backup and restore windows than adding CPUs will.

You will find that most backup devices are asynchronous rather than synchronous. An *asynchronous* device allows the backup server processes to issue I/O instructions without requiring the backup server processes to wait for the I/O to complete. An asynchronous operation, for example, allows the server process to issue a tape write instruction and, while that instruction is being performed, proceed to fill memory buffers in preparation for the next write operation. A *synchronous* device, on the other hand, would have to wait for the backup operation to complete before it could perform any other work. Thus, in our example, the synchronous process will have to wait for the tape I/O to complete before it can start filling memory buffers for the next operation. Therefore, an asynchronous device is more efficient than a synchronous one.

Because asynchronous operations are preferred, you may want to know about a few of their parameters. First, the parameter BACKUP_TAPE_IO_SLAVES (which defaults to FALSE) will cause all tape I/O to be asynchronous in nature. We suggest you set this parameter to TRUE to enable asynchronous I/O to your tape devices (if that setting is supported). Once this parameter is established, you can define the size of the memory buffers that are used by using the **parms** parameter of the **allocate channel** command or **configure channel** command.

Performance is always a concern, of course. There are views that will help you monitor performance should you be using either I/O slaves or regular I/O. If you are not using I/O slaves (the default), you can see the I/O throughput of RMAN through the V$BACKUP_SYNC_IO view. If you are using I/O slaves, you can use the V$BACKUP_ASYNC_IO views instead.

These two views can be very helpful if you are using I/O slaves to determine if enabling backup I/O slaves has any benefit and to determine how many slaves you should enable. Additionally, these views can help you determine your I/O throughput in general—which can be useful when tuning the entire backup infrastructure.

The tape buffer size is established when the channel is configured. The default value is OS specific, but is generally 64KB. You can configure this value to be higher or lower by using the **allocate channel** command. For the best performance, we suggest that you configure this value to 256KB or higher. However, this value is really dependent on the hardware and how the infrastructure is configured. Here is an example of configuring the block size for an SBT vendor:

```
allocate channel c1 device type
sbt parms="blksize=262144, ENV=(NB_ORA_CLASS=RMAN_db01)"
```

If you are backing up to disk, you need to determine whether your OS supports asynchronous I/O (most do these days). If it does, then Oracle automatically uses that feature. If it does not, then Oracle provides the parameter DBWR_IO_SLAVES, which, when set to a nonzero value, causes Oracle to simulate asynchronous I/O to disks by starting multiple DBWR processes.

When either DBWR_IO_SLAVES or BACKUP_TAPE_IO_SLAVES is configured, you may also want to create a large pool. This will help eliminate shared-pool contention and memory allocation error issues that can accompany shared-pool use when BACKUP_TAPE_IO_SLAVES is enabled. If you are using Automatic Shared Memory Management (ASMM), Oracle will manage the memory allocation of the shared pool for you. If you want to manually set the large pool, the total size of disk buffers is limited to 16MB per channel. The formula for setting the LARGE_POOL_SIZE parameter for backup is as follows:

LARGE_POOL_SIZE = (number of allocated channels) * (16MB + (4 * size of tape buffer))

NOTE
If DBWR_IO_SLAVES or BACKUP_TAPE_IO_SLAVES is not configured, RMAN will not use the large pool. Generally, you do not need to configure these parameter settings to get good performance from RMAN, unless your OS does not natively support asynchronous I/O.

Note that if you are using ASM with Oracle version 11.2 and later, ASM will automatically tune the I/O buffers for RMAN. As a result, no tuning should be required. You can review the V$BACKUP*IO views to determine the buffer sizes that ASM has configured. Usually you will find that 64 buffers will have been allocated, each at 4KB.

When either DBWR_IO_SLAVES or BACKUP_TAPE_IO_SLAVES is configured, you may also want to create a large pool. This will help eliminate shared-pool contention and memory allocation error issues that can accompany shared-pool use when BACKUP_TAPE_IO_SLAVES is enabled. If you are using Automatic Shared Memory Management (ASMM), Oracle will manage the memory allocation of the shared pool for you. If you want to manually set the large pool, the total size of disk buffers is limited to 16MB per channel.

Use the Correct Backup Strategy

In looking at the rates of backups and the time it takes to restore a database, one thing is clear—incremental backups, along with the use of the block change tracking file, are generally the way to go if throughput is your concern. That being said, the RMAN "backup once, incremental forever" backup strategy is perhaps the best of all worlds. With these types of backups you perform a level 0 base backup and then, after that, you perform incremental backups of the database. We discuss this backup strategy in more detail in Chapter 15, and the mechanics of such backups are discussed in Chapter 7.

Tune the Database

A badly tuned database can have a significant negative impact on your backup times. Certain database tuning issues can also have significant impact on your restore times. In this section, we briefly look at what some of these tuning issues are, including I/O tuning, memory tuning, and SQL tuning.

Tune I/O

Most DBAs understand the impact of I/O on basic database operations. Contention on a given disk drive for database resources (say, for example, that the online redo log and a database datafile are on the same device) can cause significant system slowdowns. Just as poor I/O distribution can impact your database performance, it can also affect your backup and restore times. This makes sense, because RMAN is going to be just another process (or, more likely, many processes due to parallel streams) that contends for I/O time on your devices.

Backing up is a read-intensive operation. If you have poor I/O distribution, not only will RMAN performance suffer, but also other users will suffer, if not even worse, during the backup operation. Recovery may be somewhat easier if all of your recoveries are full database recoveries. However, if you are just recovering a datafile or a tablespace, while the database is open and in use, you may find that poor I/O distribution impacts your recovery window, and your users. The bottom line is that bad I/O distribution impacts not only your day-to-day database users, but also your backups and recoveries, causing them to take longer.

Much has been written on distribution of I/O on an Oracle database and how to do it properly. We suggest that you take a look at the Oracle whitepaper titled "Oracle Storage Configuration Made Easy" (Juan Loaiza, Oracle Corporation, available at www.oracle.com/technology/index.html). In this paper, Mr. Loaiza makes a compelling argument for using an I/O distribution known as Stripe and Mirror Everything (SAME), discusses current disk speeds and feeds, and then demonstrates the logic of his SAME methodology. This methodology recommends that you stripe your data among the largest number of disks possible and suggests this is a much better approach than striping across a few disks or using a parity disk approach, such as RAID-5 (mirroring is, of course, more expensive). Further, this paper recommends that a stripe size of about 1MB is generally optimal and demonstrates that such a configuration in Oracle's testing resulted in a 13 percent better read/write from the disk than nonstriped systems, with an associated loss in CPU overhead. This faster disk read/write will translate into faster backup timings.

Tune Memory Usage

Like any Oracle process, RMAN uses memory. When an RMAN operation is started, a buffer is allocated to the operation for RMAN to work out of. The size of the buffer allocated depends on a number of different factors, including the following:

- RMAN backup and recovery multiplexing effects
- The device type used
- The number of channels allocated during the operation

Each of these factors affects how much memory RMAN will require. RMAN allocates memory buffers for operations. How it allocates these buffers depends on the type of device you are going to use. Let's look at the different buffer allocation methods in a bit more detail next.

Allocating Memory Buffers for Disk Devices   When backing up to disk devices, RMAN will allocate up to 16MB of memory. This memory is allocated based on the level of multiplexing (based on the **filesperset** setting). If the level of multiplexing is 4 or less, then RMAN will allocate 16 buffers of 1MB each. These 1MB buffers are divided among the number of datafiles to be backed up. So, if **filesperset** is set to 2, then each datafile will be allocated eight 1MB buffers.

If **filesperset** is between 5 and 8, then 512MB buffers are allocated and distributed evenly between the different datafiles. This way, no more than 16MB of buffers will be allocated. Finally, if the level of multiplexing is greater than 8, four buffers of 128MB will be allocated to each datafile, which amounts to 512KB per datafile.

There is a good rule of thumb with the **filesperset** parameter—less is better. We suggest that you set **filesperset** to a value around 4. This will generally result in larger buffers and better performance. What's more, in the event that there is corruption of a backup file, the loss of four datafiles is much less troublesome than the loss of, say, 64 datafiles in a single backup set.

Allocating Memory Buffers for SBT Devices   When backing up to an SBT device, RMAN allocates four buffers for each channel that is allocated. These buffers are 256KB in size generally, and thus the total memory allocated per channel is 1MB. The buffer sizes can be managed using the PARMS and BLKSIZE parameters of the **allocate** and **send** commands.

This memory is generally allocated from the PGA, but if the BACKUP_TAPE_IO_SLAVES parameter is set to TRUE, then the SGA is used unless the large pool is allocated, in which case the large pool will be used. Therefore, if you configure I/O slaves (and generally you should if you back up to SBT devices), then you should configure a large pool to reduce the overall memory requirements on the large pool.

Tune Your SQL

You might ask yourself what bad SQL running in your database has to do with performance-tuning your backup and recovery times. It's really quite simple. The negative performance impact of poor SQL statement operations has an overall negative performance impact on your database and the system the database is on. Anything that has a negative impact on your database is likewise going to have a negative impact on your backup operations. Tune your SQL operations such that they reduce the overall number of I/Os required (logical and physical), and schedule your backups to occur during times of typical low system usage (if that is possible).

Tune Your Environment

Carefully consider your backup schedules, and ensure that they do not conflict with I/O-intensive database operations such as data loads or reports. Also, if you find your backups are taking too long, consider an incremental backup strategy, and analyze your database to determine whether certain tablespaces might be made read-only, so you don't have to continue to back them up often. Further, if you are running in ARCHIVELOG mode, you can consider staggering the backups of tablespaces on different days to reduce the overall timeframe of your backups (at the cost of somewhat longer recovery times, of course).

If you are running your database using Oracle Real Application Clusters, then RMAN can take advantage of the clustered environment to parallelize your RMAN operations.

Something else to look at is your recovery catalog. You should ensure that you are running statistics on the recovery catalog, including statistics on fixed table stats.

Tune Your Backup and Recovery Strategy

We already mentioned using incremental backups as your primary backup strategy, but there are additional things you might want to do with your backup and recovery efforts.

First, don't forget that RMAN offers multisection backups, which provide the ability to back up a large datafile over more than one channel at the same time. This means that if you have several smaller datafiles and one or two large datafiles, the "single channel per backup set" rule can cause the backup or restore to take longer. Using multisection backups, you can spread the

I/O for the single datafile over more than one channel, which can significantly speed up the backup process.

Another issue to consider is the impact of your backup strategy on your recovery. One of the more painful problems with RMAN is that, depending on the platform (Unix is one example; the following three paragraphs do not apply to Oracle on Windows NT), if you restore an entire database with the **restore database** command, you must be careful to ensure that enough space is available for the restore. Everything is just fine as long as you have enough disk space, but consider for a moment a true disaster recovery situation where you do not have enough disk space in the right places. In this case, RMAN is going to spend perhaps an hour or more recovering your database. Once it runs out of disk space, you would assume that RMAN would just stop at that point, alert you to the lack-of-space problem, and then just stop the restore at that position. The truth, however, is a bit more painful.

If the datafile restore process fails, RMAN removes every incompletely restored file from that restore session. Therefore, if you spend two hours restoring all but one database datafile and then you run out of space during that restore, you are in deep trouble, because RMAN is now going to remove that one datafile, and you will have to restore it again. This equates to a very unhappy DBA.

Note that some platforms, such as Windows NT, do check for available space before you actually start an RMAN database, datafile, or tablespace restore. In this case, the issue of running out of space, while still a problem, is not as much of a time waster.

Another consideration with respect to restores is to make sure you are doing the minimal restore required by the failure you are dealing with. If you have just lost a datafile, you don't need to restore the entire database—a datafile restore is the preferred restore method in that case.

Tuning RMAN

As we stated at the beginning of the chapter, RMAN out of the box works pretty well. Still, you can do a few things to tune it so that you get better performance, which is what this section is all about. First, we discuss the tuning options in RMAN itself. Then, we discuss some MML tuning issues.

Tuning RMAN Settings

We discuss a few ways to tune RMAN in this section. Tuning RMAN itself can involve tuning parallel operations and also configuring RMAN to multiplex (or not to multiplex, that is the question). This section also covers some things that you can do to actually tune down RMAN.

Parallel Channel Operations

Perhaps the biggest impact you can make when tuning your database backups is to parallelize them by using multiple RMAN channels. Typically, you configure a channel for each device you are going to back up to. Therefore, if you back up to three different disks, configure three different channels. You will see little or no benefit of paralleling backups on the same device, of course; so if you have a D: drive and an E: drive on your Windows NT system but both are just partitioned on the same disk, you will derive no benefit from paralleling backups to those two devices.

NOTE
The memory buffering on tape systems may well make the allocation of additional channels worthwhile, so you should always do some timing tests to decide exactly how many channels you need to use on your system.

Paralleling backups is accomplished by allocating channels to the backup. Channels can have default values configured for them (along with the default degree of parallelization that will determine how many of the channels are used) with the **configure** command, discussed in Chapter 5. For example, if we have two tape devices that we are going to back up to, we'd likely configure two default channels and a default level of parallelization, as shown here:

```
CONFIGURE DEVICE TYPE DISK PARALLELISM 2;
CONFIGURE CHANNEL 1 DEVICE TYPE sbt FORMAT PARMS
'ENV=(NB_ORA_CLASS=RMAN_rs100_tape)';
CONFIGURE CHANNEL 2 DEVICE TYPE sbt FORMAT PARMS
'ENV=(NB_ORA_CLASS=RMAN_rs100_tape)';
```

This would serve to ensure that each **backup** or **recover** command is automatically allocated two channels to parallelize the process.

Of course, depending on your device, you may well be able to run parallel streams to the device. The best thing to do is run several tests and determine from those tests the performance of a varying number of backup streams from both a backup and a recovery point of view. It may be that a different number of streams will be more efficient during your backup than during your recovery, and only testing will determine this.

We have already discussed the multiplexing of backups in RMAN and how to tune this feature. Tuning multiplexing can have significant performance impacts on your backups and recoveries. As we also discussed earlier, how you configure your multiplexing will impact the amount of memory that is allocated to the RMAN backup process. The more memory, the better, as long as you do not start to induce swapping back and forth to disk.

Also, properly configuring multiplexing can make streaming to tape devices more efficient. The more memory you can allocate to RMAN, the more data that can be streamed to your I/O devices. Finally, tape streaming is rarely an issue with newer-generation tape drives. Generally, they have a great deal of onboard buffer memory that is used to ensure that the tape is written to at a constant rate.

RMAN Multiplexing

Before we dive headfirst into performance considerations, we should take a moment to discuss multiplexing in RMAN. *Multiplexing* allows a single RMAN channel to parallelize the reading of database datafiles during the backup process and to write the contents of those datafiles to the same backup set piece. Thus, one backup set piece may contain the contents of many different datafiles.

Note that the contents of a given datafile can reside in more than one backup set piece (which is evidenced by the fact that you can set **maxpiecesize** to a value smaller than that of any database datafile, but **maxsetsize** must be at least the size of the largest tablespace being backed up). However, in a given backup, a given datafile will only be backed up through one channel (or one backup set). Thus, if you allocate two channels (and, as a result, have two backup sets) and your database consists of one large datafile, the ability of RMAN to parallelize that datafile's backup will be greatly limited.

The level of RMAN's multiplexing is determined by the lesser of two RMAN parameters. The first is the **filesperset** parameter (established when you issue the **backup** command), and the second is the **maxopenfiles** parameter (established when the channel is allocated).

The **filesperset** parameter establishes how many datafiles should be included in each backup set. The number of datafiles in a given backup set will be some number less than or equivalent to **filesperset**. When you do a backup, RMAN will assign a default value for **filesperset** of either 64 or the number of input files divided by the number of allocated channels, whichever is less. You can use a nondefault value for **filesperset** by using the **filesperset** parameter of the **backup** command, as shown in this example:

```
backup database filesperset 4;
```

The **maxopenfiles** parameter establishes a limit on how many datafiles RMAN can read in parallel (the default is 8). You establish the **maxopenfiles** limit on a channel-by-channel basis. Here is an example of the use of **maxopenfiles**:

```
CONFIGURE CHANNEL 1 DEVICE TYPE DISK MAXOPENFILES 3 FORMAT
"d:\backup\recover\%U";
```

For example, if you created a backup set with **filesperset** set to 6 and **maxopenfiles** set to 3, RMAN would only be able to back up three datafiles in parallel at a time. The backup sets created would still contain at most six datafiles per backup set (assuming one channel is allocated and a degree of parallelism of 1), but only three datafiles would be written to the backup set at any time.

NOTE
*If you have your data striped on a large number of disks, you will not need to multiplex your backups, and you can set **maxopenfiles** to a value of 1. If you are striped across a smaller set of disks, consider setting **maxopenfiles** to a value between 4 and 8. If you do not stripe your data at all, **maxopenfiles** generally should be set to some value greater than 8.*

Multiplexing, and the establishment of the **filesperset** and **maxopenfiles** parameters, can have a significant impact (good and bad) on the performance of your backups. Tuning RMAN multiplexing can decrease the overall time of your backups, as long as your system is capable of the parallel operations that occur during multiplexing. As with most things, too much of a good thing is too much, and certainly you can over-parallelize your backups such that the system is overworked. In this case, you will quickly see the performance of your system diminish and your backup times increase.

Multiplexing can also have an impact on tape operations. Because tape systems are streaming devices, it's important to keep the flow of data streaming to the device at a rate that allows it to continue to write without needing to pause. Generally, once a tape has a delay in the output data stream, the tape device will have to stop and reposition the write head before the next write can occur. This can result in significant delays in the overall performance of your backups. By setting **filesperset** high and **maxopenfiles** low, you can tune your backup so that it streams to your tape device as efficiently as possible. Beware, of course, of overdoing it and bogging down your system so much that the I/O channels or CPU can't keep up with the flow of data that RMAN is providing. As always, finding the proper balance takes some patient tuning and monitoring.

Controlling the Overall Impact of RMAN Operations

Sometimes you want to tune RMAN *down* rather than up. Prior to Oracle Database 10g, you would use the RMAN parameters **rate** and **readrate** to throttle RMAN down, thus freeing system resources for other operations. These parameters would be set when you allocated channels for RMAN operations. These parameters are still available in Oracle Database, but they have been replaced.

Oracle Database makes controlling RMAN backups much easier. Now, you simply use the **duration** parameter in the **backup** command to control the duration of the backup. The **duration** parameter has an additional keyword, **minimize load**, that allows you to indicate to RMAN that it should minimize the I/O load required to back up the database over the given duration. For example, if the backup typically takes five hours and consumes 90 percent of the available I/O, you can indicate to RMAN that it should use a duration of ten hours for the backup. When this is included with the **minimize load** parameter, you might well expect to see only 45 to 50 percent of available I/O consumed, rather than the 90 percent. The negative side of this is, of course, that your backup will take longer. Here is an example of using the **duration** parameter when starting a backup; in this case, we want the backup to run ten hours:

```
Backup as copy database duration 10:00 minimize load database;
```

Of course, one problem with the use of the **duration** parameter is that the backup could actually take longer than ten hours. Any completed backup set can be used for recovery, even if the overall backup process fails due to duration issues. You can use the **partial** keyword to suppress RMAN errors in the event that the duration limit is exceeded and the backup fails.

One final thing to note about the use of the **duration** parameter is that the database files with the oldest backups will be given priority over files that have newer RMAN backup dates. Thus, if the backup of a database with 20 datafiles fails after ten are backed up, the next time the backup runs, the ten that were not backed up would get first priority.

Tuning the MML Layer

The Media Management Layer (MML) is an Oracle-provided API that interfaces with the software of various vendors who provide external backup solutions (such as tape devices). Each component of RMAN may require some tuning effort, including the MML layer. You need to consider a number of things with regard to the MML backup devices. Most are going to be running in asynchronous mode, but if they do not, that may be a big cause of your problems. Also, sometimes DBAs will set the **rate** parameter when they allocate a channel for backups. This is generally something you do not want to do, because it will create an artificial performance bottleneck.

Also, some of the MML vendors provide various configurable parameters, such as a configurable buffer size, that you can configure in vendor-specific parameter files. Look into the tuning possibilities that these parameter files offer you.

There are other factors related to the MML layer, such as the supported transfer rate of the backup device you are using, compression, streaming, and the block size. You must analyze all of these factors in an overall effort to tune the performance of your RMAN backups.

Identifying Database-Related RMAN Issues

In many ways, RMAN tuning is a lot like SQL tuning. RMAN uses the Oracle Database in much the same way that SQL statements do, such as using the buffer cache, issuing dynamic SQL calls, and calling stored PL/SQL packages. These operations, such as timed wait events, show up in the Oracle Database–generated statistics. As a result, several views are available to help give you some idea as to the kinds of problems you might be encountering and the source of those problems.

A number of views are useful for RMAN performance tuning. This book isn't a tuning book, but we can provide a few RMAN-specific insights. Some views you might be interested in with respect to RMAN tuning would include the following:

- V$RMAN_BACKUP_JOB_DETAILS
- V$ACTIVE_SESSION_HISTORY
- V$SESSION
- V$PROCESS
- V$SESSION_LONGOPS
- V$BACKUP_ASYNC_IO
- V$BACKUP_SYNC_IO

There are a number of different potential sources for performance problems. When you are performing read operations with RMAN, such as reading the control file, these components can be involved in the performance issues:

- **Control file**   RMAN frequently needs to read the control file for RMAN metadata. If the control file is experiencing slow I/O (perhaps due to slow disk response times), this can slow down RMAN operations. In the past, certain RMAN-related bugs have also caused performance problems related to the database control file, so it's important to get Oracle involved if you experience unexplainable performance problems involving the control file.

- **Recovery catalog**   If you are using the recovery catalog, RMAN will frequently access the catalog to read the RMAN metadata. If the recovery catalog is experiencing slow I/O, this can slow down RMAN operations. Keep in mind that the recovery catalog is often a separate database from the database you are backing up. Thus, performance problems can be a result of the recovery catalog database or of the database being backed up. When performance-tuning RMAN problems, then, you will need to look at the statistics of both the database being backed up and the recovery catalog database. In the past, certain RMAN-related bugs have also caused performance problems related to the recovery catalog, so it's important to get Oracle involved if you experience unexplainable performance problems involving the control file.

- **Reading memory buffers**   As with any other database operation, memory is important. The SGA should be properly configured. Typically, memory issues on the target database will surface for problems beyond RMAN. Memory issues on the recovery catalog database can cause significant performance issues.

■ **Reading database blocks** RMAN must read database blocks either from memory or from disk. If the disks are not sufficiently responsive, then I/O rates will suffer. This can cause performance impacts on RMAN operations. Likewise, if the SGA is too small, you will end up reading blocks from disk more frequently, so this can have an impact on RMAN performance.

Write operations (such as a datafile restore) can also cause performance issues. Many of the same components can be involved in write operations as with read operations. Database components that can be involved in write-related performance issues include the following:

■ Control file.
■ Recovery catalog.
■ Writing to tape/disk. As with reading from tape or disk, the I/O rates that you can achieve can make a difference with respect to performance.
■ Writing to memory buffers.

We mentioned several views in this section that can be used to monitor and tune RMAN performance. Using these views, you can determine how well the database, RMAN, and the MML are performing. You can also use these views to determine how long a backup or recovery process has taken and how much longer you can expect it to take. Let's look at these views and how you can best use them.

V$RMAN_BACKUP_JOB_DETAILS
The V$RMAN_BACKUP_JOB_DETAILS view provides some insight into each backup that occurs in your database. The view provides details on the start time, stop time, elapsed time, and bytes associated with each RMAN backup operation. Here is an example of V$RMAN_BACKUP_JOB_DETAILS:

```
select /*+ RULE */ session_key, session_recid,
start_time, end_time, output_bytes, elapsed_seconds
from v$rman_backup_job_details
where start_time >= sysdate-180
and status='COMPLETED'
And input_type='DB FULL';

SESSION_KEY SESSION_RECID START_TIM END_TIME  OUTPUT_BYTES ELAPSED_SECONDS
----------- ------------- --------- --------- ------------ ---------------
        456           456 11-JAN-14 11-JAN-14    228353024             397
        461           461 12-JAN-14 12-JAN-14    229755904             422
```

In this example, we see that two backup operations have successfully executed. Over time, we would be very interested in how long the backups were taking and whether the trend is increasing. By looking at the trends with respect to backup execution times, we can address problems before they actually become problems.

V$SESSION_LONGOPS and V$SESSION
The V$SESSION_LONGOPS view is useful during a backup or restore operation to determine how long the operation has taken and how much longer it is expected to take to complete. Join this

view to the V$SESSION view for additional information about your RMAN backup or recovery sessions. Here is an example of a join between V$SESSION_LONGOPS and V$SESSION during a database backup:

```
SQL> select a.sid, a.serial#, a.program, b.opname, b.time_remaining
from v$session a, v$session_longops b
where a.sid=b.sid
and a.serial#=b.serial#
and a.program like '%RMAN%'
and time_remaining > 0;
 SID SERIAL# PROGRAM   USERNAME  OPNAME                       TIME_REMAINING
 ---- ------- --------- --------  -------------------- ---------------------
   10       8 RMAN.EXE SYS RMAN: aggregate input                       1438
   14       3 RMAN.EXE SYS RMAN: full datafile backup                  7390
```

In this example, we have an RMAN process running a backup. It has connected to the database as SID 14. The time remaining, 7390, is the expected time in seconds that this backup will take. You can thus determine how long your backup will take by looking at this report. Note that we also did a join to V$SESSION to get some additional information on our RMAN session, such as the username and the program name.

V$ACTIVE_SESSION_HISTORY

Oracle Database offers a feature called Active Session History (ASH) that provides historical session-related information on Oracle database operations. ASH is a very powerful tool that can be used to review historical run-time information, providing information that can be effective for use when tuning RMAN operations. One use of ASH is to look at wait times that various sessions have experienced and what the associated waits are. Here is an example of such a query:

```
-- First we use V$SESSION to get the session
-- specific information if possible.
select sid, serial#, program
 from v$session
 where lower(program) like '%rman%';

   SID    SERIAL# PROGRAM
------ ---------- ----------
   125        149 rman.exe
   128        130 rman.exe
   134        164 rman.exe
-- Note that runtime session information may not always be available.
Set lines 132
Column session_id format 999 heading "SESS|ID"
Column session_serial# format 999 heading "SESS|SER|#"
Column event format a40
Column total_waits format 9,999,999,999 heading "TOTAL|TIME|WAITED|MICRO"
Select session_id, session_serial#, Event, sum(time_waited) total_waits
From v$active_session_history
Where sample_time > sysdate - 1
-- The next line can be remarked out if you don't know
-- the session information.
```

```
And session_id||session_serial# in (120102, 128102, 134129)
And program like '%rman%'
And session_state='WAITING' And time_waited > 0
Group by session_id, session_serial#, Event
Order by session_id, session_serial#, total_waits desc;
```

```
                                                         TOTAL
          SESS                                            TIME
SESS    SER                                              WAITED
  ID    #  EVENT                                          MICRO
 ----   ----  ---------------------------------------- --------------
  125   149  control file single write                   1,388,961
  125   149  control file sequential read                   45,964
  125   149  control file parallel write                     3,789
  128   130  RMAN backup & recovery I/O               192,263,005
  128   130  control file single write                   1,095,253
  128   130  control file parallel write                   529,012
```

V$BACKUP_ASYNC_IO and V$BACKUP_SYNC_IO

The V$BACKUP_ASYNC_IO and V$BACKUP_SYNC_IO views contain detailed information on RMAN asynchronous and synchronous backup operations. These views are transitory in nature and are cleared each time the database is shut down. These views contain a row for each asynchronous or synchronous backup or recovery operation. Perhaps the biggest benefit from this view is the EFFECTIVE_BYTES_PER_SECOND column in rows where the TYPE column is set to AGGREGATE. This column represents the rate at which the objects are being backed up or recovered in bytes per second. This number should be close to the listed read/write rate of your backup hardware. If the EFFECTIVE_BYTES_PER_SECOND column value is much lower than the rated speed of your backup hardware, then you should be looking for some sort of problem with your backup process. The problem could be caused by any number of things—from an overburdened CPU, to a saturated network, or perhaps a configuration issue with the MML interface to your vendor's backup solution.

NOTE
If you see data in V$BACKUP_SYNC_IO, this implies that you are not doing asynchronous backups. If this is the case, you need to investigate why your backups are occurring in synchronous fashion.

Here is an example of a query against V$BACKUP_ASYNC_IO and its results after a database backup has been completed:

```
select device_type "Device", type, filename,
to_char(open_time, 'mm/dd/yyyy hh24:mi:ss') open,
to_char(close_time, 'mm/dd/yyyy hh24:mi:ss') close,
elapsed_time ET, effective_bytes_per_second EPS
from v$backup_async_io
where close_time > sysdate - 30
order by close_time desc;
```

```
Device          TYPE
---------------- ---------
FILENAME
--------------------------------------------------------------------------------
--
OPEN                 CLOSE                  ET         EPS
-------------------- ------------------- ---------- ----------
DISK            INPUT
/oracle/app/oracle/flash_recovery_area/ROB1/backupset/2015_09_10
/o1_mf_nnndf_TAG20150910T110421_5blddpg9_.bkp
09/10/2015 11:15:35 09/10/2015 11:16:38      6300     4078836

DISK            OUTPUT
/ora01/oracle/rob1/rob1/system01.dbf
09/10/2015 11:15:35 09/10/2015 11:16:37      6200    11838761

DISK            AGGREGATE
09/10/2015 11:15:35 09/10/2015 11:16:37      6200    21986271

DISK            OUTPUT
/ora01/oracle/rob1/rob1/sysaux01.dbf
09/10/2015 11:15:36 09/10/2015 11:16:24      4800    13107200

DISK            AGGREGATE
09/10/2015 11:10:54 09/10/2015 11:11:06      1200    42269355

DISK            OUTPUT
/ora01/oracle/rob1/rob1/sysaux01.dbf
09/10/2015 11:10:55 09/10/2015 11:11:06      1100     9245789

DISK            INPUT
/oracle/app/oracle/flash_recovery_area/ROB1/backupset/2015_09_10
/o1_mf_nnndf_TAG20150910T110421_5blddpg9_.bkp
09/10/2015 11:10:54 09/10/2015 11:11:05      1100     1429132

DISK            OUTPUT
/ora01/oracle/rob1/rob1/system01.dbf
09/10/2015 11:10:54 09/10/2015 11:11:05      1100     9341114

DISK            OUTPUT
/ora01/oracle/rob1/rob1/undotbs01.dbf
09/10/2015 11:10:55 09/10/2015 11:11:00       500    58720256

DISK            OUTPUT
/ora01/oracle/rob1/rob1/users01.dbf
09/10/2015 11:10:55 09/10/2015 11:10:56       100     9175040

10 rows selected.
```

Column Name	Represents
IO_COUNT	The total number of I/O counts
READY	The number of asynchronous I/O calls for which a buffer was available immediately
SHORT_WAITS	The number of times that a buffer was requested and not available but became available after a nonblocking poll for I/O completion
LONG_WAITS	The number of times that a buffer was requested and not available and Oracle had to wait for the I/O device

TABLE 13-1.   *V$BACKUP_ASYNC_IO Column Descriptions*

In this case, we can see the effective transfer rate from the database to the backup set by RMAN. Further, we can see the name of the datafile that was backed up and the actual start and stop time of the backup itself.

Another way to measure the efficiency of your backup process is to use the V$BACKUP_ASYNC_IO view. This view has several columns of interest, which are listed and described in Table 13-1.

To determine whether there is an I/O problem, we can look at the ratio of I/Os to long waits (LONG_WAITS/IO_COUNTS), as shown in the following code segment:

```
select b.io_count, b.ready, b.short_waits, b.long_waits,
b.long_waits/b.io_count, b.filename
from v$backup_async_io b;
IO_COUNT        READY SHORT_WAITS LONG_WAITS B.LONG_WAITS/B.IO_COUNT
---------- ---------- ----------- ---------- -----------------------
FILENAME
----------------------------------------
         2          1           0          1          .5
D:\ORACLE\ADMIN\RECOVER\ARCH\ARC00052.001
         2          1           0          1          .5
D:\ORACLE\ADMIN\RECOVER\ARCH\ARC00046.001
         2          1           0          1          .5
D:\ORACLE\ADMIN\RECOVER\ARCH\ARC00051.001
         2          1           0          1          .5
D:\ORACLE\ADMIN\RECOVER\ARCH\ARC00050.001
       171        107          12         52          .304093567
D:\ORACLE\ORADATA\RECOVER\SYSTEM01.DBF
        11          8           2          1          .090909091
D:\ORACLE\ORADATA\RECOVER\RECOVER_UNDOTBS_01.DBF
         6          4           0          2          .333333333
D:\ORACLE\ORADATA\RECOVER\TOOLS01.DBF
         6          3           0          3          .5
```

```
D:\ORACLE\ORADATA\RECOVER\USERS01.DBF
        6         4         1         1                    .166666667
D:\ORACLE\ORADATA\RECOVER\RECOVER_TESTRBS_01.DBF
        3         1         0         2                    .666666667
D:\ORACLE\ORADATA\RECOVER\INDX01.DBF
        2         1         0         1                    .5
D:\ORACLE\ORADATA\RECOVER\TOOLS02.DBF
```

The numbers returned by this query clearly indicate some sort of I/O bottleneck is causing grief (in this case, it's an overly taxed single CPU).

Tracing RMAN Sessions

Sometimes using views is not enough to track down problems. Sometimes you need to get down to the nitty and the gritty. This means tracing the Oracle sessions related to the RMAN operation. This can be somewhat complex, because RMAN will actually create a number of Oracle sessions in order to complete its work. In this section, we introduce you to the notion of tracing and how to start tracing. Tracing, like tuning, is a topic unto itself. If you find yourself needing to actually trace RMAN sessions, then you have a serious problem. In these cases, you will want to do some more research on Oracle tracing and consult with Oracle.

Depending on the nature of the RMAN problem, you may need to trace one or all of those sessions. There are several ways to start tracing RMAN sessions. Generally, we try to start with the easiest method and then move to the more complicated method as required.

Tracing in Oracle is done by enabling an Oracle event. An Oracle event is something a DBA or developer "sets" in order to get Oracle to do something that it does not normally do. Each event is numbered, and in our case the event we are interested in is the 10046 event. When you set the 10046 event, you are telling the Oracle database that you want it to create a trace file and start tracing. Tracing can be enabled at the database or session level. Because of the overhead involved, you want to be cautious about tracing and only trace the sessions that need to be traced.

Reading the output of a trace file is beyond the scope of this book, and the need to do such a thing should be very rare indeed. However, you may want to investigate such things, or Oracle might ask you to trace your RMAN sessions. So, we are going to show you how to do it! Depending on your needs, you might want to enable tracing in one of these ways:

■   From the RMAN prompt, use the SQL command to enable 10046 tracing, as seen in this example. This will start tracing only on the sessions that the RMAN client is already connected to. As a result, some sessions will not be traced. Usually, this is the easiest way to trace a session, and it may produce some fruit.

```
sql "alter session set events ''10046 trace name context forever, level 12''";
RMAN> backup as compressed backupset database plus archivelog delete input;
```

■   You may also want to start tracing on the recovery catalog database. You can trace the entire database, or you can use the logon trigger demonstrated in the following bullet. Here is an example of enabling tracing for the recovery catalog database. This example would enable tracing for the whole database. If you wish to be more tactical, you could use the trigger code in the next bullet to just trace RMAN connections.

```
ALTER SESSION SET EVENTS='10046 trace name context off';
```

■ If the trace files in the first session do not help identify the problems you might be dealing with, you can create a login trigger to start tracing when a session logon occurs. This sample trigger will enable tracing for any RMAN session that connects to the database:

```
Create or replace trigger tr_rman_logon
After logon on database
Declare
    v_program    varchar2(1000);
Begin
    SELECT distinct program into v_program
    FROM v$session
    WHERE audsid = userenv('sessionid')
    and program like '%rman.exe%' and rownum < 2;
  if v_program='rman.exe'
  then
    execute immediate 'alter session set events ''10046 trace name context
    forever, level 12''';
  end if;
Exception
    when NO_DATA_FOUND then
        NULL;
End;
/
```

In Oracle Database versions 11g and later, the resulting trace file can be found in the Automatic Diagnostic Destination directory structure pointed to by the DIAGNOSTIC_DEST parameter. You can use the **show** parameter to find the setting for DIAGNOSTIC_DEST, or you can also look for the default setting for USER_DUMP_DEST to find this directory (this parameter is deprecated in Oracle Database, but is still handy to find the file paths for various files in the ADR). In Oracle Database versions previous to Oracle Database 11g, you will find the resulting trace files in the directory path pointed to by the USER_DUMP_DEST parameter.

You can find the location and name of a specific trace file if you can identify the session IDs by using the V$SESSION and V$PROCESS views. These views have a column called TRACEFILE that will give you the name and location of the trace file.

The 10046 trace files created as a result of the scripts in this book are long and complex beasts, well beyond the scope of this book. Most DBAs are aware of the tkprof tool that Oracle offers for reformatting these trace files, and many DBAs are also aware of generally how to read and interpret the resulting output. If you need more information on how to read trace files, several good sources of information are available, including books, the Web, and Oracle Metalink.

Summary

RMAN will support very fast backup and recovery schemes given that the appropriate infrastructure is in place to support it. Often, we find the reason that RMAN does not perform well is not because of the database, or because of RMAN, but because of the underlying network or insufficient numbers of backup devices.

We also talked about the times that RMAN is too fast and takes up too much CPU or floods the network. Finally, we discussed the **duration** parameter and its various options that allow you to reduce the overall run-time impact of RMAN operations.

CHAPTER
14

Using Oracle Cloud
Control for Backup
and Recovery

U p to this point, we have provided guidance on interacting with RMAN strictly from the RMAN client utility. Hopefully, this has enabled you to build some confidence using the RMAN command-line syntax. It is critical to become comfortable with this syntax because you will encounter situations in which the command-line syntax of RMAN is the only thing available to get you through a painful downtime. Oracle also provides a toolset for monitoring the entire Oracle infrastructure throughout your business, and this toolset includes a graphical user interface for taking database backups and performing recoveries. This product is Oracle Enterprise Manager Cloud Control 12c (EM12c). Coverage of everything that EM12c can do is beyond the scope of this book (we recommend *Oracle Enterprise Manager Cloud Control 12c Deep Dive* from Oracle Press). This book is about RMAN, so the coverage of EM12c is limited to how it employs RMAN to provide a backup and recovery interface from its console. However, it is worth a high-level overview to familiarize yourself with the architecture and overall function of EM12c prior to any discussion of its backup and recovery functions.

EM12c Architecture

From an architectural perspective, EM12c is composed of five main parts:

- The Oracle Management Repository
- The Oracle Management Service
- Oracle Management agents
- The Cloud Control console
- Plug-ins

Let's look at each of these in more detail.

NOTE
A discussion of the licensing for EM12c is beyond the scope of this book. (An entire licensing document is available in the Enterprise Manager documentation at http://docs.oracle.com/cd/E24628_01/ license.121/e24474/toc.htm.) However, it's worth noting that, in general, most of the basic functionality described here carries a restricted-use license and therefore is free. This restricted-use license refers specifically to Enterprise Manager, however, and many add-on options do come with license costs. Refer to the licensing documentation for full details.

Oracle Management Repository

The Oracle Management Repository (also called the repository or OMR) is an Oracle database that stores all the information collected by the various management agents. It is composed of database users, tablespaces, tables, views, indexes, packages, procedures, and database jobs. Unlike the OMS, the installation process for the OMR requires that a database already exists for the repository. This means you need to have created the database somewhere in your environment prior to installing the OMS. Again, it is typically recommended for the repository to be created in a dedicated database.

Oracle Management Service

The Oracle Management Service (OMS) is a web-based application that communicates with the agents and the Oracle Management Repository to collect and store information about all the targets on the various agents. (Note that the information itself is stored in the Oracle Management Repository, not the OMS.) The OMS is also responsible for rendering the user interface for the console. The OMS is installed into an Oracle middleware home, which also contains the Oracle WebLogic Server (including the WebLogic Server administration console), an Oracle Management agent for the middleware tier, the management service instance base directory, the Java Development Kit (JDK), and other configuration files. You can install the OMS into an existing WebLogic Server (WLS) configuration if it exists, but usually it is better from an availability perspective to have it installed in a dedicated WLS home.

Oracle Management Agents

An *Oracle Management agent* (usually referred to as simply an *agent* or abbreviated to *OMA*) is generally installed on each host that is monitored in your computing environment. (EM12*c* also introduces the capability to manage environments remotely in some cases.) These agents are deployed from the console, and they monitor all the targets that have been discovered by the agents. They are used to control blackouts on those targets, execute jobs, collect metrics, and so forth, and in turn provide details such as availability, metrics, and job statuses back to the Oracle Management Service.

For the EM12*c* release, agents were completely rewritten from the ground up for greater reliability, availability, and performance (see the upcoming section on plug-ins for details of how this was achieved). The only downside of this change is that you must use an EM12*c* agent to talk to the EM12*c* Oracle Management Service. Backward compatibility between 12*c* and earlier agents was lost because of the number of changes that were made in the new release.

The Cloud Control Console

The Cloud Control console provides the user interface that you use to access, monitor, and administer your computing environment. The console is accessed via a web browser, thus allowing you to access the central console from any location. You can customize the EM12*c* console much more than in previous releases, allowing you the following options:

- Choosing your home page from various predefined pages (or indeed setting any page you want to be your personal home page)
- Moving regions around on a target home page
- Adding regions that might be of more interest to you than the defaults
- Deleting regions that aren't of interest to you

The graphical user interface (GUI) provides a history of the most recent targets you have visited (the standard browser history is also available). In addition, you can mark pages as favorites and have them appear in a favorites list on the new menu-driven interface. Figure 14-1 shows an example of the default home page.

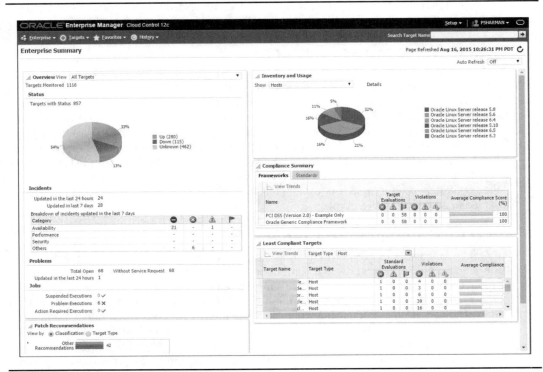

FIGURE 14-1. *The default home page in EM12c*

Plug-Ins

Plug-ins take on a whole new meaning in EM12c. In earlier releases, plug-ins were largely system-monitoring utilities used to monitor and manage non-Oracle (heterogeneous) software, including databases and middleware. Partners or Oracle Corporation itself usually built them. Some technically savvy customers built their own as well, but there weren't many plug-ins overall. In the EM12c release, a few of these monitoring plug-ins remain, but plug-ins have been greatly expanded to include every target type being managed. As such, there is now an Oracle database plug-in to manage Oracle databases, a Fusion Middleware plug-in to manage Oracle's middleware, a Fusion Applications plug-in to manage Oracle's Fusion Applications, and so on. Because new releases of the Oracle software will include plug-ins used to manage that software, this means EM12c (and later releases) will be able to monitor and manage those releases much more quickly than has been the case in the past. Plug-ins can be downloaded, applied, and deployed using the new Self Update functionality available from the Cloud Control console (if you have sufficient privileges to use it). In addition, this modular plug-in architecture means that an agent is no longer configured to be able to monitor any target type. Now, an agent will download only the plug-ins that are needed for the targets that the agent is monitoring. This means the agents themselves are smaller than they were in previous releases. This change is one of the biggest improvements in the architecture of the EM12c release.

Installing and Configuring Enterprise Manager Cloud Control 12*c* for Database Backups

A complete guide to installing and configuring EM12*c* is well beyond the scope of this book. Indeed, there are at least two manuals in the documentation set for EM12*c* that cover this specific topic (the Basic Installation Guide located at http://docs.oracle.com/cd/E24628_01/install.121/ e22624/toc.htm and the Advanced Installation and Configuration Guide located at http://docs .oracle.com/cd/E24628_01/install.121/e24089/toc.htm). Here we will restrict ourselves to covering what is needed to ensure you can back up a database using EM12*c*. The answer to that question is very straightforward—you need a standard Enterprise Manager installation (covered in the aforementioned manuals), a database to be backed up, and an agent to communicate between the two. Let's assume, for the sake of our discussion here, that EM12*c* is already installed. Let's assume further that the database to be backed up is not the first database installed on the particular host it is residing on, and in fact you have already installed an agent on the host. When that combination occurs, if you install a database using the Database Configuration Assistant (DBCA), DBCA has enough smarts built into it to realize that there is an agent already running on the host, and it will ask you if you want to add the new database to the EM12*c* configuration, and there will be little else for you to do.

However, what happens if there is no agent installed on the host? In that case, DBCA cannot determine if there is a centralized EM12*c* configuration that can manage this new database, and you will need to perform two additional steps:

1. Install an agent on the host.

2. Use EM12*c* to discover the targets that need to be monitored on that host.

Let's look at each of these in turn.

Installing an Enterprise Manager Agent

There are a variety of ways you can install the agent for Enterprise Manager. For example, you can use the Add Host Target Wizard to do the following:

- **Perform a fresh agent installation** This is probably the way most people do at least their first agent installation. The wizard walks you through a series of installation questions, including what the host name is for the agent installation, the installation directory, and so forth. If you have access to a named credential that can perform root tasks, the installation can be done without any manual intervention. If not, you will need to run some scripts as root after the software installation completes to finalize the setup of the agent.

- **Clone an existing agent** This option only appears when you are installing to a single platform, so you must have chosen one or more hosts of the same platform on an earlier screen to have this option available to you. This allows you to clone an existing well-tested, pre-patched, and running management agent.

- **Add the host to an existing shared agent** Again, this option only appears when you are installing to a single platform. In this case, it uses what is called the master agent (an existing, centrally shared agent) to install a new agent called a shared agent.

You can also install the agent in silent mode using the following items:

- **The agentDeploy script** To use this, you need to download and install EM CLI on the host being deployed to. You then use EM CLI to download the agent software before executing the agentDeploy script to perform the actual installation.

- **The AgentPull script** For a simpler installation, you can use the AgentPull script, which does not require the use of EM CLI. However, this script also only supports a few parameters, so it would be used for a more basic installation than the agentDeploy script.

- **An RPM file** Again, this requires the use of EM CLI to download an RPM file that can then be used to install the agent to an existing host or while provisioning a bare-metal host.

Each method using the Add Host Target Wizard can be performed using either the GUI or EM12c's command-line interface tool, EM CLI. EM CLI is used more frequently when you want to deploy many agents at one time (though this can be performed using the GUI as well), or when you want to perform a scripted installation.

Silent mode installations are normally used when you want to install an agent from the destination host, so you can think of this as a pull method of installing the agent as opposed to the push method of using the GUI. Silent mode requires a response file that contains the responses you would normally have given to the interview questions asked when using the GUI to install an agent.

A complete walkthrough of the installation types would take up far too much space, so if you want to see more details on these, refer to the Basic Installation Guide (for the fresh agent installation) or the Advanced Installation and Configuration Guide (for the remaining installation types), listed previously.

Discovering Targets

Once you have installed agents on a host, you then need to discover, promote, and add the remaining targets that are located on that host. As far as databases are concerned, this can be done during the creation of the database itself using Oracle's Database Configuration Assistant (DBCA), or it can be done afterward through the Enterprise Manager tool itself.

Using DBCA to Promote a Database

The DBCA is Oracle's graphical user interface (GUI) tool to walk you through the process of creating an Oracle database. It has many options available to use through the interview process, but the only one that is really relevant to the discussion in this chapter is its ability to promote the database that is being created to be managed by EM12c. This ability is only found in the advanced mode of DBCA (by selecting Advanced Mode on Step 2 of DBCA). When you select advanced mode, a more detailed interview process is begun.

Note that two options are available to you when the advanced mode interview starts:

- **Configure Enterprise Manager (EM) Database Express** This option tells you that the DBCA is running against an Oracle Database 12c home. In earlier releases of the Oracle database software, this option would have referred to Database Control, but that tool has been desupported in the Database 12c release in favor of EM Express. As EM Express contains no backup/recovery functionality, we won't cover it further here.

■ **Register with Enterprise Manager (EM) Cloud Control** The four fields underneath this option provide DBCA with enough information to register the database with EM12*c* once it is created. You need to specify the fully qualified hostname for the OMS, the port number for the OMS, and the name of an EM administrator and its password.

Using EM12*c* to Promote a Database

Although you can easily use DBCA to promote a database to be a managed target in Enterprise Manager, there are many times when you would want to use EM itself to perform this operation. Such times can be caused by simply forgetting to create the database in advanced mode so you don't even see the management options screen, deciding that you want to use EM12*c* instead of EM Express to manage the database, or more likely because you want to promote multiple databases at once. It is this final option that we want to look at in more detail here.

Provided you already have an EM agent installed on a particular host, you can promote all the databases on that host to be managed by EM12*c* in a single operation (you can, of course, also promote them one by one, which is simply a subset of the process we'll be showing you now). To add multiple databases in a single operation, you need to start by selecting Setup | Add Target | Add Targets Manually. You start the wizard by selecting the Add Targets Using Guided Process radio button, then selecting Oracle Database, Listener and Automatic Storage Management from the drop-down list, and finally clicking the Add Using Guided Process button.

This same wizard can be used to add listeners and Automatic Storage Management (ASM) targets at the same time. In this example, we'll add two databases and a single listener. On the next step of the wizard, you need to enter the hostname for the host that contains the database. To select the host on which you want to search for databases, click the magnifying glass to the right of the host or cluster field, and you will be provided a screen where you can search for the host you are interested in. The host must already have an agent installed on it to be shown in the list. Once you have selected the host, you will be returned to the Search Criteria screen, where you simply need to click the Next button.

It is when you click the Next button that the target discovery is actually performed. The OMS will communicate to the agent on the hosts you have chosen and tell it to look for any Oracle databases, listeners, or ASM targets. These will be returned to you on the next screen of the wizard.

■ Notice across the top of the screen there are two tabs: Set Global Target Properties and Specify Group for Targets. The Set Global Target Properties tab allows you to define a contact name, cost center, department, lifecycle status, line of business, and location for both the test1 and test2 databases at the same time (you cannot select different values for each database here; these must be common values). These properties allow the targets to be placed into *dynamic* groups based on the values entered into these fields (a discussion of the value of dynamic groups is beyond the scope of this book, but suffice it to say these can be very valuable for EM administrators). Likewise, the Specify Group for Targets tab can be used to specify an *administrative* group for purposes such as allowing jobs to be scheduled against all group members at once. Again, only a single group can be chosen for all the targets on this tab.

■ Across from each target name is a Target Group field. This is similar to the Specify Group for Targets tab, but here you can specify an individual group per target.

- You can also specify for each target the password for the DBSNMP account, as well as the role (NORMAL or SYSDBA) for that user. You can do this once for all targets that have just been discovered by clicking the Specify Common Monitoring Credentials button, or you can do this on a target-by-target basis by entering values in the Monitor Password and Role fields. Once you have entered values for these, it is a good idea to click the Test Connection button to ensure you haven't made any typographic errors. This will also test whether the DBSNMP account is locked or not.

- If you had selected both target names, the Configure icon would have been greyed out. If you had selected only one database target, you could click the Configure icon to not only enter the monitor password and role, but to also override the values for the ORACLE_HOME path, listener machine name, listener port number, database SID, and preferred connect string for the database. All of these except the preferred connect string are already discovered as part of the database discovery, so the only one you might want to change is the preferred connect string (for example, if you have a more complex connect string that includes failover functionality or something similar). If the connect string is left blank, the OMS automatically creates a connect string from the host name, port number, and database SID it has already discovered.

Once you have completed configuring the different options you want to use, you will be presented with the Review step of the wizard, where you just need to click the Save button to save your changes.

Configuring Backup and Recovery Settings with EM12c

Now we have a relatively simple Enterprise Manager installation built. We have the OMS and repository created, we've added a single host as a target to be monitored with EM12c, and we've discovered two databases and the listener on that host. So what's next?

Well, depending on the options you selected when you created the databases, you may or may not have the Fast Recovery Area (FRA) configured. Therefore, let's look first at how you would do that to help automate your backups. To configure the FRA, you need to start from the Databases home page, which is accessed by following the path Targets | Databases. This brings you to the Databases home page, as shown in Figure 14-2. Although it's not immediately obvious in this screenshot due to the low load in our test environment, we can see there are two databases—test1 and test2—and we can identify the load on each database separately (green in Enterprise Manager tends to indicate a healthy status and red indicates issues).

By clicking the database name in the green squares (granted, it's hard to see the green in a black-and-white book!), we can drill into the details of that particular database. If we click test1 (the database in the left of the two colored squares in Figure 14-2), we are prompted for a database username and password and are then taken to the home page for the test1 database, as shown in Figure 14-3.

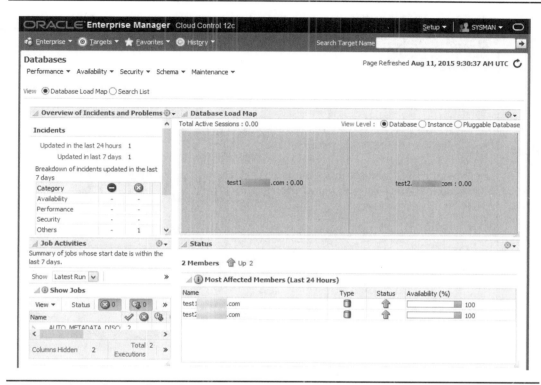

FIGURE 14-2.   *The Databases home page*

From this home page, we can follow the path Availability | Backup and Recovery | Recovery Settings to see the settings for the FRA and configure them as needed.

Once the FRA is set up, the next step is to configure ARCHIVELOG mode for the databases we want to take online backups of or to perform point-in-time recovery on. Given the database names in our example, you might think neither of those is necessary, but just for the sake of the discussion let's see how we would turn ARCHIVELOG mode on if we wanted.

Turning on ARCHIVELOG mode is done from the same Recovery Settings page as the FRA is set. In fact, the relevant section of the page appears immediately above that of the FRA setting. All we need to do is click the ARCHIVELOG Mode check box and then click the Apply button.

Once we click Apply, we see a confirmation message that the changes have been applied. We will be asked whether we want to restart the database now, so we need to click Yes for the changes to actually take place.

Before we can perform a point-in-time recovery of the database we just put into ARCHIVELOG mode, we need to make a whole database backup. To do that, there are a few more backup settings that we can customize. To access these, from the database home page

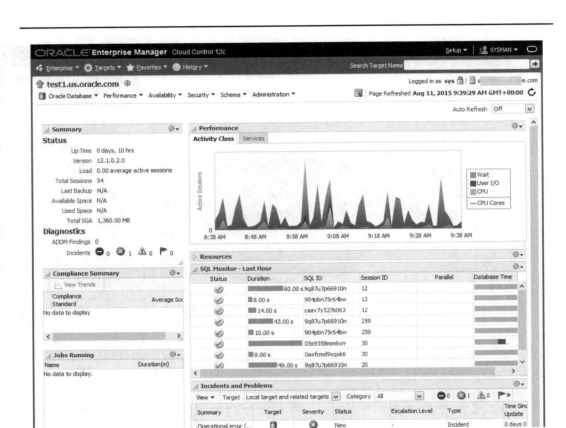

FIGURE 14-3. *The test1 database home page*

follow the path Availability | Backup and Recovery | Backup Settings. That brings us to the page shown in Figure 14-4.

On this page is a host of options we can set, most of which already have defaults:

- **Disk Settings**   Once these settings are configured, we can click the Test Disk Backup button to write some files to the disk backup location just to test our settings are okay.

    - **Parallelism**   The number of concurrent RMAN streams to write to the disk backup location.

    - **Disk Backup Location**   Defaults to the FRA, but we can override it here by specifying another directory or ASM diskgroup.

    - **Disk Backup Type**   We choose either a backup set, compressed backup set, or image copy.

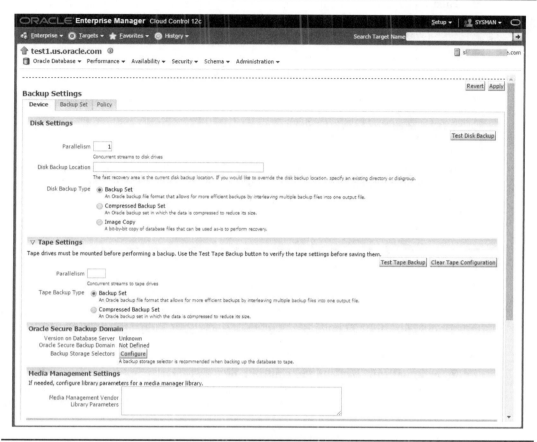

FIGURE 14-4. *The Backup Settings page*

■ **Tape Settings** Not too many people are still backing up directly to tape, but if you want to use tape drives to back up to, you can set that up here. Again, you can use the Test Tape Backup button to confirm your settings are okay.

  ■ **Parallelism** The number of concurrent RMAN streams to write to the tape drives.

  ■ **Tape Backup Type** Choose either a backup set or a compressed backup set (note that you cannot select an image copy if you are using tapes).

  ■ **Oracle Secure Backup (OSB) Domain** If you are using OSB, you can configure the OSB domain here.

  ■ **Media Management Settings** This is used if you are using a media manager library. Any parameters you would set for that library can be set here (these vary depending on the media manager library).

- **Host credentials** Though you can't see it in the screenshot shown in Figure 14-4, the host credentials we need to access the target database are set below the Tape Settings region.

Once we have set the parameters the way we want on this page, we can click the Backup Set tab to configure more settings, as required. Here are the settings we can specify:

- **Maximum Backup Piece (File) Size** The maximum size (in kilobytes, megabytes, or gigabytes) of each backup piece.
- **Compression Algorithm** This will be used for both disk and tape compressed backup sets.
  - **Algorithm Name** Depending on the current database settings and version, we can select different algorithm names. For example, in the setup in our example, we can see BASIC, LOW, MEDIUM, and HIGH as the algorithm names.
  - **Release** This will either show the DEFAULT or the current database version of the database we are backing up.
- **Tape Settings** Here, we can configure the number of copies of datafile backups and archivelog backups separately.
- **Host Credentials** The same as the Host Credentials region on the Device tab.

Finally, we can change still more backup settings on the Policy tab, which is probably the most important tab. This tab contains a number of settings, including the following:

- **Backup Policy**
  - **Automatically back up the control policy and server parameter file (SPFILE) with every backup and database structural change** We can't understand why this parameter isn't enabled by default to be honest. You should always set this by clicking the checkbox.
  - **Optimize the whole database backup by skipping unchanged files such as read-only and offline datafiles that have been backed up** You can select this option if you want to save space in the backup. We would normally recommend *not* using this unless you have space issues. The reason for that is if you set this option, when the time comes to perform a recovery, either you or the recovery process will need to hunt back through the backups you have taken to find the relevant files to restore here. Normally, recoveries are done in already stressful situations, such as when a database has crashed or otherwise needs recovery, and adding more stress to find these read-only and offline datafiles is just unnecessary.
  - **Enable block change tracking for faster incremental backups** Select this checkbox if you want to use block change tracking. In earlier releases, this put additional load on the database server, but now this is not so much of an issue.
- **Tablespaces Excluded From Whole Database Backup** If you want to exclude any tablespaces from a whole database backup, you can select them here.

- **Retention Policy** You can choose from the following:
  - Retain all backups. Do not delete any backups automatically.
  - Retain backups to meet a recovery window criterion in days.
  - Retain at least a specified number of full backups.
- **Archived Redo Log Retention Policy** Choose either None (the default) or to delete archived redo log files after they have been backed up a specified number of times.
- **Host Credentials** The same as the Host Credentials region on the Device tab.

Once we have made any changes we want on these different tabs, we just click the Apply button and are (finally!) ready to perform our backup!

Backing Up a Database with EM12c

To schedule a full backup in EM12c from a database home page, follow the path Availability | Backup and Recovery | Schedule Backup…. You have two options here: Schedule Oracle-Suggested Backup and Schedule Customized Backup. Let's look at each of these in more detail.

Schedule Oracle-Suggested Backup

This option uses the backup settings you have already set (or the defaults for ones you haven't set) to create an RMAN script to perform backups. It will back up the entire database, using a full backup first and then setting up incremental backups after that.

Let's walk through the interview process that occurs when you click this button. The first page, shown in Figure 14-5, asks you whether you are backing up to disk, tape, or both. In the current scenario, we don't have a tape drive to back up to, so we will choose to back up to disk.

On the next page, we see that a full database copy will be performed as the first backup, followed by daily incremental backups. The backups will be placed in the FRA because we have already set that up. We can also specify encryption here if we want to, but we're going to leave that unchecked.

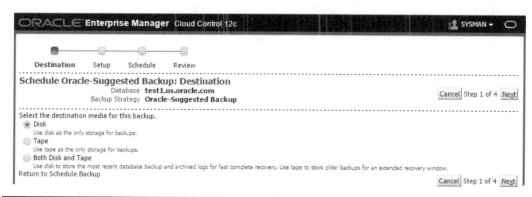

FIGURE 14-5. *Step 1 of Schedule Oracle-Suggested Backup*

The third page of the interview asks us to specify a time and date for the backup. We'll leave those at the defaults as well.

The final step of the interview, shown in Figure 14-6, provides a summary of the backup that will be scheduled, and also shows us the RMAN script that will be used to perform the backup.

Once you click the Submit Job button, a job is submitted to run the backup.

If you were to click the View Job button, depending on your timing, you might see a status that the job is either waiting or has succeeded. In the output, the wizard displays the different steps the job went through, along with timings for each step. You can also click the View Definition button to show the details of how the job runs.

Schedule Customized Backup

Now you've seen how to take a backup using the Oracle-suggested backup path, let's look at the Customized Backup path. This gives you a lot more flexibility about just what exactly you want to back up. You can still take a whole database backup using this option, but you can also back up individual tablespaces, datafiles, archived logs, or all the files in the FRA that have not been previously backed up. When you come back to the Schedule Backup screen, it will also tell you that you already have one or more backup jobs that are currently running or scheduled for this particular target—assuming you do this for the same database as the example used thus far, that is! To show you the additional flexibility you can get by choosing the Schedule Customized Backup option, let's walk through scheduling a whole database backup again, just like we did in the previous section. To do this, we start again from the database home page, follow the path Availability | Backup and

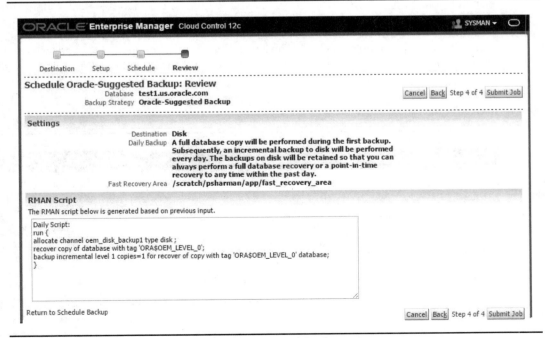

FIGURE 14-6. *Step 4 of Schedule Oracle-Suggested Backup*

Recovery | Schedule Backup…, and then click the Schedule Customized Backup button, as shown in Figure 14-7 (note that Whole Database has been chosen as the default for you).

Again, a simple interview process walks you through the different options you need to set. On the first page of the interview, you can set the following options:

- **Backup Type**

  - **Full Backup**   This is the default selection. We have also selected "Use as the base of an incremental backup strategy" to emulate the backup we took in the previous section.

  - **Incremental Backup**   This is the first option we have that is more customized than the Oracle-suggested backup. Obviously this would only be chosen if you have already taken a full backup and now just want to back up the changes since that backup.

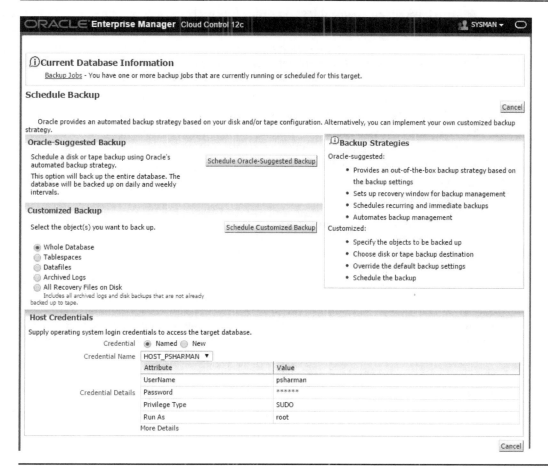

FIGURE 14-7.   *Starting the Schedule Customized Backup*

Notice the two options available to you here. The first refreshes the last backup copies on disk to the current time using the incremental backup. That saves you time when recovering because you don't need to first recover the full backup and then the incrementals. The second option allows you to take a cumulative backup, rather than just an incremental one (a cumulative backup includes all the changes since the last full or cumulative backup, whereas a simple incremental backup only backs up changes since the last incremental backup). Again, this will save you time when performing recoveries.

- **Backup Mode**
  - **Online Backup** This backup backs up the database while it is open and can only be done if the database is in ARCHIVELOG mode.
  - **Offline Backup** This backup requires the database to be shut down before the backup can take place.
- **Advanced**
  - **Also back up all archived logs on disk** This is always a good option to select because it ensures all files required for recovery are backed up at the same time.
  - **Delete all archived log files from disk after they are successfully backed up** Call us paranoid, but we just don't like this option. We would prefer to wait for two or three backups before deleting files from disk, so we leave this unchecked.
  - **Delete obsolete backups** This option deletes backups that are no longer needed to satisfy the retention policy you have set.
  - **Use proxy copy supported by media management software to perform a backup** You would only need to select this option if you are using some third-party media management software to back up the database.
- **Encryption** The options here are the same as the encryption options in the Oracle-suggested backup.

On the next page of the interview process, you are asked to select whether the backup will be sent to disk or tape. The default is disk, and the disk backup location is set to the FRA location.

On the next page of the interview process, you are asked to specify a job name (a default is chosen for you) and a schedule. The default is to schedule the backup job to occur immediately as a once-off operation. You can also specify One Time (Later) for a deferred backup or Repeating. If you select Repeating, you are given many more options:

- You can specify a frequency type (which defaults to By Minutes, which seems like a ridiculous default to us!). You can also choose By Hours, By Days, By Weeks, Weekly, Monthly, and Yearly.
- Depending on what you choose as a frequency type, the next option will vary:
  - Repeat every n minutes, hours, days, or weeks.
  - Days of Week if you specify Weekly.

- Days of Month if you specify Monthly.
- Alternatively, you can specify the month and day if you choose Yearly.
- You can specify a time zone that the backup will be taken in.
- You can specify a start date.
- You can specify a start time.
- You can specify how long to repeat the backup for (or select to repeat indefinitely).

In the example shown in Figure 14-8, we've chosen to do a weekly backup of the database to happen on Sunday at 12 A.M. U.S. Mountain Time to minimize impact on users of the database.

Finally, you are shown a review screen, such as that shown in Figure 14-9. One difference from the Oracle-Suggested Backup Review screen is that here you also have an Edit RMAN Script button, so if there are any changes you want to make, you can actually edit the RMAN script directly before submitting it.

After submitting the job, you will again be shown a screen saying the job was submitted successfully, and you can click the View Job button to drill in to see the job status.

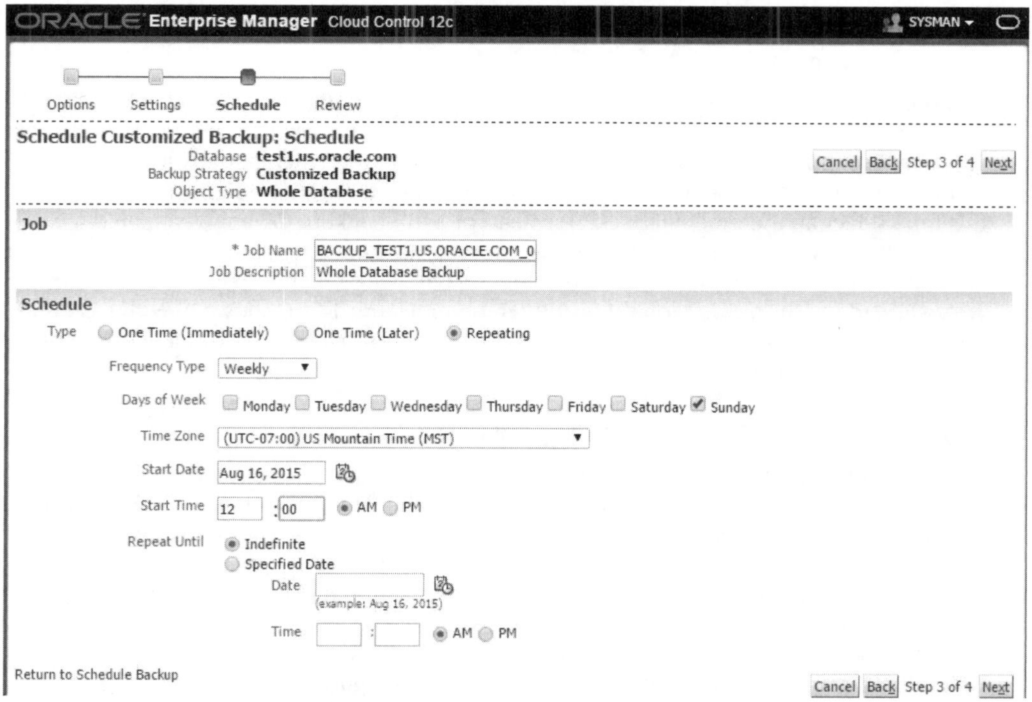

FIGURE 14-8. *Continuing to schedule the customized backup*

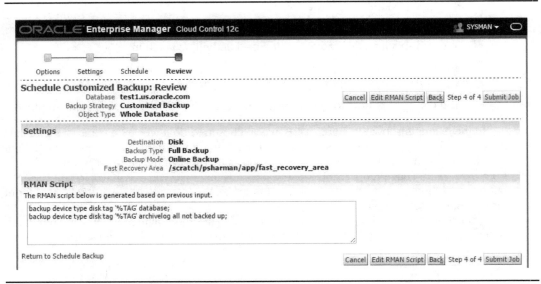

FIGURE 14-9. *Reviewing the Scheduled Customized Backup*

Incremental Backups
Of course, what we've just seen is a more flexible way of performing a full backup than using the Oracle-supplied backup path. However, what we've seen has also only done the full backup part. The Oracle-supplied backup path provides both full and incremental backups in one step. If you want to set up an incremental backup, you can go back through the steps we just performed, but this time select an incremental backup instead of a full backup. Given, we created a weekly backup. It's most likely that you would also want a daily incremental backup. The most important page in the wizard for doing that is the Schedule page (all the other pages are very similar to what we've already done, so we won't repeat them here). Figure 14-10 shows how this is done. You need to specify a frequency type of weekly and then choose each day of the week *except* the day the full backup is being done (remember, in our case that was done on Sunday).

Backing Up Multiple Databases at Once
While backing up individual databases is obviously useful to you as a DBA, using groups to back up multiple databases at once can be even more useful. Let's look at how that's done. First of all, you need to create a group. For example, you might create an administrative group of your test databases based on their lifecycle status—that they are test databases.

Now if we right-click the Test-Grp link, we can select Backup Configurations. A backup configuration contains the settings for database and file backups, and is a prerequisite before we can back up a group of databases. On the Backup Configuration page, we can click the Create button to start the configuration of a backup. When configuring a backup, we need to provide a name for the backup configuration (for example, Test Database Group Backup). Also, this page has a Storage tab, where we specify disk settings and tape settings.

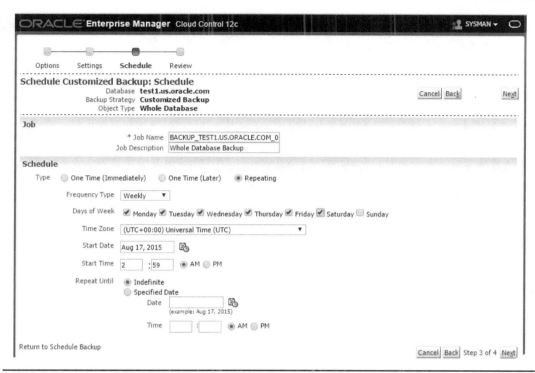

FIGURE 14-10. *Scheduling an incremental backup*

Also included is a Policy tab, where we can specify the maximum piece size, as well as the backup policy, retention, compression algorithm, and encryption. Finally, the Recovery Catalog tab is where we can specify whether to use the control file or recovery catalog.

We can save this backup configuration by clicking the Save button. We will see a confirmation window telling us that the backup configuration has been created. We are then returned to the Test-Grp definition page. From the main Group menu, we can select Schedule Backup, as shown in Figure 14-11, to start the Backup Wizard.

This time there are a few more steps to walk through. On the first page of the interview process, we are asked for the backup scope (we can select from Whole Database, All Recovery Files on Disk, or Archived Logs), and we are also asked if we want to back up all the databases in the group or just selected databases.

Clicking the Next button takes us to the Credentials page, where we are asked for both database credentials and host credentials. In this case, let's choose the option to create a new database credential using the SYS username and password that are common between the two databases. We can also specify a host credential that already exists as a named credential. The other option we'll select for both is to use preferred credentials.

Clicking Next skips the Files page, which is only relevant if we are using a media management system. Clicking Next will then take us to the Settings page. Here, we can choose to back up either

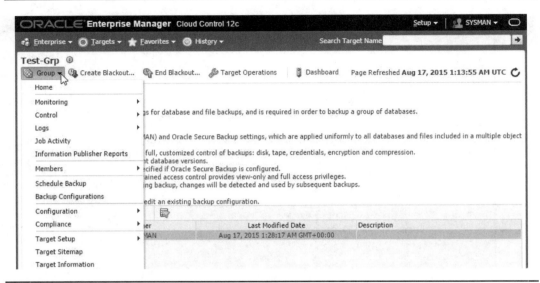

FIGURE 14-11. *Scheduling a backup for a group*

to disk (the default) or tape, and we can select the backup configuration to use. Remember, the backup configuration contains the location for both disk and tape backups, so specifying the backup configuration also selects the location for the destination media we have chosen here.

Clicking Next takes us to the Options page. These are the same options as you saw when backing up a single database, so we won't go into any details here. Let's leave the selections at the default values of Full, Online, and "Also back up all archived logs on disk that have not already been backed up." Clicking Next brings us to the Schedule page. Here, we can specify a name for the backup, along with a schedule. In this case, let's give the backup a name of BACKUP_TEST-GRP_Online and ask for it to be backed up at midnight on Saturdays. Clicking Next takes us to the Review page. Review the information on the page and then click Submit to submit the job.

After clicking the Submit button, we are returned to the Test-Grp page. Here, we can either click the BACKUP_TEST-GRP_Online link to view the backup procedure or just click the checkbox on the top right of the Information region to remove the message.

Managing Backups

Now you've seen how to schedule backups using EM12c, let's take a look at what you can do as far as managing the backups you've created is concerned. Let's start again from the test1 database home page. From here, you can follow the path Availability | Backup & Recovery | Manage Current Backups. This brings us to the Manage Current Backups page, shown in Figure 14-12.

FIGURE 14-12.   *The Manage Current Backups page*

Backup Reports

You can also view a list of all the backup jobs known to the database by going to the database home page and then following the path Availability | Backup & Recovery | Backup Reports. It will show you a list of backups, with the ability to narrow the search to jobs of a specific status, timeframe, or type, as well as to drill into the details of the backup by clicking either the backup name or status, as shown in Figure 14-13.

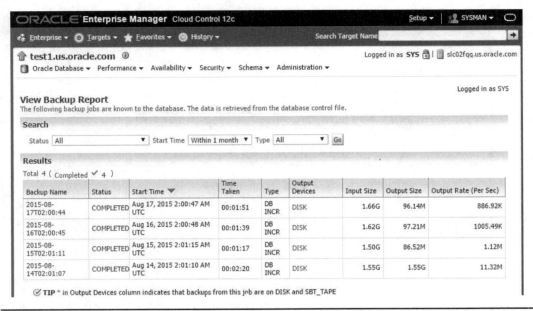

FIGURE 14-13. *The View Backup Report page*

When you drill into a particular job, you are shown some general information, such as the status, start time, time taken, input size, and output size, as well as the output log. There is a lot of output to look at, which is a good thing for backups just in case you need to troubleshoot a problem.

Using EM12*c* for Recovery

Wow, that's a lot of material on backups. You'll be pleased to know that recovery doesn't take anywhere near as much time to cover. That's largely because recovery is usually fairly straightforward—other than being a highly stressful situation to find yourself in—provided you have done all the work up front in setting up your backups.

So, what do you need to know about using EM12*c* for recovery? The first thing to understand is how to create restore points. Let's look at that in more detail.

Restore Points

A restore point is a name you give to a specific point in time. It can then be used during a recovery as the point to which you want to recover. To create a restore point for a database, from the database home page follow the path Availability | Backup & Recovery | Restore Points. That will bring you to the page shown in Figure 14-14.

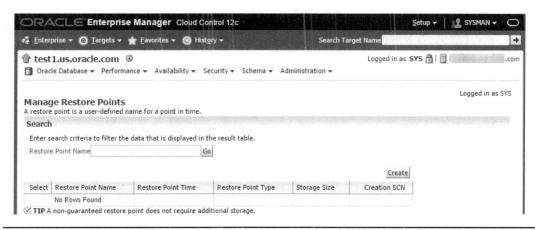

FIGURE 14-14.   *The Manage Restore Points page*

For this particular database, there are no restore points yet, so let's click the Create button to create one. That brings up the Create Restore Point page.

When creating a restore point, make sure you give it a meaningful name. Having a meaningful name makes it easier to find the restore point you want when there are lots of them.

You can also choose to create a guaranteed restore point. Guaranteed restore points ensure that a FLASHBACK DATABASE command can be used to restore the database to the restore point time. This whole process does have some prerequisites—namely, the database must have an FRA, it must be running in ARCHIVELOG mode, and it must have a value for the COMPATIBLE parameter of 10.2 or greater. Also, consider that if you are using Normal Restore Points as opposed to Guaranteed Restore Points that the Normal Restore Points can age out of the controlfile.

Clicking the OK button will bring up a screen asking you to confirm you want to create the restore point. If you click the Yes button, in a few seconds you will be returned to the Manage Restore Points page; you can see an informational message that the restore point has been created, and the restore point is listed in the table. As you can see in Figure 14-15, you now also have a button called Recover Whole Database To that allows you to recover the database to a restore point selected from the table, and you have a Delete button allowing you to delete a restore point that is no longer needed.

Performing Recovery

As mentioned before, performing a recovery is really a straightforward process in EM12c—*if* you've done the work up front in setting up the backups correctly. To start a recovery, follow the path Availability | Backup & Recovery | Perform Recovery…. That will bring you to the Perform Recovery page shown in Figure 14-16. Notice the very top part of the screen, Oracle Advised Recovery, which identifies failures for you and allows you to perform recoveries based on that. In

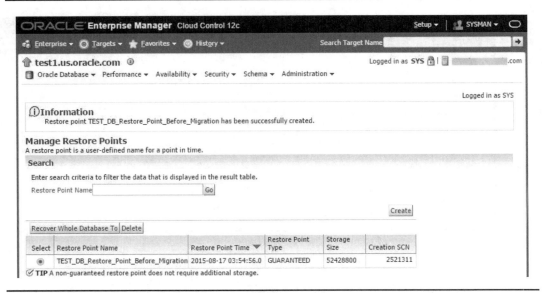

FIGURE 14-15. *The Manage Restore Points page showing a restore point*

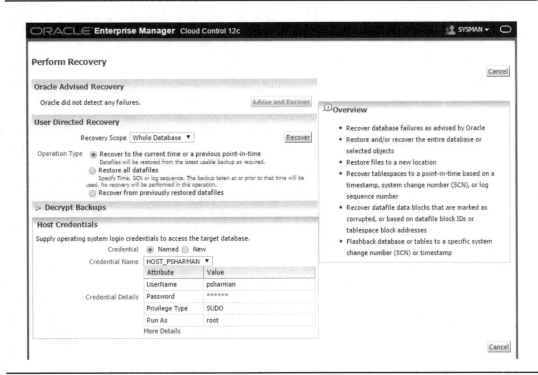

FIGURE 14-16. *The Perform Recovery page*

this case there is no failure detected automatically, so you need to look at the next section, User Directed Recovery. From here, you can specify the following:

- **The recovery scope**   The Recovery Scope drop-down list allows you to recover the whole database, specific datafiles or tablespaces, archived logs, tables, or transactions. For the example shown here, we'll perform a simple recovery of the whole database (which is the default).

- **Operation type**   You can choose to recover to the current time or a previous point in time, restore all datafiles from a previous backup (and perform no recovery after that), or recover from previously restored datafiles. Again, we've chosen the default in Figure 14-16, which is to recover to the current time or a previous point in time.

Notice that the host credentials have been picked up by default, as we already created a named credential to access this host at the operating system level. To start the recovery process, we just need to click the Recover button. This brings us to the first page of the recovery interview process. Several options will be available. For example, we can choose to recover to a prior point in time, to a particular date and time, restore point, SCN, or log sequence number.

If we click the magnifying glass to the right of that field, we can choose the restore point we want to use. Because there is only the one restore point we created earlier, we won't bother showing you that screen, so once the restore point is selected, we just need to click Next. On the next page of the interview, we are asked whether we want to use FLASHBACK DATABASE or a normal point-in-time recovery. FLASHBACK DATABASE is the default.

Clicking Next skips the Rename page, which is only needed for normal point-in-time recovery rather than using FLASHBACK DATABASE, so we move to the completely inappropriately named Schedule page (because there is no schedule we can specify here). All we can provide is a name and description for the job, not a schedule.

Clicking Next moves us to the Review page, shown in Figure 14-17, where we can review all the inputs we have provided. There's even an Edit RMAN Script button for making last-minute customizations if we want (note that if we select this option and make changes, we can't go back through the wizard interview process to make more changes).

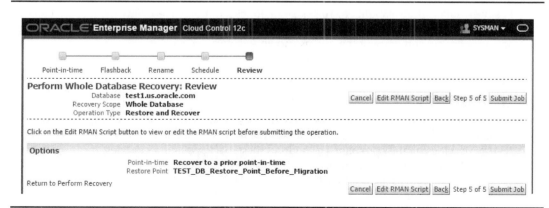

FIGURE 14-17.   *The point-in-time recovery process*

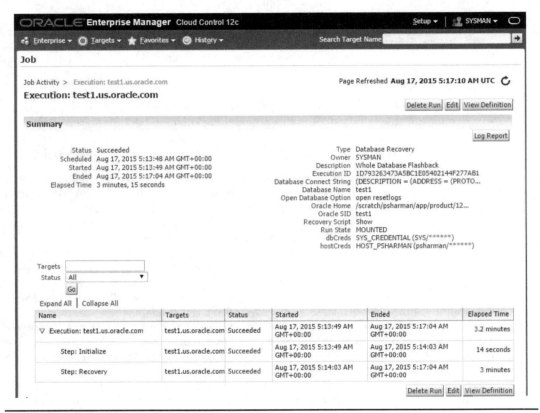

FIGURE 14-18. *Summary of a successful point-in-time recovery*

Clicking Submit Job submits a job for the recovery and presents a page indicating that the job has been successfully submitted. This page includes a button called View Job that we can click to watch the progress of the recovery. Eventually (depending on the size of the database), we should see a successful summary of the job, as shown in Figure 14-18.

And that's all there is to a successful recovery!

Summary

An Oracle database can contain a wealth of business-critical information, so it's important to be able to back up and recover that database easily, reliably, and in the least stressful way possible. While RMAN provides all the commands to perform these backups and recoveries, it can be incredibly helpful—both with less knowledgeable DBAs and to minimize stress for more experienced DBAs—to have a product such as EM12*c* to make backup and recovery as easy as possible.

PART
IV

RMAN in a Highly
Available Architecture

CHAPTER
15

RMAN Best
Practices

W e are often asked questions related to best practices when using RMAN. These are good questions because there is more to backing up a database than just backing up a database. We have spent many chapters talking about setting up RMAN and using it for backup, recovery, and other purposes. Now that we have covered the mechanics of RMAN, let's discuss best practices.

Best practices are the procedures and processes you follow that help ensure you are using RMAN in the most efficient and effective way. Best practices are guidelines and are not set in stone. Rather, these are general guidelines that are flexible, because each individual enterprise is different and has different requirements. Smaller environments have different requirements than larger ones. Therefore, the best practices you will use may vary from those that others will use.

With that in mind, we provide you with some guidelines in this chapter that might give you some ideas of some best practices you will want to consider. Here are the areas we cover:

■ Data protection
■ Service-level agreements
■ Standards and processes
■ Beyond backup and recovery
■ Best practices

However, before we dive into these subjects, let's take a detour and look at the whole backup and recovery picture from a little different perspective. We'll look at backup and recovery from the point of view of data protection.

Data Protection

We do a little bit of a disservice by trying to create a definition for something called backup and recovery, which is really a child process of something much bigger that we will call "data protection." *Data protection* recognizes that what is important for a database is the data within it. Without that data, there is no database to manage really.

In this section we'll discuss the following topics:

■ Enterprise architecture
■ Backup and recovery
■ High availability
■ Disaster recovery
■ Data governance
■ Monitoring and scheduling

Each of these disciplines (and probably more we didn't list) have many subdisciplines within them.

Enterprise Architecture

Why do we list "enterprise architecture" as the first discipline when it comes to data protection? Because it's the foundation of any successful data protection architecture. When you build your architecture thinking not only of the databases in your charge, but also about the other databases in the organization, you will craft solutions that are more scalable, easier to repeat, and easier to monitor.

Enterprise solutions, if done right, will reduce risk and improve the overall success of whatever it is you are trying to do. They offer repeatable solutions to common problems, and there is a lot about backup and recovery of a database, for example, that begs for a single, repeatable, and simple process.

Enterprise solutions require more discipline when you are designing them. They require you to coordinate with more people and collect more information. Enterprise solutions almost always take more work up front, and generally cost more up front. However, if they are built correctly, maintained correctly, and if the appropriate monitoring is put in place in the beginning, the cost of a system engineered with the enterprise in mind can be significantly less.

Finally, enterprise solutions also generally take a bit more software and can offer a bit more complexity with respect to the initial setup and configuration. Sometimes, efforts even need to be made to stabilize these infrastructures. These are normal kinds of growing pains when you are trying to create a truly enterprise architecture. All of these up-front challenges, when faced and met, will be completely offset by the long-term benefits of a stable enterprise management and monitoring platform, especially when it comes to the question of data protection.

We have largely addressed the central hub of Oracle's enterprise management infrastructure in this book when we discussed Oracle Cloud Control. When configuring a complete data protection solution, you should seriously consider using Oracle Cloud Control as your enterprise management hub.

Backup and Recovery

Of course, it's critically important to back up and then recover your Oracle databases. When you are crafting your data protection architecture and strategies, certainly backup and recovery of your databases is important.

We almost always use the phrase "backup and recovery," putting the term *backup* first. But are these terms in the right order? Certainly, chronologically they are in the right order: you have to back up a database generally before you can recover it. Also, when you are just learning how to be a DBA, the backup part is the logical beginning for that education you require. You can't, after all, restore a database unless you have a backup from which you can source that restore exercise.

However, this name betrays what should be the true order of operations that you should be following when it comes to backup and recovery impacting our thinking process when we think about database backups.

For example, how many times have you first asked yourself about how you were going to back up a database? Did it occur to you that maybe you needed to understand how you were going to restore that database first? Although it might seem like the answer to the first question depends on the answer to the second question, we would disagree. We would say that the answer to the second question is a dependency to even beginning to figure out the answer to the first question.

We are often asked to determine a DBA's skill set. One of the metrics used to determine the experience level of a DBA is to explore their thinking about recovery and backup. For example, the junior DBA will be struggling to understand backup and recovery. You can see these struggles as you question them about the mechanical rudiments of how to back up a database. Often they will struggle more on how to recover those backups. The bottom line is that the junior DBA will need help in most recovery situations. They will need the assistance of a senior DBA or Oracle Support. You would never depend on someone at this position to architect any kind of recovery solution. They simply are not ready.

As the DBA progresses in experience, they start to think about and experience various recovery situations and they learn more complex recovery techniques. At some point they have progressed past the junior level into some middle-of-the-road position. You can see this in interviews as they respond to questions about database failures with confidence, displaying a set of skills that say, "I know how to deal with this issue!"

The principal difference between the middle-of-the-road DBA and the truly senior DBA, at this point, is in how they respond to the recovery questions. The middle-of-the-road DBA usually tells me what they would do given a particular situation. They still lack experience, but they have the learning. The truly senior DBA will tell me about what they did in that (or a similar) situation. They not only have developed the skill set, but they have deployed it in real life with success.

We think it's important to answer the question "How do we back up databases?" You first need to understand the question "How do these databases need to be restored?" It's important to understand that the restore question isn't just about the mechanics of the restore; it's also about understandings the stakeholders with respect to their expectations and needs. It's about providing scalable services for the enterprise and maintaining control while also providing flexibility. In the end, it's about maturity.

So, that is the reason we've suggested that we should be saying "recovery and backup." One truly informs the other. Without exploring the first, we cannot properly implement the latter. Therefore, in the rest of this chapter, we will address these questions—which lead to an answer that we call "the enterprise recovery and backup solution."

Keep in mind that an overall solution is not going to just address backup and recovery with RMAN. In many cases, based on what you will learn, your solution may involve requirements for high availability (HA) and disaster recovery (DR). You need to keep the entire landscape of the recovery solution in your mind when you proceed to architect a solution and not get focused on just the backup and recovery aspect of it. Yes, this is a book on RMAN, but the overall architecture is more than just RMAN, of course!

Something else to consider as we start discussing architecture and infrastructure: As we describe some of the things we recommend you do, you might feel like this is an awful lot of work. You might wonder why it is that some of the details suggested, such as using SLAs, are so important. You might think that things are under control; there have been no outages, so why should you care?

There are a number of reasons you should care, of course. We've already mentioned several of them, and we'll mention several others as this chapter continues. However, there is one reason that we want to point out to you in particular. It is something that can impact even the best and seemingly most stable of infrastructures: the problem of scale. It may be that you crafted the most magnificent and well-documented backup and recovery infrastructure that has ever existed. You have SLAs, you're meeting requirements, you constantly test, and the results are flawless.

However, you might have also noticed that lately your backups are taking just a little longer. Maybe during your recovery testing the database that took an hour to restore now takes two hours. These are subtle indications that your infrastructure is starting to suffer from scaling problems. We've seen this happen a number of times. We've seen the subtle signs that no one else really noticed because things were running so well that they really didn't look at areas such as backup times at all. They didn't notice the quiet trends that were there and growing.

So, the bottom line is that every infrastructure needs to be reviewed from time to time to see not only the obvious problems you know about, but also the nasty problems that are just waiting to show up some day.

What are the things to consider when looking at the issue of backup and recovery when you are planning your architecture? You need to consider the following:

- Current and renegotiated backup and recovery SLAs (formal or informal)
- Current sizes of existing databases
- Current backup times of these databases
- Anticipated growth of existing databases
- Anticipated growth of backup times for existing databases
- New databases that will be created
- Initial sizes and anticipated growth of new databases
- Creation, removal, and refreshing of databases during various cycles such as development, testing, and QA
- Retention criteria of both the databases and the database backups

These are a few of the numerous considerations you need to make when looking at your solutions for backup and recovery.

High Availability

Along with the question of backup and recovery, there are still many other questions that need to be asked. The next logical area that needs to be addressed is high availability (HA). The primary purpose of HA is to abstract the user from the system as a whole and prevent them from suffering from any single point of failure within that system.

In the Oracle world, HA comes in many forms:

- Oracle Clusterware
- Oracle Real Application Clusters (RAC)
- Various network and hardware redundancies

HA adds additional complexities into the overall database infrastructure, and sometimes these complexities can be overlooked and lead to unexpected failures. This can be demonstrated by an experience that we had with a customer once. They thought that they had architected a very robust HA configuration (We're changing some details to protect the identity of the customer, but the general information is correct). The customer was running a RAC cluster with several instances. They had designed what they thought was a very robust HA architecture with two separate networks supporting user connections and two additional networks supporting the cluster interconnect. The disks were running ASM with triple mirroring, offering a great deal of redundancy.

However, one day, everything just stopped. Both nodes fenced and then shut down, and when they restarted, the instances would not come up. After a great deal of investigation, the truth emerged. When the disk array was installed, everyone believed that it was configured with two different disk controller cards. They believed that the array provided them with multipathing as well as redundancy should one of those cards fail.

Upon trying to recover the disk array, it was found that there was only one card active on the disk array. The second card was sitting in the array, ready to go, but it had never been connected or activated. As we looked at the Fibre Channel switch, we found that there was even a cable that had been run to the array, but it had apparently just never been connected. The moral of the story is that HA is complex, and it's so easy to just miss one little thing. We only tell this story as a cautionary tale. Architecting a robust HA solution is an incredible part of providing for data protection. It just requires a great deal of careful planning and designing, and a good peer review isn't a bad idea either.

There is another side of HA to be aware of, one that might not seem immediately apparent. Sometimes you can have a system that is so highly redundant that when something does fail, nobody notices. The thing just keeps on humming, running along—and nobody notices that a disk failed or that a network cable has become disconnected. If you are not monitoring your system and its components for failure, then you might just miss those failures.

This can result in a system that appears to be stable but in fact is becoming more and more unstable over time. This highlights the importance of monitoring as a part of an overall enterprise data protection strategy. HA strategies add a number of additional working pieces. In a way, it reminds me of when I was growing up in Oklahoma, where we used to say that the difference between a two-wheel drive and a four-wheel drive was that the four-wheel drive could get you stuck much further away from civilization. As such, a four-wheel drive can give you a bit of a sense of invulnerability. An HA architecture can have somewhat of the same impact.

Finally, adding any kind of HA infrastructure will increase the overall capital and operational costs of your infrastructure. This is something to keep in mind. You should be able to identify these costs to the stakeholders, ensuring that they understand the overall costs of their requirements. We often find that stakeholders will ask for uptimes of five 9's (99.999), but when presented with the costs of meeting such an objective, they quickly reduce those requirements to something that their budget can afford.

Disaster Recovery

Sometimes people confuse HA with disaster recovery (DR). HA is designed to hide various failures from the user in such a way that the user never sees the failure. However, there are situations that HA cannot really address very well, such as the fallout from a tornado, tsunami, or earthquake. It is for these kinds of disasters that we architect DR plans as a part of our overall data protection plan.

If there are additional costs required for HA solutions, there are even greater costs associated with providing DR services. Often this cost is taken for granted by stakeholders who ask for things, not appreciating the investment required. It is important in the overall planning process for a data protection scheme that we equate the requirements given to us by stakeholders into dollars so that they can better understand the costs of what they are requiring.

Data Governance and Security

You may think you have bought the wrong book when we mention data governance and security (in fact, one could argue that these should be treated as separate topics—but for the purposes of this chapter we can safely combine them). What do these topics have to do with backup and recovery or even HA or DR? It turns out that the answer is, quite a lot. Data governance and security cover a lot of ground, but essentially together they have to do with the integrity, ownership, and security of data within your database. How is it that this kind of responsibility intersects with backup and recovery architecture?

First, imagine the potential impacts of the loss of a backup to some competitor with little integrity. Or, perhaps, consider the relationships in the data in disparate databases that are all used by a single application. Although an Oracle database can maintain internal relational integrity within that database, often there are other databases with related data that an application will access at the same time. There is no built-in constraint mechanism to ensure the integrity of those external relationships.

Imagine that there is an application that depends on databases ABC, DEF, and XYZ. Imagine that the ABC database fails, while DEF and XYZ remain active. In this case, your backup and recovery, HA, and DR strategies need to consider these relationships, especially when it comes to recovery of the ABC database. For example, if you cannot perform a recovery to the point of failure (perhaps the online redo logs were lost), then what is the relational impact on the surviving databases? It is best to plan for such problems before they happen—and not after. Believe us, we've been there.

So, data protection and data governance are really synonymous. One of the tasks within data governance is to assign ownership to the data within the database. These owners (sometimes called governors) are responsible for all aspects of the data assigned to them, including access control. Protection of the data exceeds protection of the data within the active database. The protection of the data in the backup images, the disaster recovery databases, and any other places that the data might be stored needs to be considered when you are developing your enterprise data backup and recovery architecture and its accompanying standards and requirements.

From the security point of view, at the end of the day almost anything related to data security really is a dependency of proper data governance. In this respect, the owner of the data is responsible for all aspects of that data, including who has access to it and what kind of access. They also control how the data is used and how it is shared, and they are responsible for the classification of the sensitivity of the data. All of these elements have direct impacts on the overall data recovery solution you will need to deploy for your databases.

Notice that we have significantly increased the scope of the things you need to consider when developing enterprise backup strategies. Clearly, we are talking about more than just encrypting data as it's moved to backup media. It's about controlling who has access to and can restore backups. It's about controlling where backups can be restored to, as well as what requirements revolve around restoring backups to various destinations (requirements such as redaction or specific needs for data subsetting, for example).

All too frequently these architectural issues are almost handled in a void—each defined on the fly as the needs arise, with the wheel being reinvented numerous times. This does not happen, hopefully, when we think about backup and recovery in terms of an overall enterprise data protection environment. This approach is a huge mistake and creates huge risks that need to be avoided.

Monitoring and Scheduling

Perhaps the most overlooked aspect of the development of an overall enterprise backup and recovery architecture is monitoring and scheduling. Often the solutions chosen are not truly enterprise solutions, and these solutions do not scale well.

For example, many places will use shell scripts to execute backups. These shell scripts are sometimes stored locally on each individual server, or perhaps they are stored on a common NFS mount. Each of these solutions provides significant change management issues. The problem becomes even more complex when you try to manage different versions of the backup script, for whatever reason. In large enterprise environments, the management of large numbers of backup scripts across your infrastructure can be complex and risky.

Then there is scheduling of these shell scripts. Often we find that customers will use a local scheduling utility, such as CRON, to schedule these backups. One of the shortcomings of this solution becomes apparent if a server itself goes down and CRON is not able to start the backups. We've seen cases where databases had been created and the required CRON jobs to back up those databases did not get created. This can certainly cause all sorts of issues if these missing backups are allowed to continue unchecked.

This leads us to the topic of monitoring and reporting on backups. It is important to have ways of crosschecking the databases in your environment and their current backup status. It's important to know when backups occurred and whether they were successful or failed. It's also important to have crosschecks of all the databases in your environment and whether they have ever been backed up.

All of these issues need to be considered when creating your overall data protection solution. You can have all the tools in place, but if they don't work and you don't know they are not working, then all of your work was just wasted. With this in mind, let's move on to a discussion of just how we create a professional data protection solution.

Best Practices

Now we return to the subject at hand: best practices. In this section we discuss the following topics, suggesting some best practices you will want to consider employing:

- Service-level agreements
- Standards and processes

Service-Level Agreements

Service-level agreements (SLAs) are negotiated between people providing services (in this case, you the DBA) and those who are utilizing the services. An SLA does not define how you are providing the service, but it does define the level of service you are providing. For example, an SLA might define that you are providing support services between 8 A.M. and 5 P.M., Monday through Friday.

Some places use SLAs, some don't. We prefer SLAs because they tend to clarify expectations. They eliminate confusion and, trust us, when the chips (or the database) are down, there is already enough confusion to deal with. SLAs do not need to be complex, and it's much easier to deal with them when you have standardized your services.

Two primary parameters should be defined in an SLA. These are the recovery point objective and the recovery time objective for the databases covered by the SLA. The recovery point objective defines the amount of data loss that is allowable in the event that the database fails.

The recovery time objective indicates how long a database outage can exist. This defines the tolerance for downtime that the database can have. Together, these two parameters define the decisions made with respect to the services that will be required.

In order to standardize services, we create what is commonly called a "services menu." This menu defines the services you commonly offer to your user community. It can also define the costs of those services. The defined recovery time and recovery point objectives of an SLA will feed into the services that are selected from the services menu.

Additionally, we like to negotiate what is called a "technology menu," which defines the technologies the entire community agrees are going to be used on a regular basis. Together, these two tools make the clear definition of an SLA much easier to complete. Let's look at the services menu and the technology menu in a bit more detail.

A Services Menu

Oftentimes we ask customers open-ended questions such as, "How do you want to back up your database?" or "Do you need disaster recovery services?" These are dangerous and expensive questions. In even a moderately sized enterprise, open-ended questions like these can create a snarl of different backup and recovery requirements. Perhaps the question is one of availability.

Ask a user what kind of availability they require and they will usually answer, "We need it up all the time," or they will try to be accommodating and say they only need it from 9 to 5, when in fact they really have developers on the system at all hours of the night. We've had many times when the latter happened, only to find out when we took the database down at 6 P.M. for maintenance that we knocked 100 developers off the system.

A services menu is often a much better solution. A services menu provides a list of limited service offerings for stakeholders to choose from. It is essentially telling the stakeholders, "These are the services we can offer you, and (optionally) this is what it will cost you." A services menu may contain two or three options, or it might contain several options. It may be a fixed set of options or it might be à la carte. Here is an example of a menu for data protection services:

Service Level	Services Offered	Retention	Guaranteed RTO/RPO	Cost
Bronze	Weekly cold backup.	Four weeks.	One business day/one week.	Free.
Silver	Weekly hot backup. Daily archive log backup.	Four weeks.	One business day/48 hours.	Free.
Gold	Daily incremental hot backup. Archivelog backups every four hours.	Eight weeks.	One business day/8 hours.	$50/per month, billed to your cost center.
Platinum	Daily incremental hot backup. Archive log backups every four hours. Logging to DBLRA.	Eight weeks.	One hour per 200GB/1 min.	$500/per month, billed to your cost center.

Continued

Service Level	Services Offered	Retention	Guaranteed RTO/RPO	Cost
Level one: highest priority service	Daily incremental hot backup. Logging to DBLRA Archive log backups based on data change volume. Archivelog backups to two different locations (one local and one NFS). HA/DR services listed in "Optional Services" section. (Manual DR switchover.)	Up to one year Tier-1 retention.	Near-zero outage in non-DR cases.HA with transactional integrity if using Oracle Database 12c. Priority DR switchover with estimated five-minute outage.	
Optional Services				
Additional archive log destination (NFS)				$20/per month, billed to your cost center.
Increased backup retention	Add additional months' retention.	In units of four weeks.		$50/per month per four-week unit; billed to your cost center.
Increased availability	Add RAC cluster node.		HA includes transactional integrity with Oracle Database 12c.	$20,000 per node, up to four nodes. Annual charge, billed to your cost center once a year.
Disaster recovery services	One DR database, manual switchover.		Switch over all services: 30 minutes.Possible data loss: 30 minutes.	$25,000/per month up to 1TB and 5GB change per day. Add $X per additional 100GB and $X for each 1GB change per day. Billed to your cost center monthly.

Service Level	Services Offered	Retention	Guaranteed RTO/RPO	Cost
Backup Tier-2 and Tier-3 services	Copy backups from Tier-1 to Tier-2 and Tier-3 on an automated basis. Maintain retention of backups on Tier-1 and Tier-2. Purchase of Tier-2 without Tier-3 allowed. Purchase of Tier-3 requires purchase of Tier-2.	Tier-2: One year. Copy of backup from Tier-1 to Tier-2 is done automatically after database backup. Tier-1 to Tier-2 backup is de-prioritized. Tier 3: Five years.	Tier-1 to Tier-2 backup rate is xMB/sec. Tier-2 to Tier-3 backup rate is xMB/s. Restores from Tier-2 and Tier-3 are provided on a reduced priority Restore SLA for Tier-2 is two days per xTB. Restore SLA for Tier-3 is three days per xTB. All Tier-2 and Tier-3 SLA guarantees are deprioritized for any Tier-1 restores without management approval. All Tier-2 and Tier-3 restores to non production hardware only. This hardware must be purchased or already in place. Oracle database software must be installed. Tier-2 and Tier-3 services will not be provided if these environments are not available.	Initial configuration for Tier-2 storage: Fixed: $2000.00 (includes configuration of one environment for restores) Per MB: $X. Initial configuration for Tier-3 storage (Tier-2 storage is a prerequisite to purchase of Tier-3 storage): Fixed: $500.00 (includes configuration of one environment for restores) Per MB: $X. Note: This is only tiered storage for backups. Please see the DBA services menu for provisions for database-tiered storage and related costs.
Custom retention	Custom retention available at all tiers for an extra cost. There is a fixed annual cost and a monthly storage cost.	Unlimited at all tiers.	SLAs remain the same.	Fixed annual costs: Tier-1: $X Tier-2: $X Tier-3: $X Monthly storage costs: Tier-1: $X/MB Tier-2: $X/MB Tier-3: $X/MB

Notice that this menu provides both standardization and flexibility for the customer and the enterprise. The flexibility comes at a price that reflects the additional costs and effort required to customize those services. Note that just because we provide some customized services does not mean that significantly impacts the enterprise infrastructure we want to create. Indeed, whatever we do in the menu, we need to ensure it is easy to implement and standardize within the new infrastructure, processes, and tools we will be using. If you are going to include a service that is not easy to standardize, think twice about it and then make sure you charge sufficiently for it, reflecting the complexity it's adding to the organization.

You might look at the menu and wonder about the costing model that's demonstrated. In many cases we have added both fixed costs (well, annually recurring) and monthly recurring costs. It's often important to consider that when you sell services, you are not just selling the current hardware you have on hand. You also need to be costing your services out in such a way that you can continue to buy new hardware to support future needs, and don't forget the hardware refreshes, too. Someone needs to pay for those. Finally, don't forget that there is a cost in the initial configuration that needs to be absorbed.

A Technology Menu

You might have noticed that in the services menu we didn't mention anything about how or where we were going to provide the services. We have abstracted the mechanisms from the stakeholders. This simplifies the decision-making processes. They simply decide what services they want and how much they can pay. Sometimes it's going to be a balancing act between what they think they need and what they can pay for; however, as far as hardware, infrastructure, and such go, they really don't need to play in that space.

You and others in the IT organization do need to play in that space, however. Given that many enterprises often employ many people, and those many people have many different ideas of how to perform a task, there can be lots of confusion and even arguments over the technologies that get used. You would be amazed at how much time can be wasted just trying to decide if we are going to use shell scripts, OEM, Java, Python, or whatever for some basic project with simple deliverables. Enter the technology menu.

The technology menu clearly identifies the following for the enterprise:

- Emerging technologies
- Supported technologies
- Desupported technologies

The technology menu provides a quick list of how we do things. Let's look at each of the different sections of this list and what they mean and how technologies are allocated to these sections.

Emerging Technologies   The emerging technologies section lists new technologies that we are currently investigating but are not approved for common use. Usually these are bleeding-edge technologies that offer significant advantages over currently supported technologies. Not all technologies on the list are bleeding edge, though. New versions of the Oracle Database software, including even the security-related updates, might well appear on this part of the list for a while. Once they are tested and approved, they would be moved on to the supported technologies section.

The following rules typically exist for an emerging technology on the list:

- It goes through a process to be added to the list.
- A process exists for projects to be approved to use the technology.
- Once approved, a project may use the technology.
- A process exists to move the technology to the supported technology list.

Supported Technologies   Supported technologies are those technologies in the enterprise that have been tested and approved for use. They have standards written for them, and they have processes and procedures written around how they are used. They are stable and commonly in use. Each item is listed with specific supported versions so that the enterprise has a consistent set of software running.

With respect to data protection technologies such as the Oracle Database itself, Cloud Control, RMAN, and Data Guard, all should be listed as supported technologies. Supported technologies feed into establishing standards for the enterprise. Standards are important, especially when it comes to data protection. We will cover standards later in this chapter.

Desupported Technologies   As technologies age, they become obsolete. Versions change, vendors no longer support products, and so on. However, it is often not possible to just pull the plug on these kinds of products. Many times there are vendor dependencies on products. For example, a particular application vendor might not yet have certified on a supported version of the Oracle Database. We can't just upgrade these databases on a whim, yet we don't want new projects to start using these desupported versions of the database software either.

In most cases, these technologies will have been on the supported list. When the technology menu is created, processes are created that regularly review the supported technologies list and move any technologies that are no longer going to be supported for new projects, but still exist in the enterprise, to the desupported technologies part of the list. Once the software is permanently removed from the environment, it should be removed from the list completely.

Standards and Processes

Standards and processes are ways of defining what best practices you are following and how you will follow them. The technology menu and the services menu are both standards. How these standards are implemented (such as how you actually perform the backup of the database) is a process.

With respect to backup and recovery, there are a number of standards and processes you will want to define. These might include the following:

- The backup standards and process you will use. For example, you might decide that your standard is to use incremental backups with one full and seven incremental backups. You might also determine to perform monthly archival backups.
- Your database retention standard and the process to manage that standard you will use. For example, you might decide that your retention policy will provide the ability to do point-in-time restores for 30 days.
- Backup media management/tiering standards and processes you will use. For example, you might have a 90-day backup retention policy. You may want to keep the first 30 days on local disk storage, and you might choose to keep the remaining 60 days on cheaper

tape storage. Your policy would define how you will move these backups between these two backup tiers.

- The database restore standards and processes you will use.

- How you will schedule backups. For example, you might choose to use Oracle Cloud Control to schedule your database backups (which we strongly suggest).

Now that we've talked about standards and processes, let's talk about best practices.

RMAN Best Practices

So, we have talked SLAs, standards, and processes; now let's talk about best practices with respect to RMAN. First, it's difficult to define best practices that apply in all cases. Therefore, the best practices we discuss here are more guidelines to help get you started in defining the best practices that will apply in your situation.

That being said, here is a list of recommend RMAN best practices:

- Determine the available I/O throughput for the devices to which you will be backing up. Oracle's Orion I/O testing tool can be used for this purpose. The results of this testing will provide you with metrics required to determine exactly how fast your database can be backed up and how fast it can be restored. This testing can also determine if there are bottlenecks in your I/O subsystem that need to be addressed. Know the speeds and feeds of your entire architecture. This really is rule number one.

- Remember that the requirements of the business for recovery (with respect to both time to recover and data loss) drive the backup and recovery solution.

- Automate your database creation processes to ensure that backups are always scheduled when a database is created.

- Maintain consistency as much as possible in your database backup, recovery, and RMAN-related configurations.

- When possible, run your database in ARCHIVELOG mode and use online backups. Although it might be tempting to run development and other databases in NOARCHIVELOG mode, if at all possible, you should run all your databases in the same logging mode.

- For best performance, define an Oracle Fast Recovery Area on the local disk and back up to that set of disks first. If you wish to use less expensive or slower storage, use that as Tier-2 storage.

- Use RMAN's stored configuration capabilities. Standardize these configurations and audit them on a regular basis.

- Define your RMAN retention policies.

- Be careful not to define backup retention policies in more than one place. For example, if you back up your database to an SBT tape device, RMAN should maintain the retention alone—do not allow the tape software to also control retention of the backup media.

- To ensure optimal performance of the database and database backups, never back up to disks that contain database data.

- Carefully parallelize backups, without over consuming CPU or I/O resources.

■ Never allow RMAN to lose track of the location of your backup sets. Ensure that RMAN is always used to move backups between various backup media tiers. Also ensure that if you back up to tape that you use the RMAN MML layer, rather than tape vendor backup software that does not update the database control file or the RMAN recovery catalog.

■ Define and use a standardized set of RMAN configuration settings.

■ Use the RMAN recovery catalog. Use the virtual private catalog to separate the different backup and recovery environments (production, test, and development). This will make duplication of databases easier in your environment.

■ Keep track of all the databases you have in your environment and crosscheck that list against the RMAN recovery catalog to ensure that all the databases in your environment are actually being backed up. Oracle Cloud Control–related views can provide the source of your database configuration information.

■ If backup space availability is of greater concern than restore times, or if your backup strategy includes backups to tape, then use incremental backups. Ensure you enable block change tracking.

■ If restore times are superior to space availability, use incrementally updated backups.

■ Practice database restores from your production backups often.

■ If you are using Active Data Guard, you should offload your backups to the Active Data Guard database.

■ We strongly recommend that you back up to disks that are managed by ASM. Provision the inner sectors of the disk for backups. The outer sectors of the disk are faster and should be reserved for data. The inner sectors are slower and should be reserved for backups.

■ When backing up a database with many files of different sizes, use the **section size** parameter to further parallelize backups.

■ Encrypt your backups.

■ If you are backing up tablespaces where data needs to be encrypted, use TDE tablespace encryption rather than TDE column–level compression to eliminate double encryption in the resulting backups.

■ Remember, sometimes simpler is better. Complex architectures can complicate performance tuning.

Of course, no list is really complete. However, we feel this list gives you a good start and provides you with some things to think about.

Summary

In this chapter we tried to provide you with some nontechnical guidelines and best practices to follow with respect to RMAN. As you can see from the contents of this chapter, and from many of the other chapters in this book, there is a great deal more to database backup and recovery than just backing the database up or recovering it!

CHAPTER
16

Surviving User
Errors: Flashback
Technologies

S ometimes, don't you wish you could just take some mistake you made, roll back time, and get a do-over? Back in the day, DBAs, developers, and many users found themselves wishing for a time machine when they made terrible mistakes. Oracle answered the need for a time machine (of sorts) with the advent of the database flashback technologies. With Flashback Database features, a whole host of mistakes can be corrected.

Up until this point, this book has been focused on media recovery. Media recovery with RMAN provides critical safeguards against all kinds of unforeseeable problems—block corruption, hardware failure, even complete database loss. In this chapter, though, we want to address the Oracle Flashback Database features available in RMAN and how they can be used to correct user errors.

User errors can be roughly defined as errors caused by a human mistake (rather than a software or hardware malfunction), such as a table updated with wrong values, a table dropped, or a table truncated. Such errors are far more common than hardware failures (although, let's face it, human errors get *called* hardware errors all the time). In general, user errors are classified as logical errors—the error is logical, within the data itself, and a correction that is done using media recovery options will typically be very expensive.

In Oracle Database 12c, RMAN can assist you in the implementation of some Flashback Database operations. Other operations need to be done from the command line (which is, of course, supported by RMAN) or Oracle Enterprise Manager. In this chapter, we discuss Flashback Database in the Oracle Database. We look at the features supported by RMAN and address other Flashback Database features not supported by RMAN.

Prepared for the Inevitable: Flashback Technology

When it comes to logical errors, media recovery should not be our first line of attack. It frequently is the first line of attack, but this leads to massive outages. Typically, user error is not something we can recover from, because the action is not interpreted as an error by the database. The command **delete * from scott.emp** is not an error; it's a perfectly legitimate DML statement that is duly recorded in the redo stream. Therefore, if you restore the datafile and then perform recovery, all you will do is, well, **delete * from scott.emp** again.

Point-in-time recovery can be a solution, but such a restore can be complex, time consuming, and potentially have impacts on many users. Additionally, you have to restore the entire database, which means that a lot of other work will be lost, requiring those transactions to be reprocessed in some way.

Tablespace point-in-time recovery (TSPITR) offers a toned-down version of media recovery for user errors, but it still requires a full outage on the tablespace, has huge space demands for a temporary clone instance, and has object-level limitations (think advanced queuing tables). This can also be a time-consuming solution.

Before Flashback features were introduced in Oracle, a partial database restore could be quite time consuming and complex. First, you had to do a partial database restore to a secondary, and temporary, database. Then you used Oracle Data Pump to extract only the specific objects you wanted to restore. This had many of the same problems as the previous solutions in terms of complexity, time, resources, and potential outage time—not to mention the possible impacts of foreign key relationships and such.

Oracle Flashback Database tries to address these problems. The concept of Flashback Technology refers to a suite of features that gives you a multitude of different ways to survive user errors. These features have as a unifying concept only the simple idea that user errors occur, and recovering from them should be simple and fast. The implementation of these features within the database is often very different. Therefore, don't let yourself be confused with the term Flashback—it's more a concept than a single architecture.

Here's a list of the Flashback features:

- Flashback Query
- Flashback Table
- Flashback Transaction
- Flashback Drop
- Flashback Database
- Flashback Data Archive

We discuss each of these features in this chapter. We also discuss how Flashback Database features are impacted when you are using an Oracle Multitenant database. First, though, we want to tell you a story.

Flashback and the Undo Segment: A Love Story

The first two types of Flashback we listed—Flashback Query and Flashback Table—have their functionality based entirely on technology that has existed in the Oracle Database for years: the undo segments. When you execute a DML statement such as an insert, update, or delete, Oracle needs a way to be able to undo the results of that statement should a situation occur in which the statement needs to be rolled back. This might be because the user or application issues an explicit rollback command. Implicit rollbacks occur when a user session, or the database, crashes before the transaction is committed.

The undo generated is also used to help generate read-consistent images of a given block for other SQL statements. For example, if a long-running update is executing in one session, we don't want others to see the results of that update until it's committed. To make sure that other sessions only see the version of the data they are supposed to see, Oracle will take the current block (which may have been altered by the long-running update session) and "roll" it back using the undo to the point in time that the other transactions require. The resulting block is called a *read-consistent image*.

Back in the "old" days, once a transaction was committed, the undo information related to that transaction was immediately freed up to be overwritten—so there was no way that the before images could not be reliably found later on.

Since Oracle 9*i*, the way that the committed undo in rollback segments is managed has changed. When you start a new transaction, it first attempts to allocate undo space that has not been used. Once unused space is exhausted, Oracle starts overwriting previously used segments in a FIFO manner. This change in the way undo space is managed now makes it more likely to be able to find the undo required to reconstruct a block as it existed at a desired point in time.

The result of this changed architecture is that Oracle could introduce new functionality into the database. This new architecture started in Oracle 9*i* with the introduction of what would become Flashback Query. Over time, Oracle has significantly improved on and added to its suite of Flashback features.

The ability to query or change objects back to a certain time in the past is predicated on how long our undo extents can remain in the undo tablespace before they are overwritten. Therefore, a transaction can be flashed back as long as the undo is available to facilitate that flashback. Since Oracle will not overwrite undo extents, the database tries to preserve the undo history as long as it can so that it can be reused.

Two things control the threshold for how far back you can use a Flashback Query/Table. The first is the size of the undo tablespace. Obviously, the more space available to undo segments, the more history can be stored. Also, DML-heavy databases fill up undo segments faster than databases that are heavy on read-only activity, so the activity in a database makes a difference in terms of undo history. The period between the committing of a transaction until the undo extend is overwritten is called the *flashback window.*

As mentioned, plenty of factors go into determining the flashback window, but the most important is your transaction load. You can view statistics for undo usage with the view V$UNDOSTAT. Each row in this view represents the number of undo blocks utilized for a ten-minute period. Running a few analyses of this view through peak usage should provide a decent template to guide your settings for undo.

In normal cases, you can't be assured that the undo you need will actually be available when you need it. In some cases, you will want to ensure that flashback features dependent on redo are able to do so for a fixed period of time. In this case, a normal undo tablespace won't do, because the undo can be overwritten. In this case, you will want to use Flashback Data Archive. We discuss this feature in more detail later in this chapter.

So, what do you need to do to enable automated undo tablespace management? Your database is probably already using it. First, you need to set UNDO_MANAGEMENT = AUTO in the PFILE or SPFILE. Second, set your UNDO_TABLESPACE parameter to point to which tablespace will handle undo duties. Finally, set UNDO_RETENTION = *value in seconds*. This sets the desired length of time to keep undo segments around. Remember, though, that the value of UNDO_RETENTION is not a guarantee, it's just a target. Its value feeds into some of the values displayed in the V$UNDOSTAT view, helping you size the undo tablespace such that you can achieve your retention target.

So, now that we have discussed the mechanism used by Flashback Query and Flashback Table. Let's talk about them, as well as the rest of the Flashback Database features.

Flashback Query

Flashback Query has been around for a long time. It was among the first of the flashback-related features Oracle introduced. At first, Flashback Query was a bit complex because you had to use a PL/SQL package to set the appropriate point in time for the flashback operation.

Performing a Flashback Query of a table is simple, now that it has been integrated into SQL. All you need to know is the point in time in the past for which you would like to view the contents of a table, and then you plug it into your query:

```
select scr_id, head_config from ws_app.woodscrew as of timestamp
  to_timestamp('2009-06-27 04:27:00','YYYY-MM-DD HH:MI:SS')
  where scr_id=1001;

    SCR_ID HEAD_CONFIG
---------- --------------------
      1001 Phillips
      1001 Phillips
```

You can also use a System Change Number (SCN) qualifier, if you know the SCN of the change you are looking for:

```
select scr_id, head_config from ws_app.woodscrew
as of scn 751652 where scr_id=1001;

    SCR_ID HEAD_CONFIG
---------- -------------------
      1001 Slot
      1001 Slot
```

Although there is no strict RMAN interface into Flashback Query, you can certainly run queries using this feature from the RMAN command line. The changes in Oracle Database 12c now allow you to issue SQL queries directly from the RMAN prompt and see the results of those SQL queries. Note that you will only see SQL queries returned when connected as SYSDBA. If you are connected as SYSBACKUP, SQL queries will not return any data.

Flashback Versions Query

Flashback Versions Query provides a way to look back at a table, and specific changes to that table, over a period of time. This makes it easy to audit changes that have occurred in the table, and also it can be used should you need to roll back changes in a table.

Flashback Versions Query is dependent on undo being available. This means the undo needs to be present in the undo segments, so undo retention and possibly using guaranteed retention are considerations. Undo retention is set via the UNDO_RETENTION parameter, which is defined in seconds. By default, if the undo tablespace becomes full, then Oracle will start reusing undo segments. If you need to make sure undo retention is enforced, you can force Oracle to meet the undo retention target by using the **alter tablespace retention guarantee** command. Using guaranteed retention has its risks (such as stopping all database activity), so be careful if you choose to use it. However, the same risks are true with ARCHIVELOG mode, and it's a handy thing to use. Like everything else, you just have to measure things like space usage, availability, and requirements to get the right balance when configuring things.

Having addressed configuration, let's look at using this feature. First, let's create our test data:

```
SQL> create table test (id number, current_scn number);
Table created.
SQL> insert into test values (1, (select current_scn from v$database) );
1 row created.
SQL> commit;
Commit complete.
SQL> insert into test values(2, (select current_scn from v$database) );
1 row created.
SQL> insert into test values(3, (select current_scn from v$database) );
SQL> commit;
Commit complete.
SQL> insert into test values(4,(select current_scn from v$database) );
1 row created.
SQL> commit;
Commit complete.
SQL> update test set id=5 where id=4;
```

```
1 row updated.
SQL> commit;
Commit complete.
SQL> insert into test values(4,(select current_scn from v$database) );
1 row created.
SQL> commit;
Commit complete.
SQL>
```

Now, let's put Flashback Versions Query to work! The nice thing about this feature is that it comes with pseudo-columns you can use to identify attributes related to the rows in the table that are returned by your SQL query. Let's run a couple of queries to test this thing.

```
SQL> select id, current_scn, versions_starttime, versions_endscn,
versions_endtime, versions_operation
from test versions between scn 8845011 and 8845053
order by versions_starttime;
     ID CURRENT_SCN VERSIONS_STARTTIME     VERSIONS_ENDSCN VERSIONS_ENDTIME     V
------- ----------- ---------------------- --------------- --------------       -
      1    8845011  10-FEB-16 01.36.24 PM                                        I
      3    8845028  10-FEB-16 01.37.01 PM                                        I
      2    8845023  10-FEB-16 01.37.01 PM                                        I
      4    8845037  10-FEB-16 01.37.19 PM          8845045 10-FEB-16 01.37.28 PM I
      5    8845037  10-FEB-16 01.37.28 PM                                        U
```

In this example, we can see that, within the SCN window indicated, five records had some kind of manipulation occur to them. There are four inserts (VERSIONS_OPERATION column value of I) and one update (VERSIONS_OPERATION column value U). The VERSIONS_STARTTIME tells us the time at which that version of the column started its existence. The column VERSIONS_ENDSCN indicates when that column row had a new version. It is NULL in all but one record of our query. This is because only one record changed within the SCN window that we queried (where the ID column was changed from 4 to 5).

Flashback Table

Perhaps the most compelling function of the Flashback Technology is the ability to simply revert a table to a previous point in time in a simple and straightforward fashion. The ability to perform point-in-time recovery on a table or group of tables has often been the grounds by which entire clone databases are built—just so that a single table could be extracted and then imported back into production. With Flashback Table, unnecessary cloning operations can be put to pasture.

Flashback Table employs the same mechanisms as Flashback Query—with information stored in the undo segments, Oracle can rewind a database one transaction at a time to put the table back the way it was at a specified time in the past because the Flashback Table operation depends on undo. Thus, you can only flash back a table as far back as the undo segments allow you.

In addition to undo, the ability to flash back a table requires you to enable row movement for the table. Row movement was initially put in place as a function of partitioned tables, which allowed an updated row to move to the appropriate partition if the update changed the partition key value. Flashback Table employs row movement to assist in the rewind operations. To enable row movement, use the following **alter table** command:

```
alter table woodscrew enable row movement;
```

Flashback Table cannot save you from all user errors. Certain DDL operations that occur against a table cannot be undone. Most importantly, you cannot flash back a table to before a **truncate table** operation because a **truncate** does not produce any undo—that is why **truncate** exists, versus a **delete * from table**. Also, Flashback Table cannot be used for a dropped table (use Flashback Drop for that; see the section "Flashback Drop").

Further, Flashback Table does not follow foreign key relationships. Therefore, it will flash back a table, but if that table has established foreign key relationships to dependent tables, then the Flashback Table operation will fail with an Oracle error because the Flashback Table operation does not cascade through integrity constraints.

Performing the Flashback Table Operation from SQL

With row movement enabled, you can move forward with normal operations on the table. Then, when a user-induced corruption occurs in the table, you can use SQL at the command line to perform the Flashback Table operation:

```
flashback table matt.woodscrew to timestamp
to_timestamp('2009-06-29 13:30:00','YYYY-MM-DD HH24:MI:SS')
```

Alternatively, you can use the SCN if you have been able to determine it (through investigation via Flashback Query, for example):

```
flashback table matt.woodscrew to scn 751652;
```

Like Flashback Query, the performance of a Flashback Table operation depends on the amount of data that has to be rewound and how far back you are rewinding. The more data that has to be undone, the longer the operation will take. However, this will always be faster than trying to perform a point-in-time recovery of the table by other methods: you can try TSPITR, or you can try to restore the tablespaces to a different instance and then export the table from the clone instance and import back into production. Nothing can come close to Flashback Table in terms of performance.

Flashback Table with Oracle Enterprise Manager

The added strength of Grid Control for Flashback Table is the ability to first explore the table via Flashback Versions Query to determine exactly what time you want to flash back to. If you already know the exact time for flashback, using SQL at the command line would be just as simple as using the Flashback Table Wizard in Grid Control. Grid Control does, however, provide a way to determine what dependencies are at play.

Enabling Row Movement and Flashback Table

It is critical that you foresee possible Flashback Table candidates and enable row movement as soon as possible. You cannot enable row movement and then flash back the table to a point prior to enabling row movement. Such an operation will result in the following error:

```
ORA-08189: cannot flashback the table because row movement is not enabled.
```

In other words, you cannot wait until you need to flash back a table and then enable row movement as part of the flashback operation.

Flashback Transaction

There's always more than one way to organize a hunt for bad data in the database. Flashback Transaction allows you to look at all changes made by a specific transaction, or all transactions in a certain timeframe. Then you can go in and undo an error at the transaction level instead of rolling back the entire table. This focused level of flashback allows you to keep all other changes that have occurred since the error—that is, you are removing the smallest possible error and leaving the good data. You can also flash back a subset of the transaction instead of undoing the entire transaction as an atomic unit.

Unlike Flashback Versions Query, Flashback Transaction does not use the undo segment to understand what needs to be done to back out of an error. It utilizes the redo instead and takes advantage of the LogMiner capabilities to dig out the transaction change vectors and then determine the best way to roll back the changes.

Again, the best way to use Flashback Transaction is through Grid Control. Before you can utilize Flashback Transaction, you will need to have turned on supplemental log data for the table in question. As with enabling row movement for Flashback Table, if you don't turn on supplemental log data before you need Flashback Transaction, it's too late. The undo segment won't have the necessary information required to perform the flashback. From within Grid Control, if you try to utilize Flashback Transaction, you will see an error informing you of the actions you need to take.

Flashback Transaction Query is compelling because it allows you to review a bad transaction in its entirety, even though the window into the error may be only a single row. For instance, if we found that a row of our WOODSCREW table had been deleted, we could look up that row in Flashback Versions Query. Then, we could get the Transaction ID for the delete operation and see how many other rows were deleted at the same time. This provides a look at the full scope of the problem.

Flashback Drop

Flashback Drop allows you to "undrop" database objects. No longer will you have users desperate for the entire database to be restored to a point in the past because they thought they were on the DEV instance instead of PROD.

There's nothing all that dramatic about how Flashback Drop has been implemented. In Oracle Database 10*g*, when you drop a table, it merely gets renamed to a system-identifiable string, but the segment remains in the tablespace it was dropped from. It will remain there until you undrop the object or purge it manually, or until the tablespace runs out of space for regular objects. If space pressure exists in the tablespace, Oracle will begin to age out dropped objects from oldest to newest.

When you drop an object, Oracle doesn't just rename that object. All dependent objects move to the Recycle Bin as well: indices, triggers, and constraints. Therefore, when you undrop the table, its entire dependent chain comes back with it.

The Recycle Bin

The Recycle Bin is a virtual directory of all dropped objects in the database—simply a list of objects that have been dropped but not purged. The Recycle Bin is a logical container and does not require a specific storage location; actual storage for all dropped objects is in the tablespace the object was in prior to being dropped. Consider an example. User matt drops the table WS_

APP.WOODSCREWS. The WOODSCREWS table is in the tablespace WS_APP_DATA, but its two indices are in the WS_APP_IDX tablespace. When WOODSCREWS is dropped, the table is renamed to an internal name, and so are the two indices that existed on the table. Both appear in the DBA_RECYCLEBIN view. However, the actual WOODSCREWS table segment still exists in the WS_APP_DATA tablespace, and the indices still exist in the WS_APP_IDX tablespace. They are logically part of the Recycle Bin, but physically exist in the same place they always have.

The Recycle Bin is quickly viewed via the following two data dictionary views:

- USER_RECYCLEBIN
- DBA_RECYCLEBIN

Purging the Recycle Bin

Manually eliminating dropped objects from the Recycle Bin is not necessary. Objects are purged from the Recycle Bin as the space is required by other segments in the tablespace. In other words, dropped objects continue to take up space in a tablespace until other objects in that tablespace run out of free space elsewhere. Then, the first dropped object is the first object to be purged. Oracle automatically looks to purge indices before tables so that actual data is the last thing to be lost. Recycle Bin objects will also be dropped before a tablespace autoextends, if autoextend is on.

The new **purge** command exists to purge the Recycle Bin. You can purge by user, by object, or by tablespace, or you can purge the entire Recycle Bin:

```
purge table matt.woodscrews;
purge index matt.woodscrews_pk_idx;
purge tablespace sales;
purge recyclebin;
```

Undropping Objects in the Recycle Bin

Getting objects back from the Recycle Bin is pretty simple—a simple SQL command renames the object back to its original name, along with any dependent objects:

```
flashback table ws_app.woodscrews to before drop;
```

How Long Do Objects Live in the Recycle Bin?

A valid question, but, of course, the answer is, it depends. No, really. It depends. The real question you probably want to ask is, "Can I control how long an object lives in the Recycle Bin?" The answer to this question is no.

You cannot force an object to remain in the Recycle Bin if space pressure exists in the tablespace of the dropped object. Even with autoextend on, the dropped object is purged before the tablespace extends. Therefore, if you want to determine a certain lifespan on objects in the Recycle Bin, you are left with two choices: either make the tablespace overly large to accommodate drops, or manually manage the Recycle Bin and purge those objects you don't want to keep to leave space for those you do want to keep.

You can therefore shorten the stay of an object in the Recycle Bin. However, you cannot force something to remain, given a shortage of tablespace room.

Of course, sometimes it's not that simple. For instance, if you have multiple dropped objects with the same name, you would have to refer to the object by its new and improved Recycle Bin name:

```
SQL> select object_name, original_name, droptime,
dropscn from user_recyclebin;
OBJECT_NAME                        ORIGINAL_NAME
--------------------------------   ---------------
DROPTIME              DROPSCN
-------------------   ----------
RB$$48623$INDEX$0                  PK_WOODSCREW
2004-01-12:15:21:26    1241651
RB$$48622$TABLE$0                  WOODSCREW
2004-01-12:15:21:26    1241652
SQL> flashback table " RB$$48622$TABLE$0" to before drop;
```

Note the quotes around the Recycle Bin object name. These are required due to special symbols in the name.

If you have dropped an object and then created a new object with the same name, you can still flash back the first object. There is syntax in the flashback SQL to rename the object when you pull it from the Recycle Bin:

```
flashback table ws_app.woodscrews to before drop rename to woodscrews_history;
```

Flashback Database

The most revolutionary Flashback Technology may also be the one that gets used the least often. Flashback Database provides the ability to quickly rewind the entire database to a previous point in time. This operation has the same end result as you would get from doing point-in-time recovery using RMAN or user-managed recovery. However, Flashback Database does not require the restore of all of the database's datafiles from the most recent backup, followed by a roll-forward using all the archive logs that have accumulated since that backup. By avoiding these costly operations, Flashback Database can perform a point-in-time recovery in a fraction of the time typically required for such an operation.

Flashback Database works by incrementally recording all blocks that have changed at a timed interval. These flashback "checkpoints" then provide the points to which the database can be "rewound." After rolling back to the flashback checkpoint, you can use archive logs to then roll forward to the exact time or SCN specified by the **flashback database** command. Thus, the operation uses new technology as well as that old standby, the archive logs, to provide a fast way to perform point-in-time recovery.

Typically, there are fewer archive logs to be applied after a flashback checkpoint than must be applied to the last backup (typically taken every night, versus every few minutes for flashback logs), so the recovery stage of flashback is very quick.

Flashback Logs

Flashback Database implements a new type of log, called the *flashback log*. Flashback logs are generated by the database at regular intervals and accumulate in the FRA. You must have an FRA for Flashback Database; the logs cannot be created anywhere else. The flashback log contains a copied image of every block that has been changed since the last flashback log was generated. These blocks can then be reinstated into the database when a **flashback database** command is issued to rewind the database back to its state at the time specified in the **flashback** command.

Because entire blocks are being dumped to the flashback logs, they can accumulate very quickly in extremely active databases. Setting an appropriately sized FRA is crucial to the success of meeting your Flashback Database needs. In addition, you can manually turn off flashback logging, as follows, for certain tablespaces that could be manually re-created after a Flashback Database operation, and thereby decrease the amount of logging that occurs:

```
alter tablespace ws_app_idx flashback off;
```

You can turn flashback logging back on at any time, as follows, but it is worth noting that you cannot rewind backward through a flashback logging gap for the tablespace you turned off:

```
alter tablespace sales_idx flashback on;
```

Any tablespace that has flashback logging turned off for any period within the **flashback database** command would need to be offlined prior to performing the Flashback Database operation.

Flashback Retention Target

The lifespan of flashback logs correlates directly to how far back in time you would like to have the Flashback Database option. By default, the flashback logs are kept long enough so that you can always flash back 24 hours from the current time. If this is too long or too short a time, you can change it with an initialization parameter:

```
alter system set db_flashback_retention_target=720;
```

The value is specified in minutes (720 would be 12 hours).

RMAN Workshop: *Configure for Flashback Database*

Workshop Notes

This Workshop walks you through the primary steps required to configure the database initially to use flashback logging for Flashback Database operations.

Step 1. Shut down the database and startup mount. The database must be mounted but not open.

```
SQL> select status from v$instance;
```

In addition, check to make sure the database is in ARCHIVELOG mode, which is required for Flashback Database:

```
SQL> archive log list;
Database log mode              Archive Mode
Automatic archival             Enabled
Archive destination            USE_DB_RECOVERY_FILE_DEST
Oldest online log sequence     62
Next log sequence to archive   64
Current log sequence           64
```

Step 2. Set the flashback retention target to your desired value. We will use 12 hours as the window.

```
alter system set db_flashback_retention_target=720
SCOPE=BOTH SID='*';
```

Step 3. Set the values for DB_RECOVERY_FILE_DEST and DB_RECOVERY_FILE_DEST_SIZE (FRA parameters). Note that if you have already set these for your RMAN backup strategy, you should review the parameters now. Flashback logs increase FRA usage significantly. It would behoove you to at least double the given size of the FRA.

```
SQL> ALTER SYSTEM SET DB_RECOVERY_FILE_DEST_SIZE = 2335825920
SCOPE=BOTH SID='*';
SQL> ALTER SYSTEM SET DB_RECOVERY_FILE_DEST = '/u02/fra/'
SCOPE=BOTH SID='*';
```

Step 4. Turn flashback logging on. This is done in the same fashion as turning ARCHIVELOG mode on—with an **alter database** command when the database is mounted but not open:

```
alter database flashback on;
```

Step 5. Turn flashback logging off for any tablespaces that you deem do not require it:

```
alter tablespace sales_idx flashback off;
```

Step 6. Open the database:

```
alter database open;
```

Flashback Database: Tuning and Tweaking

So, you've determined that Flashback Database provides you with a fallback position you desire for your database, and you have determined how far back you want your fallback position to be. You've set your DB_FLASHBACK_RETENTION_TARGET. Now, the questions come up: "How do I know if I have enough space in my FRA to handle the volume of flashback logs being generated? And, for that matter, how much flashback logging is occurring?" The following sections answer those questions.

Using V$FLASHBACK_DATABASE_LOG

One thing at a time. First, Oracle provides built-in analysis for you to use in determining if you need to increase the size of your FRA. After you enable flashback logging, Oracle begins to keep track of the amount of flashback logging that is occurring and stores it in the view V$FLASHBACK_DATABASE_LOG. This view actually provides an estimate for the total flashback size:

```
select estimated_flashback_size from v$flashback_database_log;
```

Note that this view gives the size for flashback logs, not for all users in the FRA, so you need to add this value to whatever size you need for archive logs and RMAN backups. This estimated value only gets better with age, meaning that as the database runs through its day-to-day (and then month-to-month) operations, Oracle can provide a better estimate of the size. Therefore, it is a good idea to check back in with this estimator to find out if you still have the right specifications in place.

V$FLASHBACK_DATABASE_LOG also provides you with the actual oldest time that you can flash back the database to, given the current size of the FRA and the currently available flashback logs. You can use this as another indicator of space issues in the FRA. The following **select** statement will provide you with a basic understanding of the state of the flashback logs:

```
select oldest_flashback_scn, oldest_flashback_time
from v$flashback_database_log;
```

Using V$FLASHBACK_DATABASE_STAT

Oracle has built a monitoring view so that you can keep your eye on flashback logging activity. V$FLASHBACK_DATABASE_STAT provides you with information on flashback data generated over the course of a period of time (typically, a one-hour window extending back from sysdate). In addition to showing how much flashback logging occurred, this view posts the redo generated and the actual database data generated over the same period. The following **select** shows a sample output of this view:

```
select * from v$flashback_database_stat;
BEGIN_TIM  END_TIME  FLASHBACK_DATA   DB_DATA   REDO_DATA ESTIMATED_FLASHBACK_SIZE
---------  --------- --------------   ---------- --------- ------------------------
19-SEP-13  19-SEP-13        9003008   15294464   3986944                 210247680
19-SEP-13  19-SEP-13       15884288   21225472   5766144                 210247680
19-SEP-13  19-SEP-13       10248192   25772032   5162496                 210075648
```

Flashback Data Archive (Total Recall)

Oracle Total Recall is a set of functions that allows you to permanently archive all changes to a table so that you can go back to any point in time and look at the data as it was in the past. Unlike Flashback Query, which is dependent on the transitory nature of undo, Flashback Data Archive requires a specific type of tablespace to be built so that it can house the version information required to look back in time at a particular table.

Flashback Data Archive is useful for auditing and archival purposes on tables that have legal or regulatory sensitivities. You can configure the data archive to be of a set retention period that matches either the business or regulatory need, and then you assign the table to that archive. Once this is complete, you can utilize a straightforward flashback query in SQL to look back in time at the table as of months or even years ago.

You should be mindful of two architectural restrictions based on how the archive data is generated and accessed. If you put a table in a data archive mode, you cannot do the following:

- Perform an **alter table** command with an UPGRADE clause
- Perform a drop table

Either of these actions will result in an error:

```
ORA-55610: Invalid DDL statement on history-tracked table
```

Summary

In this chapter, we introduced the new means of recovering from user-induced errors, known collectively in the Oracle Database as Flashback Technology. The new Flashback Technology allows you to recover from logical errors in a faster, less intrusive way than running a full-bore media recovery. We discussed using Flashback Versions Query to determine the full scope of the logical corruption. We illustrated using the Flashback Table command to recover from a bad DML statement, as well as from a table drop. We discussed the new Flashback Transaction option that utilizes the redo logs to undo an erroneous action at the transaction level instead of at the table level. We discussed the Flashback Database functionality, which allows for a point-in-time recovery of an entire database without requiring a full restore of the datafiles from backup. We ended the chapter by reviewing Flashback Data Archive, which allows a historical point of view on a table as far back as you have space to hold the records.

CHAPTER
17

RMAN and Data Guard

Oracle Standby Database has been a database high-availability option with the Oracle Database since Oracle 7 Release 7.3. The objective of a standby database is to support the capability of maintaining a duplicate (or standby) database of a primary (or production) database for recovering from disasters at the production site. When the primary database fails (for example, because of a natural disaster), the standby database can be opened, or *activated,* and all end users can be switched to the standby database machine and continue to access the database while the previous primary database is being recovered. The goal is to be able to switch over from the primary database to the standby database in the case of a disaster in the least amount of time. The standby database started as a simple concept, and although the overall architecture is now referred to as Data Guard, the foundation is still simple: take the archive logs from your production database, move them to another computer that has a copy of that database, and apply the archive logs to the copy. In this way, Data Guard is able to provide an efficient disaster-recovery solution by maintaining transactionally consistent copies of the production database at a remote site. These copies, or standbys, can be one of two types: physical or logical. Which one you choose to include in your Data Guard configuration depends on what business needs you are trying to satisfy.

Types of Standby Databases

What is a standby database? Well, there are really two distinct types of standby databases. The first is what we call a physical standby database, and the second is called a logical standby database. Let's look at each of these two kinds of standby databases in a bit more detail.

Physical Standby Database

A standby database is called a "physical standby" if the structure of the standby database exactly matches the primary database. A *physical* standby database is kept in sync with the primary database by using media recovery to apply redo that was generated on the primary database. Because media recovery is used, we can be assured that a physical standby is a block-for-block identical copy of the primary database. Because of its nature, a physical standby database is an excellent choice for disaster recovery. In the event of a failure, we can rest assured that our data will be intact and consistent with data that existed on the primary database. We can create a physical standby database using RMAN.

Logical Standby Database

A standby database is called a "logical standby" if the physical structure of the standby does not match the primary database. A *logical* standby database is kept in sync with the primary database by transforming redo data received from the primary database into logical SQL statements and then executing those SQL statements against the standby database. Because we are applying SQL statements instead of performing media recovery, it is possible for the logical standby database to contain the same logical information as the primary database, but at the same time to have a different physical structure. Because a logical standby database is open for user access while changes are being applied, it is an ideal solution for a reporting database while maintaining its disaster recovery attributes.

You can use RMAN to create a physical standby database and then afterward, as long as the database meets all the requirements for a logical standby database, you can convert the physical standby database to a logical standby database. The requirements for logical standby databases are many, and you should carefully consider them and their implications before you decide to move toward the use of a logical standby database.

Using RMAN to Create Standby Databases

RMAN and Data Guard are complementary technologies that together make a complete Oracle solution for disaster recovery and high availability. RMAN backups can be used to create the underlying standby database, as well as provide the initial recovery phase. After you have created the standby database and configured the Data Guard broker, RMAN can connect to the standby database and take backups that can be restored to the primary database. In this way, the resources used to perform a backup can be completely removed from your production environment.

Data Guard offers several advantages. In addition to providing comprehensive disaster recovery and high-availability solutions, Data Guard offers complete data protection and efficient use of system resources. Because the redo data received from the primary database is validated at a standby database, *physical* corruptions on the primary database do not propagate to the standby database. Because the standby database is ideally a physical copy of the production environment, the database backups can be offloaded to the standby site. You can use the Data Guard database for read-only reporting and ad-hoc queries by implementing the Active Data Guard (a licensed option introduced in Oracle 11*g*), thereby maximizing Data Guard server resource utilization and increasing the return on investment (ROI) for standby servers. The key benefits of a physical standby database include faster and more efficient failover to a block-to-block copy of the primary database, offloading backups from the primary, use as a reporting database with Active Data Guard configuration, and use as a temporary test database with snapshot standby database configuration.

Obviously, this book is about RMAN and not Data Guard. If you have more questions about standby databases or Data Guard, check out the Oracle Press titles on Data Guard, as well as the Oracle documentation. Throughout the rest of this chapter, we assume that you are familiar with the basics of Data Guard standby databases and are ready to create one using RMAN.

RMAN provides different options you can use to create the standby database, including the following:

- Database backups of the primary database.
- Active database duplication from the primary database, which does not require any backups.

Active database duplication can have a bit more operational impact on the primary database, so you will want to be cautious about using it. On the other hand, using active database duplication makes creating a standby database so much easier because you don't need direct access to your database backup set pieces.

Preparing to Create a Standby Database

When you want to create a standby database, you need to complete some initial tasks first. These tasks include the following:

- Establishing a naming convention
- Putting the database in ARCHIVELOG mode and forced logging mode

- Setting database parameters
- Creating the standby database password file
- Configuring the Oracle Network
- Preparing the auxiliary instance
- Starting RMAN for the duplication

Let's look at these topics next.

Establishing a Naming Convention

When you are dealing with standby databases, an explosion of database names seems to happen. Because there are so many names, those names and how they are defined can become very confusing. However, if you get all of this naming stuff straight in your head from the beginning, you'll find it's much easier to get your standby database created with a minimum of errors.

So, what names do you need to be aware of? Well, here's a list:

- The primary database name.
- The primary database service name.
- The standby database name.
- The standby database service name.
- The database unique name.
- Your wife, husband, or significant other's name. (Okay, we threw that one in to see if you were still paying attention!)

Table 17-1 provides a list of the different database names, a description of those names, and then which names we will use in our examples throughout this chapter.

Putting the Database in ARCHIVELOG Mode and Forced Logging Mode

One of the things a standby database depends on is redo generated by the primary database. If the primary database performs an operation that does not generate redo, bad things can happen on the standby database. Therefore, to support standby database operations, the database should be in ARCHIVELOG mode and you should also put the database in forced logging mode. We have discussed putting the database in ARCHIVELOG mode several times in this book already, so by now you should be comfortable with how to do that.

NOTE
In this chapter, we assume that you are using a Fast Recovery Area (FRA), which we have discussed in a number of chapters throughout this book already.

The other thing you need to do is enable forced logging in the database. When enabled, forced logging will ensure that all operations that occur on the database generate redo. To enable

Name	Description	Example
Primary database name	Name of the primary database. Found by issuing the following command: `select name from v$database;`	Testdb
Standby database name	The name of the standby database. This name will be the *same* as the name of the primary database name.	Testdb
Database unique name	This name makes the primary and standby database names unique. Each primary and standby database will have a unique database name assigned to it. This is done through the use of the db_unique_name parameter.	Testdb_dr and testdb_pr
Primary database service name	This is the net8 service name for the primary database. In our examples and workshops, we will keep things easy and make the service name of the primary database the same as the database name of the primary database.	Testdb_pr
Standby database service name	This is the service name for the standby database. In our examples and workshops, we will make the service name of the standby database the same as the database unique name.	Testdb_dr

TABLE 17-1   *Oracle Database Names to Define when Creating a Standby Database*

forced logging, you first put the primary database in MOUNT mode. Then you use the **alter database forced logging** command to put the database in forced logging mode. Here is an example of the commands you would issue to enable forced logging:

```
Shutdown immediate
Startup mount
Alter database forced logging;
Alter database open;
```

Setting Database Parameters

Perhaps the one thing that Oracle standby databases are the most persnickety about are the parameters you set. First, a number of them need to be set just right. Second, if you don't set them correctly at the outset, things won't work and you will be pulling your hair out (then, you will look like at least one of the authors who is short a bit up top on the noggin). We don't want to be responsible for your premature baldness, so let's cover setting parameters very carefully in this section. In this section we will talk about the following topics:

- Configuring the parameters for the auxiliary instance
- Setting parameters on the primary database
- Setting parameters on standby database

Configuring the Parameters for the Auxiliary Instance

Configuring the auxiliary instance for initial use is quite easy to do. First, you need to create a text parameter file with the appropriate parameters set. For the most part, the following are the parameters you will find yourself setting:

- **DB_NAME**   This is the name of the standby database. Note that it should always be the same name as the primary database.
- **DB_CREATE_FILE_DEST**   If your primary database is using OMF-managed datafiles, you need to set the DB_CREATE_FILE_DEST parameter. You also need to make sure the directory structure pointed to by the parameter is created and that it has been granted the appropriate security privileges so that the Oracle Database OS account user can read and write to it.
- **ENABLE_PLUGGABLE_DATABASE**   If the primary database is a container database (CDB), you need to set this parameter to a value of TRUE.

In our case, the auxiliary database parameter file looks like this:

```
db_name=testdb
db_create_file_dest=/u01/app/oracle/oradata
```

You might be asking yourself, what about the other parameters that an Oracle database requires? Surely the standby must require that parameters related to memory and so on be set. In this case, you are correct.

To start the auxiliary instance, all we need is a few parameters. The auxiliary instance will mount with only the parameters we have listed. The remaining parameters will temporarily take on default values, which is just fine almost all of the time.

When the auxiliary instance is created, the SPFILE of the primary database, which defines the settings of all of the database parameters of the primary database, will be transferred to the standby database. If there are cases where we want to modify those parameter settings, we will do that when we create the standby database with RMAN. We discuss what parameters are most commonly set on the standby database later in this chapter.

One thing you want to make sure you do is create any file systems you will be using on the standby database before you start the creation of the standby database. This way, when the standby database is started, you won't get any failures because some file system or directory is missing. That is one thing that RMAN generally does not do during the standby database creation process—create directories.

Setting Parameters on the Primary Database

A few parameters we need to modify on the primary database are related to the standby database we will be creating. First, we need to configure some archive log destination directories using the parameter LOG_ARCHIVE_DEST_*n*. Typically, you set up LOG_ARCHIVE_DEST_1 to point to the FRA. Then you set up the second parameter, LOG_ARCHIVE_DEST_2, to point to the standby database service you will be creating.

You also need to set the STANDBY_FILE_MANAGMENT parameter. Typically this is set to a value of AUTO. When set to AUTO, Oracle will manage files on the standby database, such as redo log files and tablespace datafiles, automatically. For example, when a **drop tablespace including contents** command is executed on the primary database, if the STANDBY_FILE_MANAGMENT parameter is set to manual, just the tablespace would be dropped on the standby database and the physical files would need to be cleaned up manually. When STANDBY_FILE_MANAGEMENT is set to AUTO, Oracle would also delete the physical datafiles on the standby database server.

NOTE
Be careful if you are creating a standby database on the same physical server as the primary database. If you do not configure the standby database correctly, critical database files can be lost if the STANDBY_ FILE_MANAGEMENT parameter is set to AUTO.

Here is an example of the various parameter configurations for a primary database (and the ones we use in the upcoming workshop):

```
standby_file_management='AUTO';

log_archive_dest_1='location=USE_DB_RECOVERY_FILE_DEST valid_for=(all_
logfiles,all_roles)';

log_Archive_dest_2='service=testdb_dr async noaffirm reopen=15 valid_for=(all_
logfiles,primary_role) db_unique_name=testdb_dr';
```

Setting Parameters on the Standby Database
We already discussed setting parameters on the auxiliary database when you start it. The nice thing about creating the standby database with RMAN is that it will copy the SPFILE from the primary database and use it as the SPFILE for the standby database. Even better, if you want to modify some of the parameters in the SPFILE (for example, the DB_UNIQUE_NAME), you can do that on the command line when you create the standby database. We will show you examples of how to do that later in this chapter.

Creating the Auxiliary Database Password File
In order for Oracle Database to ship archived redo logs to the standby site, the standby site must have a database password file. This password file must be an exact duplicate of the password file of the primary database. When you are duplicating a database, RMAN requires that you copy the password file of the target database over to the auxiliary instance. This is not required when you are creating a standby database in Oracle Database 12*c*. When you are creating a standby database in Oracle Database 12*c*, RMAN will copy the password file to the standby database for you.

Note that if you are doing active database duplication to create your standby database, you will want to use the password file command to indicate to RMAN that it is okay to overwrite any existing password file. This option isn't available if you are creating a standby database using backup-based duplication.

Configuring the Oracle Network

Ah, Oracle Net configuration. Let's all say it together: *yuck!* Now that we are past that, let's talk about what we need to do to configure networking for a standby database configuration. First, let's talk about configuring the network on the standby database server. Then, we'll talk about configuring the network on the primary database side.

Configuring the Oracle Standby Database Server

Before we can start to create the standby database, we need to configure some things on the server where the auxiliary instance (and later the standby database) will be living. First, as is the case with database duplication, in order to connect to the auxiliary instance with RMAN, you need to create an entry in listener.ora for the auxiliary instance. Once that is done, you need to reload or restart the Oracle database listener. Here is an example of our tnsnames.ora file. The section we added is bolded:

```
LISTENER =
  (DESCRIPTION_LIST =
    (DESCRIPTION =
      (ADDRESS = (PROTOCOL = TCP)(HOST = 192.168.1.202)(PORT = 1521))
      (ADDRESS = (PROTOCOL = IPC)(KEY = EXTPROC1521))
    )
  )
SID_LIST_LISTENER =
(SID_LIST =
  (SID_DESC =
    (GLOBAL_DBNAME = testdb_dr)
    (ORACLE_HOME = /u01/app/oracle/product/12.1.0.2/dbhome_1)
    (SID_NAME = testdb)
  )
)
```

In this example, note that we added a specific listener for the testdb instance. Notice the GLOBAL_DBNAME parameter we configured. This creates a global service for this database called testdb_dr. Typically, the GLOBAL_DBNAME is a combination of the DB_NAME and DB_DOMAIN parameters. In this case, though, we have defined the DB_UNIQUE_NAME parameter, and thus GLOBAL_DBNAME is a combination of the DB_UNIQUE_NAME and DB_DOMAIN parameters. Of course, DB_DOMAIN is blank in our case. The GLOBAL_DBNAME will become the service name of our standby database. You can see this reflected when you check the status of the listener after it has been started with the modified listener.ora file, as shown here:

```
[oracle@standbytwo ~]$ lsnrctl status
Connecting to
(DESCRIPTION=(ADDRESS=(PROTOCOL=TCP)(HOST=192.168.1.202)(PORT=1521)))
… Information removed for brevity …
Services Summary...
Service "testdb_dr" has 1 instance(s).
   Instance "testdb", status UNKNOWN, has 1 handler(s) for this service...
The command completed successfully
```

Second, you need to add some entries into the tnsnames.ora file (or to whatever name-resolution method you are using). In this case, we need to configure an entry for the standby database as well as one for the standby database service. Here is an example of the tnsnames.ora entry we used:

```
TESTDB_DR =
  (DESCRIPTION =
    (ADDRESS = (PROTOCOL = TCP)(HOST = 192.168.1.202)(PORT = 1521))
    (CONNECT_DATA =
      (SERVER = DEDICATED)
      (SERVICE_NAME = testdb_dr)
    )
  )

TESTDB_PR =
  (DESCRIPTION =
    (ADDRESS = (PROTOCOL = TCP)(HOST = 192.168.1.201)(PORT = 1521))
    (CONNECT_DATA =
      (SERVER = DEDICATED)
      (SERVICE_NAME = testdb_pr)
    )
  )
```

Note in the tnsnames.ora file that we have an entry for the primary database (which is the TESTDB service) and an entry for the TESTDB_DR service (which is going to be our standby database). Note that we use the service name of the database to reference both databases.

Configuring the Oracle Primary Database Server

To configure the primary database server, the first thing we need to do is set the DB_UNIQUE_ NAME parameter on that server to uniquely identify it globally. In this case, we set the unique name to test_pr (for test primary), as shown in this example:

```
Alter system SET "db_unique_name"="testdb_pr" scope=spfile;
```

Note that if you forget this step, you probably won't notice it until you try to do a managed failover between the standby database and primary database. Next, we need to modify tnsnames.ora to point to the new standby database (using its service name). The entry is the same as it was on the standby database, and it's shown here:

```
TESTDB_DR =
  (DESCRIPTION =
    (ADDRESS = (PROTOCOL = TCP)(HOST = 192.168.1.202)(PORT = 1521))
    (CONNECT_DATA =
      (SERVER = DEDICATED)
      (SERVICE_NAME = testdb_dr)
    )
  )

TESTDB_PR =
  (DESCRIPTION =
    (ADDRESS = (PROTOCOL = TCP)(HOST = 192.168.1.201)(PORT = 1521))
    (CONNECT_DATA =
```

```
        (SERVER = DEDICATED)
        (SERVICE_NAME = testdb_pr)
    )
)
```

NOTE
You might notice that we used IP addresses instead of host names in the network configuration files. That was done just for the sake of convenience. Host names will work just as well and in most cases are preferable.

Preparing and Starting the Auxiliary Instance

We have already talked about many of the preliminary steps required to prepare the auxiliary instance, but we have a few loose ends to tie up before we can start it. We have already talked about the following requirements on the auxiliary instance:

- Figuring out the database naming schema
- Configuring the auxiliary parameter file
- Creating any needed file systems
- Configuring the networking configuration
- All of the other requirements related to duplicating a database as covered in previous chapters.

Really, at this point, all that is left for us to do is to start the auxiliary instance. To do this, we connect to the instance and issue the **startup nomount** command. Once the database instance is started, the auxiliary instance is ready to be turned into a standby database by RMAN.

Starting RMAN

Now that we are ready to create a standby database, we need to start RMAN. Because RMAN is a client program, you can really do this from anywhere that Oracle Database Server software is installed. However, typically, you will create the standby database from the target database server where the primary database lives.

When you start RMAN from the command line, you need to connect to the following:

- The primary database.
- The auxiliary database.
- The recovery catalog. (Note that this is optional but strongly advised, and we will be using one in all our examples.)

Here is an example of connecting to RMAN from the command line in preparation for the creation of a standby database:

```
rman target sys/robert auxiliary sys/robert@testdb_dr catalog rcat/rcat@rcat
```

If you want, you can connect to all the databases using Oracle networking. In this case, we connected directly to the target, as well as to the auxiliary instance and the catalog database, via the Oracle network. Here is an example where we connected to all the databases and instances involved via Oracle networking:

```
rman target sys/robert@testdb auxiliary sys/robert@testdb_dr
catalog rman/rman@rcat
```

Creating the Standby Database

We generally recommend that you use active database duplication whenever possible. In our minds, it's the easiest way to create standby databases. Also, in Oracle Database 12c, you can use the RMAN **section size** parameter of the **duplicate database** command. This can significantly speed up the creation of your standby database by making the most efficient use of all the parallel threads you have available for your duplication process.

Here is an example of the RMAN **duplicate database** command we used to create a standby database:

```
DUPLICATE TARGET DATABASE
   FOR STANDBY
   FROM ACTIVE DATABASE
   DORECOVER
   SPFILE
     SET "db_unique_name"="testdb_dr" comment "StandbyDB"
     set log_archive_dest_1='location=USE_DB_RECOVERY_FILE_DEST
valid_for=(all_logfiles,all_roles)
     SET LOG_ARCHIVE_DEST_2="service=testdb_dr ASYNC REGISTER
VALID_FOR=(online_logfile,primary_role)"
     SET FAL_SERVER="testdb" COMMENT "primary"
     SET standby_file_management="AUTO"
   NOFILENAMECHECK;
```

A few things of note: First, to create the standby database, we use the **duplicate database** command, adding the keyword **for standby**. The keywords **from active database** indicate we are using active database duplication. If we left the keywords **from active database** out of the command, the standby database would be created using backups of the database. If those RMAN backups were not available, the creation of the standby database would fail.

Next, you will notice we used the **dorecover** option (which is what we suggest); thus, RMAN will recover the standby database up to either the last online redo log or to some point in time, SCN, or log sequence number that we indicate. Once the recovery is completed, the standby database will be left in mount mode. It will not be in managed recovery mode at that point, so we would need to put it in that mode once RMAN has finished the creation of the standby database. Using the **dorecover** option also avoids problems that can occur with the standby database control file in certain cases.

The **set** keywords are followed by parameter settings. These are parameters we want to set differently in the standby database. These parameters might not be set in the primary database at all, or they may be set in some other way. In this case, we have set the two log archive destination directories to be able to properly handle standby database operations. We have indicated which database is the FAL server (discussed earlier in this chapter), and we have set the parameter **standby_file_management** to a value of AUTO. Note that this only changes the parameter settings on the new standby database. If we want to change any parameters on the primary database, we need to do that separately using the **alter system** command (which we will demonstrate later in this chapter).

Finally, the **nofilenamecheck** option is required (as it would be if we were duplicating a database to another host) to indicate to RMAN that we are using the same file paths but on different hosts. Otherwise, RMAN would generate an error in an effort to try to keep us from overwriting important files.

After the Standby Is Created

During the creation of the standby database, Oracle will create standby redo logs. These structures are used to store redo that is shipped to the standby database by the primary database. For performance reasons you may want to add more logs, or you might want to make those logs larger.

Note that when you create a standby database, certain files are not re-created by the duplication process. Among these files are flashback logs, the block change tracking file, and any backups on the FRA of the primary database.

Also, once the standby database is created, RMAN will register that standby database in the recovery catalog. You don't need (nor should you try) to register the standby database in the recovery catalog.

RMAN Workshop: *Create a Standby Database Using RMAN*

Ryan has been tasked with investigating how to create standby databases with RMAN in his test database environment so that he can determine whether they will be useful as a part of his enterprise computing strategy. In this workshop we will shadow Ryan as he proceeds to create the standby database.

Workshop Notes

To perform his tests, Ryan has configured two Oracle 64-bit Linux virtual servers running Oracle Database 12*c*. He has created the primary database already. It's sitting on a server named StandbyDBOne, and the database is called TESTDB. He has a second database on a server called StandbyDBTwo that he will also call TESTDB, because both the primary and standby database servers have to have the same database name.

Ryan has decided to make the database unique names TESTDB_PR for the primary and TESTDB_SB for the standby database site. Further, Ryan has decided to use OMF naming on both database servers and to also use the same directory structures for the database files on both servers. As a result of these decisions, Ryan created the two database servers, and he has also made sure the file systems on both of the database servers are duplicated. In addition, he has made sure the database software was properly installed on the standby database server.

Ryan has created the required network connections between the primary database server and the standby database server. The primary database server has an IP address of 192.168.1.201, and the standby database server has an IP address of 192.168.1.202.

Finally, Ryan created a recovery catalog called RCAT on the primary database server.

Step 1. The first thing Ryan needs to do is to configure the standby database site. This will involve the following tasks:

- Creating the needed directories
- Creating the auxiliary instance parameter file
- Configuring Oracle networking on the standby database server
- Starting the auxiliary instance

Step 2. Ryan needs to create the directories he needs. First, he will create the audit destination directory. Because Ryan will be using the same directory structure as the primary database, he checks the AUDIT_FILE_DEST parameter on the primary database and then creates that directory on the standby database. Here is an example of what Ryan did:

```
SQL> show parameter audit_file_dest

NAME                         TYPE      VALUE
--------------------------- ------    -----------------------------------
     audit_file_dest                  string   /u01/app/oracle/admin/testdb/adump
```

Because Ryan is also using OMF, he needs to create the base directory structure that is pointed to by the parameter DB_FILE_CREATE_DEST. He looks in the primary database to figure out what the setting is for the DB_FILE_CREATE_DEST parameter, as shown here:

```
SQL> show parameter DB_CREATE_FILE_DEST
NAME                         TYPE      VALUE
--------------------------- ------    -----------------------------------
db_create_file_dest          string    /u01/app/oracle/oradata
```

Now, he needs to create these directories on the standby database server, as shown here:

```
mkdir -p /u01/app/oracle/admin/testdb/adump
mkdir -p /u01/app/oracle/oradata
```

Step 3. Before Ryan can start to create the standby database, he needs to be able to start the auxiliary instance. To do this, he needs to create a text-based parameter file called inittestdb.ora in the $ORACLE_HOME/dbs directory. Ryan can check the location of the $ORACLE_HOME directory this way:

```
[oracle@standbytwo admin]$ echo $ORACLE_HOME
/u01/app/oracle/product/12.1.0.2/dbhome_1
```

Next, he needs to create the inittestdb.ora file, which looks like this:

```
db_name=testdb
db_create_file_dest=/u01/app/oracle/oradata
```

Step 4. Standby databases are in constant contact with the primary database so that they can keep up to date with all the changes that happen. Because of this, Ryan will need to make sure his networking configuration is correct. This involves configuring the listener.ora file and the tnsnames.ora file.

> **NOTE**
> *In this workshop we assume that network configuration files for things such as host name resolution have already been configured.*

Step 5. Ryan needs to configure the listener.ora file on the standby database server so that the listener will know how to connect to the auxiliary instance. Normally, Oracle databases register with the Oracle listener, but this is not the case for an axillary instance. Therefore, Ryan will modify the listener.ora file so that it looks like this:

```
LISTENER =
  (DESCRIPTION_LIST =
    (DESCRIPTION =
      (ADDRESS = (PROTOCOL = TCP)(HOST = 192.168.1.202)(PORT = 1521))
      (ADDRESS = (PROTOCOL = IPC)(KEY = EXTPROC1521))
    )
      )
SID_LIST_LISTENER =
(SID_LIST =
  (SID_DESC =
    (GLOBAL_DBNAME = testdb_dr)
    (ORACLE_HOME = /u01/app/oracle/product/12.1.0.2/dbhome_1)
    (SID_NAME = testdb)
  )
)
USE_SID_AS_SERVICE_LISTENER=on
```

Ryan then starts the listener after he has modified the listener.ora file.

Step 6. The tnsname.ora file needs to be updated on the standby server, too. Therefore, Ryan makes the following additions to the tnsnames.ora file:

```
TESTDB_DR =
  (DESCRIPTION =
    (ADDRESS = (PROTOCOL = TCP)(HOST = 192.168.1.202)(PORT = 1521))
    (CONNECT_DATA =
      (SERVER = DEDICATED)
      (SERVICE_NAME = testdb_dr)
    )
  )

TESTDB =
  (DESCRIPTION =
    (ADDRESS = (PROTOCOL = TCP)(HOST = 192.168.1.201)(PORT = 1521))
    (CONNECT_DATA =
```

```
      (SERVER = DEDICATED)
      (SERVICE_NAME = testdb)
    )
  )
TESTDB_PD =
  (DESCRIPTION =
    (ADDRESS = (PROTOCOL = TCP)(HOST = 192.168.1.201)(PORT = 1521))
    (CONNECT_DATA =
      (SERVER = DEDICATED)
      (SERVICE_NAME = testdb_dr)
    )
  )
```

Ryan then checks the connection between the standby database server and the primary database to make sure that part of the tnsnames.ora file and the Oracle networking are properly set up.

Step 7.   Now that Ryan has created the parameter file for the auxiliary instance, he can start the auxiliary instance. He does this by setting the database environment to point to the auxiliary instance (called testdb) and then issuing the **startup nomount** command, as shown here:

```
[oracle@standbytwo admin]$ . oraenv
ORACLE_SID = [testdb] ?

[oracle@standbytwo admin]$ sqlplus / as sysdba

SQL> startup  nomount pfile=?/dbs/inittestdb.ora
ORACLE instance started.
Total System Global Area  234881024 bytes
Fixed Size                  2922904 bytes
Variable Size             176162408 bytes
Database Buffers           50331648 bytes
Redo Buffers                5464064 bytes
```

Having started the Oracle instance, Ryan moves on to making changes on the primary database server.

Step 8.   On the primary database server, Ryan will need to modify the tnsnames.ora file. Here are the lines that he adds:

```
db_name=testdb
db_create_file_dest=/u01/app/oracle/oradata
TESTDB_DR =
  (DESCRIPTION =
    (ADDRESS = (PROTOCOL = TCP)(HOST = 192.168.1.202)(PORT = 1521))
    (CONNECT_DATA =
      (SERVER = DEDICATED)
      (SERVICE_NAME = testdb_dr)
    )
  )
```

```
TESTDB_PD =
  (DESCRIPTION =
    (ADDRESS = (PROTOCOL = TCP)(HOST = 192.168.1.201)(PORT = 1521))
    (CONNECT_DATA =
      (SERVER = DEDICATED)
      (SERVICE_NAME = testdb_dr)
    )
  )
```

Step 9. Now that Ryan has prepared both the primary and standby database servers, he is ready to create the standby database with RMAN. Ryan will start RMAN, connecting to the auxiliary database, and then connect to the target database. Here is the command he uses:

```
rman target sys/robert auxiliary sys/robert@testdb_dr
```

If Ryan had a recovery catalog, he would have used the following parameters to start RMAN:

```
rman target sys/robert auxiliary sys/robert@testdb_dr catalog rcat/password@rcat
```

Now that Ryan has started RMAN, he can begin the process of creating the standby database using the **duplicate database** command:

```
duplicate target database
  for standby
  from active database
  dorecover
  spfile
    set "db_unique_name"="testdb_dr" comment "standby"
    set log_archive_dest_1="location=use_db_recovery_file_dest
valid_for=(all_logfiles,all_roles)"
    set log_archive_dest_2="service=testdb_dr async register
valid_for=(online_logfile,primary_role)"
    set fal_server="testdb" comment "primary"
    set standby_file_management="auto"
  nofilenamecheck;
```

Step 10. Now that Ryan has created the standby database with RMAN, he needs to modify some parameters on the primary database so that it will start processing the redo logs properly. Also, he needs to set some parameters to allow for a failover, where the standby database would become the primary database and the primary database would become the standby database. Here are the parameter changes Ryan needs to make on the primary database:

```
alter system set standby_file_management='AUTO';
alter system set log_archive_dest_1='location=USE_DB_RECOVERY_FILE_DEST valid_
for=(all_logfiles,all_roles)';
alter system set db_unique_name='testdb1_pr' scope=spfile;
alter system set log_Archive_dest_2='service=testdb_dr async noaffirm
reopen=15 valid_for=(all_logfiles,primary_role) db_unique_name=testdb_dr';
```

Step 11. To finish the duplication process, Ryan switches over to the standby database. There, he makes sure he has exited SQL*Plus from any earlier connection to the standby database. Then, from the standby database, he does the following:

- Puts the database in managed recovery mode so the standby database can be open read-only
- Tests the standby database

First, Ryan will put the standby database in managed recovery mode:

```
alter database recover managed standby database disconnect from session;
```

Now, to test the standby database, Ryan will determine the current log file sequence number using the **archive log list** command, as shown here:

```
SQL> archive log list
Database log mode              Archive Mode
Automatic archival             Enabled
Archive destination            USE_DB_RECOVERY_FILE_DEST
Oldest online log sequence     49
Next log sequence to archive   51
Current log sequence           51
```

Ryan then issues a log switch on the primary database so that the log will be processed by the standby database:

```
alter system switch logfile;
```

Then, Ryan checks the standby database to ensure that the log files have been processed:

```
select process, status, sequence# from v$managed_standby;
```

Once the recovery is complete, Ryan can cancel it so that he can put the database in read-only mode. Here is how Ryan cancels managed recovery mode:

```
select process, status, sequence# from v$managed_standby;
PROCESS     STATUS        SEQUENCE#
---------   ------------  ----------
ARCH        CONNECTED     0
ARCH        CONNECTED     0
ARCH        CONNECTED     0
ARCH        CONNECTED     0
MRP0        WAIT_FOR_LOG         51
RFS         IDLE                 51
RFS         IDLE          0
RFS         IDLE          0
```

In this case, Ryan finds that log sequence number 51 has been processed by the standby database. Ryan can now take the database out of recovery mode, put the database in read-only mode, and then restart recovery, as shown here:

```
alter database recover managed standby database cancel;
alter database open;
alter database recover managed standby database disconnect from session;
```

With that, Ryan has a brand-new standby database running.

Taking Backups from the Standby Database

After creating your standby database, you can use it for a number of purposes. Its primary reason for existence, of course, is to provide a disaster recovery solution for your production database. However, you can also suspend media recovery against the standby database, open it as read-only, and perform any number of data-mining operations that would suck too many resources away from your production system.

From the RMAN perspective, there is another excellent way to put the standby database to work. As you know from Chapter 13, there is a price to pay for running RMAN against your production database in terms of resources used. You utilize precious memory, CPU, and disk I/O resources when the backup is running. Therefore, we recommend running your backups during the off-peak hours of your database. Sometimes, though, there are no off-peak hours. You could be a 24-hour operation, with constant database updates, or your database could be so large that backups are pretty much running around the clock.

If you have a physical standby database, you can take your production backups from the standby database; these backups can then be restored to the primary database if the primary database has a failure. Because the standby database has the same DBID as the primary database and is always from the same incarnation, the RMAN datafile backups are interchangeable between the standby database and the primary database. The standby database is a true clone of the primary database.

The thing to understand about using a standby database to take production backups is that RMAN will connect to the standby database as the target database. Remember, up to this point, we've encouraged you to think of the standby database as the auxiliary database. But that only holds true for duplication operations. Once the standby database is established, you can connect to it as the target database and perform **backup** commands. These backups can then be used for restore operations at the primary database.

To use the standby database in this fashion, you must have a recovery catalog set up. Without a recovery catalog, there is no way to propagate the records of the backups from the standby control file to the primary control file. With a recovery catalog, you resync with the standby control file after a backup, so the records of the backup are put in the catalog. Then, you connect to the primary database as the target and make your catalog connection. To RMAN, the primary and standby databases are indistinguishable, so it accesses the same record set in the catalog when connected to either. Therefore, you can perform a resync operation while connected to the primary database, and it will refresh the primary control file with the records of backups taken while connected to the standby database.

Other RMAN and Data Guard Topics

Data Guard and RMAN can come in handy in a number of cases. For example, if there is a loss of one or more datafiles at the primary database, and backups are not accessible, then RMAN and Data Guard can be used to recover the lost datafiles. Further, if the standby database should become seriously out of sync with the primary database, it might be easier to use RMAN to bring the standby database in sync than to spend a great deal of time applying the online redo logs. Let's quickly look at each of these cases in more detail.

Restoring a Lost Datafile, Tablespace, or Database from a Standby Database with RMAN

If the primary database should lose one or more datafiles, you can use the standby database to recover them. Assume, for example, that you have lost a datafile that is assigned to the USERS tablespace. To perform this restore, you sign into RMAN and connect to the standby database. You would take the datafile you are going to restore (in our case, datafile 6) offline:

```
Alter database datafile 6 offline;
```

With the datafile offline, you use the RMAN **restore database** command, along with the **from service** clause, to restore the datafile from the standby database. You will use the service name of the standby database in the **from service** clause, as shown in this example, where we are restoring datafile 6 from the standby database:

```
Restore datafile 6 from service testdb_stby;
```

Then, you recover the datafile with the RMAN **recover datafile** command, as shown here:

```
recover datafile 6;
```

Finally, you bring the datafile online to complete the recovery:

```
Alter database datafile 6 online;
```

Resynchronizing the Standby Database

Resynchronizing the standby database when it gets seriously out of step with the primary database is now much easier. The new **from service** clause provides the ability to directly connect to the primary database via its service name and resynchronize the standby database from the primary database.

First, you connect to the standby database on the standby database server with RMAN, as shown here:

```
Set oracle_sid=testdb
Rman target /
```

Then, you use the **recover database** command on the standby database, including the primary database service name in the **from service** clause, as shown here:

```
Recover database from service testdb_pd using compressed backupset;
```

Archive Log Backups from the Standby Database

Backing up the archive logs from the standby database is a somewhat trickier affair because of how RMAN determines which archive logs need to be backed up: it checks the view V$ARCHIVED_LOG. On the primary database, this view is incremented with each new archive log after it has been successfully created in the LOG_ARCHIVE_DEST. However, on the standby database, this view is updated only if your standby database is in MANAGED RECOVERY mode (where the archive logs are automatically applied at the standby database). If your standby database is not in MANAGED RECOVERY mode, or if due to your setup you get archive log gaps at the standby database on a regular basis, it may be hard to get all the required archive logs backed up successfully from the standby database. In this case, we recommend using your primary database for its own archive log backups and using the standby database just for datafile backups.

Summary

In this chapter, we discussed the relationship that RMAN can have with the standby database architecture. RMAN makes it quite easy to create a standby database, and it provides a number of different ways to create the standby database based on your needs. We have really only touched the surface here, and there are many other neat things RMAN can do in specific use cases. Now go out and create standby databases all over the world!

CHAPTER
18

RMAN and Real
Application Clusters

Althought it is well beyond the scope of this book to guide you through the intricacies of Oracle Real Application Clusters (RAC), we can provide some guidance on preparing your RAC configuration for backup and recovery. As with Data Guard in Chapter 17, we assume that you have a working knowledge of RAC in Oracle Database 12c, and thus our brief discussion of RAC architecture is intended more as a reminder than as an education.

Throughout this chapter, we will use a sample cluster database that has only two nodes: winrac1 and winrac2. These nodes share a disk array, which is configured with Oracle ASM as its volume manager. Each node has an instance: prod1 on winrac1, and prod2 on winrac2. Although we will limit our explanations to the simplest of RAC environments—a two-node cluster—nothing changes when you scale out to three, four, or more nodes. In our examples, you simply change the number of nodes from 2 to 3, and the number of channels from 2 to 3, and so on. The more nodes you have, the more complex your backup/recovery strategies and scripts, but the basic rules apply no matter the number of instances.

There are two basic ways to share a file system across multiple computers. The first, which was also available with Oracle 9i Database, is to use a clustered file system. This is frequently provided by a third-party vendor, such as VERITAS. On Windows and Linux, Oracle provides its own cluster file system (OCFS). A cluster file system is defined by its ability to properly handle and queue requests for files coming from multiple nodes simultaneously—which is a requirement if you are going to cluster your databases.

The second way to share a file system across multiple computers, introduced in Oracle Database 10g, is to use Automatic Storage Management (ASM). ASM is Oracle's first volume management product and can be used to manage raw disks that have no other formatting on them. Because of its architecture, ASM is built for cluster configurations and can easily handle the demands of RAC. You could say that ASM was built for RAC, because if you decide to deploy RAC on Oracle Standard Edition, ASM is the *only* file system allowed for the shared Oracle database files.

And that is all you're going to get from us on the subject, except to say this: you can no longer use raw partitions to host your RAC voting, OCR, data files, or redo log files. In 11gR2, raw partitions were only supported if upgrading from an older release, and with 12c raw partitions are completely desupported for both upgraded and new cluster installs.

Real Application Clusters: Unique Backup Challenges

Before we dig any deeper, it's helpful to consider the architectural nature of a RAC. Essentially, you have at least two different servers, each with its own memory and local disks, and each connected to a shared disk array. Oracle uses this hardware by creating two instances, one on each node, with their own SGA/PGA memory areas. Each instance has its own redo logs, but they exist on the shared disk and are accessible by the other nodes. All control files and datafiles are shared between the two instances, meaning there is only one database, with two threads accessing and updating the data simultaneously. Figure 18-1 provides an oversimplified look at RAC.

From the RMAN perspective, this architecture creates interesting challenges for taking backups. First of all, multiple instances are running, but RMAN can connect to only a single node. This shouldn't pose any problems for backing up the datafiles, but we do have a problem when it comes to archive logs. Each instance is archiving its own redo logs to a local drive rather than to the shared disks, so the issue is how we get to those other archive logs. But let's start by considering the datafile backups.

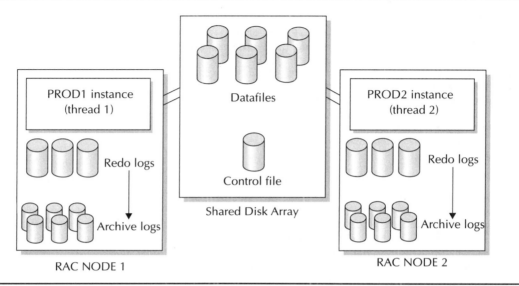

FIGURE 18-1. *RAC at its most basic*

Datafile Backups

Datafile backups in a RAC environment are pretty much the same as datafile backups in a single-node database: RMAN connects to a node and issues a **backup database** command. The memory that RMAN needs to perform the backup operation will be grabbed from that one node. If backing up to disk, the backups will be local to that node; if backing up to tape, that instance will have to be configured for integration with your MML.

The RMAN Snapshot Control File and RAC

You need to move the snapshot control file to a shared location if you plan to run backups from more than one node. If you do not move the snapshot control file to a shared file system such as OCFS or an ASM disk group, then you must make sure that the local destination is identical on all nodes. To see the snapshot control file location, use the **show** command:

```
rman> show snapshot controlfile name;
```

To change the value, use the **configure** command:

```
rman> configure snapshot controlfile name to
      '/u02/oradata/grid10/snap_grid10.scf';
```

The only problem with this scenario is that it puts quite a bit of load on a single node. This may be what you are after; if not, there is a better way. RMAN can connect to only a single node initially, but it can allocate channels at all of your nodes during an actual backup operation. The following shows an example of how this would be done:

```
configure default device type sbt;
configure device type sbt parallelism 2;
configure channel 1 device type sbt
connect 'sys/password@prod1';
configure channel 2 device type sbt
connect 'sys/password@prod2';
backup database;
```

Then, you can run your backup, and RMAN will spread the work between your two nodes. RAC datafiles sometimes have something known as *node affinity,* where a particular datafile is accessed faster from one node or the other. If this is the case for your cluster, RMAN knows about it and will back up the datafile from the node where it can be read the fastest. If there is no node affinity on your system, RMAN just distributes the work across the two channels as it would any two channels used to parallelize a backup. Obviously, you could allocate two channels at each node, or three, four, or more. How many channels each node utilizes should be based on the same performance parameters we explored in Chapter 13.

Automatic Distribution of Backup Work Across Nodes

Since Oracle Database 10g Release 2, RMAN can utilize information gleaned from Oracle's Cluster Ready Services (CRS) to provide better RAC integration. Of most importance, you no longer have to configure a channel to specifically connect at a particular node. If you have two nodes and you set parallelism to 2, RMAN will query CRS for the node information and automatically spread the two channels across the two nodes. In addition, CRS keeps track of node utilization and will spread RMAN backup jobs out to those nodes that are currently being least utilized, to avoid I/O traffic jams. This is a significant automation improvement, and the lesson to take away is simple: don't try to out-think CRS. Let it do the footwork of determining how to distribute work across your cluster. Just set your level of parallelism equal to the total number of nodes you want involved in your backup, and let CRS do the work.

Archive Log Backups

Archive log backups are far trickier than datafile backups, because each node is responsible for its own archiving, which means that each node has potentially unshared files that only it can access. If we connect to only one node and issue a **backup archivelog all** command, RMAN will look in the control file and discover the listing for the archive logs from both nodes, but when it looks at the local node, it will find only the archive logs from that node and it will error out.

Of course, the question may be posed, "Why not write archive logs to a cluster file system or ASM on the shared disk array?" The answer is, "Because that is the best and recommended solution."

RMAN, RAC, and Net Connections

RAC comes with many extremely powerful load-balancing and failover features as part of the Net configuration, but this means changes in the listener.ora file and in the tnsnames.ora files for both the cluster nodes and the clients. RMAN is a little too picky for these features. RMAN can only connect to one node and cannot fail over or be load-balanced. Therefore, the Net aliases you use for the target connection and for the **connect** clause of the channel allocation string must be configured to connect to a single node with a dedicated server. This means that you cannot use the same NET aliases configured for failover that you use for other connection purposes.

If you insist on leaving archive logs local to each node, a solution is available that allows RMAN to cope with the non shared disk locations. First, make sure that each node is archiving to a unique file location. For example, prod1 archives to a directory called /u04/prod1/arch, and prod2 archives to /u04/prod2/arch. Then, you can allocate channels at each node, as you did to load-balance the datafile backups earlier, and back up the archive logs:

```
configure default device type sbt;
configure device type sbt parallelism 2;
configure channel 1 device type sbt
connect 'sys/password@prod1';
configure channel 2 device type sbt
connect 'sys/password@prod2';
backup archivelog all delete input;
```

RMAN has a feature known as *autolocate* that identifies which archive logs belong to which node and that attempts to back them up only from that node. In this way, you don't have to specify in RMAN which logs you need backed up at which node—RMAN can figure it out for you.

Another option that would allow you to perform your archive log backup from a single node would be to NFS-mount the archive log destination of the other node. For example, at the node winrac1, you have local archive logs located at /u04/prod1/arch. Then, on winrac1, you NFS-mount the drive /u04/prod2/arch on winrac2 as /u04/prod2/arch. That way, when you run your archive log backups, RMAN checks the control file for the archive log locations, and it can find both locations while connected to only prod1. Figure 18-2 illustrates this methodology.

The only problem in the scenarios we've provided so far is that you are giving yourself a single point of failure for archive logs. If you archive your logs only to their respective nodes and you lose a node, you lose the archive logs from that node. That means you may have to perform point-in-time recovery of the entire database to the point right before the node was lost.

A better strategy is to set up each node with a LOG_ARCHIVE_DEST_2 parameter that writes to another node. One way to approach this task is to consider the NFS mount strategies already discussed in this chapter. Instead of just NFS-mounting in READ ONLY mode the archive destination of the other node, consider NFS-mounting a drive on the other node with write access, and then setting that NFS mount as a second archive destination. Take our two-node RAC

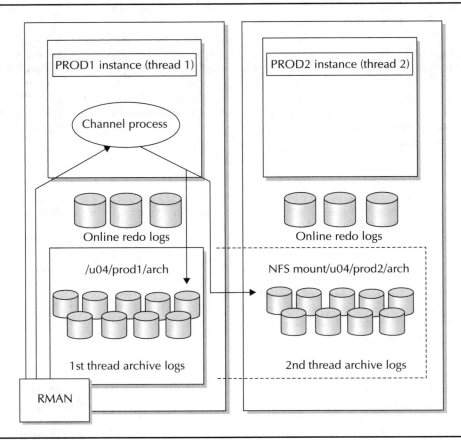

FIGURE 18-2. *Mounting the archive log destination*

database, for example. On winrac1, we could mount the shared directory /u04/prod2/arch from winrac2, and on winrac2, we could mount winrac1's /u04/prod1/arch directory. Then, we could set up the init.ora files for each node, as shown next:

```
winrac1 init.ora file:
log_archive_dest_1='location=/u04/prod1/arch'
log_archive_dest_2='location=/u04/prod2/arch'
...
winrac2 init.ora file:
log_archive_dest_1='location=/u04/prod2/arch'
log_archive_dest_2='location=/u04/prod1/arch'
```

When set up like this, Oracle writes archive logs from each node to the archive destination of the other node. This gives us an elegant solution for backing up the archive logs from a single node and provides us with fault tolerance in case a node is lost.

Avoid Archive Log Backup Complexity with ASM and the Fast Recovery Area

All of these complications can be avoided by creating a location on the shared disk array that has a volume cooked with a cluster file system, such as OCFS. Even better, you can employ ASM as your volume manager for all your RAC files. Then, you can create a second disk group and deploy your Fast Recovery Area (FRA) to the disk group. With an FRA on an ASM disk group, managing archive logs in RAC is essentially the same as managing them in a single-thread environment. If you configure the database to archive to the FRA, both nodes will deposit the logs in a single location where they are visible to both nodes at all times. Managing archive logs during cleanup operations is no different than managing them on a single-thread database.

RAC Recovery Challenges

Perhaps more confusing than getting backups done is getting restore and recovery tasks taken care of in a RAC environment. Again, this is due to the complex nature of a database that has multiple instances. The challenges can be roughly divided into three areas: restore operations, media management considerations, and recovery challenges.

Restore Operations

We must point out again that when you are performing a restore from RMAN, it can connect to only one node, but then can allocate channels at each node. This should sound pretty familiar by now, but that's not the tricky part. The part that hangs people up is keeping track of where files were backed up from.

File accessibility is the key to restore success on a RAC node. If you have been backing up to disk using channels allocated at each node, you must allocate the same channels at each node during a restore operation. This is not a problem, unless you've lost a node. If the node is down, your disk backups on that node are inaccessible and restore operations will fail. The lesson is, if you're spending all this time and money on RAC so that you don't have a single point of failure, make sure you apply this philosophy to your backup and recovery strategy as well. If you back up to disk, duplex the backup to more than one node. This might mean overriding the default autolocate feature so that you can specify where exactly you want your backups to be backed up from. You do this by specifying the channel for datafile sets:

```
configure default device type disk;
configure device type sbt parallelism 2;
configure channel 1 device type disk
connect 'sys/password@prod1';
configure channel 2 device type disk
connect 'sys/password@prod2';
backup (datafile 1,2,3,4,5 channel ORA_DISK_1)
       (datafile 6,7,8,9,10 channel ORA_DISK_2);
# then switch the channels for the datafiles
backup (datafile 1,2,3,4,5 channel ORA_DISK_2)
       (datafile 6,7,8,9,10 channel ORA_DISK_1);
```

Here, again, ASM will save you time and energy. More to the point, running an FRA on a shared ASM disk volume makes disk backups in a RAC environment simple and requires little configuration beyond what you normally do for a single-thread database. Using an FRA on ASM allows you to take advantage of job multiplexing across your nodes, yet still have all the backups end up in a location that is always accessible by other nodes during the restore. Therefore, you no longer need to fear that a disk backup might be left inaccessible on a downed node. Nor do you need to fear a single point of failure, because ASM comes with automatic redundancy, so you can mirror your FRA and have a duplexed copy of your backup without any additional work.

Media Management Considerations During a Restore

Another way to make your backups available to all nodes during a restore is to back up to tape and to use a centralized media management server to house your tape backups. If you have tape devices at each node and use them all for tape backup, you're increasing the degree of complexity unnecessarily. If you lose a node in your cluster, you then lose the media management catalog for all backups taken from that node. Chances are that your media management product has an automatic catalog backup, but then you have another restore to do, and where do you do it, and when? You need the catalogs at both of your other nodes for their backup information. So, you have a disaster that is fixable, but valuable minutes are racing by as you stick your nose in manuals, trying to figure it all out.

We prefer to use a centralized media management system so that all nodes can back up to tape devices that are all managed by the same media manager server. This way, there is a single media management catalog. Thus, when a node is lost, you can simply specify the client name in your RMAN channel and do the restores to a different node. This brings us to the most important note to remember when you use RMAN to restore your backup from tape: you must consider the node from which RMAN made the backup when doing the restore.

As an example, suppose that in our two-node cluster, we have lost node winrac2, and the disaster that took it out also corrupted some of our datafiles. We've been employing a backup strategy that allocates channels at both nodes to perform the backup, so our restore is going to have to allocate channels from both nodes. Oops! No chance of that! Instead, we can allocate two kinds of channels at winrac1: normal tape channels and channels that specify the client as winrac2. It would look something like this:

```
configure default device type sbt;
configure device type sbt parallelism 2;
configure channel 1 device type sbt
parms="env=(nb_ora_serv=rmsrv)";
configure channel 2 device type disk
parms="env=(nb_ora_serv=rmsrv, nb_ora_client=winrac2)";
restore datafile 5,12,13,18;
```

This is obviously a very simple example of what can be a complex headache. We recommend a backup approach that takes datafile backups from only a single node in the cluster. If the size of your database prohibits such a simplistic approach, try to at least restrict RMAN to a small subset of your nodes. By doing so, you keep the complexity down when it comes time to perform restore operations, because tracking which nodes participated in backups can be a time-consuming process.

Another option is to first stage your backups to a disk location using an FRA on an ASM disk volume. If you have the space on the disk array to stage your backups to disk first, your ultimate move to tape can happen from one or more nodes at a more controlled time. Using the **backup recovery area** command would allow you to take a consolidated set of backups from the FRA and move them all to tape in a separate operation. This tape operation could occur from any node or any combination of nodes. If you did the tape backup from a single node, then the SBT channel parameters would be simplified during the restore, even if a different node were responsible for the restore.

Recovery Considerations After a Restore

After you get your files restored, it's time to perform media recovery by applying archive logs. Media recovery in a RAC environment has one rule that you must never forget: *only one node can perform recovery*. Burn it into your brain. This means that one node must have access to all the archive logs on disk. Therefore, if you have been using an archive log strategy that has each node holding its own archive logs in a local disk, you must make that local disk available to the recovery node. You can do this via NFS if you followed the guidelines specified in "Archive Log Backups" earlier in this chapter. You simply mount the archive log destination of the other node and issue your recover statement from within RMAN. If you're using CFS, this is not a problem, and you can ignore all this. If you are using an FRA on ASM, again, access to all archive logs is not an issue.

If you have archive logs that you need to restore from RMAN backups, the same rules and guidelines apply to archive logs that apply to datafile restores. If you allocated channels at each node for the backup, then you need to do so for the restore as well. If you are missing a node, you have to allocate a channel that includes the client name so that the media manager can find the proper backups (see the preceding section, "Media Management Considerations During a Restore"). In addition, you may have to restore the archive logs to a directory that exists locally if the LOG_ARCHIVE_DEST parameter that existed on the missing node does not exist on the node doing the restore operation:

```
restore archivelog like '%prod2%' to '/u04/prod1/arch%';
```

Although only one node can perform recovery with RMAN, RMAN does media recovery in parallel. You cannot control this level of parallelism, other than to turn it off:

```
rman> Recover database noparallel;
```

By default, though, RMAN automatically selects the degree of recovery parallelism based on the number of available CPUs on the node performing recovery.

Advanced RMAN/RAC Topics

Once you have determined what your backup and recovery strategies will be for your RAC database, you can consider many of the same benefits that RMAN offers you in a single-node database environment: block corruption checking, null compression, block media recovery—all of these benefits are yours in a RAC environment. Advanced functionality such as database duplication exists as well. RMAN backups of RAC databases work for duplication and standby database creation, just as they would for a single-node system. We have some caveats, however, which we discuss next.

Duplication to a Single-Node System

If you administer a RAC cluster and aren't convinced yet that RMAN is the right tool for you, here's a little something to seal the deal: you can use your RMAN backups of your RAC database to create a clone of your RAC database on a single-node database. This gives you a copy of your production database without having to purchase and administer a second RAC cluster. Instead, you have a single-node database running on a cooked file system.

In fact, RMAN cannot actually duplicate from one RAC cluster to another RAC cluster. It can duplicate only to a single-thread database. However, once the database is duplicated, you can easily turn the clone database into a RAC database. Just make sure you duplicate to an ASM disk group on a node that already has CRS installed.

RMAN Workshop: *Duplicating a RAC Database to a Single-Node Database*

Workshop Notes

This Workshop creates a single-node clone of a two-node database. You can do this either to a new server or to a cooked file system on one of the nodes of the RAC cluster. This example duplicates to a file system on one of the nodes in the RAC cluster. Because duplication must perform recovery, you must remember that a recovery session has access only to the node on which the recovery is being performed, so that node must have access to all the nodes' archive logs. This Workshop assumes that you have NFS-mounted the archive destination of each node on each other node so that a full copy of each archive log stream is available at every node.

The two nodes of our cluster are opcbs01 and opcbs02, with instances of V112A and V112B, respectively. We will be connecting to V112B for all RMAN operations.

Step 1.   Build your auxiliary database directory structures:

```
mkdir /u02/32bit/app/oracle/oradata/aux1
mkdir /u02/32bit/app/oracle/oradata/aux1/arch
cd /u02/32bit/app/oracle/admin
mkdir aux1
cd aux1
mkdir pfile bdump udump cdump
ls
```

Step 2.   Copy the target init.ora file to the auxiliary location. If your target database uses an SPFILE, you need to create a PFILE from the SPFILE to capture parameters to move over.

If you use an SPFILE at your target, enter the following:

```
SQL> connect / as sysdba
create pfile='/u02/32bit/app/oracle/admin/aux1/pfile/init.ora'
from spfile;
```

If you use an init.ora file at your target, enter the following:

```
cp /u02/32bit/app/oracle/admin/V112B/pfile/init.ora
   /u02/32bit/app/oracle/admin/aux1/pfile/init.ora
```

Step 3. Make all necessary changes to your aux1 init.ora file:

```
control_files=
    '/u02/32bit/app/oracle/oradata/aux1/control01.dbf'
core_dump_dest='/u02/32bit/app/oracle/admin/aux1/cdump'
background_dump_dest='/u02/32bit/app/oracle/admin/aux1/bdump'
user_dump_dest=/u02/32bit/app/oracle/admin/aux1/udump
log_archive_dest_1=
    'location=/u02/32bit/app/oracle/oradata/aux1/arch'
db_name='aux1'
instance_name='aux1'
remote_login_passwordfile=exclusive
db_file_name_convert=
  ('/dev/vx/rdsk/usupport_dg', '/u02/32bit/app/oracle/oradata/aux1')
```

You can remove the following parameters entirely, including those that refer to the other instance:

```
cluster_database_instances=2
cluster_database=true
V112A.instance_name='V112A'
V112B.instance_name='V112B'
V112B.instance_number=2
V112A.instance_number=1
V112B.thread=2
V112A.thread=1
V112B.undo_tablespace='UNDOTBS2'
V112A.undo_tablespace='UNDOTBS1'
```

You can replace them by just having the following:

```
undo_tablespace='UNDOTBS2'
```

Step 4. Build your aux1 password file using the **orapwd** utility.

Step 5. Start the aux1 instance in NOMOUNT mode:

```
ORACLE_SID=aux1
export ORACLE_SID
SQLplus /nolog
SQL>connect / as sysdba
SQL>startup nomount
pfile=/u02/32bit/app/oracle/admin/aux1/pfile/init.ora
```

Step 6. Configure your network files for connection to aux1. After you make any changes to your listener.ora file, be sure that you bounce your listener, or the change will not take effect:

```
lsnrctl
LSNRCTL>stop
LSNRCTL>start
```

The tnsnames.ora file should have an entry like this:

```
AUX1 =
  (DESCRIPTION =
    (ADDRESS_LIST =
      (ADDRESS = (PROTOCOL = TCP)(HOST = opcbsol2)(PORT = 1526))
    )
    (CONNECT_DATA =
      (SID = aux1)
      (SERVER = DEDICATED)
    )
  )
```

The listener.ora file should have an entry like this:

```
 (SID_DESC =
    (GLOBAL_DBNAME = aux1)
    (ORACLE_HOME = /u02/32bit/app/oracle/product/11.2.0/dbhome_1)
    (SID_NAME = aux1)
)
```

Step 7.   From RMAN, connect to the target database and the auxiliary instance and run the **duplicate** command:

```
ORACLE_SID=V112B
export ORACLE_SID
rman
rman>connect target /
rman> connect auxiliary sys/password@aux1
rman>duplicate target database to aux1
  pfile=/u02/32bit/app/oracle/admin/aux1/pfile/init.ora
  logfile
  '/u02/32bit/app/oracle/oradata/aux1/redo1.dbf' size 100m,
  '/u02/32bit/app/oracle/oradata/aux1/redo2.dbf' size 100m,
  '/u02/32bit/app/oracle/oradata/aux1/redo3.dbf' size 100m;
```

The Single-Node Standby Database

Of course, if we can duplicate to a single node, then we can also use the **duplicate** command to create a standby database for our RAC cluster on a single node. Perhaps more so than even straight duplication, this feature gives us an excellent cost-to-performance strategy for providing a disaster recovery solution for our RAC database. Instead of purchasing all the hardware and software necessary to have a complete second RAC system set up but unused for a standby database, you can create the standby database on a single-node system. Obviously, it won't have the computing power or load-balancing features of the RAC database, but it gives a reasonable disaster recovery solution so that you can hobble along until the RAC database is restored.

As with the duplication process, the secret lies in using the DB_FILE_NAME_CONVERT parameter to switch the files from OCFS or ASM disk groups to normal, nonclustered file systems. In addition, the single-node standby database can receive archive logs from each of the nodes in the RAC cluster and apply them in the correct chronological order.

RMAN Workshop: *Creating a Single-Node Standby Database from a RAC Database*

Step 1.   Use RMAN to create a standby control file:

```
ORACLE_SID=V112B
export ORACLE_SID
rman
rman> connect target /
rman> backup current controlfile for standby
   format= '/u02/backup/stby_cfile.%U';
```

You need to specify a point in time after you created this standby control file, so perform a few log switches and then record the last log sequence number from V$ARCHIVED_LOG. It doesn't matter which thread you choose, because the following command will force a log switch at all nodes:

```
SQL> alter system archivelog current;
SQL> select sequence# from v$archived_log;
```

Step 2.   Build your standby database directory structures:

```
mkdir /u02/32bit/app/oracle/oradata/stby
mkdir /u02/32bit/app/oracle/oradata/stby/arch
cd /u02/32bit/app/oracle/admin
mkdir stby
cd stby
mkdir pfile bdump udump cdump
ls
```

Step 3.   Copy the target init.ora file to the auxiliary location. If your target database uses an SPFILE, you need to create a PFILE from the SPFILE to capture parameters to move over.
   If you use an SPFILE at your target, enter the following:

```
SQL> connect / as sysdba
create pfile='/u02/32bit/app/oracle/admin/stby/pfile/init.ora'
from spfile;
```

   If you use an init.ora file at your target, enter the following:

```
cp /u02/32bit/app/oracle/admin/V112/pfile/init.ora
   /u02/32bit/app/oracle/admin/stby/pfile/init.ora
```

Step 4. Make all necessary changes to your stby init.ora file:

```
control_files= '/u02/32bit/app/oracle/oradata/stby/control01.dbf'
background_dump_dest=/u02/32bit/app/oracle/admin/stby/bdump
user_dump_dest=/u02/32bit/app/oracle/admin/stby/udump
log_archive_dest_1=
    'location=/u02/32bit/app/oracle/oradata/stby/arch'
standby_archive_dest=
    'location=/u02/32bit/app/oracle/oradata/stbyarch'
lock_name_space='stby'
remote_login_passwordfile=exclusive
db_file_name_convert=
  ('/dev/vx/rdsk/usupport_dg', '/u02/32bit/app/oracle/oradata/aux1')
log_file_name_convert=
  ('/dev/vx/rdsk/usupport_dg', '/u02/32bit/app/oracle/oradata/aux1')
```

You can remove the following parameters entirely, including those that refer to the other instance:

```
cluster_database_instances=2
cluster_database=true
V112A.instance_name='V112A'
V112B.instance_name='V112B'
V112B.instance_number=2
V112A.instance_number=1
V112B.thread=2
V112A.thread=1
V112B.undo_tablespace='UNDOTBS2'
V102A.undo_tablespace='UNDOTBS1'
```

You can replace them by just having the following:

```
instance_name='V112B'
undo_tablespace='UNDOTBS2'
```

Step 5. Build your stby password file with the **orapwd** command.

Step 6. Start the stby instance in NOMOUNT mode:

```
ORACLE_SID=stby
export ORACLE_SID
SQLplus /nolog
SQL>connect / as sysdba
SQL>startup nomount
pfile=/u02/32bit/app/oracle/admin/stby/pfile/init.ora
```

Step 7. Configure your network files for connection to stby. After making any changes to your listener.ora file, be sure that you bounce your listener, or the change will not take effect:

```
lsnrctl
LSNRCTL>stop
LSNRCTL>start
```

The tnsnames.ora file should have an entry like this:

```
STBY =
  (DESCRIPTION =
    (ADDRESS_LIST =
      (ADDRESS = (PROTOCOL = TCP)(HOST = opcbsol2)(PORT = 1521))
    )
    (CONNECT_DATA =
      (SID = stby)
      (SERVER = DEDICATED)
    )
  )
```

The listener.ora file should have an entry like this:

```
  (SID_DESC =
    (GLOBAL_DBNAME = aux1)
    (ORACLE_HOME = /u02/32bit/app/oracle/product/11.2.0/dbhome_1)
    (SID_NAME = aux1)
)
```

Step 8. From RMAN, connect to the target and auxiliary instance and run the **duplicate** command:

```
ORACLE_SID=V112B
export ORACLE_SID
rman
rman>connect target /
rman> connect auxiliary sys/password@stby
rman>run {
  set until sequence = 43 thread = 1;
  duplicate target database for standby
  dorecover;}
```

Backing Up the Multinode RAC Database

Once you have created the single-node standby database, you can take all of your backups from the standby database, just as you would in a normal environment. This means that you can offload your production RAC backups from the RAC cluster itself to the node that is set up and running as a standby database. This takes the load off the cluster, gives you a disaster recovery solution, and gives you a simplified backup solution for archive logs, because all the archive logs from all nodes will necessarily exist on the standby database.

Again, the secret is in the DB_FILE_NAME_CONVERT parameter. You are taking backups from the standby database that has the datafiles on a cooked file system, but even the standby database control file knows the original location of the files (the raw system). Therefore, when you go to restore a backup taken from the standby on the production RAC database, RMAN checks with the control file, finds the raw locations, and places the files there.

For such a solution to work for you, you must use a recovery catalog. The recovery catalog acts as the transition agent for the metadata about the backups from the standby database control file to the primary database control file. After you take the backup from the standby database, RMAN resyncs with the recovery catalog, recording the backup metadata. Then, when you connect RMAN to the primary database and perform a manual resync, the backup metadata from the standby database control file is placed in the primary database control file records.

It is important to make sure you connect to the standby database as the target database when performing backups from the standby database. Then, you connect to the primary database as the target database as well, to perform the resync. RMAN can do this smoothly because it sees no functional difference between the two databases: they have the same DB_NAME, the same DBID, and the same redo stream history.

Summary

In this chapter, we discussed the means by which RMAN interacts with databases in RAC clusters. We discussed how RMAN can allocate channels on each node for backup, but that recovery requires that all backups be accessible from a single node. We discussed the complications caused in archive log backups due to multiple threads of redo being generated at different nodes. We concluded with examples for duplicating a RAC database to a single-node database and for creating a single-node standby database from a RAC database.

CHAPTER
19

Zero Data Loss Recovery
Appliance: Evolution of
RMAN to Enterprise-wide
Database Protection Solution

A s an Oracle Backup and Recovery product manager, we personally have the opportunity to work with customers worldwide on their broad and varied backup needs. And, as attested by the wealth of practical DBA experience in this book, it's clear that virtually all Oracle customers—large and small—depend on RMAN to ensure their databases are backed up properly. More importantly, it must be possible to recover these databases wherever needed and within the constraints that are provided for in SLAs and other customer-facing documents.

This book has made it clear that RMAN is incredibly feature rich and flexible—so much so that it's honestly hard to keep up with all the new bells and whistles—which is hopefully one of the reasons why you buy books like this one.

Our environments never get less complex. Where we were at one time backing up a few databases, now we back up dozens. Where we were backing up dozens, we now back up hundreds, and so forth. However, a number of problems arise as your backup infrastructure grows ever larger. Everything, including maintaining the scripts used to perform the backups, the schedules that manage the backup jobs, and all of your reporting and other functionality, becomes harder to manage as your Oracle environment grows to hundreds, thousands, or more databases. The human cost in terms of time also becomes more difficult to manage. Resources are not infinite, nor are dollars. We need a solution to this problem of scale.

Understanding these problems of scale in the enterprise, Oracle began to develop a solution that could address these and many other concerns. RMAN is a great tool, but more was needed to manage the scale problem. It was important to leverage the RMAN knowledge within the DBA community while considering a solution to deal with the problems enterprises were facing in the backup world. So it was at Oracle OpenWorld 2014 that Oracle announced a new engineered system—the "Zero Data Loss Recovery Appliance." It was the beginning of Oracle's effort to provide a truly enterprise-worthy database data protection solution, addressing the problems of scale.

The Zero Data Loss Recovery Appliance: An Overview

The Zero Data Loss Recovery Appliance is designed to dramatically reduce data loss and data protection overhead for all Oracle databases in the enterprise. Backup processing is offloaded to the appliance, boosting production performance, while data loss exposure is minimized via real-time redo transport. Oracle Enterprise Manager Cloud Control oversees administration and control of the entire environment, providing a "single pane of glass" view of the entire backup lifecycle for each database, whether backups reside on disk, tape, or a replicated appliance. The integrated hardware for the appliance, based on the industry-proven Exadata platform, is fully fault tolerant, offers extremely high performance, and scales to easily accommodate the data growth needs of the enterprise.

The key components and workflow within the environment are shown in Figure 19-1.

Architecture

The appliance is natively integrated with RMAN—at the heart of the system is an embedded Oracle Database, running Oracle Real Application Clusters (RAC), that serves as the centralized RMAN Recovery Catalog for all the protected databases. The catalog maintains all backup metadata in Automatic Storage Management (ASM) disk groups running on high-capacity disks

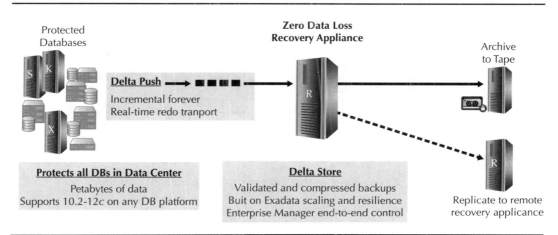

FIGURE 19-1. *Zero Data Loss Recovery Appliance environment*

using high-redundancy mode. The backup data itself is also stored in ASM disk groups, using normal redundancy. You can expand the appliance in compute and storage capacity by simply adding more racks. Backup connectivity into and out of the system is provided through standard 10GigE. For tape archival operations, the appliance comes with preinstalled Oracle Secure Backup (OSB) media management software and a 16Gb Fibre Channel adapter on each compute server to connect directly to tape hardware.

NOTE
Alternatively, other vendors' tape backup agents may be deployed on the Recovery Appliance for integration with existing tape backup software and processes. In this configuration, the agents must connect to their specialized media servers that are deployed external to the appliance.

Protected Databases

Databases supported with the Recovery Appliance can range from Oracle Database 10*g* Release 2 through Oracle Database 12*c*, on any Oracle-supported OS platform. A database is made "Recovery Appliance aware" via installation of the Recovery Appliance Backup Module that integrates with RMAN. No specialized backup agents are required.

The Recovery Appliance Backup Module allows RMAN SBT channels to be configured to back up and restore via standard HTTP to or from the Recovery Appliance, as shown in Figure 19-2.

In this example, the backup module libra.so allows SBT channels to connect over HTTP to Recovery Appliance recoveryappliance2 via the access point recoveryappliance2-ingest.company .com using credentials stored in the Oracle wallet RA_WALLET.

We will now discuss two unique architectural components of the Recovery Appliance: Delta Push and Delta Store.

```
CONFIGURE CHANNEL DEVICE TYPE SBT PARMS
'SBT_LIBRARY=/u01/app/oracle/product/12.1.0.0.0/dbhome_1/lib/libra.so,
ENV=(RA_WALLET='Location=file:/u01/app/oracle/product/12.1.0.0.0/
dbhome_1/dbs/ba
credential_alias=recoveryappliance2-ingest.company.com:1521/Recovery
Appliance2:dedicated')'
```

FIGURE 19-2. *RMAN SBT channel configuration to the Recovery Appliance*

Delta Push

Delta Push consists of two processes that are run on each protected database:

- RMAN incremental backups
- Real-time redo transport

Let's look at each of these processes in a bit more detail.

RMAN Incremental Backups

In normal operation, the Recovery Appliance receives regularly scheduled RMAN incremental level 1 backups from each protected database, which consist of the data blocks changed since the previous backup. At the Recovery Appliance, the incoming backup data is validated to ensure that there are no physical corruptions in the Oracle data blocks, then compressed using specialized block-level algorithms, and finally written to a storage pool contained within one or more preconfigured ASM disk groups.

No full backups are needed from the protected database, apart from the initial full. Thus, the Recovery Appliance implements an *incremental forever* backup strategy, eliminating traditional backup windows and the associated system impact, while boosting production server performance. More details are discussed in the section "Delta Store," later in the chapter.

Real-time Redo Transport

If the production system and storage are lost, data can only be recovered to the point in time of the last good backup and, more specifically for databases, to the last good archived log backup. Since archived logs hold records of all changes that occur in the database, these critical files must be backed up regularly, if not more frequently (for example, every few hours for active systems) than data files. Frequent backups reduce the potential data loss if the production system is indeed lost and backups need to be recovered.

In recognizing the critical nature of redo as it pertains to data loss, the Recovery Appliance supports real-time redo transport with Oracle Database 11g and 12c, the first of its kind in the industry to do so, providing sub-second data loss protection. Based on the industry-proven Oracle Data Guard redo transport technology, the Recovery Appliance receives incoming redo blocks directly from the memory (SGA) of these protected databases and writes the logs into a redo staging location, from where they are converted into compressed archived log backups and then written to the Delta Store. This means frequent resource-intensive archived log backups are no longer required on the production systems, as in a typical backup strategy. Archived log backups generated by the appliance are recorded in the recovery catalog as normal and can be restored and applied to data files via standard RMAN RECOVER commands. Figure 19-3 provides a graphic look at how real-time redo transport works.

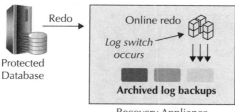

FIGURE 19-3. *Recovery Appliance real-time redo transport*

If there is an unexpected termination in the redo stream, the appliance has the ability to close the incoming redo stream and create a *partial archived redo log*, thereby preserving data loss protection. Upon detecting that the redo stream has restarted, the appliance automatically retrieves all missing archived logs from the protected database to preserve the recovery window goal.

Delta Store

The Delta Store is the key processing engine for the Recovery Appliance, creating and storing *virtual full backups*, based on the Delta Push incremental backups. Delta Store technology converts an incoming incremental level 1 backup into a virtual representation of an incremental level 0 (that is, full) backup, as of the level 1's timestamp. For example, an incremental level 1 backup **Day1_Incr** as of time **Day1** is converted into a virtual full backup called **Day1_VB**, which is simply a set of metadata maintained in the recovery catalog with references to the data file blocks from the incremental backup **Day1_Incr** and to blocks from previous incremental backups, going all the way back to the initial incremental level 0 backup. In effect, the blocks referenced by the virtual full backup make up the physical full backup set that can be restored to the point in time **Day1**. Thus, Delta Store enables the Recovery Appliance to create a "full backup" at the *cost* of only an incremental, using a fraction of the time and storage consumption of a standard full backup operation, as shown in Figure 19-4.

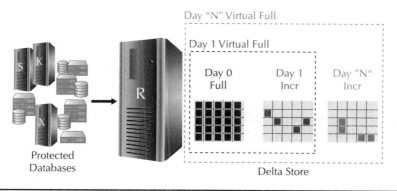

FIGURE 19-4. *Delta Store virtual full backups*

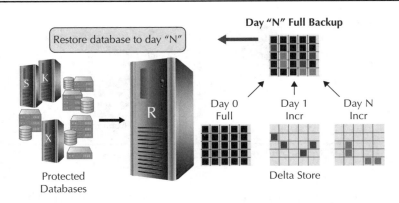

FIGURE 19-5. *Day "N" virtual full restore*

Since the protected database uses familiar RMAN BACKUP commands, all virtual full backups show up as normal incremental level 0 backups in the recovery catalog and can be used by future RMAN restore operations as needed. When a protected database issues an RMAN RESTORE, the Recovery Appliance responds by reading the appropriate virtual full backup blocks, constructing the physical full backup sets, and then sending the backup sets to the database, where they are restored. Figure 19-5 illustrates how a physical full backup set at Day "N" is created from its virtual full backup, which references blocks from Day 1, 2, and N incremental backups.

Virtual full backups are completely transparent to RMAN and the protected database—DBAs continue to utilize their existing RMAN skill set with the Recovery Appliance.

Replication

The RMAN transparency model also holds when replicating a local Recovery Appliance's backups to a secondary Recovery Appliance for protection against server or site outage. After an incremental backup is received by the local Recovery Appliance, it is automatically queued for forwarding to a secondary Recovery Appliance—that is, just the changed blocks are replicated, not full backups. When the incremental is received at the replica Recovery Appliance, a virtual full is created on the system as normal, with new backup records created in its own recovery catalog and propagated back to the local Recovery Appliance's catalog. You can see examples of the various replication models the Recovery Appliance supports in Figure 19-6.

Since records of the replicated backups in the secondary Recovery Appliance are also maintained in the local Recovery Appliance, any virtual full backup requests that cannot be satisfied by the local Recovery Appliance are automatically forwarded to the replica Recovery Appliance, where the physical backup sets are constructed as normal and sent back to the protected database. Again, DBAs continue to utilize RMAN as normal, without needing to understand where or how the backup sets originated.

Autonomous Tape Archival

In contrast to disk-only backup systems, the Recovery Appliance is an excellent fit in IT organizations that have continued to rely on tapes for long-term retention and archival purposes. As previously

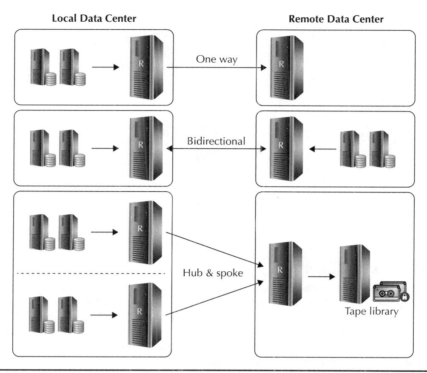

FIGURE 19-6. *Recovery Appliance replication models*

discussed, the Recovery Appliance comes with preinstalled Oracle Secure Backup software and a 16Gb Fibre Channel adapter on each compute server to connect directly to tape hardware. When the Recovery Appliance executes a tape archival job for a virtual full backup, the physical backup sets are first constructed, then pushed to tape via the built-in SBT interface. Once the tape backups complete, the appropriate backup metadata is written to the recovery catalog. All tape copy operations are performed by the Recovery Appliance with *zero* impact on the production system. That means tape operations can run 24/7 on the appliance, unlike production systems, thereby reducing tape hardware requirements. Figure 19-7 provides a graphic demonstration of these features.

A RESTORE request that requires backups from tape is automatically retrieved by the Recovery Appliance—no special action is needed by the DBA. Furthermore, because the backups on tape are physical backup sets, these backups can be restored *directly* by the protected databases if needed. The protected database simply needs to be configured with the SBT plug-in module that is included with the Oracle Secure Backup installation, and then SBT channels are allocated as normal to perform the restore operations directly from tape.

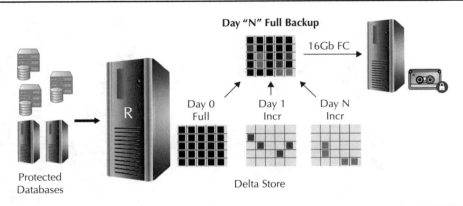

FIGURE 19-7. *Copy virtual full backup Day "N" to tape*

Backup Validation

One of the basic principles of a well-rounded backup and recovery strategy is to ensure that the backups created can be restored and used successfully. To ensure that there are no physical corruptions within the backed-up data blocks and that they can be properly restored, backups must be validated on a regular basis. This typically means running an RMAN RESTORE VALIDATE job regularly, along with running periodic full restore and recovery operations to a separate machine. All of these add overhead to an already taxed production system. With Recovery Appliance, incoming backups are automatically validated in-line for Oracle block correctness. Similarly, backups that are replicated to a secondary Recovery Appliance and/or copied to tape are also validated. Furthermore, virtual full backups themselves are periodically validated in-place by a background task running on the appliance. Another benefit is that backup validation operations are now *offloaded* from the production system to the Recovery Appliance, thus improving production system performance. Finally, because ASM is used for storing the backup data on the appliance, it is also made fully redundant through ASM mirrored copies, where corrupted blocks discovered by ASM on the primary disk can be automatically repaired by a mirrored copy.

Protection Policy

Recovery Appliance introduces the concept of a protection policy, which defines granular recovery window goals that are enforced on a per-database basis for backups on the local or replica Recovery Appliance and/or tape. Using protection policies, databases can be easily grouped by recovery service tier; for example, "Gold" tier databases require backups kept for a 35-day recovery window goal on the local Recovery Appliance and 90 days on tape, whereas "Silver" tier databases only require 10 days on the local Recovery Appliance and 45 days on tape. An optional maximum disk retention (for example, in days, weeks, or months) can be defined within a policy, to hard-limit the amount of space consumed by the policy's databases. Separate protection policies can also be set up at the replica Recovery Appliance, which will govern the

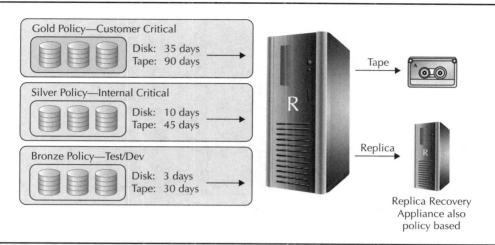

FIGURE 19-8. *Recovery Appliance: Database Protection as a Service*

space management of the replicated backups. Figure 19-8 illustrates how the Recovery Appliance provides protection services.

With this unique implementation, Recovery Appliance introduces the concept of *Database Protection as a Service,* through which database protection strategies can easily be implemented based on the criticality of the business application, rather than simply on the availability of storage space.

Cooperative Space Management

Once a protection policy is created, a database can then be assigned to it, along with a minimum *space reservation* (for example, in GB or TB) that is used by the Recovery Appliance to provision backup space per the defined recovery window goals. The database space reservation defines the minimum amount of space that is always available for use by the database's backups. Space is provisioned by first using any free space and, if needed, by purging *obsolete virtual full backups* (that is, backups no longer needed to meet a database's recovery window goal). Figure 19-9 illustrates the use of protection policies.

For example, if the HR database requires 1TB space today to support a three-week recovery window (shown in the grey bar), and its backup space needs increase to 2TB tomorrow due to higher workloads, then the storage location will attempt to meet the additional 1TB space need by utilizing any available free space and, if necessary, by purging obsolete virtual full backups and their corresponding archived log backups from other databases (for example, FIN and CRM). Conversely, after the workloads on HR subside and it once again requires just 1TB space to support a three-week recovery window, then any of its *obsolete virtual full backups* may be purged by the Recovery Appliance if other databases need additional space to meet their respective recovery window goals. Backups may also be *proactively* purged as needed in anticipation of future space needs—this "predictive purging" background process is based on historical space usage patterns.

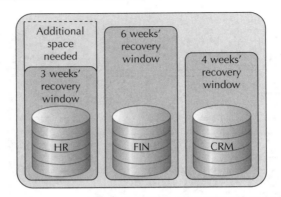

FIGURE 19-9. *Protection policy–based space management*

In the event that all obsolete backups have been purged and certain databases still require additional space to meet their recovery window, then the storage location will begin purging the oldest virtual full backups for each database that is consuming more than its minimum space reservation, prioritized in order of databases with the highest percentage of space overage. Note that in some cases, this action can compromise a database's recovery window goal. If this occurs, the system can alert the administrator that additional capacity is needed in order to maintain the stated recovery windows. The administrator can then take action to add disk capacity and increase space reservation to allow the system to return to a balanced state, where all recovery windows can be satisfied.

Recovery Appliance fully manages all backup space in order to meet each database's recovery window goal, automatically re provisioning space as needed and proactively purging backups in advance of future space needs.

Monitoring and Administration

Oracle Enterprise Manager Cloud Control provides a complete end-to-end view into the backup lifecycle managed by the Recovery Appliance, from the time the RMAN backup is initiated on the database, to when it is stored on disk, tape, and/or replicated to a secondary appliance. All appliance monitoring and administration functions are enabled via installation of the Enterprise Manager Recovery Appliance plug-in.

Standard metrics such as overall backup volume/performance and aggregate/per-database space consumption are easily accessed from the console, as seen in Figure 19-10 and Figure 19-11.

Because database recovery window goals form a core component of Recovery Appliance, administrators can immediately see whether any databases are currently not meeting their goals from the Recovery Appliance home page, as shown in Figure 19-12.

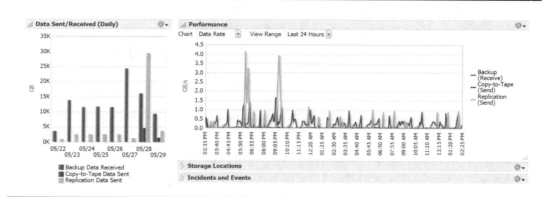

FIGURE 19-10. *Recovery Appliance Enterprise Manager home page: overall performance and storage metrics*

FIGURE 19-11. *Storage location detail: per-database backup space needed to meet recovery window goal*

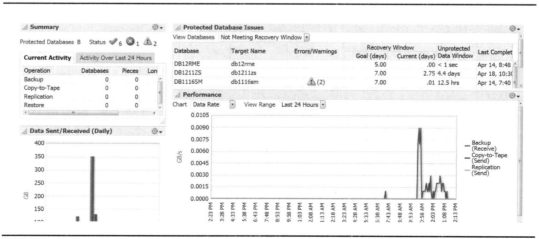

FIGURE19- 12. *Recovery Appliance Enterprise Manager: "STORE26" not meeting recovery window goal*

Scale-out Hardware

The Recovery Appliance can easily scale to accommodate growing amounts of protected databases, backup traffic, and storage usage: you simply add more compute and storage servers. The Base Rack includes two compute servers and three storage servers, providing up to 94TB usable capacity for backups. The Base Rack can be upgraded in increments of one storage server up to a maximum of 18 storage servers with 580TB of usable capacity, providing an effective capacity of up to 5.8PB (petabytes) of virtual full backups with a 120TB/hr virtual backup rate (12TB/hr sustained delta ingest). If additional compute servers are required, a second Base Rack can be connected via Infiniband to the first rack—storage capacity can then be easily expanded, as done in the first rack. Up to 18 fully configured racks can be connected together, providing up to 10PB of usable capacity, effectively storing 100PB of virtual full backups, with a 2PB/hr virtual backup rate (216TB/hr delta ingest rate). A full rack can restore up to 12TB/hr, and 18 fully configured racks can restore up to 216TB/hr.

Summary

The Zero Data Loss Recovery Appliance heralds a new era in Oracle data protection technology. Key innovations include an incremental-forever strategy to reduce production overhead, real-time redo transport for reducing data loss exposure down to the sub second, end-to-end data validation and database recoverability status, and, finally, scale-out hardware and storage built on the proven Exadata platform. The Recovery Appliance directly targets the challenges of managing backup and recovery at-scale in large Oracle environments. For more information, including data sheets, white papers, and videos, visit oracle.com/recoveryappliance.

CHAPTER
20

RMAN in the Workplace:
Case Studies

We included this chapter in our very first RMAN book way back in Oracle 9*i*. We felt it was important to not only provide you with the mechanics of doing RMAN backup and recovery, but also to give you some practical examples to follow so that you could improve your backup and recovery knowledge. It is with this purpose in mind that we present the case studies in this chapter.

Based on both reading through this book and your own experience, we are sure you have figured out that you face an almost infinite number of recovery combinations. Recovery can be simple, and it can be complex. Sometimes, it's not about recovering the database at all, but about getting the database to perform. Yes, in some respects even performance tuning can be a form of database recovery. However, you don't do database performance tuning with RMAN, so we will save that topic for other books.

What we will do in this chapter is provide you with various case studies to help you review your knowledge of backup and recovery (see if you can figure out the solution before you read it). When you do come across these situations, the case studies may well help you avoid some mistakes you might otherwise make when trying to recover your database. You can even use these case studies to practice performing recoveries so that you become an RMAN backup and recovery expert.

We hope that you will go through this chapter and make a list of the case studies that apply to you. It might be that some of them won't. If you are running your database in NOARCHIVELOG mode, for whatever reason, then restoring from an online backup isn't going to be possible for you. Once you have identified the case studies in this chapter that apply to you, you might want to make a list of situations you might face that are not contained in this chapter. For example, we don't provide a case study on restoring your OS from scratch, since we can't possibly know which OS you are using. This seems like a reasonable thing to practice.

Once you have that list, we strongly suggest that you practice these case studies on a regularly scheduled basis. Also, use this list to help your more junior DBAs improve their skills with RMAN backup and recovery. They need to practice these things over and over—so that it's second nature to them. Even if you are an experienced DBA, keep practicing so it stays fresh in your mind. Heck, we wrote this book and we still practice backup and recovery all the time.

Before we get into the case studies, though, the following section provides a quick overview about facing the ultimate disaster—a real-life failure of your database.

Before the Recovery

Disaster strikes. Often, when you are in a recovery situation, everyone is in a big rush to recover the database. Customers are calling, management is panicking, and your boss is looking at you for answers, all of which is making you nervous, wondering if your résumé is up to date. When the real recovery situation occurs, stop. Take a few moments to collect yourself and ask these questions:

- What is the exact nature of the failure?
- What are the recovery options available to me?
- Might I need Oracle Support?
- Is there anyone who can act as a second pair of eyes for me during this recovery?

Let's address each of these questions in detail.

What Is the Exact Nature of the Failure?

Here's some firsthand experience from one of the authors. Back in the days when I was contracting, I was paged one night (on Halloween, no less!) because a server had failed, and once they got the server back up, none of the databases would come up. Before I received the page, the DBAs at this site had spent upward of eight hours trying to restart the 25 databases on that box. Most of the databases would not start. The DBAs had recovered a couple of the seemingly lost databases, yet even those databases still would not open. The DBAs called Oracle, and Oracle seemed unsure as to what the problem was. Finally, the DBAs paged me (while I was out trick-or-treating with my kids).

Within about 20 minutes after arriving at the office, I knew what the answer was. I didn't find the answer because I was smarter than all the other DBAs there (I wasn't, in fact). I found the answer for a couple of reasons. First, I approached the problem from a fresh perspective (after eight hours of problem solving, one's eyes tend to become burned and red!). Second, I looked to find the nature of the failure rather than just assuming the nature of the failure was a corrupted database.

What ended up being the problem, pretty clearly to a fresh pair of eyes, was a set of corrupted Oracle libraries. Once we recovered those libraries, all the databases came up quickly, without a problem. The moral of the story is that when you have a database that has crashed, or that will not open, do not assume that the cause is a corrupted datafile or a bad disk drive. Find out for sure what the problem is by investigative analysis. Good analysis may take a little longer to begin with, but, generally, it will prove valuable in the long run.

This also implies that one of the more important skills a DBA should possess is the ability to do research. Develop a list of resources you will use when a problem occurs and develop your understanding of how to use those resources. For example, you might know how to log onto Oracle's support portal and open an SR—but do you know what to do if you feel like your severity 1 SR is not moving fast enough or if the support analyst does not seem to be "getting" your problem? Oracle Support has some great training available online to teach you how to effectively use this support mechanism. Take advantage of that training and learn how to "work the system" before you actually need to do so.

What Recovery Options Are Available?

Recovery situations can offer a number of solutions. Again, back when I was a consultant, I had a customer who had a disk controller drive fail over a weekend, and the result was the loss of file systems on the box, including files belonging to an Oracle database in ARCHIVELOG mode. The DBA at the customer site went ahead and recovered the entire database (about 150GB), which took, as I recall, a couple of hours.

The following Monday, the DBA and I had a discussion about the recovery method he selected. The corrupted file systems actually impacted only about five database datafiles (the other file systems contained web server files that we were not concerned with). The total size of the impacted database datafiles was no more than 8 or 10GB. The DBA was pretty upset about having to come into the office and spend several hours recovering the database. When I asked the DBA why he hadn't just recovered the five datafiles instead of the entire database, he replied that it just had not occurred to him.

The moral of this story is that it's important to consider your recovery options. The type of recovery you do may make a big difference in how long it takes you to recover your database. Another moral of this story is to really become a backup and recovery expert. Part of the reason the DBA in this case had not considered datafile recovery, I think, is that he had never done such a recovery. When facing a stressful situation, people tend not to consider options they are not familiar with. Therefore, we strongly suggest you set up a backup and recovery lab and practice recoveries until you can do them in your sleep.

Might Oracle Support Be Needed?

You might well be a backup and recovery expert, but even the experts need help from time to time. This is what Oracle Support is there for. Even though I feel like I know something about backup and recovery, I ask myself if a failure looks to be something that I might need Oracle Support for. Generally, if the failure is something odd, even if I think I can solve it on my own, I "prime" support by opening a service request on the problem. That way, if I need help, I have already provided Oracle with the information they need (or at least some initial information) and have them ready to support me should I need it. If you are paying for Oracle Support, use it now, don't wait for later.

We mentioned earlier the benefit of learning how to effectively use Oracle Support. This one thing is so important that we opted to mention it again here.

Who Can Act as a Second Pair of Eyes During Recovery?

When I'm in a stressful situation, first of all it's nice to have someone to share the stress with. Somehow I feel a bit more comfortable when someone is there just to talk things out with. Further, when you are working on a critical problem, mistakes can be costly. Having a second experienced pair of eyes there to support you as you recover your database is a great idea!

Recovery Case Studies

Now to the meat of the chapter—the recovery case studies. In this section, we provide you with a number of case studies, listed next in the order they appear:

1. Recovering from complete database loss in NOARCHIVELOG mode with a recovery catalog
2. Recovering from complete database loss in NOARCHIVELOG mode without a recovery catalog
3. Recovering from complete database loss in ARCHIVELOG mode without a recovery catalog
4. Recovering from complete database loss in ARCHIVELOG mode with a recovery catalog
5. Recovering from the loss of the SYSTEM tablespace
6. Recovering online from the loss of a datafile or tablespace
7. Recovering from loss of an unarchived online redo log
8. Recovering through **resetlogs**
9. Completing a failed duplication manually
10. Using RMAN duplication to create a historical subset of the target database
11. Recovering from a lost datafile in ARCHIVELOG mode using an image copy in the Fast Recovery Area

12.   Recovering from running the production datafile out of the Fast Recovery Area

13.   Using Flashback Database and media recovery to pinpoint the exact moment to open the database with **resetlogs**

In each of these case studies, we provide you with the following information:

- ■   **The Scenario**   Outlines the environment for you
- ■   **The Problem**   Defines a problem that needs to be solved
- ■   **The Solution**   Outlines the solution for you, including RMAN output solving the problem

Now, let's look at our case studies!

Case #1: Recovering from Complete Database Loss (NOARCHIVELOG Mode) with a Recovery Catalog

The Scenario

Thom is a new DBA at Unfortunate Company. Upon arriving at his new job, he finds that his databases are not backed up at all and that they are all in NOARCHIVELOG mode. Because Thom's manager will not shell out the money for additional disk space for archived redo logs, Thom is forced to do offline backups. Thom manages to find disk space to back up the database to, and he configures space as an FRA. Thom also turns on autobackups of his control file and has converted the database so that it is using an SPFILE. Thom also decides that he should create and use a recovery catalog database. After all this configuration, Thom manages to perform a cold backup of the database by logging into RMAN and issuing the following commands:

```
rman target sys/password catalog rcat_user/rcat_password@catalogdb
shutdown immediate
startup mount;
backup database;
startup force;
```

The Problem

Unfortunate Company's cheap buying practices catch up to it in the few days following Thom's initial work, when the off-brand (cheap) disks that it has purchased all become corrupted due to a bad controller card. Thom's database is lost.

Thom's offline database backup strategy includes tape backups to a local tape drive. Once the hardware problems are solved, the system administrator quickly rebuilds the lost file systems, and Thom quickly gets the Oracle software installed. Now, Thom needs to get the database back up and running immediately.

The Solution

Thom's only recovery option in this case is to restore from the last offline backup. In this case, Thom's recovery catalog database was not lost (it was on another server), and his file systems are in place, so all he needs to do is recover the database. First, Thom needs to recover the database SPFILE, followed by the control file. Then, he needs to recover the database datafiles to the file systems.

The Solution Revealed   Based on the preceding considerations, Thom devises and implements the following recovery plan:

1. Restore a copy of the SPFILE. Note that in this case, Thom is able to start the Oracle Database instance without having to create a parameter file first. Once Thom is able to start the instance, he will proceed to restore the SPFILE.

    Because Thom does not yet have a parameter file or a control file set up, the persistent settings that he would normally need are not available. As a result, he will need to add some special parameters to the **restore spfile** command. Here, he has used the **db_name** and **recovery_area** parameters of the **restore** command. These parameters indicate the name of the database and the location for the FRA. The end result is an easy recovery of the SPFILE. Here are the commands Thom used:

    ```
    rman target sys/password catalog rcat_user/rcat_password@catalogdb
    startup force nomount;
    restore spfile from autobackup db_name='ROBT' recovery area='/u01/app/
    oracle/fast_recovery_area';
    shutdown immediate;
    startup nomount;
    ```

NOTE
If you are not using the FRA or a recovery catalog, there will be additional steps you will need to follow to restore the database parameter file.

2. Now, Thom will restore a copy of the control file. He will use the same RMAN session as in Step 1. After previously restoring the SPFILE, Thom restarted the instance so that the SPFILE parameters will be in effect. The result is that RMAN now knows the name of the database and the location of the SPFILE. As a result, the **restore controlfile** command is much simpler than the **restore spfile** command was. Once Thom restores the control file, he mounts the database in preparation to restore the database datafiles:

    ```
    restore controlfile from autobackup;
    alter database mount;
    ```

3. Since Thom has restored the control file, the settings that configure the FRA are now correctly set for the database instance. So, now he is ready to restore the database files and then recover the database. When he runs the restore, RMAN will automatically catalog the files in the FRA. Therefore, if Thom would have had to restore these files from some other backup media, RMAN would have automatically located and cataloged the backup files in the FRA before starting the restore.

    ```
    restore database;
    recover database noredo;
    alter database open resetlogs;
    ```

NOTE
*Thom used the **alter database open resetlogs** command. He could have used the SQL command (**sql "alter database open resetlogs"**), too. However, one benefit of using the RMAN **alter** command is that the catalog and the database will both be reset. Using the SQL version, only the database is reset.*

Case #2: Recovering from Complete Database Loss (NOARCHIVELOG Mode) Without a Recovery Catalog

The Scenario

Elys is the DBA of a development OLTP system. Because it is a development system, the decision was made to do RMAN offline backups and to leave the database in NOARCHIVELOG mode. Elys did not decide to use a recovery catalog when doing her backups. Further, she has configured RMAN to back up the control file backups to disk by default, rather than to tape. Finally, Elys has recorded the DBID of the database from the V$DATABASE view, which she will use should she need to perform a database restore.

The Problem

Sevi, a developer, developed a piece of PL/SQL code designed to truncate specific tables in the database. However, due to a logic bug, the code managed to truncate all the tables in the schema, wiping out all test data.

The Solution

If there were a logical backup of the database, this would be the perfect time to use it. Unfortunately, there is no logical backup of the database, so Elys is left with performing an RMAN recovery. Because her database is in NOARCHIVELOG mode, Elys has only one recovery option in this case, which is to restore from the last offline backup. Because all the pieces to do recovery are in place (the RMAN disk backups, the Oracle software, and the file systems), all that needs to be done is to fire up RMAN and recover the database.

The Solution Revealed   Based on the preceding considerations, Elys devises and implements the following recovery plan:

1. Restore the control file. When doing a recovery from a cold backup, it is always a good idea to recover the control file associated with that backup (this prevents odd things from happening). In this case, Elys will be using the latest control file backup (because she doesn't back up the control file at other times). Because Elys uses the default location to create control file backup sets to, she doesn't need to allocate any channels. If Elys is not using the Oracle Fast Recovery Area and not using a recovery catalog, she will need to set the DBID of the system before she can restore the control file. If Elys were using

a recovery catalog or the FRA, then setting the DBID would not be required. To start the restore, Elys begins restoring the control file and then she mounts the database:

```
rman target sys/password
startup nomount
set dbid=2540040039;
restore controlfile from autobackup;
sql 'alter database mount';
```

NOTE
If you are using the FRA, you will not need to set the database DBID.

2. The control file that Elys restored has the correct default persistent parameters already configured in it, so all she needs to do is perform the restore and recovery:

```
restore database;
recover database noredo;
sql "alter database open resetlogs";
```

Case #3: Recovering from Complete Database Loss (ARCHIVELOG Mode) Without a Recovery Catalog

The Scenario
We meet Thom from Case #1 again. Thom's company finally has decided that putting the database in ARCHIVELOG mode seems like a good idea. (Thom's boss thought it was his idea!) Unfortunately for Thom, due to budget restrictions, he was forced to use the space that was allocated to the recovery catalog to store archived redo logs. Thus, Thom no longer has a recovery catalog at his disposal.

In addition to space for the archived redo logs that Thom's company has provided, a tape backup system has been put into place. Thom has configured this tape backup infrastructure and is using it to store his backups on. The controlfile autobackups are backed up to tape as well.

The Problem
As if things have not been hard enough on Thom, we also find that Unfortunate Company is an unfortunately located company. The server room, located in the basement of the company's headquarters, suffered the fate of a broken water main nearby. The entire room was flooded, and the server on which Thom's database resides has been completely destroyed.

Thom's backup strategy has improved. It now includes tape backups to an offsite media management server. Also, he's sending his automated control file/SPFILE backups to tape rather than to disk. Again, he's salvaged a smaller server from the wreckage, which already has Oracle installed on the system, and now he needs to get the database back up and running immediately.

The Solution
Again, Thom has lost the current control file and the online redo logs for his database, so it's time to employ the point-in-time recovery skills. Thom still has control file autobackups turned on, so he can use them to get recovery started. In addition, he's restoring to a new server, so he wants to

be aware of the challenges that restoring to a new server brings; there are media management, file system layout, and memory utilization considerations.

Media Management Considerations   Because he's restoring files to a new server, Thom must first make sure that the MML file has been properly set up for use on his emergency server. This means having the media management client software and Oracle Plug-In installed prior to using RMAN for restore/recovery.

Next, Thom needs to configure his tape channels to specify the client name of the server that has been destroyed. Thom will need to specify the name of the client from which the backups were taken. In addition, he needs to ensure that the media management server has been configured to allow for backups to be restored from a different client to his emergency server.

File System Layout Considerations   Thom's new system has a different file system structure from his original server. The production database had files manually striped over six mount points: /u02, /u03, /u04, /u05, /u06, and /u07. His new server has only two mount points: /u02 and /u03. Fortunately, Thom employed directory structure standards across his enterprise, and all data directories are /oradata/prod/ on all mount points. In addition, he has a standard that always puts the ORACLE_HOME on the same mount point and directory structure on every server.

Memory Utilization Considerations   Thom's emergency server has less physical memory than his lost production server. This means he will have to significantly scale back the memory utilization for the time being in order to at least get the database up and operational.

The Solution Revealed   Based on the preceding considerations, Thom devises and implements the following recovery plan:

1.   Determine the DBID of the target database. Thom can do this by looking at the file handle for his control file autobackup. He needs to be able to view the media management catalog to do so. Even easier, Thom has every DBID for all his databases stored somewhere in a log—a notebook, a PDA, whatever. (Whatever you decide to use, just make sure it's accessible in an emergency.) If Thom were using the FRA, he would not need to worry about the DBID of the target database.

2.   Restore a copy of the SPFILE. To start this process, he will issue the **startup nomount** command to start the Oracle instance. Then he can restore the correct SPFILE from backup. Because Thom changed the default location for his control file/SPFILE autobackups to tape, he needs to manually configure the channel for this backup because he doesn't have a control file yet; thus, he cannot configure channels permanently. Instead, he has to imbed **channel allocation** commands in a **run** block, and then issue the **startup** command to start the database with the correct SPFILE.

```
rman target /
set dbid=204062491;
startup force nomount;
run {
allocate channel tape_1 type sbt
parms='env=(nb_ora_serv=rmsrv, nb_ora_client=cervantes)';
restore spfile from autobackup;}
shutdown immediate;
startup nomount;
```

NOTE
If you are using the FRA, you will not need to set the database DBID.
Also, if Thom were using a recovery catalog, this step and Step 3
would have been much easier to do.

3. Make changes to the SPFILE. Thom must modify his SPFILE to take into account the new server configuration. This means changing memory utilization parameters and setting filename conversion parameters. He must connect to the newly started instance from SQL*Plus and make the necessary changes.

```
alter system set control_files= '/u02/oradata/prod/control01.dbf',
'/u03/oradata/prod/control02.dbf' scope=spfile;
alter system set db_file_name_convert= ('/u04' , '/u02' ,
'/u05' , '/u02' ,
'u06' , ' u03' ,
'u07' , 'u03') scope=spfile;
alter system set log_file_name_convert= ('/u04' , '/u02' ,
'/u05' , '/u02' ,
'u06' , ' u03' ,
'u07' , 'u03') scope=spfile;
alter system set log_archive_dest_1=
'location=/u02/oradata/prod/arch' scope=spfile;
alter system set db_cache_size=300m scope=spfile;
alter system set shared_pool_size=200m scope=spfile;
shutdown immediate;
startup nomount;
```

NOTE
*You could also choose to use the **set newname** option here.*

4. Restore a copy of the control file. Using the same RMAN session as the preceding, Thom can do this quite simply (he has already set the DBID). Then, mount the database using the restored control file. Again, if Thom had used the FRA, then no DBID would be needed.

```
run {
allocate channel tape_1 type sbt
parms='env=(nb_ora_serv=rmsrv, nb_ora_client=Cervantes)';
restore controlfile from autobackup; }
alter database mount;
```

5. Configure permanent channel parameters. Now that Thom has a control file restored, he can update the persistent parameters for channel allocation to include the name of the lost server as the media management client. This serves two purposes: it allows RMAN to access the backups that were taken from the lost server, and RMAN will pass this client name to the media management server when any backups are taken from the new server. That way, when the lost server is rebuilt, any backups taken from this stopgap system will be accessible at the newly reconstructed production server.

```
configure default device type to sbt;
configure device type sbt parallelism 2;
configure auxiliary channel 1 device type sbt parms
```

```
= "env=(nb_ora_serv=mgtserv, nb_ora_client=cervantes)";
configure auxiliary channel 2 device type sbt parms
= "env=(nb_ora_serv=mgtserv, nb_ora_cient=cervantes)";
```

6. Determine the last archive log for which there is a copy. Because Thom lost the entire server, he also lost any archive logs that had not yet been backed up by RMAN. So, he must query RMAN to determine what the last archive log is for which a backup exists.

```
list backup of archivelog from time = 'sysdate-7';
```

7. With the last log sequence number in hand, Thom performs his restore. Note that because the **until sequence** recovers up to but not including the listed sequence number, Thom will add 1 to the log sequence number. He will then recover and open the database:

```
restore database;
recover database until sequence=<number+1>;
alter database open resetlogs;
```

Case #4: Recovering from Complete Database Loss (ARCHIVELOG Mode) with a Recovery Catalog

The Scenario

Charles is taking over for Thom because management recognized that Thom was a hero of a DBA and therefore sent him and his wife to Hawaii for two weeks of R and R. Before Thom left, his company added more disk storage and decided that using the RMAN recovery catalog was probably a good idea.

Unfortunately for Charles, disaster seems to follow him around. At his last company, a huge electrical fire caused all sorts of mayhem, and this time, it's gophers. Yes, gophers. Somewhere outside the computer room, a lone gopher ate through the power cable leading to the computer room. This resulted in an electrical fire and a halon release into the computer room. As a result of the electrical fire, the server and disks on which his database resides have been completely destroyed…again.

The Problem

Charles reviews Thom's backup strategy. Like Thom, Charles has salvaged a smaller server that survived the fiasco, which already has Oracle installed, and now he needs to get the database back up and running immediately. Fortunately, the recovery catalog server is intact, so Charles can use it during the recovery.

The Solution

It seems that Charles has lost the current control file and the online redo logs for his database, so it's time to employ his point-in-time recovery skills. The backup strategy still has control file autobackups turned on, so Charles can use them to get recovery started. In addition, he's restoring to a new server, so he wants to be aware of the challenges that restoring to a new server brings; there are media management, file system layout, and memory utilization considerations.

Media Management Considerations   Because Charles is restoring files to a new server, he must first make sure that the MML file has been properly set up for use on his emergency server. This means having the media management client software and Oracle Plug-In installed prior to using

RMAN for restore/recovery. Charles uses sbttest to check to make sure the media manager is accessible.

Next, Charles needs to configure his tape channels to specify the client name of the server that has been destroyed. Charles will need to specify the name of the client from which the backups were taken. In addition, he needs to ensure that the media management server has been configured to allow for backups to be restored from a different client to his emergency server.

File System Layout Considerations   On Charles's new system, the file system structure is different from that on his original server. The production database had files manually striped over six mount points: /u02, /u03, /u04, /u05, /u06, and /u07. His new server has only two mount points: /u02 and /u03. Luckily, directory structure standards exist across his enterprise, and all data directories are /oradata/prod/ on all mount points. In addition, he has a standard that always puts the ORACLE_HOME on the same mount point and directory structure on every server.

Memory Considerations   Charles's emergency server has less physical memory than his lost production server. This means he has to significantly scale back the memory utilization for the time being in order to at least get the database up and operational.

The Solution Revealed   Based on the preceding considerations, Charles devises and implements the following recovery plan:

1. Get a copy of the SPFILE restored. First, Charles will nomount the database instance without a parameter file, since Oracle supports this. Then, he will restore the correct SPFILE from backup. Because he doesn't have a control file yet, he cannot configure channels permanently. Instead, he has to embed **channel allocation** commands in a **run** block, and then issue the **startup** command to start the database with the correct SPFILE. Because he has a recovery catalog, he doesn't need to set the machine ID as he did earlier.

```
rman target / catalog rcat_user/rcat_password@catalog
startup force nomount;
run {
allocate channel tape_1 type sbt
parms='env=(nb_ora_serv=rmsrv, nb_ora_client=cervantes)';
restore spfile from autobackup;}
shutdown immediate;
startup nomount;
```

2. Make changes to the SPFILE. Charles must modify his SPFILE to take into account the new server configuration. This means changing memory utilization parameters and setting filename conversion parameters. He must connect to the newly started instance from SQL*Plus and make the necessary changes.

```
alter system set control_files= '/u02/oradata/prod/control01.dbf',
'/u03/oradata/prod/control02.dbf' scope=spfile;
alter system set db_file_name_convert= "('/u04' , '/u02' ,
'/u05' , '/u02' ,
'/u06' , '/u03' ,
```

```
'/u07' , '/u03')" scope=spfile;
alter system set log_file_name_convert= "('/u04' , '/u02' ,
'/u05' , '/u02' ,
'/u06' , '/u03' ,
'/u07' , '/u03')" scope=spfile;
alter system set log_archive_dest_1=
'location=/u02/oradata/prod/arch' scope=spfile;
alter system set db_cache_size=300m scope=spfile;
alter system set shared_pool_size=200m scope=spfile;
shutdown immediate;
startup nomount;
```

3. Restore a copy of the control file. Using the same RMAN session, Charles can do this quite simply (he's already set the DBID). Then, he must mount the database using the restored control file.

```
run {
allocate channel tape_1 type sbt
parms='env=(nb_ora_serv=rmsrv, nb_ora_client=Cervantes)';
restore controlfile from autobackup; }
sql 'alter database mount';
```

4. Configure permanent channel parameters. Now that Charles has a control file restored, he can update the persistent parameters for channel allocation to include the name of the lost server as the media management client. This serves two purposes: it allows RMAN to access the backups that were taken from the lost server, and RMAN will pass this client name to the media management server when any backups are taken from the new server. That way, when the lost server is rebuilt, any backups taken from this stopgap system will be accessible at the newly reconstructed production server.

```
configure default device type to sbt;
configure device type sbt parallelism 2;
configure auxiliary channel 1 device type sbt parms
= "env=(nb_ora_serv=mgtserv, nb_ora_client=cervantes)";
configure auxiliary channel 2 device type sbt parms
= "env=(nb_ora_serv=mgtserv, nb_ora_cient=cervantes)";
```

5. Determine the last archive log for which there is a copy. Because Charles lost the entire server, he also lost any archive logs that had not yet been backed up by RMAN. So, he must query RMAN to determine what's the last archive log for which a backup exists:

```
list backup of archivelog from time = 'sysdate-7';
```

6. With the last log sequence number in hand, Charles performs his restore and recovery. Note that because the **until sequence** recovers up to but not including the listed sequence number, Charles adds 1 to the sequence number. He then opens the database:

```
restore database;
recover database until sequence=<number+1>;
alter database open resetlogs
```

Case #5: Recovering from the Loss of the SYSTEM Tablespace

The Scenario
Nancy, an awesome DBA, is in charge of a large database installation. She shut down her database so the system administrators of her Unix system could do some file system maintenance.

The Problem
Unfortunately, during the maintenance operation, the system administrators at her company managed to drop a file system her database is sitting on. They have since restored the file system, but none of the files from her database are on it, so she must recover them. Nancy lost all datafiles from the following tablespaces: USERS, SYSTEM, and INDEX.

The Solution
Fortunately for Nancy, this is not a complete loss of her system. Her online redo logs and control file are all intact. Because she has to recover the SYSTEM tablespace, she has to do her recovery with the database closed, not open. Otherwise, the recovery is a pretty easy one.

The Solution Revealed   Based on the preceding considerations, the recovery plan that Nancy devises and implements simply requires her to restore the database, as follows:

```
rman target / catalog rcat_user/rcat_password@catalog
startup force mount;
restore tablespace users, system, index;
recover tablespace users, system, index;
alter database open;
```

Case #6: Recovering Online from the Loss of a Datafile or Tablespace

The Scenario
Yang was working on his database the other day when a power surge caused a media failure.

The Problem
Unfortunately for Yang, he lost one file system. This file system contained the following:

- All the datafiles for a tablespace called WORKING_DATA
- One datafile for a tablespace called HISTORICAL_DATA

Several other tablespaces in this database are not related to the tablespace he is recovering, so Yang needs to do this recovery with the database up and running.

The Solution
Yang will restore the WORKING_DATA tablespace and the lone datafile missing from the HISTORICAL_DATA tablespace via RMAN. He first will take offline the tablespace and datafile so that others may continue to work.

The Solution Revealed   Based on the preceding considerations, Yang devises and implements the following recovery plan:

NOTE
*In Oracle Database 12c you no longer have to proceed SQL statements with the RMAN **sql** command.*

1. Take offline the WORKING_DATA tablespace:

    ```
    alter tablespace working_data offline;
    ```

2. Take offline the HISTORICAL_DATA datafile needed to recover (Yang has already queried the V$DATAFILE view to determine that it is datafile 13):

    ```
    alter database datafile 13 offline;
    ```

3. Restore and recover the tablespace and datafile using RMAN and then bring them online:

    ```
    restore tablespace working_data;
    restore datafile 13;
    recover tablespace working_data;
    recover datafile 13;
    alter tablespace working_data online;
    alter database datafile 13 online;
    ```

NOTE
If either tablespace contains active rollback segments, this recovery case may not work. In the event of the loss of active rollback segment tablespaces, you may well be required to do an offline recovery of that tablespace or datafile.

Case #7: Recovering from Loss of an Unarchived Online Redo Log

The Scenario
Today is not Bill's day. A large thunderstorm is raging outside, and Bill has forgotten that his car's soft top is down. To make Bill's day worse, a strike of lightning hits the datacenter and fries several disk drives that Bill's database calls home.

The Problem
Once the hardware is repaired, Bill is horrified to find that he has lost all of his online redo logs, in addition to some of his datafiles. Fortunately, his control file is intact.

The Solution
Bill needs to restore his database by using incomplete recovery. Because the online redo logs are not available, Bill has to accept that there will be some data loss as a result of the recovery.

The Solution Revealed   Based on the preceding considerations, Bill devises and implements the following recovery plan:

1. Determine the last archive log for which there is a copy. Because Bill has to do incomplete recovery, he must query RMAN to determine the last archive log for which a backup exists.

   ```
   startup mount;
   List backup of archivelog from time = 'sysdate-7';
   ```

   The output will look something like the following—note the log sequence number (log sequence number 3 in bold at the bottom of the report). Because this is the oldest backed up archived redo log, this is as far as Bill can recover to.

   ```
   List of Backup Sets
   ===================
   BS Key   Size         Device Type Elapsed Time Completion Time
   -------  ----------   ----------- ------------ ---------------
   216      48K          DISK           00:00:03     16-JUL-15
            BP Key: 247    Status: AVAILABLE    Tag: TAG20150716T095848
            Piece Name: D:\BACKUP\RECOVER\75E08R2P_1_1

     List of Archived Logs in backup set 216
     Thrd Seq     Low SCN    Low Time    Next SCN    Next Time
     ---- ------- ---------- --------- ---------- ---------
     1    2       1271924    16-JUL-15 1272223    16-JUL-15

   BS Key   Size         Device Type Elapsed Time Completion Time
   -------  ----------   ----------- ------------ ---------------
   218      2K           DISK           00:00:02     16-JUL-15
            BP Key: 249    Status: AVAILABLE    Tag: TAG20150716T100344
            Piece Name: D:\BACKUP\RECOVER\77E08RC1_1_1

     List of Archived Logs in backup set 218
     Thrd Seq     Low SCN    Low Time    Next SCN    Next Time
     ---- ------- ---------- --------- ---------- ---------
     1    3       1272223    16-JUL-15 1272321    16-JUL-15
   ```

2. With the last log sequence number in hand, perform the restore and recovery and open the database. Bill first restores the database using the **until sequence** parameter. This ensures that all database datafiles will be restored to a point in time no later than log sequence 3. Also note the use of the **force** parameter, which ensures that all datafiles are restored. Recall that one of the requirements for point-in-time recovery is that all database datafiles must be restored to the same consistent point in time. Thus, it's important to restore all datafiles to at least a point in time prior to the point in time to which Bill wants to recover.

   ```
   restore database until sequence=4 thread=1 force;
   ```

3. Recover the database until sequence 4 (because the **until sequence** recovers up to but not including the listed sequence number, Bill added one number to the last sequence number, and thus gets 4):

   ```
   recover database until sequence=4 thread=1;
   ```

4. Open the database:

   ```
   alter database open resetlogs
   ```

NOTE
*If Bill's database had been shut down normally (via **shutdown normal**, **immediate**, or **transactional**) before the online redo logs were lost, he may well have been able to open the database without needing to recover it.*

Case #8: Recovering Through resetlogs

The Scenario
Bill spent all night doing his recovery and then called in Tim to monitor the restore and finish the database recovery. Once the recovery was done, Tim was supposed to back up the database. One problem is that the business requirement demanded that the database be open and available during the backup.

Tim came in and finished the recovery. Following that, he opened the database using the **resetlogs** command (as previously described in Case #7). Following the business requirements, Tim began the backup, but allowed users access to the database.

The Problem
Unfortunately, on this troubled day, a power surge hit Tim's system, and one of the disk drives of Tim's database was damaged. After another hardware repair, Tim finds that several datafiles were lost. To make matters worse, he has no complete backup of these datafiles since he issued the **resetlogs** command. Fortunately for Tim, this database was upgraded about three months ago. So, Tim is in luck. Since Oracle Database 10g, Oracle has made recovery through the **resetlogs** command much easier.

When the database was upgraded to Oracle Database 11g, the LOG_ARCHIVE_FORMAT parameter was changed. The DBA added the new %R parameter so that LOG_ARCHIVE_FORMAT now looks like this:

```
SQL> show parameter log_archive_format
NAME                                 TYPE        VALUE
------------------------------------ ----------- -----------
log_archive_format                   string      ARC%S_%R.%T
```

Now the LOG_ARCHIVE_FORMAT parameter includes the %R placeholder, which means the resetlogs ID is contained in the archived redo logs' filenames. This will save our intrepid DBAs much time during this recovery!

The Solution
Tim is going to use RMAN to recover the database through **resetlogs**. For the most part, this is a recovery that is easy to complete since Oracle Database 10g.

The Solution Revealed   Based on the preceding considerations, Tim devises and implements the following recovery plan:

1. Mount the database:

```
Rman target=/
startup mount
```

2. Tim knows that datafile 4 is missing. It is part of the USERS tablespace. He therefore restores datafile 4:

```
restore datafile 4;
```

NOTE
Tim didn't even have to reset the incarnation of the database! This is new since Oracle Database 10g and makes cross-incarnation recovery so much easier.

3. Having restored the datafile, Tim now recovers it and then opens the database:

```
recover datafile 4;
alter database open resetlogs;
```

NOTE
Did it occur to you that Tim could have opened the database by just taking the datafile offline? He then could have restored the datafile and brought it online after the recovery. Here is an example of the commands he would have used to do an online recovery:

```
startup mount
alter database datafile 4 offline
alter database open;
restore datafile 4;
recover datafile 4;
alter database datafile 4 online
```

Case #9: Completing a Failed Duplication Manually

The Scenario
Tim decided to use RMAN duplication to create a clone of his production database on a different server. He ran the **duplicate** command, and the datafiles were successfully restored to the new server. The database is very large, and this file restore process took six hours to complete.

The Problem
Tim forgot to move the archive logs over to the auxiliary server for media recovery, so the duplication failed. This means that the cloned database is not fully recovered and does not have a new DBID.

The Solution
Tim isn't worried, though, and he certainly isn't going to take another six hours to perform the file restore. Tim can manually perform the media recovery and then use the DBNEWID utility on the clone database to create a new DBID and finish the duplication process without RMAN's assistance.

The Solution Revealed   Based on the solution he decided upon, Tim will implement the following action plan to complete his failed duplication:

1. Move the archive logs from the production to the auxiliary site:

```
cd /space/oracle_user/OraHome1/oradata/sun92
tar -cvf arch.tar arch
gzip arch.tar
```

2. Use FTP to move the arch.tar file to the auxiliary system, and then enter the following:

```
cd /space/oracle_user/OraHome1/oradata/sun92
gunzip arch.tar.gz
tar -xvf arch.tar
```

3. Perform manual recovery on the database. Tim needs to note the sequence number of the last archive log available on his target database and then set the recovery to stop at that sequence number. The %s variable in the LOG_ARCHIVE_FORMAT parameter signifies the sequence number and will be in the archive log name. Tim will perform manual recovery from SQL*Plus, connecting locally to his auxiliary database (at the auxiliary site).

```
ORACLE_SID=aux1
export ORACLE_SID
Sqlplus /nolog
SQL> connect / as sysdba
SQL> recover database using backup controlfile until sequence 11 thread 1;
```

4. Use DBNEWID (**nid**) to create a new DBID for the clone database. Tim's auxiliary database has been mounted, but it has not yet been opened. This is the right state in which to use DBNEWID. (If you are unsure of the database state, you can go ahead and remount it without doing any harm.)

```
Shutdown immediate;
startup mount;
exit
$ nid target=/
$ sqlplus /nolog
connect / as sysdba
Shutdown immediate;
startup mount;
alter database open resetlogs
```

Case #10: Using RMAN Duplication to Create a Historical Subset of the Target Database

The Scenario

Svetlana is a DBA at an online toy-train reseller. Her production database is under heavy load, with constant updates, inserts, and deletes. Over time, Svetlana has noticed that performance is starting to trail off for data-mining operations against certain inventory-tracking tables.

The Problem
She suspects foul play from the Cost-Based Optimizer, thinking that the Explain Plan might be changing in an adverse way. To test things, she is looking for a way to get a historical snapshot of a subset of production tables. She's considered duplication in the past, but doesn't have enough room on any server to clone the entire production database.

The Solution
Svetlana can use the Oracle RMAN feature of being able to specify tablespaces to skip during duplication. In this way, she can include only tablespaces that are part of the subset that she needs to test. In addition to skipping tablespaces, she can specify an **until** clause in the **duplication** command itself to set the historical point in time that she would like to test against.

The Solution Revealed   Svetlana will be duplicating to the same server that runs her target database, so she needs to make sure that she has her file-renaming strategy worked out. Then, she needs to get an auxiliary database started in NOMOUNT mode. After that, she runs her duplication code:

```
rman log=/space/backup/pitrdup.out
connect target /
connect auxiliary sys/password@aux1
duplicate target database to aux1
 pfile=/space/oracle_user/OraHome1/admin/aux1/pfile/init.ora
 skip tablespace 'CWMLITE' , 'USERS' , 'ODM' , 'TOOLS'
 until sequence = 11 thread = 1
 logfile
 '/space/oracle_user/OraHome1/oradata/aux1/redo01.dbf' size 5m,
 '/space/oracle_user/OraHome1/oradata/aux1/redo02.dbf' size 5m,
 '/space/oracle_user/OraHome1/oradata/aux1/redo03.dbf' size 5m;
```

RMAN would then generate the script required to duplicate the database as requested and then execute that script. Remember that when you set an **until sequence** clause in RMAN, the sequence you specify is not included as part of the recover set. So, in Svetlana's code, she has archive logs through sequence 10, but not sequence 11.

Case #11: Recovering from a Lost Datafile (ARCHIVELOG Mode) Using an Image Copy in the Fast Recovery Area

The Scenario
Tim, a senior DBA for a large manufacturing firm, has long lived by the maxim "Just because you are paranoid doesn't mean they aren't out to get you." In this vein, he has fought hard up the management chain to garner the resources to keep a full database backup on disk instead of streaming directly to tape. There is not enough room for every datafile backup on disk, so he has chosen those datafiles that represent the data that is most important to operations and that would be the most impacted by a prolonged outage.

After the database was migrated, Tim set up his Fast Recovery Area and created an image copy of his most important files in the FRA. He now takes a nightly incremental backup and applies the incremental to the image copy of those files.

The Problem

Disaster strikes, as it invariably does, near the end of month, when massive data processing is taking place. Tim's cell phone starts chirping with alert text messages only moments before a deluge of angry department heads start calling him. Tim turns off his phone and checks the database. He finds that one of the critical tablespaces has a corrupt datafile, file number 5. The file shows up on disk as 0 bytes. The end-of-month processing cannot continue until the file is recovered.

The Solution

Tim will switch to the datafile running in the FRA, which is current as of the level 1 incremental backup the night before. Then it's just a matter of applying archive logs to the file to bring it up to the current point in time.

The Solution Revealed   Tim's preparation means his outage will be significantly minimized. Here is his action plan:

1. Switch datafile 5 to the copy in the FRA:

   ```
   target /
   switch datafile 5 to copy;
   ```

2. Recover datafile 5:

   ```
   recover datafile 5;
   ```

3. Bring datafile 5 online:

   ```
   alter database datafile 5 online
   ```

Case #12: Recovering from Running the Production Datafile Out of the Fast Recovery Area

The Scenario

Tim used his FRA setup to significantly minimize the outage due to a corrupted datafile 5. However, now he is running a production datafile out of the FRA, the bad disk has been replaced, and it is time to get the datafile properly restored to its normal location.

The Problem

Using the datafile switch methodology to decrease MTTR is, of course, a very good thing. But it means that the production database is running live with a datafile that is in the Fast Recovery Area. This can hold for a short period, but ultimately the file has to be switched back to the correct standard location.

The Solution

Tim needs to make a new backup of datafile 5, restore it to the original file location, and then take a temporary outage while he switches back to this datafile and recovers it.

For Tim to restore the production datafile to the production environment, he has to plan a temporary outage. One of the trade-offs of a quick recovery time is this preplanned temporary outage. However, Tim can plan for it to occur deep in the night, when few users will be affected, and can absolutely minimize the amount of time the outage requires.

The Solution Revealed Tim will use the following action plan:

1. Take a new image copy backup of datafile 5. (Alternatively, Tim could use a previous backup of datafile 5 from tape, but Tim felt that taking a new backup of the file and restoring it from disk would actually be faster than trying to get the tape loaded and restored.)

    ```
    backup as copy datafile 5 format
    '/u01/app/oracle/oradata/v102/payroll01.dbf';
    ```

2. Restore datafile 5 to the original file location. In the code displayed previously, the file was backed up directly to the original location, so the restore is not required.

3. Switch datafile 5 to the copy in the original location:

    ```
    switch datafile 5 to copy;
    ```

4. Recover datafile 5 and bring the file online:

    ```
    recover datafile 5;
    ```

Case #13: Using Flashback Database and Media Recovery to Pinpoint the Exact Moment to Open the Database with resetlogs

The Scenario

Farouk did not notice the problem for all of Monday and part of Tuesday morning, because it was not brought to his attention. Finally, Tuesday morning, one of the managers for the woodscrew department called him to say that the Woodscrew database was missing records for some of the most popular woodscrew models. Farouk checked the database and, sure enough, found that someone had deleted rows from a primary table.

The Problem

Finding out who did it, and why, would have to wait. First, it was time to act. The manager said he had noticed the problem around lunchtime on Monday. Farouk checked his Flashback Query option, but found that the transaction was already older than his undo segments. He checked his Flashback Database option and found that he could still flash back nearly 48 hours.

The Solution

Farouk will use Flashback Database to do a point-in-time recovery of his entire database. There is no other option at this time. However, Farouk does not know the exact moment of failure, so he needs to be able to move back and forth in time to pinpoint the very last transaction before the failure. He will use Flashback Database and archive log recovery to scroll back and forth until he finds the correct moment to open the database. He will open the database in READ ONLY mode to check the table.

The Solution Revealed   Farouk devises the following plan:

1. He flashes back the database to the approximated first point of the failure:

```
RMAN> run {
2> flashback database to time "to_date('2015-03-19 13:30:00',
'YYYY-MM-DDHH24:MI:SS')";
3> }
```

2. He selects from the affected table to see if the values are in place:

```
alter database open read only;
select count(*) from ws_app.woodscrew where thread_cnt=30;
```

3. Farouk finds the values are not there, so he flashes back again:

```
shutdown immediate;
startup mount;

rman> run {
flashback database to time "to_date('2015-04-16 13:20:00',
'YYYY-MM-DD HH24:MI:SS')";}
```

4. He checks the values again:

```
alter database open read only;
select count(*) from ws_app.woodscrew where thread_cnt=30;
```

5. The values are there, but are missing a few rows that can be gained. So Farouk can shut down the database again and recover a bit further.

```
shutdown immediate;
startup mount;
recover database until sequence=227 thread=1;
alter database open read only;
select count(*) from ws_app.woodscrew where thread_cnt=30;
```

6. The values are the best they can be, under the circumstances. Farouk opens the database in read/write mode:

```
shutdown immediate;
startup mount;
alter database open resetlogs;
```

Summary

We hope you found these case studies helpful. We have done our best to provide you with a number of different circumstances that might come your way and solutions you can practice on a test system so that you will be ready to implement them in real life, should the occasion arise.

PART
V

RMAN Media
Management

CHAPTER
21

Media Management
Considerations

T he RMAN utility in Oracle Database 12c focuses on the best way to leverage disk backups as the media recovery solution. With the price of disks falling, massive storage area networks (SANs) have found a permanent place in many datacenters. With the business evolving toward cheaper and larger disks, upgrades in RMAN functionality (such as the Fast Recovery Area) were implemented to make best use of the available storage space.

It's a logical progression for the RMAN backup utility, and, of course, writing to disk is something that the Oracle Database is extremely good at. Therefore, any time it gets to leverage its disk-writing muscle, the RDBMS will do so for performance improvements.

But, for many customers, the world of unlimited disk storage has not arrived. For many, the size of the database, or its location, keeps it from being backed up to disk. Or, there still may be a business requirement to make a copy of the data and archive it offsite. So what does RMAN do if it needs to write to good, old-fashioned tape?

Tape backups of the Oracle database require third-party assistance. This is primarily due to the disparate nature of the different sequential media subsystems that are on the market and that are used every day. Instead of trying to employ different system calls for each different type of tape device, RMAN's development team decided to employ those software vendors that already earn a living by selling products that can read and write from tape.

Oracle has its own media management software solution, Oracle Secure Backup (OSB). OSB is a fully integrated RMAN-to-tape solution that does not require any third-party vendor software plug-in, and OSB has come a long way since its introduction in 10gR2. However, many customers will continue to purchase a license from any of the number of certified backup providers that have an Oracle RMAN plug-in (more on this in a minute).

This chapter covers the conceptual architecture of employing a media manager to back up your database directly to disk. It does so from a generic standpoint, by staying focused on the RMAN side of the equation and speaking in sweeping generalizations about the media management products themselves. We will talk about the setup from the RMAN side, how it all works, and what changes when you use tape for your output device. Several chapters in this book go into detail about many of the most popular media management products on the market and talk about configuring and using them specifically.

In Oracle Database 12c, you can utilize OSB to provide free backup-to-tape functionality, provided that you have a single tape head and it is attached directly to the server that contains the Oracle database that you want to back up. In other words, you will pay for centralized tape farms. To get additional backup-to-tape functionality, you will have to purchase the full version of OSB or buy a product from a media management vendor.

Tape Backups in a Disk Backup World

In the world of Oracle databases, size does matter. In fact, less than a decade ago, a database of a few gigabytes was considered very large. Now, databases range upward into the terabytes, the first petabyte database has been reported, and the average database is 100GB and growing. So when it comes to backups, trying to find enough contiguous space on disk to get the thing backed up can be difficult, even with the massive number of SANs being deployed in the enterprise.

Therefore, the first reason for considering tape backups is the size of the database. The size of a database determines whether you need to back up to tape: buying more hard drives can get pricey. But even with disk prices dropping radically, tapes are still cheaper and reliable, considering their purpose is to hold copies of data—copies that likely will rarely get used. Of course, sometimes disk backups become a critical piece of a strategy that stresses quick recovery, and using tape backups is much slower than using disks on both the backup and the restore. The price point of a tape, compared with disks, remains a compelling reason for tape backups.

The second reason to use tape backups is manageability. Typically, enterprise-wide backup strategies are implemented and executed by one person on a centralized system. And this allows your company to invest in large tape storage jukeboxes that can stream data from multiple sources. Then, the data backups can be catalogued and removed without having someone trek all over the enterprise distributing tapes, troubleshooting individual tape devices, or training users on new software rollouts.

A third and frequently disregarded reason for tape backups is their portability. A pile of tapes can easily be moved offsite for archiving and disaster-proofing. Hard drives just don't transport that well.

The drawback to pooling backup resources is that it leads to complications, especially in regard to Oracle databases. The complexity of Oracle datafiles, log files, and control files means that we cannot simply let an OS job step in and copy the files at its leisure. Instead, we have to prepare the database for the backup job, signal the copy to begin, and afterward reconfigure the database—or, so it was in the old-school world (refer to Chapter 2).

Using RMAN means that this kind of database configuration is eliminated and that backups can occur anytime, under any circumstance. However, to get the backups to stream to your centralized tape backup location, you have to do some RMAN-specific configuration.

RMAN and the Media Manager: An Overview

RMAN streams backups to tape by engaging a media manager. A *media manager* is software provided by a third-party vendor that takes the data stream of blocks passed from the RMAN channel process and redirects it to the appropriate tape. Most often, a media management server exists in an enterprise network. A *media management server* is a centralized system that handles all enterprise-wide backup operations to tape devices that it manages.

To engage a media manager, a computer system must have the corresponding media management client software installed on it. This is the software that makes the connection to the media management server and passes the data to it over the network. For RMAN to engage the media management server, an additional software component is needed. After you install the client software, you must also install the Oracle module for the media manager. The *Oracle module* is a software plug-in for the Oracle RDBMS that connects RMAN to the client media management software, which can then make the pass to the media management server. This plug-in for Oracle is referred to as the *Media Management Library* (MML). Figure 21-1 shows a generalized overview of the backup topology when a media manager is used to back up to tape.

The Media Manager Catalog

The media manager is a separate subsystem in the overall backup system you will use. It has three essential components, as previously described: the Media Management Library that integrates with Oracle, the media management client, and the media management server. The media management server has multiple components, the specifics of which depend upon the vendor. But all media management servers must have a few similar components, the most important of which (from the perspective of this chapter) is the media manager catalog.

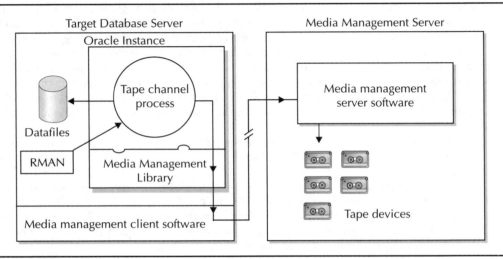

FIGURE 21-1. *Network topology when backing up to tape*

The media manager catalog is the database at the media management server that holds information about the physical tapes, who has access to those tapes, and what is being stored on those tapes. This catalog records the RMAN file handle when a backup is complete. The *handle* refers to the name of the backup piece that gets created when you perform a backup with RMAN. When you back up to disk, the handle is the physical filename. When you back up to tape, the handle is used in the media manager catalog to refer to the location on tape where the backups can be located.

RMAN completes a backup to tape by providing the handle name to the media manager, which records that handle in the catalog. When a restore is required, RMAN requests a specific handle (based on its own catalog) from the media manager. The media manager looks for that handle, associates it with a specific tape, and determines if that tape is available. If the tape is available, the media manager engages the tape and begins to stream the data back to RMAN so that you can rebuild the datafiles.

The Media Manager: Other Software Components

In addition to the catalog, the media management server comprises two essential pieces:

- **Device agent**   The component responsible for engaging the actual tape device and passing data to and from it.

- **Robotic interface**   The software that controls any robotics that are responsible for changing tapes when they are full or for retrieving a tape that has been filled.

From the Oracle perspective, RMAN is blind to these components. RMAN simply sends a command request to its MML, and the media management software handles the coordination of all events after that. However, it is important to be familiar with these software components because your backup and recovery success depends on them. Many problems that come from using RMAN are related to the device agent or the robotic interface, but from the RMAN interface these problems are nearly impossible to discern.

Media Management Library

The MML is simply a library file that interprets generic requests from RMAN for a particular backup or restore operation, and translates that request into the specific system call necessary at the media management server to turn that request into reality. The MML is provided by the same vendor that supplies the media management client and server software, but you purchase and license the MML separately from the client and server software.

   The MML is loaded into the Oracle memory space as an integrated library file when a tape channel is first allocated; it is logically part of the Oracle RDBMS software so that RMAN can make the correct calls to the media management client software. The integration is simple: When a channel to tape is allocated, Oracle loads a file called libobk.so. This file, located in the ORACLE_HOME/lib directory, is just a symbolic link to whichever MML file you will be using. On the Windows platform, Oracle looks for a file called orasbt.dll in the searchable path. Regardless of which media management provider you use, its media management DLL will be named orasbt .dll, and media management providers usually write it to the WINDOWS\system32 directory. If your media management provider does not do this, it will append to the system path environment variable a searchable path that leads to orasbt.dll.

   In the next several chapters, we discuss the linking process by which you can establish your vendor's MML file as the one RMAN initiates when a channel is allocated. For testing purposes, Oracle provides a test MML file. This library file allows you to allocate a channel to tape but then to write the backup to disk. In the following RMAN Workshop, we show you how to use this test MML.

RMAN Workshop: *Test Tape Channels with the Oracle Default SBT Interface*

Workshop Notes

You need access to a sufficient amount of disk space, and you need to create a directory in which to place the backup piece. In our example, we use the mount point u04, on which we created a directory called *backup*. Make sure you have sufficient memory available for the backup, as outlined in Chapter 3, and be aware of the disk I/O that goes to the backup location. Try to allocate space on a controller other than those that house your actual database.

Step 1.   Build your backup directory:

```
$>cd /u01
mkdir backup
```

Step 2.   Make sure permissions are established so that the Oracle Database, which operates as the user that installed the software, can write to this location:

```
ls -al backup
```

Step 3. Initiate RMAN and connect to the target. In the following example, we are connecting locally to the target PROD. This means that if you check the environment on a Linux system, the environment variable ORACLE_SID would point to PROD.

```
$>Rman
Rman> connect target
```

Step 4. Run your backup by using the PARMS parameter during channel allocation to specify the Oracle test library file. You also need to specify a BACKUP_DIR directory, which is the location that RMAN will write the backup to. Here, we specify this as /u04/backup:

```
run {
allocate channel x1 type 'sbt_tape'
PARMS="SBT_LIBRARY=oracle.disksbt,
ENV=(BACKUP_DIR=/u01/backup)";
backup datafile 1 format='%U';}
```

Alternatively, you can use a permanent configuration command to set the Oracle library (but remember that you've done it, and don't leave it lying around for too long):

```
CONFIGURE CHANNEL DEVICE TYPE 'SBT_TAPE' PARMS
'SBT_LIBRARY=oracle.disksbt,ENV=(BACKUP_DIR=/u04/backup)';
```

This is a great test if you are trying to troubleshoot possible problems with your media manager backup solution and cannot get the backups to work. By allocating a "fake" tape channel, you can see that RMAN is configured correctly.

CAUTION
Do not use the test MML file for production backups. If you will be backing up to disk in a production environment, allocate a disk channel. The performance of the fake MML is terrible because RMAN is allocating memory buffers for tape, not disk, and therefore is not taking advantage of the speed of disk writes versus tape writes.

If you have not successfully loaded your vendor's MML file and you do not specify in the PARMS section of the channel allocation that you want to use Oracle's disk SBT interface, you will receive an error when you try to allocate a channel to tape:

```
RMAN-00571: ===========================================================
RMAN-00569: =============== ERROR MESSAGE STACK FOLLOWS =====
RMAN-00571: ===========================================================
RMAN-03009: failure of allocate command on x channel
         at 12/05/2014 21:26:43
ORA-19554: error allocating device, device type: SBT_TAPE, device name
ORA-27211: Failed to load Media Management Library
```

Interfacing with the MML

When you are linking Oracle and the MML, you are establishing the means by which RMAN can pass a command that engages the MML and, by extension, the media management client software installed on the database server. But how do you know which media management server to engage?

To specify the media management server, you must pass an environment variable within the RMAN session to specify the server name. We specify the server name as an environment variable when we allocate our tape channel. As you saw in the previous RMAN Workshop, you pass the environment variable by using the PARMS option of the **allocate channel** command. Different media management products have different environment variables that they accept. VERITAS NetBackup, for example, requires the parameter NB_ORA_SERV:

```
Allocate channel t1 type 'sbt_tape'
PARMS="ENV=(NB_ORA_SERV=storage1)";
```

In the preceding example, the name of the media management server is storage1, and our database server has already been registered in this server and has permission to write to its tape devices.

In addition to passing the name of the server, we can pass numerous other parameters at the time of the channel allocation to take advantage of management functions at the server. For instance, NetBackup offers the ability to specify the class or the schedule to use for this backup, whereas EMC Networker allows you to specify the resource pool.

The SBT API

RMAN can engage different media managers with impunity because it sends the same marching orders no matter what MML has been loaded. Oracle developed RMAN with a generic API called the SBT API, which is provided to third-party vendors that wish to write integration products for Oracle database backups. This API is the means by which RMAN sends commands to the media manager.

The SBT API is responsible for sending the commands to the media management server to initiate the creation of backup files on tape. It also sends commands to search for previous backups based on the file handle in the media manager catalog. It can send commands to remove these backups, as well as write new backups and, of course, read from the backup location. There are two versions of the Oracle RMAN SBT API: 1.1 and 2.0. Version 1.1 was published and used with Oracle 8.0.x, and that's it. Since then, RMAN has made calls to the media manager by using the specifications of version 2.0. You can see this version in RMAN's output when you run a backup:

```
channel x1: finished piece 1 at 25-SEP-14
piece handle=05kq4cfd_1_1 tag=TAG20140925T102902
comment=API Version 2.0,MMS Version 8.1.3.0
channel x1: backup set complete, elapsed time: 00:00:02
Finished backup at 25-SEP-14
```

RMAN also returns the version of the MML that it initializes at channel allocation time. This is seen during channel allocation in the RMAN output:

```
allocated channel: x
channel x: sid=12 devtype=SBT_TAPE
channel x: VERITAS NetBackup for Oracle.....
```

Not only is this a good way to determine your MML version, but it also means that you have successfully linked in your MML with RMAN—otherwise, it would not be able to extract the version information.

Back Up to Tape: From Start to Finish

In this section, we do a walkthrough of a backup to tape and show the different calls made to the SBT API and how they are handled by the media manager. Again, please note that we are giving you a very generic overview, and the specifics are handled by the vendor that writes the integration MML.

When you allocate a tape channel, RMAN spawns a server process at your target database. This server process then makes a call to the SBT API of sbtinit(). This call initializes the MML file and loads it into memory. It also returns to RMAN the version of SBT API supported by that MML. After calling sbtinit(), RMAN calls sbtinit2(), which supplies further configuration details to the media manager software.

After RMAN has parsed your backup command, it executes the RPC that makes the call to sys.dbms_backup_restore.backuppiececreate. At this time, the channel process calls sbtbackup(), which handles the creation of the backup piece at the specified tape location. This call informs the media manager that Oracle will begin pushing the flow of data blocks to it, so it should prepare the tape device for the onslaught.

The RMAN input buffers fill up and make the memory-to-memory write to the output buffer. When the output buffer fills, the channel process calls sbtwrite2(), which performs the write of filled output buffers to the tape location (for more on input buffers, see Chapter 3). Typically, this means engaging the device agent at the media management server in order to access the tape itself.

When all the output buffers for a particular backup set have been cleared out and there is no more work for sbtwrite2(), the channel session calls sbtclose2(). This flushes out any media manager buffers and commits the backup piece to tape.

After we complete the backup piece, the channel process invokes sbtinfo2() to make sure the media manager catalog has documented the backup piece. It requests the tape, the tape location, and the expiration time of the backup from the catalog. Then, it writes the backup piece handle to the catalog.

After confirming the backup piece location, the channel process calls sbtend(), which cleans up any remaining resources and releases them for other database use. The final action performed is the deallocation of the channel process, which is terminated at the target database.

Restore from Tape: From Start to Finish

Of course, sooner or later, all that backing up you've been doing will get put to the test, and you will need to perform a restore. As with a backup, the SBT API has a specific series of steps that it goes through during a restore operation in order to get the backups on tape back into place for your database. In this section, we briefly run through the SBT API during a restore operation.

When you allocate the tape channel for restore, RMAN creates a server process at the target database. This channel then calls sbtinit() to initialize the media manager software. This is identical to the initialization that would take place for a backup: the MML file is loaded into memory.

Based on the parameters of our **restore** command in RMAN, RMAN will have checked its catalog to determine the handle name of the backup required for the restore. It then takes this requested backup piece handle and passes it to the media manager by using sbtrestore(). The sbtrestore() function instructs the media manager to prepare the appropriate tape for a restore operation. This means engaging the media manager catalog and finding the appropriate tape, and then (if necessary) passing the command to the robotic instruction set to get the tape. After the tape is loaded, it will need to be rewound to the backup piece starting point.

After preparing the tape for the restore, the channel process calls the sbtread2() function to read the data from the tape device and stream it to the Oracle process. This data is loaded into the input buffers, written to the output buffers, and finally written to the datafile locations as specified by the control file.

When the end of a backup piece is detected on tape, the tape channel process calls the sbtclose() function to disengage the particular tape that had that piece on it. This signals that Oracle is done with the tape. If there are more backup pieces that need to be read for the restore operation, then the channel process returns to the second step and calls sbtrestore() for a different backup piece.

After the restore is complete and RMAN requests no more backup pieces, the channel process calls the sbtend() function, which cleans up the channel resources and releases them for other use. Then the channel process is terminated, after which the media manager is free to unload any tapes that had been requested.

Using sbttest and loadsbt.exe

As we mentioned previously, there are always indications as to whether you have successfully linked your MML with Oracle. The information from the channel allocation shows the MML version, for instance. However, these sorts of indicators do not guarantee success, because a failure may occur further down the topology: at the media management client level or at the media management server. Oracle provides a utility called sbttest that can test to make sure that RMAN will be able to perform backups to tape by using your media management configuration. This utility is called from a command line and performs a complete test: it writes a block to tape and then requests a read of that block. In this way, it runs through the entire gamut of SBT API functions that would occur during backup and makes sure they will all be successful.

Using sbttest is simple. After making sure that you have completed the full configuration of your media management configuration, go to the command prompt within the environment from which you will run RMAN and type **sbttest** and a test filename. The following code walks you through each of the sbt() calls previously listed in the "Restore from Tape: From Start to Finish" section and provides output on whether each call succeeded:

```
/u02/home/usupport> sbttest oratest_061915
The sbt function pointers are loaded from libobk.so library.
NetWorker: Cannot contact nsrexecd service on horatio.hadba.com,
Service not available.-- sbtinit succeeded
NetWorker: Cannot contact nsrexecd service on horatio.hadba.com,
Service not available.-- sbtinit (2nd time) succeeded
sbtinit: Media manager supports SBT API version x.0
sbtinit: vendor description string=NMO vx.x
sbtinit: allocated sbt context area of 536 bytes
sbtinit: Media manager is version x.x
sbtinit: proxy copy is supported
sbtinit: maximum concurrent proxy copy files is 0
-- sbtinit2 succeeded
-- regular_backup_restore starts ................................
```

```
MMAPI error from sbtbackup: 7501, nwora_index_ssinfo:
index connect to cervantes.windba.com failed for client
horatio.hadba.com: Program not registered
-- sbtbackup failed
```

The sbttest utility has matured impressively since its inception as a simple binary indicator of success or failure. Now, a number of parameters can be passed to tweak the exact test you would like to take your media management system through. This includes naming the database you want to test, changing the number of blocks that are written by sbttest, and specifying how to further handle the file that sbttest writes to tape. Simply typing **sbttest** at the command prompt will give you all the switches you can use, along with simple text descriptions.

The sbttest utility is only available for Unix platforms; on Windows, you can request the utility loadsbt.exe from Oracle Support. Unfortunately, this utility does not have the same capabilities as sbttest and instead simply checks the searchable path for a file called orasbt.dll. If it finds this file, it will try to load it the same way that Oracle will during a tape backup. It will tell you if it can be loaded, but it will not attempt to write a block to tape, so it does not "swim downstream" very far to see if the entire configuration works. As such, it is not as useful as sbttest.

Media Management Errors

Error reporting in RMAN looks much the same when reporting media management problems as it does when reporting any other problem, and this can lead to some confusion. It is critical when troubleshooting RMAN errors to be able to determine where exactly the error is coming from: is it RMAN, the target database, the catalog database, or the media manager?

There are specific ways to determine if an error that is being returned in RMAN is related to the media manager. Some of them are obvious, particularly if you have not linked the MML correctly. We've shown examples of these errors already. However, if you have properly linked the MML with your Oracle installation, how can you tell if an error is related to the MML?

There are a number of different errors, but the most common error you will see related to the media manager is ORA-19511. This error is actually a *blank error,* meaning that Oracle supplies no text; instead, Oracle provides this as an error trap for media management errors. So if you see the following error, there is no doubt that you have linked your MML correctly and that the problem you are having is irrefutably a problem with the media manager:

```
ORA-19511: sbtbackup: Failed to process backup file
```

Other indicators of media management problems are not so clear, but just as telling. For instance, if you ever see in the error stack RMAN referring to a "sequential file," then you are dealing with a tape backup, and the problem is due to a failed read or write to the sequential file on tape. Another common error is ORA-27206:

```
RMAN-10035: exception raised in RPC: ORA-27206: requested file
not found in media management catalog
```

Again, the wording indicates a problem communicating with the media management catalog, which is where you would need to look to resolve the problem.

In addition to actual errors, any hang you might encounter in RMAN is *usually* related to media management problems. *Usually.* When RMAN makes an sbtwrite() call to the media manager, for instance, RMAN cannot possibly know how long this will take to complete. Therefore, RMAN does not provide any sort of timeout for the operation—it will wait indefinitely for the media manager to return with either a successful write or an error. If the media manager is waiting on a particular event that has no timeout, such as a tape switch or a tape load, the media manager waits, and so RMAN waits. And so you wait. And wait. As we said, RMAN will not time out, so if you notice that RMAN is taking a particularly long time to complete and you see no progress in V$SESSION_LONGOPS (see Chapter 3), then your first instinct should be to check the media manager for an untrapped error or for an event such as a tape load or tape switch.

Summary

In this chapter, we discussed the concepts behind how RMAN utilizes the media management software of a third-party vendor to make backups to tape. We walked through the specific steps that RMAN makes using the SBT API. We also briefly discussed media management errors in RMAN.

CHAPTER
22

Oracle Secure Backup

Oracle Secure Backup (OSB) is a reliable, complete, and centralized tape backup management solution. OSB provides heterogeneous data protection in distributed, mixed-platform environments. It protects Oracle Database and file system data, such as the contents of Oracle Home. In addition to tape backup, OSB delivers an integrated Oracle database backup to third-party cloud (Internet) storage, through the Oracle Secure Backup Cloud Module. Oracle Secure Backup offers two tape management editions: OSB and OSB Express.

This chapter discusses features of OSB, its interfaces, components of OSB, and how to install and configure OSB.

Features of Oracle Secure Backup

Oracle Secure Backup (OSB) is an Oracle product that integrates tightly with RMAN. OSB provides a conduit between Oracle databases, RMAN, and a number of major table drives and table libraries. Additionally, OSB supports the most common TCP/IP protocols, including Internet Protocol v4 (IPv4), Internet Protocol v6 (IPv6), and mixed IPv4/IPv6 environments on all platforms that support IPv6. In association with TCP/IP support, OSB provides support for NFS (network file system) or CIFS (Common Internet File System) file systems. Additionally, support for fibre-attached devices is provided by OSB.

With Oracle Database 12*c*, OSB offers the ability to back up directly to local disks as well as a host of other features:

- Ability to use wildcards and exclusion lists to specify the files for backup
- Support for multilevel incremental backups, duplexed database backups, and backups that span multiple volumes
- Automatic tape-drive sharing to reduce idle tape-drive write periods
- Use of direct-to-block positioning and direct access restore to avoid unnecessarily reading tape blocks to locate files

Additional features of OSB include the following:

- Highly configurable encryption for file system backups
- Support for fast backup compression.
- Support for ACSLS (Automated Cartridge System Library Software) and vaulting
- Reports on the progress of backup or restore jobs during the operations
- Offers tight RMAN integration
- Integrated with Oracle Cloud Control
- Allows direct backup to cloud storage using the Oracle Secure Backup Cloud Module
- Acts as single point of contact for issues involving Recovery Manager (RMAN) and the media manager
- Includes Oracle Secure Backup Express, available free with the Oracle Database and Oracle Applications, which may be employed for the backup and restore of one server to a single tape drive

Oracle Secure Backup and Recovery Manager

Oracle Secure Backup is a media management layer for RMAN, and it supplies an SBT interface that RMAN can use to back up database files to tape. The OSB SBT library is the only interface that supports RMAN encrypted backups and unused block compression directly to tape. The RMAN ability to eliminate backup of committed undo is exclusive to OSB and is not available with other media management products. In Oracle Database 11g, CPU overhead is reduced by using a shared buffer for SBT (System Backup to Tape) and tape to eliminate the copy process from SBT to the tape buffer. OSB is better integrated with Oracle Enterprise Manager (OEM) as compared with other media managers, and managing tapes, media servers, and tape devices using OEM is exclusive to OSB.

Differences Between OSB and OSB Express

The following are the common features with Oracle Secure Backup and Oracle Secure Backup Express:

- Integrated with RMAN for online tape backup and restore of Oracle Database
- Backs up and restores file system data
- Integrated with Oracle Enterprise Manager (Oracle Database 10gR2 and higher)

These features are available only with Oracle Secure Backup:

- Backs up Real Application Clusters (RAC) environments
- Integrated with Oracle Enterprise Manager Grid Control (Oracle Database 10gR2 and higher)
- Enables multiple tape drive usage within the backup environment
- Provides Fibre-attached device support
- Offers backup encryption to tape
- Includes Oracle fast backup compression
- Supports ACSLS and vaulting
- Features networked backup of distributed servers and/or tape devices

Backup Encryption

Oracle Secure Backup encryption is available for both RMAN and file system backup operations. The data is encrypted on the server before transport over the network, or written to a locally attached tape device. Database data is encrypted after RMAN has passed the data through the SBT to OSB. If the RMAN data from the SBT is encrypted, then no further encryption occurs. Backup encryption is normally available only with the purchase of the Oracle Advanced Security Option (ASO).

Fast Database Backup Compression

Fast database backup compression is normally available only with the purchase of the Oracle Advanced Compression Option (ACO).

Oracle Secure Backup Cloud Module

The Oracle Secure Backup Cloud Module is independent of the OSB tape management editions. The module has been qualified only with Amazon S3 (Simple Storage Service) for now, but it might be expanded to other cloud storage vendors in the future. The number of Oracle Secure Backup Cloud Module licenses depends on the number of RMAN channels for backup to the cloud and does not depend on the number of Oracle database backups. For example, four OSB Cloud Module licenses could be used to back up two Oracle databases using two RMAN channels for each or used to back up one Oracle database using four RMAN channels.

Oracle Secure Backup Interfaces

Figure 22-1 illustrates the interfaces you may use to access Oracle Secure Backup, described here:

- **Oracle Enterprise Manager Database Control and Grid Control** This is the preferred graphical user interface (GUI) for managing OSB. Most OSB tasks can be performed via OEM. The OSB administrative server can be configured as a target in OEM Grid Control and can be used to perform file system backup and restore operations.

- **Oracle Secure Backup Web tool** This interface is a browser-based GUI that enables you to configure an administrative domain, browse the backup catalog, manage backup and restore of file system data, and perform certain other tasks not possible in OEM. It exposes all functions of obtool. The Web tool employs an Apache web server running on the administrative server.

- **Oracle Secure Backup command-line interface (obtool)** This command-line program is the primary interface to OSB and is in the bin subdirectory of the OSB home. Using obtool, you may log into the administrative domain to back up and restore file system data, as well as to perform configuration and administrative tasks. You may run obtool on any host within the administrative domain.

- **Recovery Manager command-line interface** The RMAN command-line interface may be used to configure and initiate database backup and restore operations for utilization of OSB. The RMAN utility is located in the bin directory of an ORACLE_HOME directory.

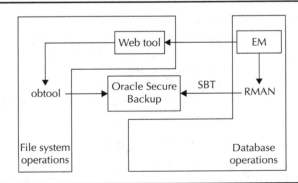

FIGURE 22-1. *OSB interfaces*

The RMAN command-line client will run on any database host, as long as the client is able to connect to the target database. The OSB SBT library must exist on the same host as the target database in order for RMAN to make backups using OSB.

Oracle Secure Backup Components

An administrative domain is a group of hosts managed as a common unit for performing backup and restore operations. When configuring OSB, you assign roles to each host in the domain. A single host may consist of one or more of the following roles:

- **Administrative server**   Starting and monitoring backup and recovery jobs is accomplished by the administrative server running within an administrative domain. The administrative server may also run other applications in addition to OSB.

- **Media server**   Houses secondary storage devices such as tape drives or tape libraries. At least one media server will be defined for each administrative domain.

- **Client**   A host whose local data is backed up by OSB. One or more clients will be defined in each administrative domain. Most hosts in the administrative domain are clients.

Figure 22-2 illustrates an OSB administrative domain. The domain includes an administrative server, a media server with an attached tape library, three clients, and five hosts.

Figure 22-3 demonstrates an OSB administrative domain containing a single Linux host. This Linux host assumes the roles of administrative server, media server, and client. An Oracle database and a locally attached tape library are configured for the Linux host.

Oracle Secure Backup Daemons

An administrative domain uses seven types of OSB daemons:

- **Service daemon**   This daemon runs on the administrative server, media server, and client. Access to OSB configuration data on the administrative server is provided by the service daemon. It also runs jobs requested by the schedule daemon. On a media server or a client, the daemon handles membership in an administrative domain.

- **Schedule daemon**   This runs only on the administrative server. It is the OSB scheduler.

- **Index daemon**   This daemon runs only on the administrative server, to manage the backup catalog. It starts when a backup is completed or the catalog is accessed for restore or browsing operations.

- **Apache web server daemon**   This runs only on the administrative server and provides the Web tool interface.

- **NDMP daemon**   This daemon runs on a media server and a client, and provides data communication between them.

- **Robot daemon**   This runs on a media server and manipulates tapes in a tape library. The service daemon starts one robot daemon for each tape library when a tape manipulation is needed.

- **Proxy daemon**   This daemon runs on a client to verify user access for SBT backup and restore operations.

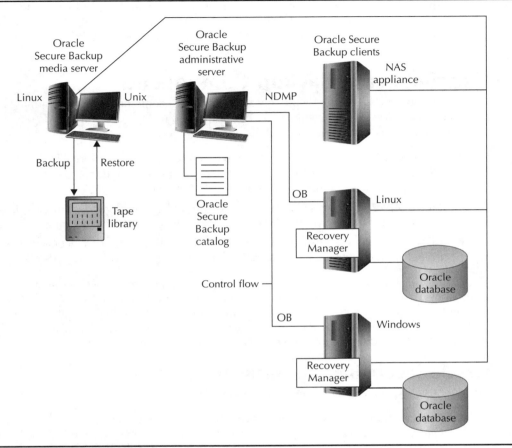

FIGURE 22-2. *OSB administrative domain*

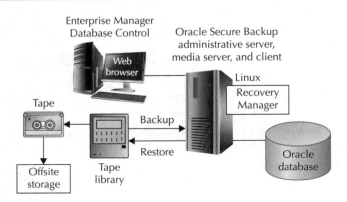

FIGURE 22-3. *OSB administrative domain with a single host*

Host Access Modes

Communicating to a host in an administrative domain is possible through two access modes:

- **Primary** For primary access mode, OSB is installed on a host. The access mode is used by OSB daemons. An Oracle database typically exists on a host accessed via this mode. In OEM, it is referred to as "native" access mode. In OSB Web tool, it is called "OB" access mode.

- **NDMP** The Network Data Management Protocol host is a storage appliance provided by third-party vendors, such as DinoStor, Mirapoint, and Network Appliance. Using a vendor-specific implementation, the NDMP host uses the NDMP protocol to back up and restore file systems. OSB is accessible via NDMP, although OSB software is not installed on an NDMP host.

Administrative Data

OSB arranges information for the administrative domain as a hierarchy of files in the OSB home on the administrative server. The directory that OSB is installed into is the OSB home.

Figure 22-4 illustrates the directory structure for an OSB home. All platforms have the same directory structure, although the default home is /usr/local/oracle/backup for Unix and Linux systems, but is C:\Program Files\Oracle\Backup for Microsoft Windows systems.

Domain-wide entities, such as media families, classes, and devices, are included within the administrative data. Figure 22-4 illustrates how the config directory contains several subdirectories. These subdirectories each represent an object maintained by OSB. For each object directory, OSB creates files describing the characteristics for the corresponding object.

Only in rare circumstances would it be necessary to access the administrative database directly from the file system. The OEM, Web tool, and obtool interfaces are commonly used to access catalogs and configuration data.

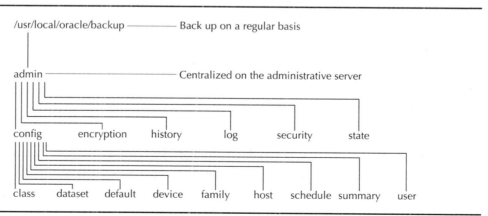

FIGURE 22-4. *Administrative server directories*

Oracle Secure Backup Users and Classes

To enable OSB to maintain consistent user identities across the administrative domain, OSB saves information for OSB users, as well as their rights, on the administrative server.

On the administrative server, each OSB user has an account and an encrypted password. Using Web tool or obtool, operating system users may enter their username and password. Using an encrypted SSL connection, the client program transmits the password to the administrative server.

The admin user is created by default during OSB installation on the administrative server. Also during the installation, you can create the oracle user to back up and recover Oracle databases. The installer assigns a random password to the oracle user. Usually, it is unnecessary to log into OSB by using this user.

Operating System Accounts

For OSB users, the namespace is distinct from the namespaces for Linux, Unix, and Microsoft Windows users. Therefore, if you access a host in the administrative domain as, for example, the operating system user backup_usr, and if the OSB user in the domain is named backup_usr, these accounts will be managed separately, though the names are identical. You may find it convenient to create the OSB user with the same name and password as an operating system user.

At the time you create an OSB user, you may associate the user with Unix and Microsoft Windows accounts. Accounts of this type are used with an unprivileged backup, which is a backup that is not run with root privileges. Privileged backup and restore operations use a client with root (Unix) or Local System (Microsoft Windows) permissions.

If you were to create an OSB user named backup_usr and associate it with Unix account ubackup_usr and Microsoft Windows account wbackup_usr, when backup_usr uses the **backup --unprivileged** command to back up a client, the jobs will run under the operating system account associated with backup_usr. Therefore, backup_usr is only able to back up files on a Unix client accessible to ubackup_usr, and able to back up files on a Microsoft Windows client accessible to wbackup_usr.

With the "modify administrative domain's configuration" right, you may configure the preauthorization attribute for an OSB user. This right allows you to preauthorize operating system users to create RMAN backups or to access the OSB command-line utilities.

NDMP Hosts

When setting up an OSB user account, you may configure user access to Network Data Management Protocol (NDMP). You may set up the host to use a user-defined text password, a null password, or the default NDMP password. A password for an NDMP host is associated with the host, not the user. You may configure a password authentication method such as MD5-encrypted or text.

Oracle Secure Backup Rights and Classes

A defined set of rights granted to an OSB user is considered an OSB class. Though similar to a Unix group, an OSB class has a finer granularity of access rights specific for the needs of OSB. As shown in Figure 22-5, multiple users may be assigned to a class, while each user is a member of a single class.

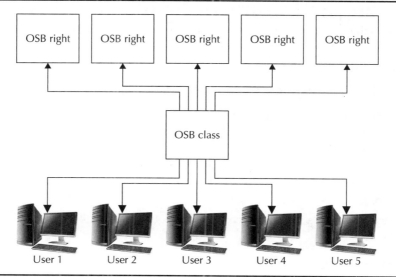

FIGURE 22-5. *Rights and classes*

These classes are important to understanding the rights of an OSB user:

■ **admin** Utilized for overall administration of a domain, it consists of all rights necessary to change domain configurations and to complete backup and restore operations.

■ **monitor** Does not allow users to receive e-mail notifications, change domain configurations, or to complete backup and restore operations. The users can only access backups, see information about storage devices and domain configuration, and list scheduled jobs.

■ **operator** For standard day-to-day operations, it has no configuration rights, but consists of all the rights needed for backup and restore operations. This class allows the user to control and query the state of primary and secondary storage devices.

■ **oracle** Much like the operator class, but with rights enabling the user to change Oracle database configuration settings and to perform Oracle database backups. Members of this class usually are OSB users mapped to operating system accounts of an Oracle database installation.

■ **reader** Allows members to browse the OSB catalog. Readers may modify only the name and password for their OSB user accounts.

■ **user** Assigned to users to allow them rights to interact in limited ways with their domains. This class allows users to browse their own data within the OSB catalog and to perform user-based restores.

Installing and Configuring Oracle Secure Backup

OSB is available for delivery on CD-ROM or may be downloaded from the Oracle Technology Network (OTN) website at the following address:

http://www.oracle.com/technology/products/secure-backup/index.html

The following are requirements for installing and configuring OSB:

- Each host in the OSB administrative domain must run TCP/IP. Static IP addresses should be assigned to all hosts, or it should be ensured that the DHCP server always assigns the same IP address.
- There should be no duplicate host names in the OSB administrative domain because index catalog data is based on the client host name.
- For Linux media servers, the SCSI Generic (SG) driver needs to be installed.
- Each node of a RAC cluster using OSB requires an installation of OSB.

RMAN Workshop: *Install and Configure Oracle Secure Backup*

Workshop Notes

The following example uses the Linux operating system. OSB is downloaded from OTN. The recommended directory for the installation of OSB on Linux is /usr/local/oracle/backup. To simplify the example, the administrative server, media server, and client are all installed on the same machine.

Step 1. As the root user, check whether the uncompress utility is installed on the system. If it is not, create a symbolic link pointing to the gunzip utility:

```
[root@lin32 ~]# uncompress
-bash: uncompress: command not found
[root@lin32 ~]# ln -s /bin/gunzip /bin/uncompress
```

Step 2. Create a directory for the download and then issue the **cd** (change directory) command to that directory:

```
[root@lin32 ~]# mkdir download
[root@lin32 ~]# cd download/
```

Step 3. Download OSB into the download directory and then unzip the product:

```
[root@lin32 download]# unzip osb*.zip
```

Step 4. Create the directory where the install will place OSB files:

```
[root@lin32 download]# mkdir -p /usr/local/oracle/backup
```

Step 5.   Issue the **cd** (change directory) command to the OSB destination and run **setup**:

```
[root@lin32 download]# cd $OSB_INSTALL_LOCATION
[root@lin32 backup]# ./setup
```

The following output is returned:

```
Welcome to Oracle's setup program for Oracle Secure Backup. This program loads
Oracle Secure Backup software from the CD-ROM to a filesystem directory of your
choosing.
Please wait a moment while I learn about this host... done.
- - - - - - - - - - - - - - - - - - - - - - - - - - - - - - - - - -
    1. linux32
        administrative server, media server, client
- - - - - - - - - - - - - - - - - - - - - - - - - - - - - - - - - -
Loading Oracle Secure Backup installation tools... done.
Loading linux32 administrative server, media server, client... done.
- - - - - - - - - - - - - - - - - - - - - - - - - - - - - - - - - -
Oracle Secure Backup has installed a new obparameters file.
Your previous version has been saved as install/obparameters.savedbysetup.
Any changes you have made to the previous version must be made to the new obparameters file.
Would you like the opportunity to edit the obparameters file
Please answer 'yes' or 'no' [no]:
```

Step 6.   Leaving the default parameters for now, press ENTER to choose the default answer. The
following output is returned:

```
- - - - - - - - - - - - - - - - - - - - - - - - - - - - - - - - - -
Loading of Oracle Secure Backup software from CD-ROM is complete.
You may unmount and remove the CD-ROM.
Would you like to continue Oracle Secure Backup installation with 'installob' now?
(The Oracle Secure Backup Installation Guide contains complete information about installob.)
Please answer 'yes' or 'no' [yes]:
```

Step 7.   Again, press ENTER to choose the default answer. The following output is returned:

```
- - - - - - - - - - - - - - - - - - - - - - - - - - - - - - - - - -
Welcome to installob, Oracle Secure Backup's installation program.
For most questions, a default answer appears enclosed in square brackets.
Press Enter to select this answer.
Please wait a few seconds while I learn about this machine... done.
Have you already reviewed and customized install/obparameters for your Oracle
Secure Backup installation [yes]?
```

Step 8.   Again, press ENTER to choose the default answer and to leave the default parameters. The
following output is returned:

```
- - - - - - - - - - - - - - - - - - - - - - - - - - - - - - - - - -
Oracle Secure Backup is not yet installed on this machine.
Oracle Secure Backup's Web server has been loaded, but is not yet configured.
```

```
Choose from one of the following options. The option you choose defines the
software components to be installed.
Configuration of this host is required after installation completes.
You can install the software on this host in one of the following ways:
    (a) administrative server, media server and client
    (b) media server and client
    (c) client
If you are not sure which option to choose, please refer to the Oracle Secure
Backup Installation Guide. (a,b or c) [a]?
```

Step 9. You are going to install all three components of OSB on the same server, so again press ENTER to choose the default answer. The following output is returned:

```
Beginning the installation.  This will take just a minute and will produce
several lines of informational output.
Installing Oracle Secure Backup on lin32 (Linux version 2.6.18-53.el5)
You must now enter a password for the Oracle Secure Backup encryption key store.
Oracle suggests you choose a password of at least 8 characters in length,
containing a mixture of alphabetic and numeric characters.
Please enter the key store password:
Re-type password for verification:
```

Step 10. Enter the OSB encryption key twice. The key is not displayed. You will see the following output:

```
You must now enter a password for the Oracle Secure Backup 'admin' user. Oracle
suggests you choose a password of at least 8 characters in length, containing a
mixture of alphabetic and numeric characters.
Please enter the admin password:
Re-type password for verification:
```

Step 11. Enter the admin password twice. The password is not displayed. You will see the following output:

```
You should now enter an email address for the Oracle Secure Backup 'admin' user.
Oracle Secure Backup uses this email address to send job summary reports and to
notify the user when a job requires input. If you leave this blank, you can set it
later using the obtool's 'chuser' command.
Please enter the admin email address:
```

Step 12. Leave the e-mail address blank for now. The following output is returned:

```
    generating links for admin installation with Web server
    updating /etc/ld.so.conf
    checking Oracle Secure Backup's configuration file (/etc/obconfig)
    setting Oracle Secure Backup directory to /usr/local/oracle/backup in /etc/obconfig
    setting local database directory to /usr/etc/ob in /etc/obconfig
    setting temp directory to /usr/tmp in /etc/obconfig
    setting administrative directory to /usr/local/oracle/backup/admin in /etc/obconfig
    protecting the Oracle Secure Backup directory
```

```
creating /etc/rc.d/init.d/observiced
activating observiced via chkconfig
initializing the administrative domain
****************************** N O T E ******************************
On Linux systems Oracle recommends that you answer no to the next two questions.
The preferred mode of operation on Linux systems is to use the /dev/sg devices for
attach points as described in the 'ReadMe' and in the 'Installation and
Configuration Guide'.
Is lin32 connected to any tape libraries that you'd like to use with Oracle Secure Backup [no]?
Is lin32 connected to any tape drives that you'd like to use with Oracle Secure Backup [no]?
```

Step 13.   Since, in this example, you use a Linux system, answer "no," as recommended by Oracle, and configure the media server later. The following summary is returned:

```
Installation summary:
    Installation  Host                    OS           Driver      OS Move    Reboot
        Mode      Name                    Name         Installed?  Required?  Required?
    admin         lin32                   Linux        no          no         no
Oracle Secure Backup is now ready for your use.
```

The OSB administrative server, media server, and client are now installed. The OSB Web tool is used to configure the tape library and tape drives. Let's add the oracle user and a Database Backup Storage Selector to enable backup of an Oracle database.

Step 14.   Connect and log into the OSB Web tool using the https://<administrative server> link as the admin user. Go to the Configure page, click the Users link, click the Add button, and add the oracle user, as shown next.

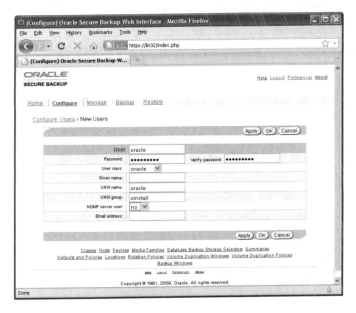

Step 15. After the oracle user is added, click the Edit button and change Preauthorized Access.

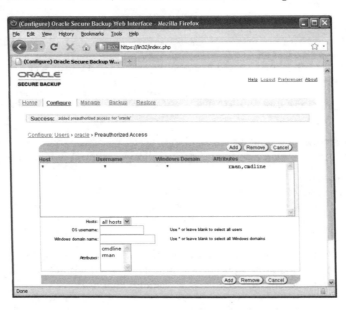

Step 16. As a result, you will have the admin and oracle users.

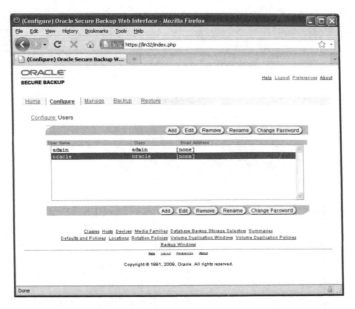

Step 17. Go to Configure: Hosts, and make sure that the server has the mediaserver role, as shown here.

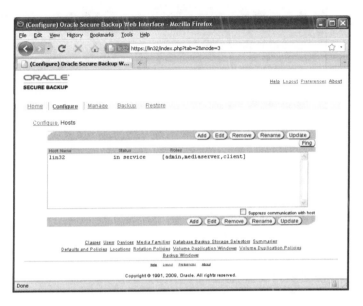

Step 18. To add a storage selector, click the Database Backup Storage Selectors link at the bottom of the Configure page, click Add, and fill in the fields, as shown in the illustration.

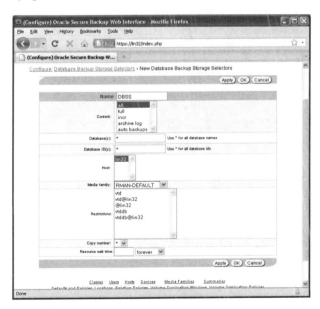

Step 19.   Click OK and the storage will be created, as shown.

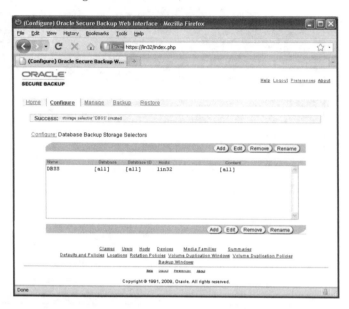

Step 20.   Now, let's configure OEM for OSB usage. Connect to the database and go to the Availability tab in OEM. Click Backup Settings and go to the end of the page shown in this illustration.

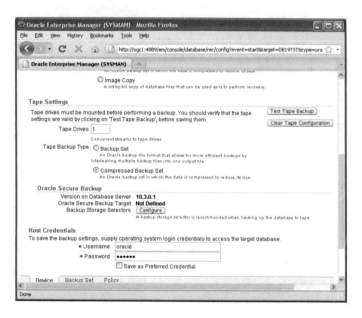

Step 21. Click Configure to specify your OSB target, and on the Specify Oracle Secure Backup Target page, click the Add button and then enter the host.

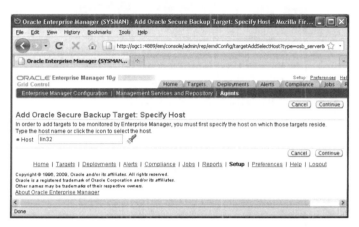

Step 22. Click Continue and enter the values shown here.

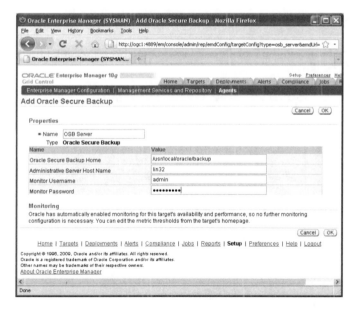

Step 23. After clicking two OK buttons, you will see the Backup Storage Selectors page, shown next.

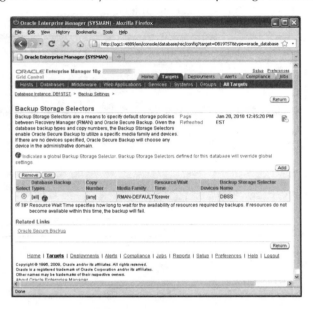

Step 24. Click Return, and the OSB Server target is ready for backing up Oracle databases to tape, as shown in the illustration.

The OSB administrative server is configured as an OEM target and can be managed by OEM.

Chapter 22: Oracle Secure Backup

Step 25. Find the OSB server on the All Target page in OEM, and click it to see what is shown next.

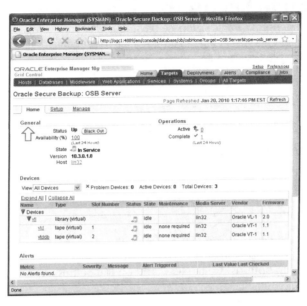

Step 26. Click the Setup tab to configure the OSB server. The OSB devices can be configured on the Devices page, as shown in the illustration.

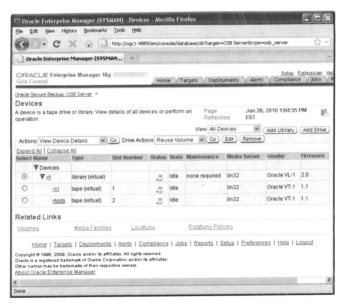

If you click the Manage tab, file system data backup and restore jobs can be scheduled.

Oracle Database and File System Data Backup Using Oracle Secure Backup

It is not possible to perform Oracle database backup and restore using the OSB Web tool. Therefore, we recommend using OEM as a centralized interface to schedule backup and restore jobs for Oracle database and file system data.

RMAN Workshop: *Schedule Oracle Database and File System Data Backups*

Workshop Notes

This workshop schedules OSB Oracle database and file system data backups. First, let's take a full Oracle database backup.

Step 1.   Connect to the database, go to the Availability tab in OEM, and click Schedule Backup. Then, choose Whole Database and click Schedule Customized Backup. On this page, you can choose different backup options. Click Next, and on the Settings page, choose Tape and click Next.

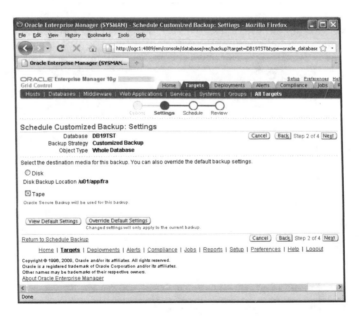

Step 2. Choose the job as a one-time job and review the scheduled job. Click Submit Job, as shown here.

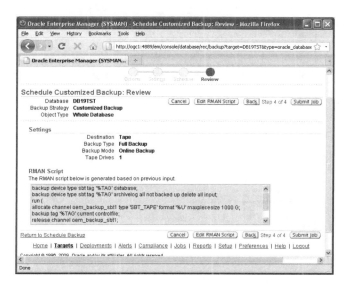

Step 3. OEM will indicate that the job has been submitted. You can click View Job to see the status, as shown in the illustration.

Step 4. The executed job can be found on the Jobs tab.

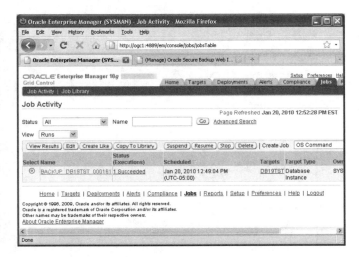

Now, let's take a backup of the listener.ora file.

Step 5. On the Manage page of OEM OSB Server, click Schedule Backup and then choose Specify Hosts, Directories and Files.

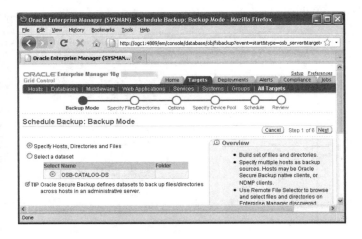

Step 6. Add the listener.ora file to be included in the backup, as shown.

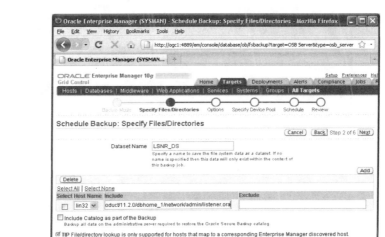

Step 7. Click Next, check Privileged user to have the job run by the root user, and click Next again. On the Specify Device Pool page, the tape device can be specified for the backup, as the illustration shows.

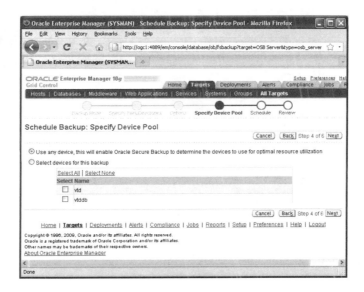

Step 8. Click Next, select the job schedule, and click Next again. Review the backup job.

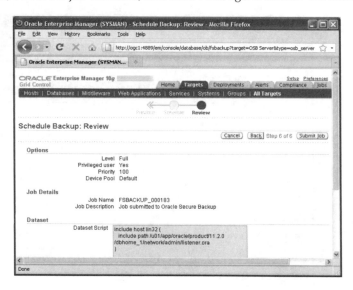

Step 9. After the job is submitted, you can see the OEM confirmation. The job execution status can be seen on the Jobs page.

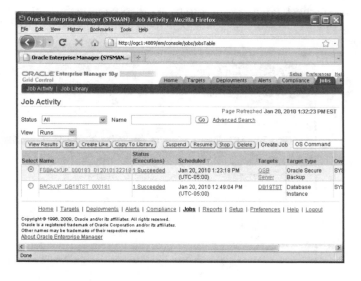

Oracle Database Backup Using Oracle Secure Backup Cloud Module

OSB provides the ability to use storage clouds, such as Amazon S3, as offsite backup storage destinations. To utilize Amazon S3 as backup storage, you need to sign up for Amazon S3 service and get the Access Key ID and the Secret Access Key. After the access identifiers are collected, they can be used to configure OSB during the OSB Cloud Module installation. The OSB Cloud Module install tool can be downloaded from OTN at the following address:

http://www.oracle.com/technology/software/tech/cloud/index.html.

RMAN Workshop: *Installing OSB Cloud Module and Using It for OSB Backups*

Workshop Notes

This workshop installs the OSB Cloud Module and schedules an OSB Oracle database backup.

Step 1. Download and install OSB Cloud Module:

```
[oracle@lin32 distrib]$ ls -al
total 2428
-rw-r--r-- 1 oracle oinstall 2480195 Jan 19 18:13 osbws_installer.zip
[oracle@lin32 distrib]$ unzip osbws_installer.zip
Archive:  osbws_installer.zip
  inflating: osbws_readme.txt
  inflating: osbws_install.jar
[oracle@lin32 distrib]$ vi osbws_install.sh
[oracle@lin32 distrib]$ cat osbws_install.sh
java -jar osbws_install.jar -AWSID <Access Key ID> -AWSKey <Secret Access Key> -
otnUser alisher.yuldashev@<mail_server>.com -otnPass <OTN password> -walletDir
$ORACLE_HOME/dbs/osbws_wallet
[oracle@lin32 distrib]$ chmod u+x osbws_install.sh
[oracle@lin32 distrib]$ ./osbws_install.sh
Oracle Secure Backup Database Web-Service Install Tool
OTN userid is valid.
AWS credentials are valid.
Creating new registration for this S3 user.
Created new log bucket.
Registration ID: <Registration ID>
S3 Logging Bucket: oracle-log-alisher-1
Validating log bucket location ...
Validating license file ...
Create credential oracle.security.client.connect_string1
OSB web-services wallet created in directory /u01/app/oracle/product/12.1.0/dbhome_1/dbs/
osbws_wallet.
OSB web-services initialization file /u01/app/oracle/product/12.1.0/dbhome_1/dbs/osbwsDB19TST
.ora created.
```

Step 2. Connect to the database, go to the Availability tab in OEM, and click Schedule Backup. Then, choose Whole Database and click Schedule Customized Backup. We recommend you encrypt the backup to keep it in offsite storage.

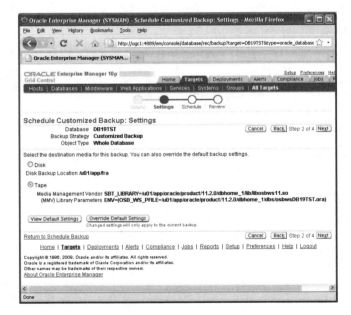

Step 3. On the Settings page, choose Tape and click Next.

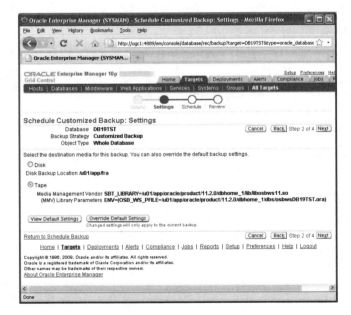

Step 4. Choose the job as a one-time job, review the scheduled job, and click Submit Job.

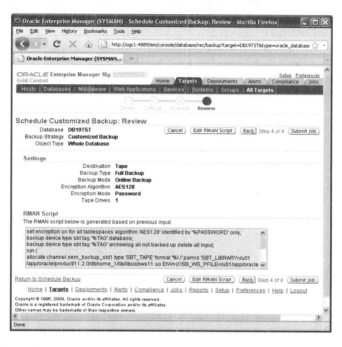

Step 5. OEM will show that the job has been submitted. The executed job can be found on the Jobs tab, as shown here.

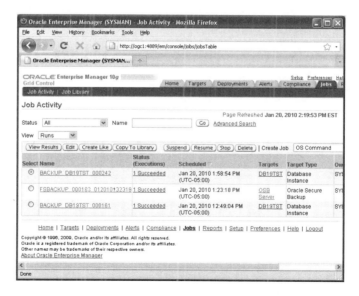

Summary

Oracle Secure Backup delivers high performance and secure data protection crucial for both offsite and local storage of mission-critical data. Complete product support from Oracle Support Services, integration with Oracle Enterprise Manager, the ability to use the cloud as a next-generation offsite backup storage, and excellent pricing are only a few of the many reasons for employing OSB to meet your file system and Oracle database backup requirements. For a centralized backup tape management system in mixed distributed environments that provides a complete backup solution for the enterprise, OSB is a strong contender.

CHAPTER
23

Backing Up to Amazon Web Services Using the Oracle Secure Backup Cloud Module

O racle and Amazon.com have provided a media management library for RMAN that allows Oracle databases to be backed up directly to the Amazon Web Services cloud. This chapter provides an overview of cloud computing and how Amazon's cloud works, how Oracle can be used in a cloud computing context, and why backing up using the OSB Cloud Module and Amazon S3 may be a good idea for some sites. Additionally, we provide detailed instructions on installing and deploying the OSB Cloud Module and Amazon S3 as a backup solution.

Conventional Backups: Assumptions and Limitations

Two key requirements for robust Oracle backup and recovery are a scalable high-capacity onsite backup infrastructure and regular offsite storage of backups in a location separate from the database.

Traditionally, an onsite backup infrastructure has consisted of large tape libraries or disk arrays. Offsite storage has been accomplished by physically moving tapes to a secure remote facility. Offsite tape storage companies provide transport and remote facilities for a fee.

These traditional approaches have a number of disadvantages:

- High cost of enterprise backup infrastructure
- Limited capacity of enterprise backup infrastructure
- High cost of offsite media transport and storage
- Long time to recovery (TTR) for offsite backups
- Reliance on physical security for offsite backups

The Oracle Secure Backup Cloud Module

The OSB Cloud Module is a media management library (MML) for Recovery Manager (RMAN) that allows backups to be written directly to Amazon.com's Simple Storage Service (S3) over the Internet as if it were a tape library. S3 is a component of Amazon Web Services, Amazon's *cloud computing* platform.

Cloud computing, an emerging infrastructure model being pioneered by Amazon.com and others, offers a viable alternative to both physical hosting infrastructure and offsite data storage. The cloud backup model addresses many of the drawbacks of traditional backups. Additionally, storing backups in a cloud storage service offers several potential advantages.

NOTE
While we are specifically covering Amazon's S3 cloud offerings in this chapter, numerous cloud backup storage offerings are available. The general instructions here will apply to any of those vendors—with slight variations on implementation.

What Is Cloud Computing?

The term *cloud computing* suffers from having been appropriated for use by numerous technology vendors to apply in various ways to their own products or services. This diffusion of the term's meaning has led to confusion among many in the technology field.

Generally, cloud computing refers to a remote pool of storage and computing resources available to the public over the Internet at as small or as large a scale as users require. The cloud resources of one user are discrete and secure from those of other users. Users manage cloud resources using a uniform, published software API (application program interface). A computing cloud conforms to set availability and performance service levels published by the provider.

More simply, from a user's perspective, a computing cloud is an Internet service on which users can deploy applications and services on a professionally managed enterprise-class infrastructure.

In the case of Google, software such as visualization and mapping tools is available to be integrated into a user's web pages or applications as a component.

In the case of Amazon, users can deploy virtual server hosts and virtual storage. From the perspective of the users and applications, cloud services look and behave similarly to stand-alone server and storage equipment.

Oracle and the Amazon Cloud

Oracle and Amazon.com have worked together to provide a way to deploy several components of Oracle technology on *Amazon Web Services* (AWS), Amazon.com's cloud computing platform. Currently, Oracle supports two classes of services on AWS:

- Running Oracle software on AWS Elastic Compute Cloud (EC2)
- Backing up Oracle databases to AWS Simple Storage Service (S3)

Elastic Compute Cloud (EC2) and Elastic Block Store (EBS)

Amazon EC2 and EBS allow users to deploy virtual hosts running Windows or Linux and highly available volume storage to support virtually any application that runs on those operating systems. EC2 provides virtual hosts, and EBS provides storage volumes.

Simple Storage Service (S3): Oracle's Cloud Backup Solution

Yet another component of Amazon's cloud is S3, a low-cost, reliable, redundant mass-storage service. Popular software packages such as Jungle Disk use S3 as an inexpensive way to back up your personal computer or just to get some extra storage space. Oracle has followed suit, providing the Oracle Secure Backup (OSB) Cloud Module, an RMAN media management library (MML) for S3. The OSB Cloud Module allows Oracle databases on the Amazon cloud *and at customer sites* to back up directly to S3 on the Amazon cloud from RMAN.

RMAN Backup to S3: The Oracle Secure Backup Cloud Module

The OSB Cloud Module is essentially a MML that provides access to Amazon S3 storage via the SBT channel interface of RMAN. Just as with tape MMLs, the OSB Cloud Module is implemented as a shared library for Linux/Unix and as a DLL for Windows.

The OSB Cloud Module is available for Oracle versions 9*i* and higher on 32- and 64-bit Linux, 32-bit Windows, and Solaris (SPARC 64-bit). Oracle has offered to port it to any other brand of Unix upon customer request.

S3 Backup over the Internet or from Amazon EC2

A database hosted somewhere other than on Amazon Web Services can back up over the public Internet to S3. As such, performance may be variable. In contrast, a database hosted on AWS can back up to S3 over Amazon's internal network, where performance will be predictably good.

For Amazon cloud-hosted databases, the decision to use the OSB Cloud Module is easy. It is a cheap, reliable way to store backups. It is also among the only options for cloud-hosted databases.

For databases hosted somewhere other than AWS, such as in the customer's own datacenter, it is necessary to determine first whether acceptable speed and performance can be achieved. This is discussed later in this chapter.

Oracle Cloud Backup Advantages

There are several benefits to using cloud backup instead of local or offsite disk or tape storage. Chief among these are the following:

- **No up-front equipment costs** Tape libraries and mass storage arrays are major capital expenses and require ongoing maintenance and upkeep. When physical storage capacity is exceeded, new equipment must be purchased and deployed. In contrast, deploying backups on cloud storage is affordable and requires no additional equipment, even as scale increases.

- **Low ongoing storage costs** Amazon S3 costs vary, but are reasonable. The cost of the investment in S3 storage can be very competitive with other forms of storage.

- **Elasticity** With cloud computing, you can use as few or as many resources as you need. As requirements grow, there is no need to replace equipment such as tape libraries with new equipment of larger capacity.

- **Reliability** Amazon provides redundancy and availability within their internal architecture and meets a published SLA (service-level agreement) of 99.99 percent availability for S3. One of the key features of S3 is geographic replication. S3 replicates data to three availability zones within an Amazon Web Services region. Availability zones are analogous to separate datacenters. Similar redundancy and availability within a customer's own datacenter would have to be architected as part of an enterprise backup infrastructure at significant expense and effort.

- **Time to recovery** Unlike offsited tapes, which must be ordered and loaded into libraries, RMAN backups to Amazon S3 are always online and available for recoveries.

- **No third-party MML license costs** The Oracle Secure Backup Cloud Module is licensed through Oracle and is priced per channel. That means that customers can leverage their preexisting license relationship with Oracle.

RMAN Workshop: *Deploying RMAN Backups to Amazon S3*

Workshop Notes

A few prerequisites and credentials are required to use the OSB Cloud Module:

- An Oracle.com single sign-on account (the same one used to log into the Oracle Technology Network)
- An Amazon Web Services account

Step 1. Establish an Oracle single sign-on account, if needed. If you already have an Oracle .com or Oracle Technology Network account, you can skip this step. Otherwise:

    a. In a browser, navigate to http://www.oracle.com/admin/account.

    b. Click **Create your Oracle account now**.

Step 2. Establish an Amazon Web Services account:

    a. In a browser, navigate to http://aws.amazon.com.

    b. Click **Sign Up Now**. You will be prompted to sign into Amazon.com. Your AWS account is accessed via your Amazon.com retail account. If you do not have an existing account at Amazon.com, select **I am a new customer**.

    c. Once you are logged in, you must check a box and click **Continue** to accept the terms of the AWS Customer Agreement.

Step 3. When you successfully establish an account with AWS, you still need to sign up for Amazon's Simple Storage Service (S3):

    a. In a browser, navigate to http://aws.amazon.com/s3.

    b. Click **Sign up for Amazon s3**.

    c. On subsequent web pages, Amazon will prompt you to provide a credit card for payment and a billing address. Finally, you will be prompted to review your selections and to click **Complete Sign Up**.

Step 4. To store and retrieve data on S3, you will need your private access identifiers. The link to obtain these values should be sent to you in an e-mail from Amazon.com upon signing up for Amazon S3. If you do not have the URL handy, you can do the following:

    a. In a browser, navigate to http://aws.amazon.com.

    b. Hover your cursor over **Your Account**.

    c. Click **Security Credentials**.

    d. Note the values for **Access Key ID** and **Secret Access Key**. Keep these values in a safe place. They are the keys for charging AWS services to your account.

Step 5. Download and install the Oracle Secure Backup Cloud Module installer.

> **NOTE**
> *If you are performing backups for an Oracle database running on Amazon EC2 using one of Oracle's Amazon Machine Images (AMIs), you do not need to install the OSB Cloud Module. It has already been installed for you under /home/oracle/scripts/.*

The OSB Cloud Module installer can be downloaded from the Oracle Technology Network Cloud Computing Center:

a. In a browser, navigate to http://www.oracle.com/technology/software/tech/cloud.

b. Review the license agreement and then click **All Supported Platforms**.

c. The download is a .zip file containing a .jar file and a readme. Place the .zip file on the database server that you will be backing up under the user that runs the Oracle software (usually oracle).

d. Verify that you have the appropriate version of Java installed.

```
$ java -version
java version "1.5.0_16"
```

e. Install the OSB Cloud Module by running the installer and providing the appropriate arguments for your environment. You must pass these arguments to the installer:

Argument	Description
-awsid	Your Amazon Web Services access key ID
-awskey	Your Amazon Web Services secret access key
-otnuser	Your Oracle.com single sign-on account login
-otnpass	Your Oracle.com single sign-on password
-walletdir	Where to store the preceding login credentials

Linux Example

```
$ java -jar osbws_install.jar \
> -awsid 3HKFEHKTI6JW4R88GB72 -awskey  KjsopcHzhVMAoXpPs8d0jPCa4hspbrHbssRbspbq \
> -otnuser larry_e@gmail.com -otnpass i1uvb0at$ \
> -walletdir $ORACLE_HOME/dbs/osbws_wallet -libdir $ORACLE_HOME/lib
OTN userid is valid.
AWS credentials are valid.
Creating new registration for this S3 user.
Created new log bucket.
Registration ID: 0f0a8aac-dad0-6254-7d70-be4ac4f112c4
S3 Logging Bucket: oracle-log-jane-doe-1
Create credential oracle.security.client.connect_string1
```

```
OSB web-services wallet created in directory /u01/oracle/product/11.1/db_1/dbs/osbws_wallet.
OSB web-services initialization file /u01/oracle/product/11.1/db_1/dbs/osbwst1.ora created.
Downloading OSB Web Services Software Library.
Downloaded 13165919 bytes in 204 seconds. Transfer rate was 64538 bytes/second.
Download complete.
Extracted file /u01/oracle/product/11.1/db_1/lib/libosbws11.so
```

Performing Backups by Using the OSB Cloud Module

RMAN backups to Amazon S3 work like backups to traditional MML products. From within RMAN

- Allocate one or more channels of type SBT.
- Issue backup commands to the SBT channels.

RMAN must specify the location of the S3 SBT library and OSB Cloud Module parameter file (both created during install) when allocating the SBT channel to S3. You can specify this information persistently for the database by using the RMAN **configure** command, or each time you allocate a channel. If you also use other media management libraries such as NetWorker, NetBackup, and Oracle Secure Backup, you should not configure S3 persistently to be the default MML unless you really mean to do that.

To Persistently Store S3 as the Default SBT Channel

The following RMAN code snippet demonstrates how to persistently configure the default settings for RMAN's SBT I/O channels to use Amazon S3 using the OSB Cloud Module. Using this method, the default destination for SBT I/O will be Amazon S3. If other RMAN backup jobs need to write to or read from local tape, for instance, they will have to specify their local tape MML libraries in the **allocate channel** command.

```
RMAN> configure channel device type sbt
2>   parms 'ENV=(OSB_WS_PFILE=/u01/oracle/product/11.1/db_1/dbs/osbwst1.ora),
3>   SBT_LIBRARY=/u01/oracle/product/11.1/db_1/lib/libosbws11.so';
```

To Specify the OSB Cloud Module Each Time You Allocate a Channel

The following RMAN code snippet demonstrates how to manually configure each channel to use the OSB Cloud Module at script run time. The default SBT channel configuration will remain unchanged. If there is a local tape MML in place, jobs that use that service will continue to function normally without modification.

```
RMAN> allocate channel t1 type sbt
2>   parms='ENV=(OSB_WS_PFILE=/u01/oracle/product/11.1/db_1/dbs/osbwst1.ora),
3>   SBT_LIBRARY=/u01/oracle/product/11.1/db_1/lib/libosbws11.so';
```

The following RMAN script demonstrates how to manually allocate an SBT I/O channel to S3 using the OSB Cloud Module and then perform a full backup of the database, including the archived redo logs:

```
RMAN> run {
2>   allocate channel t1 type sbt
3>   parms='ENV=(OSB_WS_PFILE=/u01/oracle/product/11.1/db_1/dbs/osbwst1.ora),
4>   SBT_LIBRARY=/u01/oracle/product/11.1/db_1/lib/libosbws11.so';
5>   backup database plus archivelog;
6>   }
allocated channel: t1
channel t1: SID=133 device type=SBT_TAPE
channel t1: Oracle Secure Backup Web Services Library
Starting backup at 27-OCT-09
channel t1: starting full datafile backup set
channel t1: specifying datafile(s) in backup set
input datafile file number=00002 name=+DG1/t1/datafile/sysaux.257.700422031
input datafile file number=00001 name=+DG1/t1/datafile/system.256.700422031
input datafile file number=00003 name=+DG1/t1/datafile/undotbs1.258.700422031
input datafile file number=00004 name=+DG1/t1/datafile/users.259.700422031
channel t1: starting piece 1 at 27-OCT-09
channel t1: finished piece 1 at 27-OCT-09
piece handle=03ksrndv_1_1 tag=TAG20091027T133142 comment=API Version 2.0,MMS Version 2.0.0.0
channel t1: backup set complete, elapsed time: 00:02:35
...
Finished backup at 27-OCT-09
released channel: t1
```

The exact syntax for allocating the SBT channel to S3 varies between Oracle versions. For instance, Oracle 11gR2 does not accept the ENV keyword. Instead, you must use an alternate channel allocation syntax using the SBT_PARMS keyword. On some versions, you may also have to create a symbolic link in ORACLE_HOME/lib called libobk.so pointing to libosbws11.so:

```
$ ln -s $ORACLE_HOME/lib/libosbws11.so $ORACLE_HOME/lib/libobk.so
```

Listing RMAN Backups and Backup Sets Stored on S3

As with all RMAN backups, all management of stored backups must be performed with RMAN. If you manually delete backup sets, future RMAN recoveries will continue to assume that they exist. RMAN must be used to mark as obsolete and to purge all RMAN backups.

Similarly, listing and reporting existing backups is best performed via RMAN. For example, the following command lists all backups stored on an SBT device (such as S3 via the OSB Cloud Module) in the past 24 hours:

```
RMAN> list backup device type sbt completed after 'sysdate-1';
List of Backup Sets
===================
BS Key  Type LV Size        Device Type Elapsed Time Completion Time
1       Full    1.17G        SBT_TAPE    00:02:34     27-OCT-09
        BP Key: 2   Status: AVAILABLE   Compressed: NO   Tag: TAG20091027T133142
        Handle: 03ksrndv_1_1   Media:
   List of Datafiles in backup set 2
```

```
File LV Type Ckp SCN    Ckp Time   Name
1       Full 1515937    27-OCT-09  +DG1/t1/datafile/system.256.700422031
2       Full 1515937    27-OCT-09  +DG1/t1/datafile/sysaux.257.700422031
3       Full 1515937    27-OCT-09  +DG1/t1/datafile/undotbs1.258.700422031
4       Full 1515937    27-OCT-09  +DG1/t1/datafile/users.259.700422031
```

Several third-party tools exist for browsing the contents of your S3 buckets, where the OSB Cloud Module stores RMAN backups. One such popular tool is a Firefox browser add-on called S3fox. Using S3fox, you can browse the backup pieces RMAN stores in S3.

Optimizing Backups and Recoveries over the Internet Using the OSB Cloud Module and Amazon S3

The effectiveness of backing up and restoring Oracle database backups over the Internet to Amazon S3 depends on a number of factors:

- Size of database
- Redo generation rate
- Internet bandwidth between the Oracle server and Amazon S3
- Backup strategy
- RMAN options
- Requirements for time to recovery (TTR)

Very large databases not hosted in the Amazon cloud may be poor candidates for backup to Amazon S3 over the Internet, depending on your network performance. It could simply take too long to complete a backup and too long to restore in the event of a recovery. For the same reason, databases that generate very large amounts of redo per day may be poor candidates for this backup strategy. Amazon Web Services has reliable fast connectivity to S3, so databases hosted on Amazon EC2 can use the OSB Cloud Module without as much tuning and optimization.

For example, a level 0 backup of a database of 500GB that generates 50GB of redo per day might compress to 250GB. With a single T1, it might take over 50 hours to back up to S3, using most of the available network capacity. For this reason, you must carefully consider and test network throughput and compressed backup size when contemplating moving to an S3-based backup strategy over the Internet. The longest backup window in the backup cycle must be able to accommodate a level 0 backup, while using a percentage of the network resources that is acceptable to the enterprise. *Additionally, organizations must determine if the amount of time to perform a complete restore from S3 is acceptable to the enterprise.*

Because of the many caveats associated with deploying backups over the Internet to S3, any organization contemplating it should rigorously test both backup and recovery performance before embarking on a large-scale migration to this architecture.

Regardless of database size, customers using the OSB Cloud Module can optimize backup capacity and performance using a variety of means. By improving backup efficiency, customers can back up larger databases to S3 over the Internet than would otherwise have been possible. The main approaches are as follows:

- Using multiple SBT channels
- Backing up during times of minimal Internet use

- Using compressed backup sets
- Using an incremental backup strategy
- Backing up archive logs frequently

Sites contemplating an Oracle backup strategy over the Internet to Amazon S3 must have sufficient Internet bandwidth to back up the databases in question within an acceptable backup window. If sufficient bandwidth is available, the challenge becomes configuring RMAN to consume those resources. An effective way to maximize the use of network resources is opening multiple SBT channels. In testing, the goal should be to use sufficient network resources to complete the backup within the required timeframe, while leaving resources available for other services and purposes.

To minimize the impact to other users and services, Oracle backups to Amazon S3 should be scheduled for periods of minimal network use. The quantity of data transferred can be further reduced with compressed backup sets.

An incremental backup strategy can additionally reduce the daily backup size that must be written to Amazon S3. In most databases, only a small portion of the data changes on a daily, weekly, or even monthly basis. Therefore, full or level 0 backups can conceivably be taken very infrequently and can even be spread over the period of a whole night or a whole weekend. On a nightly or weekly basis, differential and incremental backups can be used to maintain recoverability while keeping the backup size small.

Example with Multiple Channels and Compressed Backup Sets

The following RMAN script demonstrates typical syntax for opening multiple channels to Amazon S3 using the OSB Cloud Module and then performing a full (level 0) compressed backup, including archived redo logs over those channels:

```
RMAN> run {
2>   allocate channel t1 type sbt
3>   parms='ENV=(OSB_WS_PFILE=/u01/oracle/product/11.1/db_1/dbs/osbwst1.ora),
4>   SBT_LIBRARY=/u01/oracle/product/11.1/db_1/lib/libosbws11.so';
5>   allocate channel t2 type sbt
6>   parms='ENV=(OSB_WS_PFILE=/u01/oracle/product/11.1/db_1/dbs/osbwst1.ora),
7>   SBT_LIBRARY=/u01/oracle/product/11.1/db_1/lib/libosbws11.so';
8>   allocate channel t3 type sbt
9>   parms='ENV=(OSB_WS_PFILE=/u01/oracle/product/11.1/db_1/dbs/osbwst1.ora),
10> SBT_LIBRARY=/u01/oracle/product/11.1/db_1/lib/libosbws11.so';
11> backup as compressed backupset incremental level 0 database plus archivelog;}
```

Because archive log generation is periodic, it is possible to distribute the impact of archive log backup throughout the day and night. Frequently backing up archive logs reduces the amount of data to be backed up during the nightly database backup window. This approach has the added benefit of improving point-in-time recoverability because more recent archive logs are available offsite for more recent points in time.

Licensing Considerations

Most media management library (MML) software packages for Oracle RMAN require licensing with a third party, such as EMC or Symantec. In the case of the OSB Cloud Module, the Oracle

Secure Backup Licensing Information documentation (P/N E10310-02) states that customers must obtain a license "for each RMAN channel simultaneously used by the backup domain to an Amazon S3 destination."

Customers should thoroughly consult the documentation, any written license agreements, and their own legal counsel in order to determine the correct number of licenses to obtain for the OSB Cloud Module.

Summary

The OSB Cloud Module provides a compelling solution for secure offsite backup storage and vaulting, especially for Oracle databases hosted on Amazon's cloud. Cloud storage has the potential for lower cost, better time to recovery (TTR), and more geographically distributed disaster recovery properties, when compared to traditional magnetic tape vaulting.

Careful testing for performance of both backup and restore functions in a range of scenarios is a prerequisite before deploying backups to S3. In addition, those considering using the OSB Cloud Module must carefully review their licensing obligations with Oracle for the package.

CHAPTER
24

Enhancing RMAN
with Veritas NetBackup
for Oracle

eritas NetBackup Server software and Database Agent software work in collaboration with RMAN to manage enterprise backup, recovery, and storage administration. The products run on many operating systems, support popular databases, and integrate easily with an assortment of storage devices. NetBackup's tantalizing features, coupled with the vendor's close partnership with Oracle, make it a desirable choice. The information and downloads in this chapter are available on Symantec's website, as Veritas is now part of Symantec.

Key Features

NetBackup for Oracle has many features and benefits that augment the functionality of RMAN. A summary of the key features is listed in Table 24-1.

Some specialty add-ons worth looking into are NetBackup Advanced Client, NetBackup Vault, and NetBackup Bare Metal Restore.

Feature	Benefit
Back up to disk staging area	Provides faster backups and restores by avoiding the overhead of tape latency.
Synthetic backups	Conserves network bandwidth by allowing incremental backups.
Inline copy	Provides data redundancy by writing multiple copies of the data at the same time.
Tape multiplexing	Improves performance by writing parallel streams of data from one or more clients to a single tape drive. Multiplexing the database backups can reduce the time necessary to complete the operation.
Automatic tape device configuration	Reduces the time and effort that would otherwise be required to manually configure tape drives.
Data encryption	Secures data as it is written to tape by offering multiple levels of data protection.
Backup templates	Simplifies the effort of writing RMAN backup and recovery scripts by providing a graphical tool to assist with script generation and sample scripts preconfigured to run with NetBackup.
Proxy copy	Offloads processing power from the database server to a separate media server when doing backups and restores.
Checkpoint restart	Allows backups to resume where they left off in the case of a failure.

TABLE 24-1. *Key Features of NetBackup for Oracle*

Feature	Benefit
Scheduling facilities	NetBackup scheduling facilities on the master server can be used to schedule automatic and unattended Oracle backups. This feature also lets the DBA or backup administrator choose the times when the backup operations can occur. For example, if DBAs would like to prevent interference with normal daytime operations (business hours), they can schedule the backups for the database to occur only at night.
Templates	NetBackup for Oracle database can create backup and recovery templates. The backup and recovery templates are platform independent and contain configuration information that the software uses when performing backups and restores. The wizard-generated templates do not support all the features native to Oracle, but the DBA can use the script generated by a template to customize it as desired.
Compression	Compression increases backup performance over the network and reduces the size of the backup image that NetBackup writes to the storage unit.

TABLE 24-1.   *Key Features of NetBackup for Oracle (Continued)*

Necessary Components

The following elements enable successful communication exchanges between RMAN, the NetBackup servers, and the storage devices:

- NetBackup Server software
- NetBackup for Oracle agent software—includes a required interface library file (libobk.*)
- Oracle Database software—includes the RMAN utility and the Oracle Call Interface (OCI)
- NetBackup licenses—needed for all software, options, and agents being used

Storage/Media Device Configuration

Setting up tape drives, host bus adapters, SCSI IDs, and tape robots (see *NetBackup Media Manager Device Configuration Guide*) is usually left up to Unix or storage administrators. We will not discuss those vendor-specific steps here, but will instead provide a few commands to verify proper configuration of tape media devices.

NOTE
Hardware devices should be set up and tested for proper working order prior to installing the NetBackup for Oracle agent software.

Use the following command to query the master server from the client server to verify communications:

 `/<install_path>/netbackup/bin/bpclntcmd -pn`

Next, query the master server from the client server to verify the version:

 `/<install_path>/netbackup/bin/bpclntcmd -sv`

View which storage server will be servicing the client server by issuing the following:

 `cat /<install_path>/netbackup/bp.conf`

Finally, verify that the NetBackup communication daemons are listening for requests:

```
netstat -a |grep bpcd
netstat -a |grep vnetd
```

NetBackup Installation

Multiple tiers make up a networked backup environment. Every layer needs some amount of software configuration to enable component interoperability. The installations are straightforward and should take less than 20 minutes each. Besides doing local installations, you can run remote installs, installs from the Administration Console, and software propagation to the clients from a central master server.

NOTE
NetBackup software should not be installed on a network file system– mounted directory. Doing so could cause interference with its file- locking mechanisms.

NetBackup Server software gets installed on the following servers:

- Master server
- Media server (optional)
- Client (database) server

The NetBackup for Oracle agent software gets installed on the client (database) server. The following list defines the server types just mentioned:

- **Master server**   Orchestrates the NetBackup environment. It is placed in a layer referred to as Tier 1 (top server tier). *Tiers* are labels for each of the different architectural layers or groupings of architectural components. The role of the master server is to schedule backups, track job progress, manage tape devices, and store backup metadata in a repository. Since the master server plays such a critical role, it is a good idea to cluster this server for high availability (and greater peace of mind).

- **Media servers**   Occupy Tier 2 (middle tier) and are used to back up a group of files locally while other files are being backed up across the network. Media servers are introduced into the environment to boost performance, but they are not required.

- **Client servers**   Reside in Tier 3 (client tier) and are usually the database servers that house the databases to be backed up.

Pre-Installation Tasks for NetBackup for Oracle Agent

Before you install NetBackup for Oracle, you need to complete the following tasks:

1. Verify that the system administrator has installed and properly configured the NetBackup software on the master server, media servers (optional), and the client database servers.

2. Ensure that the proper license keys for all NetBackup servers, clients, agents, and options have been purchased and are registered on the master server. You can do this from either the Administration Console or the command line. From the Administration Console, launch the following and then choose Help | License Keys:

   ```
   /<install_path>/netbackup/bin/jnbSA &
   ```

   From the command line, run

   ```
   /<install_path>/netbackup/bin/admincmd/get_license_key
   ```

3. Obtain the NetBackup for Oracle agent software CD, or ask a Unix system administrator to push the software to the client database machine from the master server.

NOTE
On the database server, both the NetBackup Server software and NetBackup for Oracle agent software need to be the same version. The software on the master server needs to be the same or a higher version as that on the database server.

NetBackup for Oracle Agent Installation Steps

To install the NetBackup for Oracle agent, follow these steps:

1. Insert and mount the installation CD.
2. Log in as **root** to the client (database) server.
3. Change to the directory where the CD is mounted.
4. Run the ./install script.
5. Choose NetBackup Database Agent.
6. You are asked whether you want to do a local installation. Enter **y**.
7. Choose NetBackup for Oracle.
8. Enter **q** (Done Selecting Agents).
9. Enter **y** to verify your selection.
10. Installation proceeds as follows:
    A. A script called /<install_path>/netbackup/dbext/install_dbext is generated.
    B. The file /<install_path>/netbackup/bp.conf is updated with server names.
    C. Entries are added to /etc/services.
    D. Entries are added to the NIS services map if NIS is running on the server.

E. Entries are added to the server /etc/initd.conf file for bpcd, vopied, and bpjava-msvc.

F. Startup and shutdown scripts are copied to the /etc/init.d directory.

G. Installation output is written to /<install_path>/netbackup/ext.

NOTE
In most cases, look for NetBackup to be installed in the /usr/openv/ netbackup directory.

How to Link Oracle to NetBackup Media Manager

After installing the NetBackup for Oracle agent, you need to link Oracle Database software with the NetBackup Media Management Library. The link allows RMAN to write files to the media devices or to pull files from them. The NetBackup Media Management Library or API often is found in /<install_path>/netbackup/bin, whereas the Oracle library is located in $ORACLE_HOME/lib. Both files are named libobk*.

Linking can be done either automatically or manually, as described next.

Automatic Link Method

NetBackup for Oracle includes a script to automate the library link process. Since all steps are automated, using the script is preferred over a manual method. The oracle_link script performs the following actions:

- Retrieves the database version
- Retrieves the operating system version
- Warns if the database is not shut down
- Checks environment variable settings
- Applies the appropriate library based on its assessment

The steps to automatically link Oracle 9i Database, Oracle Database 10g, Oracle Database 11g, and Oracle Database 12c with NetBackup for Oracle follow:

1. Log into the Unix server as the Oracle Database owner account, usually *oracle*.

2. Set the variables $ORACLE_SID and $ORACLE_HOME.

3. Shut down each Oracle database instance:

```
sqlplus "/ as sysdba"
shutdown immediate
exit
```

4. Run the <install_path>/netbackup/bin/oracle_link script.

5. View the output that is written to /tmp/make_trace.pid for errors.

Manual Link Method

If you prefer more control over the link process, you may opt for the manual method. The following are the steps to manually link Oracle 9*i* Database and Oracle Database 10*g* with NetBackup for Oracle:

1. Log into the Unix server as the oracle account.

2. Set the variables $ORACLE_SID and $ORACLE_HOME.

3. Shut down each Oracle database instance:

```
sqlplus "/ as sysdba"
shutdown immediate
exit
```

4. Perform the applicable linking steps in Table 24-2.

For OS version...	...do these steps	If this file exists in ${ORACLE_HOME}/lib...	...then create a symbolic link from the Oracle library to the new NetBackup library

AIX 64-bit using 64-bit Oracle 9*i* Release 9.0.1 and 9.2, Oracle 10*g* Release 10.1	n/a	libobk.a	`mv libobk.a libobk.a.orig`
			`ln -s /<install_path>/`
			`netbackup/bin/libobk.a64`
			`libobk.a`

Compaq Tru64/ Digital Unix (OSFI)	Put ${ORACLE_HOME}/lib in search path. On Digital Unix, set LD_LIBRARY_PATH.	libobk.so
		libobk.a
			`mv libobk.so libobk`
			`.so.orig`
			`mv libobk.a libobk.a.orig`
			`ln -s /<install_path>/`
			`netbackup/bin/`
			`libobk.so.1 libobk.so.1`
			`ln -s libobk.so.1 libobk`
			`.so`

HP-UX 64-bit using 64-bit Oracle 9*i* Release 9.0.1 and 9.2, Oracle 10*g* Release 10.1	n/a	libobk.sl
		libobk.a
			`mv libobk.sl libobk`
			`.sl.orig`
			`mv libobk.a libobk.a.orig`
			`ln -s /<install_path>/`
			`netbackup/bin/`
			`libobk.sl64 libobk.sl`

TABLE 24-2. *Manual Link Process*

For OS version...	...do these steps	If this file exists in ${ORACLE_HOME}/lib...	...then create a symbolic link from the Oracle library to the new NetBackup library
Linux	Put ${ORACLE_HOME}/lib in search path. On Digital Unix, set LD_LIBRARY_PATH.	libobk.so	`ln -s /<install_path>/ netbackup/bin/ libobk.so libobk.so`
Solaris (32-bit or 64-bit) using 32-bit Oracle 9*i* Release 9.0.1 and 9.2, Oracle 10*g* Release 10.1	n/a	libobk.so	`mv libobk.so libobk .so.orig` `ln -s /<install_path>/ netbackup/bin/ libobk.so.1 libobk.so`

TABLE 24-2. *Manual Link Process (Continued)*

> **NOTE**
> *Starting with Oracle 9i, making a new Oracle executable is no longer required.*

Architecture

Now that the hardware is configured, the server and agent programs are installed, the daemons are running, and the libraries are linked, we've built a solid foundation (see Figure 24-1) upon which to run RMAN.

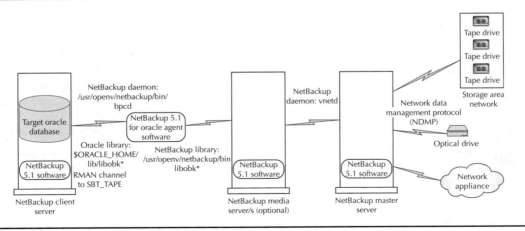

FIGURE 24-1. *NetBackup architecture*

Configuring NetBackup Policies

You need to give NetBackup instructions on how and when to execute the backups. These instructions are organized into special groupings called *policies*. Here are some points to be aware of when configuring policies:

- An RMAN job must be associated with at least one policy in order for it to execute.
- A default policy is provided with the agent software.
- Multiple policies can be created for a single database server.

The NetBackup Administration Console provides a nice and easy interface for configuring the following policy information:

- Attributes
- Schedule
- Clients on which the policy is implemented
- Backup selection

Adding New Policies

Here's how to add a new policy:

1. Start the NetBackup program on the storage server where the policy will be created.
2. Click the Policies tab. Expand NetBackup Management | Policies, as shown in Figure 24-2.
3. In the All Policies pane, right-click Master Server and then choose New.
4. Type a unique name in the Add a New Policy dialog box, shown in Figure 24-2. Once you add the name of the new policy in the dialog box, the Change Policy dialog box will appear.

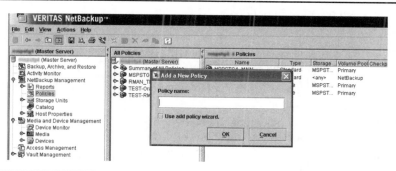

FIGURE 24-2. *Adding new policies*

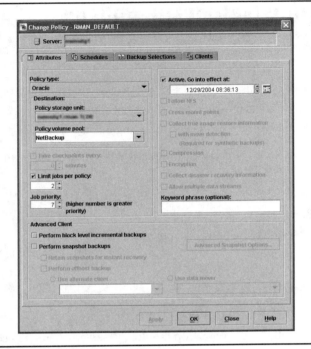

FIGURE 24-3. *NetBackup policy configuration*

As part of the policy definition, choose the policy attributes, shown on the Attributes tab in Figure 24-3, as follows:

- **Policy Type** This drop-down list contains many options; for Oracle RMAN backups, you can choose the Oracle policy type. The following are the various policy options with the intended use of each option:

Oracle	Use when the policy will contain only clients with the NetBackup for Oracle option.
DB2	Use when the policy will have only clients with the NetBackup for DB2 option.
DataStore	A policy type reserved for use by Veritas or its partners to provide agents for new applications or databases.
Lotus-Notes	Use when the policy will contain only clients with the NetBackup for Lotus Notes option.
MS-Windows-NT	Use when the policy will contain only Windows 2000, NT, XP, or Windows Server 2003 clients.

MS-Exchange-Server	Use when the policy will contain only clients with the NetBackup for MS-Exchange-Server option.
MS-SQL-Server	Use when the policy will contain only clients with the NetBackup for MS-SQL-Server option.
NCR-Teradata	Use when the policy will contain only clients with the NetBackup for Teradata option.
NetWare	Use when the policy will contain only NonTarget NetBackup Novell NetWare clients.
NDMP	Use when the policy will contain only clients with the NetBackup for NDMP option.
AFS	Use when the policy will be backing up only AFS file systems on clients.
DataTools-SQL-BackTrack	Use when the policy will contain only clients with the NetBackup for DataTools-SQL-BackTrack option.
FlashBackup-Windows	Applies only to NetBackup Enterprise Server; use when the policy will contain only NetBackup FlashBackup-Windows clients on Windows. This policy is available only when the NetBackup Advanced Client is installed.
FlashBackup	Use when the policy will contain only NetBackup FlashBackup clients on Unix.
Informix-On-BAR	Use when the policy will contain only clients that are running the NetBackup for Informix option.
MS-SharePoint	Use to configure a policy for NetBackup for SharePoint Portal Server.
Split-Mirror	Use when the policy will contain only clients with the NetBackup for EMC option.
SAP	Use when the policy will contain only clients with the NetBackup for SAP option.
Sybase	Use when the policy will contain only clients with the NetBackup for Sybase option.
Standard	Use when the policy will contain any combination of the following:

- NetBackup Novell NetWare clients that have the target version of NetBackup software

- Unix clients (including Mac OS X clients), except those covered by a specific policy, such as Oracle

- **Destination**   Choose settings for Policy Storage Unit and Policy Volume Pool.
- **Limit Jobs Per Policy**   Check this box to restrict the number of jobs that can be run in parallel.
- **Active. Go into Effect At**   Check this box and specify a date and time to turn on, at a later date and time, a policy that you create in advance.

Defining Schedules

If you are using the NetBackup scheduler, you must define when the jobs should run. A single policy can contain more than one job schedule and can be shared by multiple database servers (clients).

The *Oracle* policy type has options for Application Backup Schedule and Automatic Backup Schedule, as described next. One or more automatic backup schedules will be required depending on the job frequency.

Configure an Application Backup Schedule

Whenever the policy type is "Oracle," NetBackup creates an *Application Backup* schedule. This schedule defines the overall timeframe when any backup job can occur. Unscheduled Oracle backups will default to using this schedule. Special processes, needed for the execution of RMAN jobs, are initiated as part of the Application Backup schedule.

To configure an Application Backup schedule, follow these steps:

1. In the Change Policy dialog box, click the Schedules tab.

2. Double-click Default Application Backup Schedule.

3. Click the Attributes tab, shown in Figure 24-4, and make sure that the Retention option is set.

4. Click the Start Window tab. The Start Window defines the time limits during which a backup job can begin. It is a more granular subschedule within the overall Application Backup schedule. A backup job must start within the time limits of the Start Window, but will continue to run until it finishes.

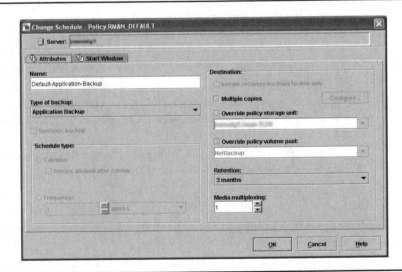

FIGURE 24-4. *Application Backup schedule*

NOTE
Set the backup window for the Application Backup schedule to 24 hours a day, seven days a week, in order to perform any unscheduled or scheduled backup at any time and for any duration.

Configure an Automatic Backup Schedule

To configure an Automatic Backup schedule, follow these steps:

1. In the Change Policy dialog box, click the Schedules tab.
2. Click the New button to open the Add Schedule window.
3. On the Attributes tab (refer to Figure 24-5), enter a unique name for the schedule.
4. Select from four different backup types in the Type of Backup drop-down list:

   - **Application Backup** Runs when an Oracle backup is started manually. Each Oracle policy must be configured with one Application Backup schedule.
   - **Automatic Full Backup** Backs up all the database blocks that have been allocated or that are in use by Oracle.
   - **Automatic Differential Incremental Backup** Backs up database blocks that have changed since the most recent full or incremental backup at level *n* or lower.
   - **Automatic Cumulative Incremental Backup** Backs up database blocks that have changed since the most recent full or incremental backup at level *n* – 1 or lower.

5. Select from two different schedule types:

   - **Calendar** Specifies exact dates, recurring days of the week, or recurring days of the month.

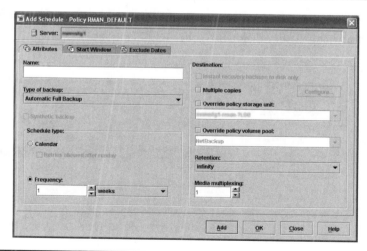

FIGURE 24-5. *Automatic Backup schedule*

■ **Frequency** Specifies the period that will elapse until the next backup operation can begin on this schedule. Options are hourly, daily, and weekly.

6. Select an appropriate retention period from the Retention drop-down list, which controls how long NetBackup retains the records for scheduled backups.

To add other schedules, repeat Steps 1 through 6.

Defining a Backup Selection

When running backup jobs, NetBackup will call any custom scripts or templates that are placed in the *backup selection list*. These files will be executed in the order they are listed. In NetBackup, two options can be used to define commands for Oracle RMAN backup or recovery:

■ **Templates** Stored in a known location on the central master server so that they do not need to be put on each database server. The filename is entered without a path.

■ **Scripts** Located on each database server listed and must be entered with a full pathname.

To add scripts or templates to the backup selections list, follow these steps:

1. From the Administration Console, double-click the policy name in the Policies list.
2. In the Change Policy dialog box, click the Backup Selections tab.
3. Click New.
4. In the Add Backup Selection dialog box, shown in Figure 24-6, enter the shell script or template name. Use the Add button to add the script or template to the selection list.
5. Click OK.

Defining Policy Clients

To add a database server (client) to a policy, follow these steps:

1. From the Administration Console, double-click the policy name in the Policies list.
2. In the Change Policy dialog box, click the Clients tab.

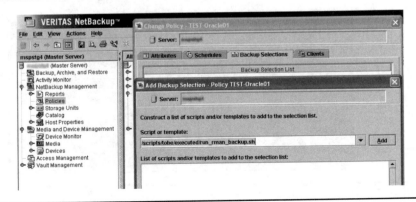

FIGURE 24-6. *Backup selection*

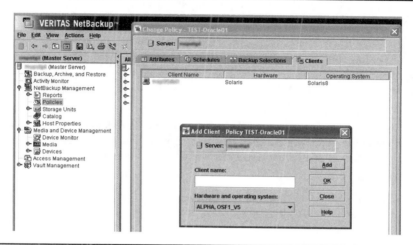

FIGURE 24-7. *Define policy clients*

3. Click New to open the Add Client dialog box, shown in Figure 24-7.
4. In the Client Name box, type the name of the client you are adding.
5. Choose the hardware and operating system type from the drop-down list.
6. Click OK or click Add to set up another client.

Managing Expired Backup Images

The NetBackup Media Manager and RMAN both have the ability to manage backup retention periods. This can be a problem if their retention settings don't match. Automatic expiration of backup images from both repositories is not supported. A workaround is to use the Retention setting in the Application Backup schedule and then to synchronize the NetBackup and RMAN repositories.

Delete Expired Backups Using NetBackup Repository

NetBackup controls the expiration of the Oracle backup images from its repository by using the Retention setting in an Application Backup schedule. The setting specifies the length of time before the backup image expires and is deleted. When you use NetBackup retention to delete backup images, you must do regular Oracle repository maintenance to remove references to expired backup files.

Delete Expired Backups Using RMAN

RMAN has a manual command to remove all database and archive log backups that have reached their retention limits. You can use this command to delete database backups from both the RMAN catalog and the NetBackup repository. When a request is issued to delete a backup file from the

RMAN repository, RMAN sends the request to NetBackup to delete the corresponding images from its repository, regardless of the retention level. The code for deleting expired backups is shown next:

```
RMAN> allocate channel for maintenance type 'SBT_TAPE';
RMAN> crosscheck backup;
RMAN> delete expired backup;
```

The **crosscheck** command should be used only in cases where files marked with the status "Available" that no longer exist can be expired and marked deleted. RMAN should control the retention using the following command. If you configure the channel with the tape parameters, there is no need to allocate channels. This feature is available in Oracle 9*i* Database and newer versions.

```
RMAN> allocate channel for maintenance type 'SBT_TAPE';
RMAN> delete noprompt obsolete;
```

RMAN Sample Scripts

Something particularly clever about the NetBackup for Oracle agent installation is that it includes RMAN backup and recovery sample scripts that are pre-instrumented (that is, they already include code snippets or templates) with code for using NetBackup. Look for the sample scripts in /<install_path>/netbackup/ext/db_ext/oracle/samples/rman.

These sample scripts will be included:

```
cold_database_backup.sh
hot_database_backup_proxy.sh
cold_duplex_database_backup_full.sh
hot_tablespace_backup.sh
database_restore.sh
hot_tablespace_backup_proxy.sh
hot_database_backup.sh
pit_database_restore.sh
```

New scripts can be generated from the Administration Console. For anyone who has suffered through the time-consuming effort of trying to locate elusive punctuation errors, these scripts come as a pleasant surprise.

The following is an RMAN code snippet for calling NetBackup:

```
rman target / catalog <user>/<password>@rman_cat_db log=<my_output.log>
run
{
allocate channel t1 type 'SBT_TAPE'
parms="ENV=(NB_ORA_SERV=<storage_server>,
NB_ORA_POLICY=RMAN_DEFAULT, NB_ORA_CLIENT=<db_server>)";
backup database format 'db_%d%U%t'
}
```

The *NetBackup Administrator's Guide* recommends adding **%t** at the end of the format string, since NetBackup uses a timestamp as part of its search criteria for catalog images. You can also do this by using **configure**.

The following is an RMAN code snippet for calling NetBackup that uses **configure** commands:

```
rman target / catalog <user>/<password>@rman_cat_db log=<my_output.log>
rman> CONFIGURE CHANNEL DEVICE TYPE 'SBT_TAPE' PARMS
'SBT_LIBRARY=/<install_path>/netbackup/bin/libobk.so64.1,
ENV=(NB_ORA_SERV=<storage_server>, NB_ORA_POLICY=<policy_name>,
NB_ORA_CLIENT=<db_server>)';
rman> CONFIGURE DEVICE TYPE 'SBT_TAPE' FORMAT 'db_%d%U%t'
rman> backup database;
```

Troubleshooting

Inevitably, something will break in the environment. Knowing how to prioritize problems in advance helps to resolve them more smoothly. This section highlights steps to help troubleshoot issues.

The following are general troubleshooting steps to take:

1. Verify Oracle agent installation by making sure that the proper libraries exist in /<install_path>/netbackup/bin. Refer to Table 24-2 earlier in the chapter to determine which library (for example, libobk.a) corresponds to your operating system.

2. Check the database server (client) to ensure that the bphdb executable exists. This is used by both the NetBackup scheduler and the GUI to start backups.

3. Check that the following executables exist:
   - /<install_path>/netbackup/bin/bpdbsbora
   - /<install_path>/netbackup/bin/bpubsora
   - /<install_path>/lib/libdbsbrman.so
   - /<install_path>/lib/libnbberman.so

4. Check that the following /<install_path>/netbackup/logs directories exist with 777 permissions:
   - On the database server (client): bpdbsbora, dbclient, bphdb, and bpcd
   - On the master server: bprd and bpdbm
   - On the media server: bpbrm and bptm

Use NetBackup Logs

NetBackup generates logs for backup and restore operations. These logs can be used to investigate media manager problems, but RMAN errors will be written to the RMAN logs. There are two types of NetBackup logs:

- **Progress logs**   Located in /<install_path>/netbackup/logs/user_ops/username/logs, these logs are generated for any backup or restore operations. These files can sometimes be large and cumbersome. They contain sizable amounts of data. The key here is knowing how to extract the data you need. There are basically two error types: numbers 16 and 32, where 16 is an error failure and 32 is a critical failure. The best way to find them is to search the log files for <16> and <32>.

- **Debug logs**   Each debug log corresponds to a NetBackup process and executable. When debugging is turned on, the logs are written to /<install_path>/netbackup/logs. These logs can grow quickly in size, so use debugging only when necessary.

To enable logging on the database server (client), modify the /<install_path>/netbackup/bp.conf file with this line:

```
VERBOSE = #
```

is a value of 1 to 5 to indicate the level of logging. Keep in mind that a higher value generates a lot of information and could cause the directory to run out of space.

NOTE
Make sure that the debug file permissions are set to 777. Verify that libobk is linked properly if log files are not being created.

Determine Which Library Is in Use

You can find out which NetBackup library is interfacing with Oracle, as follows:

```
ls -l $( echo $LD_LIBRARY_PATH | sed -e "s/:/ /g")/libobk* | grep libobk
```

Security Best Practices

Since the NetBackup software runs in a networked environment, it is susceptible to vulnerabilities such as denial of service attacks. To prevent these situations from happening, the following best practices are recommended by Veritas, which is now Symantec:

- Allow administrative access to privileged users only.
- Allow remote access only from trusted servers.
- Apply the latest patches.
- Install NetBackup behind a firewall.
- Ensure virus protection is running on the servers.
- Monitor network traffic for malicious activity.

- Block external access to the default ports used by NetBackup.
- NetBackup server and clients should face toward the internal network.

Cost Justification

It's not always easy to justify the costs of purchasing expensive software and licenses for an information technology department, which is traditionally considered to be a non-revenue-generating part of an organization. This section provides some ideas for demonstrating to management the value of purchasing Veritas NetBackup for Oracle.

The NetBackup for Oracle software extends the capabilities of RMAN. Since the software allows RMAN to speak directly to storage servers, it automates processes that would otherwise be done by people. It shortens backup and recovery time by eliminating some steps altogether and by cutting out process variation. Essentially, this translates into better overall application performance (since backups take less time), reduced business outages during recovery events, more error-free recoveries, and greater productivity of database and storage administrators.

The NetBackup software could easily pay for itself during just one significant business outage where productivity and revenue are negatively impacted.

Summary

We have explored how NetBackup software is used to facilitate a networked backup and recovery environment. We outlined the ways in which it extends existing RMAN functionality. We described how to configure each layer for direct component communication, which eliminates the need for manual intervention. We discovered that using NetBackup to enhance RMAN results in faster backup and recovery, reduced process variation, and shorter business outages during recovery events. NetBackup for Oracle software has been thoughtfully developed for those of us who are excited about easily deployed and feature-rich backup and recovery solutions.

CHAPTER
25

Configuring HP Data
Protector for Oracle

I n large environments, it's hard for database administrators to schedule, manage, monitor, and report all database backups centrally. Another challenge for DBAs is managing the backup media: setting the protection, monitoring the usage, and checking on the backup history. For HP customers, using a backup user interface with RMAN such as HP Data Protector overcomes all these issues.

This chapter begins with a discussion of the integration between Oracle RMAN 12c and HP Data Protector 9.0. It then describes the configuration of Oracle backups with Data Protector. You will learn how to back up and restore an Oracle database with Data Protector. Finally, you will learn how to set up synchronization between Oracle RMAN Metadata and Data Protector Media Management Database.

Integration of Oracle and Data Protector

You must properly integrate Oracle and Data Protector in order to run successful backup/restore operations. To integrate them, therefore, you'll now learn about the support matrix and the integration components, and do a workshop on integration configuration.

Support Matrix

At the time of writing, HP Data Protector 9.0 supports Oracle 12c (64-bit) Recovery Manager on the following operating systems:

- Windows Server 2008 (64-bit; x64)
- Windows Server 2008 R2 (64-bit; x64)
- Windows Server 2012 (64-bit; x64)
- Windows Server 2012 R2 (64-bit; x64)
- RHEL Advanced Server 6.4 (64-bit; x64)
- Oracle Enterprise Linux 6.4 (64-bit; x64)
- CentOS 6.4 (64-bit; x64)

Integration Components

For Oracle and Data Protector integration, RMAN and the Data Protector Oracle Integration software work together to accomplish backup, copy, restore, recovery, and duplication operations.

The Data Protector Oracle Integration agent uses the information in the recovery catalog or in the control file to determine how to execute the requested backup and restore operations. By using this integration, you can perform Oracle full and incremental backups. Oracle incremental backups can be differential or cumulative. By default, Data Protector performs Oracle differential incremental backups. By changing the default RMAN script created by Data Protector, you can specify a cumulative backup.

With Data Protector, both online and offline database backups can be performed. However, successful backups require proper configurations. For an online database backup, the database instance must be in ARCHIVELOG mode, and for an offline database backup, the database needs to be prepared for backup with the Pre-exec and Post-exec options in the backup specification. You can use these options for shutting down the database or taking a tablespace offline before backup, and then reverse operations after backup.

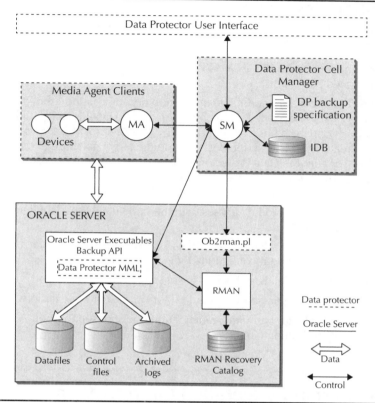

FIGURE 25-1. *Integration architecture of Oracle and Data Protector*

Here are the components of this integration, as shown in Figure 25-1:

- **SM** The Data Protector Session Manager, which manages the backup and restore sessions.

- **MA** The Data Protector General Media Agent, which reads and writes data from and to media devices.

- **Data Protector MML** The Data Protector Oracle Integration Media Management Library, which is a set of routines that enables data transfer between the Oracle server and Data Protector. The Data Protector MML links Data Protector and Oracle server software.

- **Ob2rman.pl** The Data Protector Oracle Integration agent, which works with RMAN to manage all aspects of the backup/recovery operations on the Oracle target database.

- **Backup API** The Oracle-defined application programming interface.

- **IDB** The Internal Database, where all the information about Data Protector sessions, including session messages, objects, data, used devices, and media, is written.

- **RMAN** The Oracle Recovery Manager.

Integration Restrictions

There are a number of restrictions with respect to the use of Data Protector. These restrictions include the following:

- You cannot use the RMAN MAXPIECESIZE option in Data Protector and Oracle integrated backups.

- The Data Protector and Oracle integration does not support the RMAN disk backup of a target database to the Fast Recovery Area. The Data Protector and Oracle integration supports only backups from the Fast Recovery Area to a backup device. However, you can create an RMAN script that backs up the target database to the Fast Recovery Area before or after the Data Protector backs up files from the Fast Recovery Area to a backup device. The script can be set up using the Pre-exec or Post-exec option when creating a backup specification.

- It's not possible to add databases with the same database identifiers (DBIDs) into a Data Protector Cell.

- In a Data Guard configuration, you cannot add only one standby database to Data Protector Cell without configuring the primary database.

- Logical standby database backup is not supported.

- Recovery Catalog database is required for Data Guard integrations.

- The Data Protector and Oracle integration does not support non-ASCII characters in backup specification names.

RMAN Workshop: *Integration Configuration*

Workshop Notes

To run a successful RMAN backup of an Oracle Database using Data Protector Integration, you should have the Oracle target database mounted or opened, the recovery catalog database configured and opened (if being used), Oracle Net Services properly configured, and Data Protector Disk Agent, Media Agent, and Oracle Integration installed on the server the target database resides on.

NOTE
In RAC databases with Oracle version 11.2.0.2 and later, the control file must be created on a shared disk and be accessible from all RAC nodes, and the OB2_DPMCTL_SHRLOC environment variable must point to this location, from where the control file is backed up.

In this Workshop, it is assumed that devices and media are ready for use and that Data Protector Cell Manager is installed and properly configured. HP Data Protector Manager software, which may reside in a PC, will be used to configure the integration. Oracle Database is on a Linux host.

Step 1.   First you must install the Data Protector agent to the target database server. This can be done locally or remotely if an installation server is ready for the necessary operating system. In this Workshop we'll install the Data Protector agent locally.

    a.   Insert and mount the Unix installation DVD-ROM or ISO image.

    b.   Run omnisetup.sh, which is under the LOCAL_INSTALL directory.

NOTE
You can use the **[-server name]** *syntax to import the client to the Cell Manager, where* name *is a full hostname of the Cell Manager. If you don't use the* **-server** *option, you can still import the client after the installation, as specified in Step 2.*

    c.   Installer will ask for the components you want to install. Select Disk Agent (da), Media Agent (ma), and Oracle Integration (oracle8) components.

    d.   Setup informs you if the installation was completed.

Step 2.   When the agent is installed locally and not imported to the Cell Manager using the **-server** option, execute this step to import the target database server as a client to the Cell Manager.

    a.   Run HP OpenView Storage Data Protector Manager Software and connect the Cell Manager.

    b.   In the context list, select Clients, and in the Scoping pane, right-click Clients and then click Import Client.

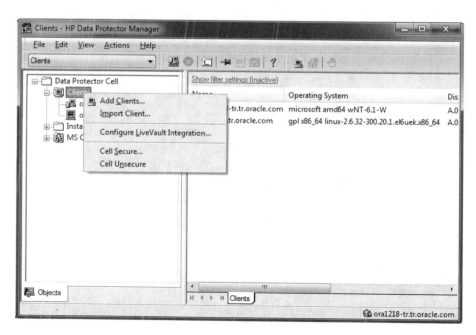

   c. Type the IP or host name (if it can be resolved) of the target server in the Name box and click Finish.

Step 3. You must add the Oracle database software owning account (typically with username *oracle*) to the Data Protector *admin* user group.

   a. Run HP OpenView Storage Data Protector Manager Software and connect the Cell Manager.

   b. In the context list, select Users, and in the Scoping pane, right-click the *admin* group and then click Add/Delete Users.

   c. In the Add/Delete Users interface, select Type as UNIX. Then type the username and select <Any> as the UNIX Group.

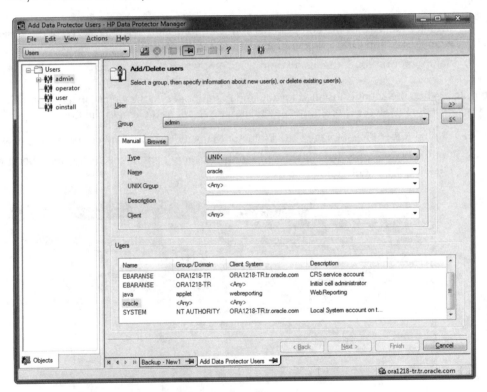

   d. Click the right double arrows and then click Finish.

NOTE
You do not need to link Oracle Server with the Data Protector MML manually, which is required in former releases. When you start backups or restores using the Data Protector GUI or CLI, Data Protector automatically links Oracle Server with the correct platform-specific Data Protector MML.

RMAN Backup Configuration on Data Protector

To configure an Oracle RMAN backup configuration on Data Protector, decide which devices, media pool, and media will be used for that backup operation. Then you can create the Data Protector Oracle backup specification.

Data Protector offers database backup templates that can be used when creating the backup specification. You can also create templates tailored to your needs.

RMAN Workshop: *Backup Configuration*

Workshop Notes

Now that you have added the target host to Data Protector successfully, you can define a backup specification. Using this specification, you will be able to start the backup immediately or to schedule it to run within a specific period.

Step 1. Run HP OpenView Storage Data Protector Manager and connect the Cell Manager.

Step 2. In the context list, select Backup; in the Scoping pane, expand Backup Specifications. Then, right-click Oracle Server and click Add Backup.

Step 3. In the Create New Backup window, you can select one of the predefined backup templates, or select Blank Backup to specify backup operation details later. Select Blank Oracle Backup and click OK.

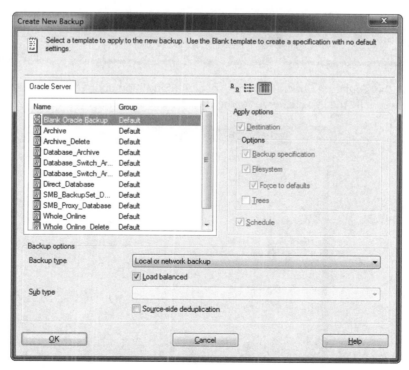

Step 4. In the next window, Data Protector asks for client, application database, username, and group name information. Specify the client on which the target database resides, the SID of the target database, the username, and the name of the group that owns the Oracle instance, as shown here. Click Next.

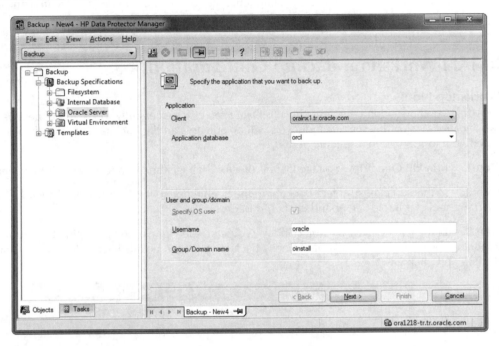

Step 5. In the Configure Oracle window, specify information about the target database. On the General tab, specify the Oracle Server home directory, as shown here.

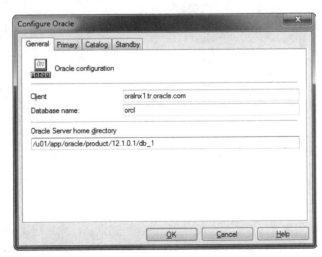

On the Primary tab, specify username, password, and service information. Don't forget that this user must have been granted Oracle SYSDBA privilege. Service is the name used to identify a SQL*Net server process for the target database. The Catalog tab requires the username, password, and service information for the Catalog database if it's being used. The last tab, Standby, is necessary to fill if the Oracle Data Guard environment is in use and will be backed up. Click OK.

Step 6. This step asks you to specify which components of the database you want to back up. Because you selected Blank Backup in Step 3, you will see all components unchecked. Select the components you want to back up and then click Next.

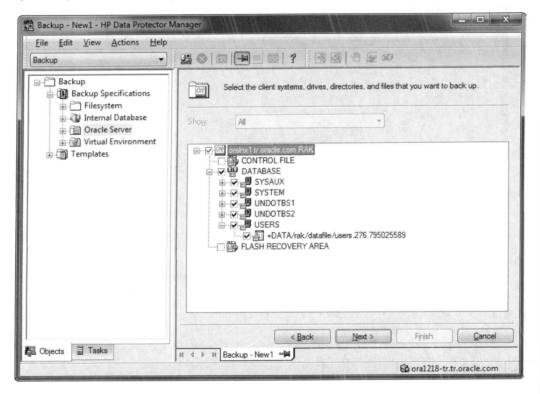

Step 7. Now, Data Protector asks you which hardware will be used for this backup. Select the drive you want to use, as shown here. If you defined it earlier, you can also specify the media pool

that will be used for the backup. Select the drive and click Properties. You'll see a drop-down menu to select a media pool. Make your choice and click Next.

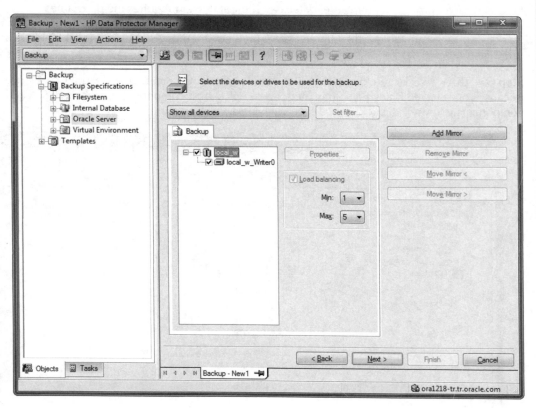

Step 8. This step allows you to specify detailed configuration. As you can see in the following illustration, the three categories each have an Advanced button. You can define pre- and post-execution scripts under Backup Specification Options. You can define backup objects' protection and report level under Common Application Options. Lastly, you can see an overview of the

prepared RMAN script and disable/enable Data Protector–managed control file backup under Application Specific Options. Make your selections and click Next.

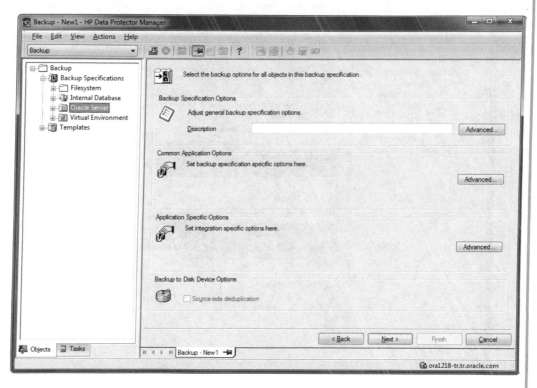

Step 9. You can schedule the configured backup in this step. Specify the dates and times that you want backups performed. You can also configure the incremental level of backups in this stage. For example, create two schedule tasks by clicking Add:

- Level 0 backup on Sundays
- Level 1 incremental backup on the other days

The schedule will look like what's shown here.

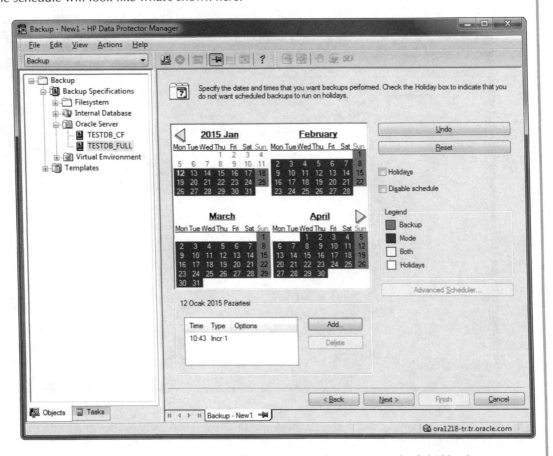

Select the Holiday box if you want to indicate that you do not want scheduled backups to run on holidays. When you want to disable the whole schedule for a backup, you can use the Disable Schedule checkbox.

Step 10.   This last step gives you three options:

- **Save As**   Save the newly created backup/template.
- **Start Backup**   Begin an interactive backup with the current backup specification.
- **Start Preview**   Begin an interactive preview (test) of the backup with the current backup specification.

If you choose to save the backup specification, you can also preview or start the backup later.

Editing the RMAN Script

You can edit the RMAN script section only after the Data Protector Oracle backup specification has been saved.

To manually edit the RMAN script, in the context list, select Backup; in the Scoping pane, expand Backup Specifications. Then expand Oracle Server and click the backup specification you will edit. On the Options tab, click Advanced in the Application Specific Options box. The RMAN script appears with an Edit button.

Click Edit and manually configure the script. You can save the configuration by clicking OK, OK, and Apply.

By default, RMAN scripts automatically created by Data Protector contain instructions for backing up one or more of the following objects:

- Databases, tablespaces, or datafiles
- Archive logs
- Fast Recovery Area
- Control files

When you edit manually, the RMAN scripts with all combinations of the aforementioned backup objects are recognized by Data Protector as its own scripts, and it is still possible to modify the selection of objects that will be backed up in the Source tab by clicking the appropriate button.

If the RMAN script contains additional manually entered backup commands (for example, a second backup command for backing up a database that is already listed in the first backup command), the object selection is disabled, and it is only possible to browse the Source tab.

NOTE
Single quotes should be used when editing the RMAN script. Double quotes (") must not be used.

Example of the RMAN Script

The following is an example of the RMAN script created by Data Protector based on the Blank Oracle Backup template, after the whole database selection:

```
run {
allocate channel 'dev_0' type 'sbt_tape'
 parms 'ENV=(OB2BARTYPE=Oracle8,OB2APPNAME=ORCL,OB2BARLIST=TESTDB_FULL)';
allocate channel 'dev_1' type 'sbt_tape'
 parms 'ENV=(OB2BARTYPE=Oracle8,OB2APPNAME=ORCL,OB2BARLIST=TESTDB_FULL)';
allocate channel 'dev_2' type 'sbt_tape'
 parms 'ENV=(OB2BARTYPE=Oracle8,OB2APPNAME=ORCL,OB2BARLIST=TESTDB_FULL)';
backup incremental level <incr_level> format 'TESTDB_FULL<ORCL_%s:%t:%p>.dbf'
 database;
backup format 'TESTDB_FULL<ORCL_%s:%t:%p>.dbf' archivelog all;
backup format 'TESTDB_FULL<ORCL_%s:%t:%p>.dbf' current controlfile;
}
```

Running an RMAN Backup

Now that you've integrated Oracle with Data Protector and configured an RMAN backup on Data Protector, you'll learn how to run an RMAN backup of a Data Protector integrated Oracle database.

Backup Methods

To start an RMAN backup of a Data Protector integrated Oracle database, you can choose from these three methods:

- Use either the Data Protector GUI or the Data Protector CLI to start an interactive backup of a predefined Oracle backup specification.
- Use the Data Protector Scheduler to schedule a backup of a predefined Oracle backup specification.
- Use either Oracle Recovery Manager or Oracle Enterprise Manager to start a backup on the Oracle server.

Running an Interactive Backup

To start an interactive backup of an Oracle database using the Data Protector GUI, follow these steps:

1. In the HP OpenView Storage Data Protector Manager (Data Protector GUI), select Backup in the drop-down menu.
2. In the left pane, choose Backup | Backup Specifications | Oracle Server.
3. Right-click the backup specification you want to start and select Start Backup.

Scheduling a Backup

To schedule an Oracle backup specification, follow these steps:

1. In the HP OpenView Storage Data Protector Manager, select Backup in the drop-down menu.
2. In the left pane, choose Backup | Backup Specifications | Oracle Server.
3. Double-click the backup specification you want to schedule and click the Schedule tab.
4. In the Schedule page, select a date in the calendar and then click Add to open the Schedule Backup dialog box.
5. Specify the necessary scheduling options.

Starting Oracle Database Backup Using RMAN or Enterprise Manager

You can also use the RMAN CLI or Enterprise Manager to perform backups of Data Protector integrated databases. To use Data Protector backup media in Oracle database backups, you must set the channel type as SBT_TAPE and specify the OB2BARTYPE, OB2APPNAME, and OB2BARLIST variables:

```
allocate channel 'dev_0' type 'sbt_tape'
  parms 'ENV=(OB2BARTYPE=Oracle8,OB2APPNAME=ORCL,OB2BARLIST=TESTDB_FULL)';
```

Backup Procedure

When a backup is started with Data Protector, the following happens in the background:

1. Data Protector executes ob2rman.pl, which starts RMAN on the client and sends the preconfigured RMAN script.

2. RMAN contacts the Oracle server, which contacts Data Protector via the MML interface and initiates the backup.

3. During the backup session, the Oracle server reads data from the disk and sends it to Data Protector for writing to the backup device.

At these stages, messages from the Data Protector backup session and messages generated by Oracle are logged to the Data Protector database.

Restoring Oracle Using the Data Protector GUI

You can restore the following database objects by using both the Data Protector GUI and RMAN:

- Control files
- Datafiles
- Tablespaces
- Databases
- Recovery catalog databases

You can also duplicate a database by using the Data Protector GUI. You need to create an Oracle instance in order to restore or duplicate a database.

Before you restore any database item or you duplicate a database, ensure that the database is in the correct state:

Item to Restore	Database State
Control file, duplicating a database	Nomount (started)
All other items	Mount

NOTE
When you are restoring only a few tablespaces or datafiles, the database can be open with the tablespaces or datafiles to be restored offline.

For a restore, RMAN scripts are generated and executed, depending on selections made in the GUI. If you want to perform additional actions, you cannot edit the RMAN restore script, but you can perform the actions manually from RMAN itself.

Restoring the Control File

To restore the control file, follow these steps:

1. Open the SQL*Plus window and put the database in the nomount state.

2. In the Data Protector GUI, switch to the Restore context.

3. Under Restore Objects, expand Oracle Server, expand the system on which the database for which you want to restore the control file resides, and then click the database.

4. In the Restore Action drop-down list, select Perform RMAN Repository Restore. In the Results area, select the preferred control file restore option, as shown in Figure 25-2.

Depending on the type of the control file backup, the types of restore described in the following sections are possible when you are restoring the control file.

Restoring from Data Protector Managed Control File Backup

When you restore a control file that was backed up with Data Protector, you should know a few things. First, a recovery catalog is not required. Also, the control file will be restored to the default

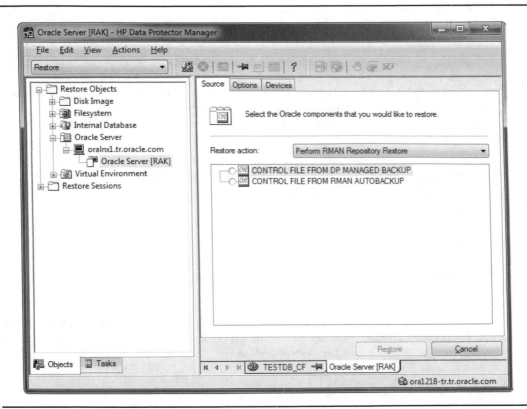

FIGURE 25-2. *Control file restore options*

Data Protector temporary files directory. Then, you will need to execute the following RMAN script to complete the restore:

```
run {
allocate channel 'dev0' type disk;
restore controlfile from 'TMP_FILENAME';
release channel 'dev0';
}
```

Here, TMP_FILENAME is the location to which the file was restored.

Restoring from RMAN Autobackup

■ The control file must be automatically backed up by RMAN.

■ The recovery catalog is not required.

Restoring from RMAN Backup Set

■ The recovery catalog is required.

Restoring Standby Control File from RMAN Backup Set

If you restore a standby database (not using duplication), you must restore this type of control file. A backup session can contain more than one type of the control file backup. Here are the steps to follow:

1. In the Options page, from the Client drop-down list, select the system on which the Data Protector Oracle Integration agent (ob2rman.pl) will be started. To restore the control file to a different database than is selected, click Settings and specify the login information for the target database.

2. Set the other restore options.

3. Click Restore.

4. Proceed with restoring the Oracle database objects.

Restoring Oracle Database Objects

To restore Oracle database objects, follow these steps:

1. Put the database in the mount state.

2. In the Data Protector GUI, switch to the Restore context.

3. Under Restore Objects, expand Oracle Server, expand the client on which the database for which you restore the database objects resides, and then click the database.

4. In the Restore Action drop-down list, select the type of restore you want to perform.

5. In the Results area, select objects for restore. If you are restoring datafiles, you can restore the files to a new location. Right-click the database object, click Restore As, and in the Restore As dialog box specify the new datafile location.

NOTE
When you are restoring to a new location, current datafiles will be switched to the restored datafile copies only if you have selected Perform Restore and Recovery from the Restore Action drop-down list.

6. In the Options page, from the Client drop-down list, select the client on which the Data Protector Oracle Integration agent will be started. To restore the database objects to a different database than is selected, click Settings and specify the login information for the target database.

7. In the Devices page, select the devices to be used for the restore.

8. Click Restore.

Oracle RMAN Metadata and Data Protector Media Management Database Synchronization

The RMAN metadata, which can be stored either in the recovery catalog database or in the control files, contains information about the target database. RMAN uses this information for all backup, restore, and maintenance operations.

Data Protector has its own data protection policy that is not automatically synchronized with Oracle RMAN metadata. To have both catalogs synchronized, run the following command using RMAN:

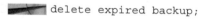

```
allocate channel for maintenance type 'sbt_tape' parms
'SBT_LIBRARY=Path_to_Data_Protector_MML, ENV=(OB2MAINTENANCE=1)';
crosscheck backup completed after
"TO_DATE('01/13/15 12:00:00', 'MM/DD/YY HH24:MI:SS')";
release channel;
```

RMAN will check all backup information in its repository and query the Data Protector Internal Database for the availability of the backup pieces. RMAN then marks the backup piece as expired or available, depending on media availability. RMAN will not delete the backup information in its repository if it is expired in the Data Protector Internal Database, but instead marks it as expired in the RMAN repository as well.

In order to delete expired backup objects from the recovery catalog database, run the following command using RMAN:

```
delete expired backup;
```

Summary

This chapter has given you an overview of using HP Data Protector software for Oracle RMAN operations. After configuring the integration properly, as well as preparing and scheduling backup configurations that meet your backup needs, you will find it easy to manage the backup/restore operations.

CHAPTER
26

RMAN and Tivoli
Storage Manager

I f you already use Tivoli Storage Manager (TSM) for backing up files in your enterprise, taking the next step and using TSM to back up your Oracle database makes a lot of sense: you not only can leverage an existing data protection asset, but also get a seamless connection from Oracle's RMAN utility to TSM. With only a few minor modifications to your RMAN scripts and a straightforward one-time TSM client installation, you won't even know that the tape or disk drive you're using for backup is on a different server. In your DBA role, you may never even have to run a TSM console command.

In this chapter we'll cover a number of topics related to TSM, the TSM client in general, and the add-on module known as *Tivoli Data Protection for Oracle* (TDPO). First, we'll give you a brief overview of the TSM architecture and how an Oracle client connects to it. Your in-depth involvement with TSM begins when you must test and configure TDPO on the server where you will perform the RMAN backup commands.

Throughout this chapter, we'll briefly cover a couple of TSM and Oracle client utilities that you will use to perform initial and routine configuration and monitoring tasks. We'll next perform a couple of backups using RMAN and see the effect of these backups in the storage pool assigned to your TSM Oracle client. At the end of the chapter, we will cover a couple common problems you might encounter in backing up Oracle databases with TSM and TDPO and how to resolve them.

Overview of Tivoli Storage Manager

TSM is a multitiered architecture: when you use it to back up an Oracle database, you may have as many as four tiers. In contrast, you could host all tiers on a single server, but this is not recommended in a distributed environment where you want to keep your backup server separate from the server whose data you want to back up.

Figure 26-1 is a diagram of a typical TSM environment. In the next few sections we'll drill down into a few of the components shown in Figure 26-1 and explain some TSM concepts along the way.

Table 26-1 outlines the nodes shown in Figure 26-1. These nodes are used in the examples throughout this chapter to show you how you can distribute the TSM components across your network.

TSM Server System Objects

The multilevel structure of system objects in a TSM server makes it easy to optimally configure your backups for each of the various data sources in your environment. For the same reason, this flexible hierarchy also makes it easy to assign a specific configuration to unrelated data sources! Figure 26-2 shows the relationship between TSM system objects as well as the types and number of objects that a client uses on any given TSM server.

At the highest level is the policy domain: a policy domain consists of one or more policy sets, and each policy set consists of one or more management classes. Each management class can have one archive copy group and one backup copy group. We'll tell you more about each of these objects in the following sections.

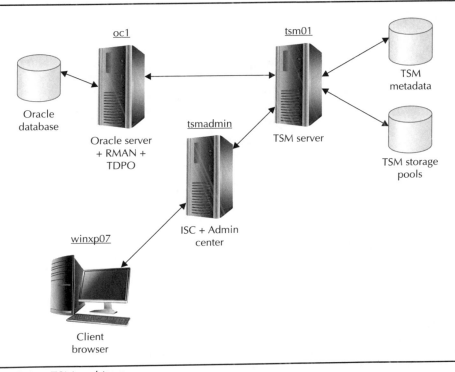

FIGURE 26-1. *TSM architecture*

Policy Domain

A *policy domain* is a group of clients with similar requirements for backing up and archiving data. You might use a policy domain for everyone in a particular department, a particular building or floor, or all users of a specific file server.

A default TSM installation includes one default policy domain called **standard**. For the examples later in this chapter, we will use the **standard** policy domain. You assign backup clients to a policy domain.

Node Name	Operating System	Role
tsm01	Linux	TSM server
oc1	Linux	Oracle database, Tivoli Data Protection for Oracle, TSM client

TABLE 26-1. *TSM Node Names and Roles*

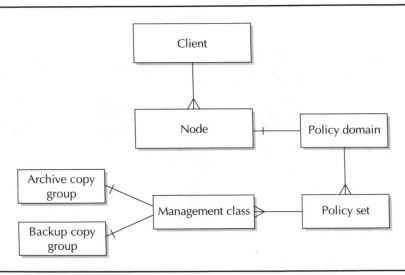

FIGURE 26-2. *Client/TSM relationship and TSM system objects*

Policy Set

A *policy set* is a group of management classes. Each policy domain can contain one or more policy sets, but only one policy set in a policy domain can be active at any given time. You use policy sets to easily switch between available management classes.

Management Class

A *management class* is a collection of zero, one, or two copy groups. You designate one management class within a policy set as the default management class. You typically use management classes to partition client data based on its criticality to the business, how frequently it changes, or whether the data must be retained indefinitely. A management class can have at most one backup copy group and at most one archive copy group.

Backup Copy Groups and Archive Copy Groups

A *copy group* specifies the common attributes that control these characteristics of a backup or archive file:

- **Generation** How many copies of each file are retained
- **Destination** Which storage pool will contain the backup
- **Expiration** When a file will be deleted because the expiration date or retention period has passed

A *backup copy group* contains attributes that control whether a file that has changed since the last backup is backed up again, how many days must elapse before a file is backed up again, and how a file is processed if it is in use during a backup. In contrast, an *archive copy group* contains attributes that control whether a file is archived if it is in use, where the server stores archived copies of the files, and how long the server keeps archived copies of the files. TDPO only uses backup copy groups for Oracle backups.

TSM Client

You install the client piece of TSM, which includes the TSM API, on any server that needs to use a TSM server for backup or recovery. Also included in an installation on an Oracle server is the RMAN library interface to TSM: Tivoli Data Protection for Oracle (TDPO).

Using TDPO, RMAN can back up these database objects to TSM:

- Databases
- Tablespaces
- Datafiles
- Archived log files
- Control files
- Spfiles

Plus, you can perform a full database restoration while the database is offline; you can perform tablespace or datafile restores while the database is either online or offline.

The server oc1 is a client node in an Oracle Real Application Clusters (RAC) database in Figure 26-1 and is a client of TSM on server tsm01.

RMAN Workshop: *Configuring TDPO for Oracle*

For this Workshop you will need an operational TSM server and client environment and Oracle database home installed. The latest and greatest version available is the IBM Tivoli Storage Manager for Databases: Data Protection for Oracle Version 7.1.

Step 1. To install TDPO on your Oracle server, you need to install the following RPM packages:

- **Data Protection for Oracle Linux x86_64 base code, license, utilities: TDP-Oracle .x86_64.bin** This contains the libraries and link definitions that Oracle RMAN will use to connect to TSM.
- **Tivoli Storage Manager API Linux x86_64: TIVsm-API64.i386.rpm** This installs the application program interface (API) libraries to support TDPO or any other application that will programmatically access TSM.

```
# mount <device name> /cdrom
# cd <cdrom>/oracle/linux86_64/api
# rpm -i TIVsm-API64.x86_64.rpm

# cd <cdrom>/oracle/linux86_64
# TDP-Oracle.x86_64.bin -i silent
```

Step 2. The next step is to register the client oc1 on the TSM server using the TSM console:

```
tsm> reg node oc1_oracle orabakpw maxnummp=2
```

Note that we're setting **maxnummp=2**, which specifies the maximum number of parallel sessions that the client can use when backing up to tape. Even though we're using disk drives for backup in these examples, it's a good idea to define the parallelism you need on those occasions when you do back up to tape. Note that orabakpw is the password for this node.

Registering a client node also creates an administrative account that you can use to connect to the TSM server; however, creating individual server accounts for each administrator gives you more control over privileges assigned to each administrator, as well as more precise auditing information when an administrator changes the TSM server's configuration.

Step 3. Define TDPO options. On the Oracle client node oc1, change to the directory /opt/ tivoli/tsm/client/oracle/bin64 and then copy tdpo.opt.smp (the sample file) to tdpo.opt. The file tdpo.opt, as you might expect, defines the TDPO-specific options, such as how TDPO will connect to the TSM server. Uncomment the line beginning with TDPO_NODE and replace <hostname> with the name of the TSM client node. In this example, we will use oc1_oracle. In addition, uncomment the lines beginning with DSMI_ORC_CONFIG and DSMI_LOG if you installed TDPO in a directory different from the default location. Your tdpo.opt file should now look like this:

```
*****************************************************************
* IBM Tivoli Storage Manager for Databases
*    Data Protection for Oracle
*
* Sample tdpo.opt for the Linux Data Protection for Oracle
*****************************************************************

*DSMI_ORC_CONFIG      /opt/tivoli/tsm/client/oracle/bin64/dsm.opt
*DSMI_LOG             /opt/tivoli/tsm/client/oracle/bin64

*TDPO_FS              /adsmorc
TDPO_NODE             oc1_oracle
*TDPO_OWNER           <username>
*TDPO_PSWDPATH        /opt/tivoli/tsm/client/oracle/bin64

*TDPO_DATE_FMT        1
*TDPO_NUM_FMT         1
*TDPO_TIME_FMT        1

*TDPO_MGMT_CLASS_2    mgmtclass2
*TDPO_MGMT_CLASS_3    mgmtclass3
*TDPO_MGMT_CLASS_4    mgmtclass4
```

Step 4. Create dsm.sys. The file dsm.sys defines how to connect to each TSM server, specifying the port number, TCP/IP address, and so forth. Copy the file /opt/tivoli/tsm/client/api/bin64/dsm .sys.smp to /opt/tivoli/tsm/client/oracle/bin64/dsm.sys and change the values as follows:

```
**********************************************************************
* Tivoli Storage Manager                                            *
*                                                                   *
* Sample Client System Options file for Linux (dsm.sys.smp)    *
**********************************************************************

*   This file contains the minimum options required to get started
*   using TSM.  Copy dsm.sys.smp to dsm.sys.  In the dsm.sys file,
*   enter the appropriate values for each option listed below and
*   remove the leading asterisk (*) for each one.

*   If your client node communicates with multiple TSM servers, be
*   sure to add a stanza, beginning with the SERVERNAME option, for
*   each additional server.
**********************************************************************

SErvername          tsm01
COMMmethod          TCPip
TCPPort             1500
TCPServeraddress    192.168.2.69
Passwordaccess      generate
```

The IP address 192.168.2.69 is the address of the server tsm01. To avoid manually entering a password for every backup, you will use the **tdpoconf** utility later in this chapter to create a password file that TDPO will use to authenticate with the TSM server.

Step 5. Create dsm.opt. The file dsm.opt defines the TSM server name you will use for backups on this node. In the directory /opt/tivoli/tsm/client/oracle/bin64, create a file with one line, as follows:

```
SERVERNAME tsm01
```

Step 6. To enable the RMAN catalog's archiving and expiration settings to control backup retention on the TSM server, update the configuration for node oc1_oracle on the TSM node by using this console command:

```
tsm> update node oc1_oracle backdelete=yes
```

Step 7. Configure TSM copy group options. Since RMAN creates different backup filenames for each backup file it creates, all backup objects saved to the TSM backup storage pool have unique filenames, and therefore they will never expire. As a result, you must set the copy group attribute **verdeleted** to **0** so that TDPO can remove unwanted backup objects from the TSM backup storage pool when an RMAN command or policy sets the backup object to an inactive or expired state. The parameter **verdeleted** specifies the maximum number of backup versions to retain for files that have been deleted from the client; therefore, setting this value to **0** ensures that the expired backup files on the TSM server are deleted the next time expiration processing occurs.

In this example, you are using the default copy group for your TDPO backups, so you set the option **verdeleted** as follows using TSM console:

```
tsm> update copygroup standard verdeleted=0
```

Step 8. Generate the tdpo password file. To ensure that you do not have to interactively specify a password for every RMAN backup to the TSM server, use the **tdpoconf** utility as follows:

```
# tdpoconf password
IBM Tivoli Storage Manager for Databases:
Data Protection for Oracle
Version 7, Release 1, Level 0.0
(C) Copyright IBM Corporation 1997, 2013. All rights reserved.

*************************************************************
*        IBM Tivoli Storage Manager for Databases Utility *
*   Password file initialization/update program          *
*      ROOT privilege needed to update value             *
*************************************************************

Please enter current password:
Please enter new password:
Please reenter new password for verification:

ANU0260I Password successfully changed.
```

The **tdpoconf** utility creates or updates an encrypted password file called /opt/tivoli/tsm/client/oracle/bin64/TDPO.oc1_oracle.

Step 9. You need to create a symbolic link to the TSM library functions in Oracle's default library directory, as follows:

```
ln /opt/tivoli/tsm/client/oracle/bin64/libobk.so
   $ORACLE_HOME/lib/libobk.so
```

The RPM utility has no way of knowing where your Oracle executables and libraries are stored, so you must define this link manually. If you have multiple Oracle homes, you need to create the link in each home that you want to be able to use TDPO in.

Libobk is the generic name for the library file. Each backup vendor that wants to interface with RMAN will provide a library file that is linked to the libobk file.

Step 10. Test TDPO connectivity. To ensure that you can establish a connection to the TSM server, use the sbttest utility. You can find sbttest in the directory $ORACLE_HOME/bin. Here, tdpo_check is the backup_file_name created by this program:

```
$ sbttest tdpo_check -libname /opt/tivoli/tsm/client/oracle/bin64/libobk.so
The sbt function pointers are loaded from libobk.so library.
..
..
```

Performing an RMAN Backup Using TDPO

Now that the TDPO setup is complete, you're ready to perform your first RMAN backup. You'll use the **allocate channel** command in an RMAN session to define the backup location; even though your channel type is always **sbt_tape**, the actual backup device on the TSM server could be a disk, a writable DVD, or a physical tape drive; RMAN doesn't know and you don't care what physical device will contain the backup, as long as you can recover the database when disaster strikes!

In this first example, you back up just the USERS tablespace to TSM:

```
$ rman target /
Recovery Manager: Release 12.1.0.2.0 - Production on Sat Jan 24 07:30:18 2015
Copyright (c) 1982, 2014, Oracle and/or its affiliates.  All rights reserved.
connected to target database: RAC (DBID=2170964680)
RMAN> run
2> { allocate channel t1 type 'sbt_tape' parms
3>     'ENV=(TDPO_OPTFILE=
4>        /opt/tivoli/tsm/client/oracle/bin64/tdpo.opt)';
5>   backup tablespace users;
6>   release channel t1;
7> }

using target database control file instead of recovery catalog
allocated channel: t1
channel t1: sid=293 instance=rac1 devtype=SBT_TAPE
channel t1: Tivoli Data Protection for
    Oracle: version 7.1.0.0

Starting backup at 24-JAN-15
channel t1: starting full datafile backupset
channel t1: specifying datafile(s) in backupset
input datafile fno=00004
    name=+DATA/rac/datafile/users.259.582982545
channel tdpo: starting piece 1 at 24-JAN-2015
channel tdpo: finished piece 1 at 24-JAN-2015
piece handle=02horjvc_1_1 tag=TAG20150124T212604
channel t1: backup set complete, elapsed time: 00:00:03
Finished backup at 24-JAN-15

released channel: t1
RMAN>
```

The only bit of extra work you need to do to back up to TSM is to specify the location of the TDPO options file in the RMAN **env** parameter. In this second example, you back up the entire database:

```
RMAN> run
2> { allocate channel t1 type 'sbt_tape' parms
3>     'ENV=(TDPO_OPTFILE=
4>           /opt/tivoli/tsm/client/oracle/bin64/tdpo.opt)';
5>   backup database;
```

```
6>    release channel t1;
7> }

allocated channel: t1
channel t1: sid=293 instance=rac1 devtype=SBT_TAPE
channel t1: Tivoli Data Protection for Oracle: version 7.1.0.0

Starting backup at 24-JAN-15
channel t1: starting full datafile backupset
channel t1: specifying datafile(s) in backupset
input datafile fno=00003 name=+DATA/rac/datafile/sysaux.257.582982545
input datafile fno=00001 name=+DATA/rac/datafile/system.256.582982545
input datafile fno=00002 name=+DATA/rac/datafile/undotbs1.258.582982545
input datafile fno=00005 name=+DATA/rac/datafile/example.264.582982703
input datafile fno=00006 name=+DATA/rac/datafile/undotbs2.265.582982943
input datafile fno=00007 name=+DATA/rac/datafile/undotbs3.266.582983003
input datafile fno=00004 name=+DATA/rac/datafile/users.259.582982545
channel t1: starting piece 1 at 24-JAN-2015
channel t1: finished piece 1 at 24-JAN-2015
piece handle=03hork9s_1_1 tag=TAG20150124T213140
channel t1: backup set complete, elapsed time: 00:03:26
channel t1: starting full datafile backupset
channel t1: specifying datafile(s) in backupset
including current control file in backupset
including current SPFILE in backupset
channel t1: starting piece 1 at 24-JAN-2015
channel t1: finished piece 1 at 24-JAN-2015
piece handle=04horkga_1_1 tag=TAG20150124T213140 comment=API
channel t1: backup set complete, elapsed time: 00:00:06
Finished backup at 24-JAN-2010

released channel: t1

RMAN>
```

Note that you do not have to specify where the backup goes or what disk device to use. TSM automatically puts the backup files into one or more of the storage pool's volumes.

By querying the RMAN catalog, you can see both of the backups you just created:

```
RMAN> list backup;

using target database control file instead of recovery catalog

List of Backup Sets
===================

BS Key  Type LV Size        Device Type Elapsed Time Completion Time
------- ---- -- ---------- ----------- ------------ ---------------
```

```
1        Full    2.00M      SBT_TAPE    00:00:02     24-JAN-2015
         BP Key: 1    Status: AVAILABLE  Compressed: NO  Tag:
                                          TAG20150124T212604
         Handle: 02horjvc_1_1    Media:
  List of Datafiles in backup set 1
  File LV Type Ckp SCN    Ckp Time  Name
  ---- -- ---- ---------- --------- ----
    4       Full 8772169     24-JAN-2015
                            +DATA/rac/datafile/users.259.582982545


BS Key  Type LV Size       Device Type Elapsed Time Completion Time
------- ---- -- ---------- ----------- ------------ ---------------
2        Full    1.24G      SBT_TAPE    00:03:24     24-JAN-2015
         BP Key: 2    Status: AVAILABLE  Compressed: NO  Tag:
                                          TAG20150124T213140
         Handle: 03hork9s_1_1    Media:
  List of Datafiles in backup set 2
  File LV Type Ckp SCN    Ckp Time  Name
  ---- -- ---- ---------- --------- ----
    1       Full 8772449     24-JAN-2015
                            +DATA/rac/datafile/system.256.582982545
    2       Full 8772449     24-JAN-2015
                            +DATA/rac/datafile/undotbs1.258.582982545
    3       Full 8772449     24-JAN-2015
                            +DATA/rac/datafile/sysaux.257.582982545
    4       Full 8772449     24-JAN-2015
                            +DATA/rac/datafile/users.259.582982545
    5       Full 8772449     24-JAN-2015
                            +DATA/rac/datafile/example.264.582982703
    6       Full 8772449     24-JAN-2015
                            +DATA/rac/datafile/undotbs2.265.582982943
    7       Full 8772449     24-JAN-2015
                            +DATA/rac/datafile/undotbs3.266.582983003


BS Key  Type LV Size       Device Type Elapsed Time Completion Time
------- ---- -- ---------- ----------- ------------ ---------------
3        Full    14.75M     SBT_TAPE    00:00:05     24-JAN-2015
         BP Key: 3    Status: AVAILABLE  Compressed: NO  Tag:
                                          TAG20150125T213140
         Handle: 04horkga_1_1    Media:
  Control File Included: Ckp SCN: 8772600      Ckp time: 24-JAN-2015
  SPFILE Included: Modification time: 24-JAN-2015

RMAN>
```

And finally, you can see how much disk space the backups are using in the storage pool by looking at the properties of the storage pool volumes, as shown in Figure 26-3. You access this page by clicking the ORACLEPOOL storage pool link in Figure 26-4 and then clicking the Volumes link in Figure 26-5.

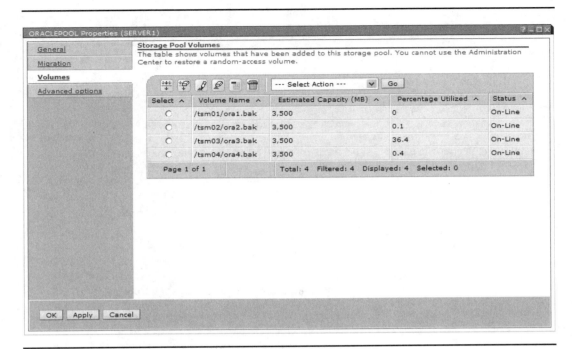

FIGURE 26-3. *Querying storage pool volumes*

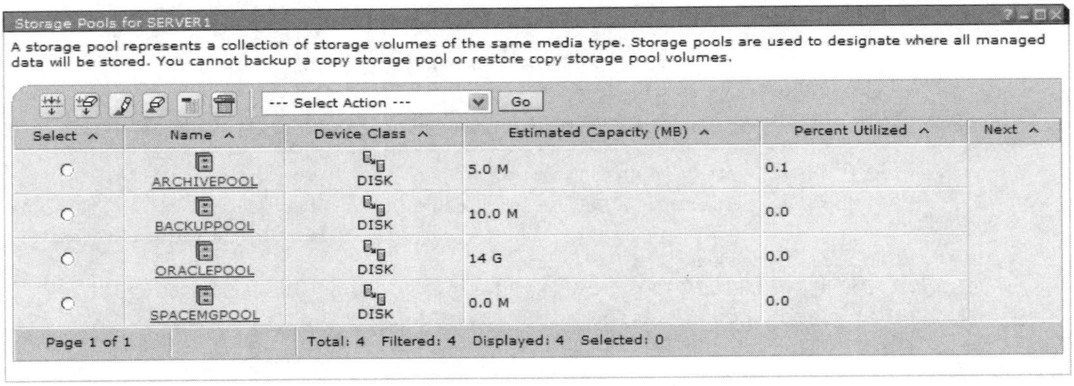

FIGURE 26-4. *Displaying storage pools and capacity*

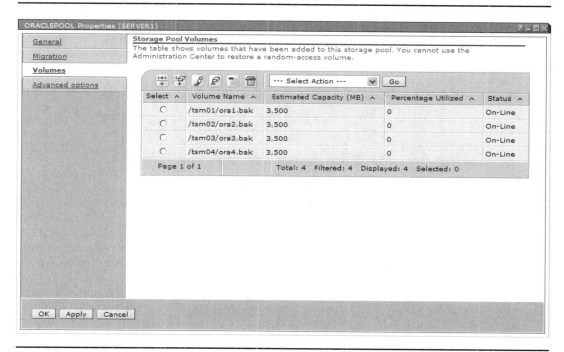

FIGURE 26-5. *Client displaying storage pool volumes*

What's in a Name?

TDPO_NODE can be called almost anything. In environments with many Oracle databases that are using TSM and TDPO for backups, TDPO_NAME could be the root of why backups and restores aren't working. If backups were done with a TDPO_NODE of oc1_oracle and then a new TDPO_NODE (oc2_oracle) is created, and if the tdpo file is changed to use the new TDPO_NAME, RMAN would be unable to access any backups taken under oc1_oracle until the TDPO_NODE is changed in the tdpo file to oc1_oracle. Another common problem is that the password file for the TDPO_NODE that is being used isn't on the database server. This will cause both backups and restore operations to fail.

Default Channels

Although every DBA should know how to manually allocate channels, it can involve a lot of error-prone typing, and if you have many databases, you may not know which tdpo file to use. By setting one parameter, you can back up a database with a simple backup database command with no manual channel allocation. Running a **show all** command from the RMAN> prompt will show the various RMAN options that are configured. To back up to TSM with automatic channel allocation, we are interested in only two options: CONFIGURE DEFAULT DEVICE TYPE TO 'SBT_ TAPE' and CONFIGURE CHANNEL DEVICE TYPE 'SBT_TAPE' PARMS.

By running the following commands from the RMAN prompt, we can set default channels:

```
RMAN> CONFIGURE DEFAULT DEVICE TYPE TO 'SBT_TAPE';
RMAN> CONFIGURE CHANNEL DEVICE TYPE 'SBT_TAPE' PARMS
ENV=(TDPO_OPTFILE=/opt/tivoli/tsm/client/oracle/bin64/tdpo.opt)' FORMAT %U';
```

After the configuration commands have been run, backups are even easier:

```
RMAN> backup database;
```

Deleting Database Backups

One of the main advantages of using RMAN is a common interface in deleting backups. It doesn't matter if the backups are on disk or tape; the same commands are used to delete expired backups. Even though the commands to delete backups are the same when using TSM and TDPO, there are times when additional cleanup may be needed. When you delete backups, you will notice they are deleted very quickly regardless of their size. When RMAN tells TSM to delete backup files, TSM does not immediately delete the files because the tape may not be available at the moment, or all the tape drives could be busy. Therefore, TSM marks the files to be deleted and returns a success code to RMAN. The TSM administrator will run a purge process that actually deletes the files. If you are using a catalog with the tdposync tool provided by TSM, it is possible to compare what the RMAN catalog shows as deleted and what TSM has actually deleted.

To launch tdposync from the default location using the sample tdpo file, run the following:

```
/opt/tivoli/tsm/client/oracle/bin64/tdposync SYNCDB
-TDPOfile=/opt/tivoli/tsm/client/oracle/bin64/tdpo.opt
```

You must have the tdpo file that was used to take the backups for the comparison to work. After launching, tdposync will ask for a username, password, and a connection string to the RMAN catalog. If more than one RMAN catalog holds backup records, add the following parameter:

```
-NUMCATALOGS=number
```

If any discrepancies are found after the comparison, tdposync will provide a list and ask for confirmation before deleting the files from TSM.

Troubleshooting Common Backup Scenarios

Backing up an Oracle database using TSM involves four parts: RMAN, Oracle, O/S, and TSM— each of which can fail and report errors. When you use the RMAN console at first, it can be difficult to know which of the four parts is reporting the error because errors from all sources are returned to the RMAN console. In the next example, O/S, Oracle, and RMAN errors are returned after a simple backup database was issued:

```
RMAN> backup database;

RMAN-00571: ===========================================================
RMAN-00569: =============== ERROR MESSAGE STACK FOLLOWS ===============
```

```
RMAN-00571: ============================================================
RMAN-03002: failure of backup command at 07/17/2009 10:34:31
RMAN-03014: implicit resync of recovery catalog failed
RMAN-06403: could not obtain a fully authorized session
ORA-01034: ORACLE not available
ORA-27101: shared memory realm does not exist
Linux-x86_64 Error: 2: No such file or directory
RMAN>
```

It is usually best to take a bottom-up approach when reading the error messages:

6. RMAN-03002: failure of backup command

5. RMAN-03014: implicit resync of recovery catalog failed

4. RMAN-06403: could not obtain a fully authorized session

3. ORA-01034: ORACLE not available

2. ORA-27101: shared memory realm does not exist

1. Linux-x86_64 Error: 2: No such file or directory

Line 1 is an O/S error that was returned to Oracle. In this case, it doesn't prove too helpful in resolving the problem. Lines 2 and 3 provide the answer and should be recognizable to Oracle DBAs. "ORA-27101: shared memory realm does not exist" means the database instance was not running, and therefore RMAN could not connect to the database.

The first example could happen whether or not you are using TSM. The next scenario will introduce an error only if you are using TSM. We begin with an RMAN run block that allocates a channel, backs up the archive logs, deletes them, and then releases the channel.

```
RMAN> RMAN> run
2> { allocate channel t1 type 'sbt_tape' parms
3>      'ENV=(TDPO_OPTFILE=
4>             /opt/tivoli/tsm/client/oracle/bin64/tdpo.opt)';
5>    backup database;
6>    release channel t1;
7> }


RMAN-00571: ============================================================
RMAN-00569: =============== ERROR MESSAGE STACK FOLLOWS ===============
RMAN-00571: ============================================================
ORA-19506: failed to create sequential file, name="rac_9ikk7ac3_1_1", parms=""
ORA-27028: skgfqcre: sbtbackup returned error
ORA-19511: Error received from media manager layer, error text:
ANS1353E (RC53) Session rejected: Unknown or incorrect ID entered

RMAN>
```

Again, starting with the bottom-up approach, we read the error messages starting with 1:

4. ORA-19506: failed to create sequential file, name="a400_9ikk7ac3_1_1", parms=""

3. ORA-27028: skgfqcre: sbtbackup returned error

2. ORA-19511: Error received from media manager layer, error text:

1. ANS1353E (RC53) Session rejected: Unknown or incorrect ID entered

ANS and ANU are errors returned by the TDPO library. Line 3 indicates RMAN received an error from the media management layer (TDPO library). Lines 2 and 1 are again RMAN saying that it failed to create the backup file of the archive logs. ANU and ANS errors can be time consuming to troubleshoot because many configuration and parameter files and settings have to be checked, as well as many different TSM errors that can be returned. From the error message returned in Step 1, "Session rejected," we can assume a connection was made from RMAN to TSM and TSM rejected the session. Many different causes may result in a session being rejected; in this case, it is a lack of a password file for the tdpo node. As mentioned earlier in the chapter, to back up or restore an RMAN backup, a tdpo node name and password are supplied to TSM. To quickly troubleshoot this error, check the tdpo options file for the tdpo name that RMAN is using, and then also check to ensure RMAN can access the password file for the tdpo name. Also look in the dsm.sys file for the parameter ERRORLOGNAME. This will tell you the path to the file where TDPO will save error information and may provide more details. Your storage administrator may also be able to see if the session rejection message in the TSM logs fails and may be able to provide additional details.

Additional Troubleshooting

To turn on or off debug involves a simple **debug on;** or **debug off;** command. Once debug is on, we need to inform RMAN what additional debug information is to be collected. On the **allocate channel** command, trace=1 is used to create trace files in the user_dump_destination directory. Also on the **allocate channel** command, the debug=2 instructs RMAN to send additional information to the sbtio.log file.

Summary

Once you perform the initial installation and setup of TSM and TDPO in a few easy steps, it's a case mostly of "set it and forget it," allowing you, the DBA, to focus more on the RMAN scripts themselves than on managing where and how TSM stores the backups. When problems do arise, by properly reading out an error, you will quickly be able to diagnose backup failures and whether the problem lies with the database or with TSM.

TSM and TDPO not only make it easy to back up your Oracle database using the familiar RMAN interface, but they also reduce your enterprise's storage management administrative costs because you can use a single storage manager—Tivoli Storage Manager—for all of your backup, recovery, and archival needs.

CHAPTER
27

RMAN and
CommVault Simpana

CommVault's Simpana software is an enterprise-wide data management and backup solution. Multiple options are available for solving your company's backup, storage, and archiving requirements for critical Oracle database applications as well as other types of data, such as e-mail, SharePoint, virtual servers, and file systems.

The Simpana interface was designed to provide some of the most robust support for the widest range of backup situations in most datacenters. The GUI interface is a complete management system that allows total backup and restore management of all the protected data. The entire Oracle database environment can be protected with this same interface in a consistent, familiar method. There are many tightly integrated features supporting the most important RMAN functionality.

Configuration is simple and flexible and provides easy access to complete data backup and protection needs. Whether the requirement is for simple backup and restore to an original source server instance or as complex as out-of-place restore, Duplicate Database, RAC backup and restore, snapshot protection, or Data Guard backup, Simpana has many tightly integrated functions to provide support to complete these actions.

Many corporate IT environments have invested a large amount of resources developing RMAN scripts specific to their operations. These existing scripts can still be utilized with minimal modification upon implementation of the Simpana software. Other organizations may choose to utilize the Oracle Enterprise Manager to execute backup and recovery. This does not pose a problem utilizing Simpana software for ongoing maintenance should continuing use of this already-established method to protect the database be desired. Simpana completely supports these non-Simpana GUI methods of backup protection.

Backups can be scheduled for regular protection at specific intervals through the GUI. The choice for ad-hoc backup on as-needed basis can also be utilized through the GUI interface provided by Simpana.

CommVault storage and data retention management provides flexible options for the most complex retention needs. Backups can be generated through different options and utilize different retention criteria. Different requirements within the enterprise are all supported as a part of the core design of the Simpana software.

If complex business processes should be involved with variable business rules for backup and restore, CommVault Simpana provides an interface such as Workflow management. Workflow is an activity task process interface with multiple predefined activities. These activities utilize a graphic interface for designing groups of functions together. These workflows are available to complete business operation support for many tasks that require some logic before an action is taken.

Snapshot technology is supported through the GUI to allow complete control of snapshots from a wide range of storage vendors through the same interface. This allows you to use the GUI as a "single pane of glass," standardizing the management of different backup technologies and making them easier to use.

Although CommVault itself is designed for a wide range of functionality and protection of various data types, this chapter will focus specifically on how to use Simpana in protecting the Oracle database applications in a day-to-day support and protection process. Some advanced protection options will be reviewed, but a comprehensive review of all supported options would require a complete book dedicated to the functionality built into the Simpana Oracle interface itself. For the purposes of this focused discussion, installation, configuration, backup and restore, plus some advanced topics that are typically encountered in regular protection of Oracle data will be covered.

Simpana Overview

In its most basic form, the structure of a Simpana CommCell consists of three components. There is one CommServe, which acts to manage the various services in the cell. There are also one or more media agents to manage the total data to be protected, and, finally, all the clients (that is, the database servers) with the organization's key data to be protected.

Software installations can be performed and controlled from the CommServe. Software can also be installed from local software packages, including silent install packages. This single server is capable of managing thousands of clients from a console interface that can be used by multiple administrators through a common web interface. Data generated by backups of clients are stored on media agent servers.

Together, these three components—CommServe, the media agent, and the client—make up what is referred to as a CommCell.

Installation

When installing the CommVault software, you must have a couple of key items of information available that will be utilized for proper configuration. The installation of the agent is well diagramed and explained in the CommVault documentation and will only be referred to here. Use the web address http://documentation.commvault.com/commvault/v10/article for the Simpana 10 documentation, and navigate to the specific instructions for the deployment steps of the agent itself. As outlined earlier, there are multiple possible installation methods.

Specific items of note for the installation on each platform are discussed here. For a Windows platform, installation must be performed on a server where the database has been shut down and the database instance services have been stopped. With Unix installations, there is no equivalent requirement of shutdown necessary for deployment.

For both platforms, the appropriate user accounts must be installed correctly. With Windows, the user account must be a domain user with local administrator access rights. This will configure the service to run with the appropriate rights after installation. For Unix deployments, the installation must be completed as a root user and will require the primary group of the Unix user profile to be identified. This identification allows association of the CommVault Simpana binaries to the same group. This association is necessary to allow the execution of the RMAN executables from CommVault processes.

With the core CommServe installation and configuration complete and the appropriate CommVault Oracle software installed on the client, the application interface will appear similar to what's shown in Figure 27-1.

The GUI layout, by default, uses a navigational browser on the left with context-specific detail of the items selected in the browser on the right. The hierarchy displayed will allow a user to modify functionality by using right-click context menus. These menus are used to configure the various object properties that define a complete client application structure and thus define the actions taken during backups.

All CommVault software that is installed to clients for data protection is referred to as an iDA. This iDA (or Intelligent Data Agent) will contain a hierarchy of objects relevant to the type of data being protected.

All agents have a similar look and feel to the others. The subclient is an object structure that exists across all iDA installations. This is one of the most important objects to understand functionally. The subclient contains an association with other key CommVault objects and allows

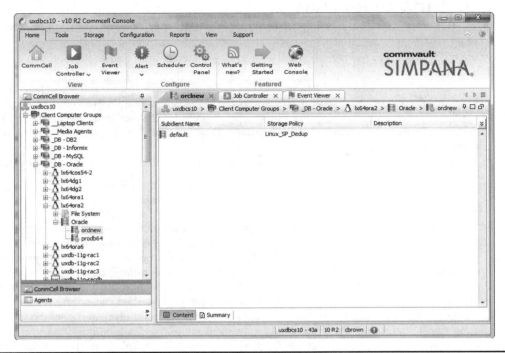

FIGURE 27-1. *CommServe GUI with a client, agent, and subclient*

options to be set that are to be used during a backup of the data being protected. This subclient is associated with a schedule policy that's used to initiate a backup job, using the definitions set in the properties of the subclient. It is also associated with a storage policy that identifies retention for the data backed up and the location of its storage.

As applicable to the Oracle iDA, each of the important objects, including the subclient configuration, will be identified and discussed here.

Data Retention

Data retention is probably one of the stronger, more flexible attributes of the Simpana software package. Retention logic is provided through the object known as a *storage policy*. These storage policies can be shared among subclients for use in backups of many different data types, or they can be more specifically defined for intricately complex business rules.

This flexibility is one of the most robust and useful functions within the CommVault environment. A storage policy is utilized within a subclient by being identified as an associated attribute. A storage policy may be utilized by as many subclients as makes sense given the storage requirements for the backups generated. From this perspective, they are reusable. A storage policy provides significant flexibility for managing multiple data sets generated from different data-protection operations.

Data retention definitions in the storage policy are managed through an object referred to as a *copy*. Within a storage policy definition there will always be at least one copy of type "primary." There can only be one primary copy in each storage policy definition. This primary copy manages data that is created from a backup job run on the client. Multiple copies may be defined. These other copies identify how all data generated from backup jobs is managed. All copies, whether primary or secondary, have attributes for what CommVault refers to as basic retention and extended retention.

Each copy also identifies the location of the data storage. Secondary copies or auxiliary copies are used to manage an exact copy of the data managed by the primary copy. This allows a disaster recovery copy of the primary backup data to be stored in a different location for a different retention. This also allows many copies of the data to be managed without multiple primary backup jobs being run against the client. The destination location of auxiliary copies can be any media agent and data library defined within the CommCell, thus allowing the backup storage administrator to spread the backup data across various datacenters.

Within each copy, retention definitions exist for basic and extended retention. The basic retention is defined with a combination of days and cycles. Cycles are the amount of time between full backups. A typical retention definition of two cycles, 15 days, can be interpreted as identifying two full backups and all subsequent incremental backups leading to the next full backup *and* at least 15 days of age. This retention definition identifies how long data must be retained to maintain the minimum required backup data to properly support the desired business rules. Extended retention defines the number of days all full backups must be retained and can be used to extend the retention of full backups for a longer period of time than the basic retention.

Through the combination of basic and extended retention and utilizing primary and auxiliary copies, the business requirements for backup data storage can be matched with extremely precise accuracy.

Schedule Policies

Schedule policies are definitions of when individual backup jobs will run. They are independent objects that define the time and type of backup to be utilized. Schedule policies are also objects that are associated with a subclient, and they can be associated with as many subclients as necessary. When specific data types are being backed up, the schedule policies contain advanced configuration attributes for the backup of that data.

In the case of Oracle backups, an example of these advanced attributes may identify how to manage archived redo log backups on the primary Oracle log destination. Multiple advanced attributes can be utilized to completely define the backup desired.

CommVault Oracle iDA: What Is It?

The software that is installed on an Oracle server is called an Intelligent Data Agent, or iDA. This software installation provides access to the data on the Oracle database and is identified in the CommServe GUI as a client of the CommCell.

Once the iDA is installed, a number of tasks may be performed, depending on the protection desired. Within the GUI construct of an iDA or Oracle client, there will be a representation of the client server, the Oracle iDA object, an instance, and one or more subclients. Each of these objects has properties that can be set to help configure the backup desired.

CommVault Oracle instances must be identified to the GUI interface. This can be done manually through an entry wizard, or automatic instance discovery can be turned on with the properties of the Oracle iDA, depending on environmental requirements.

An instance will identify the Oracle SID, Oracle owner, Oracle Home, and connection properties for the database being protected. Subclients are the objects whose properties are modified to identify what objects are to be backed up and various other settings that correspond to RMAN commands during a regular backup. See Figure 27-2 for a view of the CommCell GUI, an Oracle client, and the object properties for the contents of an Oracle subclient.

As can be seen in Figure 27-2, the object hierarchy starts with a CommVault group (Client Computer Groups), followed by a group name (DB-Oracle), the host client name (lx64Ora2), the iDA used (Oracle), the Oracle instance (orclnew), and, finally, the subclient (Default).

To this point in the chapter, our discussion has given you an overview of CommVault and its structures so that you understand the real point of why we are here—to configure a backup of an

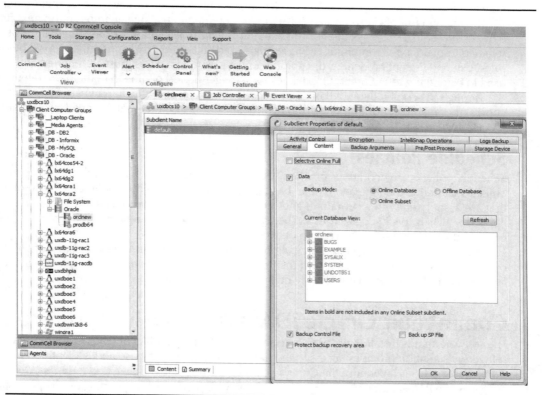

FIGURE 27-2. *Default subclient content properties*

Oracle database using the CommVault software. With this basic understanding of the CommVault interface and functionality, we will outline the definition in CommVault of an Oracle instance and subsequent GUI definitions that govern a backup job.

Configure an Oracle Instance

After the agent is installed, you must configure an instance. This step is necessary to allow CommVault to communicate with the Oracle instance you are to protect. Begin by selecting either New Instance or Discover Instance from the context menu on the Oracle iDA object within the context of the host server you are working with.

The option chosen should match the desired effort. With the New Instance selection, an open entry screen is used to manually enter all important connection information for the instance. The Discover Instance option uses the /etc/oratab file to determine the Oracle instances running on a given host server (see Figure 27-3).

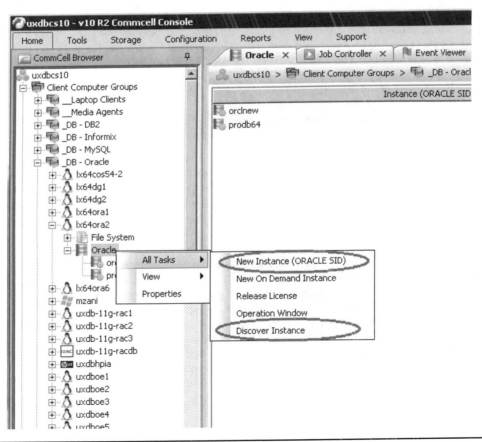

FIGURE 27-3. *The CommServe GUI option Discover Instance*

If the Discover Instance option is selected, information will be prepopulated in each field based on an automatic discovery by CommVault of the Oracle instance. You must validate the information that has been discovered by the CommVault process in order to ensure the correct information for the various fields.

Next, you enter the correct connection information on the Details tab of the instance screen. Note that it is preferred that you connect to the Oracle instance through the network and the complete service name using a user account that has SYSDBA privileges.

It is also possible to connect using the OS authentication method (/) in the first field of the connection string and leave the password and service name blank. This method will allow connections to utilize privileged user status as if connecting to the PL/SQL interface using the following syntax:

```
$ sqlplus / as sysdba
```

This method allows CommVault to connect to the instance and utilize standard backup and restore options.

NOTE
Some advanced features such as Duplicate Database require connections to be configured with a named user that has the sysdba privilege assigned, the password, and the service name. Determine the method accordingly for your application and process. You can find a full discussion on advanced user and password management related to Commvault at the following link: http://docs.commvault.com/commvault/v10/article?p=features/user_account_password/user_account_password_how_to.htm.

Closely associated with this topic of Oracle privileges is the fact that under Oracle 12c, the new privilege SYSBACKUP will be available. In the past, backups could only be performed with an Oracle user profile that had been associated with the sysdba privilege. Using this new role, SYSBACKUP, will allow a DBA to perform RMAN backup commands without additional access to the sysdba role. Effectively, Oracle has separated these two functions, Administration and Backup, with this new Oracle 12c role.

As of this writing, the SYSBACKUP privilege is not yet supported through the CommVault GUI. It is scheduled to be applicable in the GUI in a very short time and may be supported after this volume goes to print. Check with Books Online for the latest support information.

If a recovery catalog is to be used, enter the connect string information next. Be sure to use name, password, and service name. A recovery catalog stores RMAN metadata, and we discuss the recovery catalog in several places in this book in great detail.

Enter the TNS_ADMIN folder location only if you have changed the default location. Set the Block Size to 1048576 to allocate more memory to each backup RMAN channel. This extra memory could help improve backup performance in larger databases.

NOTE
Clearly, memory is an important factor in overall database performance, as well as performance of database backups. We discuss a number of performance-related features and tuning options throughout this book. Additionally, CommVault provides a page on performance tuning backups with CommVault at the following URL: http://docs.commvault.com/commvault/v10/article?p=features/ agents/ora_perf_tuning.htm.

After completing the information entry on the Details tab, choose the Storage Device tab and select the desired storage policy. The Command Line Backup storage policy selection is specific to data generated from RMAN command-line backups outside of the CommVault GUI. The Log Backup storage policy selection determines the destination for archived redo log backup data sets. Storage policies can be chosen independently for each type of data to be protected. Later in this chapter we discuss backups utilizing a direct connection through the terminal session and the RMAN interface.

Click the OK button, and the instance will be saved.

Configure the Subclient

After the instance is configured and the connection to the database has been successful, configure the subclient for the type of backup you wish to complete. The minimum of suggested subclients would be two. The first, the subclient named default, should be configured to back up the database and the archived redo logs. The second subclient should be configured to protect archived redo logs only. This subclient would be scheduled as required such that the archived redo logs will be backed up to meet any service-level agreements.

The default subclient is suggested to be used as the main subclient for backing up the database. The option to back up the database is achieved by clicking the Data checkbox and then selecting the desired backup method. To provide Oracle best practice protection, the option for Online Database should be selected for databases in archived redo log mode. Databases running in NOARCHIVE mode can only be backed up offline and must use the option Offline Database when backups are performed. Databases in NOARCHIVE mode limit the options available for database protection.

Continuing with our setup of the backup, next you enable the option to back up the control file. The SP file protection option should also be set if there is an SPFILE initialization file used by the Oracle instance. Otherwise, clear this option because RMAN will report an inability to find an SPFILE and the backup will not succeed. In the event the older PFILE initialization file is utilized, the file system agent will protect the file. Verify the file system agent is active and the contents of the $ORACLE_HOME/dbs (the default location) are included in any protection jobs.

Continuing with the configuration, you will configure the options available in the subtab Backup Arguments under the main tab Backup Arguments for performance improvements. Then under the Storage Device tab you will set the storage policy and choose the number of channels involved in the backup. Finally, set the options for managing archived redo logs on the Logs Backup tab.

It is important to note that the logs can be managed from this location as well as the advanced options under the schedule policy option of the schedule task screen. If set on this tab, the archived redo logs will be set to be backed up. They can be identified for deletion from the operating system at the same time by clicking the Archive Delete option. However, this option will take precedence if the options in the schedule policy are also used. Checking the backup and delete boxes on the subclient's Logs Backup tab will issue the RMAN command BACKUP ARCHIVELOG ALL DELETE ALL INPUT; when the backup job is executed.

Options in the Advanced Schedule screen allow conditions to be met before RMAN deletes archived redo logs from the operating system, such as number of times backed up and age of the logs. These extra options will be ignored if the option to delete is set on the subclient. Figure 27-4 provides one illustration of how CommVault allows you to modify

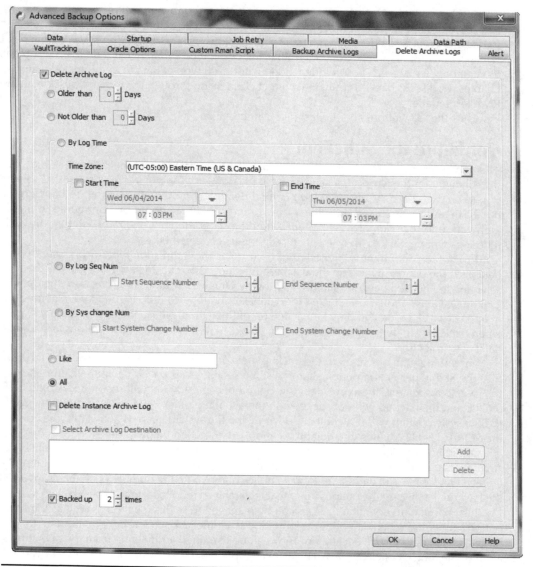

FIGURE 27-4. *The Delete Archive Logs tab*

RMAN-related backup settings. In this case, this screen allows you to configure settings related to the deletion of the archived redo logs.

Initiate a Backup

You have two ways to initiate a backup from the CommVault GUI for Oracle. First, right-click a subclient to select the context-sensitive menu option Backup to execute a backup from the subclient, as previously defined. This option allows you to run a backup immediately (see Figure 27-5).

After you select Backup, a dialog appears in which you can set the type of backup to occur and even preview the RMAN code being generated (see Figure 27-6).

This RMAN script has some code inserted into it that is used by Simpana to communicate through the SBT interface, but otherwise the code in the script is exactly what any DBA may have configured into an RMAN run block to execute a backup. Click OK on the dialog, and a backup will run using the options set in the subclient.

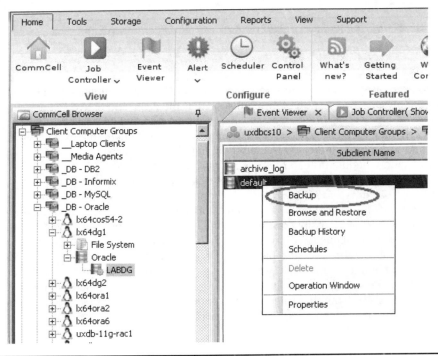

FIGURE 27-5. *Immediate backup from subclient*

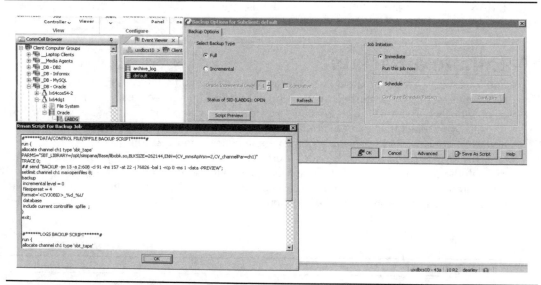

FIGURE 27-6. *Immediate backup options with RMAN Preview*

You can also initiate backups from the Simpana GUI by creating a schedule policy. A schedule policy allows for the creation of properties such as the dates and times backups should execute, as well as the type of backup to create, such as a full or incremental backup.

A schedule can be created and associated with the subclient that executes the backup on the days and at the times indicated in the schedule policy. This also creates the desired backup, but on a specific schedule instead of immediately, as displayed earlier.

Schedule policies should always be associated with individual subclients when you are scheduling backups for Oracle. During the configuration for best practices, multiple subclients are created. Selecting any context higher than a subclient will automatically include all subclients in the schedule created, possibly resulting in multiple backups being generated at once. You will find various options available to you when scheduling a backup.

The CommCell browser also provides a way to scan a current list of saved schedules. When the list of schedules is displayed, you can execute a schedule for an immediate backup of all associated subclients by right-clicking the schedule and selecting the Run Immediately option (see Figure 27-7). Note that selecting this option will execute a backup for all associated subclients that have been added to that schedule policy.

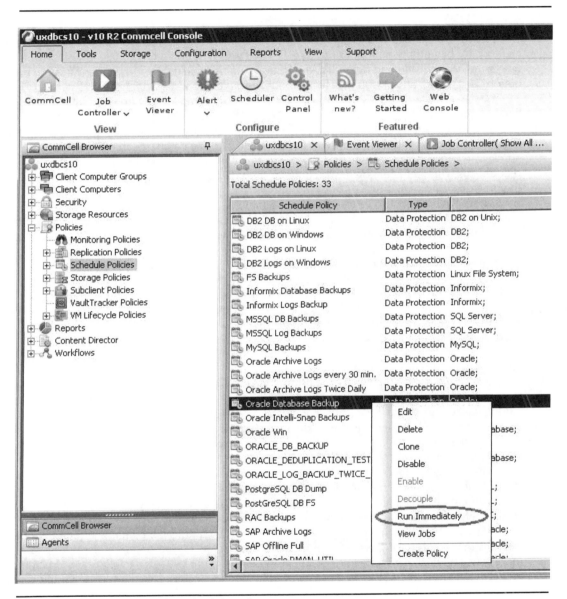

FIGURE 27-7. *Executing the schedule policy*

Restore

To begin restoring a database, you must have created backups with relevant data. There are two methods for beginning the restore process. The first is to drill down on the CommCell browser where the host is listed and right-click the instance name to select the Browse and Restore menu option. This option allows you to select various restore criteria.

You can also start your restore by using the selection Backup History from the subclient where backups are defined and scheduled. When you start a restore with this option, the process will display a similar search criteria dialog, as well as a list of backups in which the desired backup should be selected. When the desired backup is selected, the database/tablespace view will appear after you choose Browse and Restore from a context menu on the display of the backup record. This will open a dialog in which the desired database/tablespaces may be selected, as in the previous restore method.

When this browse and restore view is available, you can select the entire database by checking the box next to the database. You can also restore individual datafiles or tablespaces using this method. Once you have selected what you want to restore, click the button labeled Restore All Selected. The Restore dialog will open with the restore options selected.

Some restrictions are enforced from these checkboxes. The duplicate DB option is a separate function. Selecting the Duplicate DB checkbox will clear all other options because they are mutually exclusive to the operation of duplicating a database.

The options Restore Archive Log and Recover are mutually exclusive. In both of these cases, RMAN will retrieve backup pieces containing archived redo logs, but in the first case the logs will be restored to a specific host server mount location, whereas in the case of the Recover option, the archived redo logs will be read and applied during the recovery but the logs will not be restored to any file location on the host server.

Select the desired number of streams from the option in the upper-right corner of the screen. Streams and channels are the same. This Stream setting is restricted by the number of streams used during backup. RMAN will allocate channels with this setting. During backup, these channels are used to create backup pieces and they dictate how many channels could be used for restore. If restore is desired with a larger number of channels/streams, then the backup should use that same desired number.

When using the recovery catalog, enter the appropriate connection information in the upper area of the dialog to connect to the recovery catalog.

With the desired options selected, click the Advanced button at the bottom of this screen. The Oracle Advanced Restore dialog will open. On this dialog are several options that must be considered before allowing the restore to complete. The Options tab contains several important settings that could have great effect on any restore operation. The option in the middle of the page, Switch Database Mode for Restore, must be selected if you want to allow CommVault to perform actions such as shutting down or starting up the database, as appropriate for the action to be completed. Without this option set, you must place the database into the correct mode before continuing. These options provide great flexibility for the process to complete as desired.

After you have completed your restore and recovery, you can use the Open DB option to open the database. If you have performed an incomplete recovery, the option Reset Logs must be set to Yes in the drop-down list. This will cause the command **alter database open resetlogs** to be issued during the opening of the database. You can choose to open the database manually if required.

The Restore tab also provides options to validate or modify the backup used to restore the database.

Advanced Configurations

CommVault supports some advanced Oracle configurations. The RAC database is a powerful configuration that can provide improved utilization balance, as well as failover protection. RAC database backups are supported through the CommVault interface in addition to the single-instance configurations already discussed.

Installation and configuration of the RAC database are extremely similar as well. Installation requires an individual CommVault iDA to be installed on each physical node of the RAC database instance. Upon completion of the installation, the configuration to identify the instance is different. CommVault is RAC aware through the use of a CommVault RAC pseudo-client. The pseudo-client is created through the context menu in the CommCell browser under the Computers group. Right-click the Computers group, and a new menu option will appear, as shown in Figure 27-8.

Upon selection of the Oracle RAC option from the New Client menu option, a wizard opens in which the same options are available as if you were using a single database instance. The difference is that you will now see each of the RAC nodes. This provides the ability to configure operations using one or more of the nodes of the cluster. You can see that each RAC node is listed individually in the GUI in Figure 27-9.

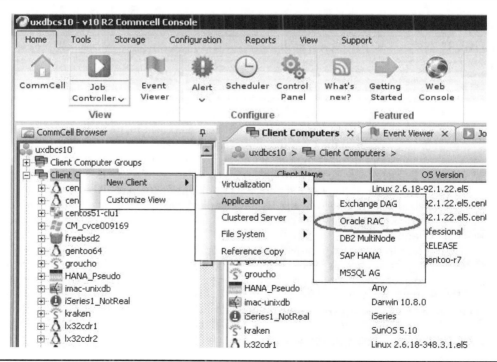

FIGURE 27-8. *Selecting the Oracle RAC pseudo-client*

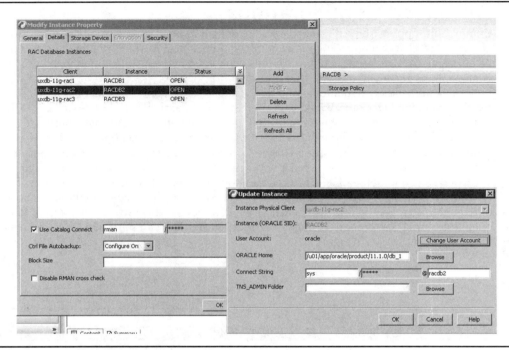

FIGURE 27-9. *RAC pseudo-client detail*

Figure 27-10 shows an example where each RAC node is being used to perform a backup and that the nodes are sharing the load of the backup equally. With CommVault, a stream is an equivalent object to an RMAN channel. It is the defined object that is responsible for moving the stream of data to and from the CommVault storage devices.

CommVault supports other important Oracle constructs natively. Backups can be performed on standby databases for use in restoring a primary database. The standby database is essentially a clone of production. Backups of the primary control file are completed along with backups of the standby database itself. In this way, RMAN has complete copies of the data it requires to restore a database. The load of the backup can continue on the standby database, leaving the primary database to fulfill its primary function.

CommVault Intellisnap can provide RMAN-supported snapshot backup of Oracle databases. Various storage array vendors have specific methods of interaction with the CommVault application and Oracle database. CommVault is aware of and tightly integrated with most major array vendors.

These arrays are managed from within configuration in the CommServe and allow the snapshot to be created natively through the control function of the array. CommVault manages these snaps with its retention and also provides a mechanism for reading the data from the snapshot through a proxy server and into storage media.

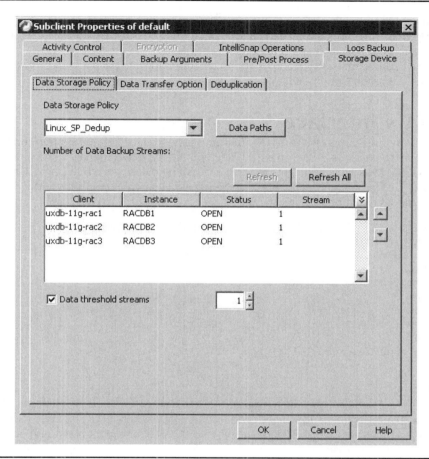

FIGURE 27-10. *RAC data storage policy definition*

A combination of snapshots and archived redo log backups can protect a database. This is especially well suited for large databases that would otherwise take too long to create a backup and pose an unreasonable load on the primary database.

Intellisnap will quiesce the database using hot backup mode, perform the snapshot, un-quiesce the database by taking the database out of hot backup mode and allow it to continue its primary function, and then mount the snapshot to a proxy server where the data is read from the snapshot into CommVault media—all while the primary function of the database continues to function as normal. Everything would be offloaded to the proxy server.

CommVault supports other advanced configurations as well. Oracle's incrementally merged backup is supported through the CommVault GUI. Another function available through the GUI is the option where individual user tables can be restored independently of the entire database utilizing the backups created during ongoing protection.

Finally, an open interface allows you to create custom scripts that will be executed and monitored through CommVault.

RMAN Interface

CommVault fully supports the RMAN SBT interface. Because of this support, backups can be made in multiple ways. A DBA who is fluent with the syntax of the SBT interface can write his or her own RMAN scripts and execute them against the databases while CommVault ingests and becomes responsible for the backup data generated. A sample script illustrating the SBT interface and its required composition follows:

```
run {
allocate channel ch1 type 'sbt_tape'
PARMS="SBT_LIBRARY=/opt/simpana/Base/libobk.so,BLKSIZE=262144"
TRACE 0;
setlimit channel ch1 maxopenfiles 8;
backup
 incremental level = 1
 filesperset = 4
database
 include current controlfile  spfile  ;
}
exit;
```

This script demonstrates the typical RMAN backup syntax. For Unix platforms, the key is in the **allocate channel** statement, which identifies the type of channel as sbt_tape, indicating we are using the MML layer, as opposed to backing to disk. Additional parameters and options specifically related to the CommVault SBT library are included in the **parms** portion of the statement.

In the Windows interface, the statement identifying the libobk interface is not necessary. Simply identifying the channel with the sbt_tape keyword will indicate that the data being generated from the backup goes through the MML layer (and in our case, to CommVault). During the installation, DLL software initiated in the operating system will handle the routing of data to the CommVault media agent and its storage accordingly. This serves the same function as the libobk library in Unix.

Troubleshooting

When it comes to troubleshooting backup problems within the CommVault interface, you have multiple logs available to review for clues. CommVault logs can be reviewed either by selecting View Logs From an Active Backup or by selecting View Logs from a backup history listing generated from all the backup jobs that have run against a specific subclient.

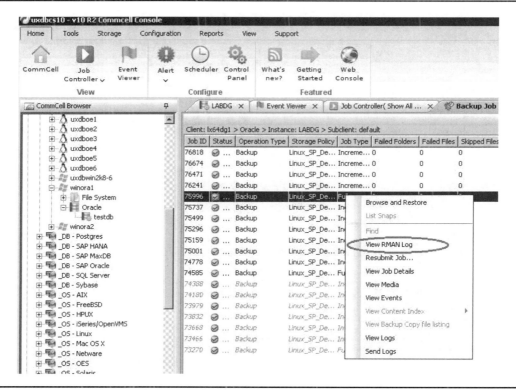

FIGURE 27-11. *Selecting the RMAN log from backup history*

The logs generated by CommVault are separated by function and are unique to each individual machine where a backup has been run. The default names for the principle CommVault logs are CLOraAgent.log and ORASBT.log.

Utilizing these logs can be difficult at first because there are messages and logs relayed to CommVault directly from RMAN, as well as messages and logs generated by CommVault as it operates its backup. When you are troubleshooting backups through CommVault, it is likely best (or easiest) to simply view the RMAN log. This log is generated by RMAN, but captured by CommVault during a backup. It can be seen generating in real time from a running backup. In Figure 27-11, the option to select the RMAN log from a backup history is shown, and the actual log itself is shown in Figure 27-12.

This RMAN log is maintained within the CommVault job history for seven days by default, but it can be stored for extended periods of time depending on the requirements of the DBA.

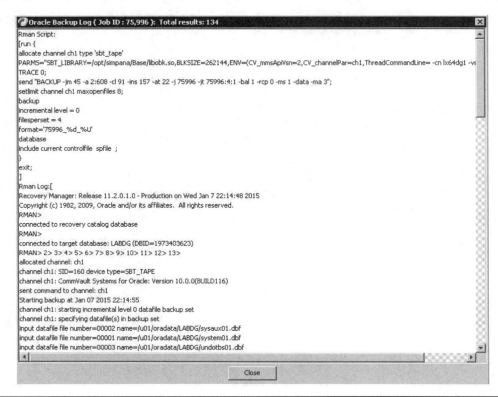

FIGURE 27-12. *Sample RMAN log*

Summary

CommVault and RMAN are woven tightly together to provide a friendly GUI interface along with a robust feature set. RMAN is the key focus of CommVault, and CommVault fully supports the RMAN interface. CommVault storage and retention management are designed to enhance the ability of the administrator to support the backup and storage requirements of the organization.

This chapter provided a quick overview of many CommVault Oracle features. The most widely used features along with basic configuration were covered, but there are many more features supported by CommVault through the SBT interface in Oracle.

The CommVault Oracle archiving feature allows you to identify data for archiving and move it out of the primary database, but later you can retrieve it back into the database as necessary. The ability to restore individual tables that have been dropped is a useful function. This functionality is outside of the features found within the Flashback functions native to Oracle. Multiple methods of the Duplicate Database function are supported. These Duplicate Database methods support a scheduled refresh of test and dev databases utilizing the backups from production. Strong reporting functionality helps you to determine what's working successfully and to identify problem areas in protecting the database environment. You can find many more features by reviewing the CommVault Books Online documentation website at www.documentation.commvault.com.

PART
VI

Appendixes

APPENDIX

A

RMAN Scripting
Examples

W e have gotten a number of requests for scripts related to RMAN. The nice thing about RMAN is that scripting it is a pretty straightforward process. In this chapter, we provide you with some basic scripts for both Windows and Linux to get you started.

These scripts assume that you are using the Oracle Fast Recovery Area (FRA), which will manage disk space and backup retention for you. If you are not using the FRA, perhaps you might want to customize these scripts for your own needs. We will leave that to your ingenuity and skill!

RMAN Scripts for Windows

These scripts were written and tested using Windows XP. First, we give you a sample batch script that calls RMAN for a backup of the database and the archived redo logs. We then show you a method of scheduling these scripts from the operating system. Note that this is just one method of scheduling automated backups. You might also choose to use Oracle Enterprise Manager (OEM) to schedule and manage your backups. We suggest that you use OEM's scheduling facilities to schedule your backups rather than the OEM Backup Wizard.

Creating a Windows Script to Schedule Backups

This is a pretty basic script; you might want to augment it for incremental backups, backup validation, or other operations. Note that the script will return an error message if the backup fails. To create this script, you might use Notepad, or some other text editor, and call this script something like backup.bat.

```
rem *******************************************************************
rem * Script Name: backup.bat
rem * Script Purpose: This script will call RMAN and execute the command
rem * file specified on the command line.
rem * Usage backup.bat <oracle_sid> <backup|arch>
@echo off
rem
rem RMAN BACKUP SCRIPT
rem For WIN XP
rem
echo %1
set oracle_sid=%1
if "%2" == "backup" rman target=/ cmdfile=c:\oracle\scripts\backup.scr
if not ERRORLEVEL 0 echo "WARNING - FAILURE OCCURRED"
if "%2" == "arch" rman target=/ cmdfile= c:\oracle\scripts\arch.scr
if not ERRORLEVEL 0 echo "WARNING - FAILURE OCCURRED"
```

Note that this script calls two command files, backup.scr and arch.scr, which in this case are located in the c:\oracle\scripts directory.

Here is the backup.scr script:

```
Backup as compressed backupset database plus archivelog delete input;
```

This is the arch.scr script:

```
Backup as compressed backupset archivelog all delete input;
```

Again, each of these scripts would be created using a text editor and placed in the c:\oracle\ scripts directory. If you put them somewhere else, you will need to edit the backup.bat script to point to the correct location of these scripts.

Scheduling the Backup

Now, we want to schedule the backup. We will use the Windows schtasks utility to perform this operation. In our experience, schtasks is a rarely used but powerful scheduling utility. In this example, we are scheduling a daily database backup using the backup.bat file. We also have an example of scheduling the archived redo log backup and an example of how to remove a scheduled task:

```
schtasks /create /tn "database_backup" /sc weekly /d SUN /st 14:50:00 /tr
"c:\bc\rman\backup.bat rob10r2 backup>\>c:\bc\rman\backup.output"
rem schtasks /delete /tn "database_backup"
schtasks /create /tn "archivelog_backup" /sc daily /st 14:50:00 /tr
"c:\bc\rman\backup.bat rob10r2 arch>\>c:\bc\rman\backup.output"
```

You have a number of scheduling options when using the schtasks scheduler. The schtasks scheduler will request the login ID of the user running the job.

RMAN Scripts for Unix

These scripts were written and tested on Red Hat Linux Version 5. In this section, we have a backup script (backup.ksh) and the related command-line files that will be used to execute the actual backup. You can use **cron** or **at** to schedule this script in Unix. First, here is our sample shell script for our Unix backup:

```
#/bin/ksh
# Script name: backup.ksh
# Usage: backup.ksh <ORACLE_SID> <backup|arch>
# Note: We assume the oracle environment is already setup except for
# ORACLE_HOME. If not, you will need to setup your environment correctly.
set ORACLE_SID=$1
if [ "$2"="backup" ]; then
    rman target=/ cmdfile=/home/oracle/scripts/backup.scr
fi
if [ "$2"="arch" ]; then
    rman target=/ cmdfile=/home/oracle/scripts/arch.scr
fi
```

The backup.scr script is the same as you saw earlier:

```
Backup as compressed backupset database plus archivelog delete input;
```

As is the arch.scr script:

```
Backup as compressed backupset archivelog all delete input;
```

APPENDIX B

Setting Up an RMAN Test Environment

As the complexity of production enterprise environments grows with each passing year, we DBAs are finding the same complexity creeping into our test environments. For example, in *Oracle9i RMAN Backup & Recovery*, the test environment was seemingly complex for us: a Windows laptop for minor tweaks and screenshots, another Windows server for more robust testing, and a Sun Blade 150 for multi-OS interaction and Unix commands. Among these three machines, we were able to do all technical reviews (combined with years of actual experience in the workplace, of course).

For the 10*g* RMAN book, the test environment included two Linux boxes with a shared FireWire disk drive (running RAC, of course), Matthew's trusty Windows laptop, that old Sun Blade, and a stand-alone Linux box. And Matthew still went hunting with his colleagues looking for other RAC clusters, tape storage jukeboxes, and Oracle Enterprise Manager repositories.

That being said, things have taken an interesting turn since the last book. We authors had to travel significantly during the production of this book, so the needs changed dramatically from a tactical standpoint. Because of the up and down, thrashed and trashed nature of B&R testing, testing from a remote location can be difficult. In addition, this was the first time we wrote against beta code (long story), so there are plenty of hiccups that simply prevented traditional solutions.

So, what did our test environment look like this time? One recent Dell laptop, running Oracle Virtual Machine, and lots of disk space. This time also involved quite a bit of time on various Oracle Exadata Database Machines…or a dozen. We also used various virtual machines that Oracle provides for your use.

Of course, there are a ton of platforms you might be using. The nice thing is that RMAN tends to work the same regardless of which platform you are running on. Whatever lab environment you construct, it's probably not going to run as fast as the one you have at work, but if you are going to become an expert at RMAN backup and recovery, you need a test environment. Not just to learn in, but to practice in, time and time again. With backup and recovery, practice truly does make perfect.

We suggest you try to make your test environment mimic your actual environment as much as possible. So, if you are running Linux where you work, your test environment would best be served running Linux. If your shop is running additional database products, such as GoldenGate, you will want to consider setting those environments up on your test environment too. That's because these products can have impacts on your databases and how you back them up. It's also possible that your backups might impact those products in some way. You will want to know about these things sooner rather than later.

A test environment for backup and recovery is different from other testing environments. First of all, you have to be able to remove datafiles, or even the entire database, on a whim, without having to clear it with other users. In other words, you need your own database…or two. If you begin testing RMAN functionality on a shared database, pretty soon you'll either start getting angry phone calls from other users or find yourself locked out of the machine by the SA.

A backup and recovery test environment is simply too volatile to share. Think about it from the other end: you're busy testing a backup yourself when suddenly the backup aborts because someone started removing datafiles in order to test their own restore and recovery.

On the other hand, you need to test your strategies in an environment that most closely matches that of your production databases. Therefore, you can't always run in isolation because you might need to tune your backup on a large, production-grade server that has the same kind of load as production.

What we suggest, then, is that you approach RMAN backup and recovery testing as a two-tiered investigation: First, get comfortable with functionality and behavior in the isolation of a small test server. Second, take the lessons you've learned, and schedule time to test on a larger, production-grade database server. That way, you can schedule time on a test box for a backup/recovery test outage, and avoid spending that valuable time trying to learn lessons that you could have figured out on your workstation.

So, what does this approach look like more specifically? The answer is provided in this appendix.

The Test Box

The first-level test machine for RMAN functionality doesn't need to be a supercomputer. In fact, you should think of the first level of testing as just a rehearsal—you're reading through your lines, getting the placement right, and talking through the steps with the other actors and the director.

Match Your Production Environment

If possible, your RMAN testing should take place on the same operating system that you run in production. This is a rather humorous thing to say, we know: who has a single OS in their environment anymore? Anyway, if you will be backing up only Solaris servers, it makes sense to invest a little money in a Sun workstation. That way, you can begin production environment matching as soon as possible.

Go Cheap—At a Price

Everyone is concerned about price. The problem is that the Oracle database can be very resource intensive. Although you can run Oracle on a slower system, with less memory, slow I/O throughput, and slow networking, the speed of backups and restores can be frustratingly slow. It's hard to really get quality time with the database when the backup or restore takes 30 minutes to complete. It's also hard to stand up a duplicate database when you have limited disk space, memory, or I/O throughput.

There are a number of websites that can provide a great deal of help with respect to setting up the environment you might want to create. Web sites such as www.oracle-base.com have many pages that offer various ways you can configure Oracle databases using different versions and different configurations such as Real Application Clusters (RAC) technology and other Oracle options.

The nice thing is that RMAN acts the same on all platforms, and the exercises in this book work on all platforms. So, if you can't afford the Cadillac, then certainly you can practice on a smaller scale. Practice is the important thing here!

That being said, what kind of hardware do you need for a decent test platform? At a minimum we'd suggest the following advice:

- **Processor speed**   You will need enough processors that are fast enough to support at least three databases and the connections required to support RMAN operations. RMAN will run better if you have more CPUs to parallelize across when you are performing tasks such as creating duplicate databases. Also, if you are going to be using compression or encryption, CPU power will make a difference.

- **Memory**   This really depends on how many databases you will be running. You will want sufficient memory to run at least three Oracle instances at the same time: one each for the target database, the recovery catalog, and an auxiliary database. You need enough memory to run three Oracle instances simultaneously, along with your media management software. At a minimum we'd recommend that you allocate 8GB, and it's likely that will be rather slow. Of course, if you add requirements, such as using Cloud Control, you will need even more memory. Don't cut corners on memory, or you will get sucked down into time-consuming swap rat holes from which there is no escape.

■ **Disk space**   You've probably heard that disks are cheap. Well, this might be true, but that does not ensure that they are fast. Although at first blush it might seem that speed isn't important, disk I/O speeds and memory are likely to be the chief limiting factors on how long your backups or restores take. While you don't need blazing fast backup and restore times, sitting for an hour waiting to see if your test restore worked can be more than frustrating. Find yourself a fast disk and sacrifice storage for speed. You will want at least 250GB to start with, though if you run lots of tests you can eat up that amount of space pretty easily.

The Oracle Configuration

After you get your test box up and running, you need to think about your Oracle installation and configuration. This step depends on what you need to test: Will you be backing up multiple versions of Oracle? Will you be using OEM?

Multiple Homes

If you will be installing multiple versions of Oracle, remember to install them starting with the oldest version first. Also, Oracle will make you install each in its own ORACLE_HOME location, so you will need more disk space for each install image. You will also want to make sure you are running on the most current patch set.

Creating Databases

Obviously, you need at least one database created in each ORACLE_HOME that you have installed. These databases may be default databases created during Oracle installation, but an even better scenario would be to use databases that are configured somewhat like production databases. From a size perspective, that may not be possible, but you can scale datafile sizes down while keeping the same number of datafiles and tablespaces.

In addition, you might be able to scale down the memory utilization of these test boxes, but this can have negative consequences. Adjust your SGA allocations based on the recommendations of the various memory advisors. It's likely that you won't need a great deal of memory unless you plan on using your test environment for something beyond backup and recovery.

If you are going to create a recovery catalog database, make sure that it's using the more current version of Oracle that you will be putting on your test system. Although you can share the recovery catalog schema with a database doing other kinds of work, we recommend that you keep the recovery catalog database separate—this is a best practice and the configuration you are most likely to come across. You might also want to put it on a different server (virtual or otherwise) to protect it from loss of the server where other databases live.

The RMAN Configuration

Now that you have your system set up with Oracle installed and databases built, we have a few hints on the testing process:

- *Have a cold backup that remains untouched.* Before you do any RMAN testing, shut down your database, take a cold OS copy backup, and place it in a folder that doesn't get touched. This is your last line of defense if you completely mess everything up during your RMAN testing.

- *Switch your redo logs a lot.* One of the biggest mistakes that happens with RMAN testing is that the timeframe between the backup and restore is unrealistically short. Confusion sets in because there is no space between the completion time of the backup and the "until time" of the restore operation. Therefore, after any backup, make sure you switch the log file three or four times, just to put a little "distance" between operations.

- *Set the* NLS_DATE_FORMAT *environment variable.* This is good advice for RMAN in general, but particularly in a test situation, where the timeframe between a backup and a restore will be unrealistically short and you will want to know the timeframe of a backup to the second. Therefore, before starting RMAN, be sure to run the following:

```
export NLS_DATE_FORMAT='mon-dd-yyyy hh24:mi:ss'
```

    Then, when you start RMAN and issue a **list backup** command, the time will always show details to the minute and second.

- *Leave your catalog database alone.* You will be tempted to use the database that houses your catalog as a target and to perform some tests with it. That is fine—that's why it's called a test environment. But you can seriously undermine your testing if you foul up your catalog. Do yourself a favor and leave the catalog database alone. Also, export your catalog schema with a user-level export before any new test session begins.

- *Keep up with catalog maintenance.* This may be your test environment, but you will be creating a lot of backups over time, and you have a limited amount of space on your little test box. Take the opportunity to test using retention policies to get rid of old backups.

- *Remove clones as soon as possible.* Attack of the clones! If you use the **duplicate** command, you can end up with numerous different instances running and taking up precious memory and disk space. Hey, it's a clone, and you're in a test environment—get rid of it as soon as you make it.

- *Leave a clone file system in place.* You don't need to go through the steps of building the file system and the init.ora file for your duplicate database every time you want to test the **duplicate** or **duplicate for standby** command. Leave the file system and supporting files in place, and use the same DB_NAME and SID. On Windows, be sure to leave the Oracleservice<sid> in place in the Services control panel.

- *Don't get attached to your test environment.* Sometimes you need to just blow everything away and start over from scratch, particularly if you don't have good maintenance habits. Eventually, your database will get to the point that it has had tablespaces dropped; has had re-created, dropped, and forgotten files placed in the wrong directory; has had archive logs stored all over the place—basically it's a rambling mess. Don't worry.

That's why they call it testing. Don't get too wrapped up in the environment you have; just whack everything and start over from the cold backup you took prior to testing.

■ *Have FUN!* Where else can you get a job where you are paid to have fun. Disneyland, perhaps? Have fun becoming a backup and recovery expert!

You'll surely find some of your own valuable lessons after you've done a bit of testing. After you go through the conceptual learning, take the scripts you've built and the knowledge you've gained, and schedule some time on a production-grade system to make sure that everything is going to scale up to your enterprise. You'll be glad you took the time to learn it before you went live.

Index

G

H

P

Join the Largest Tech Community in the World

 Download the latest software, tools, and developer templates

 Get exclusive access to hands-on trainings and workshops

 Grow your professional network through the Oracle ACE Program

 Publish your technical articles – and get paid to share your expertise

Join the Oracle Technology Network
Membership is free. Visit oracle.com/technetwork

@OracleOTN   facebook.com/OracleTechnologyNetwork

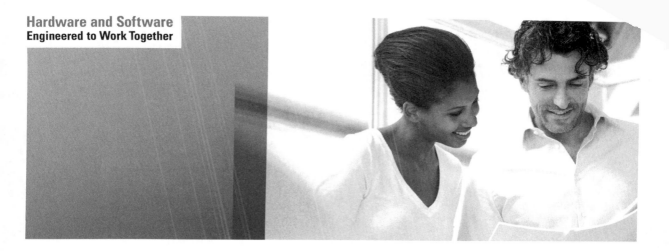

Reach More than 700,000 Oracle Customers with Oracle Publishing Group

Connect with the Audience that Matters Most to Your Business

Oracle Magazine
The Largest IT Publication in the World
Circulation: 550,000
Audience: IT Managers, DBAs, Programmers, and Developers

Profit
Business Insight for Enterprise-Class Business Leaders to
Help Them Build a Better Business Using Oracle Technology
Circulation: 100,000
Audience: Top Executives and Line of Business Managers

Java Magazine
The Essential Source on Java Technology, the Java
Programming Language, and Java-Based Applications
Circulation: 125,000 and Growing Steady
Audience: Corporate and Independent Java Developers,
Programmers, and Architects

For more information
or to sign up for a FREE
subscription:
Scan the QR code to visit
Oracle Publishing online.

Beta Test Oracle Software

Get a first look at our newest products—and help perfect them. You must meet the following criteria:

✓ **Licensed Oracle customer or Oracle PartnerNetwork member**

✓ **Oracle software expert**

✓ **Early adopter of Oracle products**

Please apply at: pdpm.oracle.com/BPO/userprofile

ORACLE®

If your interests match upcoming activities, we'll contact you. Profiles are kept on file for 12 months.